Essentials of Business Communication

NELSON

Essentials of Business Communication, Ninth Canadian Edition

Mary Ellen Guffey, Dana Loewy, and Richard Almonte

VP, Product Solutions, K–20:
Claudine O'Donnell

Publisher:
Alexis Hood

Executive Marketing Manager:
Amanda Henry

Content Manager:
Lisa Peterson

Photo and Permissions Researcher:
Jessica Freedman

Senior Production Project Manager:
Natalia Denesiuk Harris

Production Service:
MPS Limited

Copy Editor:
Kate Unrau

Proofreader:
Lakshmi

Indexer:
Edwin Durbin

Design Director:
Ken Phipps

Higher Education Design PM:
Pamela Johnston

Interior Design:
Dave Murphy

Cover Design:
John Montgomery

Compositor:
MPS Limited

Printed and bound in Canada
2 3 4 5 22 21 20 19

For more information contact Nelson Education Ltd., 1120 Birchmount Road, Toronto, Ontario, M1K 5G4. Or you can visit our Internet site at nelson.com

Library and Archives Canada Cataloguing in Publication

Guffey, Mary Ellen, author
Essentials of business communication / Mary Ellen Guffey, Professor Emerita of Business, Los Angeles Pierce College, Dana Loewy, Business Communication Program, California State University, Fullerton, Richard Almonte, George Brown College. — Ninth Canadian edition.

Includes bibliographical references and index.
Issued in print and electronic formats.
ISBN 978-0-17-672124-4 (softcover).
—ISBN 978-0-17-682714-4 (PDF)

1. Business writing—Textbooks. 2. English language—Business English—Textbooks. 3. Business communication—Textbooks. 4. Textbooks. I. Loewy, Dana, author II. Almonte, Richard, author III. Title.

HF5718.3.G84 2018   808.06'665
C2017-906968-3
C2017-906969-1

ISBN-13: 978-0-17-672124-4
ISBN-10: 0-17-672124-X

Essentials of Business Communication

Mary Ellen Guffey
Professor Emerita of Business
Los Angeles Pierce College

Dana Loewy
Business Communication Program
California State University, Fullerton

Richard Almonte
George Brown College

NELSON

Learning With Guffey...

From the emphasis on writing in an increasingly digital workplace to updated model documents, Guffey, Loewy, and Almonte have updated tools and created new ways to keep you interested and engaged.

The following six pages describe features that will help you succeed in today's technologically enhanced workplace.

Essentials of Business Communication offers a three-in-one learning package that gets results:

- Authoritative textbook
- Practical workbook
- Self-teaching Grammar/Mechanics Handbook

EMPHASIS ON GRAMMAR

Throughout the text, you are encouraged to build on your basic grammar skills. The Grammar/Mechanics Handbook coupled with the Web-based Grammar/Mechanics Checkups and Grammar/Mechanics Challenges help you practise and sharpen your skills.

EMPHASIS ON PROFESSIONALISM

The Ninth Canadian Edition increases its emphasis on professional workplace behaviours and illustrates the importance of professionalism. Businesses have a keen interest in a professional workforce that effectively works together to deliver positive results that ultimately boost profits and bolster a company's image. In this edition, you'll discover the professional characteristics most valued in today's competitive workplace.

CAREER RELEVANCE

Because employers often rank communication skills among the most requested competencies, the Ninth Canadian Edition emphasizes the link between excellent communication skills and career success—helping you see for yourself the critical role business communication will play in your life.

It's Just That Easy!

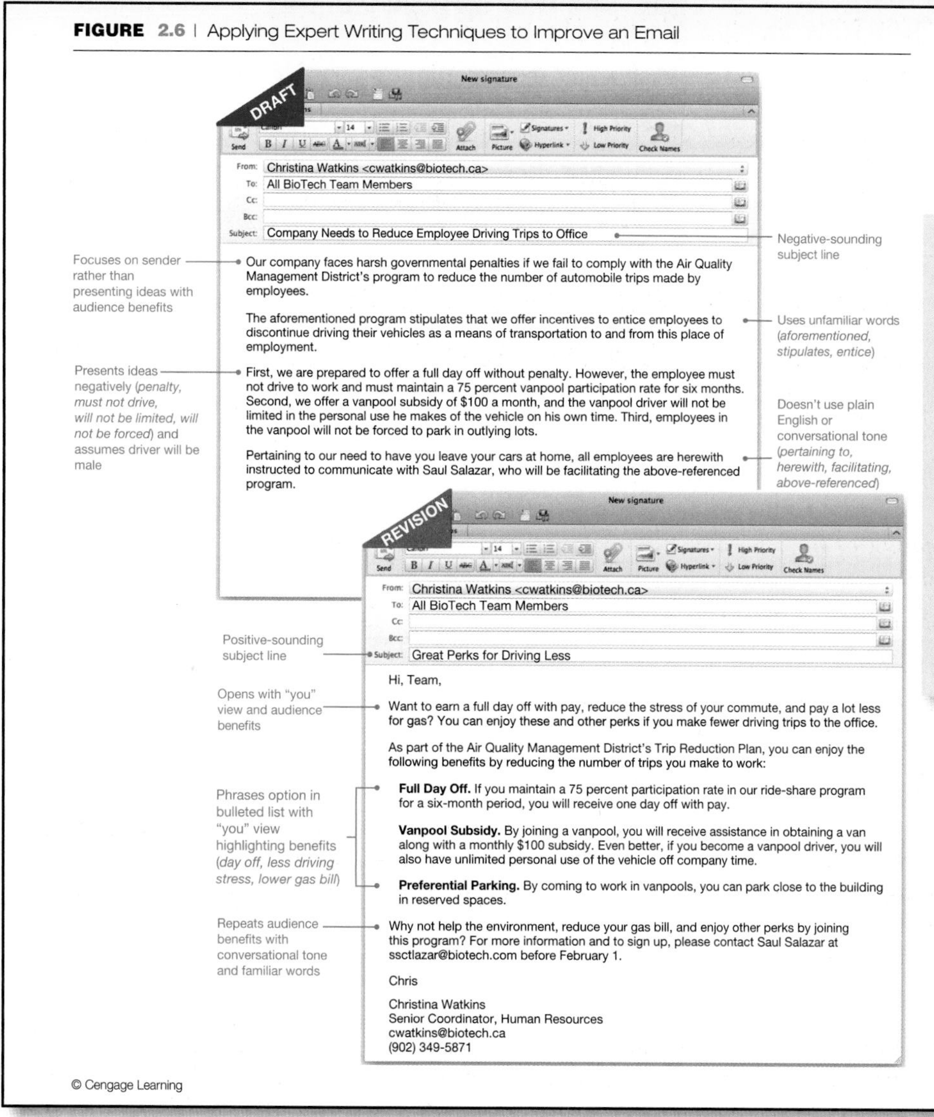
FIGURE 2.6 | Applying Expert Writing Techniques to Improve an Email
DRAFT
New signature
From: Christina Watkins <cwatkins@biotech.ca>
To: All BioTech Team Members
Cc:
Bcc:
Subject: Company Needs to Reduce Employee Driving Trips to Office
Negative-sounding subject line
Focuses on sender rather than presenting ideas with audience benefits
Our company faces harsh governmental penalties if we fail to comply with the Air Quality Management District's program to reduce the number of automobile trips made by employees.
The aforementioned program stipulates that we offer incentives to entice employees to discontinue driving their vehicles as a means of transportation to and from this place of employment.
Uses unfamiliar words (aforementioned, stipulates, entice)
Presents ideas negatively (penalty, must not drive, will not be limited, will not be forced) and assumes driver will be male
First, we are prepared to offer a full day off without penalty. However, the employee must not drive to work and must maintain a 75 percent vanpool participation rate for six months. Second, we offer a vanpool subsidy of $100 a month, and the vanpool driver will not be limited in the personal use he makes of the vehicle on his own time. Third, employees in the vanpool will not be forced to park in outlying lots.
Doesn't use plain English or conversational tone (pertaining to, herewith, facilitating, above-referenced)
Pertaining to our need to have you leave your cars at home, all employees are herewith instructed to communicate with Saul Salazar, who will be facilitating the above-referenced program.
REVISION
New signature
From: Christina Watkins <cwatkins@biotech.ca>
To: All BioTech Team Members
Cc:
Bcc:
Positive-sounding subject line
Subject: Great Perks for Driving Less
Hi, Team,
Opens with "you" view and audience benefits
Want to earn a full day off with pay, reduce the stress of your commute, and pay a lot less for gas? You can enjoy these and other perks if you make fewer driving trips to the office.
As part of the Air Quality Management District's Trip Reduction Plan, you can enjoy the following benefits by reducing the number of trips you make to work:
Phrases option in bulleted list with "you" view highlighting benefits (day off, less driving stress, lower gas bill)
Full Day Off. If you maintain a 75 percent participation rate in our ride-share program for a six-month period, you will receive one day off with pay.
Vanpool Subsidy. By joining a vanpool, you will receive assistance in obtaining a van along with a monthly $100 subsidy. Even better, if you become a vanpool driver, you will also have unlimited personal use of the vehicle off company time.
Preferential Parking. By coming to work in vanpools, you can park close to the building in reserved spaces.
Repeats audience benefits with conversational tone and familiar words
Why not help the environment, reduce your gas bill, and enjoy other perks by joining this program? For more information and to sign up, please contact Saul Salazar at ssctlazar@biotech.com before February 1.
Chris
Christina Watkins
Senior Coordinator, Human Resources
cwatkins@biotech.ca
(902) 349-5871
© Cengage Learning

More Before-and-After Model Documents

Before-and-after sample documents and descriptive callouts create a road map to the writing process, demonstrating the effective use of the skills being taught, as well as the significance of the revision process.

Learning With Guffey...

Office Insider

To accentuate how excellent communication skills translate into career success, the *Office Insider* demonstrates the importance of communication skills in real-world practice.

OFFICE INSIDER

"Civility on the job creates an atmosphere of respect and appreciation that ultimately translates to a better reputation and, hence, to better business."

—Ronald M. Bosrock, founder and director of The Global Institute, a research centre

Workplace in Focus Photo Essays

Vivid photos with intriguing stories demonstrate real-world applications of business communication concepts. Each photo essay concludes with a critical thinking question.

WORKPLACE IN FOCUS

At credit card company Amex's Canadian headquarters in Toronto, brainstorming and informal research is built right into the office architecture. In a recent head-office move, Amex decided to devote 20 percent of its office floor space—on every floor—to "open, collaborative spaces so employees can set up meetings in the conference room, grab a couch by a window, or enjoy a whiteboard brainstorming session over lunch with a colleague—all without compromising their connectivity."[1] Encouraging employees to seek out information in this way, instead of sitting in a cubicle or office all day, has a double impact: it encourages the type of research gathering necessary in an ideas-based economy, and it suits the preferences of Millennial workers who appreciate collaboration and informality in the workplace. *What type of collaborations have you participated in at work?*

It's Just That Easy!

WRITING PLAN FOR PROFESSIONAL EMAILS

- **Subject line:** Summarize the main information/request in condensed form.
- **Greetings:** Say hello and goodbye politely.
- **Opening:** Reveal the reason for writing immediately in a more expanded form than in the subject line.
- **Body:** Explain or justify the reason using headings, bulleted lists, and other high-skim techniques when appropriate.
- **Closing:** Include (a) action information, dates, or deadlines; (b) a summary of the message; or (c) a closing thought.

Writing Plans

Ample step-by-step writing plans help you get started quickly on organizing and formatting messages.

Closes with forward look

A number of other payroll services offer outstanding programs. I'm sure we can find the perfect partner to enable you to outsource your payroll responsibilities, thus allowing your company to focus its financial and human resources on its core business. I look forward to our next appointment when you may choose from a number of excellent payroll outsourcing firms.

Sincerely,

Jane Moffatt

Jane Moffatt
Partner

Tips for Resolving Problems and Following Up

- Whenever possible, call or see the individual involved.
- Describe the problem and apologize.
- Explain why the problem occurred.
- Take responsibility, if appropriate.
- Explain what you are doing to resolve it.
- Explain what you are doing to prevent recurrence.
- Follow up with a message that documents the personal contact.
- Look forward to positive future relations.

Tips for Preparing Business Messages

Tips boxes summarize practical suggestions for creating effective business messages. Study them before completing your writing assignments.

Learning With Guffey...

Chapter Review and Critical Thinking Exercises

End-of-chapter questions reinforce concepts covered in each chapter.

CHAPTER REVIEW

1. Define *communication*. When is it successful? (Obj. 1)
2. List the five steps in the communication process. (Obj. 1)
3. In what ways is business writing different from high school writing and private messages? (Obj. 2)
4. Describe the components in each stage of the 3-×-3 writing process. (Obj. 2)
5. What does *WIIFM* mean? Why is it important to business writers? (Obj. 3)
6. What seven factors should writers consider in selecting an appropriate channel to deliver a message? (Obj. 3)
7. What is the "you" view? When can the use of the pronoun *you* backfire? (Obj. 4)
8. How can a business writer sound conversational but also be professional? (Obj. 4)
9. Why is positive wording more effective in business messages than negative wording? (Obj. 5)
10. What are three ways to avoid biased language? Give an original example of each. (Obj. 5)

CRITICAL THINKING

1. Has digital transmission changed the nature of communication? (Obj. 1)
2. Why do you think employers prefer messages that are not written like high school writing? (Obj. 2)
3. Why should business writers strive to use short, familiar, simple words? Does this "dumb down" business messages? (Obj. 5)
4. A wise observer once said that bad writing makes smart people look dumb. Do you agree or disagree, and why? (Objs. 1–5)
5. In a letter to the editor, a teacher criticized a newspaper article on autism because it used the term *autistic child* rather than *child with autism*. She championed *people-first* terminology, which avoids defining individuals by their ability or disability.[6] For example, instead of identifying someone as a *disabled person*, one would say, *she has a disability*. What does *people-first language* mean? How can language change perceptions? (Obj. 5)

It's Just That Easy!

ACTIVITIES AND CASES

5.1 EMAIL THAT INFORMS AND REQUESTS: DRESS CODE CONTROVERSY (OBJ. 1)

As the Montreal-based director of Human Resources at Sensational, you have not had a good week. The national media recently reported the fact that Sensational—a leading women's fashion chain—has been taken before the Nova Scotia Human Rights Commission to defend against a claim by a young woman. The young woman recently applied for a job at a Halifax Sensational location and was told in a pre-interview with a manager that "she'd never be hired if she wore her headdress to work." Citing the Commission's website claim that "It's against the law to fire an employee because he wears clothing that is required by his religion," the young woman lodged a complaint.[44] Head office in Vancouver has been in damage-control mode ever since.

Your Task. Quickly realizing the effects the negative media reporting will have, you draft an email to all employees. The purpose of the email is to reaffirm that Sensational abides by and supports all Canadian human rights legislation and, at the same time, that employees should not talk to any media that may ask them for comments. You realize that these two messages are somewhat contradictory (one positive, one negative), but you feel time is of the essence.

Related website: Nova Scotia Human Rights Commission (www.gov.ns.ca/humanrights).

Activities and Cases

Chapter concepts are translated into action as you try out your skills in activities designed to mirror real-world experiences.

Brief Contents

Contents

Appendixes 327

Grammar/Mechanics Handbook 359

Preface

Today's graduates enter working environments with ever-increasing demands. As a result of growing emphasis on team management and employee empowerment, they will be expected to gather data, solve problems, and make decisions independently. They will be working with global trading partners and collaborating with work teams in an increasingly diverse workplace. And they will be using sophisticated technologies to communicate.

Surprisingly, writing skills are becoming more and more important. In the past businesspeople may have written a couple of business letters a month, but now they receive and send hundreds of emails and texts weekly. Their writing skills are showcased in every message they send. To help students develop the skills they need to succeed in today's technologically enhanced workplace, we have responded with a thoroughly revised Ninth Canadian Edition of *Essentials of Business Communication*.

Effective Features That Remain Unchanged

The Ninth Canadian Edition maintains the streamlined, efficient approach to communication that has equipped past learners with the skills needed to be successful in their work. It is most helpful to postsecondary and adult learners preparing themselves for new careers, planning a change in their current careers, or wanting to upgrade their writing and speaking skills. The aim of this edition is to incorporate more of the comments, suggestions, and insights provided by adopters and reviewers over the past few years. For those new to the book, some of the most popular features include the following:

- **Text/Workbook Format.** The convenient text/workbook format presents an all-in-one teaching–learning package that includes concepts; workbook application exercises; writing, speaking, and interpersonal challenges; and a combination handbook/reference manual.
- **Comprehensive but Concise Coverage.** An important reason for the enormous success of *Essentials of Business Communication* is that it practises what it preaches. The Ninth Canadian Edition follows the same strategy, concentrating on essential concepts presented without wasted words.
- **Writing Plans and Writing Improvement Exercises.** Step-by-step writing plans structure the writing experience so that novice writers get started quickly—without struggling to provide unknown details to unfamiliar, hypothetical cases. Many revision exercises build confidence and skills.
- **Wide Coverage of Communication Technology.** All relevant chapters build technology skills by including discussions and applications involving email, instant messaging, texting, cellphones, Web research, contemporary software, online employment searches, and electronic presentations. The Ninth Canadian Edition stays on top of the use of mediated communication within organizations, including the use of social media sites, like Twitter, and blogs for both business and marketing communication.
- **Challenging Cases.** The reality of the work world is that communication situations will not always easily fit the models provided in a business communication textbook. As a result, we have threaded ambiguity and complexity into the tasks

so that students have a chance to use their critical thinking skills as well as their business communication skills regularly.

- **Workplace in Focus Feature.** Chapters contain a Workplace in Focus feature that connects the content being discussed in the chapter to a real-world example. These features make ideal starting points for in-class discussion.
- **Communication Technology in the News Feature.** Units open with articles from Canadian media outlets that bring home the relevance of business communication to today's technology-driven workplace. Topics covered range from texting lingo in the workplace to mastering anger when sending email.
- **Plagiarism.** An unfortunate reality of the Internet age is the difficulty today's students have in understanding the need for proper citation and documentation, as well as the difficulty in understanding the seriousness of plagiarism and its difficult repercussions. We address the issue of plagiarism by offering concrete examples of the real-world ramifications of this behaviour.

Revision Highlights

The following features were updated for the Ninth Canadian Edition:

- **Situational Focus.** The reality of business communication is that people need to be able to respond effectively and professionally in a variety of workplace situations. This is different from memorizing a number of genres or formats. For this reason, while the Ninth Canadian Edition includes a rich introductory chapter covering a multitude of daily forms of communication (e.g., text, email, Web conference, social media), it expands on this generic way of thinking by considering important, realistic, and recurring business situations divided into three categories: daily, persuasive, and negative.
- **New and Revised End-of-Chapter Exercises and Activities.** This edition features a significant revision of the end-of-chapter exercises, activities, and cases. The *Chapter Review, Critical Thinking* questions, and *Activities and Cases* feature more than 15 percent new content. As with the last edition, these new cases recognize the pedagogical usefulness of scripting, role play, and performance as effective means of practising business communication skills.
- **New Technology in the News Boxes.** Every unit opens with a new and current Canadian newspaper article focusing on technology and communication in the workplace. Covering a wide range of topics, from creating online profiles for job seekers to the rise of incivility in the increasingly technological workplace, these articles are timely and relevant, and they will enhance students' understanding of how communication can be influenced by shifts in technology.
- **New Workplace in Focus Boxes.** These boxes have been refreshed to reflect current trends in communication in the workplace.
- **Increased Analysis of New Communication Technologies.** Technology manufacturers' ability to innovate can seem to outstrip teachers' ability to contextualize the changes happening to communication. This edition stays ahead of the curve by contextualizing podcasts, Twitter, LinkedIn, Facebook, wikis, blogs, and other of-the-moment technologies in more detail than any other business communication textbook.

Other Features That Enhance Teaching and Learning

Although the Ninth Canadian Edition of *Essentials of Business Communication* packs considerable information into a small space, it covers all of the critical topics necessary in a comprehensive business communication course; it also features many teaching–learning devices to facilitate instruction, application, and retention.

- **Focus on Writing Skills.** Most students need a great deal of instruction and practice in developing basic and advanced writing techniques, particularly in view of today's increased emphasis on communication by email. Writing skills have returned to the forefront since so much of today's business is transacted through written messages.
- **Realistic Emphasis.** *Essentials* devotes a chapter to the writing of email, texts, and instant messages, plus other daily forms of communication, recognizing that the business world no longer operates via letter or memo except in certain specialized situations (e.g., direct-mail sales letter, collection letters, cover letters for job applications, etc.).
- **Listening, Speaking, and Nonverbal Skills.** Employers are increasingly seeking well-rounded individuals who can interact with fellow employees as well as represent the organization effectively. *Essentials* provides professional tips for managing nonverbal cues; overcoming listening barriers; developing speaking skills; planning and participating in meetings; and making productive telephone calls.
- **Coverage of Formal and Informal Reports.** Two chapters develop functional report-writing skills. Chapter 8 provides detailed instruction in the preparation of six types of informal reports, while Chapter 9 covers proposals and formal reports. For quick comprehension, all reports contain marginal notes that pinpoint writing strategies.
- **Employment Communication Skills.** Successful résumés, cover letters, and other employment documents are among the most important topics in a good business communication course. *Essentials* provides the most realistic and up-to-date résumés in the field. The models show chronological, functional, combination, and computer-friendly résumés.
- **Focus on Oral Communication Skills.** Chapter 10 looks at oral interpersonal skills: person-to-person conversations, telephone communication (including cellphone etiquette), and business meeting skills, while Chapter 11 specifically discusses business presentation skills.
- **Employment Interviewing.** *Essentials* devotes a chapter to effective interviewing techniques, including a discussion of screening interviews and hiring interviews. Chapter 13 also teaches techniques for fighting fear, answering questions, and following up.
- **Models Comparing Effective and Ineffective Documents.** To facilitate speedy recognition of good and bad writing techniques and strategies, *Essentials* presents many before-and-after documents. Marginal notes spotlight targeted strategies and effective writing. We hope that instructors turn this before-and-after technique into effective pedagogy whereby all their students' written assignments undergo the scrutiny of an editing and revising process before being handed in as final products.
- **Variety in End-of-Chapter Activities.** An amazing array of review questions, critical-thinking questions, activities, and realistic case problems holds student attention and helps them apply chapter concepts meaningfully.
- **Grammar/Mechanics Handbook.** A comprehensive Grammar/Mechanics Handbook supplies a thorough review of English grammar, punctuation, capitalization style, and number usage. Its self-teaching exercises may be used for classroom instruction or for supplementary assignments. The handbook also serves as a convenient reference throughout the course and afterwards.

Student Resources

MindTap

Stay organized and efficient with **MindTap**—a single destination with all the course material and study aids students need to succeed. The MindTap that accompanies this textbook includes the following:

- Animated model documents
- Videocases and interviews with Canadian industry professionals
- Aplia™ offers high-quality, auto-graded assignments that ensure students put forth effort on a regular basis throughout the term.
- YouSeeU is an interactive platform where students can record and upload videos using easy-to-use recording tools that are accessible on multiple devices. Instructors can easily view and grade submitted video assignments and offer valuable commentary at a precise frame for targeted feedback.
- Study tools like practice quizzes, chapter PowerPoint summaries, and flashcards
- ReadSpeaker will read the text aloud.
- Highlight the text and make notes in the MindTap Reader. Notes will flow into Evernote, the electronic notebook app that is accessible anywhere when it's time to study for the exam.
- All written assignments can be uploaded into Pathbrite, our e-portfolio app. Access to Pathbrite continues after the MindTap access expires.

Visit nelson.com/student to start using MindTap. Enter the Online Access Code from the card included with the textbook. If a code card is not provided, instant access can be purchased at NELSONbrain.com.

Instructor Resources

The **Nelson Education Teaching Advantage (NETA)** program delivers research-based instructor resources that promote student engagement and higher-order thinking to enable the success of Canadian students and educators. Visit Nelson Education's **Inspired Instruction** website at nelson.com/inspired/ to find out more about NETA.

The following instructor resources have been created for *Essentials of Business Communication*, Ninth Canadian Edition. Access these ultimate tools for customizing lectures and presentations at nelson.com/instructor.

NETA Test Bank

This resource was written by Karen McLaren, Cambrian College. It includes over 325 multiple-choice questions written according to NETA guidelines for effective construction and development of higher-order questions. Also included are over 195 true/false questions and over 130 fill-in-the-blank questions.

The NETA Test Bank is available in a new, cloud-based platform. **Nelson Testing Powered by Cognero®** is a secure online testing system that allows instructors to author, edit, and manage test bank content from anywhere Internet access is available. No special installations or downloads are needed, and the desktop-inspired interface, with its drop-down menus and familiar, intuitive tools, allows instructors to create and manage tests with ease. Multiple test versions can be created in an instant, and content can be imported or exported into other systems. Tests can be delivered from a learning management system, the classroom, or wherever an instructor chooses. Nelson Testing Powered by Cognero for *Essentials of Business Communication*, Ninth Canadian Edition, can be accessed through nelson.com/instructor.

NETA PowerPoint

Microsoft® PowerPoint® lecture slides for every chapter have been created by Lisa Jamieson, Red River College. There is an average of 30 slides per chapter, many featuring key figures, tables, and photographs from *Essentials of Business Communication*, Ninth Canadian Edition. The Notes feature also includes additional activities and ideas for discussion. NETA principles of clear design and engaging content have been incorporated throughout, making it simple for instructors to customize the deck for their courses.

Image Library

This resource consists of digital copies of figures, short tables, and photographs used in the book. Instructors may use these jpegs to customize the NETA PowerPoint or create their own PowerPoint presentations. An Image Library Key describes the images and lists the codes under which the jpegs are saved.

NETA Instructor Guide

The Instructor's Manual to accompany *Essentials of Business Communication*, Ninth Canadian Edition, has been prepared by Karen McLaren, Cambrian College. This manual contains sample lesson plans, learning objectives, and suggested classroom activities to give instructors the support they need to engage their students within the classroom.

Instructor's Solutions Manual

This manual, prepared by Karen McLaren of Cambrian College, contains complete solutions to Critical Thinking Questions, Chapter Review Questions, and Activities and Cases.

Media Guide

The Media Guide includes teaching materials for all video cases selected to accompany *Essentials of Business Communication*, Ninth Canadian Edition.

Acknowledgments

The Ninth Canadian Edition of *Essentials of Business Communication* includes many of the constructive suggestions and timely advice provided by professional communicators, educators, and students who use the book across Canada. These dedicated reviewers include the following:

Bob Ackroyd, Northern Alberta Institute of Technology
Marie Brodie, Nova Scotia Community College Truro
Katherine Dyck, Saskatchewan Polytechnic
Lara Loze, Durham College
Heather Lundy, RCC Institute of Technology
Catrina McBride, Algonquin College
John McLean, Humber College
Tetiana Seredynska, HEC Montréal
Panteli Tritchew, Kwantlen Polytechnic University

A new edition like this would not be possible without the development team at Nelson. Special thanks go to Alexis Hood, Lisa Peterson, Amanda Henry, and Natalia Denesiuk Harris. We would also like to thank Megha Bhardwaj and the team at MPS. Thanks also go to the copy editor, Kate Unrau.

Mary Ellen Guffey
Dana Loewy
Richard Almonte

Business Communication in the Digital Age

UNIT 01

CHAPTER 1
Communicating in the Digital-Age Workplace

LDprod/Shutterstock

COMMUNICATION TECHNOLOGY IN THE NEWS

The next big thing in video communications

Gillian Shaw, Vancouver Sun, *May 6, 2015*

Vancouver start-up Perch launched with a video-messaging service but it has morphed into an always-on video portal that allows companies with employees around the globe to create virtual offices.

It's the third incarnation for Perch's product, first conceived as a security system that turned old iPods into home monitoring cameras. That was before the company's cofounder and CEO Danny Robinson's kids started using the system to leave him video messages, turning beta testing into video messaging.

As with many tech start-ups, that turned out to be only a stepping stone to the commercial product that's now being used by employees at hundreds of companies around the globe and most recently had Perch named of one of five Cool Vendors in Unified Communications for 2015 by industry analyst Gartner.

"The aha moment was when my daughter came home and held up her report card to the iPad to show Danny," said Maura Rodgers, Robinson's wife. She is founder of the social promotions platform Strutta and Perch's vice-president of marketing. "We thought, this is very cool, the kids are using it to communicate directly. What if it could be live."

The way Perch works is by using a dedicated iPad mounted at work or at home with the Perch app (though you can use Perch anywhere you have an Internet connection with an iPad or iPhone). You can set up a Perch portal using your email (although for security reasons not free online services like Gmail and others) and once that's verified you can invite colleagues.

Users can control their availability. The can opt to turn Perch on and let others in their network use the iPad's camera to see that they're available to chat. If you want to talk to someone, walk up to the Perch screen and the face detection automatically unmutes the microphone.

"You can use it in live mode, where you essentially create a virtual window to connect spaces or you can use it where it's online but more of an ambient mode, where there are images that broadcast your availability and let people know that you are available to talk," said Rodgers.

Unlike video calling services such as Skype or FaceTime, Perch doesn't require a call—you can just walk up to it and start talking.

That's what Carman Neustaedter's one-and-a-half-year-old son does when he wants to get grandma's attention—or at least his version of talking. Grandma's in Kelowna, but connected via a portal in the family's kitchen.

"When my one-and-a-half-year-old was born, we had already started using Perch," said Neustaedter, an assistant professor in Simon Fraser University's School of Interactive Arts & Technology, whose research focuses on human-computer interaction and interaction design. "He can push a stool to the kitchen counter and when he climbs up to look at the screen, he knows he's looking at grandma's house.

"He'll start squawking to get her attention."

Neustaedter said video calling and connection services such as Skype, FaceTime and Google Hangout are designed with a calling mode.

"To me what Perch is doing that's really smart is changing the connection model that people use," he said.

Neustaedter said the traditional calling mode "is growing stale," and while people will try leaving connections open on other video calling services, they're not designed for it and the result he said is "clunky."

"Perch is designed for that purpose to leave a connection open for a long period of time and so I see this as a transition to this new way of connecting that makes more sense for people as they begin to rethink the way they connect with their family and friends and coworkers."

Perch is based on a freemium model. It's free for download but with added features at a fee for large corporate users that want to use the system to keep their employees connected.

Rodgers, who uses Perch to stay connected with her mother in Boston, said she is also increasingly hearing from companies and individuals who are using Perch to connect to elderly parents and relatives.

"It's so simple for my Mom to use," said Rodgers. "She knows when I'm there and she'll just pop in and say 'I haven't see you in a couple of days, what have you been up to?'

"It lets me know how she's doing and I get to see how she's doing."

Summarize the article you've just read in a two- to three-sentence paragraph. Answer the following questions, either on your own or in a small group. Be prepared to give your answers in a short presentation or in an email to your instructor.

QUESTIONS:

1. How does what you've learned in this article change your perception of what business communication is or is not?
2. How might what you've learned in this article be useful in changing your own school or workplace communication?
3. Come up with pro and con arguments for the following debate/discussion topic: In the digital age, should employees who work from home expect the same kind of privacy as people who are not working from home? In other words, is it reasonable for an employer to expect an employee working from home to have an application like Perch installed so they can be available at all times?

CHAPTER

1 Communicating in the Digital-Age Workplace

OBJECTIVES

After studying this chapter, you should be able to

1.1 Describe how solid communication skills will improve your career prospects.

1.2 Confront barriers to effective listening.

1.3 Explain the importance of nonverbal communication.

1.4 Understand five common dimensions of culture and how they affect communication.

1.5 Use intercultural communication strategies to prevent miscommunication.

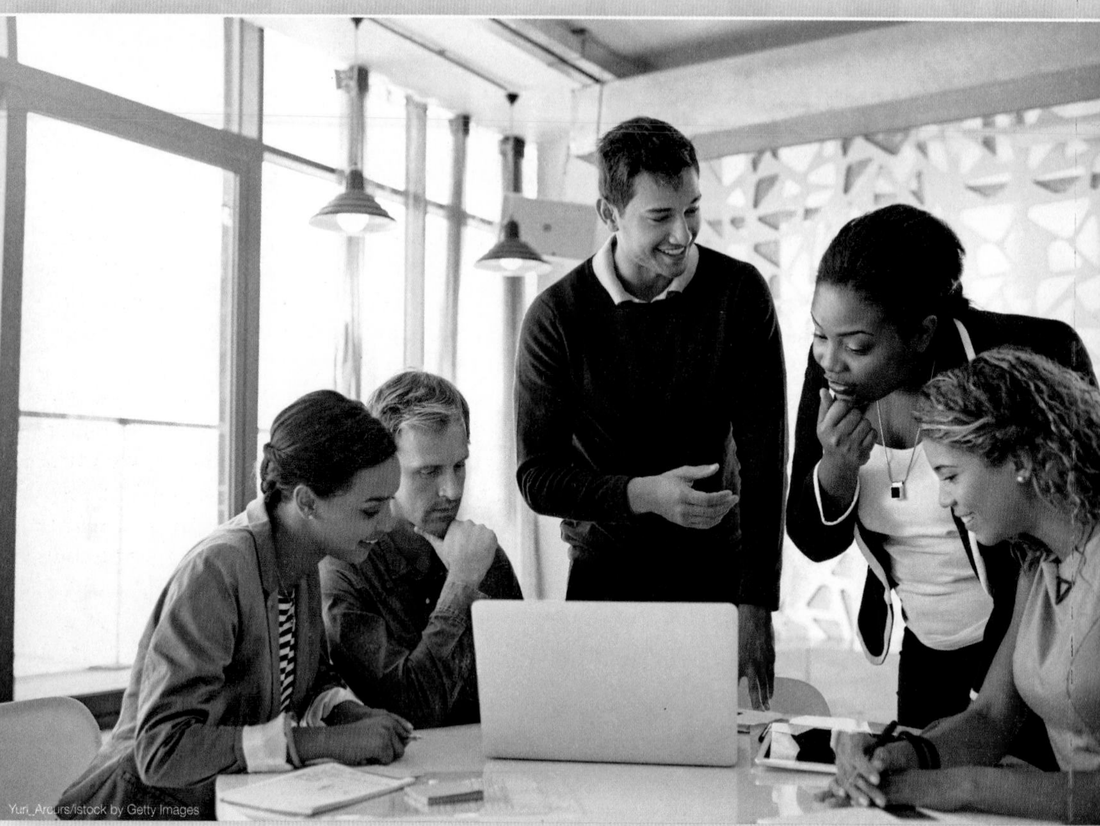
Yuri_Arcurs/istock by Getty Images

1.1 The Relationship Between Solid Communication Skills and Workplace Success

You may wonder what kind of workplace you will enter when you graduate and which skills you will need to be successful in it. Expect a fast-moving, competitive, and information-driven digital environment. Communication technology provides unmatched mobility and connects individuals anytime and anywhere in the world. Today's communicators interact using mobile electronic devices and access information stored on remote servers, in the cloud. This mobility and instant access explain why increasing numbers of workers must be available practically around the clock and must respond quickly.

1.1a Solid Communication Skills: Your Path to Success

Your ability to communicate is a powerful career sifter.[1] Strong communication skills will make you marketable even in a tough economic climate. When jobs are few and competition is fierce, superior communication skills will give you an edge over other job applicants. Recruiters rank communication high on their wish lists.[2] In a poll, 1,000 executives cited writing, critical-thinking, and problem-solving skills along with self-motivation and team skills as their top choices in new hires. Effective writing skills can be a stepping stone to great job opportunities; poorly developed writing skills, on the other hand, will derail a career. Given the increasing emphasis on communication, Canadian corporations are paying millions of dollars to communication coaches and trainers to teach employees the very skills that you are learning in this course. For example, Toronto-based Livewire, a leading provider of business communication services, and the winner of a 2017 International Association of Business Communicators Award of Excellence, lists among its clients well-known Canadian companies like BMO, Four Seasons, McCain Foods, and Telus.[3]

Because communication skills are learned, you control how well you communicate.

1.1b The Digital Revolution: Why Writing Skills Matter More Than Ever

People in today's workforce communicate more, not less, since information technology and the Internet have transformed the world of work. Thanks to technology, messages travel instantly to distant locations, reaching potentially huge audiences with a minimum of expense and effort. Work team members collaborate even when they are physically apart. Moreover, social media are playing an increasingly prominent role in business. In such a hyperconnected world, writing matters more than ever. Digital media require written communication, and workers' skills are always on display.[4]

As a result, employers seek employees with a broader range of skills and with higher levels of knowledge in their field than in the past.[5] Unfortunately, a great number of workers can't deliver.[6] A survey of corporations revealed that two thirds of salaried employees have some writing responsibility. About one third of them, however, do not meet the writing requirements for their positions.[7] "Businesses are crying out—they need to have people who write better," said Gaston Caperton, business executive and former College Board president.[8]

Not surprisingly, many job listings mention the need for excellent oral and written communication skills. In a poll of recruiters, oral and written communication skills were, by a large margin, the top skill set sought.[9] Among the top choices in two other surveys were teamwork, critical-thinking, analytical-reasoning, and oral and written communication skills.[10] In addition, as you will learn in later chapters, recruiters will closely examine your social media presence to learn about your communication skills and professionalism. Naturally, they will not hire candidates who write poorly or post inappropriate content online.[11]

OFFICE INSIDER

"Communicating clearly and effectively has NEVER been more important than it is today. Whether it's fair or not, life-changing critical judgments about you are being made based solely on your writing ability."

—Victor Urbach, management consultant

Office Insider based on Canavor, N. (2012). *Business writing in the digital age*. Los Angeles: Sage, p. 4.

Note: Small superscript numbers in the text announce information sources. Full citations begin on page 4 near the end of the book. This edition uses a modified APA reference format.

TECHIES WRITE TOO. Even in technical fields such as accounting and information technology, you will need strong communication skills. An Accountemps poll of 1,400 chief financial officers revealed that 75 percent said that verbal, written, and interpersonal skills are more important today than they were in the past.[12] Technical experts must be able to communicate with others and explain their work clearly, says an IBM systems specialist.[13] A survey of Web professionals showed that those with writing and copyediting skills were far less likely to have their jobs sent offshore.[14] Another survey conducted by the Society for Information Management revealed that network professionals ranked written and oral communication skills among the top five most desired skills for new hires.[15]

BUSINESSES GENERATE A WIDE RANGE OF MESSAGES. Be prepared to use a variety of media. In addition to occasional traditional letters and memos, expect to communicate with the public and within the company by email,* instant messaging and texting, company blogs, collaboration software such as wikis, and social media sites such as Facebook, Twitter, Instagram, and YouTube. You will learn more about workplace communication technology in Chapter 5.

---

*The usage standard in this book is *Canadian Oxford Dictionary*, Second Edition. Words such as *email* and *Web* are in a state of flux, and a single standard has yet to establish itself. The *Canadian Oxford Dictionary* continues to show conventional usage patterns.

FIGURE 1.1 | Professional Email Message

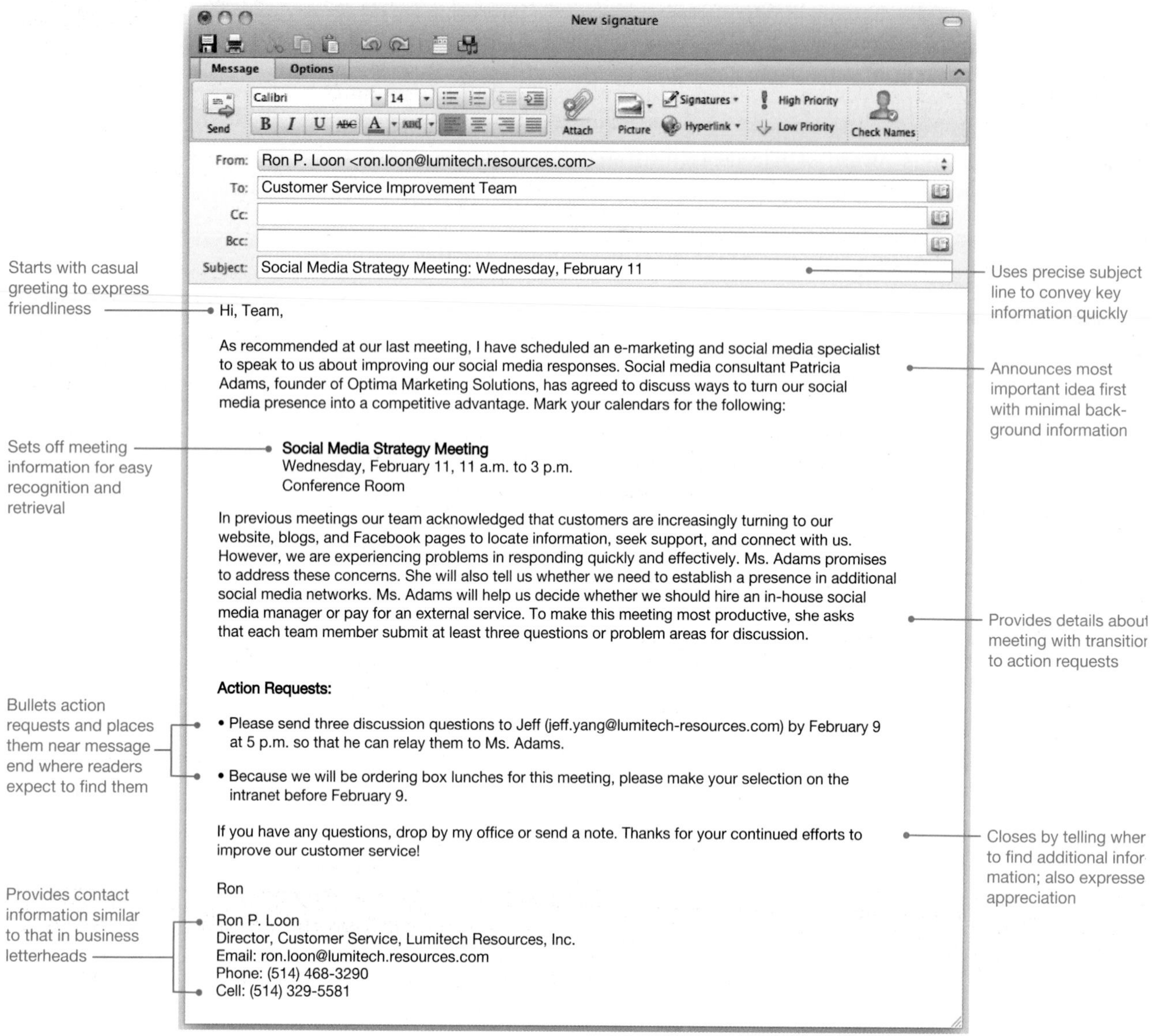

WRITING IS IN YOUR FUTURE. Regardless of career choice, you will probably be sending many digital messages, such as the email shown in Figure 1.1. In fact, email is "today's version of the business letter or interoffice memo."[16] Because email and other digital media have become important channels of communication in today's workplace, all digital business messages must be clear, concise, and professional. Notice that the message in Figure 1.1 is more professional than the quick email or text you might send socially. Learning to write professional digital messages will be an important part of this course.

1.1c What Employers Want: Professionalism

Your future employer will expect you to show professionalism and possess what are often referred to as "soft skills" in addition to your technical knowledge. Soft skills are essential career attributes that include the ability to communicate, work well with others, solve problems, make ethical decisions, and appreciate diversity.[17] Sometimes called employability skills or key competencies, these soft skills are desirable in all business sectors and job positions.[18]

Not every job seeker is aware of the employer's expectations. Some new hires have no idea that excessive absenteeism or tardiness is grounds for termination. Others are surprised to learn that they are expected to devote their full attention to their duties when on the job. One young man wanted to read novels when things got slow.[19] Some recent graduates had unrealistic expectations about their salaries and working hours.[20] Moreover, despite well-publicized warnings, some people continue to post racy photos and otherwise questionable content online, thus sabotaging their careers.[21]

Projecting and maintaining a professional image can make a real difference in helping you obtain the job of your dreams. Figure 1.2 reviews areas you will want to check to be sure you are projecting professionalism. You will learn more about soft skills and professionalism in Chapter 10.

OFFICE INSIDER

"The ability to write well is unquestionably a skill necessary for 21st-century success in college and the workplace.... Strong writing skills are essential."

—Gaston Caperton, former president, College Board

Office Insider based on Lewin, T. (2008, April 25). Informal Style of Electronic Messages Is Showing Up in Schoolwork, Study Finds. Retrieved from http://www.nytimes.com/2008/04/25/education/25writing.html?mcubz=1

1.1d How Your Education Drives Your Income

As tuition rises steeply and student debt mounts, you may wonder whether going to college or university is worthwhile. Yet the effort and money you invest in earning your degree or diploma will most likely pay off. Graduates earn more, suffer less unemployment, and can choose from a wider variety of career options than workers without a postsecondary education. Moreover, graduates have access to the highest-paying and fastest-growing careers, many of which require a degree.[22] As Figure 1.3 on page 8 shows, graduates with college diplomas and bachelor's degrees earn significantly higher salaries than high school diploma earners, and are much less likely to be unemployed.[23]

Writing is one aspect of education that is particularly well rewarded. A survey of employers confirms that soft skills such as communication ability can tip the scales in favour of one job applicant over another.[24] Your ticket to winning in a tight job market and launching a successful career is good communication skills.

FIGURE 1.2 | Projecting Professionalism When You Communicate

	UNPROFESSIONAL	PROFESSIONAL
Speech habits	Speaking in *uptalk*, a singsong speech pattern that has a rising inflection making sentences sound like questions; using *like* to fill in mindless chatter; substituting *go* for *said*; relying on slang; or letting profanity slip into your conversation.	Recognizing that your credibility can be seriously damaged by sounding uneducated, crude, or adolescent.
Email	Writing emails with incomplete sentences, misspelled words, exclamation points, IM slang, and senseless chatting. Sloppy, careless messages send a nonverbal message that you don't care or don't know what is correct.	Employers like to see subjects, verbs, and punctuation marks. They don't recognize IM abbreviations. Call it crazy, but they value conciseness and correct spelling, even in brief emails.
Internet	Using an email address such as *hotbabe@hotmail.com, supasnugglykitty@yahoo.com,* or *buffedguy@aol.com.*	An email address should include your name or a relevant, positive, businesslike expression. It should not sound cute or like a chat room nickname.
Voice mail	An outgoing message with strident background music, weird sounds, or a joke message.	An outgoing message that states your name or phone number and provides instructions for leaving a message.
Telephone	Soap operas, thunderous music, or a TV football game playing noisily in the background when you answer the phone.	A quiet background when you answer the telephone, especially if you are expecting a prospective employer's call.
Cellphones and smartphones	Taking or placing calls during business meetings or during conversations with fellow employees; raising your voice (cell yell) or engaging in cell calls that others must reluctantly overhear; using a PDA during meetings.	Turning off phone and message notification, both audible and vibrating, during meetings; using your cell only when conversations can be private.

FIGURE 1.3 | The Education Bonus: Higher Income, Lower Unemployment

EDUCATION	EARNINGS*	UNEMPLOYMENT RATE**
High School Graduate	$38,808	6.5%
Trades Certificate/Diploma	$46,176	6%
College/CEGEP	$46,176	5%
Bachelor's Degree or Above	$70,779	5%

*Average employment income, for graduates of Ontario postsecondary institutions, 25 to 64 year olds, by location of study, 2011.

**Unemployment rate for Ontarians 25 years of age and over, by educational attainment from Statistics Canada, Labour Force Survey.

Source: http://cou.on.ca/wp-content/uploads/2015/06/COU-University-Works-Report-2015.pdf

1.1e Meeting the Challenges of the Information-Age Workplace

Today's digital workplace is changing profoundly and rapidly. As a business communicator, you will be affected by many trends, including new communication tools such as social media, the "anytime, anywhere" office, and team-based projects. Other trends are flattened management hierarchies, global competition, and a renewed emphasis on ethics. The following overview reveals how communication skills are closely tied to your success in a constantly evolving networked workplace.

- **Rapidly changing communication technologies.** New communication technology is dramatically affecting the way workers interact. In our always-connected world, businesses exchange information by email, instant messaging, text messaging, smartphones, fax, voice mail, powerful laptop computers, and tablets. Satellite communications, wireless networking, teleconferencing, and videoconferencing help workers conduct meetings with associates around the world. Social media sites such as Facebook, Twitter, Instagram, and YouTube as well as blogs, wikis, forums, and peer-to-peer tools help businesspeople collect information, serve customers, and sell products and services. Figure 1.4 on pages 10–11 illustrates many new technologies you will encounter in today's workplace.
- **"Anytime, anywhere" and nonterritorial offices.** High-speed and wireless Internet access has freed millions of workers from nine-to-five jobs in brick-and-mortar offices. Flexible working arrangements allow them to work at home or on the road. Meet the "work shifter," a telecommuter or teleworker who largely remains outside the territorial office. The "anytime, anywhere" office requires only a mobile electronic device and a wireless connection.[25] Teleworkers now represent almost 20 percent of the working adult population.[26] To save on office real estate, some industries provide "nonterritorial" workspaces, or "hot desks." The first to arrive gets the best desk and the corner window.[27] At the same time, 24/7 availability has blurred the line between work and leisure, so some workers are always "on duty."
- **Self-directed work groups and virtual teams.** Teamwork has become a reality in business. Many companies have created cross-functional teams to empower employees and boost their involvement in decision making. You can expect to collaborate with a team in gathering information, finding and sharing solutions, implementing decisions, and managing conflict. You may even become part of a virtual team whose members are in remote locations. Increasingly, organizations are also forming ad hoc teams to solve particular problems. Such project-based teams disband once they have accomplished their objectives.[28] Moreover, parts of our future economy may rely on "free agents" who

will be hired on a project basis, a far cry from today's full-time and relatively steady jobs.

- **Flattened management hierarchies.** To better compete and to reduce expenses, businesses have for years been trimming layers of management. This means that as a front-line employee, you will have fewer managers. You will be making decisions and communicating them to customers, to fellow employees, and to executives.
- **Heightened global competition.** Because many Canadian companies continue to move beyond domestic markets, you may be interacting with people from many cultures. To be a successful business communicator, you will need to learn about other cultures. You will also need to develop intercultural skills including sensitivity, flexibility, patience, and tolerance.
- **Renewed emphasis on ethics.** Ethics is once again a hot topic in business. On the heels of the banking crisis and the collapse of the real estate market, a calamitous recession followed, caused largely, some say, by greed and ethical lapses. The government now requires greater accountability. As a result, businesses are eager to regain public trust by building ethical environments. Many have written ethical mission statements, installed hotlines, and appointed compliance officers to ensure strict adherence to their high standards and the law.

These trends mean that your communication skills will constantly be on display. Those who can write clear and concise messages contribute to efficient operations and can expect to be rewarded.

OFFICE INSIDER

"Rare is the new college hire who lacks skills involving Facebook, texting, or any other form of electronic communication. But face to face, many of these same people have difficulty reading interpersonal signals and communicating, especially in the increasingly multigenerational workplace. Most of the gaps I see are on the social, soft skills side."

—Cindy Warkentin, CIO, Maryland Automobile Insurance Fund

Office Insider based on King, J. (2009, September 21). Crossing the skills gap. *Computerworld*, p. 30. Retrieved from http://search.ebscohost.com

1.2 Developing Listening Skills

In an age that thrives on information and communication technology, listening is an important skill. However, by all accounts most of us are not very good listeners. Do you ever pretend to be listening when you are not? Do you know how to look attentive in class when your mind wanders far away? How about "tuning out" people when their ideas are boring or complex? Do you find it hard to focus on ideas when a speaker's clothing or mannerisms are unusual?

You probably answered *yes* to one or more of these questions because many of us have poor listening habits. In fact, some researchers suggest that we listen at only 25 to 50 percent efficiency. Such poor listening habits are costly in business, and they affect professional relationships. Messages must be rewritten, shipments reshipped, appointments rescheduled, contracts renegotiated, and directions restated.

To develop better listening skills, we must first recognize barriers that prevent effective listening. Then we need to focus on specific techniques for improving listening skills.

1.2a Overcoming Barriers to Effective Listening

As you have seen, bad habits and distractions can interfere with effective listening. Have any of the following barriers and distractions prevented you from hearing what has been said?

- **Physical barriers.** You cannot listen if you cannot hear what is being said. Physical impediments include hearing disabilities, poor acoustics, and noisy surroundings. It is also difficult to listen if you are ill, tired, or uncomfortable.
- **Psychological barriers.** Everyone brings to the communication process a unique set of cultural, ethical, and personal values. Each of us has an idea of what is right and what is important. If other ideas run counter to our preconceived thoughts, we tend to "tune out" speakers and thus fail to receive their messages.
- **Language problems.** Unfamiliar words can destroy the communication process because they lack meaning for the receiver. In addition, emotion-laden, or "charged," words can adversely affect listening. If the mention of words or phrases

OFFICE INSIDER

Did you know?

- *It is estimated that more than 50 percent of our work time is spent listening.*
- *Immediately following a ten-minute presentation, average people retain about half of what they hear and only one quarter after 48 hours.*
- *Sixty percent of all management problems are related to listening.*
- *We misinterpret, misunderstand, or change 70 to 90 percent of what we hear.*

—Valarie Washington, CEO, Think 6

Office Insider based on Washington, V. (n.d.). The high cost of poor listening. EzineArticles.com. Retrieved from http://ezinearticles.com/?The-High-Cost-of-Poor-Listening&id=163192

FIGURE 1.4 | Communication and Collaborative Technologies

Communication Technologies Reshaping the World of Work

Becoming familiar with modern communication technology can help you be successful on the job. Today's digital workplace is changing dramatically as a result of innovative software; social media networks; superfast broadband and wireless access; and numerous technologies that allow workers to share information, work from remote locations, and be more productive in or away from the office. With today's tools you can exchange ideas, solve problems, develop products, forecast performance, and complete team projects any time of the day or night anywhere in the world.

Cloud Computing and Web 2.0

Increasingly, applications and data are stored in remote locations online, in the cloud. *Cloud computing* means that businesses and individuals no longer need to maintain costly hardware and software in-house; instead, they can pay for digital storage space and software applications offered by providers online. Photo- and video-sharing sites such as 500 Pixels and Flickr keep your photos in the cloud. Similarly, Dropbox, a popular file-synchronization service, and Carbonite, an online backup provider, allow users to edit and sync files online independent of the device used to access them. Websites and Web applications have moved from "read only" to "read–write," thus enabling users to participate, collaborate, and network in unprecedented ways.

Telephony: VoIP

Savvy businesses are switching from traditional phone service to voice over Internet protocol (VoIP). This technology allows callers to communicate using a broadband Internet connection, thus eliminating long-distance and local telephone charges. Higher-end VoIP systems now support unified voice mail, email, click-to-call capabilities, and softphones (phones using computer networking). Free or low-cost Internet telephony sites, such as the popular Skype, are also increasingly used by businesses, although their sound and image quality is often uneven.

Voice Recognition

Computers equipped with voice recognition software enable users to dictate up to 160 words a minute with accurate transcription. Voice recognition is particularly helpful to disabled workers and to professionals with heavy dictation loads, such as physicians and attorneys. Users can create documents, enter data, compose and send emails, browse the Web, and control their desktops—all by voice. Smart devices can also execute tasks as directed through voice command apps.

Voice Conferencing

Telephone "bridges" join two or more callers from any location to share the same call. *Voice conferencing* (also called *audio conferencing, teleconferencing,* or just plain *conference calling*) enables people to collaborate by telephone. Communicators at both ends use enhanced speakerphones to talk and be heard simultaneously.

Open Offices

The widespread use of laptop computers, tablets, and other smart devices; wireless technology; and VoIP have led to more fluid, flexible, and open workspaces. Smaller computers and flat-screen monitors enable designers to save space with boomerang-shaped workstations and cockpit-style work surfaces rather than space-hogging corner work areas. Smaller breakout areas for impromptu meetings are taking over some cubicle space, and digital databases are replacing filing cabinets. Mobile technology allows workers to be fully connected and productive on the go.

Smart Mobile Devices and Digital Convergence

A new generation of lightweight, hand-held devices provide phone, email, Web browsing, and calendar options anywhere there is a cellular or Wi-Fi network. Tablets and smartphones such as Android devices, iPhones, and iPads now allow workers to tap into corporate databases and intranets from remote locations. They can check customers' files, complete orders, and send out receipts without returning to the office. Increasingly, businesses are issuing smartphones to their workforces, abandoning landlines completely. At the same time, the need for separate electronic gadgets is waning as digital smart devices are becoming multifunctional and highly capable. With streaming video on the Web, connectivity between TVs and computers, and networked mobile devices, technology is converging, consolidating into increasingly powerful devices. Many smart devices today are fully capable of replacing digital point-and-shoot still photography and video cameras. Mobile smart devices are also competing with TVs and computers for primacy.

Photos, top to bottom: Bangkokhappiness/Shutterstock; © Jochen Tack/Alamy; Asia Images Group/Getty Images; © photos.com; Hero Images/Getty Images; Oleksiy Maksymenko Photography/Alamy

Presence Technology

Presence technology makes it possible to locate and identify a computing device as soon as users connect to the network. This technology is an integral part of communication devices including smartphones, laptop computers, tablets, and GPS devices. Collaboration is possible wherever and whenever users are online.

Web Conferencing

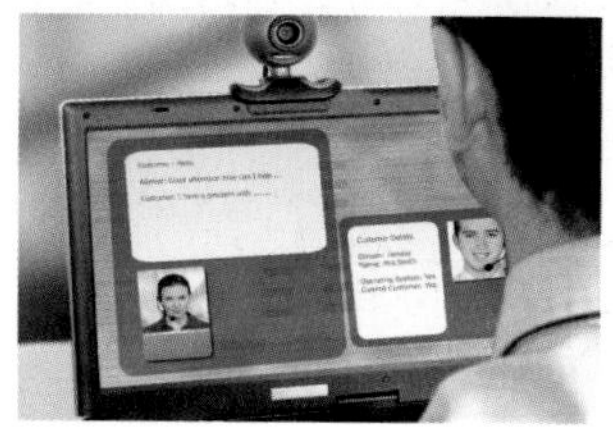

With services such as GoToMeeting, WebEx, and Microsoft Live Meeting, all you need is a computer or a smart device and an Internet connection to hold a meeting (*webinar*) with customers or colleagues in real time. Although the functions are constantly evolving, Web conferencing currently incorporates screen sharing, chats, slide presentations, text messaging, and application sharing.

Videoconferencing

Videoconferencing allows participants to meet in special conference rooms equipped with cameras and television screens. Individuals or groups see each other and interact in real time, although they may be far apart. Faster computers, rapid Internet connections, and better cameras now enable 2 to 200 participants to sit at their own computers or mobile devices and share applications, spreadsheets, presentations, and photos. The technology extends from the popular Internet applications Skype and FaceTime to sophisticated videoconferencing software that delivers HD-quality audio, video, and content sharing.

Electronic Presentations

Business presentations in PowerPoint, Keynote, SlideRocket, or Prezi can be projected from a laptop or tablet or posted online. Sophisticated presentations may include animation, sound effects, digital photos, video clips, or hyperlinks to Internet sites. In some industries, electronic slides ("decks") are replacing or supplementing traditional hard-copy reports.

Social Media

Never before in history have so many people been connected in online communities called social networks. Broadly speaking, the term *social media* describes technology that enables participants to connect and participate in social networks online. For example, tech-savvy companies and individuals send *tweets*, short messages of up to 140 characters, to other users to issue up-to-date news about their products, to link to their blogs and websites, or to announce events and promotions. The microblogging service Twitter also allows businesses to track what is being said about them and their products. Similarly, businesses use social networks such as Facebook, YouTube, and Instagram to build their brands and interact with their customers. Companies may also prospect for talent using social media networks.

Collaboration With Blogs, Podcasts, and Wikis

Businesses use *blogs* to keep customers and employees informed and to receive feedback. Company news can be posted, updated, and categorized for easy cross-referencing. An audio or video file streamed online or downloaded to a digital music player is called a *podcast*. A *wiki* such as Google Docs is a real-time website that allows multiple users to collaboratively create and edit pages. Information can get lost in emails, but a wiki provides an easy way to communicate and keep track of what has been said.

such as *bankruptcy* or *real estate meltdown* has an intense emotional impact, a listener may be unable to focus on the information that follows.

- **Nonverbal distractions.** Many of us find it hard to listen if a speaker is different from what we view as normal. Unusual clothing or speech mannerisms, body twitches, or a radical hairstyle can cause enough distraction to prevent us from hearing what the speaker has to say.
- **Thought speed.** Because we can process thoughts at least three times faster than speakers can say them, we can become bored and allow our minds to wander.
- **Faking attention.** Most of us have learned to look as if we are listening even when we are not. Such behaviour was perhaps necessary as part of our socialization. Faked attention, however, seriously threatens effective listening because it encourages the mind to engage in flights of unchecked fancy. Those who fake attention often find it hard to concentrate even when they want to.
- **Grandstanding.** Would you rather talk or listen? Naturally, most of us would rather talk. Because our own experiences and thoughts are most important to us, we grab the limelight in conversations. We sometimes fail to listen carefully because we are just waiting politely for the next pause so that we can have our turn to speak.

1.2b Building Powerful Listening Skills

You can reverse the harmful effects of poor habits by making a conscious effort to become an active listener. This means becoming involved. You can't sit back and hear whatever a lazy mind happens to receive. The following keys will help you become an active and effective listener:

- **Stop talking.** The first step to becoming a good listener is to stop talking. Let others explain their views. Learn to concentrate on what the speaker is saying, not on what your next comment will be.
- **Control your surroundings.** Whenever possible, remove competing sounds. Close windows or doors, turn off TVs and smartphones, and move away from loud people, noisy appliances, or engines. Choose a quiet time and place for listening.
- **Establish a receptive mindset.** Expect to learn something by listening. Strive for a positive and receptive frame of mind. If the message is complex, think of it as mental gymnastics. It is hard work but good exercise to stretch and expand the limits of your mind.
- **Keep an open mind.** We all sift through and filter information based on our own biases and values. For improved listening, discipline yourself to listen objectively. Be fair to the speaker. Hear what is really being said, not what you want to hear.
- **Listen for main points.** Heighten your concentration and satisfaction by looking for the speaker's central themes. Congratulate yourself when you find them!
- **Capitalize on lag time.** Make use of the quickness of your mind by reviewing the speaker's points. Anticipate what is coming next. Evaluate evidence the speaker has presented. Don't allow yourself to daydream. Try to guess what the speaker's next point will be.
- **Listen between the lines.** Focus both on what is spoken and what is unspoken. Listen for feelings as well as for facts.
- **Judge ideas, not appearances.** Concentrate on the content of the message, not on its delivery. Avoid being distracted by the speaker's looks, voice, or mannerisms.
- **Hold your fire.** Force yourself to listen to the speaker's entire argument or message before responding. Such restraint may enable you to understand the speaker's reasons and logic before you jump to false conclusions.
- **Take selective notes.** In some situations thoughtful note taking may be necessary to record important facts that must be recalled later. Select only the most important points so that the note-taking process does not interfere with your concentration on the speaker's total message.
- **Provide feedback.** Let the speaker know that you are listening. Nod your head and maintain eye contact. Ask relevant questions at appropriate times. Getting involved improves the communication process for both the speaker and the listener.

1.3 Learning Nonverbal Communication Skills

Understanding messages often involves more than merely listening to spoken words. Nonverbal cues, in fact, can speak louder than words. These cues include eye contact, facial expression, body movements, time, space, territory, and appearance. All of these nonverbal cues affect how a message is interpreted, or decoded, by the receiver.

WHAT IS NONVERBAL COMMUNICATION? Nonverbal communication includes all unwritten and unspoken messages, whether intended or not. These silent signals have a strong effect on receivers. However, understanding them is not simple. Does a downward glance indicate modesty? Fatigue? Does a constant stare reflect coldness? Dullness? Aggression? Do crossed arms mean a person is defensive or withdrawn, or just that the person is shivering?

WHAT IF WORDS AND NONVERBAL CUES CLASH? Messages are even harder to decipher when the verbal and nonverbal cues do not agree. What will you think if Scott says he is not angry, but he slams the door when he leaves? What if Alicia assures the hostess that the meal is excellent, but she eats very little? The nonverbal messages in these situations speak more loudly than the words. In fact, researchers believe that the bulk of any message we receive is nonverbal.

OFFICE INSIDER

"Listening is hard work. Unlike hearing, it demands total concentration. It is an active search for meaning, while hearing is passive."

—Alfonso Bucero, consultant and author

Office Insider based on Bucero, A. (2006, July). Listen and learn. *PM Network*. Retrieved from http://search.ebscohost.com

1.3a Your Body Sends Silent Messages

Psychologist and philosopher Paul Watzlawick claimed that we cannot not communicate.[29] In other words, it's impossible to not communicate. This means that every behaviour is sending a message even if we don't use words. The eyes, face, and body convey meaning without a single syllable being spoken.

EYE CONTACT. The eyes have been called the windows to the soul. Even if they don't reveal the soul, the eyes are often the best predictor of a speaker's true feelings. Most of us cannot look another person straight in the eyes and lie. As a result, in Canadian culture we tend to believe people who look directly at us. Sustained eye contact suggests trust and admiration; brief eye contact signals fear or stress. Good eye contact enables the message sender to see whether a receiver is paying attention, showing respect, responding favourably, or feeling distress. From the receiver's viewpoint, good eye contact reveals the speaker's sincerity, confidence, and truthfulness.

FACIAL EXPRESSION. The expression on a person's face can be almost as revealing of emotion as the eyes. Experts estimate that the human face can display over 250,000 expressions.[30] To hide their feelings, some people control these expressions and maintain "poker faces." Most of us, however, display our emotions openly. Raising or lowering the eyebrows, squinting the eyes, swallowing nervously, clenching the jaw, smiling broadly—these voluntary and involuntary facial expressions can add to or entirely replace verbal messages.

POSTURE AND GESTURES. A person's posture can convey anything from high status and self-confidence to shyness and submissiveness. Leaning toward a speaker suggests attentiveness and interest; pulling away or shrinking back denotes fear, distrust, anxiety, or disgust. Similarly, gestures can communicate entire thoughts via simple movements. However, the meanings of some of these movements differ across cultures. Unless you know local customs, such differences can get you into trouble. In Canada and the U.S., for example, forming the thumb and forefinger in a circle means everything is OK. But in parts of South America, the OK sign is obscene.

To take stock of the kinds of messages being sent by your body, ask a classmate to critique your use of eye contact, facial expressions, and body movements. Another way to analyze your nonverbal style is to record yourself making a presentation. Then study your performance. This way you can make sure your nonverbal cues send the same message as your words.

1.3b Time, Space, and Territory Send Silent Messages

In addition to nonverbal messages transmitted by your body, three external elements convey information in the communication process: time, space, and territory.

TIME. How we structure and use time tells observers about our personalities and attitudes. For example, when Prem Watsa, famous Canadian investor and philanthropist, gives a visitor a prolonged interview, he signals his respect for, interest in, and approval of the visitor or the topic to be discussed.

SPACE. How we order the space around us tells something about ourselves and our objectives. Whether the space is a bedroom, a dorm room, or an office, people reveal themselves in the design and grouping of their furniture. Generally, the more formal the arrangement, the more formal and closed the communication style. An executive who seats visitors in a row of chairs across from his desk sends a message of aloofness and a desire for separation. A team leader who arranges chairs informally in a circle rather than in straight rows conveys her desire for a more open exchange of ideas.

TERRITORY. Each of us has a certain area that we feel is our own territory, whether it is a specific spot or just the space around us. Your father may have a favourite chair in which he is most comfortable, a cook might not tolerate intruders in the kitchen, and veteran employees may feel that certain work areas and tools belong to them. We all maintain zones of privacy in which we feel comfortable. Figure 1.5 categorizes the four zones of social interaction among Americans, as formulated by anthropologist Edward T. Hall.[31] Notice that North Americans are a bit standoffish; only intimate friends and family may stand closer than about 45 centimetres. If someone violates that territory, North Americans feel uncomfortable and may step back to reestablish their space.

1.3c Appearance Sends Silent Messages

Much like the personal appearance of an individual, the physical appearance of a business document transmits immediate and important nonverbal messages. Ideally, these messages should be pleasing to the eye.

EYE APPEAL OF BUSINESS DOCUMENTS. The way an email, letter, memo, or report looks can have either a positive or a negative effect on the receiver. Sloppy emails send a nonverbal message that you are in a terrific hurry or that you do not care about the receiver. Envelopes—through their postage, stationery, and printing—can suggest that they are routine, important, or junk mail. Letters and reports can look neat, professional, well organized, and attractive—or just the opposite. In succeeding chapters you will learn how to create business documents that send positive nonverbal messages through their appearance, format, organization, readability, and correctness.

PERSONAL APPEARANCE. The way you look—your clothing, grooming, and posture—telegraphs an instant nonverbal message about you. Based on what they see, viewers make quick judgments about your status, credibility, personality, and potential. If you want to be considered professional, think about how you present yourself. One marketing manager said, "I'm young and pretty. It's hard enough to be taken seriously, and if I show up in jeans and a T-shirt, I don't stand a chance."[32]

WORKPLACE IN FOCUS

One of the latest fads is body art in the form of tattoos and piercings. Once seen primarily on bikers, prisoners, and sailors, inked images increasingly adorn the bodies of Canadians today. A Pew Research study found the highest incidence of tattoos in 18- to 29-year-olds (38 percent). Canadian HR site HRM Canada points out that at least one major Canadian employer has changed its dress code requiring employees to cover up all large tattoos.[33] *Conspicuous body art may make you feel distinctive and slightly daring, but how might it affect your career?*

Workplace in Focus based on Papiernik, R. L. (1995, October 30). Diversity demands new understanding. *Nation's Restaurant News, 29*(43), 54. Retrieved from http://www.nrn.com. © Cengage Learning

Hero Images/Getty Images

FIGURE 1.5 | Four Space Zones for Social Interaction

Zone	Distance	Uses
Intimate	0 to 45 cm (1.5 feet)	Reserved for members of the family and other loved ones.
Personal	45 to 122 cm (1.5 to 4 feet)	For talking with friends privately. The outer limit enables you to keep someone at arm's length.
Social	122 to 366 cm (4 to 12 feet)	For acquaintances, fellow workers, and strangers. Close enough for eye contact yet far enough for comfort.
Public	366 cm and over (12 feet and over)	For use in the classroom and for speeches before groups. Nonverbal cues become important as aids to communication.

1.3d Building Strong Nonverbal Skills

Nonverbal communication can outweigh words in the way it influences how others perceive us. You can harness the power of silent messages by reviewing the following tips for improving nonverbal communication skills:

- **Establish and maintain eye contact.** Remember that in Canada appropriate eye contact signals interest, attentiveness, strength, and credibility.
- **Use posture to show interest.** Encourage interaction by leaning forward, sitting or standing erect, and looking alert.
- **Reduce or eliminate physical barriers.** Move out from behind a desk or lectern; arrange meeting chairs in a circle.
- **Improve your decoding skills.** Watch facial expressions and body language to understand the complete verbal and nonverbal messages being communicated.

- **Probe for more information.** When you perceive nonverbal cues that contradict verbal meanings, politely seek additional cues (*I'm not sure I understand, Please tell me more about . . .* , or *Do you mean that . . .*).
- **Interpret nonverbal meanings in context.** Make nonverbal assessments only when you understand a situation or a culture.
- **Associate with people from diverse cultures.** Learn about other cultures to widen your knowledge and tolerance of intercultural nonverbal messages.
- **Appreciate the power of appearance.** Keep in mind that the appearance of your business documents, your business space, and yourself sends immediate positive or negative messages to receivers.
- **Observe yourself on video.** Ensure that your verbal and nonverbal messages are in sync by recording and evaluating yourself making a presentation.
- **Enlist friends and family.** Ask friends and family to monitor your conscious and unconscious body movements and gestures to help you become an effective communicator.

1.4 Recognizing How Culture Affects Communication

Global business, new communication technologies, the Internet, and social media span the world, shrinking distances. However, cultural differences still exist and can cause significant misunderstandings. Comprehending the verbal and nonverbal meanings of a message can be difficult even when communicators are from the same culture. When they come from different cultures, special sensitivity and skills are necessary.

Verbal and nonverbal meanings are even more difficult to interpret when people are from different cultures.

WHAT IS CULTURE? For our purposes, *culture* may be defined as "the complex system of values, traits, morals, and customs shared by a society, region, or country." Culture is a powerful operating force that moulds the way we think, behave, and communicate.

So that you will better understand your culture and how it contrasts with other cultures, we will describe five key dimensions of culture: context, individualism, time orientation, power distance, and communication style. The section closes with a look at the interaction between culture and social media.

1.4a Context

Context is probably the most important cultural dimension and also the most difficult to define. In a model developed by cultural anthropologist Edward T. Hall, context refers to the stimuli, environment, or ambience surrounding an event. Hall arranged cultures on a continuum, shown in Figure 1.6, from low to high in relation to context. This figure also summarizes key comparisons for today's business communicators.

Communicators in low-context cultures (such as those in North America, Scandinavia, and Germany) depend little on the context of a situation to convey their meaning. They assume that messages must be explicit, and listeners rely exclusively on the written or spoken word. Low-context cultures tend to be logical, analytical, and action oriented. Business communicators stress clearly articulated messages that they consider to be objective, professional, and efficient. Words are taken literally.

Communicators in high-context cultures (such as those in China, Japan, and Arab countries) assume that the listener does not need much background information.[34] Communicators in high-context cultures are more likely to be intuitive and contemplative. They may not take words literally. Instead, the meaning of a message may be implied from the social or physical setting, the relationship of the communicators, or nonverbal cues. For example, a Japanese communicator might say *yes*

FIGURE 1.6 | Comparing Low- and High-Context Cultures

Culture has a powerful effect on business communicators. The following observations point out selected differences. However, these are simplifications and practices within a given culture vary considerably. Moreover, as globalization expands, low- and high-context cultures are experiencing change and differences may be less pronounced.

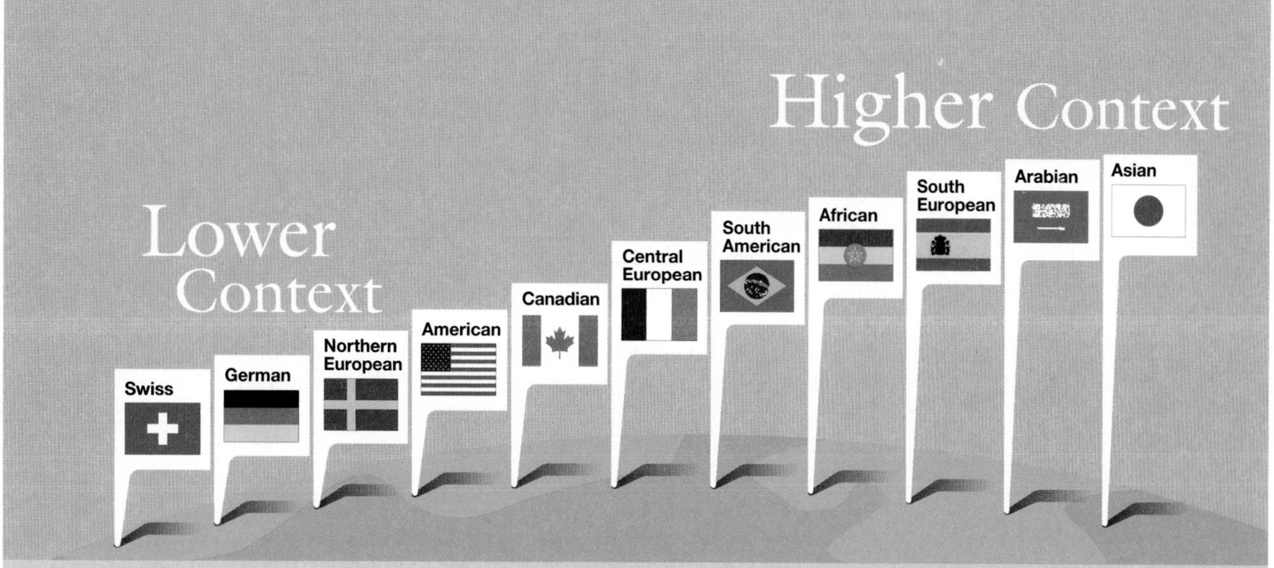

- Tend to prefer direct verbal interaction
- Tend to understand meaning at only one sociocultural level.
- Are generally less proficient in reading nonverbal cues
- Value individualism
- Rely more on logic
- Say *no* directly
- Communicate in highly structured, detailed messages with literal meanings
- Give authority to written information

- Tend to prefer indirect verbal interaction
- Tend to understand meanings embedded at many sociocultural levels
- Are generally more proficient in reading nonverbal cues
- Value group membership
- Rely more on context and feeling
- Talk around point, avoid saying *no*
- Communicate in sometimes simple, sometimes ambiguous messages
- Understand visual messages readily

when he really means *no*. From the context of the situation, his Japanese conversation partner would conclude whether *yes* really meant *yes* or whether it meant *no*. The context, tone, time taken to answer, facial expression, and body cues would convey the meaning of *yes*.[35] Communication cues are transmitted by posture, voice inflection, gestures, and facial expression.

Context means it's not just what's said or written that's important, but *how* it's said or written, as well as the posture, voice, and facial expression of the communicator.

1.4b Individualism

An attitude of independence and freedom from control characterizes individualism. Members of low-context cultures, particularly North Americans, tend to value individualism. They believe that initiative and self-assertion result in personal achievement. They believe in individual action and personal responsibility, and they desire much freedom in their personal lives.

Members of high-context cultures are more collectivist. They emphasize membership in organizations, groups, and teams; they encourage acceptance of group values, duties, and decisions. They typically resist independence because it fosters competition and confrontation instead of consensus. In group-oriented cultures such as those in many Asian societies, for example, self-assertion and individual decision making are discouraged. "The nail that sticks up gets pounded down" is

While Canadians value both individualism and collectivism, as well as personal responsibility, other cultures emphasize group- and team-oriented values.

a common Japanese saying.[36] Business decisions are often made by all who have competence in the matter under discussion. Similarly, in China managers also focus on the group rather than on the individual, preferring a consultative management style to an autocratic style.[37]

Many cultures, of course, are quite complex and cannot be characterized as totally individualistic or group oriented. For example, European Americans are generally quite individualistic, whereas African Americans are less so, and Latinos are closer to the group-centred dimension.[38]

1.4c Time Orientation

Canadians consider time a precious commodity. They correlate time with productivity, efficiency, and money. Keeping people waiting for business appointments is considered a waste of time and also rude.

In other cultures time may be perceived as an unlimited resource to be enjoyed. A Canadian businessperson, for example, was kept waiting two hours past a scheduled appointment time in South America. She wasn't offended, though, because she was familiar with South Americans' more relaxed concept of time.

The perceptions of time and how it is used are culturally learned. In some cultures time is perceived analytically. People account for every minute of the day. In other cultures time is holistic and viewed in larger chunks. People in Western cultures tend to be more analytical, scheduling appointments at 15- to 30-minute intervals. Those in Eastern cultures tend to be more holistic, planning fewer but longer meetings. People in one culture may look at time as formal and task oriented. In another culture time may be seen as an opportunity to develop interpersonal relationships.

Canadians equate time with productivity, efficiency, and money.

1.4d Power Distance

One important element of culture is power distance, a concept first introduced by influential social psychologist Geert Hofstede. The Power Distance Index measures how people in different societies cope with inequality; in other words, how they relate to more powerful individuals. In high power distance countries, subordinates expect formal hierarchies and embrace relatively authoritarian, paternalistic power relationships. In low power distance cultures, however, subordinates consider themselves as equals of their supervisors. They confidently voice opinions and participate in decision making. Relationships between high-powered individuals and people with little power tend to be more democratic, egalitarian, and informal in these cultures.

As you probably guessed, in Western cultures people are more relaxed about social status and the appearance of power.[39] Deference is not generally paid to individuals merely because of their wealth, position, seniority, or age. In many Asian cultures, however, these characteristics are important and must be respected. Walmart, facing many hurdles in breaking into the Japanese market, admits having had difficulty training local employees to speak up to their bosses. In the Japanese culture, lower-level employees do not question management. Deference and respect are paid to those in authority and power. Recognizing this cultural pattern, Marriott Hotel managers learned to avoid placing a lower-level Japanese employee on a floor above a higher-level executive from the same company.

1.4e Communication Style

People in low- and high-context cultures tend to communicate differently with words. To Canadians, for example, words are very important, especially in contracts and negotiations. People in high-context cultures, on the other hand, place more emphasis on the surrounding context than on the words describing a negotiation. A Greek may see a contract as a formal statement announcing the intention to build a business for the future. The Japanese may treat contracts as statements of intention, and they assume changes will be made as projects develop. Mexicans may treat contracts as artistic exercises of what might be accomplished in an ideal world. They do not necessarily expect contracts to apply consistently in the real world. An Arab may be insulted by merely mentioning a contract; a person's word is more binding.[40]

In communication style Canadians value straightforwardness, are suspicious of evasiveness, and distrust people who might have a "hidden agenda" or who "play their cards too close to the chest."[41] We also tend to be uncomfortable with silence and impatient with delays. Some Asian businesspeople have learned that the longer they drag out negotiations, the more concessions impatient Canadians are likely to make.

1.4f Intercultural Communication, Social Media, and Communication Technology

Canadians tend to be direct and to understand words literally.

Much has been made of the connectedness that social media and communication technology provide today. With minimal resources, communicators can reach out to larger and more varied audiences than ever before.

SOCIAL NETWORKING: BRIDGING CULTURAL DIVIDES? What we make of the potential for intercultural connectedness online is as much up to us as it would be at a dinner party where we don't know any of the other guests. "Digital media is an amplifier. It tends to make extroverts more extroverted and introverts more introverted," says Clay Shirky, a social media expert.[42] At the same time, the online environment may deepen feelings of isolation; it can make interpersonal contact more difficult because all contact is mediated electronically.[43]

In real life, as online, we instinctively tend to gravitate toward people who seem similar to us, believes Gaurav Mishra, a social media strategist: "[H]uman beings have a strong tendency to prefer the familiar, so we pay attention to people with a shared context and treat the rich Twitter public stream as background noise."[44] Twitter and other social media can boost intercultural communication; however, we must be willing to reach out across the boundaries that separate us. Yet, the public around the world is witnessing first-hand, real-time accounts of political unrest and natural and human-caused disasters on social media—often long before traditional media reporters arrive on the scene.

SOCIAL NETWORKING: ERASING CULTURAL DIFFERENCES? Despite the equalizing influence of globalization, regional and cultural differences persist, as

Cienpies Design/Shutterstock.com

Whether social media networks will allow business communicators to engage across cultures and bridge intercultural differences will depend on the users' attitudes and openness.

those who design media for markets in other countries know. Asian users may prefer muted pastel colours and anime-style graphics that North Americans would find unusual. Conversely, Korean and Japanese employees may balk at being compelled to post photos of themselves on company intranet pages. They opt for avatars or pictures of pets instead, possibly as an expression of personal modesty or due to expectations of privacy; whereas, North Americans believe photos promote cohesion and make them seem accessible.

It remains to be seen whether social networking will slowly erase many of the cultural differences present today or whether distinct national, even local, networks will emerge.[45]

1.5 Building Intercultural Workplace Skills

Being aware of your own culture and how it contrasts with others is a first step in learning intercultural skills. Another important step involves recognizing barriers to intercultural accommodation and striving to overcome them. The digital-age economy needs workers who can thrive on diverse teams and interact effectively with customers and clients at home and abroad.

1.5a Curbing Ethnocentrism and Stereotyping

Two barriers often hamper the process of successfully understanding and interacting with people from other cultures: ethnocentrism and stereotyping. These barriers, however, can be overcome by developing tolerance, a powerful and effective aid to communication.

ETHNOCENTRISM. The belief in the superiority of one's own culture is known as *ethnocentrism.* This natural attitude is found in all cultures. Ethnocentrism causes us to judge others by our own values. If you were raised in Canada, values such as punctuality and directness described previously probably seem "right" to you, and you may wonder why the rest of the world doesn't function in the same sensible fashion.

STEREOTYPES. Our perceptions of other cultures sometimes cause us to form stereotypes about groups of people. A *stereotype* is an oversimplified perception of a behavioural pattern or characteristic applied to entire groups. For example, the Swiss are hardworking, efficient, and neat; Germans are formal, reserved, and blunt; Americans are loud, friendly, and impatient; Canadians are polite, trusting, and tolerant; Asians are gracious, humble, and inscrutable. These attitudes may or may not accurately describe cultural norms. Look beneath surface stereotypes and labels to discover individual personal qualities.

Ethnocentrism is the belief in the superiority of one's own culture and group.

TOLERANCE. As global markets expand and as our society becomes increasingly multiethnic, tolerance is critical. *Tolerance* here means learning about and appreciating beliefs and practices different from our own. It means being open-minded and receptive to new experiences. One of the best ways to develop tolerance is to practise *empathy*, defined as trying to see the world through another's eyes. It means being less judgmental and more eager to seek common ground.

A stereotype is an oversimplified perception of a behavioural pattern applied to entire groups.

For example, BMW Group and the United Nations Alliance of Civilizations jointly award projects around the world that promote international understanding and the overcoming of religious and cultural boundaries. A pair of recent finalists, a Palestinian school principal and an Israeli school principal, joined forces to counter the political turmoil in Jerusalem."[46] Students at both schools collaborate on environmental protection activities and study each other's languages. Getting along well with others is always a good policy, but doubly so in the workplace. Some job

Developing intercultural tolerance means practising empathy, being nonjudgmental, and being patient.

descriptions now include statements such as *Must be able to interact with ethnically diverse workforce.*

1.5b Successful Spoken Communication With Intercultural Audiences

When you have a conversation with someone from another culture, you can reduce misunderstandings by following these tips:

- **Use simple English.** Speak in short sentences (under 20 words) with familiar, short words. Eliminate puns, sports and military references, slang, and jargon (special business terms). Be especially alert to idiomatic expressions that can't be translated, such as *burn the midnight oil* and *throw a curve ball.*
- **Speak slowly and enunciate clearly.** Avoid fast speech, but don't raise your voice. Overpunctuate with pauses and full stops. Always write numbers for all to see.
- **Encourage accurate feedback.** Ask probing questions, and encourage the listener to paraphrase what you say. Don't assume that a *yes*, a nod, or a smile indicates comprehension or assent.
- **Check frequently for comprehension.** Avoid waiting until the end of a long explanation to request feedback. Instead, make one point at a time, pausing to check for comprehension. Don't proceed to B until A has been grasped.
- **Observe eye messages.** Be alert to a glazed expression or wandering eyes. These tell you the listener is lost.
- **Accept blame.** If a misunderstanding results, graciously accept the responsibility for not making your meaning clear.
- **Listen without interrupting.** Curb your desire to finish sentences or to fill out ideas for the speaker. Keep in mind that North Americans abroad are often accused of listening too little and talking too much.
- **Smile when appropriate.** The smile is often considered the single most understood and most useful form of communication. In some cultures, however, excessive smiling may seem insincere.[47]
- **Follow up in writing.** After conversations or oral negotiations, confirm the results and agreements with written messages—if necessary, in the local language.

1.5c Successful Written Communication With Intercultural Audiences

When you write to someone from a different culture, you can improve your chances of being understood by following these suggestions:

- **Consider local styles and conventions.** Learn how documents are formatted and how letters are addressed and developed in the intended reader's country. Decide whether to use your organization's preferred format or adjust to local styles. Observe titles and rank. Be polite.
- **Hire a translator.** Engage a professional translator if (a) your document is important, (b) your document will be distributed to many readers, or (c) you must be persuasive.
- **Use short sentences and short paragraphs.** Sentences with fewer than 20 words and paragraphs with fewer than 8 lines are most readable.
- **Avoid ambiguous wording.** Include relative pronouns (*that, which, who*) for clarity in introducing clauses. Stay away from contractions (especially ones such as *here's the problem*). Avoid idioms (*once in a blue moon*), slang (*my presentation really bombed*), acronyms (*ASAP* for *as soon as possible*), abbreviations (*DBA* for *doing business as*), jargon (*ROI, bottom line*), and sports references (*play ball, slam dunk*). Use action-specific verbs (*buy a printer* rather than *get a printer*).

OFFICE INSIDER

"Not everyone can travel, but since we live and work in a global economy, we should expect undergraduate programs to prepare students with a fundamental understanding of the cultural differences, historical perspectives, and common business practices employed by all the major countries within it."

—Craig Cuyar, CIO, Omnicom

Office Insider based on King, J. (2009, September 21). Crossing the skills gap. *Computerworld*, p. 32. Retrieved from http://search.ebscohost.com

- **Cite numbers carefully. In international trade learn and use the metric system.** In citing numbers, use figures (*15*) instead of spelling them out (*fifteen*). Always convert dollar figures into local currency. Spell out the month when writing dates. In North America, for example, *March 5, 2018*, might be written as *3/5/18*, whereas in Europe the same date might appear as *5.3.18*.

1.5d Globalization and Workplace Diversity

While Canadian companies like Shopify are expanding global operations and adapting to a variety of emerging markets, the domestic workforce is also becoming more diverse. This diversity has many dimensions—race, ethnicity, age, religion, gender, national origin, physical ability, sexual orientation, and other qualities.

No longer will the workplace be predominantly male or Caucasian. According to Douglas Quan of the *National Post*, "In 2011, the percentage of visible minorities was 19.1 percent, according to Statistics Canada. By 2031, that number is expected to grow to 30.6 percent, with South Asian and Chinese immigrants driving much that growth. Vancouver and Toronto are expected to become 'majority-minority' cities with three out of five people—60 percent—belonging to a visible minority group by then."*[48] In the near future, women will comprise nearly 50 percent of the workforce, and the number of workers aged 55 and older will grow to 20 percent.[49]

What do all these changes mean for you? Simply put, your job will require you to interact with colleagues and customers with backgrounds from around the world. You will need to cooperate with individuals and teams. What's more, your coworkers may differ from you in race, ethnicity, gender, age, and other ways.

1.5e Benefits of a Diverse Workforce

As society and the workforce become more diverse, successful communication among various identity groups brings distinct advantages. Customers want to deal with companies that respect their values. They are more likely to say, "If you are a company whose ads do not include me, or whose workforce does not include me, I will not buy from you."

A diverse staff is better able to respond to the increasingly diverse customer base in local and world markets. "We find that more and more of our clients are demanding that our partners and staff—involved in securing new business as well as delivering the work—reflect diversity within their organizations," said an employee at accounting giant PricewaterhouseCoopers.[50] Theo Fletcher, a vice president at IBM, agrees: "It is important that we have a supply base that looks like our employee base and that looks like the market we are trying to attract."[51]

Most important, though, is the growing realization among organizations that diversity is a critical bottom-line business strategy to improve employee relationships and to increase productivity. Developing a diverse staff that can work together cooperatively is one of the biggest challenges facing business organizations today.

OFFICE INSIDER

"I need to find the best set of skills to do the assignment rather than someone who looks like me, acts like me, or went to the same school or fits into the old mould."

—Ken Henderson, former managing director of IMCOR, a national executive search firm

Office Insider based on Papiernik, R. L. (1995, October 30). Diversity demands new understanding. *Nation's Restaurant News, 29*(43), 54. Retrieved from http://www.nrn.com

1.5f Tips for Communicating With Diverse Audiences on the Job

Harmony and acceptance do not happen automatically when people who are dissimilar work together. This means that companies must commit to diversity. Harnessed effectively, diversity can enhance productivity and propel a company to success. Mismanaged, it can become a drain on a company's time and resources. The following suggestions can help you find ways to improve communication and interaction:

- **Seek training.** Look upon diversity as an opportunity, not a threat. Intercultural communication, team building, and conflict resolution are skills that can be learned in diversity training programs.

- **Understand the value of differences.** Diversity makes an organization innovative and creative. Sameness fosters an absence of critical thinking called *groupthink*. Real-world examples like the Lac-Mégantic derailment disaster suggest that groupthink may prevent alternatives from being considered. Even smart people working collectively can make dumb decisions if they do not see different perspectives.[52]
- **Learn about your cultural self.** Begin to think of yourself as a product of your culture, and understand that your culture is just one among many. Try to look at yourself from the outside. Do you see any reflex reactions and automatic thought patterns that are a result of your upbringing? These may be invisible to you until challenged by people who are different from you. Be sure to keep what works and yet be ready to adapt as your environment changes.
- **Make fewer assumptions.** Be careful of seemingly insignificant, innocent workplace assumptions. For example, don't assume that everyone wants to observe the holidays with a Christmas party and a decorated tree. Moreover, in workplace discussions don't assume anything about others' sexual orientations or attitudes toward marriage. For invitations, avoid phrases such as *managers and their wives*. Using *spouses* or *partners* is more inclusive. Valuing diversity means making fewer assumptions that everyone is like you or wants to be like you.
- **Build on similarities.** Look for areas in which you and others not like you can agree or at least share opinions. Be prepared to consider issues from many perspectives, all of which may be valid. Although you can always find differences, it is much harder to find similarities. Look for common ground in shared experiences, mutual goals, and similar values.[53] Concentrate on your objective even when you may disagree on how to reach it.

SUMMARY OF LEARNING OBJECTIVES

1.1 Describe how solid communication skills will improve your career prospects.

- Employers hire and promote job candidates who have excellent communication skills; writing skills make or break careers.
- Because workers interact more than ever using communication technology, even technical fields require communication skills.
- New hires and other employees must project a professional image and possess soft skills.
- Job challenges in the information age include changing communication technologies, mobile 24/7 offices, flatter management, an emphasis on teams, and global competition.

1.2 Confront barriers to effective listening.

- Most of us are poor listeners; we can learn active listening by removing physical and psychological barriers, overlooking language problems, and eliminating distractions.
- A fast processing speed allows us to let our minds wander; we fake attention and prefer to talk than to listen.
- Poor listening can be overcome as long as we stop talking, focus fully on others, control distractions, keep an open mind, and listen for the speaker's main ideas.
- Capitalizing on lag time, listening between the lines, judging ideas instead of appearances, taking good notes, and providing feedback are other methods for building listening skills.

1.3 Explain the importance of nonverbal communication.

- Be aware of nonverbal cues such as eye contact, facial expression, and posture that send silent, highly believable messages.
- Understand that how you use time, space, and territory is interpreted by the receiver, who also "reads" the eye appeal of your business documents and your personal appearance.
- Build solid nonverbal skills by keeping eye contact, maintaining good posture, reducing physical barriers, improving your decoding skills, and probing for more information.
- Interpret nonverbal meanings in context, learn about other cultures, and understand the impact of appearance—of documents, your office space, and yourself.

1.4 Understand five common dimensions of culture and how they affect communication.

- Culture is a complex system of values, traits, and customs shared by a society; culture moulds the way we think, behave, and communicate both offline and online.
- Culture can be described using key dimensions such as context, individualism, time orientation, power distance, and communication style.
- Today's communicators need to be aware of low- and high-context cultures, individualistic versus collectivist societies, differing attitudes toward time, clashing perceptions of power, and varying reliance on the written word.
- Whether social media and technology can bridge cultural divides and erase differences will depend on the users as much as it would among strangers who meet at a dinner party.

1.5 Use intercultural communication strategies to prevent miscommunication.

- Beware of ethnocentrism and stereotyping; instead, embrace tolerance and keep an open mind.
- When communicating orally, use simple English, speak slowly, check for comprehension, observe eye messages, accept blame, don't interrupt, smile, and follow up in writing.
- When writing, consider local styles, hire a translator, use short sentences, avoid ambiguous wording, and cite numbers carefully.
- As the domestic workforce becomes more diverse, appreciate diversity as a critical business strategy.
- To communicate well with diverse audiences, seek training, understand the value of diversity, learn about your own culture, make fewer assumptions, and look for similarities.

CHAPTER REVIEW

1. Based on what you have learned in this chapter, describe the kind of work environment you can expect to enter when you graduate. (Obj. 1)
2. Why are writing skills more important in today's workplace than ever before? (Obj. 1)
3. List six trends in the information-age workplace that affect business communicators. Be prepared to discuss how they might affect you in your future career. (Obj. 1)
4. List bad habits and distractions that can act as barriers to effective listening. (Obj. 2)
5. List 11 techniques for improving your listening skills. Be prepared to discuss each. (Obj. 2)
6. What is nonverbal communication, and are nonverbal cues easy to read? (Obj. 3)
7. How do we send messages to others without speaking? (Obj. 3)
8. What is culture, and what are five key dimensions that can be used to describe it? (Obj. 4)
9. List seven or more suggestions for enhancing comprehension when you are talking with non-native speakers of English. Be prepared to discuss each. (Obj. 5)

CRITICAL THINKING

1. Do you consider your daily texting, Facebook updates, blog entries, emails, and other informal writing to be "real writing"? How might such writing differ from the writing done in business? (Obj. 1)
2. Why do executives and managers spend more time listening than do workers? (Obj. 2)
3. What arguments could you give for or against the idea that body language is a science with principles that can be interpreted accurately by specialists? (Obj. 3)
4. Consider potential culture clashes in typical business situations. Imagine that businesspeople from a high-context culture, say, China, meet their counterparts from a low-context culture, Canada, for the first time to negotiate and sign a manufacturing contract. What could go wrong? How about conflicting perceptions of time? (Obj. 4)
5. A stereotype is an oversimplified perception of a behavioural pattern or characteristic applied to entire groups. For example, Germans are formal, reserved, and blunt; Americans are loud, friendly, and impatient; Asians are gracious, humble, and inscrutable. In what way are such stereotypes harmless or harmful? (Obj. 5)

ACTIVITIES AND CASES

1.1 INTRODUCE YOURSELF (OBJ. 1)

Your instructor wants to know more about you, your motivation for taking this course, your career goals, and your writing skills.

Your Task. Send an email or write a memo of introduction to your instructor. See Chapter 5 for formats and tips on drafting emails. In your message include the following:

a. Your reasons for taking this class
b. Your career goals (both short term and long term)
c. A brief description of your employment, if any, and your favourite activities
d. An evaluation and discussion of your current communication skills, including your strengths and weaknesses

For online classes, write a message of introduction about yourself with the preceding information. Post your message (memo or letter) to your discussion board. Read and comment on the posts of other students. Think about how people in virtual teams must learn about each other through online messages.

Alternatively, your instructors may assign this task as a concise individual voice mail message to establish your telephone etiquette and speaking skills.

1.2 SMALL-GROUP PRESENTATION: INTRODUCE EACH OTHER (OBJS. 1, 2)

Many organizations today use teams to accomplish their goals. To help you develop speaking, listening, and teamwork skills, your instructor may assign team projects. One of the first jobs in any team is selecting members and becoming acquainted.

Your Task. Your instructor will divide your class into small groups or teams. At your instructor's direction, either (a) interview another group member and introduce that person to the group or (b) introduce yourself to the group. Think of this as an informal interview for a team assignment or for a job. You will want to make notes from which to speak. Your introduction should include information such as the following:

a. Where did you grow up?
b. What work and extracurricular activities have you engaged in?
c. What are your interests and talents? What are you good at doing?
d. What have you achieved?
e. How familiar are you with various computer technologies?
f. What are your professional and personal goals? Where do you expect to be five years from now?

To develop listening skills, practise the listening techniques discussed in this chapter and take notes when other students are presenting. In addition to mentioning details about each speaker, be prepared to discuss three important facts about each speaker.

1.3 REMEMBERING A TIME WHEN SOMEONE DIDN'T LISTEN TO YOU (OBJ. 2)

Think of a time when you felt that someone didn't listen to you—for example, on the job, at home, at the doctor's office, or at a store where you shop. Your instructor will split the class into pairs of speakers and listeners. The speakers will share their stories. The listeners must try to recognize two things: (a) what the poor listener in the story did that demonstrated nonlistening and (b) what impact this had on the speaker's feelings. The speakers and listeners then reverse roles. After this second round, the class compares notes to debrief. All ideas are collected to identify patterns of nonlistening behaviour and its negative impact on the speakers.

Your Task. In pairs or individually, identify behaviour that would reverse what happened in the stories told in class. Based on your insights, write an email or memo that describes several principles of good listening illustrated with brief examples. You could end by concisely telling of an encounter that shows ideal active listening.

Visit **MindTap** for a variety of videos, additional exercises, activities, and quizzes to support your learning.

UNIT 02

The Business Writing Process

CHAPTER 2
Planning Your Message

CHAPTER 3
Organizing and Drafting Your Message

CHAPTER 4
Revising Your Message

Chris Schmidt/istockphoto

COMMUNICATION TECHNOLOGY IN THE NEWS

Editorial: STM needs to work on communication

The 10-hour service disruption on the Orange Line on Saturday was the first test of the Société de transport de Montréal's new proactive strategy for communicating with passengers when the métro goes down.

To the public at large, it seemed like an abysmal failure.

The promise that service would be restored within 30 minutes stretched longer and longer before the time frame was finally classified as being undetermined. There was conflicting information about how much of the Orange Line was down. Stranded passengers who stuck around hoping the métro would resume faced long waits and lengthy lineups for shuttle buses.

All the while, transit users waited for the STM to make good on chairman Philippe Schnobb's recent pledge to update passengers in real time about the nature of problems when they arise.

For the full explanation, transit users had to wait until Monday. Then the STM held a technical briefing about the incident with pictures of damaged equipment.

Monday's PR blitz included statistics about the STM's exemplary service record (12 stoppages per million kilometres compared to the world average of 22) as well as how many halts can be attributed to métro clientele (43 percent). Fair enough. But Coderre admonishing those who dared question the state of public transit, be they political opponents or frustrated métro riders, was unhelpful. Suggesting problems are being blown out of proportion does nothing for those left in the lurch.

Saturday's debacle was a perfect storm for the STM. It happened on a weekend, which meant staff had to be called in to work. And the technical issue itself was one the STM had never experienced before. In fact, the reason for the damage to the contact shoes on both the new AZUR trains and the legacy MR-73 vehicles remains a mystery.

Circumstances surely hampered efforts to communicate more effectively.

But the bottom line is the STM still has work to do. This includes equipping more stations with Wi-Fi so métro riders can access reliable information, ensuring the messages it broadcasts to the public are timely and accurate, and continuing the transparency it has just shown itself capable of.

Summarize the article you've just read in a two- to three-sentence paragraph. Answer the following questions, either on your own or in a small group. Be prepared to give your answers in a short presentation or in an email to your instructor.

QUESTIONS:

1. How does what you've learned in this article change your perception of what business communication is or is not?
2. How might what you've learned in this article be useful in changing your own school or workplace communication?
3. Come up with pro and con arguments for the following debate/discussion topic: In the digital age of communication when people expect timely and accurate communication, is an organization that offers services to the public being unethical or negligent if it doesn't offer timely and accurate communication? Feel free to provide other examples you've experienced.

CHAPTER

2

Planning Your Message

OBJECTIVES

After studying this chapter, you should be able to

2.1 Explain the steps in the communication process.

2.2 Recognize the goals and process of business writing.

2.3 Know the purpose of a message, anticipate its audience, and select the best communication channel for it.

2.4 Incorporate audience adaptation techniques.

2.5 Use additional expert writing techniques.

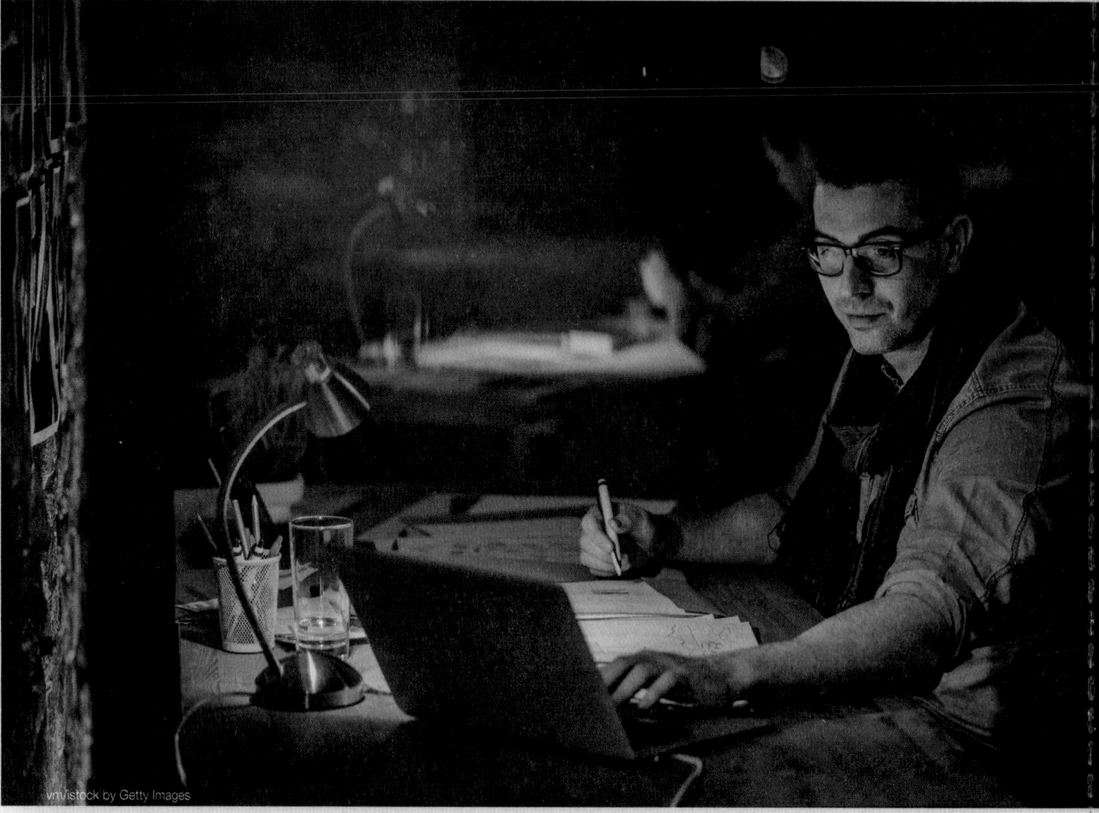
vm/iStock by Getty Images

2.1 Understanding the Communication Process

The digital revolution has profoundly changed the way we live our lives, do business, and communicate. People are sending more and more messages, and they are using new media as the world becomes increasingly interconnected. However, even as we become accustomed to new channels like email, messaging, Facebook, Twitter, and other social media, the nature of communication remains largely unchanged. No matter how we create or send our messages, the communication process remains a human process of interaction, in which an idea is shared and reacted to.

In its simplest form, *communication* may be defined as "the transmission of information and meaning from a sender to a receiver." The crucial element in this definition is *meaning*. The process is successful once the receiver understands an idea as the sender intended it. The process is shown as a diagram in in Figure 2.1, but keep in mind that what the diagram doesn't show is that at each "step" of the process, "noise" such as distraction, boredom, or frustration can get in the way and cause miscommunication.

2.1a Sender Has Idea

The communication process begins when a sender has an idea, like a request or something to share. The form of the idea may be influenced by complex factors surrounding the sender. These factors may include mood, frame of reference, background, culture, and physical makeup, as well as the context of the situation and many other factors.

2.1b Sender Encodes Idea

The next step in the process is *encoding*. This means converting the idea into words or gestures to convey meaning: mostly this is done through words, though sometimes it's done through images. Recognizing how easy it is to be misunderstood, skilled communicators choose familiar, concrete words. In choosing proper words and symbols, senders must be alert to the receiver's communication skills, attitudes, background, experiences, and culture. Including a smiley face in an email to stockholders may turn them off.

2.1c Sender Selects Channel and Transmits Message

The medium over which the message travels is the *channel*. Messages may be delivered by email, text, smartphone, letter, memo, report, announcement, image, conversation, fax, Web page, or some other channel. Today's messages are increasingly carried over digital networks, which may cause distraction and a breakdown in communication. Receivers may be overloaded with incoming messages or unable to receive messages clearly on their devices. Anything that interrupts the transmission of a message in the communication process is called *noise*. Channel noise may range

FIGURE 2.1 | The Communication Process

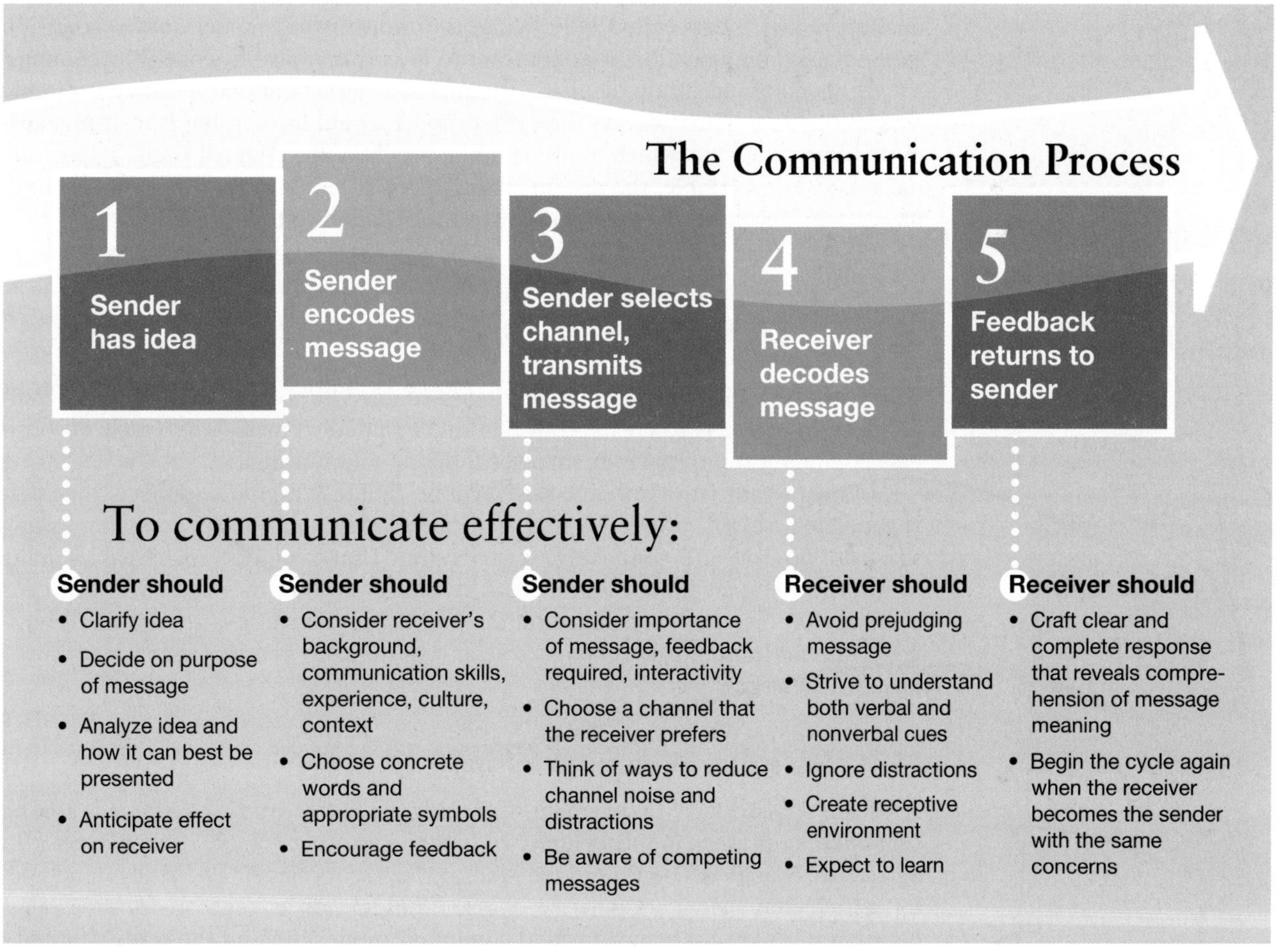

from a weak Internet signal to sloppy formatting and typos in emails. Noise may even include the annoyance a receiver feels when the sender chooses an improper channel for transmission or when the receiver is overloaded with messages and information.

2.1d Receiver Decodes Message

The individual for whom the sender's message is intended is the *receiver*. Decoding takes place when the receiver reads or listens to—that is, internalizes—the sender's message. Only when the receiver understands the meaning intended by the sender—that is, successfully decodes the message—does communication take place. Such success is often difficult to achieve because of a number of barriers that block the process.

2.1e Feedback Returns to Sender

The receiver usually creates *feedback*, a vital part of the communication process. Sometimes lack of feedback—that is, ignoring a message—is its own type of feedback (though not a productive type). Feedback helps the sender know that the message was received and understood. Senders can encourage feedback by asking questions such as *Am I making myself clear?* and *Is there anything you don't understand?* Senders can further improve feedback by timing the delivery appropriately and by providing only as much information as the receiver can handle. Receivers improve the communication process by providing clear and complete feedback. In the business world, one of the best ways to advance understanding is to paraphrase the sender's message with comments such as *Just to confirm what you're requesting....*

The communication process theorized above is sometimes known as the "transmission model" (Lasswell, 1948). While the transmission model does a good job explaining communication, it's important to note that it also has one shortcoming.[1]

Other communication theorists (McLuhan, 1964) claim that meaning isn't only transmitted in a linear way, as the earlier model would have it, but is instead transmitted in a "field" in which multiple inputs, such as the channel itself, help create meaning.[2] For example, the instantaneous speed of texting could be seen as eliminating the "decoding" step—receivers tend to respond to texts instantly.

2.2 Using the 3-×-3 Writing Process as a Guide

Today's new media and digital technologies enable you to choose from many communication channels to create, transmit, and respond to messages. Nearly all business communication, however, involves thinking and writing.

Many of your workplace messages will be digital. A *digital message* is "one that is generated, stored, processed, and transmitted electronically by computers using strings of positive and nonpositive binary code." That definition encompasses many forms, including email, Facebook posts, tweets, and other messages. We will focus primarily on messages exchanged on the job. Because writing is central to all business communication, this chapter presents a systematic plan for preparing written business messages.

2.2a Defining Business Writing Goals

A recent Canadian Management Centre/Ipsos Reid study conducted among Canadian employees indicates that "only 42 percent of Canadian employees . . . agree that change is communicated well in their workplace." The study concludes by stating that managers must recognize "building an engaged workforce relies heavily on leadership behaviour and communication."[3] Behind the study's findings lies a sometimes-unacknowledged reality about communication: it's not just *what* you want to say that's important; it's also *how* your audience will react upon seeing/reading/hearing your communication. In other words, all workplace communicators need to think about their audience.

One thing you should immediately recognize about business writing is that it differs from other writing you have done. Business writing is different than high school writing; it also differs from personal texts you may exchange with your friends and family. These messages enable you to stay connected and express your feelings. In the workplace, however, you will want your writing to be:

- **Purposeful.** You should write only to solve problems and convey information.
- **Economical.** You should present ideas clearly but concisely. Length is not rewarded.
- **Audience oriented.** You should solve problems and convey information with the receiver's perspective—not your own—in mind.

These distinctions ease your task. You won't be searching your imagination for creative topic ideas or stretching your ideas to make them appear longer. Get over the notion that longer is better. Whether you are presenting your message in an email, in a business report, or at a wiki site, conciseness and clarity are what count in business.

The ability to prepare purposeful, concise, and audience-centred messages doesn't come naturally. Very few people, especially beginners, can sit down and compose an effective email, letter, or report without training. However, following a systematic process, studying model messages, and practising the craft can make you a successful business writer or speaker.

OFFICE INSIDER

"Writing in the** Harvard Business Review, **David Silverman blasts 'an educational system that rewards length over clarity.' Students learn to overwrite, he says, in hopes that at least some of their sentences 'hit the mark.' Once on the job, they continue to act as if they were paid by the word, a perception that must be unlearned."

—David Silverman, businessman, entrepreneur, and blogger

Office Insider from February 2009 *Harvard Business Review* Digital article, "Why Is Business Writing So Bad?" by David Silverman. https://hbr.org/2009/02/why-is-business-writing-so-bad

2.2b Introducing the 3-×-3 Writing Process

Regardless of what you are writing, the process will be easier if you follow a systematic plan. The 3-×-3 writing process breaks the entire task into three phases: *prewriting*, *drafting*, and *revising*, as shown in Figure 2.2.

Following a systematic process helps beginning writers create effective messages and presentations.

To illustrate the writing process, let's say that you own a successful local Tim Hortons franchise. At rush times, you face a problem. Customers complain about the chaotic multiple waiting lines to approach the service counter. You once saw two customers nearly get into a fist fight over cutting into a line. What's more, customers often are looking for ways to improve their positions in line and fail to examine the menu. Then they are undecided when their turn arrives. You've also taken note of your competitor's (McDonald's) move into self-ordering via touch screen. You want to convince other franchise owners that a single-line (serpentine) system with touch screens would work better. You want to present a serious argument that they will remember and be willing to act on when they gather for their next district meeting. You decide to send a persuasive email.

The writing process has three parts: prewriting, writing, and revising.

PREWRITING. The first phase of the writing process involves analyzing the audience and your purpose for writing. The audience for your message will be other franchise owners, some highly educated and others not. Your purpose in writing is to convince them that a change in policy would improve customer service. You think that a single-line system, such as that used in banks, would reduce chaos and make customers happier because they would not have to worry about where they are in line.

The first phase of the writing process involves analyzing and anticipating the audience and then adapting to that audience.

Prewriting also involves *anticipating* how your audience will react to your message. You're sure that some of the other owners will agree with you, but others might fear that customers seeing a long single line might go elsewhere. In *adapting* your message to the audience, you try to think of the right words and tone that will win over skeptics.

DRAFTING. The second phase involves researching, organizing, and then drafting the message. In *researching* information for this message, you would probably

FIGURE 2.2 | The 3-×-3 Writing Process

1 Prewriting

Analyze

- What is your purpose?
- What do you want the receiver to do or believe?
- What channel should you choose: face-to-face conversation, group meeting, email, memo, letter, report, blog, wiki, tweet, etc.

Anticipate

- Profile the audience.
- What does the receiver already know?
- Will the receiver's response be neutral, positive, or negative? How will this affect your organizational strategy?

Adapt

- What techniques can you use to adapt your message to its audience?
- How can you promote feedback?
- Strive to use positive, conversational, and courteous language.

2 Drafting

Research

- Gather data to provide facts.
- Search company files, previous correspondence, and the Internet.
- What do you need to know to write this message?
- How much does the audience already know?

Organize

- Organize direct messages with the big idea first, followed by an explanation in the body and an action request in the closing.
- For persuasive or negative messages, use an indirect, problem-solving strategy.

Draft

- Prepare a first draft, usually quickly.
- Focus on short, clear sentences using the active voice.
- Build paragraph coherence by repeating key ideas, using pronouns, and incorporating appropriate transitional expressions.

3 Revising

Edit

- Edit your message to be sure it is clear, concise, conversational, readable.
- Revise to eliminate wordy fillers, long lead-ins, redundancies, and trite business phrases.
- Develop parallelism.
- Consider using headings and numbered and bulleted lists for quick reading.

Proofread

- Take the time to read every message carefully.
- Look for errors in spelling, grammar, punctuation, names, and numbers.
- Check to be sure the format is consistent.

Evaluate

- Will this message achieve your purpose?
- Does the tone sound pleasant and friendly rather than curt?
- Have you thought enough about the audience to be sure this message is appealing?
- Did you encourage feedback?

The second phase of the writing process includes researching, organizing the message, and actually drafting it.

investigate other kinds of businesses that use single lines for customers. You can research how successful your competitors have been with their touch-screen ordering. You can call to see whether other franchise owners are concerned about chaotic lines. Before writing to the entire group, you can brainstorm with a few owners to see what ideas they have for solving the problem.

Once you've collected enough information, you should focus on *organizing* your message. Should you start out by offering your solution? Or should you work up to it slowly, describing the problem, presenting your evidence, and then ending with the solution? The final step in the second phase of the writing process is actually *drafting* the letter. At this point many writers write quickly, realizing that they will polish their ideas when they revise.

The third phase of the writing process includes revising for clarity and readability, proofreading for errors, and evaluating for effectiveness.

REVISING. The third phase of the process involves editing, proofreading, and evaluating your message. After writing the first draft, you should spend time *editing* the message for clarity, conciseness, tone, and readability. Could parts of it be rearranged to make your point more effectively? This is when you look for ways to improve the organization and tone of your message. Next you should spend time *proofreading* to ensure correct spelling, grammar, punctuation, and format. The final step is *evaluating* to decide whether the message accomplishes your goal. Only now should you press "send"!

2.3 Analyzing and Anticipating the Audience

Many people begin writing and discover only as they approach the end of a message what they are trying to accomplish. If you analyze your purpose *before* you begin, you can avoid backtracking and starting over. The remainder of this chapter covers phase one of the writing process: knowing the purpose for writing, anticipating how the audience will react, and adapting the message to the audience.

2.3a Know Your Purpose

As you plan a workplace message, ask yourself two important questions: (a) Why am I sending this message? and (b) What do I hope to achieve? Your responses will determine how you organize and present your information.

Your message may have primary and secondary purposes. The primary purposes for sending business messages are typically to inform and to persuade. A secondary purpose is to promote goodwill. You and your organization want to look good in the eyes of your audience.

The primary purpose of most business messages is to inform or to persuade; the secondary purpose is to promote goodwill.

Many business messages simply *inform*. They explain procedures, announce meetings, answer questions, and transmit findings. Other business messages are meant to *persuade*. These messages sell products, convince managers, motivate employees, and win over customers. Persuasive and informative messages are developed differently.

2.3b Anticipate and Profile the Audience

A good writer anticipates the audience for a message: What is the reader or listener like? How will that person react to the message? Although we can't always know exactly who the receiver is, it is possible to imagine some of that person's characteristics. A copywriter at Hudson's Bay Company may picture his sister-in-law whenever he writes product descriptions for the website.

Profiling your audience is a pivotal step in the writing process. The questions in Figure 2.3 will help you do so.

How much time you devote to answering these questions depends on your message and its context. A report that you write for management or an oral presentation

FIGURE 2.3 | Asking the Right Questions to Profile Your Audience

Primary Audience

- Who is my primary reader or listener?
- What are my personal and professional relationships with this person?
- What position does this person hold in the organization?
- How much does this person know about the subject?
- What do I know about this person's education, beliefs, culture, and attitudes?
- Should I expect a neutral, positive, or negative response to my message?

Secondary Audience

- Who might see or hear this message in addition to the primary audience?
- How do these people differ from the primary audience?
- Do I need to include more background information?
- How must I reshape my message to make it understandable and acceptable to others to whom it might be forwarded?
- What risk is involved in saying what I'm about to say?

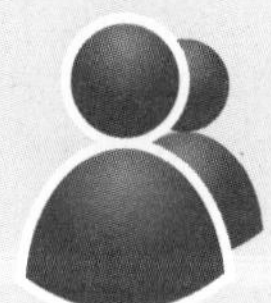

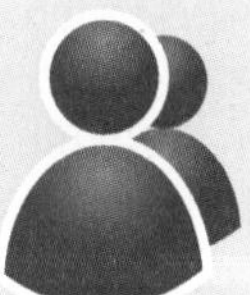

that you deliver to a big group will demand considerable audience anticipation. An email to a coworker or a message to a familiar supplier might require only a few moments of planning. That said, both types of message, once they've been published, attract the same type of risk: that something insensitive, belligerent, misleading, or politically incorrect might become known by the outside world and perhaps embarrass or cost your company.

No matter how routine or seemingly inconsequential your message, spend some time thinking about the audience so that you can tailor your words to your readers. Remember that they will be thinking *What's in it for me (WIIFM)?* One of the most important writing tips you can take away from this book is to recognize that every message you write should begin with the notion that your audience is thinking WIIFM. Another important tip is to realize that the audience for anything you write, in the digital age, is potentially much larger than you think (and perhaps less forgiving than your coworkers)—keep all audiences in mind, not just internal ones, when you write.

2.3c Make Choices Based on Your Audience Profile

After profiling the audience, you can decide whether the receiver will be neutral, positive, or hostile toward your message.

Profiling your audience helps you make decisions about shaping the message. You will discover what language is appropriate, whether you are free to use specialized technical terms, whether you should explain the background, and so on. Profiling the audience helps you decide whether your tone should be formal or informal and whether the receiver is likely to feel neutral, positive, or negative about your message.

Another advantage of profiling your audience is considering the possibility of a secondary audience. For example, let's say you start to write an email to your supervisor, Sheila, describing a problem you are having. Halfway through the message you realize that Sheila will probably forward this message to her boss, the vice president. Sheila will not want to summarize what you said; instead she will take the easy route and merely forward your email.

When you realize that the vice president will probably see this message, you decide to use a more formal tone. You remove your inquiry about Sheila's family, you reduce your complaints, and you tone down your language about why things went wrong. Instead, you provide more background information, and you are more specific in explaining issues with which the vice president is unfamiliar.

2.3d Select the Best Channel

Choosing an appropriate channel depends on the importance of the message, the feedback required, the need for a permanent record, the cost, the formality needed, and the best practices of your company.

After identifying the purpose of your message, you'll want to select the most appropriate communication channel. In the digital age, the number of channels continues to expand, as shown in Figure 2.4. Whether to send an email, schedule a videoconference, or have a face-to-face conversation or group meeting depends on some of the following factors:

- Importance of the message
- Amount and speed of feedback and interactivity required
- Necessity of a permanent record
- Cost of the channel
- Degree of formality desired
- Confidentiality and sensitivity of the message
- Receiver's preference and level of technical expertise

In addition to these practical issues, you will also consider how *rich* the channel is. The *richness* of a channel involves the extent to which it conveys all the information available in the original message. A richer medium, such as a face-to-face conversation, permits more interactivity and feedback. A leaner medium, such as a letter or an email, presents a flat, one-dimensional message. Richer media enable the sender to provide more verbal and visual cues (e.g., facial gestures), whereas lean messages must resort to substitutes such as emojis to help fill this gap.

WORKPLACE IN FOCUS

Employee retention is a big issue these days: how do employers ensure their workers like where they're working and want to continue working there? To address this issue, a new job category, Employee Communications, has been created. Employee Communications coordinators and managers are sometimes part of the Human Resources team and sometimes part of the Marketing team. Their job is to create employee engagement within their organization. Sara Presutto of Starbucks Canada creates employee engagement through various types of specialized meetings, as she describes in a YouTube interview at www.hrreporter.com/videodisplay/249-employee-communications-at-starbucks. *Why might organizations use multiple communication channels to transmit messages to employees? As an employee, how do you like to be engaged by your employer?*

Jeff Greenberg 2 of 6/Alamy

FIGURE 2.4 | Comparing Rich and Lean Communication Channels

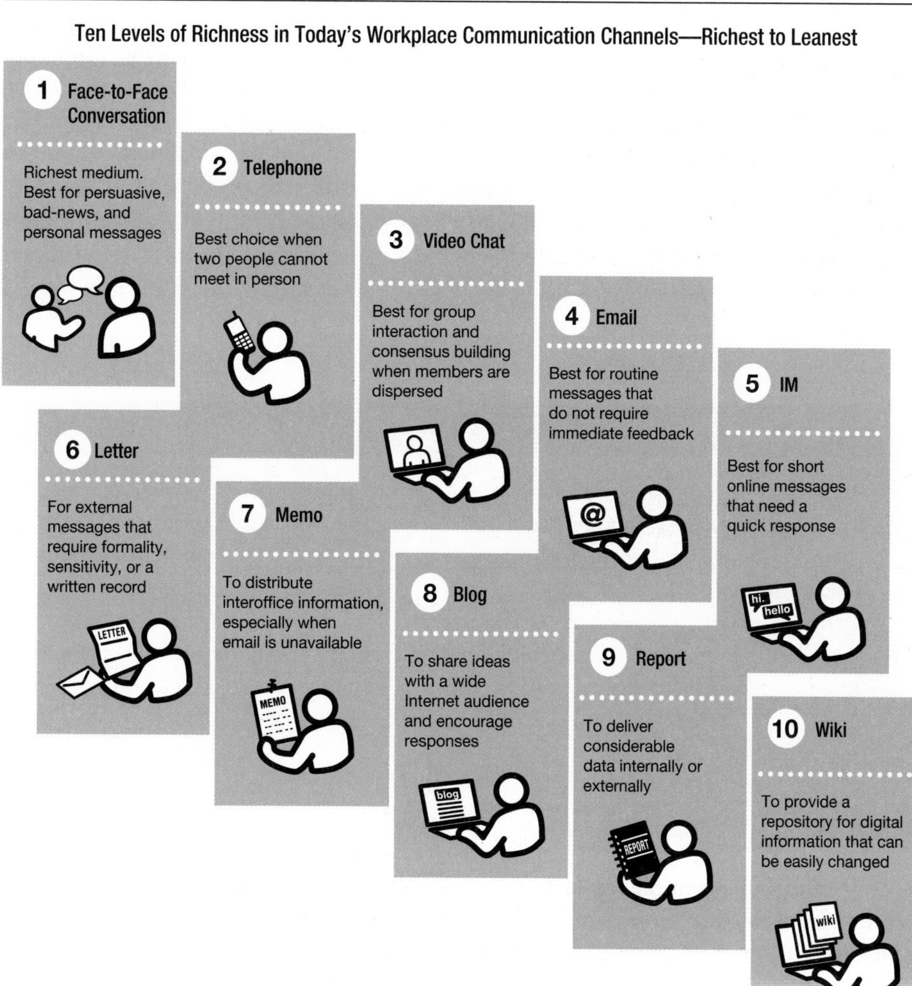

Ten Levels of Richness in Today's Workplace Communication Channels—Richest to Leanest
1 Face-to-Face Conversation
Richest medium. Best for persuasive, bad-news, and personal messages
2 Telephone
Best choice when two people cannot meet in person
3 Video Chat
Best for group interaction and consensus building when members are dispersed
4 Email
Best for routine messages that do not require immediate feedback
5 IM
Best for short online messages that need a quick response
hi. hello
6 Letter
For external messages that require formality, sensitivity, or a written record
LETTER
7 Memo
To distribute interoffice information, especially when email is unavailable
MEMO
8 Blog
To share ideas with a wide Internet audience and encourage responses
blog
9 Report
To deliver considerable data internally or externally
REPORT
10 Wiki
To provide a repository for digital information that can be easily changed
wiki

Choosing the wrong medium can result in the message being less effective or even misunderstood. A marketing manager must motivate his sales force to increase sales in the fourth quarter and is unlikely to achieve his goal if he merely posts an announcement on the office bulletin board, writes a memo, or sends an email. He could be more persuasive with a richer channel such as individual face-to-face conversations or a group meeting to stimulate sales. Keep in mind the following tips for choosing a communication channel:

- Use the richest media available.
- Employ richer media for more persuasive or personal communications.

2.4 Use Expert Writing Techniques to Adapt to Your Audience

After analyzing the purpose and anticipating the audience, writers begin to think about how to adapt a message to the task and the audience. Adaptation is the process of creating a message that suits the audience. Expert writers employ a number of techniques such as spotlighting audience benefits, cultivating a "you" view, and sounding conversational but professional.

2.4a Spotlight Audience Benefits

Adapting your written and spoken messages to the needs of their receiver means putting yourself in that person's shoes. It's a skill known as *empathy*. Empathic senders think about how a receiver will decode a message. They always try to give something to the receiver, solve the receiver's problems, save the receiver time or money, or just understand the feelings and position of that person. Such communicators are experts at what they do because they realize that by writing in this way (i.e., thinking about the receiver) they are more likely to have that person on their side in future, which is invaluable in business.

Which version of each of the following messages is more appealing to the audience?

OFFICE INSIDER

"When it comes to writing engaging content, 'you' is the most powerful word in the English language, because people are ultimately interested in fulfilling their own needs."

—Brian Clark, founder of a top marketing blog called Copyblogger

DON'T Sender Focus	DO✓ Audience Focus
✘ All employees are instructed herewith to fill out the enclosed questionnaire so that we can allocate our training funds to employees.	✓ By filling out the enclosed questionnaire, you can be one of the first employees to sign up for our training funds.
✘ Our warranty becomes effective only when we receive an owner's registration.	✓ Your warranty begins working for you as soon as you return your owner's registration.

2.4b Cultivate a "You" View

Because receivers are most interested in themselves, emphasize *you* whenever possible.

In concentrating on audience benefits, skilled communicators naturally develop a habit known as the "you" view. They emphasize second-person pronouns (*you, your*) instead of first-person pronouns (*I/we, us, our*). Whether your goal is to inform, persuade, or promote goodwill, the catchiest words you can use are *you* and *your*, because this signals that you have the receivers' needs uppermost in your mind.

Compare the following examples.

DON'T "I/We" View	DO "You" View
✗ We are requiring all employees to respond to the attached survey about health benefits.	✓ Because your ideas count, please complete the attached survey about health benefits.
✗ I need your account number before I can do anything.	✓ Please give me your account number so that I can locate your records and help you solve this problem.

Although you want to focus on the reader or listener, don't overuse or misuse the second-person pronoun *you*. The authors of some sales messages, for example, are guilty of overkill when they include *you* dozens of times in a direct-mail promotion. What's more, the word can sometimes create the wrong impression. Consider this statement: *You cannot return merchandise until you receive written approval.* The word *you* appears twice, but the reader may feel singled out for criticism. In the following version, the message is less personal and more positive: *Customers may return merchandise with written approval.*

Another difficulty in emphasizing the "you" view and de-emphasizing *we/I* is that it may result in overuse of the passive voice. For example, to avoid writing *We will give you* (active voice), you might write *You will be given* (passive voice). The active voice in writing is generally preferred because it identifies who is doing the acting. You will learn more about active and passive voice in Chapter 3.

In recognizing the value of the "you" view, however, you don't have to sterilize your writing and totally avoid any first-person pronouns or words that show your feelings. Don't be afraid of phrases such as *I'm happy* or *We're delighted* if you truly are. When speaking face to face, you can show sincerity and warmth with nonverbal cues such as a smile and a pleasant voice tone. In letters, emails, and memos, however, only expressive words and phrases can show your feelings. These phrases suggest hidden messages that say, *You are important, I hear you*, and *I'm honestly trying to please you.*

Emphasize *you* but don't eliminate all *I* and *we* statements.

2.4c Sound Conversational but Professional

Most business messages replace conversation. That's why they are most effective when they convey an informal, conversational tone instead of a formal, pretentious tone. Just how informal you can be depends greatly on the workplace. At Google, casual seems to be preferred. In a short message to users describing changes in its privacy policies, Google recently wrote, "we believe this stuff matters."[4] In more traditional organizations, that message probably would have been more formal. The dilemma, then, is knowing how casual to be in your writing. We suggest that you strive to be conversational but professional, especially until you learn what your organization prefers.

Strive for conversational expression, but also remember to be professional.

Email, instant messaging, texting, Twitter, and other short messaging channels enable you and your coworkers to have spontaneous conversations. Don't, however, let your messages become sloppy, unprofessional, or even dangerous.

To project a professional image, you want to sound educated and mature. Overuse of expressions such as *totally awesome, you know*, and *like*, as well as a reliance on unnecessary abbreviations (BTW for *by the way*), make a businessperson sound like a teenager. Professional messages do not include texting abbreviations, slang, sentence fragments, and chit-chat. Strive for a warm, conversational tone

WORKPLACE IN FOCUS

While addressing a panel at the 2014 Consumer Electronics Show, Ford marketing chief Jim Farley stirred controversy in comments meant to showcase the automaker's advanced GPS features. Instead of selling consumers on the benefits of in-dash computers, Farley confirmed their worst suspicions: "We know everyone who breaks the law, and we know when you're doing it," he said. "We have GPS in your car, so we know what you're doing." The remark startled listeners and violated nearly every rule of audience-focused communication. Ford quickly denounced the comments. *How might automakers adopt the "you" view to emphasize the benefits of in-dash navigation services to customers?*

Workplace in Focus based on Henkel, K. and Shepardson, D. Ford exec apologizes for saying company tracks customers with GPS. Published Jan. 9, 2014 by *The Detroit News*.

Jeff Kowalsky/Bloomberg/Getty Images

that avoids low-level diction. Levels of diction, as shown in Figure 2.5, range from unprofessional to formal:

DON'T Unprofessional	DO Professional
✗ Hey, boss, Gr8 news! Firewall now installed!! BTW, check with me b4 announcing it.	✓ Mr. Smith, our new firewall software is now installed. Please check with me before announcing it.
✗ Look, dude, this report is totally bogus. And the figures don't look kosher. Show me some real stats. Got sources?	✓ Because the figures in this report seem inaccurate, please submit the source statistics.

FIGURE 2.5 | Levels of Diction

Unprofessional (Low-level diction)	Conversational (Middle-level diction)	Formal (High-level diction)
badmouth	criticize	denigrate
guts	nerve	courage
pecking order	line of command	dominance hierarchy
ticked off	upset	provoked
rat on	inform	betray
rip off	steal	expropriate
If we just hang in there, we'll snag the contract.	If we don't get discouraged, we'll win the contract.	If the principals persevere, they will secure the contract.

DON'T Overly Formal	DO✓ Conversational
✘ All employees are herewith instructed to return the appropriately designated contracts to the undersigned.	✓ Please return your contracts to me.
✘ Pertaining to your order, we must verify the sizes that your organization requires prior to consignment of your order to our shipper.	✓ We will send your order as soon as we confirm the sizes you need.

2.5 Using Additional Expert Writing Techniques

As you continue to improve your writing skills, you can start integrating expert techniques that improve the clarity, tone, and effectiveness of a message. These techniques include using a positive and courteous tone, bias-free language, simple expression, and precise words. Take a look at Figure 2.6 to see how a writer can improve an email by applying numerous expert writing techniques.

2.5a Be Positive Rather Than Negative

One of the best ways to improve the tone of a message is to use positive rather than negative language. Positive language generally conveys more information than negative language does. Moreover, positive messages are uplifting and pleasant to read. Positive wording tells what *is* and what *can be done* rather than what *isn't* and what *can't be done*. For example, *Your order cannot be shipped by January 10* is not nearly as informative as *Your order will be shipped January 15*. An office supply store adjacent to an ice cream parlour posted a sign on its door that reads: *Please enjoy your ice cream before you enjoy our store*. That sounds much more positive and inviting than *No food allowed!*[5]

Using positive language also involves avoiding negative words that create ill will. Some words appear to blame or accuse your audience. For example, opening a letter to a customer with *You claim that* suggests that you don't believe the customer. Other loaded words that can get you in trouble are *complaint, criticism, defective, failed, mistake*, and *neglected*. Also avoid phrases such as *you are apparently unaware of* or *you did not provide* or *you misunderstood* or *you don't understand*. Often you may be unaware of the effect of these words. Notice in the following examples how you can revise the negative tone to create a more positive impression.

Positive language creates goodwill and gives more options to receivers.

DON'T Negative	DO✓ Positive
✘ This plan definitely cannot succeed if we don't obtain management approval.	✓ This plan definitely can succeed if we obtain management approval.
✘ You failed to include your credit card number, so we can't mail your order.	✓ We look forward to completing your order as soon as we receive your credit card number.

OFFICE INSIDER

"Negative tone can hurt your company in many ways. It can lose customers, it can generate lawsuits, and if inflammatory rhetoric is found in a discoverable email or log notes, a few words might cost your company a whopping settlement and punitive damages in a bad-faith lawsuit."

—Gary Blake, national underwriter life & health-financial services

2.5b Express Courtesy

A courteous tone involves not just guarding against rudeness but also avoiding words that sound demanding or preachy. Expressions such as *you should, you must*, and *you have to* cause people to instinctively react with *Oh, yeah?*

FIGURE 2.6 | Applying Expert Writing Techniques to Improve an Email

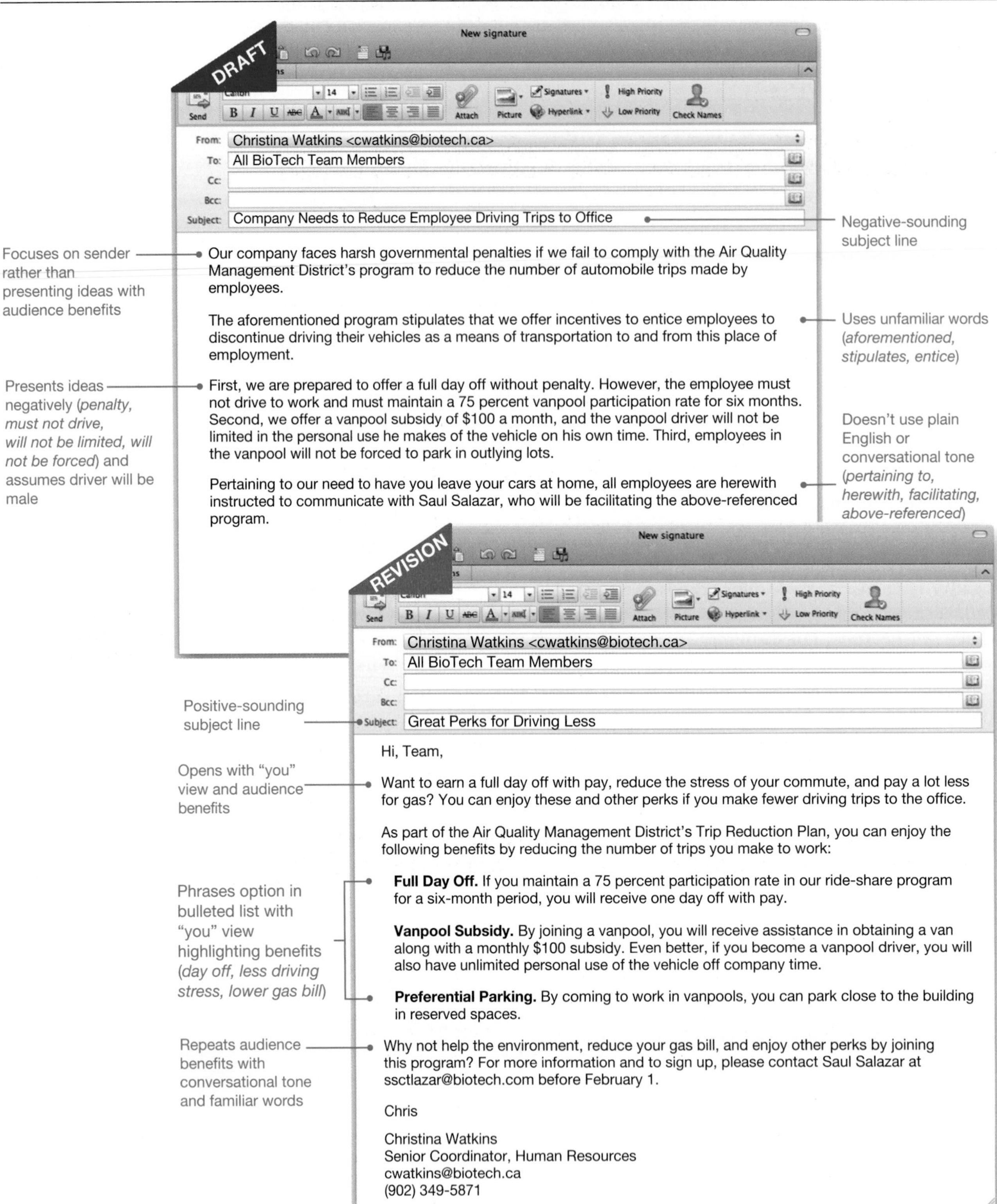
DRAFT
New signature
From: Christina Watkins <cwatkins@biotech.ca>
To: All BioTech Team Members
Cc:
Bcc:
Subject: Company Needs to Reduce Employee Driving Trips to Office
Our company faces harsh governmental penalties if we fail to comply with the Air Quality Management District's program to reduce the number of automobile trips made by employees.
The aforementioned program stipulates that we offer incentives to entice employees to discontinue driving their vehicles as a means of transportation to and from this place of employment.
First, we are prepared to offer a full day off without penalty. However, the employee must not drive to work and must maintain a 75 percent vanpool participation rate for six months. Second, we offer a vanpool subsidy of $100 a month, and the vanpool driver will not be limited in the personal use he makes of the vehicle on his own time. Third, employees in the vanpool will not be forced to park in outlying lots.
Pertaining to our need to have you leave your cars at home, all employees are herewith instructed to communicate with Saul Salazar, who will be facilitating the above-referenced program.
Negative-sounding subject line
Focuses on sender rather than presenting ideas with audience benefits
Uses unfamiliar words (aforementioned, stipulates, entice)
Presents ideas negatively (penalty, must not drive, will not be limited, will not be forced) and assumes driver will be male
Doesn't use plain English or conversational tone (pertaining to, herewith, facilitating, above-referenced)
REVISION
New signature
From: Christina Watkins <cwatkins@biotech.ca>
To: All BioTech Team Members
Cc:
Bcc:
Subject: Great Perks for Driving Less
Hi, Team,
Want to earn a full day off with pay, reduce the stress of your commute, and pay a lot less for gas? You can enjoy these and other perks if you make fewer driving trips to the office.
As part of the Air Quality Management District's Trip Reduction Plan, you can enjoy the following benefits by reducing the number of trips you make to work:
Full Day Off. If you maintain a 75 percent participation rate in our ride-share program for a six-month period, you will receive one day off with pay.
Vanpool Subsidy. By joining a vanpool, you will receive assistance in obtaining a van along with a monthly $100 subsidy. Even better, if you become a vanpool driver, you will also have unlimited personal use of the vehicle off company time.
Preferential Parking. By coming to work in vanpools, you can park close to the building in reserved spaces.
Why not help the environment, reduce your gas bill, and enjoy other perks by joining this program? For more information and to sign up, please contact Saul Salazar at ssctlazar@biotech.com before February 1.
Chris
Christina Watkins
Senior Coordinator, Human Resources
cwatkins@biotech.ca
(902) 349-5871
Positive-sounding subject line
Opens with "you" view and audience benefits
Phrases option in bulleted list with "you" view highlighting benefits (day off, less driving stress, lower gas bill)
Repeats audience benefits with conversational tone and familiar words

Even when you feel justified in displaying anger, remember that losing your temper or being sarcastic will seldom accomplish your goals as a business communicator: to inform, to persuade, and to create goodwill. When you are irritated, frustrated, or infuriated, keep cool and try to defuse the situation. In telephone conversations with customers, use polite phrases such as: *I would be happy to assist you with that, Thank you for being so patient*, and *It was a pleasure speaking with you.*

DON'T Less Courteous	DO✓ More Courteous and Helpful
✗ Can't you people get anything right? This is the second time I've written!	✓ Please credit my account for $340. My latest statement shows that the error noted in my letter of May 15 has not yet been corrected.
✗ Stewart, you must complete all performance reviews by Friday.	✓ Stewart, will you please complete all performance reviews by Friday?

2.5c Employ Bias-Free Language

In adapting a message to its audience, be sure your language is sensitive and bias-free. Sometimes we say things that we never thought could be hurtful. The real problem is that we don't think about the words that stereotype groups of people, such as *the boys in the mailroom* or *the girls in the front office*. Be cautious about expressions that might be biased in terms of gender, race, ethnicity, age, and disability.

Generally, you can avoid gender-biased language by choosing alternate language for words involving *man* or *woman*, by using plural nouns and pronouns, or by changing to a gender-free word (*person* or *representative*). Avoid the *his or her* option whenever possible. It's wordy and conspicuous.

Sensitive communicators avoid language that excludes people.

Specify age only if it is relevant, and to avoid disability bias, do not refer to an individual's disability unless it is relevant. The following examples give you a quick look at a few problem expressions and possible replacements. The real key to bias-free communication, though, lies in your awareness and commitment. Be on the lookout to be sure that your messages do not exclude, stereotype, or offend people.

DON'T Gender Biased	DO✓ Bias Free
✗ female doctor, woman attorney, cleaning woman	✓ doctor, attorney, cleaner
✗ waiter/waitress, authoress, stewardess	✓ server, author, flight attendant
✗ mankind, man-hour, man-made	✓ humanity, working hours, artificial
✗ office girls	✓ office workers
✗ the doctor ... he	✓ doctors ... they
✗ the teacher ... she	✓ teachers ... they
✗ executives and their wives	✓ executives and their spouses
✗ foreman, flagman, workman, craftsman	✓ lead worker, flagger, worker, artisan
✗ businessman, salesman	✓ businessperson, sales representative

DON'T Racially or Ethnically Biased	DO✓ Bias Free
✘ An Indian accountant was hired.	✓ An accountant was hired.
✘ Jim Nolan, an African Canadian, applied.	✓ Jim Nolan applied.

DON'T Age Biased	DO✓ Bias Free
✘ The law applied to old people.	✓ The law applied to people over sixty-five.
✘ Sally Kay, 55, was transferred.	✓ Sally Kay was transferred.
✘ a sprightly old gentleman	✓ a man
✘ a little old lady	✓ a woman

DON'T Disability Biased	DO✓ Bias Free
✘ afflicted with arthritis, crippled by arthritis	✓ has arthritis
✘ confined to a wheelchair	✓ uses a wheelchair

2.5d Choose Plain Language and Familiar Words

In adapting your message to your audience, use plain language and familiar words that audience members will recognize. Don't, however, avoid a big word that conveys your idea efficiently and is appropriate for the audience. Your goal is to shun pompous and pretentious language. If you mean *begin*, don't say *commence* or *initiate*. If you mean *pay*, don't write *compensate*. By substituting everyday, familiar words for unfamiliar ones, as shown here, you help your audience comprehend your ideas quickly.

DON'T Unfamiliar	DO✓ Familiar
✘ commensurate	✓ equal
✘ interrogate	✓ question
✘ materialize	✓ appear
✘ obfuscate	✓ confuse
✘ remuneration	✓ pay, salary
✘ terminate	✓ end

At the same time, be selective in your use of jargon. *Jargon* describes technical or specialized terms within a field. These terms enable insiders to communicate complex ideas briefly, but to outsiders they mean nothing. Human resources professionals, for example, know precisely what's meant by *cafeteria plan* (a benefits option program), but most of us would be thinking about lunch. Geologists refer to *plate tectonics*, and physicians discuss *metastatic carcinomas*. These terms mean little to most of us. Use specialized language only when the audience will understand it. In addition, don't forget to consider secondary audiences: Will those potential receivers understand any technical terms used?

2.5e Use Precise, Vigorous Words

Strong verbs and concrete nouns give receivers more information and keep them interested. Don't overlook the thesaurus (also available online or on your computer) for expanding your word choices and vocabulary. Whenever possible, use precise, specific words, as shown here:

DON'T Imprecise, Dull	DO✓ More Precise
✗ a change in profits	✓ a 25 percent hike in profits a 10 percent plunge in profits
✗ to say	✓ to promise, confess, understand to allege, assert, assume, judge
✗ to think about	✓ to identify, diagnose, analyze to probe, examine, inspect

SUMMARY OF LEARNING OBJECTIVES

2.1 Explain the steps in the communication process.

- A sender encodes (selects) words or symbols to express an idea in a message.
- The message travels over a channel (such as email, website, tweet, letter, or smartphone call).
- "Noise" (loud sounds, misspelled words, other distractions) may interfere with the transmission.
- The receiver decodes (interprets) the message and responds with feedback.

2.2 Recognize the goals and process of business writing.

- Business writing should be purposeful, economical, and audience oriented.
- The 3-×-3 writing process helps writers create efficient and effective messages.
- Phase 1 (prewriting): analyze the message, anticipate the audience, and consider how to adapt the message to the audience.
- Phase 2 (drafting): research the topic, organize the material, and draft the message.
- Phase 3 (revising): edit, proofread, and evaluate the message.

2.3 Know the purpose of a message, anticipate its audience, and select the best communication channel for it.

- Before composing, decide what you hope to achieve.
- Select the appropriate channel to inform, persuade, or convey goodwill.
- After identifying the purpose, visualize both the primary and secondary audiences.
- Remember that receivers will usually be thinking, *What's in it for me (WIIFM)?*
- Select the best channel by considering (a) the importance of the message, (b) the amount and speed of feedback required, (c) the necessity of a permanent record, (d) the cost of the channel, (e) the degree of formality desired, (f) the confidentiality and sensitivity of the message, and (g) the receiver's preference and level of technical expertise.

2.4 Incorporate audience adaptation techniques.

- Look for ways to shape the message from the receiver's view rather than the sender's.
- Apply the "you" view without attempting to manipulate.
- Use conversational but professional language.

2.5 Use additional expert writing techniques.

- Use positive language that tells what can be done rather than what can't be done (The project will be successful with your support rather than The project won't be successful without your support).
- Be courteous rather than rude, preachy, or demanding.
- Provide reasons for a request to soften the tone of a message.
- Avoid biased language that excludes, stereotypes, or offends people (lady lawyer, spry old gentleman, confined to a wheelchair).
- Strive for plain language (equal instead of commensurate), familiar terms (end instead of terminate), and precise words (analyze instead of think about).

CHAPTER REVIEW

1. Define *communication*. When is it successful? (Obj. 1)
2. List the five steps in the communication process. (Obj. 1)
3. In what ways is business writing different from high school writing and private messages? (Obj. 2)
4. Describe the components in each stage of the 3-×-3 writing process. (Obj. 2)
5. What does *WIIFM* mean? Why is it important to business writers? (Obj. 3)
6. What seven factors should writers consider in selecting an appropriate channel to deliver a message? (Obj. 3)
7. What is the "you" view? When can the use of the pronoun *you* backfire? (Obj. 4)
8. How can a business writer sound conversational but also be professional? (Obj. 4)
9. Why is positive wording more effective in business messages than negative wording? (Obj. 5)
10. What are three ways to avoid biased language? Give an original example of each. (Obj. 5)

CRITICAL THINKING

1. Has digital transmission changed the nature of communication? (Obj. 1)
2. Why do you think employers prefer messages that are not written like high school writing? (Obj. 2)
3. Why should business writers strive to use short, familiar, simple words? Does this "dumb down" business messages? (Obj. 5)
4. A wise observer once said that bad writing makes smart people look dumb. Do you agree or disagree, and why? (Objs. 1–5)
5. In a letter to the editor, a teacher criticized a newspaper article on autism because it used the term *autistic child* rather than *child with autism*. She championed *people-first* terminology, which avoids defining individuals by their ability or disability.[6] For example, instead of identifying someone as a *disabled person*, one would say, *she has a disability*. What does *people-first language* mean? How can language change perceptions? (Obj. 5)

ACTIVITIES AND CASES

2.1 CHANNEL SELECTION: VARIOUS BUSINESS SCENARIOS (OBJ. 3)

Your Task. Using Figure 2.4 on page 35, suggest the best communication channels for the following messages. Assume that all channels shown are available, ranging from face-to-face conversations to instant messages, blogs, and wikis. Be prepared to justify your choices based on the richness of each channel.

a. As part of a task force to investigate cell phone marketing, you need to establish a central location where each team member can see general information about the task as well as add comments for others to see. Task force members are located throughout the country.
b. You're sitting on the couch in the evening watching TV when you suddenly remember that you were supposed to send Jeremy some information about a shared project. Should you text him right away before you forget?
c. As an event planner, you have been engaged to research sites for a celebrity golf tournament. What is the best channel for conveying your findings to your boss or planning committee?
d. You want to persuade your manager to change your work schedule.
e. As a sales manager, you want to know which of your sales reps in the field are available immediately for a quick teleconference meeting.
f. You need to know whether Amanda in Reprographics can produce a rush job for you in two days.
g. Your firm must respond to a notice from the Canada Revenue Agency announcing that the company owes a penalty because it underreported its income in the previous fiscal year.

2.2 RESEARCH AND REPORT: GENERATIONAL COMMUNICATION (OBJ. 4)

In the past five years or so, a discussion has arisen about how different generations behave differently in the workplace, based mostly on the varying expectations younger and older people have of their jobs and the workplace. For example, it is generally agreed that Millennials (people born in the 1990s) communicate differently than GenXers (people born in the 1970s).

Your Task. Using your college or university library's research databases, find two to three reputable articles (i.e., from well-known newspapers or magazines) on the topic of generational communication differences in the workplace. Summarize your findings in a brief email/memo to your instructor. In your email/memo offer some "adaptive" suggestions for how workers from different generations can communicate effectively with each other (and their clients/customers) in the workplace.

2.3 TURNING NEGATIVES INTO POSITIVES (OBJ. 5)

There has been a lot of bad business news in the past couple of years. Between the lingering recession and the catastrophic train derailment and explosion in Lac-Mégantic, Quebec, the world has witnessed large corporations going bankrupt or having to be bailed out by taxpayers, CEOs losing their jobs due to mismanagement of corporate disasters, and national governments negotiating bailouts (e.g., Ireland, Greece). From the point of view of one of the bailed-out companies or governments or corporations suffering from bad media publicity, how do you move the focus away from the negative news and toward a more positive perspective?

Your Task. In your school's library databases or on the Internet, using a search term such as "bad publicity," see if you can find a source that gives good advice on how companies or governments can turn negatives into positives. Then, imagine that your college or university has just experienced a horrible health or environmental disaster, or some large-scale scandal that has been reported in the media. Create some business communications for various stakeholders (e.g., students, parents, media, government, corporate partners) that turn negatives into positives. Present your communications to your instructor or to the class.

Visit **MindTap** for a variety of videos, additional exercises, activities, and quizzes to support your learning.

CHAPTER

3

Organizing and Drafting Your Message

OBJECTIVES

After studying this chapter, you should be able to

3.1 Research to collect background information for messages.

3.2 Organize information into strategic relationships.

3.3 Compose a first draft using a variety of sentence types.

3.4 Improve your message by using style effectively.

3.5 Organize paragraphs effectively.

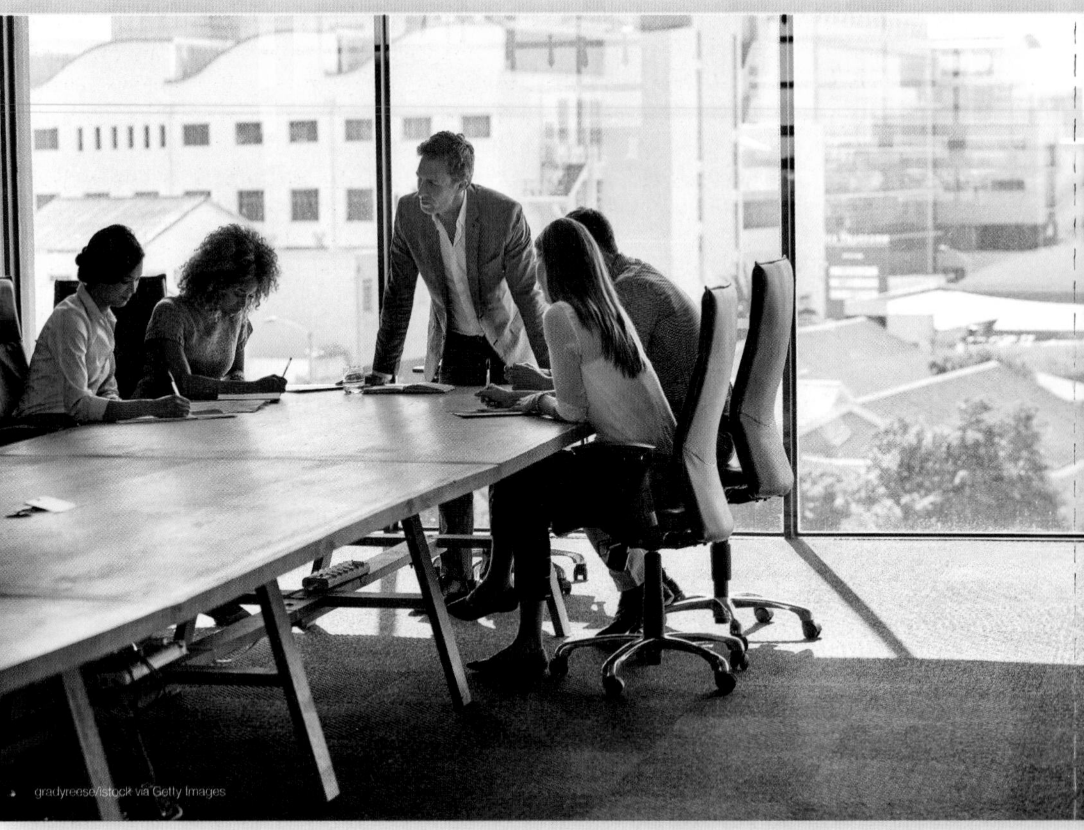
gradyreese/istock via Getty Images

OFFICE INSIDER

"With the fast pace of today's electronic communications, one might think that the value of fundamental writing skills has diminished in the workplace. Actually the need to write clearly and quickly has never been more important than in today's highly competitive, technology-driven global economy."

—Joseph M. Tucci, president and chief executive officer of EMC Corporation

Office Insider based on Tucci, J. M. (2004, September 1). Quoted in the National Writing Project, Writing: A ticket to work . . . or a ticket out. Retrieved from http://www.nwp.org/cs/public/print/resource/2154

3.1 Drafting Workplace Messages

Who me? Write on the job? With today's advances in technology, lots of people believe they will never be required to write on the job. The truth is that business, technical, and professional people in this digital age are exchanging more messages than ever before. The more quickly you can put your ideas down and the more clearly you can explain what needs to be said, the more successful you will be in your career.

3.1a Researching Background Information

No smart businessperson would begin drafting a message before doing research. For our purposes *research* simply means "collecting information about a certain topic." This is an important step in the writing process because that information helps the writer shape the message and build credibility. Business writers collect information to answer several questions:

- What does the receiver need to know?
- What is the receiver to do?
- How is the receiver to do it?
- When must the receiver do it?
- What will happen if the receiver doesn't do it?

Whenever your message requires more information than you have in your head or at your fingertips, you must conduct research. This research may be informal or formal.

The second stage of the writing process involves research, which means collecting the necessary information to prepare a message.

3.1b Informal Research Methods

Many routine messages—such as emails, memos, letters, informational reports, and oral presentations—require information that you can collect informally. The following informal research techniques are useful at work:

- **Search your company's files.** If you are responding to an inquiry or drafting a routine message, you often can find background information such as previous correspondence in your own files or those of the company. You might consult the company wiki or other digital and manual files. You might also consult colleagues.
- **Talk with your manager.** Get information from the individual to whom you report. Your superior will probably know something about the topic and what slant should you take. Your manager can also point you to other sources.
- **Interview the target audience.** Consider talking with individuals at whom the message is aimed. They can provide clarifying information that tells you what they want to know and how you should shape your remarks. Suggestions for conducting interviews are presented in Chapter 9.
- **Conduct an informal survey.** Gather unscientific but helpful information through questionnaires, telephone surveys, or online surveys. In preparing a report predicting the success of a proposed company fitness centre, for example, circulate a questionnaire asking for employee reactions.
- **Brainstorm for ideas.** Alone or with others, discuss ideas for the writing task at hand, and record at least a dozen ideas without judging them. Small groups are especially fruitful in brainstorming because people spin ideas off one another.

3.1c Research Methods

Complex business problems lead to longer reports and generally require formal research methods. Let's say you are part of the management team for an international

FIGURE 3.1 | The 3-×-3 Writing Process

1 Prewriting	2 Drafting	3 Revising
Analyze: Decide on the message purpose. What do you want the receiver to do or believe? **Anticipate:** What does the audience already know? How will it receive this message? **Adapt:** Think about techniques to present this message most effectively. Consider how to elicit feedback.	**Research:** Gather background data by searching files and the Internet. **Organize:** Arrange direct messages with the big idea first. For persuasive or negative messages, use an indirect, problem-solving strategy. **Draft:** Prepare the first draft, using active-voice sentences, coherent paragraphs, and appropriate transitional expressions.	**Edit:** Eliminate wordy fillers, long lead-ins, redundancies, and trite business phrases. Strive for parallelism, clarity, conciseness, and readability. **Proofread:** Check carefully for errors in spelling, grammar, punctuation, and format. **Evaluate:** Will this message achieve your purpose? Is the tone pleasant? Did you encourage feedback?

WORKPLACE IN FOCUS

At credit card company Amex's Canadian headquarters in Toronto, brainstorming and informal research is built right into the office architecture. In a recent head-office move, Amex decided to devote 20 percent of its office floor space—on every floor—to "open, collaborative spaces so employees can set up meetings in the conference room, grab a couch by a window, or enjoy a whiteboard brainstorming session over lunch with a colleague—all without compromising their connectivity."[1] Encouraging employees to seek out information in this way, instead of sitting in a cubicle or office all day, has a double impact: it encourages the type of research gathering necessary in an ideas-based economy, and it suits the preferences of Millennial workers who appreciate collaboration and informality in the workplace. *What type of collaborations have you participated in at work?*

GaudiLab/Shutterstock

retailer such as Roots, and you have been asked to help launch a new store in Japan. Or let's assume you must write a term paper for a college class. Both tasks require more data than you have in your head or at your fingertips. To conduct formal research, consider the following research options:

- **Access electronic sources.** University, college, and public libraries provide digital catalogues that permit access to a wide array of books, journals, magazines, newspapers, and other online literature. You also could conduct a Google search, but expect to be deluged with torrents of information, presenting a troubling paradox: research seems to be far more difficult to conduct in the digital age than in previous times.[2] With so much data drowning today's researchers, they struggle to sort through it all, trying to decide what is current, relevant, and credible.
- **Search manually.** Valuable background information is sometimes still available through manual searching of resources in public and college libraries. These traditional paper-based sources include books and newspaper, magazine, and journal articles. Other sources are encyclopedias, reference books, handbooks, dictionaries, directories, and almanacs.
- **Investigate primary sources.** To develop firsthand, primary information for a project, go directly to the source. In helping to launch a new Roots location in Tokyo, you might travel to possible sites and check them out. If you need information about how many shoppers pass by a location or visit a shopping centre, you might conduct a traffic count. If you need information about consumers, you could search blogs, Twitter, wikis, and Facebook fan pages. To learn more about specific shoppers, you could use questionnaires, interviews, or focus groups. Formal research includes scientific sampling methods that enable investigators to make accurate judgments and valid predictions.
- **Conduct scientific experiments.** Instead of merely asking for the target audience's opinion, scientific researchers present choices with controlled variables. Imagine, for example, that the management team at Roots wants to know at what price and under what circumstances consumers would purchase sweatpants from Roots instead of from H&M. Or let's say that management wants to study

the time of year and type of weather conditions that motivate consumers to begin purchasing sweaters, jackets, and cold-weather gear. The results of such experimentation would provide valuable data for managerial decision making.

3.2 Organizing Information to Show Relationships

Once you have collected data, you must find some way to organize it. Organizing includes two processes: grouping and strategizing. Well-organized messages group similar items together, and ideas follow a sequence that helps the reader understand relationships and accept the writer's views. Unorganized messages jump from one thought to another. Such messages fail to emphasize important points. Puzzled readers can't see how the pieces fit together, and they become frustrated and irritated. Many communication experts regard poor organization as the greatest failing of business writers. Two simple techniques can help you organize data: the scratch list and the outline.

Some writers make a quick scratch list of the topics they wish to cover in a message. They then write the message directly from the scratch list. Most writers, though, need to organize their ideas—especially if the project is complex—into a hierarchy such as an outline. The beauty of preparing an outline is that it gives you a chance to organize your thinking before you get bogged down in word choice and sentence structure. Figure 3.2 shows an outline format.

A simple way to organize data is the outline.

DIRECT ORGANIZATION FOR RECEPTIVE AUDIENCES. After preparing a scratch list or an outline, think about how the audience will respond to your ideas. When you expect the reader to be pleased, mildly interested, or, at worst, neutral—use the direct strategy. That is, put your main point—the purpose of your message—in the first or second sentence. Dianna Booher, a writing consultant, points out that typical readers begin any message by thinking, "So what am I supposed to do with this information?" In business writing you have to say, "Reader, here is my point!"[3]

Business messages typically follow either (1) the direct pattern, with the main idea first, or (2) the indirect pattern, with the main idea following explanation and evidence.

FIGURE 3.2 | Format for an Outline

Title: Major Idea or Purpose

I. First major component
  A. First subpoint
    1. Detail, illustration, evidence
    2. Detail, illustration, evidence
    3. Detail, illustration, evidence
  B. Second subpoint
    1.
    2.
II. Second major component
  A. First subpoint
    1.
    2.
  B. Second subpoint
    1.
    2.
    3.

Tips for Writing Outlines

- Define the main topic in the title.
- Divide the main topic into major components or classifications (preferably three to five).
- Break the components into subpoints.
- Don't put a single item under a major component; if you have only one subpoint, integrate it with the main item above it or reorganize.
- Strive to make each component exclusive (no overlapping).
- Use details, illustrations, and evidence to support subpoints.

Compare the direct and indirect strategies in the following email openings. Notice how long it takes to get to the main idea in the indirect opening.

DON'T Indirect Opening	DO✓ Direct Opening
✗ Bombardier is seeking to improve the process undertaken in producing its annual company awards ceremony. To this end, the Marketing Department, which is in charge of the event, has been refining last year's plan, especially as regards the issue of rental costs and food and beverage costs.	✓ The Marketing Department at Bombardier suggests cutting costs for the annual awards ceremony by adjusting the way we order food and the way we handle rentals.

Frontloading saves the reader time, establishes the proper frame of mind, and prevents frustration.

Explanations and details follow the direct opening. What's important is getting to the main idea quickly. This direct method, also called *frontloading*, has at least three advantages:

- **Saves the reader's time.** Many of today's businesspeople can devote only a few moments to each message.
- **Sets a proper frame of mind.** Without a clear opening, the reader may be thinking, "Why am I being told this?"
- **Reduces frustration.** Readers forced to struggle through wordy language before reaching the main idea can become frustrated and begin to resent the writer.

Typical business messages that follow the direct strategy include routine requests and responses, orders and acknowledgments, non-sensitive memos, emails, informational reports, and informational oral presentations. All these tasks have one element in common: none has a sensitive subject that will upset the reader.

The indirect pattern works best when the audience may be uninterested, unwilling, displeased, or even hostile.

INDIRECT ORGANIZATION FOR UNRECEPTIVE AUDIENCES. When you expect the audience to be uninterested, unwilling, displeased, or perhaps even hostile, the indirect strategy is more appropriate. In this strategy you reveal the main idea only after you have offered an explanation and evidence. This approach works well with three kinds of messages: (a) bad news, (b) ideas that require persuasion, and (c) sensitive news, especially when being transmitted to superiors. The indirect strategy has these benefits:

- **Respects the feelings of the audience.** Bad news is always painful, but preparing the receiver for it can lessen the pain.
- **Facilitates a fair hearing.** Messages that may upset the reader are more likely to be read when the main idea is delayed.
- **Minimizes a negative reaction.** A reader's reaction to a negative message is generally improved if the news is delivered gently.

Typical business messages that are organized indirectly include messages that refuse requests, deny claims, and disapprove credit. Persuasive requests, sales letters, sensitive messages, and some reports and oral presentations may also benefit from the indirect strategy.

In summary, business messages may be organized directly (with the main idea first) or indirectly. How you expect the audience to respond determines which strategy to use, as illustrated in Figure 3.3. Although these two methods cover many communication problems, they should not be considered universal. Some messages are mixed: part good news, part bad; part goodwill, part persuasion. In upcoming chapters you will practise applying the direct and indirect organization in typical situations.

FIGURE 3.3 | Audience Response Determines Direct or Indirect Organization

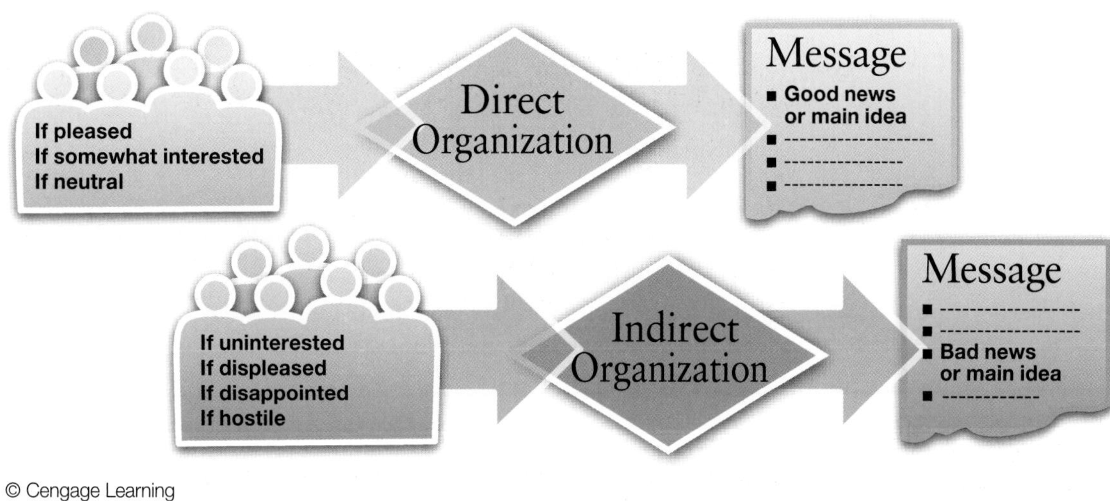

3.3 Composing Drafts With Effective Sentences

Once you've researched your topic, organized the data, and selected an organization method, you're ready to begin drafting. Many writers have trouble getting started, especially if they haven't completed the preparatory work. Organizing your ideas and working from an outline are very helpful in overcoming writer's block. Writing is also easier if you have a quiet environment in which to concentrate, if you set aside time to concentrate, and if you limit interruptions.

As you begin writing, think about what style fits you best. Some experts suggest that you write quickly (*freewriting*). Get your thoughts down now and refine them in later versions. As you begin each idea, imagine that you are talking to the reader. If you can't think of the right word, insert a substitute or type *find perfect word later*. Freewriting works well for some writers, but others prefer to move more slowly and think through their ideas more deliberately. Whether you are a speedy or a deliberate writer, keep in mind that you are writing the first draft. You will have time later to revise and polish your sentences.

3.3a Achieve Variety With Four Sentence Types

Messages that repeat the same sentence pattern soon become boring (e.g., We need to keep growing market share. We also need to increase shareholder satisfaction. Finally, we need to nurture ethical responses…) To avoid monotony and add spark to your writing, use a variety of sentence types.

Use a variety of sentence types to avoid boring, monotonous writing.

SIMPLE SENTENCE. Contains one complete thought (an independent clause) with a subject and predicate verb:

> The entrepreneur saw an opportunity.

COMPOUND SENTENCE. Contains two complete but related thoughts. May be joined by (a) a conjunction such as *and, but*, or *or;* (b) a semicolon; or (c) a conjunctive adverb such as *however, consequently*, or *therefore*:

> The entrepreneur saw an opportunity, and she responded immediately.
>
> The entrepreneur saw an opportunity; she responded immediately.
>
> The entrepreneur saw an opportunity; consequently, she responded immediately.

COMPLEX SENTENCE. Contains an independent clause (a complete thought) and a dependent clause (a thought that cannot stand by itself). Dependent clauses are often introduced by words such as *although, since, because, when*, and *if*. When dependent clauses precede independent clauses, they are always followed by a comma:

> When the entrepreneur saw the opportunity, she responded immediately.

COMPOUND-COMPLEX SENTENCE. Contains at least two independent clauses and one dependent clause:

> When the entrepreneur saw the opportunity, she responded immediately; however, she needed capital.

OFFICE INSIDER

"If you think an apostrophe was one of the 12 disciples of Jesus, you will never work for me. If you think a semicolon is a regular colon with an identity crisis, I will not hire you. If you scatter commas into a sentence with all the discrimination of a shotgun, you might make it to the foyer before we politely escort you from the building."

—Kyle Wiens, CEO, iFixit, the largest online repair community

Office Insider from July 2012 *Harvard Business Review* Digital article, "I Won't Hire People Who Use Poor Grammar. Here's Why" by Kyle Wiens. https://hbr.org/2012/07/i-wont-hire-people-who-use-poo.html

3.3b Avoid Three Common Sentence Faults

As you craft your sentences, beware of three common traps that lessen your credibility: fragments, run-on (fused) sentences, and comma-splice sentences.

One of the most serious errors a writer can make is punctuating a fragment as if it were a complete sentence. A *fragment* is usually a broken-off part of a complex sentence. Fragments often can be identified by the words that introduce them—words such as *although, as, because, even, except, for example, if, instead of, since, such as, that, which*, and *when*. These words introduce dependent clauses, as italicized in the following fragment examples. They should not be punctuated as sentences. Make sure such clauses always connect to independent clauses, as shown in the revisions.

DON'T Fragment	DO✓ Revision
✘ *Because most transactions require a permanent record.* Good writing skills are critical.	✓ Because most transactions require a permanent record, good writing skills are critical.
✘ The recruiter requested a writing sample. *Even though the candidate seemed to communicate well.*	✓ The recruiter requested a writing sample even though the candidate seemed to communicate well.

Fragments are broken-off parts of sentences and should not be punctuated as sentences.

A second serious writing fault is the *run-on (fused) sentence*. A sentence with two independent clauses must be joined by a coordinating conjunction (*and, or, nor, but*) or by a semicolon (;) or separated into two sentences. Without a conjunction or a semicolon, a run-on sentence results.

When two independent clauses are run together without punctuation or a conjunction, a run-on (fused) sentence results.

DON'T Run-on Sentence	DO✓ Revision
✘ Many job seekers prepare traditional résumés some also use websites as electronic portfolios.	✓ Many job seekers prepare traditional résumés. Some also use websites as electronic portfolios.
✘ One candidate sent an email résumé another sent a link to her Web portfolio.	✓ One candidate sent an email résumé; another sent a link to her Web portfolio.

A third sentence fault is a *comma splice*. It results when a writer joins (splices together) two independent clauses with a comma. Independent clauses may be joined with a coordinating conjunction (*and, or, nor, but*) or a conjunctive adverb (*however, consequently, therefore*, and others). Notice that clauses joined by coordinating conjunctions require only a comma. Clauses joined by a conjunctive adverb require a semicolon and a comma. To rectify a comma splice, try one of the possible revisions shown here:

DON'T Common Splice	DO✓ Revision
✘ Some employees prefer their desktop computers, others prefer their tablets.	✓ Some employees prefer their desktop computers, but others prefer their tablets. ✓ Some employees prefer their desktop computers; however, others prefer their tablets. ✓ Some employees prefer their desktop computers; others prefer their tablets.

3.3c Consider Short Sentences

Because your goal is to communicate clearly, you should strive for sentences around 20 words. Some sentences will be shorter; some will be longer. One authoritative source reports that reader comprehension drops off markedly as sentences become longer.[4] Therefore, in crafting your sentences, think about the relationship between sentence length and comprehension.

Sentence Length	Comprehension Rate
8 words	100%
15 words	90%
19 words	80%
28 words	50%

Instead of stringing together clauses with *and, but*, and *however*, break some of those complex sentences into separate segments. Business readers want to grasp ideas immediately. They can do that best when thoughts are separated into short sentences. On the other hand, too many monotonous short sentences will sound unintelligent and may bore or even annoy the reader. Strive for a balance between longer sentences and shorter ones.

OFFICE INSIDER

On the topic of comma splices, one well-known writing coach says, "Why do intelligent people make the error? I think people worry that they will come across too informally or too plainly if they use [two] short sentences. They believe using four-to-six-word sentences, especially two of them in a row, can't be professional. But two short, crisp, clear sentences in a row are professional and punchy."

—Lynn Gaertner-Johnston, business writing trainer, coach, blogger

3.4 Developing Business Writing Techniques

Business writers can significantly improve their messages by working on a few writing techniques like emphasis and voice.

3.4a Show Emphasis

When you are talking with someone, you can emphasize your main ideas by saying them loudly or by repeating them slowly. You can even pound the table if you want to show real emphasis! Another way you can signal the relative importance of an idea is by raising your eyebrows, by shaking your head, or by whispering in a low voice. But when you write, you must rely on other means to tell your readers which ideas are more important than others. Emphasis in writing can be achieved mechanically or stylistically.

EMPHASIS THROUGH MECHANICS. To emphasize an idea in print, a writer may use any of the following devices:

Underlining	Underlining draws the eye to a word.
Italics and boldface	Using *italics* or **boldface** conveys special meaning.
Font changes	Selecting a large, small, or different font draws interest.
All caps	Printing words in ALL CAPS is like shouting them.
Dashes	Dashes—used sparingly—can be effective.
Listing	Listing items vertically makes them stand out: 1. First item 2. Second item 3. Third item

Other means of achieving mechanical emphasis include the arrangement of space, colour, lines, boxes, columns, titles, headings, and subheadings. Today's software and colour printers provide an array of capabilities for highlighting ideas.

EMPHASIS THROUGH STYLE. Although mechanical devices are occasionally appropriate, more often a writer achieves emphasis stylistically, by choosing words carefully and constructing sentences skillfully to emphasize main ideas and de-emphasize minor or negative ideas. Here are four suggestions for emphasizing ideas stylistically:

Use vivid, not general, words. Vivid words are emphatic because the reader can picture ideas clearly.

DON'T General	DO✓ Vivid
✗ The way we seek jobs has changed.	✓ The Internet has dramatically changed how job hunters search for positions.
✗ Someone will contact you as soon as possible.	✓ Ms. Rivera will telephone you before 5 p.m. tomorrow, May 3.

Label the main idea. If an idea is significant, tell the reader.

DON'T Unlabelled	DO✓ Labelled
✗ Consider looking for a job online, but also focus on networking.	✓ Consider looking for a job online; but, *most important*, focus on networking.
✗ We shop here because of the customer service and low prices.	✓ We like the customer service, but the *primary reason* for shopping here is the low prices.

Place the important idea first or last. Ideas have less competition from surrounding words when they appear first or last in a sentence. Observe how the concept of productivity can be emphasized by its position in the sentence:

DON'T Main Idea Lost	DO✓ Main Idea Emphasized
✗ Profit-sharing plans are more effective in increasing *productivity* when they are linked to individual performance rather than to group performance.	✓ *Productivity* is more likely to be increased when profit-sharing plans are linked to individual performance rather than to group performance.

Give the important idea the spotlight. Don't dilute the effect of the main idea by making it share the stage with other words and clauses. Instead, put it in a simple sentence or in an independent clause.

DON'T Main Idea Lost	DO✓ Main Idea Clear
✗ Although you are the first trainee we have hired for this program, we had many candidates and expect to expand the program in the future. (The main idea is lost in a dependent clause.)	✓ You are the first trainee we have hired for this program. (Simple sentence)

DE-EMPHASIZING WHEN NECESSARY. To de-emphasize an idea, such as bad news, try one of the following stylistic devices:

Use general words.

DON'T Emphasizes Harsh Statement	DO✓ De-Emphasizes Harsh Statement
✗ Our records indicate that you were recently fired.	✓ Our records indicate that your employment status has recently changed.

Place the bad news in a dependent clause connected to an independent clause that contains something positive. In sentences with dependent clauses, the main emphasis is always on the independent clause.

DON'T Emphasizes Bad News	DO✓ De-Emphasizes Bad News
✗ We cannot issue you credit at this time, but we have a special plan that will allow you to fill your immediate needs on a cash basis.	✓ Although credit cannot be issued at this time, you can fill your immediate needs on a cash basis with our special plan.

3.4b Use the Active and Passive Voice Effectively

In active-voice sentences, the subject performs the action. In passive-voice sentences, the subject receives the action. Active-voice sentences are more direct because they reveal the performer immediately. They are easier to understand and usually shorter. Most business writing should be in the active voice. However, passive voice is useful to (a) emphasize an action rather than a person, (b) de-emphasize negative news, and (c) conceal the doer of an action.

Active Voice

Actor → Action
Justin must submit a tax return.

Actor → Action
Officials reviewed all tax returns.

Actor → Action
We cannot make cash refunds.

Actor → Action
Our CPA made a big error in the budget.

Passive Voice

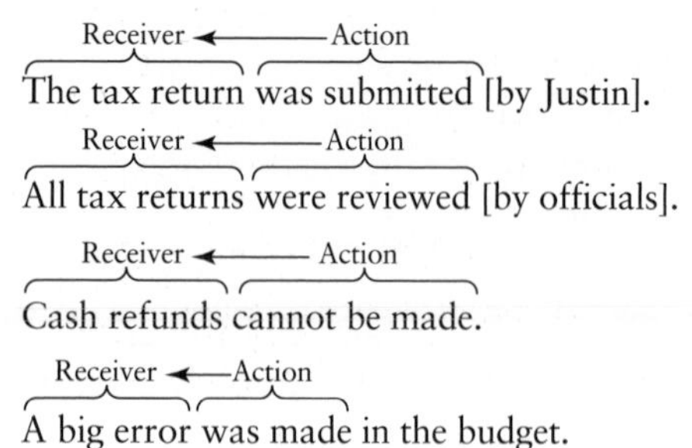

Receiver ← Action
The tax return was submitted [by Justin].
Receiver ← Action
All tax returns were reviewed [by officials].
Receiver ← Action
Cash refunds cannot be made.
Receiver ← Action
A big error was made in the budget.

3.4c Develop Parallelism

Parallelism is a technique that creates balanced writing. Sentences written so that their parts are balanced, or parallel, are easy to read and understand. To achieve parallelism, use similar structures to express similar ideas. For example, the words *computing, coding, recording*, and *storing* are parallel because the words all end in *-ing*. To express the list as *computing, coding, recording*, and *storage* is disturbing because the last item is not what the reader expects. Try to match nouns with nouns, verbs with verbs, and clauses with clauses. Avoid mixing active-voice verbs with passive-voice verbs.

DON'T Lacks Parallelism	DO✓ Illustrates Parallelism
✘ The policy affected all vendors, suppliers, and *those involved with consulting*.	✓ *Productivity* is more likely to be increased when profit-sharing plans are linked to individual performance rather than to group performance.
✘ Our primary goals are to increase productivity, reduce costs, and *the improvement of product quality.*	✓ Our primary goals are to increase productivity, reduce costs, and *improve product quality*. (Matches verbs.)
✘ We are scheduled to meet in Atlanta on January 5, *we are meeting in Montreal on the 15th of March*, and in Vancouver on June 3.	✓ We are scheduled to meet in Atlanta on January 5, *in Montreal on March 15*, and in Vancouver on June 3. (Matches phrases.)
✘ Shelby audits all accounts lettered A through L; accounts lettered M through Z are audited by Andrew.	✓ Shelby audits all accounts lettered A through L; Andrew audits accounts lettered M through Z. (Matches clauses.)
✘ Our Stanley Cup ads have three objectives: 1. We want to increase product use. 2. Introduce complementary products. 3. Our corporate image will be enhanced.	✓ Our Stanley Cup ads have three objectives: 1. Increase product use 2. Introduce complementary products 3. Enhance our corporate image (Matches verbs in listed items.)

3.4d Escape Dangling and Misplaced Modifiers

A modifier dangles when the word or phrase it describes is missing from its sentence—for example, *After working overtime, the report was finally finished*. This sentence says that the report was working overtime! Revised, the sentence contains a logical subject: *After working overtime, we finally finished the report.*

A modifier is misplaced when the word or phrase it describes is not close enough to be clear—for example, *Firefighters rescued a dog from a burning car that had a broken leg*. Obviously, the car did not have a broken leg. The solution is to position the modifier closer to the word(s) it describes or limits: *Firefighters rescued a dog with a broken leg from a burning car.*

DON'T Dangling or Misplaced Modifier	DO✓ Clear Modification
✘ Working together as a team, the project was finally completed.	✓ Working together as a team, we finally completed the project.
✘ To meet the deadline, your Excel figures must be sent by May 1.	✓ To meet the deadline, you must send your Excel figures by May 1.
✘ The recruiter interviewed candidates who had excellent computer skills in the morning.	✓ In the morning the recruiter interviewed candidates with excellent computer skills.
✘ As an important customer to us, we invite you to our spring open house.	✓ As you are an important customer to us, we invite you to our spring open house. *OR*: ✓ As an important customer to us, you are invited to our spring open house.

OFFICE INSIDER

Good writers don't let their modifiers dangle in public. "Always suspect an -ing word of dangling if it's near the front of a sentence; consider it guilty until proved innocent."

—Patricia T. O'Conner, author, *Woe Is I: The Grammarphobe's Guide to Better English in Plain English*

Office Insider based on O'Conner, P. (1996). *Woe is I*. New York: Putnam, p. 161.

3.5 Drafting Well-Organized, Effective Paragraphs

Good business writers develop well-organized paragraphs by focusing on a single main idea. The sentences in their paragraphs cohere, or stick together, by using transitional expressions.

3.5a Craft a Topic Sentence

A paragraph is unified when it develops a single main idea, usually expressed in a topic sentence. Business writers generally place the topic sentence first in the paragraph. It tells readers what to expect and helps them understand the paragraph's central thought immediately (e.g., This report investigates consumer confidence changes in Canada in the past 10 years.)

3.5b Develop Support Sentences

Support sentences illustrate, explain, or strengthen the topic sentence. One of the hardest things for beginning writers to remember is that all support sentences in the paragraph must relate to the topic sentence. Any other topics should be treated separately. The following example starts with a topic sentence about flexible work scheduling and is followed by three support sentences that explain how flexible scheduling could function. Transitional expressions are italicized:

> **Topic sentence:** Flexible work scheduling could immediately increase productivity and enhance employee satisfaction in our organization.
>
> **Support sentences:** Managers would maintain their regular hours. For many other employees, *however*, flexible scheduling provides extra time to manage family responsibilities. Feeling less stress, employees are able to focus their attention better at work; *therefore*, they become more relaxed and more productive.

3.5c Build Paragraph Coherence

Paragraphs are coherent when ideas are linked—that is, when one idea leads logically to the next. Well-written paragraphs take the reader through a number of steps. When the author skips from Step 1 to Step 3 and forgets Step 2, the reader is lost. Several techniques allow the reader to follow the writer's ideas:

- **Repeat a key idea by using the same expression or a similar one: Employees treat guests as VIPs.** These VIPs are never told what they can or cannot do.
- **Use pronouns to refer to previous nouns: All new employees receive a two-week orientation.** They learn that every staffer has a vital role.
- **Show connections with transitional expressions: Hospitality is our business; consequently, training is critical.** (Use transitions such as consequently, however, as a result, and meanwhile. For a complete list, see Figure 3.4.)

3.5d Control Paragraph Length

Business writers recognize the value of short paragraphs. Paragraphs with eight or fewer printed lines look inviting and readable. Longer, solid chunks of print appear formidable. If a topic can't be covered in eight or fewer printed lines (not sentences), consider breaking it into smaller segments.

FIGURE 3.4 | Transitional Expressions to Build Coherence

To Add or Strengthen	To Show Time or Order	To Clarify	To Show Cause and Effect	To Contradict	To Contrast
additionally	after	for example	accordingly	actually	as opposed to
accordingly	before	for instance	as a result	but	at the same time
again	earlier	I mean	consequently	however	by contrast
also	finally	in other words	for this reason	in fact	conversely
beside	first	put another way	hence	instead	on the contrary
indeed	meanwhile	that is	so	rather	on the other hand
likewise	next	this means	therefore	still	previously
moreover	now	thus	thus	yet	similarly

SUMMARY OF LEARNING OBJECTIVES

3.1 Research to collect background information for messages.

- Shape messages and increase credibility by collecting information. Collect information by answering questions about what the receiver needs to know and what the receiver is to do.
- Conduct informal research for routine messages by looking in the company's digital and other files, talking with the boss, interviewing the target audience, organizing informal surveys, and brainstorming for ideas
- Conduct formal research for long reports and complex problems by searching electronically or manually, investigating primary sources, and organizing scientific experiments.

3.2 Organize information into strategic relationships.

- For simple messages, make a quick scratch list of topics; for more complex messages, create an outline.
- To prepare an outline, divide the main topic into three to five major components.
- Break the components into subpoints consisting of details, illustrations, and evidence.
- Organize the information using *direct organization* (with the main idea first) when audiences will be pleased, mildly interested, or neutral.
- Organize information using the *indirect organization* (with explanations preceding the main idea) for audiences that will be unwilling, displeased, or hostile.

3.3 Compose a first draft using a variety of sentence types.

- Decide whether to compose quickly (*freewriting*) or to write more deliberately—but remember that you are writing a first draft.
- Employ a variety of sentence types including simple (one independent clause), complex (one independent and one dependent clause), compound (two independent clauses), and compound-complex (at least two independent clauses and one dependent clause).
- Avoid fragments (broken-off parts of sentences), run-on sentences (two clauses fused improperly), and comma splices (two clauses joined improperly with a comma).
- Remember that sentences are most effective when they are short (20 or fewer words).

3.4 Improve your message by using style effectively.

- Emphasize an idea mechanically by using underlining, italics, boldface, font changes, all caps, dashes, tabulation, and other devices.
- Emphasize an idea stylistically by using vivid words, labelling it, making it the sentence subject, placing it first or last, and removing competing ideas.
- For most business writing, use the active voice by making the subject the doer of the action (*the company hired the student*).
- Use the passive voice (*the student was hired*) to de-emphasize negative news, to emphasize an action rather than the doer, or to conceal the doer of an action.
- Employ parallelism for balanced construction (*jogging, hiking, and biking* rather than *jogging, hiking, and to bike*).
- Avoid dangling modifiers (*sitting at my computer, the words would not come*) and misplaced modifiers (*I have the report you wrote in my office*).

3.5 Organize paragraphs effectively.

- Build well-organized, unified paragraphs by focusing on a single idea.
- Always include a topic sentence that states the main idea of the paragraph.
- Develop support sentences to illustrate, explain, or strengthen the topic sentence.
- Build coherence by repeating a key idea, using pronouns to refer to previous nouns, and showing connections with transitional expressions (*however, therefore, consequently*).
- Control paragraph length by striving for eight or fewer lines.

CHAPTER REVIEW

1. What is *research*, and how do informal and formal research methods differ? (Obj. 1)
2. Before drafting a message, what questions should writers ask as they collect information? (Obj. 1)
3. Why do writers need to outline complex projects before beginning? (Obj. 2)
4. What business messages are better organized directly, and which are better organized indirectly? (Obj. 2)
5. What are the four sentence types? Provide an original example of each. (Obj. 3)
6. What is the relationship between sentence length and comprehension? (Obj. 3)

7. What is the difference between active-voice and passive-voice sentences? Give an original example of each. When should business writers use each? (Obj. 4)
8. How are topic sentences different from support sentences? (Obj. 5)
9. Name three techniques for building paragraph coherence. (Obj. 5)

CRITICAL THINKING

1. What trends in business and developments in technology are forcing workers to write more than ever before? (Obj. 1)
2. Molly, a twenty-three-year-old college graduate with a 3.5 GPA, was hired as an administrative assistant. She was a fast learner on all the software, but her supervisor had to help her with punctuation. On the ninth day of her job, she resigned, saying: "I just don't think this job is a good fit. Commas, semicolons, spelling, typos—those kinds of things just aren't all that important to me. They just don't matter."[5] For what kind of job is Molly qualified? (Objs. 1–5)
3. Why is audience analysis so important in the selection of the direct or indirect organization strategy for a business message? (Obj. 2)
4. How are speakers different from writers in the way they emphasize ideas? (Obj. 4)
5. Now that you have studied the active and passive voice, what do you think when someone in government or business says, "Mistakes were made"? Is it unethical to use the passive voice to avoid specifics?

Visit **MindTap** for a variety of videos, additional exercises, activities, and quizzes to support your learning.

CHAPTER 4

Revising Your Message

Monkey Business Images/Shutterstock.com

OBJECTIVES

After studying this chapter, you should be able to

4.1 Revise business messages for conciseness.

4.2 Improve clarity in business messages.

4.3 Enhance readability through effective document design.

4.4 Proofread and apply effective techniques to find mistakes in routine and complex documents.

4.5 Evaluate messages to judge overall effectiveness.

4.1 Taking Time to Revise: Applying Phase 3 of the Writing Process

In this digital age of emailing, texting, and tweeting, the idea of stopping to revise a message seems almost alien to productivity. Stop to proofread? Crazy idea! No time! However, sending quick but sloppy business messages (especially over a period of time) not only fails to enhance productivity but produces the opposite result. Those rushed messages can be confusing and frustrating and take away from your credibility. They often set into motion a frustrating series of back-and-forth messages seeking clarification. To avoid messages that waste time, create confusion, and reduce credibility, take time to slow down and revise—even for short messages.

The final phase of the 3-×-3 writing process focuses on editing, proofreading, and evaluating. Editing means improving the content and sentence structure of your message. Proofreading is correcting its grammar, spelling, punctuation, format, and mechanics. Evaluating involves analyzing whether your message achieves its purpose.

The revision stage is your chance to make sure your message says what you mean and makes you look good.

OFFICE INSIDER

"Regardless of what you may have been taught in school, writing more doesn't necessarily equate to writing better—especially in a business environment, where time is precious. Don't bury your important points under unnecessary verbiage."

—Edwin Powell, business writing expert and senior editor, *Office Solutions* magazine

Office Insider based on Powell, E. (2003, November/December). Ten tips for better business writing. *Office Solutions, 20*(6), 36.

Whether you revise immediately or after a break, you will want to examine your message critically. You should be especially concerned with ways to improve its conciseness, clarity, and readability.

4.1a Tighten Your Message by Revising for Conciseness

In business, time is indeed money. Translated into writing, this means that concise messages save reading time and, thus, money. In addition, messages that are written directly and efficiently are easier to read and comprehend. In the revision process, look for more efficient ways to say what you mean. Could the thought be conveyed in fewer words? Your writing will be more concise if you eliminate wordy expressions, drop unnecessary introductory words, get rid of redundancies, and purge empty words.

ELIMINATE WORDY EXPRESSIONS. As you revise, focus on eliminating wordy expressions. This takes conscious effort. For example, notice the wordiness in this sentence: *Due to the fact that sales are booming, profits are strong.* It could be said more concisely: *Because sales are booming, profits are strong.* Many wordy expressions can be shortened to one concise word as shown here and illustrated in Figure 4.1. Notice in this figure how you can revise digital documents with strikethrough formatting and colour. If you are revising print documents, use proofreading marks.

A wordy phrase can often be reduced to a single word.

DON'T Wordy	DO✓ Concise
✗ as a general rule	✓ generally
✗ at a later date	✓ later
✗ at this point in time	✓ now, presently
✗ despite the fact that	✓ although
✗ due to the fact that, inasmuch as, in view of the fact that	✓ because
✗ feel free to	✓ please
✗ for the period of, for the purpose of	✓ for
✗ in addition to the above	✓ also
✗ in all probability	✓ probably
✗ in the event that	✓ if
✗ in the near future	✓ soon
✗ in very few cases	✓ seldom, rarely
✗ until such time as	✓ until

LIMIT LONG LEAD-INS. Another way to create concise sentences is to delete unnecessary introductory words. Consider this sentence: *I am sending you this*

FIGURE 4.1 | Revising Digital and Print Documents

Revising Digital Documents Using Track Changes

~~This is a short note to let you know that, as~~ As you requested, I ~~made an investigation of~~ investigated several of our competitors' websites. Attached ~~hereto~~ is a summary of my findings. ~~of my investigation.~~ I was ~~really~~ most interested in ~~making a comparison of the employment of strategies for~~ comparing marketing strategies as well as ~~the use of~~ navigational graphics ~~used~~ to guide visitors through the sites. ~~In view of the fact that~~ Because we will be revising our own website ~~in the near future~~ soon, I was ~~extremely~~ intrigued by the organization, ~~kind of~~ marketing tactics, and navigation at each ~~and every~~ site I visited.

When revising Word documents, you can use Word's easy Track Changes feature which strikes out (in red) what you'd like to delete, and adds in (also in red) what you'd like to add. Track Changes can be enabled by going to the "Review" tab at the top of any Word document and clicking on "Track Changes."

Revising Printed Documents Using Proofreading Symbols

When revising printed documents, use proofreading symbols to manually show your revisions.

~~This is a short note to let you know that,~~ as you requested, I ~~made an~~ investigat~~ion of~~ several of our competitors' websites. Attached ~~hereto~~ is a summary of my findings ~~of my investigation.~~ I was ~~really~~ most interested in ~~making a comparison of the employment of~~ strategies ~~for marketing~~ as well as ~~the use of~~ navigational graphics ~~used~~ to guide visitors through the sites. ~~In view of the fact that~~ we will be revising our own website ~~in the near future,~~ I was ~~extremely~~ intrigued by the organization, ~~kind of~~ marketing tactics, and navigation at each ~~and every~~ site I visited.

Popular Proofreading Symbols

- Delete
- Capitalize
- Insert
- Insert comma
- Insert period
- Start paragraph

email to announce that a new manager has been hired. A more concise and more direct sentence deletes the long lead-in: *A new manager has been hired.* The meat of the sentence often follows the long lead-in.

Avoid long lead-ins that delay the reader from reaching the meaning of the sentence.

DON'T Wordy	DO Concise
✗ We are sending this announcement to let everyone know that we expect to change Internet service providers within six weeks.	✓ We expect to change Internet service providers within six weeks.
✗ This is to inform you that you may find lower airfares at our website.	✓ You may find lower airfares at our website.
✗ I am writing this letter because Professor Brian Wilson suggested that your organization was hiring trainees.	✓ Professor Brian Wilson suggested that your organization was hiring trainees.

DROP UNNECESSARY *THERE IS/ARE* AND *IT IS/WAS* FILLERS. In many sentences the expressions *there is/are* and *it is/was* function as unnecessary fillers. In addition to taking up space, these fillers delay getting to the point of the sentence. Eliminate them by tweaking the sentence. Many—but not all—sentences can be revised so that fillers are unnecessary.

DON'T Wordy	DO✓ Concise
✗ *There are* more women than men enrolled in college today.	✓ More women than men are enrolled in college today.
✗ *There* is an aggregator that collects and organizes blogs.	✓ An aggregator collects and organizes blogs.
✗ *It was* the *Globe and Mail* that first reported the story.	✓ The *Globe and Mail* first reported the story.

REJECT REDUNDANCIES. Expressions that repeat the same idea or include unnecessary words are redundant. Saying *unexpected surprise* is like saying *surprise surprise* because *unexpected* carries the same meaning as *surprise*. Excessive adjectives, adverbs, and phrases often create redundancies and wordiness. Redundancies do not add emphasis, as some people think. Instead, they identify a writer as inexperienced. As you revise, look for redundant expressions such as the following:

DON'T Redundant	DO✓ Concise
✗ absolutely essential	✓ essential
✗ adequate enough	✓ adequate
✗ basic fundamentals	✓ fundamentals *or* basics
✗ big in size	✓ big
✗ combined together	✓ combined
✗ exactly identical	✓ identical
✗ each and every	✓ each *or* every
✗ necessary prerequisite	✓ prerequisite
✗ new beginning	✓ beginning
✗ refer back	✓ refer
✗ repeat again	✓ repeat
✗ true facts	✓ facts

PURGE EMPTY WORDS. Familiar phrases roll off the tongue easily, but many contain expendable parts. Be alert to these empty words and phrases: *case, degree, the fact that, factor, instance, nature*, and *quality*. Notice how much better the following sentences sound when we remove all the empty words:

> *~~In the case of~~ GO Transit, ~~they~~ improved customer satisfaction by adding more trips between Kitchener-Waterloo and Toronto.*
>
> *Because of ~~the degree of~~ support from upper management, the plan worked.*
>
> *We are aware ~~of the fact~~ that sales of new products soar when pushed by social networking.*
>
> *Except for ~~the instance of~~ Toyota, Japanese imports sagged.*
>
> *She chose a career in a field that was analytical ~~in nature~~. [OR: She chose a career in an analytical field.]*
>
> *Student writing in that class is excellent ~~in quality~~.*

Also avoid saying the obvious. In the following examples, notice how many unnecessary words we can omit through revision:

> *~~When it arrived,~~ I cashed your cheque immediately. (Announcing the cheque's arrival is unnecessary. That fact is assumed in its cashing.)*
>
> *As consumers learn more about ingredients ~~and as they become more knowledgeable~~, they are demanding fresher foods. (Avoid repeating information.)*

Look carefully at clauses beginning with *that, which*, and *who*. They can often be shortened without loss of clarity. Search for phrases such as *it appears that*. These phrases often can be reduced to a single adjective or adverb such as *apparently*.

> *Changing the name of a successful company ~~that is successful~~ is always risky.*
>
> *All employees ~~who are among those~~ completing the course will be reimbursed.*
>
> *Our final proposal, ~~which was~~ slightly altered ~~in its final form~~, was approved.*
>
> *We plan to schedule weekly meetings ~~on a weekly basis~~.*

4.1b Write Concisely When Microblogging and Posting on Social Media

Concise expression is especially important in microblogging. As its name suggests, *microblogging* consists of short messages exchanged on social media such as Twitter, Facebook, and Tumblr. Many businesses are eagerly joining these microblogging networks to hear what's being said about them and their products. When they hear complaints, they can respond immediately and often solve customer problems. Companies are also using microblogging to make marketing announcements, improve their image, and sell their products.

Microblogging may be public or private. Twitter and similar social networks are predominantly public channels with messages broadcast externally to the world. Twitter limits each post ("tweet") to 140 characters, including spaces, punctuation, and links. Recognizing the usefulness of microblogging but desiring more confidentiality and security, some companies prefer to keep their messaging internal. IBM, for example, employs Blue Twit, a tool that enables IBM employees to share real-time news and get help from colleagues without going outside the organization. Blue Twit extends the length of messages to 400 characters.

Your messages must be short—without straying too far from conventional spelling, grammar, and punctuation. Sound difficult? It is, but it can be done, as shown in the following 140-character examples of workplace tweets:

Sample Response to Customer Complaint

@complainer Our manual can be confusing about that problem. Call me at 800-123-4567 or see http://bit.ly/xx for easy fix. Thanks, Henry

Frank + Oak CEO Announces Meeting

Livestreaming the Frank + Oak Family quarterly all hands meeting 4-6 PM EST today! Tune in: http://on.fb.me/allhandslive

Air Canada Explains

Air Canada responds to loss of pressurization event on flight from YYC to YHZ [with a link to an Air Canada statement about the event]

Starbucks Thanks Customers

Throughout April, you contributed 231,000+ hours of community service in 34 countries across five continents. Thank You! #monthofservice

When microblogging, (a) include only main ideas, (b) choose descriptive but short words, (c) personalize your message if possible, and (d) be prepared to write several versions striving for conciseness, clarity, and, yes, even correctness.

OFFICE INSIDER

"Good writing is brevity, and brevity is marketing. Want to lose me as a customer, forever, guaranteed? Have a grammar error on any form of outward communication."

—Peter Shankman, founder of Geek Factory, blogger, angel investor, author

Office Insider based on Shankman, P. (2011, May 20). I will never hire a "social media expert," and neither should you. Retrieved from http://shankman.com/i-will-never-hire-a-social-media-expert-and-neither-should-you

4.2 Making Your Message Clear

A major revision task is assessing the clarity of your message. A clear message is one that's immediately understood. Employees, customers, and investors increasingly want to be addressed in a clear and genuine way. Fuzzy, long-winded, and unclear writing prevents comprehension. Readers understand better when information is presented clearly and concisely, as a study about drug facts illustrates in Figure 4.2. Three techniques can improve the clarity of your writing: applying the KISS formula (Keep It Short and Simple), dumping trite business phrases, and avoiding clichés and slang.

4.2a Keep It Short and Simple

To achieve clarity, resist the urge to show off or be fancy. As a business writer, your goal is to *express*, not *impress*. One way to achieve clear writing is to apply the KISS formula: active-voice sentences that avoid indirect, pompous language.

DON'T Wordy and Unclear	DO✓ Improved
✗ Employees have not been made sufficiently aware of the potentially adverse consequences regarding the use of these perilous chemicals.	✓ Warn your employees about these dangerous chemicals.
✗ In regard to the matter of obtaining optimal results, it is essential that employees be given the implements that are necessary for jobs to be completed satisfactorily.	✓ To get the best results, give employees the tools they need to do the job.

FIGURE 4.2 | Conciseness Aids Clarity in Understanding Banking Facts

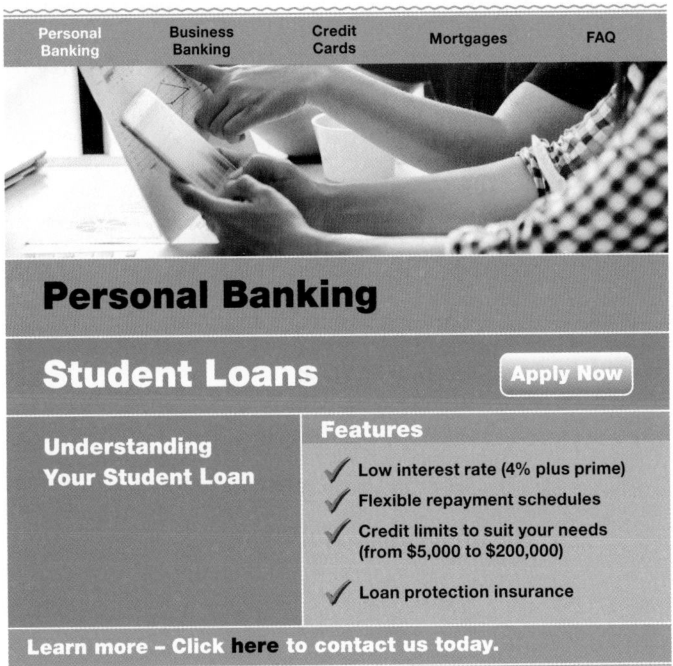

Personal Banking
Business Banking
Credit Cards
Mortgages
FAQ
Personal Banking
Student Loans
Apply Now
Understanding Your Student Loan
Features
Low interest rate (4% plus prime)
Flexible repayment schedules
Credit limits to suit your needs (from $5,000 to $200,000)
Loan protection insurance
Learn more – Click here to contact us today.

Consumers understand banking better when detailed information is presented concisely and clearly, as in the clear bulleted style from this banking website.

4.2b Dump Trite Business Phrases

To sound "businesslike," some business writers repeat the same stale expressions that others have used over the years. Your writing will sound fresher and more vigorous if you eliminate these trite phrases or find more original ways to convey the ideas.

DON'T Trite Phrase	DO✓ Improved
✗ as per your request	✓ as you request/asked
✗ pursuant to your request	✓ at your request
✗ enclosed please find	✓ enclosed is
✗ every effort will be made	✓ we'll try
✗ in accordance with your wishes	✓ as you requested
✗ in receipt of	✓ have received
✗ please do not hesitate to	✓ please
✗ respond forthwith	✓ respond immediately
✗ thank you in advance	✓ thank you
✗ under separate cover	✓ separately
✗ with reference to	✓ about

4.2c Drop Clichés

Clichés are dull and sometimes ambiguous.

Clichés are expressions that have become exhausted by overuse. Many cannot be explained, especially to those who are new to our culture. Clichés lack not only freshness but also clarity. Instead of repeating clichés such as the following, try to find another way to say what you mean.

below the belt	last but not least
better than new	make a bundle
beyond a shadow of a doubt	pass with flying colours
easier said than done	quick as a flash
exception to the rule	shoot from the hip
fill the bill	step up to the plate
first and foremost	think outside the box
good to go	true to form

4.2d Avoid Slang and Buzzwords

Slang is informal words with arbitrary and extravagantly changed meanings. Slang words quickly go out of fashion because they are no longer appealing when everyone begins to understand them. If you want to sound professional, avoid slangy expressions such as *snarky, lousy, blowing the budget, bombed,* and *getting burned.*

Buzzwords are technical expressions that have become fashionable and often are meant to impress rather than express. Business buzzwords include empty terms such as *optimize, incentivize, innovative, leveraging, scale*, and *paradigm shift.* Countless businesses today use vague rhetoric in the form of phrases such as *cost effective, positioned to perform, solutions-oriented*, and *value-added services with end-to-end fulfillment.*

Consider the following statement by a government official who had been asked why his department was dropping a proposal to lease offshore oil lands: *The Administration has an awful lot of other things in the pipeline, and this has more wiggle room, so they just moved it down the totem pole.* He added, however, that the proposal might be offered again since *there is no pulling back because of hot-potato factors.* What exactly does this mean? The official could simply have said: "We won't be leasing the offshore lands at this time, though we may consider doing so in future."

OFFICE INSIDER

"If you could taste words, most corporate websites, brochures, and sales materials would remind you of stale, soggy rice cakes: nearly calorie free, devoid of nutrition, and completely unsatisfying. Unfortunately, years of language dilution by lawyers, marketers, executives, and HR departments have turned the powerful, descriptive sentence into an empty vessel optimized for buzzwords, jargon, and vapid expressions."

—Jason Fried, software developer and cofounder of the company 37signals

Office Insider based on Fried, J. (2010, May 1). Why is business writing so awful? Inc. magazine. Retrieved from http://www.inc.com/magazine/20100501/why-is-business-writing-so-awful.html

4.2e Rescue Buried Verbs

Buried verbs have been needlessly converted to wordy noun expressions. Verbs such as *acquire, establish*, and *develop* are made into nouns such as *acquisition, establishment*, and *development.* Such nouns often end in *-tion, -ment*, and *-ance.* Sometimes called *zombie nouns* because they cannibalize and suck the life out of active verbs,[2] these nouns increase sentence length, slow the reader, and muddy the thought. You can make your writing cleaner and more forceful by avoiding buried verbs and zombie nouns:

WORKPLACE IN FOCUS

Ever heard of Internet content that is "snackable"? Do you prefer websites that deliver an "immersive experience"? Have you seen the latest pet photos that have "gone viral" because of their "click-ability"? Do you know what any of this means? You do if you work in the world of digital marketing, according to technology blog Mashable, which included these words in a list of the most overused buzzwords in the digital media profession. While people use buzzwords to sound smart or trendy, such words are inappropriate in most—but not all—business settings. *In what situations should communicators avoid using buzzwords and slang?*[3]

serato/Shutterstock.com

DON'T Buried Verbs	DO✓ Unburied Verbs
✘ conduct a discussion of	✓ discuss
✘ create a reduction in	✓ reduce
✘ engage in the preparation of	✓ prepare
✘ give consideration to	✓ consider
✘ make an assumption of	✓ assume
✘ make a discovery of	✓ discover
✘ perform an analysis of	✓ analyze
✘ reach a conclusion that	✓ conclude
✘ take action on	✓ act

4.2f Control Exuberance

Occasionally, we show our exuberance with words such as *very, definitely, quite, completely, extremely, really, actually*, and *totally*. These intensifiers can emphasize and strengthen your meaning. Overuse, however, makes your writing sound unbusinesslike. Control your enthusiasm and guard against excessive use.

DON'T Excessive Exuberance	DO✓ Businesslike
✗ The manufacturer was *extremely* upset to learn that its smartphones were *definitely* being counterfeited.	✓ The manufacturer was upset to learn that its smartphones were being counterfeited.
✗ We *totally* agree that we *actually* did not give his proposal a *very* fair trial.	✓ We agree that we did not give his proposal a fair trial.

4.2g Choose Clear, Precise Words

As you revise, make sure your words are precise so that the audience knows exactly what you mean. Clear writing creates meaningful images in the mind of the reader. Such writing is sparked by specific verbs, concrete nouns, and vivid adjectives. Foggy messages are marked by sloppy references that may require additional inquiries to clarify their meaning.

DON'T Less Precise	DO✓ More Precise
✗ She requested that everyone help out.	✓ Our manager asked each team member to volunteer.
✗ They will consider the problem soon.	✓ Our steering committee will consider the recruitment problem on May 15.
✗ We received many responses.	✓ The Sales Division received 28 job applications.
✗ Someone called about the meeting.	✓ Russell Vitello called about the June 12 sales meeting.

4.3 Enhancing Readability Through Document Design

Well-designed documents improve your messages in two important ways. First, they enhance readability and comprehension. Second, they make readers think you are a well-organized and intelligent person. In the revision process, you have a chance to adjust formatting and make other changes so that readers grasp your main points quickly. Design techniques to improve readability include appropriate use of white space, margins, typefaces, fonts, numbered and bulleted lists, and headings for visual impact.

4.3a Use White Space

Empty space on a page is called *white space*. A page crammed full of text or graphics appears busy, cluttered, and unreadable. To increase white space, use headings, bulleted or numbered lists, and effective margins. Remember that short sentences

(20 or fewer words) and short paragraphs (eight or fewer printed lines) improve readability and comprehension. As you revise, think about shortening long sentences. Consider breaking long paragraphs into shorter chunks.

4.3b Understand Margins and Text Alignment

Margins determine the white space on the left, right, top, and bottom of a block of type. They define the reading area and provide important visual relief. Business letters and memos usually have side margins of 2.5 to 3.8 centimetres (1 to 1.5 inches).

Your writing software (e.g., Microsoft Word) probably offers four forms of margin alignment: (a) lines align only at the left, (b) lines align only at the right, (c) lines align at both left and right *(justified)*, and (d) lines are centred. Nearly all text in Western cultures is aligned at the left and reads from left to right. The right margin may be either *justified* or *ragged right*. The text in books such as this one, magazines, and other long works is usually justified on the left and right for a formal appearance.

On the other hand, as you type your own work in your writing software, you'll notice that while it is left-justified, it is ragged on the right. This makes sense for academic assignments or for drafts of documents that might later be published (e.g., reports, websites, etc.). Finally, centred text is appropriate only for headings and short invitations, not for complete messages.

4.3c Choose Appropriate Typefaces

Business writers may choose from a number of typefaces in their writing software. A typeface defines the shape of text characters. A wide range of typefaces, as shown in Figure 4.3, is available for various purposes. Some are decorative and useful for special purposes. For most business messages, however, you should choose from *serif* or *sans serif* categories.

Serif typefaces have small features at the ends of strokes. The most common serif typeface is Times New Roman. Serif typefaces suggest tradition, maturity, and formality. They are frequently used for body text in business messages and longer documents. Because books, newspapers, and magazines favour serif typefaces, readers are familiar with them.

Sans serif typefaces include Arial, Calibri, Gothic, Tahoma, Helvetica, and Univers. These clean characters are widely used for headings, signs, and material that does not require continuous reading. Web designers often prefer sans serif

FIGURE 4.3 | Typefaces With Different Personalities for Different Purposes

All-Purpose Sans Serif	Traditional Serif	Happy, Creative Script/Funny	Assertive, Bold Modern Display	Plain Monospaced
Arial	Century	Brush Script	Britannic Bold	Courier
Calibri	Garamond	Comic Sans	Broadway	Letter Gothic
Helvetica	Georgia	Gigi	Elephant	Monaco
Tahoma	Goudy	Jokerman	Impact	Prestige Elite
Univers	Palatino	Lucinda	Bauhaus 93	
Verdana	Times New Roman	Kristen	SHOWCARD	

typefaces for simple, pure pages. For longer documents, however, sans serif typefaces may seem colder and less appealing than familiar serif typefaces.

For less formal messages or special decorative effects, you might choose one of the "happy" fonts such as Comic Sans or a bold typeface such as Impact. You can simulate handwriting with a script typeface. Despite the wonderful possibilities available in your writing software, don't get carried away with fancy typefaces (there has been a backlash against the use of Comic Sans for some time now, for example). All-purpose sans serif and traditional serif typefaces are most appropriate for your business messages. Generally, use no more than two typefaces within one document.

4.3d Capitalize on Type Fonts and Sizes

Font refers to a specific style within a typeface family. Here are examples of font styles in the Verdana font family:

CAPITALIZATION	underline
SMALL CAPS	Outline
boldface	Shadow
italics	Emboss

Font styles are a mechanical means of adding emphasis to your words. ALL CAPS, SMALL CAPS, and **bold** are useful for headings, subheadings, and single words or short phrases in the text. ALL CAPS, HOWEVER, SHOULD **NEVER** BE USED FOR LONG STRETCHES OF TEXT BECAUSE ALL THE LETTERS ARE THE SAME HEIGHT. This makes it difficult for readers to differentiate words. In addition, excessive use of all caps feels like shouting and irritates readers.

Boldface, *italics*, and underlining are effective for calling attention to important points and terms. Be cautious, however, that your use of fancy font styles is not excessive. Don't use them if they will confuse, annoy, or delay readers.

As you revise, think about type size. Readers are generally most comfortable with 10- to 12-point type for body text. Smaller type enables you to fit more words into a space. Tiny type, however, makes text look dense and unappealing. Slightly larger type makes material more readable. Overly large type (14 points or more) looks amateurish and out of place for body text in business messages. Larger type, however, is appropriate for headings.

4.3e Number and Bullet Lists for Quick Comprehension

Numbered lists represent sequences; bulleted lists highlight items that may not show a sequence.

One of the best ways to ensure rapid comprehension of ideas is through the use of numbered or bulleted lists. Lists provide high "skim value": readers can browse quickly and grasp main ideas. By breaking up complex information into smaller chunks, lists improve readability, understanding, and retention. They also force the writer to organize ideas and write efficiently.

When revising, look for ideas that could be converted to lists, and follow these techniques to make your lists look professional:

- **Numbered lists:** Use for items that represent a sequence or reflect a numbering system.
- **Bulleted lists:** Use to highlight items that don't necessarily show a chronology.
- **Capitalization:** Capitalize the initial word of each line.
- **Punctuation:** Add end punctuation only if the listed items are complete sentences.
- **Parallelism:** Make all the lines consistent; for example, start each with a verb.

In the following examples, notice that the list on the left presents a sequence of steps with numbers. The bulleted list does not show a sequence of ideas; therefore, bullets are appropriate. Also notice the parallelism in each example. In the numbered list, each item begins with a verb. In the bulleted list, each item follows an adjective/noun sequence. Business readers appreciate lists because they focus attention and save time.

Numbered List	Bulleted List
Our recruiters follow these steps when hiring applicants: 1. Examine the application. 2. Interview the applicant. 3. Check the applicant's references.	To attract upscale customers, we feature the following: • Quality fashions • Personalized service • Generous return policy

4.3f Add Headings for Visual Impact

Headings help the reader separate major ideas from details. They enable a busy reader to skim familiar or less important information. They also provide a quick preview or review. Headings appear most often in reports, which you will study in Chapters 9 and 10. However, headings can also improve readability in emails, memos, and letters. In the following example, notice how a *category heading* highlights each listing:

> Our company focuses on the following areas in the employment process:
>
> - **Attracting applicants.** We advertise for qualified applicants, and we also encourage current employees to recommend good people.
> - **Interviewing applicants.** Our specialized interviews include simulated customer encounters as well as scrutiny by supervisors.
> - **Checking references.** We investigate every applicant thoroughly. We contact former employers and all listed references.

In Figure 4.4 the writer converts a dense, unappealing email into an easier-to-read version by applying professional document design. Notice that the all-caps font shown earlier makes its meaning difficult to decipher. Lack of white space further reduces readability. In the revised version, the writer changed the all-caps font to upper- and. One of the best document design techniques in this message is the use of headings and bullets and white space to help the reader see chunks of information in similar groups. All of these improvements are made in the revision process.

4.4 Proofreading to Find Errors

Even the best writers sometimes make mistakes. The problem, however, is not making the mistakes; the real problem is not finding and correcting them. Documents with errors affect your credibility and the success of your organization, as illustrated by the infographic in Figure 4.5.

Once the message is in its final form, it's time to proofread. Don't proofread earlier because you may waste time checking items that eventually will be changed or omitted. Important messages—such as those you send to management or to customers—deserve careful revision and proofreading. When you finish a first draft of an important document, put the document aside and return to it after a break, preferably 24 hours or longer. Proofreading is especially difficult because most of us read what we *thought* we wrote. That's why it's important to look for specific problem areas.

FIGURE 4.4 | Document Design Improves Readability

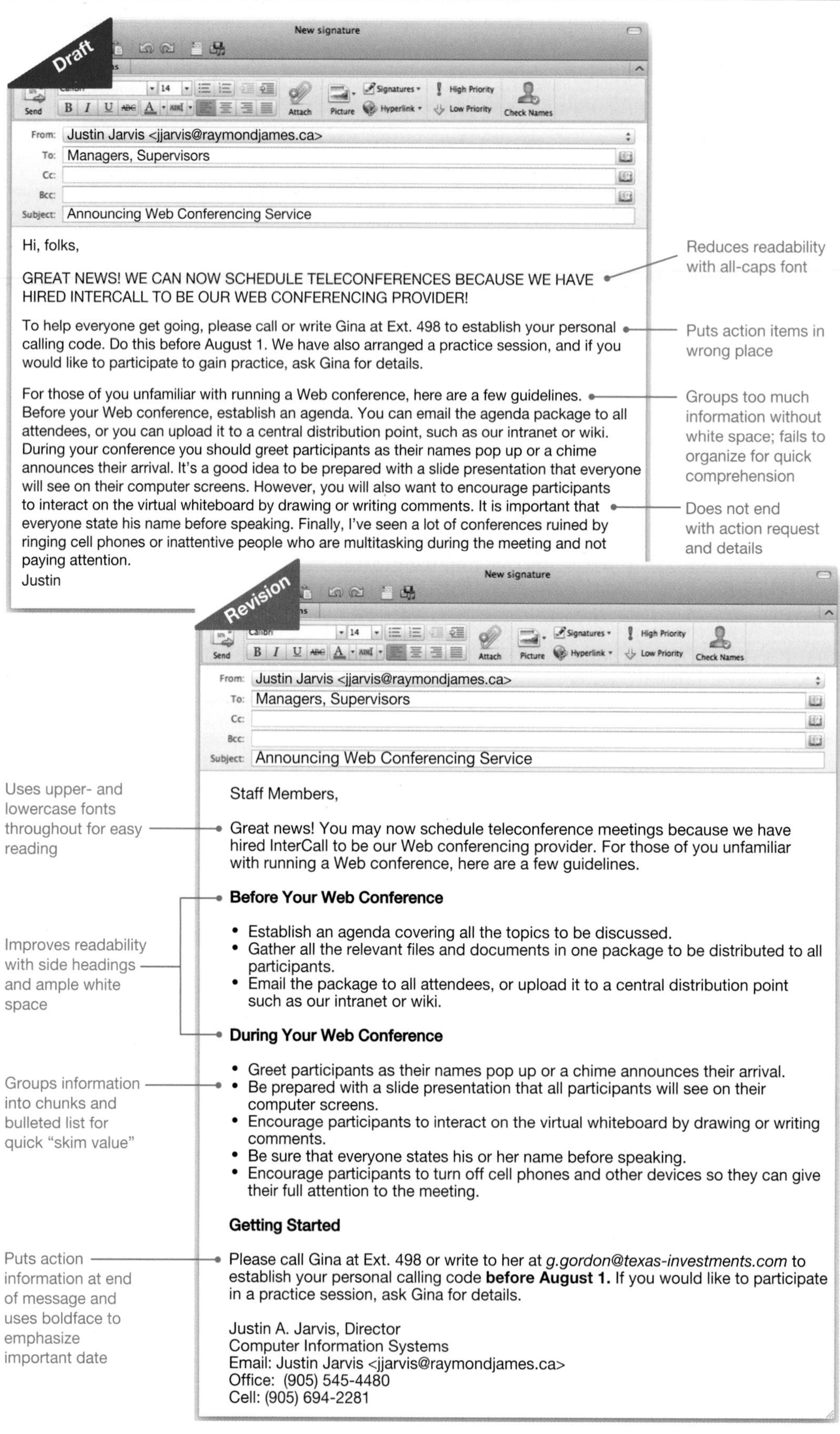

FIGURE 4.5 | Why Proofread?

WHY PROOFREAD? IN BUSINESS, ACCURACY MATTERS

A survey of business professionals revealed the following:

100% said that writing errors influenced their opinions about a business.

57% will stop considering a company if its print brochure has one writing error.

77% have eliminated a prospective company from consideration in part because of writing errors.

75% thought misspelled words were inexcusable.

30% of Web visitors will leave if a website contains writing errors.

Goodluz/Shutterstock.com

© Cengage Learning

4.4a What to Watch for in Proofreading

Careful proofreaders check for problems in the following areas:

- **Spelling.** Now is the time to consult the dictionary. Is *recommend* spelled with one or two *c*'s? Do you mean *affect* or *effect*? Use your computer spell-checker, but don't rely on it totally.
- **Grammar.** Locate sentence subjects; do their verbs agree with them? Do pronouns agree with their antecedents? Review the principles in the Grammar/Mechanics Handbook if necessary. Use your computer's grammar checker, but be suspicious. It's not always correct.
- **Punctuation.** Make sure that introductory clauses are followed by commas. In compound sentences put commas before coordinating conjunctions *(and, or, but, nor)*. Double-check your use of semicolons and colons.
- **Names and numbers.** Compare all names and numbers with their sources because inaccuracies are not always visible. Especially verify the spelling of the names of individuals receiving the message. Most of us immediately dislike someone who misspells our name.
- **Format.** Be sure that your document looks balanced on the page. Compare its parts and format with those of standard documents shown in Appendix A. If you indent paragraphs, be certain that all are indented and that their spacing is consistent.

4.4b How to Proofread Routine Documents

Most routine documents require a light proofreading. If you read on screen, use the down arrow to reveal one line at a time. This focuses your attention at the bottom of the screen. A safer proofreading method, however, is reading from a printed copy. Regardless of which method you use, look for typos and misspellings. Search for easily confused words, such as *to* for *too* and *then* for *than*. Read for missing words and inconsistencies. For handwritten or printed messages, use standard proofreading marks, shown briefly in Figure 4.6 or completely in Appendix B. For digital documents and collaborative projects, use the simple word processing tools also shown in Figure 4.1 or use the **Comment** and **Track Changes** functions discussed above and in the Communication Workshop in the MindTap.

4.4c How to Proofread Complex Documents

Long, complex, or important documents demand careful proofreading. Apply the previous suggestions but also add the following techniques:

- Print a copy, preferably double-spaced, and set it aside for at least a day. You will be more alert after a breather.
- Allow adequate time to proofread carefully. A common excuse for sloppy proofreading is lack of time.
- One student confessed, "I can find other people's errors, but I can't seem to locate my own." Psychologically, we don't expect to find errors, and we don't want to find them. You can overcome this obstacle by anticipating errors and congratulating, not criticizing, yourself each time you find one.
- Read the message at least twice—once for word meanings and once for grammar and mechanics. For very long documents, read a third time to verify consistency in formatting.
- Reduce your reading speed. Concentrate on individual words rather than ideas.

FIGURE 4.6 | Common Proofreading Marks

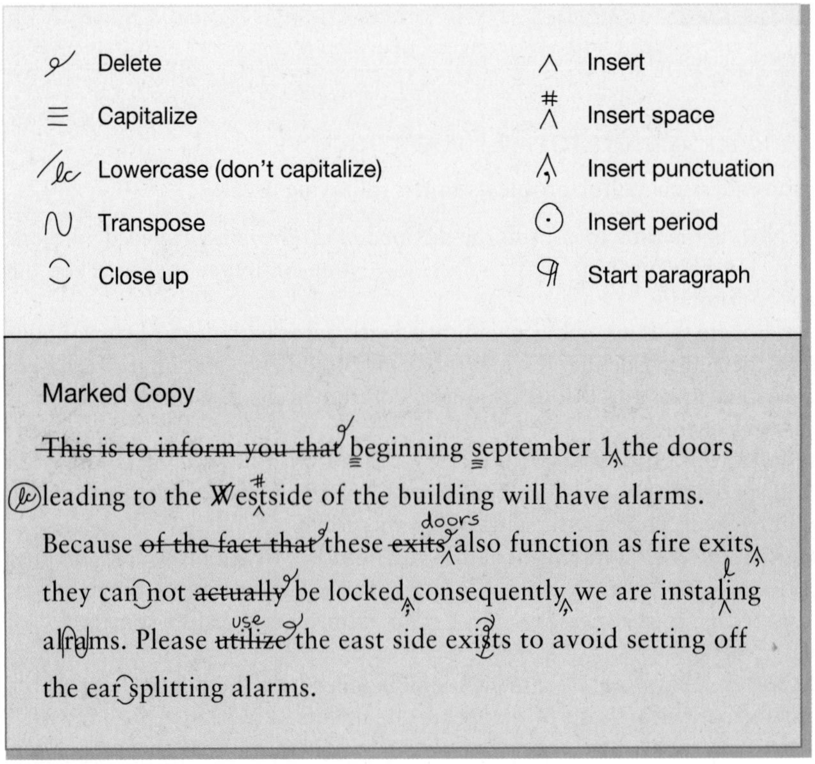

Mark	Meaning	Mark	Meaning
⁄ (delete mark)	Delete	∧	Insert
≡	Capitalize	# ∧	Insert space
/ lc	Lowercase (don't capitalize)	∧ with comma	Insert punctuation
∩∪	Transpose	⊙	Insert period
⁀‿	Close up	¶	Start paragraph

Marked Copy

~~This is to inform you that~~ beginning september 1 the doors leading to the Westside of the building will have alarms. Because ~~of the fact that~~ these ~~exits~~ doors also function as fire exits they can not ~~actually~~ be locked consequently we are instaling alrams. Please ~~utilize~~ use the east side exists to avoid setting off the ear splitting alarms.

- For documents that must be perfect, enlist a proofreading buddy. Have someone read the message aloud, spelling names and difficult words, noting capitalization, and reading punctuation.
- Use the standard proofreading marks shown in Appendix A to indicate changes.

Many of us struggle with proofreading our own writing because we are seeing the same information over and over. We tend to see what we expect to see as our eyes race over the words without looking at each one carefully. We tend to know what is coming next and glide over it. To change the appearance of what you are reading, you might print it on a different coloured paper or change the font. If you are proofing on screen, enlarge the page view or change the background colour of the screen.

4.5 Evaluating the Effectiveness of Your Message

Remember that everything you write, once it's sent out, takes the place of a personal appearance. If you were meeting in person, you would be certain to dress appropriately and professionally. The same standard applies to your writing.

The best way to judge the success of your communication is through feedback. For this reason you should encourage the receiver to respond to your message. This feedback will tell you how to modify future efforts to improve your communication technique.

Your instructor will also be evaluating some of your writing. Although any criticism is painful, don't be defensive. Look on these comments as valuable advice tailored to your specific writing weaknesses—and strengths. Many businesses today spend thousands of dollars bringing in communication consultants to improve employees' writing skills. You are getting the same training in this course.

SUMMARY OF LEARNING OBJECTIVES

4.1 Revise business messages for conciseness.

- Revise for conciseness by eliminating wordy expressions (*as a general rule, at a later date, at this point in time*).
- Exclude opening fillers (*there is, there are*), redundancies (*basic essentials*), and empty words (*in the case of, the fact that*).
- In microblogging messages, include only main ideas, choose descriptive but short words, personalize your message if possible, and be prepared to write several versions striving for conciseness, clarity, and correctness.

4.2 Improve clarity in business messages.

- To be sure your messages are clear, apply the KISS formula: Keep It Short and Simple.
- Avoid foggy, indirect, and pompous language.
- Do not include trite business phrases (*as per your request, enclosed please find, pursuant to your request*), clichés (*better than new, beyond a shadow of a doubt, easier said than done*), slang (*snarky, lousy, bombed*), and buzzwords (*optimize, paradigm shift, incentivize*).
- Avoid burying nouns (*to conduct an investigation* rather than *to investigate, to perform an analysis* rather than *to analyze*).
- Don't overuse intensifiers that show exuberance (*totally, actually, very, definitely*) but sound unbusinesslike.
- Choose precise words (*the report was well-organized rather than the report was great*).

4.3 Enhance readability through effective document design.

- Enhance readability and comprehension by using ample white space, appropriate side margins, and ragged-right (not justified) margins.
- Use serif typefaces (fonts with small features at the ends of strokes, such as Times New Roman, Century, and Palatino) for body text; use sans serif typefaces (clean fonts without small features, such as Arial, Helvetica, and Tahoma) for headings and signs.
- Choose appropriate font styles and sizes for business messages.
- Provide high "skim value" with numbered and bulleted lists.
- Include headings to add visual impact and aid readability in business messages as well as in reports.

4.4 Proofread and apply effective techniques to find mistakes in routine and complex documents.
- In proofreading be especially alert to spelling, grammar, punctuation, names, numbers, and document format.
- Proofread routine documents immediately after completion by reading line by line on the computer screen or, better yet, from a printed draft.
- Proofread more complex documents after a breather.
- Allow adequate time, reduce your reading speed, and read the document at least three times—for word meanings, for grammar and mechanics, and for formatting.

4.5 Evaluate messages to judge overall effectiveness.
- Encourage feedback from the receiver so that you can determine whether your communication achieved its goal.
- Welcome any advice from your instructor on how to improve your writing skills.

CHAPTER REVIEW

1. What's involved in the revision process? Is revision still necessary in a digital age when workplace messages fly back and forth in split seconds? (Obj. 1)
2. What's wrong with a message that begins, *I am writing this announcement to let everyone know that...*? (Obj. 1)
3. What is microblogging, and why is conciseness especially important in microblogging messages and social media posts? (Obj. 1)
4. What's wrong with familiar business phrases such as *as per your request* and *enclosed please find*? (Obj. 2)
5. Why should writers avoid expressions such as *first and foremost* and *think outside the box*? (Obj. 2)
6. What are buried verbs and zombie nouns? Give an original example of each. Why should they be avoided? (Obj. 2)
7. How do bulleted and numbered lists improve readability? (Obj. 3)
8. In proofreading, why is it difficult for writers to find their own errors? How could they overcome this barrier? (Obj. 4)
9. What are five items to check in proofreading? Be ready to discuss methods you find useful in spotting these errors. (Obj. 4)
10. How can you overcome defensiveness when your writing is criticized constructively? (Obj. 5)

CRITICAL THINKING

1. In this digital age of rapid communication, how can you justify the time it takes to stop and revise a message? (Objs. 1–5)
2. Assume you have started a new job in which you respond to customers by using boilerplate (previously constructed) paragraphs. Some of them contain clichés such as *pursuant to your request* and *in accordance with your wishes*. Other paragraphs are wordy and violate the principle of using concise and clear writing that you have learned. What should you do? (Obj. 2)
3. Because business writing should have high "skim value," why not write everything in bulleted lists? (Obj. 3)
4. Conciseness is valued in business. However, can messages be too short? (Obj. 1)
5. What advice would you give in this ethical dilemma? Brittany is serving as interim editor of the company newsletter. She receives an article written by the company president describing, in abstract and pompous language, the company's goals for the coming year. Brittany thinks the article will need considerable revising to make it readable. Attached to the president's article are complimentary comments by two of the company vice presidents. What action should Brittany take and why? (Obj. 5)

Visit **MindTap** for a variety of videos, additional exercises, activities, and quizzes to support your learning.

UNIT 03

Writing at Work

Rawpixel.com/Shutterstock.com

COMMUNICATION TECHNOLOGY IN THE NEWS

Email on vacation? There's help for that. It takes a directive from the very top of an organization before employees can feel safe unplugging while they're away.

You are on the beach. You tell your partner you need to nip up to the cottage to retrieve, oh, a book. You are lying.

Once inside the cottage, you grab any old book off the shelf, then proceed to your secret main task, which is, of course, to check your email. Your partner believes that you, as promised, have not brought your smartphone on holiday. This, too, is an untruth.

Jennifer Deal has you figured out. The senior research scientist at the Center for Creative Leadership in San Diego says you and your brethren suffer from the Zeigarnik effect, a topic she wrote about in the *Wall Street Journal* last week.

"The Zeigarnik effect is what happens when you haven't been able to finish a task—it sort of keeps bugging you. It keeps pinging you, pinging your brain," Deal says in an interview. "Email's a task that never finishes for most people. It's just never done."

The Zeigarnik effect is named after Bluma Zeigarnik, a Lithuanian-born psychologist whose research into memory and what she deemed "states of tension" dates to the late 1920s. Unfinished tasks, she found, are remembered approximately twice as well as completed ones, a finding complicated by an individual's unquantifiable feelings about tasks deemed completed, but inadequately so.

You can see the potential benefits of this to the corporation. And, in contemporary culture, its demerits. "The price is paid beyond the individual," Deal says. "It's all of the people who the individual isn't attending to who are also affected by the situation."

Your partner waiting for you on the beach, for example.

"People need time to reset their brain," Deal says. "We all wander around with a sort of buffer that we use to keep going and if the buffer gets worn down to nothing, disappears, we have real problems coping, being creative, getting things done, not overreacting, being efficient with processes."

The remedy may seem as simple as leaving the phone at home while on vacation.

But no. "The bottom line is, an individual works in a particular position within an org structure, and within a particular network within the organization," Deal notes. "So an individual can say, 'I just choose to turn my smartphone off.' Period. But there are implications for that person's career that they won't necessarily like. And then there are implications for how everybody else within the organization works."

So the true remedy lies at the top of the organization.

Example: Two summers ago, the German automaker Daimler AG announced the launch of its "mail on holiday" email policy. Instead of receiving the standard and often meaningless out-of-office advisory (physically out of office but mentally hyper attentive), the sender is notified that the email is headed for the trash bin. Not in those words. The name of an alternate contact is offered.

"Our employees should relax on holiday and not read work-related emails," a Daimler human resources representative told the *Financial Times*. "With 'mail on holiday' they start back after the holidays with a clean desk. There is no traffic jam in their inbox. That is an emotional relief."

And a political one, too, as the endorsement from the very top relieves the vacationer of the stigma of being labelled a slacker, slouch, avoider, etc.

A media relations representative at the company's headquarters in Stuttgart confirms that the policy is still in place.

How do other companies measure up?

The current cover story in the *Harvard Business Review* suggests that "accepters"—those high-intensity employees who prioritize their work identities over any other sense of self—"can become the main drivers of organizational pressure for round-the-clock availability." Managers can rewrite this script, the story's authors insist, by "actively protecting employees' non-work time and identities."

We know, because the evidence on this is building mountain high, that companies can reap the richest rewards from multifaceted employees with rich out-of-office lives. Progressive email policies can help enable that because, really, left to our own devices, how successful can we possibly be?

In her *Wall Street Journal* piece, Deal suggests that one to way to beat, or at least rein in the Zeigarnik effect is to lock your phone in a safe. "If you can't look at it—that is, you can't without going to substantial trouble—the brain itch will eventually die off because you can't scratch it."

Really? Does this not seem a strategy vulnerable to compulsion? Deal responds: "It depends on how difficult you make the retrieval." The better solution is to take the responsibility out of the hands of the employee altogether. And stay on the beach.

Summarize the article you've just read in a two- or three-sentence paragraph. Answer the following questions, either on your own or in a small group. Be prepared to present your answers in a short presentation or in an email to your instructor.

QUESTIONS:

1. How does what you've learned in this article change your perception of what business communication is or is not?
2. How might what you've learned in this article be useful in changing your own school or workplace communication?
3. Come up with pro and con arguments for the following debate/discussion topic: "Digital communication such as email is as much an addiction as it is a communication channel." Make sure to reference the Zeigarnik effect in your arguments.

CHAPTER

5

Daily Workplace Writing Channels

OBJECTIVES

After studying this chapter, you should be able to

5.1 Demonstrate professional standards in the use and formatting of major daily workplace writing channels.

5.2 Instant message and text professionally.

5.3 Create professional podcasts and wikis.

5.4 Design professional internal and external blogs.

5.5 Use social media networks professionally.

Rawpixel.com/Shutterstock.com

5.1 Writing at Work in the Digital Age

Today's workplaces are far from paperless, but increasingly, written information is exchanged electronically and on the go. Writing has become a dynamic, interactive activity. This is quite different from writing before the Internet, which was a more static exchange between sender and receiver, as per the model of communication we looked at in Chapter 2. Writers today are empowered by their devices to be active participants who correspond (often in real-time) with colleagues and outsiders, but who also create content, review products, and edit and share all kinds of information, among other activities.

Today, virtual private networks (VPNs) offer secure access to company information from any location in the world that provides an Internet connection. In addition, in many businesses, desktop computers are fast becoming obsolete with the adoption of ever-smaller laptops, netbooks, smartphones, tablets, and other compact mobile devices. As a result, mobile and cloud computing are the two most important technological trends impacting business communication today.

Businesspeople today are connected—and writing—at all times. Many of them are expected to respond to messages on their smartphones wherever they are, even on weekends or while on vacation. As a result, some argue that the communications technology revolution of the past 20 years has resulted in amazing productivity gains, while others point out that technological advances have perhaps created more (unnecessary) work.

You are already sharing pictures and music and messages digitally with your friends and family. Even though "personal" technology has entered the workplace, *this does not mean your workplace messages should look and sound the same as your personal messages*. The main difference is that a higher level of structure and formality should be apparent at work than at home. The importance of maintaining this difference is perhaps the most important lesson in business communication today.

5.1a Email: Love It or Hate It—But It's Not Going Away

Critics say that email is outdated, inefficient, and slowly dying. They complain that it takes too much time, increases stress, and leaves a dangerous "paper" trail. However, email in the workplace is here to stay. Statistics Canada reports that 81 percent of Canadian private-sector enterprises use email, while 100 percent of Canadian public-sector workplaces do so.[1] Companies acknowledge that email has become an indispensable means of internal communication as well as an essential link to customers and suppliers. Despite the substantial attention that social media receive in the news, most business messages are still sent by email.[2] In the next three to five years, we may see more business messages being sent by social media platforms, predicts Dr. Monica Seeley, author of *Brilliant Email*. "But email will remain a bedrock of businesses for some time to come," she maintains.[3] Typical businesspeople spend at least two hours a day—perhaps much more—writing and replying to email.

Because you can expect to use email extensively to communicate at work, it's smart to learn how to do it expertly.

OFFICE INSIDER

"Email is not dead, it's just evolving. It's becoming a searchable archive, a manager's accountability source, a document courier.... Three-quarters of all email is junk, and we're wasting lots of time dealing with less important messages. But it remains the mule of the information age—stubborn and strong."

—Barry Gill, chief of staff, Simply Migrate

5.1b Why People Complain About Email

Although email is recognized as the mainstay of business communication, in a recent study of 1,800 global knowledge workers, 40 percent confessed that "they had received emails that made no sense whatsoever."[4] A *Wall Street Journal* article reports that many business schools are ramping up their writing programs or hiring writing coaches because of complaints about their graduates' skills.[5] Adding to the complaints, Chris Carlson, former recruiting officer at the consulting firm of Booz Allen Hamilton Inc., says that new MBA graduates exchange more than 200 emails a day, and some look like text messages. "They're not [even] in complete sentences," he says.[6]

EMAIL OVERLOAD. In addition to complaints about confusing and poorly written emails, many workers are overwhelmed by too many messages. Currently, the average employee receives 11,680 emails per year.[7] The unfortunate use of "Reply All" often adds to the inbox, irritating those who have to plow through dozens of messages that barely relate to them. Others blame email for eliminating the distinction between work life and home life. They feel an urgency to be available 24/7 and respond immediately.

EMAIL—EVERLASTING EVIDENCE. Still other emailers fail to recognize how dangerous email can be. After deletion, email files still leave trails on servers within and outside organizations. Messages are also backed up on other servers, making them traceable and recoverable by forensic experts. Even writers with nothing to hide should be concerned about what may come back to haunt them. Your best bet is to put nothing in an email that you wouldn't post on your office door. Also, be sure that you know your organization's email policy before sending personal messages. Estimates suggest that as many as a quarter of bosses have fired an employee for an email violation.[8]

Despite the above, email has many advantages and remains the prime communication channel. Therefore, it's to your advantage to learn when and how to use it efficiently and safely.

5.1c When Email Is Appropriate

Email is appropriate for short messages that request information and respond to inquiries. It is especially effective for messages to multiple receivers and messages that must be archived (saved). Emails are also used as cover documents when sending longer attachments.

However, email is not a substitute for face-to-face conversations or phone calls. These channels are much more successful if your goal is to convey enthusiasm or warmth, explain a complex situation, present a persuasive argument, or smooth over disagreements. One expert gives this wise advice: "Sometimes it's better to get off the computer and make a phone call. If emails are ... just not getting the job done, call or walk over to that colleague."[9] Managers and employees echo this advice, as revealed in recent research. They are adamant about using face-to-face contact, rather than email, for critical work situations such as human resources annual reviews, discipline, and promotions.[10]

5.1d How to Draft a Professional Email

Professional emails are different from messages you may send to friends. Instead of casual words tossed off in haste, professional emails are well-considered messages that usually carry non-sensitive information unlikely to upset readers. Therefore, these messages should be organized directly and contain five elements, as described in the following writing plan.

WRITING PLAN FOR PROFESSIONAL EMAILS

- **Subject line:** Summarize the main information/request in condensed form.
- **Greetings:** Say hello and goodbye politely.
- **Opening:** Reveal the reason for writing immediately in a more expanded form than in the subject line.
- **Body:** Explain or justify the reason using headings, bulleted lists, and other high-skim techniques when appropriate.
- **Closing:** Include (a) action information, dates, or deadlines; (b) a summary of the message; or (c) a closing thought.

A subject line must be concise but meaningful.

CRAFT A COMPELLING SUBJECT LINE. The most important part of an email is its subject line. Avoid meaningless statements such as *Help*, *Important*, or *Meeting*. Summarize the purpose of the message clearly and make the receiver want to open the message. Try to include a verb (*Need You to Attend Mississauga Trade Show*). Remember that in some instances the subject line can be the entire message (*Meeting Changed from May 3 to May 10*). Also be sure to adjust the subject line if the topic changes after repeated replies. Subject lines should appear as a combination of uppercase and lowercase letters—never in all lowercase letters.

INCLUDE GREETINGS AND A SIGN-OFF. To help receivers see the beginning and end of your message and to help them recognize whether they are the primary or secondary receiver, include greetings and a sign-off. The greeting sets the tone for the message and reflects your audience analysis. For friends and colleagues, try friendly greetings (*Hi, Julie; Thanks, Julie; Good morning, Julie;* or *Greetings, Julie*). For more formal messages and those to outsiders, include an honorific (usually "dear") and last name (e.g., *Dear Ms. Stevens*). At the end of your message, again depending on your audience analysis, sign off with a "Cheers," "Best," "Regards," or "Sincerely" plus your name and signature block.

DON'T Poor Subject Lines	DO Improved Subject Lines
✗ Trade Show	✓ Need You to Showcase Two Items at Our Next Trade Show
✗ Staff Meeting	✓ Staff Meeting Rescheduled for May 12

OPEN WITH THE MAIN IDEA. Open emails by frontloading—reveal your main idea (information, instruction, request, concern, question) immediately. Even though the purpose of the email is summarized in the subject line, that purpose should be restated—and amplified—in the first sentence. Busy readers want to know immediately why they are reading a message. As you learned in Chapter 3, most messages should begin directly. Notice how the following indirect opening can be improved by frontloading.

Indirect Opening	Direct Opening
For the past six months, the Human Resources Development Department has been considering changes in our employee benefit plan.	Please review the following proposal regarding employee benefits and let me know by May 20 if you approve these changes.

ORGANIZE THE BODY FOR READABILITY AND TONE. After drafting an email, ask yourself how you can make your message more readable. Did you start directly? Did you group similar topics together? Could some information be presented with bulleted or numbered lists? Could you add headings—especially if the message is more than a few paragraphs? Do you see any phrases or sentences that could be condensed? To convey the best tone, read the message aloud. If it sounds curt, it probably is. See below for email body best practice examples.

Designed for easy comprehension, the body explains one topic.

Instead of This	Try This
Here are the instructions for operating the copy machine. First, you insert your copy card in the slot. Then you load paper in the upper tray. Last, copies are fed through the feed tray.	Follow these steps to use the copy machine: 1. *Insert* your copy card in the slot. 2. *Load* paper in the upper tray. 3. *Feed* copies through the feed tray.

Instead of This	Try This		
	Date	City	Speaker
On May 16 we will be in Regina, and Dr. Susan Dillon is the speaker. On June 20, we will be in Saskatoon, and Dr. Diane Minger is the speaker.	May 16	Regina	Dr. Susan Dillon
	June 20	Saskatoon	Dr. Diane Minger

Instead of This	Try This
To keep exercising, you should make a written commitment to yourself, set realistic goals for each day's workout, and enlist the support of a friend.	To keep exercising, you should (a) make a written commitment to yourself, (b) set realistic goals for each day's workout, and (c) enlist the support of a friend.

CLOSE EFFECTIVELY. Generally, close emails with action information or questions, dates, or deadlines. For certain emails it may be appropriate to close with a summary of the message or a closing thought. The closing is where readers look for deadlines and action language. An effective memo or email closing might be *Please send me the PowerPoint deck by June 15 so that we can have your data before our July planning session.*

In some messages a summary of the main points may be an appropriate closing. If no action request is made and a closing summary is unnecessary, you might end with a simple concluding thought *(I'm glad to answer your questions* or *This sounds like a useful project).* You don't need to close messages to coworkers with goodwill statements such as those found in letters to customers or clients. However, a closing thought is often necessary to prevent a feeling of abruptness.

Closings can show gratitude or encourage feedback with remarks such as *I sincerely appreciate your help* or *What are your ideas on this proposal?* Other closings look forward to what's next, such as *How would you like to proceed?* Avoid closing with overused expressions such as *Please let me know if I may be of further assistance.* This ending sounds mechanical and insincere. Figure 5.1 illustrates an employee's revision of a typical problematic email draft into a highly professional final version email.

5.1e Control Your Inbox

Business communicators love to complain about email, and some young people even deny its existence. In the business world, however, email writing IS business writing.[11] Instead of letting your inbox consume your time and ruin your productivity, control it by implementing a few time management strategies.

The most important strategy is checking your email at set times, such as first thing in the morning and again after lunch or at 4 p.m. To avoid being distracted, be sure to turn off your audio and visual alerts. If mornings are your best working times, check your email later in the day. Let your boss and colleagues know about your schedule for responding. Another excellent time saver is the two-minute rule. If you can read and respond to a message within two minutes, then take care of it immediately. For messages that require more time, add them to your to-do list or schedule them on your calendar. To be polite, send a quick note telling the sender when you plan to respond.

5.1f Reply Efficiently With Down-Editing

When answering email, especially ones that request information, a useful skill to develop is *down-editing*. This involves inserting your responses into parts of the incoming message instead of drafting a brand new email. After a courteous opening, your reply will include only the parts of the incoming message to which you are responding. Delete the sender's message headers, signature, and all unnecessary parts. If more than one person will be seeing the response, your responses can be identified with your initials. Another trick is to use a different colour for your down-edits. It takes a little practice to develop this skill, but the down-edited reply reduces confusion, saves writing and reading time, and makes you look savvy.

Figure 5.2 shows a number of additional best practices for managing your email.

5.1g Writing Memos and Letters

Hard-copy memos are useful for internal messages that require a permanent record or formality.

Before email, interoffice memos (along with phone calls and face-to-face discussions) were the primary communication channel for delivering information within organizations. Memos are still useful for important internal messages that require a permanent record or formality. For example, organizations use memos to explain and enforce changes in procedures and for new official instructions.

FIGURE 5.1 | Creating a Professional Email

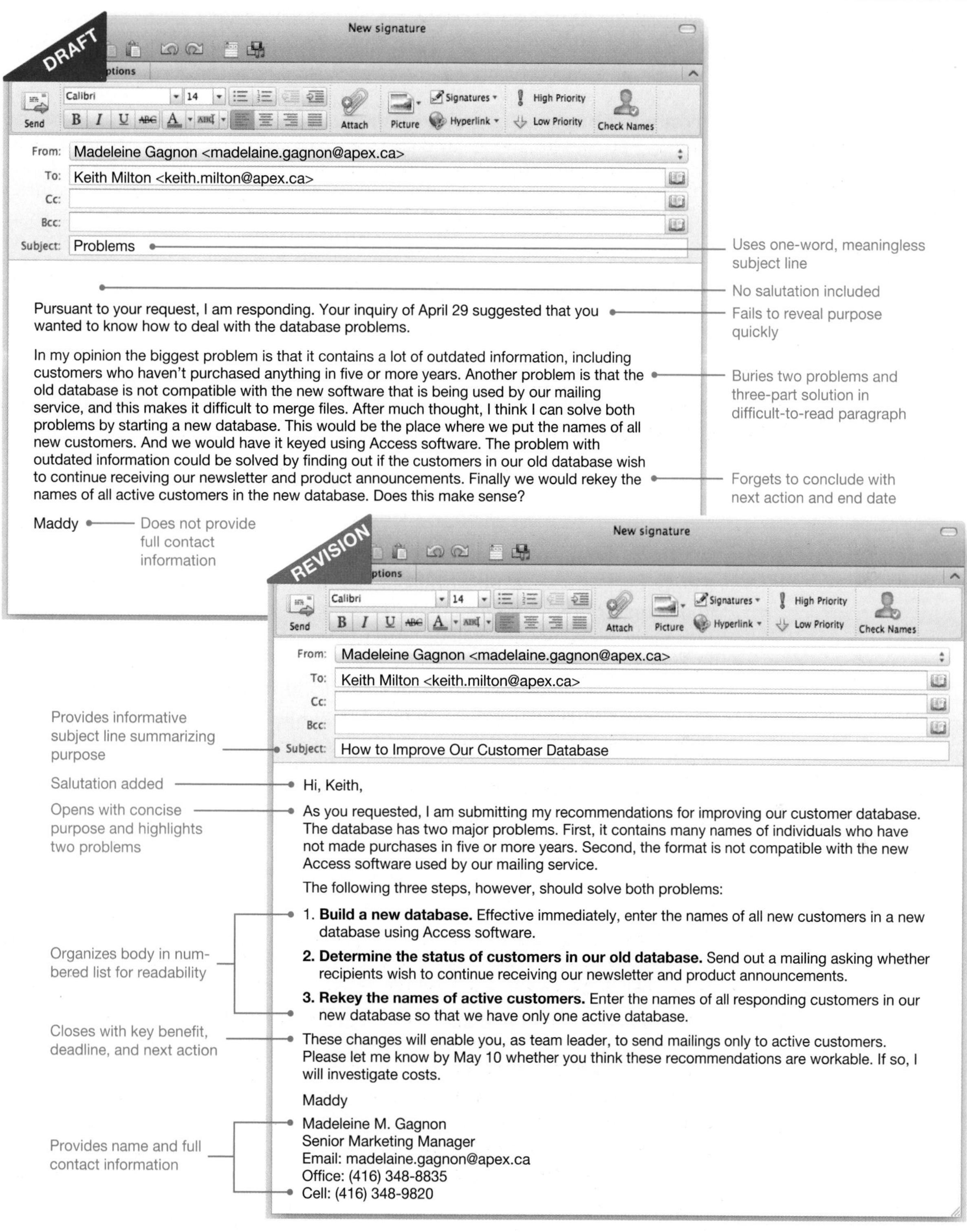

DRAFT
New signature
Send
Calibri
14
Attach
Picture
Signatures
Hyperlink
High Priority
Low Priority
Check Names
From: Madeleine Gagnon <madelaine.gagnon@apex.ca>
To: Keith Milton <keith.milton@apex.ca>
Cc:
Bcc:
Subject: Problems
Uses one-word, meaningless subject line
No salutation included
Pursuant to your request, I am responding. Your inquiry of April 29 suggested that you wanted to know how to deal with the database problems.
Fails to reveal purpose quickly
In my opinion the biggest problem is that it contains a lot of outdated information, including customers who haven't purchased anything in five or more years. Another problem is that the old database is not compatible with the new software that is being used by our mailing service, and this makes it difficult to merge files. After much thought, I think I can solve both problems by starting a new database. This would be the place where we put the names of all new customers. And we would have it keyed using Access software. The problem with outdated information could be solved by finding out if the customers in our old database wish to continue receiving our newsletter and product announcements. Finally we would rekey the names of all active customers in the new database. Does this make sense?
Buries two problems and three-part solution in difficult-to-read paragraph
Forgets to conclude with next action and end date
Maddy
Does not provide full contact information
REVISION
New signature
From: Madeleine Gagnon <madelaine.gagnon@apex.ca>
To: Keith Milton <keith.milton@apex.ca>
Cc:
Bcc:
Subject: How to Improve Our Customer Database
Provides informative subject line summarizing purpose
Salutation added
Hi, Keith,
Opens with concise purpose and highlights two problems
As you requested, I am submitting my recommendations for improving our customer database. The database has two major problems. First, it contains many names of individuals who have not made purchases in five or more years. Second, the format is not compatible with the new Access software used by our mailing service.
The following three steps, however, should solve both problems:
1. Build a new database. Effective immediately, enter the names of all new customers in a new database using Access software.
2. Determine the status of customers in our old database. Send out a mailing asking whether recipients wish to continue receiving our newsletter and product announcements.
3. Rekey the names of active customers. Enter the names of all responding customers in our new database so that we have only one active database.
Organizes body in numbered list for readability
Closes with key benefit, deadline, and next action
These changes will enable you, as team leader, to send mailings only to active customers. Please let me know by May 10 whether you think these recommendations are workable. If so, I will investigate costs.
Maddy
Madeleine M. Gagnon
Senior Marketing Manager
Email: madelaine.gagnon@apex.ca
Office: (416) 348-8835
Cell: (416) 348-9820
Provides name and full contact information

MEMO FEATURES. Some organizations have their own memo templates. In addition to the name of the organization, these templates include the basic elements of *Date*, *To*, *From*, and *Subject*. Large organizations may include other identifying headings, such as *File Number*, *Floor*, *Extension*, *Location*, and *Distribution*.

FIGURE 5.2 | Best Practices for Professional Email

Getting Started

- Don't write if another channel—such as IM, social media, or a phone call—might work better.
- Send only content you would want published.
- Write compelling subject lines, possibly with names and dates: *Jake: Can You Present at January 10 Staff Meeting?*

Replying

- Scan all emails, especially those from the same person. Answer within 24 hours or say when you will.
- Change the subject line if the topic changes. Check the threaded messages below yours.
- Practise down-editing; include only the parts from the incoming email to which you are responding.
- Start with the main idea.
- Use headings and lists.

Observing Etiquette

- Obtain approval before forwarding.
- Soften the tone by including a friendly opening and closing.
- Resist humour and sarcasm. Absent facial expression and tone of voice, humour can be misunderstood.
- Avoid writing in all caps, which is like SHOUTING.
- Don't copy everyone—send replies only to necessary people.

Closing Effectively

- End with due dates, next steps to be taken, or a friendly remark.
- Add your full contact information including social media addresses.
- Edit your text for readability. Proofread for typos or unwanted auto-corrections.
- Double-check before hitting **Send**.

If your company or organization doesn't have its own template for memos, simply open a new Word document, go to Templates (usually in the File menu), and search for memos. Word offers a number of memo templates you can use. Start writing in the template, making sure to save as you go. A typical memo is shown in Figure 5.3.

Notice the following important elements: there are spaces between the title and the guide words, and spaces among the guide words—this increases readability. Next, notice that memos follow the writing pattern discussed earlier for emails: specific subject line, opening with main idea, body that explains the main idea, closing. Finally, notice that a memo is the only type of business correspondence form that does not include an opening or a closing salutation (i.e., *Hi* or *Dear* or *Sincerely* or *Cheers*). This is because memos were developed to save time and to be impersonal. See Appendix A for more details on memo and fax (a form of memo) formatting.

WRITING PLAN FOR MEMOS

- **Subject line:** Summarizes the content of the memo.
- **Opening:** Expands the subject line by stating the main idea concisely in a full sentence.
- **Body:** Provides background data and explains the main idea. Consider using lists, bullets, or headings to improve readability. In describing a procedure or giving instructions, use command language (*do this, don't do that*).
- **Closing:** Requests a specific action, summarizes the message, or presents a closing thought. If appropriate, includes a deadline and a reason.

To deliver a long or formal document, send a cover email with an attachment.

SENDING MEMOS AS EMAIL ATTACHMENTS. Because email is inappropriate for writing overly long documents or for items that require formality or permanence, with such messages, writers may prepare the information in standard memo format and send the memo as an attachment with a cover email.

FIGURE 5.3 | Professional Business Memo

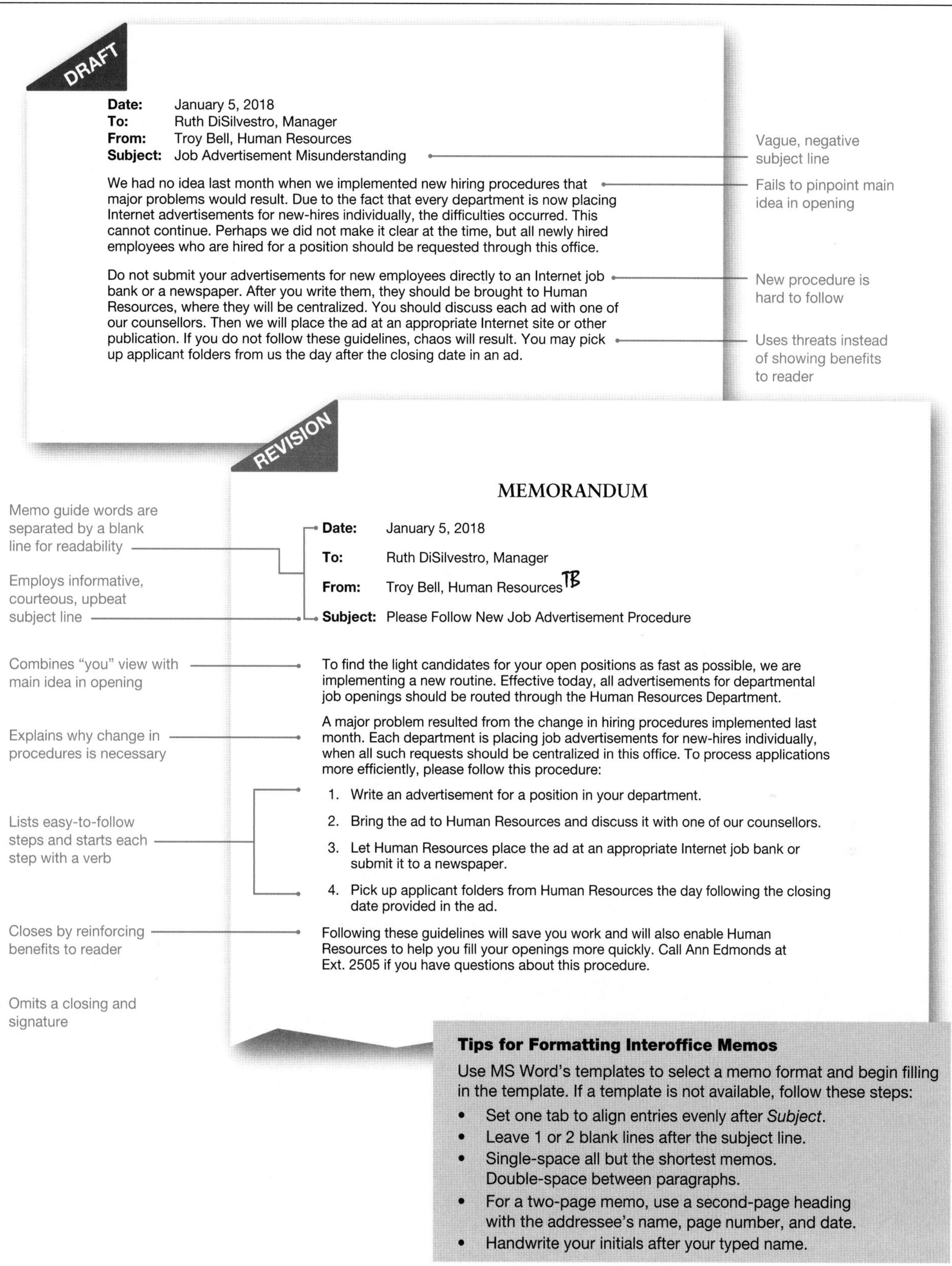

DRAFT
Date: January 5, 2018
To: Ruth DiSilvestro, Manager
From: Troy Bell, Human Resources
Subject: Job Advertisement Misunderstanding
We had no idea last month when we implemented new hiring procedures that major problems would result. Due to the fact that every department is now placing Internet advertisements for new-hires individually, the difficulties occurred. This cannot continue. Perhaps we did not make it clear at the time, but all newly hired employees who are hired for a position should be requested through this office.
Do not submit your advertisements for new employees directly to an Internet job bank or a newspaper. After you write them, they should be brought to Human Resources, where they will be centralized. You should discuss each ad with one of our counsellors. Then we will place the ad at an appropriate Internet site or other publication. If you do not follow these guidelines, chaos will result. You may pick up applicant folders from us the day after the closing date in an ad.
Vague, negative subject line
Fails to pinpoint main idea in opening
New procedure is hard to follow
Uses threats instead of showing benefits to reader
REVISION
MEMORANDUM
Date: January 5, 2018
To: Ruth DiSilvestro, Manager
From: Troy Bell, Human Resources TB
Subject: Please Follow New Job Advertisement Procedure
To find the light candidates for your open positions as fast as possible, we are implementing a new routine. Effective today, all advertisements for departmental job openings should be routed through the Human Resources Department.
A major problem resulted from the change in hiring procedures implemented last month. Each department is placing job advertisements for new-hires individually, when all such requests should be centralized in this office. To process applications more efficiently, please follow this procedure:
1. Write an advertisement for a position in your department.
2. Bring the ad to Human Resources and discuss it with one of our counsellors.
3. Let Human Resources place the ad at an appropriate Internet job bank or submit it to a newspaper.
4. Pick up applicant folders from Human Resources the day following the closing date provided in the ad.
Following these guidelines will save you work and will also enable Human Resources to help you fill your openings more quickly. Call Ann Edmonds at Ext. 2505 if you have questions about this procedure.
Memo guide words are separated by a blank line for readability
Employs informative, courteous, upbeat subject line
Combines "you" view with main idea in opening
Explains why change in procedures is necessary
Lists easy-to-follow steps and starts each step with a verb
Closes by reinforcing benefits to reader
Omits a closing and signature

Tips for Formatting Interoffice Memos

Use MS Word's templates to select a memo format and begin filling in the template. If a template is not available, follow these steps:

- Set one tab to align entries evenly after *Subject*.
- Leave 1 or 2 blank lines after the subject line.
- Single-space all but the shortest memos. Double-space between paragraphs.
- For a two-page memo, use a second-page heading with the addressee's name, page number, and date.
- Handwrite your initials after your typed name.

When attaching a document to an email, be sure to include identifying information in the attachment. This is because the cover email message may become separated from the attachment, and the receiver won't know who sent the attachment. If your email attachment is a memo, there shouldn't be any problems, as memos identify the date, sender, receiver, and subject.

Business letters are important for messages requiring a permanent record, confidentiality, formality, sensitivity, and a well-considered presentation.

LETTER FEATURES. Before memos and email, business was carried on for centuries using letters. Despite the widespread use of email and other digital channels, in certain situations letters are still the preferred channel for communicating *outside* an organization. Such letters are sent to suppliers, government agencies, other businesses, and most important, customers. Letters to customers receive a high priority because they are seen as important by receivers (not surprisingly, given how rarely we get actual letters in the mail anymore), encourage product feedback, project a favourable image of the organization, and promote future business.

A letter remains a powerful and effective channel for businesspeople to get their message across. Business letters are particularly necessary when (a) a permanent record is required; (b) confidentiality is paramount; (c) formality and sensitivity are essential; and (d) a persuasive, well-considered presentation is important.

Many organizations will have their own letter templates, including their logo and company name and address. Unless instructed not to, always use your company's letter template when drafting a letter.

If your company or organization doesn't have its own template for letters, simply open a new Word document, go to Templates (usually in the File menu), and search for letters. Word offers a number of letter templates you can use. Choose one that looks professional and formal, not informal or too busy. Start writing in the template, making sure to save as you go. A typical business letter is shown in Figure 5.4.

Notice the following important elements: the letter begins with your company's letterhead—the company name and any logo associated with the company, plus your address. The date of the letter goes a few spaces underneath the letterhead. A few spaces further down are the name and address of the person to whom you're writing. Then, there is an opening salutation (like in an email), which usually begins with *Dear*. The letter opens after the salutation. It has a body that explains the main point of the letter. The letter closes politely, and ends with a closing salutation (usually *Sincerely*) plus a signature and title. See Appendix A for more details about letter formatting.

WRITING PLAN FOR LETTERS

- **Letterhead:** Your company name, logo, and address.
- **Date and address:** The date of the letter followed by the name and address to which it is being sent.
- **Body:** Three sections: an opening, the body that explains your main reason for writing, and a polite closing.
- **Closing salutation and signature:** A polite "goodbye" with your signature and title.

OFFICE INSIDER

"[B]ear in mind that messaging sessions can be stored, then copied and pasted elsewhere.... The term 'confidential' is somewhat rubbery these days, so ... think before you hit that enter key."

—Michael Bloch, Taming the Beast, e-commerce development and Web marketing consultant

Office Insider based on Bloch, M. (n.d.). Instant messaging and live chat etiquette tips. Taming the Beast. Retrieved from http://www.tamingthebeast.net/articles6/messaging-chat-etiquette.htm

5.2 Workplace Messaging and Texting

Instant messaging (IM) and text messaging have become powerful communication tools, not only among teens and twentysomethings. IM enables two or more individuals to use the Internet or an intranet (an internal corporate communication platform) to "chat" in real time by exchanging brief text-based messages. One such intranet chat window is captured in Figure 5.5.

Companies large and small now provide live online chats with customer service representatives, in addition to the usual contact options, such as telephone and email. The free IM apps most popular among mobile device users are Skype, Facebook Messenger, WhatsApp, and Hangouts.

Text messaging, or texting, is another popular means for exchanging brief messages in real time. Usually delivered by or to a smartphone, texting requires a short

FIGURE 5.4 | Professional Business Letter

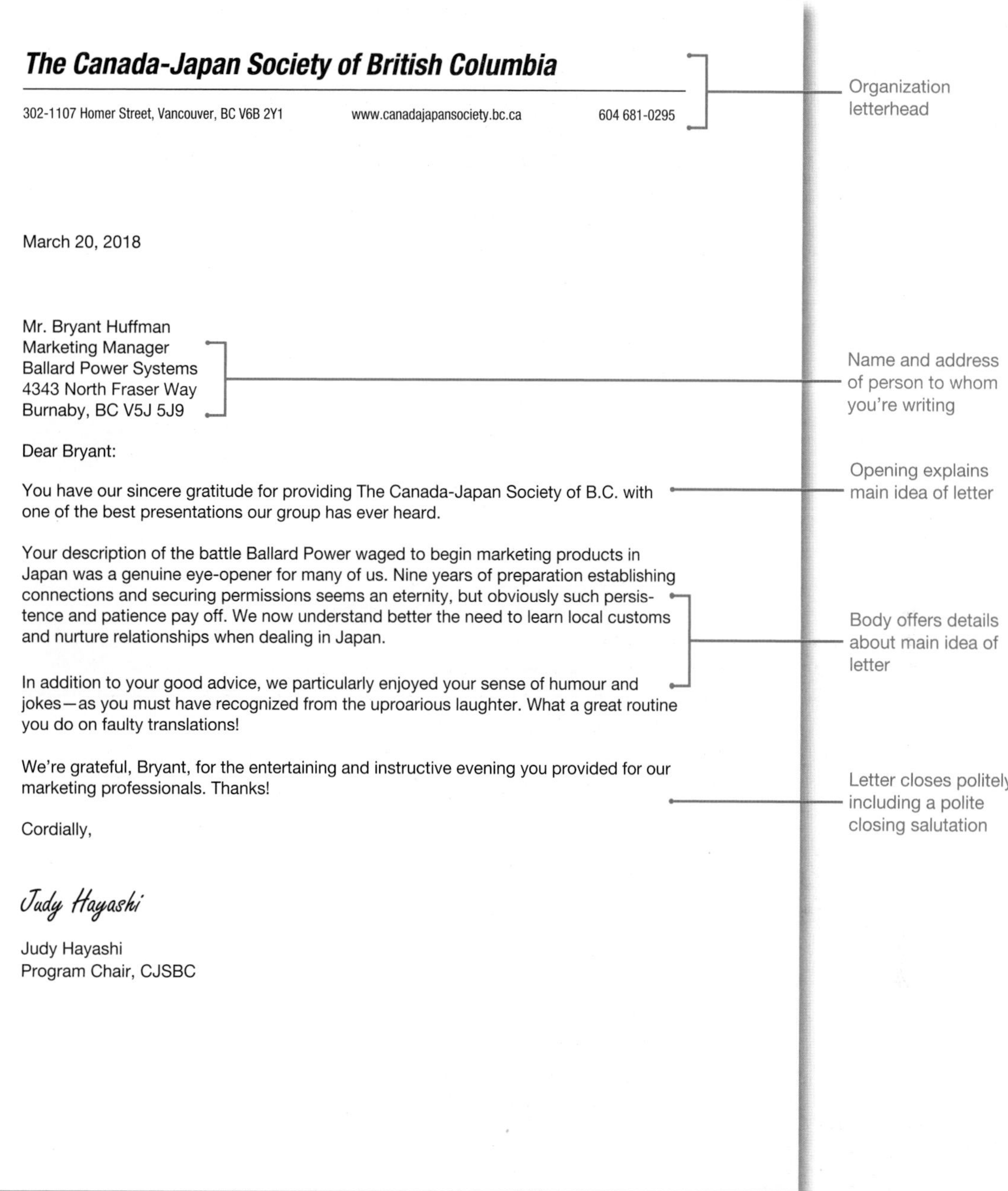

The Canada-Japan Society of British Columbia

302-1107 Homer Street, Vancouver, BC V6B 2Y1 www.canadajapansociety.bc.ca 604 681-0295

March 20, 2018

Mr. Bryant Huffman
Marketing Manager
Ballard Power Systems
4343 North Fraser Way
Burnaby, BC V5J 5J9

Dear Bryant:

You have our sincere gratitude for providing The Canada-Japan Society of B.C. with one of the best presentations our group has ever heard.

Your description of the battle Ballard Power waged to begin marketing products in Japan was a genuine eye-opener for many of us. Nine years of preparation establishing connections and securing permissions seems an eternity, but obviously such persistence and patience pay off. We now understand better the need to learn local customs and nurture relationships when dealing in Japan.

In addition to your good advice, we particularly enjoyed your sense of humour and jokes—as you must have recognized from the uproarious laughter. What a great routine you do on faulty translations!

We're grateful, Bryant, for the entertaining and instructive evening you provided for our marketing professionals. Thanks!

Cordially,

Judy Hayashi

Judy Hayashi
Program Chair, CJSBC

Organization letterhead
Name and address of person to whom you're writing
Opening explains main idea of letter
Body offers details about main idea of letter
Letter closes politely, including a polite closing salutation

message service (SMS) supplied by a cellphone service provider or a voice over Internet protocol (VoIP) service. Some of the most common apps for unlimited mobile text messaging are Facebook Messenger, WhatsApp, and WeChat.

Texting requires a smartphone, and users pay for the service, often choosing a flat rate for a certain number of text or media messages per month. VoIP providers such as Skype also offer texting. For a small fee, subscribers can send text messages to SMS-enabled cellphones and IM messages both domestically and internationally.

5.2a Impact of Instant Messaging and Texting

Texting and IM are convenient alternatives to the telephone and are replacing email for short internal communication. French IT giant Atos switched its in-house communication entirely from email to a Facebook-style interface and instant messaging.[12]

FIGURE 5.5 | Instant Messaging for Brief, Fast Communication

Brief instant messages or texts can provide quick answers to coworkers who need responses immediately. For security reasons, most large companies use proprietary communication systems behind firewalls. These enterprise-grade communication platforms—for example, Adobe's Unicom—combine functions such as IM, email, voice mail, phone directory, video chat, and presence technology.

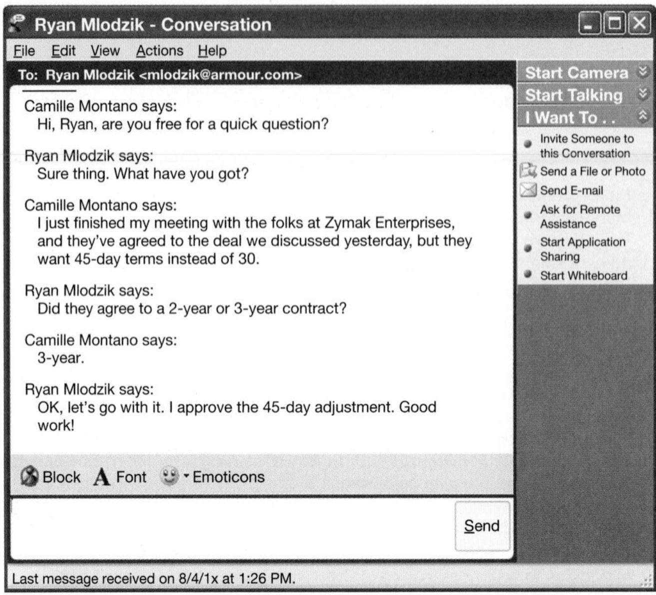

More than 2.7 billion IM accounts worldwide[13] attest to IM's popularity. Sixty-four percent of business professionals use IM.[14]

BENEFITS OF IM AND TEXTING. The major attraction of instant messaging is real-time communication with colleagues anywhere in the world—so long as a cellphone signal or a Wi-Fi connection is available. Because IM allows people to share information immediately and make decisions quickly, its impact on business communication has been dramatic. Group online chat capabilities in enterprise-grade IM applications allow coworkers on far-flung project teams to communicate instantly. Many people consider instant messaging and texting productivity boosters because they enable users to get answers quickly and allow multitasking.[15]

LOW COST, SPEED, AND UNOBTRUSIVENESS. Both IM and texting can be low-cost substitutes for voice calls, delivering messages between private mobile phone users quietly and discreetly. Organizations around the world provide news alerts, financial information, and promotions to customers via text. Credit card accounts can be set up to notify account holders by text or email of approaching payment deadlines. Wireless providers send automated texts helping customers track their data usage. At the same time, public sector organizations that often send out public service announcements, may be retreating from the use of texting. A recent announcement by the University of Waterloo in Ontario states that "emergency alerts/notifications will no longer be sent to members of the campus community via SMS (text message) as these messages were becoming unreliable and were no longer received in a timely manner."[16] A sample of corporate text alerts is shown in Figure 5.6.

IMMEDIACY AND EFFICIENCY. The immediacy of instant and text messaging has created many fans. A user knows right away whether a message was delivered.

Messaging avoids phone tag and eliminates the downtime associated with personal telephone conversations. Another benefit includes *presence functionality*. Coworkers can locate each other online, thus avoiding wasting time trying to reach someone who is out of the office.

RISKS OF IM AND TEXTING. Despite their popularity among workers, some organizations forbid employees to use instant and text messaging for a number of reasons. Employers consider instant messaging yet another distraction in addition to the telephone, email, and the Web. Some organizations also fear that employees using free instant messaging systems will reveal privileged information and company records. One UK study found that 72 percent of businesses have banned IM, although 74 percent of the respondents believed that IM could boost collaboration in their organizations. IT directors worried about security risks posed by free consumer IM services, with loss of sensitive business data a primary concern.[17]

FIGURE 5.6 | Wireless Provider Text Alert

This Canadian wireless provider sends texts to its customers whenever they have crossed an international border: roaming charges will apply if the customer texts or makes a phone calls outside of his or her coverage area.

Georgejmclittle/Shutterstock.com

LIABILITY BURDEN. A worker's improper use of mobile devices while on company business can expose the organization to staggering legal liability. A jury awarded $18 million to a victim struck by a transportation company's big rig, the driver of which had been checking text messages. Another case resulted in a $21 million verdict to a woman injured by a trucker who had used a cellphone while driving a company truck.[18]

Organizations may ban instant messaging because of fears around productivity, security, litigation, and compliance.

SECURITY AND COMPLIANCE. Companies also worry about *phishing* (fraudulent schemes), viruses, *malware* (malicious software programs), and *spim* (IM spam). Like email, instant and text messages as well as all other electronic records are subject to discovery (disclosure); that is, they can become evidence in lawsuits. Businesses must track and store messaging conversations to comply with legal requirements. Finally, IM and texting have been implicated in inappropriate uses such as bullying and the notorious *sexting*.

5.2b How to Use Instant Messaging and Texting on the Job

In today's workplace instant messaging and texting can definitely save time and simplify communication with coworkers and customers. If your organization does allow IM or texting, you can use it efficiently and professionally by following these best practices:

- Follow company policies: netiquette rules, code of conduct, and ethics guidelines as well as harassment and discrimination policies.
- Don't disclose sensitive financial, company, customer, employee, or executive data.
- Don't forward or link to inappropriate photos, videos, and art.
- Don't text or IM while driving a car; pull over if you must read or send a message.
- Separate business contacts from family and friends.
- Avoid unnecessary chit-chat and know when to say goodbye.
- Keep your presence status up-to-date, and make yourself unavailable when you need to meet a deadline.
- Use good grammar and correct spelling; shun jargon, slang, and abbreviations, which can be confusing and appear unprofessional.

FIGURE 5.7 | Texting Etiquette

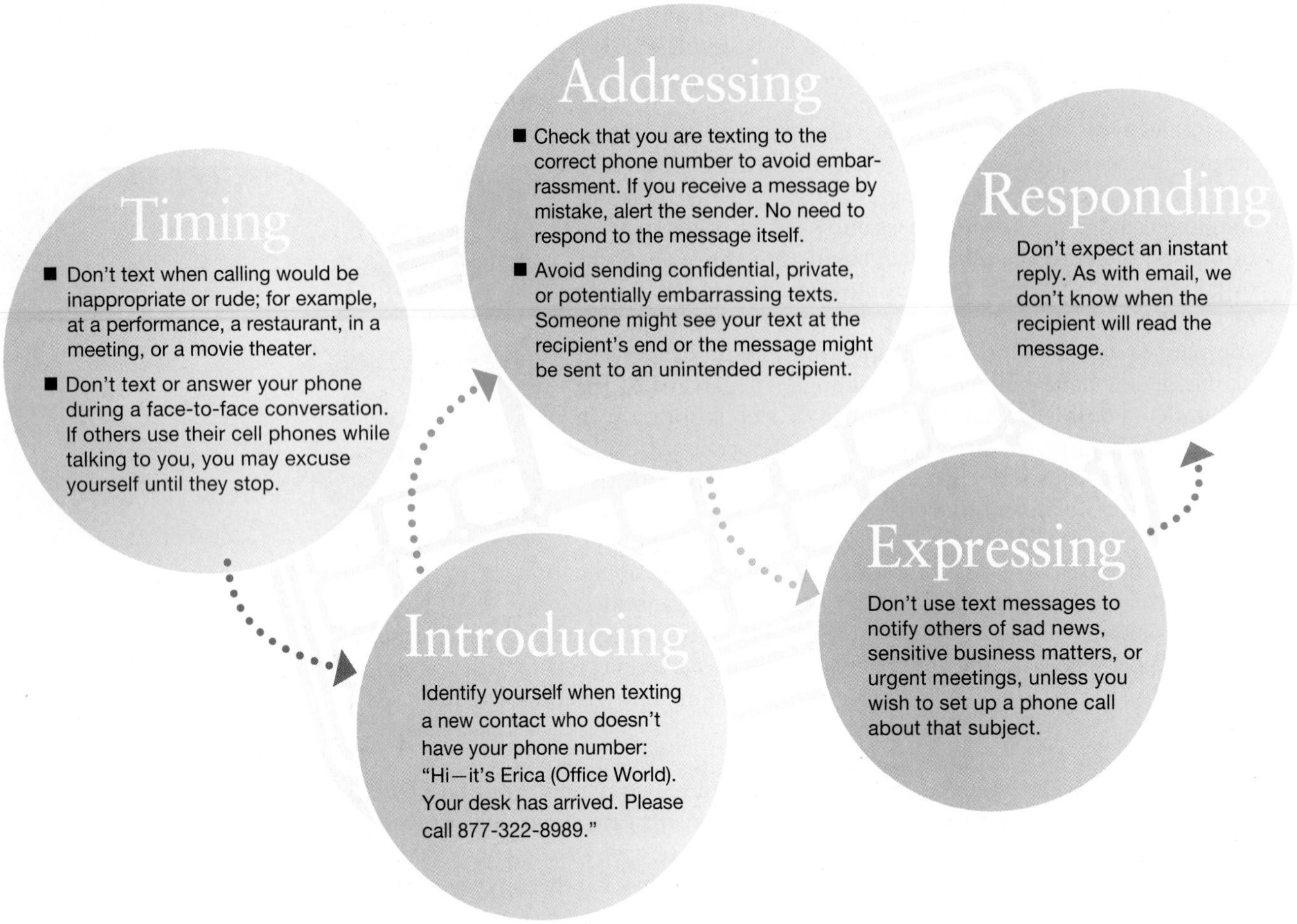

Timing
■ Don't text when calling would be inappropriate or rude; for example, at a performance, a restaurant, in a meeting, or a movie theater.
■ Don't text or answer your phone during a face-to-face conversation. If others use their cell phones while talking to you, you may excuse yourself until they stop.
Addressing
■ Check that you are texting to the correct phone number to avoid embarrassment. If you receive a message by mistake, alert the sender. No need to respond to the message itself.
■ Avoid sending confidential, private, or potentially embarrassing texts. Someone might see your text at the recipient's end or the message might be sent to an unintended recipient.
Responding
Don't expect an instant reply. As with email, we don't know when the recipient will read the message.
Introducing
Identify yourself when texting a new contact who doesn't have your phone number: "Hi—it's Erica (Office World). Your desk has arrived. Please call 877-322-8989."
Expressing
Don't use text messages to notify others of sad news, sensitive business matters, or urgent meetings, unless you wish to set up a phone call about that subject.

5.2c Text Messaging and Business Etiquette

Texting is quick and unobtrusive, and for routine messages it is often the best alternative to a phone call or email. Given the popularity of text messaging, etiquette experts are taking note.[19] Figure 5.7 summarizes the suggestions they offer for the considerate and professional use of texting.

5.3 Using Podcasts and Wikis in Business

In the digital age, individuals wield enormous influence because they can potentially reach huge audiences. Far from being passive consumers, today's Internet users have the power to create Web content; interact with businesses and each other; review products, self-publish, or blog; contribute to *wikis*; or tag and share images and other files. Many businesses rightly fear the wrath of disgruntled employees and customers, or they curry favour with influential plugged-in opinion leaders, the so-called *influencers*.

5.3a Business Podcasts or Webcasts

Perhaps because podcasts are more elaborate to produce and require quality hardware, their use is lagging behind that of other digital media. However, they have their place among digital business communication strategies. Although the terms *podcast* and *podcasting* have caught on, they are somewhat misleading. The words *broadcasting* and *iPod* combined to create the word *podcast*; however, audio and video files can be played on any number of devices, not just Apple's. *Webcasting* for audio and *vcasting* for video content would be more accurate terms. Podcasts can extend from short clips of a few minutes to 30-minute or longer digital files. Most are recorded, but some are live. They can be streamed on a website or downloaded as media files.

HOW ORGANIZATIONS USE PODCASTS. Podcasting is popular among various user groups online. Major news organizations and media outlets podcast radio shows (e.g., CBC Radio) and TV shows, from CBC to TVO. You may have heard of TED Talks. These thought-provoking podcasts on any imaginable topic in technology, entertainment, and design (TED) are delivered by an intriguing mix of entrepreneurs, scientists, and other opinion leaders. Podcasts are also common in education. You can access instructors' lectures, interviews, and other media files. Apple's iTunes U is perhaps the best-known example of free educational podcasts from prestigious universities.

DELIVERING AND ACCESSING PODCASTS. Businesses have embraced podcasting for sending audio and video messages that do not require a live presence yet offer a friendly human face. Because they can broadcast repetitive information that does not require interaction, podcasts can replace costlier live teleconferences. Podcasts are featured on media websites and company portals or shared on blogs and social networking sites, often with links to YouTube and Vimeo.

For example, Royal Bank of Canada has a series of podcasts called "The Sound of Small Business" on its website, featuring professionally produced videos highlighting entrepreneurs across Canada. Canadian universities such as McGill and the University of Alberta have strong podcast sites. Check out McGill University's series of podcasts on contemporary issues in business at http://podcasts.mcgill.ca/business-leadership.

To browse and learn from popular favourites, search on the Podcast Awards website for podcasts in various categories, including business, science, and technology.

5.3b Collaborating With Wikis

Wikis are another important feature of the interactive, participatory digital environment. A wiki is a Web-based tool that employs easy-to-use collaborative software to allow multiple users collectively to create, access, and modify documents. Think of Wikipedia, the well-known online encyclopedia. You will find wikis in numerous subject categories on the Internet. Wiki editors may be given varying access privileges and control over the cloud-based material.

ADVANTAGES OF WIKIS. Two major advantages of wikis come to mind. First, wikis capitalize on *crowdsourcing*, which can be defined as the practice of tapping into the combined knowledge of an online community to solve problems and complete assignments. Second, working on the same content jointly eliminates the infamous problem of version confusion. Most wikis store all changes and intermediate versions of files so that users can return to a previous stage if necessary. A survey found that benefits of corporate wikis include enhancing the reputation of expert contributors, making work flow more easily, and improving an organization's processes.[20]

HOW BUSINESSES USE WIKIS. An enterprise-level wiki serves as an easy-to-navigate, efficient central repository of company information, complete with hyperlinks and keywords pointing to related subjects and media. IBM, for example, uses

FIGURE 5.8 | Four Main Uses for Business Wiki

The global wiki

For companies with a global reach, a wiki is an ideal tool for information sharing between headquarters and satellite offices. Far-flung team members can easily edit their work and provide input to the home office and each other.

The wiki knowledge base

Teams or departments use wikis to collect and disseminate information to large audiences creating a database for knowledge management. For example, human resources managers may update employee policies, make announcements, and convey information about benefits.

Wikis for meetings

Wikis can facilitate feedback from employees before and after meetings and serve as repositories of meeting minutes. In fact, wikis may replace some meetings, yet still keep a project on track.

Wikis for project management

Wikis offer a highly interactive environment for project information with easy access and user input. All participants have the same information, templates, and documentation readily available.

wikis to publish documentation for its WebSphere and Lotus products and to interact with the community of adopters. The four main uses of wikis in business are shown in Figure 5.8.[21]

Popular simple-to-use wiki hosting services, called *wiki farms*, are PBworks (Project Hub), Wikispaces, and Wikia. Some are noncommercial and offer free hosting. Consider starting a wiki for your next classroom project requiring teamwork. Alternatively, explore Google Docs and Google Sites, a page of which is shown in Figure 5.9.

5.4 Blogging for Business

A business blog is a website with journal entries on any imaginable business topic. It is usually written by one person; although, most corporate blogs feature multiple contributors. Typically, readers leave comments. Businesses use blogs to keep customers, employees, and the public at large informed and to interact with them.

Marketing firms and their clients are looking closely at blogs because blogs invite spontaneous consumer feedback faster and more cheaply than such staples of consumer research as focus groups and surveys. Businesses use blogs to communicate externally with the public but also internally with employees. Currently, 171 of Fortune 500 companies (34 percent) are blogging, and researchers note a rise in the number of corporations with active blogs.[22]

5.4a How Companies Blog

Like other digital media, corporate blogs help create virtual communities, build brands, and develop relationships. In other words, blogs are part of a social media strategy to create engagement, resulting in customers' goodwill and brand loyalty. Companies use blogs for public relations, customer relations, crisis communication, market research, viral marketing, internal communication, and recruiting. For example, the Canadian food company McCain's blog—"the all smiles blog" shown in Figure 5.10—promotes itself as a place to share what inspires the company.

Blogs are online journals used by companies to communicate internally with employees and externally with customers.

PUBLIC RELATIONS, CUSTOMER RELATIONS, AND CRISIS COMMUNICATION. One of the prominent uses of blogs is to provide up-to-date company information to the media and the public. Blogs can be written by junior employees or by top managers. Consider these examples: Executive chairman Bill Marriott is an avid and astute blogger. His Marriott on the Move blog feels personal and honest. Just one of several General Electric blogs, Edison's Desk addresses industry insiders and the interested public. Under the heading Best Buy Blogger Network, the electronics retailer operates a number of niche blogs targeting various constituencies and actively soliciting customer input.[23]

Social media experts believe that brands should embrace negative blog posts and turn them into opportunities to reach out to the customer and strengthen the relationship.[24] Whether businesses choose to respond angrily or surprise and delight customers, "the world is watching."[25]

An organization's blog is a natural forum for late-breaking news, especially when disaster strikes. Although a blog cannot replace other communication channels in an emergency, it should be part of the overall effort to soothe the public's

FIGURE 5.9 | Creating a Wiki With Google Sites and Google Docs

This screenshot shows a template available for customization in Google Sites, a free, user-friendly wiki and website creator. Google Sites and the document editing and revision tool Google Docs allow users to create, edit, share, and manage documents online in real time. Unlike in typical wikis, here multiple editors can modify files simultaneously.

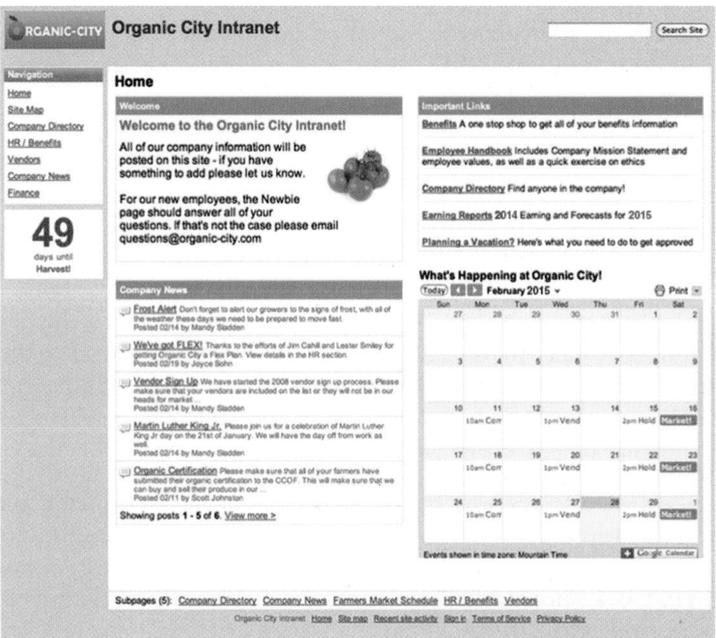

FIGURE 5.10 | A Corporate Blog: McCain

Passion & Potatoes: 60 Years of Partnership with Canadian Farmers

Courtesy of McCain.ca

emotional reaction with a human voice of reason. In the aftermath of hugely devastating fires in Fort McMurray, Alberta, in 2016, various corporate blogs like Allstate's "Good Hands" blog, chronicled recovery and rebuilding efforts, offering vital information to the public.[26]

OFFICE INSIDER

"I make [blogging] work because it's a great way to communicate with our customers and stakeholders.... When your family's name is on the building or you are the person clearly identified with the company, everything you say or do affects the business, good or bad. In this fascinating information age, you have to be transparent."

—J. W. "Bill" Marriott, Jr., executive chairman, Marriott International, Inc.

MARKET RESEARCH AND VIRAL MARKETING. Because most blogs invite feedback, they can be invaluable sources of opinion and bright ideas from customers as well as industry experts. Mountain Equipment Co-op understands blogging. The outdoor retailer's "MEC Blog" (https://www.mec.ca/en/blog) contains sections where MEC's community members offer skills and tips, personal stories, and information on community events. The blog is curated by a mix of employees, co-op members, and other people who interact with MEC. Many companies now have employees who scrutinize the blogosphere for buzz and positive and negative postings about their organizations and products.

The term *viral marketing* refers to the rapid spread of messages online, much like infectious diseases that pass from person to person. Marketers realize the potential of getting the word out about their products and services in the blogosphere. There, their messages are often picked up by well-connected bloggers, the so-called *influencers*, who boast large audiences. Viral messages must be authentic and elicit an emotional response, but for that very reason they are difficult to orchestrate. People resent being co-opted by companies using overt hard-sell tactics.

ONLINE COMMUNITIES. Company blogs can attract a devoted community of participants who want to keep informed about company events, product updates, and other news. In turn, those enthusiasts can contribute new ideas. Few companies enjoy the brand awareness and customer loyalty of Coca-Cola. With its blog Coca-Cola Conversations, the soft drink maker shares its rich past ("Life without Coca-Cola") and thus deepens Coke fans' loyalty. Coke's marketing is subtle; the blog is designed to provide a unique experience to fans.

INTERNAL COMMUNICATION AND RECRUITING. Blogs can be used to keep virtual teams on track and share updates on the road. Members in remote locations can stay in touch by smartphone and other devices, exchanging text, images, sound, and video clips. In many companies, blogs have replaced hard-copy publications for sharing late-breaking news or tidbits of interest to employees. Blogs can create a sense of community and stimulate employee participation. Furthermore, blogs mirror the company culture and present a priceless opportunity for job candidates to size up a potential employer and the people working there.

5.4b Blog Best Practices: Seven Tips for Master Bloggers

As with any public writing, your blog posts will be scrutinized; therefore, you want to make the best impression possible.

CRAFT A CATCHY BUT CONCISE TITLE. The headline is what draws online readers to even open your post. Some will be intriguing questions or promises. Online writers often use numbers to structure their posts. Here are some examples: *Six Apps You Don't Want to Miss; Five Tips to Keep Spear Phishers Out of Your Inbox; Create Powerful Imagery in Your Writing; How Financially Sexy is Your Household?; The False Choice of Mediocrity.*

ACE THE OPENING PARAGRAPH. The lead must deliver on the promise of the headline. Identify a need and propose to solve the problem. Ask a relevant question. Say something startling. Tell an anecdote or use an analogy to connect with the reader. The author of "How Many Lives Does a Brand Have?" opened with this:

> *It's said that cats have nine lives, but how many lives does a brand have? The answer, it seems, is definitely more than one. Recently, in Shanghai, a friend took me to one of the city's most sophisticated luxury malls....*[27]

PROVIDE DETAILS IN THE BODY. Mind the *So what?* and *What's in it for me?* questions. Use vivid examples, quotations and testimonials, or statistics. Structure the body with numbers, bullets, and subheadings. Use expressive action verbs (*buy* for *get*; *own* for *have*; *travel* or *jet* for *go*). Use conversational language to sound warm and authentic. Use contractions (*can't* for *cannot*; *doesn't* for *does not*; *isn't* for *is not*).

CONSIDER VISUALS. Add visual interest with relevant images and diagrams. Keep paragraphs short and use plenty of white space around them. Aim to make the look simple and easy to scan.

INCLUDE CALLS TO ACTION. Call on readers in the title to do something or provide a take-away and gentle nudge at the end. Chris Brogan, writing in his blog post "Become a Dream Feeder," had this to say: "So, how will you make your blog into a dream feeder? Or do you do that already? What dreams do your readers have?"[28] Ask open-ended questions or tell the reader what to do: *So be sure to ask about 360-degree security tactics that aim to stop inbound attacks, but also to block outbound data theft attempts.*

EDIT AND PROOFREAD. Follow the revision tips in Chapter 4 of this book. Cut any unneeded words, sentences, and irrelevant ideas. Fix awkward, wordy, and repetitious sentences. Edit and proofread as if your life depended on it. Your reputation might. The best blogs are error free.

RESPOND TO POSTS RESPECTFULLY. Build a positive image online by posting compelling comments on other bloggers' posts. Politely and promptly reply to comments on your site. When a customer asked a question about WestJet's blog posting about why it doesn't overbook seats, WestJet responded. The reply begins by making a positive observation about the post and adds a valuable thought, albeit with some questionable punctuation:

> *Great question. Here's a common example: a business traveller books three fully-refundable tickets on three different flights for one single trip. If that traveller only intends to use one flight, but isn't sure exactly when they'll be able to depart, they may book multiple itineraries, then cancel all but one at the last minute. In this case, the airline would not receive the revenue from the refundable cancelled bookings, and would likely not be able to sell the now-available seat(s) at the last minute, before the flight departs.*[29]

Don't ramble. If you disagree with a post, do so respectfully. Remember, your comments may remain online practically forever and could come back to haunt you long after posting.

5.5 Social Networking in Business

Popular social networking sites such as Facebook and Twitter are used by businesses for similar reasons and in much the same way as podcasts, blogs, and wikis: to market services and products, to solidify company image, and to reach out to customers with news and with problem resolutions, as can be seen in Figure 5.11. Social networking sites enable businesses to connect with customers and employees, share company news, and exchange ideas.

Social networking sites allow businesses to connect with customers and employees, sell products and services, share company news, and exchange ideas.

5.5a Tapping Into Social Networks

Business interest in social networking sites is not surprising if we consider that 93 percent of Millennials, also called Generation Y, go online several times a day. They are most likely to access the Internet wirelessly with mobile phones, laptops,

FIGURE 5.11 | Corporate Twitter Feed: Airline Industry

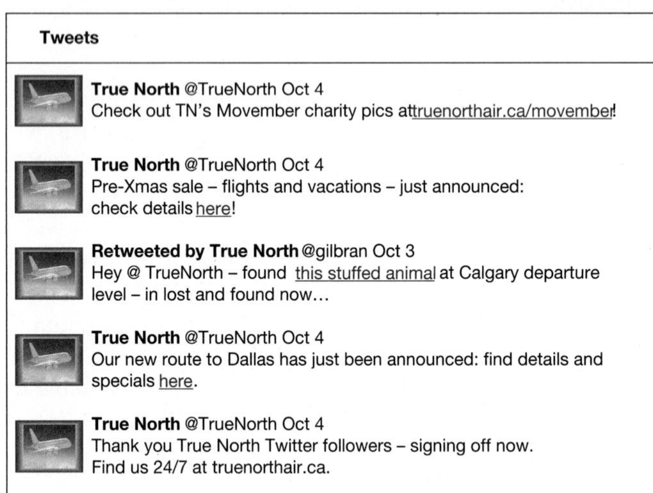

and tablets.[30] Young adults lead in instant messaging, blog reading, listening to music, playing online games, and participating in virtual worlds. However, older age groups are gaining on them and even pulling ahead in some categories; for example, in Facebook growth.

Tweets
True North @TrueNorth Oct 4
Check out TN's Movember charity pics at truenorthair.ca/movember!
True North @TrueNorth Oct 4
Pre-Xmas sale – flights and vacations – just announced: check details here!
Retweeted by True North @gilbran Oct 3
Hey @ TrueNorth – found this stuffed animal at Calgary departure level – in lost and found now…
True North @TrueNorth Oct 4
Our new route to Dallas has just been announced: find details and specials here.
True North @TrueNorth Oct 4
Thank you True North Twitter followers – signing off now.
Find us 24/7 at truenorthair.ca.

As for Twitter, the heaviest users are people in the 18-to-24 age bracket (31 percent), followed by 25- to 34-year-olds (17 percent).[31] Predictably, businesses are trying to adapt and tap the vast potential of social networking. About 70 percent of the Fortune 500 companies are now on Facebook, and 77 percent have corporate Twitter accounts.[32] Excluding celebrities and news media, Facebook (the corporation) leads in the number of Twitter followers with 10.9 million, with Google coming in second (6.7 million), and Samsung Mobile US in third place (4.6 million), followed by Starbucks (4.2 million).[33]

5.5b How Businesses Use Social Networks

Companies harness the power of very public online communities to boost brand image or to provide a forum for collaboration. However, the social Web has also spawned internal networking sites safely located behind corporate firewalls. For example, with almost 600,000 likes, Wells Fargo, a U.S. bank, is a popular company on Facebook with about 50,000 Twitter followers, a comparatively modest number. However, the bank's private social network, Teamworks, connects 280,000 team members worldwide.[34] Insurer MetLife runs MetConnect, an internal networking tool. Similarly, a digital ad agency by the name of Possible turned to its own social network to share a new brand identity with its 20 offices from Cincinnati to Guangzhou, China.[35]

That said, studies have shown that actual *use* of internal social networks is low. In "Why No One Uses the Corporate Social Network," *Harvard Business Review* contributor Charlene Li shows that unless managers model the use of social networks, employees will intuit that they are just the latest in a string of online tools that no one uses.[36]

CROWDSOURCING CUSTOMERS. Social networks and blogs also help companies invite customer input at the product design stage. On its IdeaStorm site, Dell has solicited over 26,000 new product ideas and suggested improvements, including a USB port that also acts as a charger (see Figure 5.12).[37] Canadian fast food restaurant A&W has used Facebook to let followers know about the quality of its ingredients. According to a testimonial at Facebook Business, this campaign led to a 23 percent increase in burger sales.[38]

5.5c Potential Risks of Social Networks for Businesses

Most managers want plugged-in employees with strong tech skills. They like to imagine their workers as brand ambassadors. They fantasize about their products becoming overnight sensations thanks to viral marketing. However, they also fret about incurring productivity losses, compromising trade secrets, attracting the wrath of huge Internet audiences, and facing embarrassment over inappropriate and damaging employee posts.[39] Moreover, network administrators fear security breaches from the unauthorized private use of work-issued devices.[40]

Businesses take different approaches to the "dark side" of social networking. Some, such as Zappos, take a hands-off approach and encourage employee online activity. Others, such as IBM, have drafted detailed policies to cover all forms of self-expression online. According to one survey, 50 percent of businesses block Web access to social networking sites; 61 percent, to gaming sites; and 40 percent, to entertainment sites.[41] However, some experts believe that organizations should embrace positive word-of-mouth testimonials from employees about their jobs, not quash them with rigid policies.[42]

5.5d Using Social Networking Sites and Keeping Your Job

Most professionals agree that, as with any public online activity, users of social networking sites would do well to exercise caution. Privacy online is a myth, and sensitive information should not be shared lightly, least of all risqué photographs. Furthermore, refusing *friend requests* or *unfriending* individuals could jeopardize professional relationships.

OFFICE INSIDER

"Security risks rise in businesses because many employees adopt 'my way' work lifestyles in which their devices, work, and online behaviour mix with their personal lives virtually anywhere—in the office, at home and everywhere in between."

—Cisco Annual Security Report

Office Insider based on Cisco annual security report: Threats step out of the shadows. (2013). Cisco: The Network. [Press release]. Retrieved from http://newsroom.cisco.com/release/1133334

FIGURE 5.12 | How Companies Use Crowdsourcing

USB Port

Jul 10, 2017
Posted By parshys
Status: Acknowledged

1 VOTE

How about having a USB port on the Power Adaptor of DELL E5470 laptop which would act as a charger for the USB devices as well. It can be made into a Power Bank as well by implementing a long battery into it.

1 Votes | *1 Comment*

Categories: Accessories (Keyboards, etc.), Desktops and Laptops, IdeaStorm,

The advice to think twice before posting online applies to most communication channels used on the job. Many users leave their pages open and risk trouble with their employers by assuming that online comments are hidden.[43] Even privacy settings, however, do not guarantee complete protection from prying eyes.

Among the many risks in the cyber world are inappropriate photographs and tagging. Tags make pictures searchable so that an embarrassing college incident may resurface years later. The dos and don'ts in Figure 5.13 sum up best practices for all digital media.

FIGURE 5.13 | Using Media Professionally: Dos and Don'ts

DON'T — AVOIDING QUESTIONABLE CONTENT, PERSONAL DOCUMENTS, AND FILE SHARING	DO✓ — KNOWING WORKPLACE POLICIES AND AVOIDING PRIVATE USE OF MEDIA AT WORK
✘ **Don't spread rumours, gossip, and negative defamatory comments.** Because all digital information is subject to discovery in court, avoid unprofessional content and conduct, including complaints about your employer, customers, and employees.	✓ **Learn your company's rules.** Some companies require workers to sign that they have read and understand Internet and digital media use policies. Being informed is your best protection.
✘ **Don't download and share cartoons, video clips, photos, and art.** Businesses are liable for any recorded digital content regardless of the medium used.	✓ **Avoid sending personal email, instant messages, or texts from work.** Even if your company allows personal use during lunch or after hours, keep it to a minimum. Better yet, wait to use your own electronic devices away from work.
✘ **Don't open unfamiliar attachments.** Attachments with executable files or video files may carry viruses, spyware, or other malware (malicious programs).	✓ **Separate work and personal data.** Keep information that could embarrass you or expose you to legal liability on your personal storage devices, on hard drives, or in the cloud, never on your office computer.
✘ **Don't download free software and utilities to company machines.** Employees can unwittingly introduce viruses, phishing schemes, and other cyber "bugs."	✓ **Be careful when blogging, tweeting, or posting on social networking sites.** Unhappy about not receiving a tip, a Beverly Hills waiter lost his job for tweeting disparaging remarks about an actress. Forgetting that his boss was his Facebook "friend," a British employee was fired after posting, "OMG, I HATE MY JOB!" and calling his supervisor names.
✘ **Don't store your music and photos on a company machine (or server), and don't watch streaming videos.** Capturing precious company bandwidth for personal use is a sure way to be shown the door.	✓ **Keep sensitive information private.** Use privacy settings, but don't trust the "private" areas on Facebook, Twitter, Flickr, and other social networks.
✘ **Don't share files, and avoid file-sharing services.** Clarify whether you may use Google Docs and other services that offer optional file sharing. Stay away from distributors or pirated files such as LimeWire.	✓ **Avoid pornography, sexually explicit jokes, or inappropriate screen savers.** Anything that might "poison" the work environment is a harassment risk and, therefore, prohibited.

SUMMARY OF LEARNING OBJECTIVES

5.1 Demonstrate professional standards in the use and formatting of major daily workplace writing channels.

- Although sometimes annoying, email will likely remain a mainstream communication channel.
- Email is especially effective for informal messages to multiple receivers and as a cover document for attachments.
- Business emails should feature a compelling subject line, include a greeting, be organized for readability, and close effectively.
- Memos, which include a subject line, a dateline, and the names of senders and receivers, are sometimes used for internal messages that are too long for email, require a lasting record, demand formality, or inform workers who don't have email.
- Letters, which include letterhead, the date, an inside address, opening salutation, message opening, body and close, and closing salutation, are used when a permanent record and confidentiality are required; when formality and sensitivity are essential; and when a persuasive presentation is important.

5.2 Instant message and text professionally.

- Individuals use the Internet or corporate intranets to exchange brief text-based messages, which requires a cellular connection or a VoIP service.
- The benefits of messaging are low cost, high speed, unobtrusiveness, immediacy, and efficiency.
- The risks of messaging include legal liability, security breaches, and compliance issues.
- Best practices for messaging include minding policies, protecting sensitive data, pulling over to message, separating personal and work contacts, and using correct language.

5.3 Create professional podcasts and wikis.

- Whether as short clips or longer digital files, business podcasts offer a friendly human face and can replace costlier live teleconferences.
- A wiki is a Web-based collaborative software tool that allows multiple users to create, access, and modify documents.
- Wikis can help online groups solve problems and complete assignments while preventing version confusion.

5.4 Design professional internal and external blogs.

- External or internal corporate blogs help create virtual communities, build brands, and develop relationships.
- Companies use blogs for public relations, customer relations, crisis communication, market research, viral marketing, building online communities, internal communication, and recruiting.
- Best practices include crafting a catchy title and intriguing opening, providing details in the body, using visuals, calling for action, editing carefully, and commenting respectfully.

5.5 Use social media networks professionally.

- Social networking sites enable businesses to connect with customers and employees, share news, exchange ideas, and boost their brand images.
- In addition to Facebook, Twitter, and other very public social media, many businesses also run private social networks behind corporate firewalls.
- The risks of social media use in business include productivity losses, leaked trade secrets, angry Internet audiences, security breaches, and damaging employee posts.
- Savvy users should keep privacy settings up-to-date, avoid risqué images, handle friend requests tactfully, and beware of tagging.

CHAPTER REVIEW

1. Why do some businesspeople criticize email? (Obj. 1)
2. When is email appropriate? (Obj. 1)
3. Describe the writing plan for business emails. (Obj. 1)
4. What are the risks of instant messaging and texting? (Obj. 2)
5. List five best practices for using IM and texting that you consider most important. (Obj. 2)
6. How do organizations use and deliver podcasts? (Obj. 3)
7. Explain what a wiki is and list its advantages. (Obj. 3)
8. How do companies use blogs? (Obj. 4)
9. What tips would you give to a beginning blogger? (Obj. 4)
10. Name potential risks of social networks for businesses. (Obj. 5)

CRITICAL THINKING

1. Some people are concerned that privacy is increasingly rare in our hyperconnected world as our online presence leaves a lasting footprint. To what degree do you fear that disclosing personal matters online will hamper your job search? Why? (Objs. 1–5)
2. Experts have argued that social media fool us into thinking that we are connected when in reality they do not help us develop true friendships. To what degree do you agree that technology diminishes personal relationships rather than bringing us closer together? Why? (Objs. 1–5)
3. Are texting abbreviations such as *lol* and *imho* and other all-lowercase writing acceptable in texting or instant messaging for business? Why or why not? (Obj. 2)
4. Traditional media act as *gatekeepers* that decide what kind of content gets published or broadcast. However, social media networks have changed the game. Now anyone with an Internet connection can potentially publish or broadcast anything and reach vast audiences. What are the benefits and dangers of this unprecedented access? (Obj. 5)
5. Some marketers employ machines to inflate the number of likes and fans online. So-called Facebook bot networks (*botnets*) operate large numbers of fake accounts around the world. For example, a big-city rental agency based in went from two fans to almost 15,000 within a few days. How do you feel about companies and their brands pretending they have actual traffic on their sites and buying *likes*? (Obj. 5)

ACTIVITIES AND CASES

5.1 EMAIL THAT INFORMS AND REQUESTS: DRESS CODE CONTROVERSY (OBJ. 1)

As the Montreal-based director of Human Resources at Sensational, you have not had a good week. The national media recently reported the fact that Sensational—a leading women's fashion chain—has been taken before the Nova Scotia Human Rights Commission to defend against a claim by a young woman. The young woman recently applied for a job at a Halifax Sensational location and was told in a pre-interview with a manager that "she'd never be hired if she wore her headdress to work." Citing the Commission's website claim that "It's against the law to fire an employee because he wears clothing that is required by his religion," the young woman lodged a complaint.[44] Head office in Vancouver has been in damage-control mode ever since.

Your Task. Quickly realizing the effects the negative media reporting will have, you draft an email to all employees. The purpose of the email is to reaffirm that Sensational abides by and supports all Canadian human rights legislation and, at the same time, that employees should not talk to any media that may ask them for comments. You realize that these two messages are somewhat contradictory (one positive, one negative), but you feel time is of the essence.

Related website: Nova Scotia Human Rights Commission (www.gov.ns.ca/humanrights).

5.2 MEMO THAT INFORMS: CHANGE IN INSURANCE PREMIUMS (OBJ. 1)

You are the benefits manager for a national furniture retail chain, The Home Centre, headquartered in Richmond, British Columbia. Most of the full-time employees who work for the chain pay into an employee benefits plan. This plan includes dental and vision care, prescription drug coverage, and other benefits. One of the most expensive benefits employees pay for is long-term disability (LTD) insurance. Recently, your insurance provider, Cansafe, has informed you that due to the high number of recent long-term disability claims, premiums for long-term disability insurance will have to rise substantially, on the order of 15 percent. For the average employee, this means an increase of more than $20 per month.

Your Task. Your job requires you to write a well-organized memo informing The Home Centre employees about the impending increase. From past experience, you know that employees who are closer to retirement are big supporters of long-term disability insurance, whereas younger employees tend to be frustrated by the high premiums.

Related website: Manulife's site has a useful description of LTD insurance. Google "Manulife LTD" to find the page.

5.3 LETTER THAT REQUESTS: DONATION FOR ANNUAL AUCTION (OBJ. 1)

A common business-to-business writing situation is the donation letter. Not-for-profit organizations, for example, often hold high-profile fundraising events for which they need to solicit prizes, donations, and other gifts-in-kind.

Your Task. Casey House, a health services provider for people living with HIV/AIDS, has been holding a successful fundraiser for over 20 years, lately in conjunction with TD Canada Trust. The fundraiser, called Art With Heart, supports the activities of Casey House and is structured as an art auction. In order for the event to be successful each year, staff at Casey House and TD Canada Trust must secure roughly 100 art donations from commercial galleries and artists around Canada. As a staff member at one of these organizations, write a letter to dc3 Art Projects, a commercial gallery in Edmonton, asking for a donation of a work by Travis McEwen, one of the gallery's artists.

Related websites: http://www.dc3artprojects.com, http://artwithheart.ca

Visit **MindTap** for a variety of videos, additional exercises, activities, and quizzes to support your learning.

CHAPTER 6

Persuasive Writing Situations

OBJECTIVES

After studying this chapter, you should be able to

6.1 Explain digital-age persuasion and the time-proven AIRA persuasive technique.

6.2 Write persuasive messages to request help.

6.3 Write persuasive messages to make claims or complaints.

6.4 Write persuasive messages to get things done within your organization.

6.5 Write persuasive direct-mail, email, and online messages to sell goods and services.

Peopleimages/istock by Getty Images

6.1 Persuasion in the Digital Age

In the digital age, businesses have moved toward leaner corporate hierarchies, simultaneously relying on teams, dismantling division walls, and blurring the lines of authority. Persuasive skills are becoming ever more important at work as teams and managers abandon the traditional command structure and focus instead on *influencing* others.[1] However, getting others to do what we want isn't easy. Persuasion is needed when we are making more than routine demands and facing skeptical audiences.

Experts say that the average adult endures between 300 and 1,500 ads and other persuasive appeals a day.[2] As citizens and consumers, we need to be alert to persuasive practices and how they influence behaviour. Being informed is our best defence. On the other hand, social media networks have put power into the hands of many. Persuasion guru B. J. Fogg points out that social media enable individuals or groups to reach virtually limitless audiences and practise "mass interpersonal persuasion."[3]

In Chapter 4 you studied techniques for writing routine messages that require minimal persuasion. This chapter focuses on messages that require deliberate and skilled persuasion in the workplace. It also addresses selling, both offline and online. Perhaps the most persuasive writing situation of all—that of the cover letter—is dealt with separately in Chapter 12.

6.1a How Has Persuasion Changed in the Digital Age?

The ability to persuade is a primary factor in personal and business success.

The preoccupation with persuasion is not new. From the days of Aristotle in ancient Greece and Niccolò Machiavelli in Renaissance Italy, philosophers, politicians, and businesspeople have longed to understand the art of influencing others. However, persuasion in the 21st century is different from persuasion in previous historic periods in distinct ways.[4] The most striking developments, summarized below, are less than three decades old.

PERSUASIVE MESSAGES HAVE EXPLODED IN VOLUME AND REACH. The Internet, mobile phones, and TV blast a huge volume of messages around the world. This can be positive, as when popular culture trends, whether fashion or music or art, spread over Instagram from somewhere like Japan or China to Canada; or, it can be negative, as when incitements to terrorism spread via social media from the Middle East to North America and Europe.

PERSUASIVE MESSAGES SPREAD AT WARP SPEED. Popular TV shows such as *The X Factor* and their corporate sponsors use social media to engage the fans, whose more than half a million social media comments instantly influence the contestants' dance routines, songs, and wardrobes. *American Idol* now clocks one million posts during a single show,[5] and citizen reporters deliver instant updates from disaster areas on Twitter and other social media networks.

ORGANIZATIONS OF ALL STRIPES ARE IN THE PERSUASION BUSINESS. Companies, ad agencies, PR firms, social activists, lobbyists, marketers, and more spew persuasive messages. Although outspent by corporations that can sink millions into image campaigns, activists use social networks to rally their followers.

PERSUASIVE TECHNIQUES ARE SUBTLER AND MORE MISLEADING. Instead of a blunt, pushy hard-sell approach, persuaders play on emotions by using flattery, empathy, nonverbal cues, and likability appeals. They are selling images and lifestyles, not products.[6] In this age of spin, the news media are increasingly infiltrated by partisan interests, and they spread messages masquerading as news.

PERSUASION IS MORE COMPLEX AND IMPERSONAL. North American consumers are diverse and don't necessarily think alike. To reach them, marketers carefully study various target groups and customize their appeals. Technology has increased the potential for distortion. People can "mash up" content, give it meanings the original source never intended, and blast it into the world in seconds.

You probably recognize how important it is not only to become a skilled persuader, but also to identify devious messages and manipulation attempts directed at you. The delivery channels may have changed, but the principles of effective, time-tried persuasion still apply today.

When you want your ideas to prevail, start thinking about how to present them. Listeners and readers will be more inclined to accept what you are offering if you focus on important strategies, outlined in Figure 6.1 and further discussed throughout this chapter.

6.1b A Time-Proven Persuasion Technique

Despite these changes in persuasion, a traditional indirect persuasion strategy is still necessary in your day-to-day relations with busy coworkers, managers, people in outside organizations, and the general public because you will meet resistance when trying to persuade. This resistance is natural because most people who are trying to persuade others are asking for something that is valuable: money (e.g., in a sales presentation; in a charity solicitation), time (e.g., in a negotiation over increased vacation time), or goods (e.g., in a situation when a donation is requested).

FIGURE 6.1 | The Persuasion Process

Establish credibility

- Show that you are truthful, experienced, and knowledgeable.
- Use others' expert opinions and research to support your position.

Make a reasonable, specific request

- Make your request realistic, doable, and attainable.
- Be clear about your objective. Vague requests are less effective.

Tie facts to benefits

- Line up plausible support such as statistics, reasons, and analogies.
- Convert the supporting facts into specific audience benefits.

Recognize the power of loss

- Show what others stand to lose if they don't agree.
- Know that people dread losing something they already possess.

Expect and overcome resistance

- Anticipate opposition from conflicting beliefs, values, and attitudes.
- Be prepared to counter with well-reasoned arguments and facts.

Share solutions and compromise

- Be flexible and aim for a solution that is acceptable to all parties.
- Listen to people and incorporate their input to create buy-in.

Knowing that you will encounter resistance, it only makes sense that you should reduce or counter the resistance of the person you're trying to persuade before actually asking for what you want. For example, if after eight years of working for a furniture manufacturing company as a territory sales manager, with six straight years of growth in your sales but no growth to speak of in your vacation time, you may decide to ask your manager for more time off. Knowing that your company overall has had a slow sales period (not in your territory, however), you know you can't simply make a direct request to your boss: "Ken, I've been thinking it's time I received an increase in my vacation time!"

Instead, you'll need an *indirect* strategy that begins with countering resistance: "Ken, I've got some ideas the other territory managers can use to emulate my reps' success in growing business in these tough times. Can we talk about the ideas over lunch this week? When we meet, I'd also like to make a formal request for two extra days of vacation time going forward. After eight years with the company and a lot of success in my job, I feel this is an appropriate time for me to see a small bump in my vacation time. Let me know a time that works for you."

The indirect strategy requires more practice and experience than the direct strategy you used in the previous chapter to deal with routine writing situations. For this reason, pay close attention to the writing plans in this chapter as they show you how to perform the "persuasive moves" necessary to make things happen in the world of work. Also try the end-of-chapter Activities and Cases to build your persuasive writing skills.

6.1c The AIRA Technique

The indirect strategy used by Ken in the example above contains separate strategies, but to be successful all four should appear together as a unified whole. This unified strategy for persuasive writing is called AIRA, which stands for attention, interest, resistance, and action. These are the four crucial elements of any persuasive message. The order of the four elements isn't set in stone; for example, not every persuasive situation will require you to build interest before you reduce resistance. However, most persuasive messages begin by gaining attention and end by motivating action.

A: GAIN ATTENTION. In the brief opening of the message, gain the reader's attention by describing a problem, making an unexpected statement, mentioning a reader benefit, paying the reader a compliment, or posing a stimulating question. For example, in a persuasive voice mail message left by a local theatre company to its current subscribers, the speaker might begin by mentioning a listener benefit: *All of our returning subscribers will be able to take advantage of special access to our subscribers' lounge and attend after-show talks by members of the cast and creative team!*

I: BUILD INTEREST. The message's body is intended to keep the reader's attention and persuade him or her that the request is reasonable. This section is often the longest part of the message, as it includes the use of facts and statistics, expert opinion, direct benefits to the receiver, examples, and specific details, as well as indirect benefits to the receiver. Together, these facts create desire, which is especially important when your persuasive message is a sales message. In the theatre subscription example, the person leaving the voice mail may build interest by stating, *We rely on our subscribers to join us year after year because your subscription helps generate the largest part of our revenue. Government grants and donations currently make up only 30 percent of our revenue. This is why we need subscribers to keep coming back....*

R: REDUCE RESISTANCE. A crucial step in preparing the body of a persuasive message, yet one that is often left out by novice writers, is that of putting oneself in the receiver's shoes and asking, *What kinds of problems might the receiver have with my request?* For example, the person selling theatre subscriptions may be instructed to reduce the argument that people have many other important uses for their time and money. She may do this by arguing that, while people are busy and have many priorities, supporting the arts is important for the cultural life of the city and the quality of life of those enjoying the theatre. To counter this perceived resistance, the speaker anticipates and names this resistance in her voice mail and then counters it with a benefit: *Even though we understand you have competing priorities for your hard-earned money, we also know that supporting the arts is good for our city and good for our health. An evening at the theatre is a surefire way to leave the pressures and worries of everyday life behind for a few hours.*

A: MOTIVATE ACTION. Finally, no persuasive message is complete without the sender closing by telling the receiver exactly what he or she wants, and when he or she wants it. The goal is to sound confident but not pushy, and to motivate the reader to say yes. In essence, a persuasive message should end with a specific request that is confident but not demanding. In the theatre subscription example, the voice mail might end: *I'm sorry I missed you tonight, but I'll try you again tomorrow after dinnertime. In the meantime, feel free to give me a call at (416) 922-0018 and ask for Helen if you'd like to re-subscribe immediately. I can offer you the special access to the subscribers' lounge and after-show talks until March 15.*

6.2 Persuasive Situation: Asking for Help

On occasion, everyone needs to ask a favour. Small favours, such as asking a coworker to lock up the office for you on Friday, can be straightforward and direct. Little resistance is expected. Larger favours, though, require careful planning and an indirect strategy. A busy executive is asked to serve on a committee to help disadvantaged children; a florist is asked to donate table arrangements for a charity fundraiser; a well-known author is asked to speak before a local library group—why should they agree to do so? In each instance, persuasion is necessary to overcome the recipient's natural resistance.

Requests for large favours generally require persuasive strategies.

People are more likely to grant requests if they see direct or indirect benefits to themselves.

Fortunately, many individuals and companies are willing to grant requests for time, money, information, cooperation, and special privileges. They grant these favours for a variety of reasons. They may be interested in your project, or they may see goodwill potential for themselves. Often, though, they comply because they see that others will benefit from the request. Professionals sometimes feel obligated to contribute their time or expertise to "give back to the community."

Figure 6.2 shows a persuasive help request from Michelle Moreno. Her research firm seeks to persuade other companies to complete a questionnaire regarding

FIGURE 6.2 | Persuasive Help Request

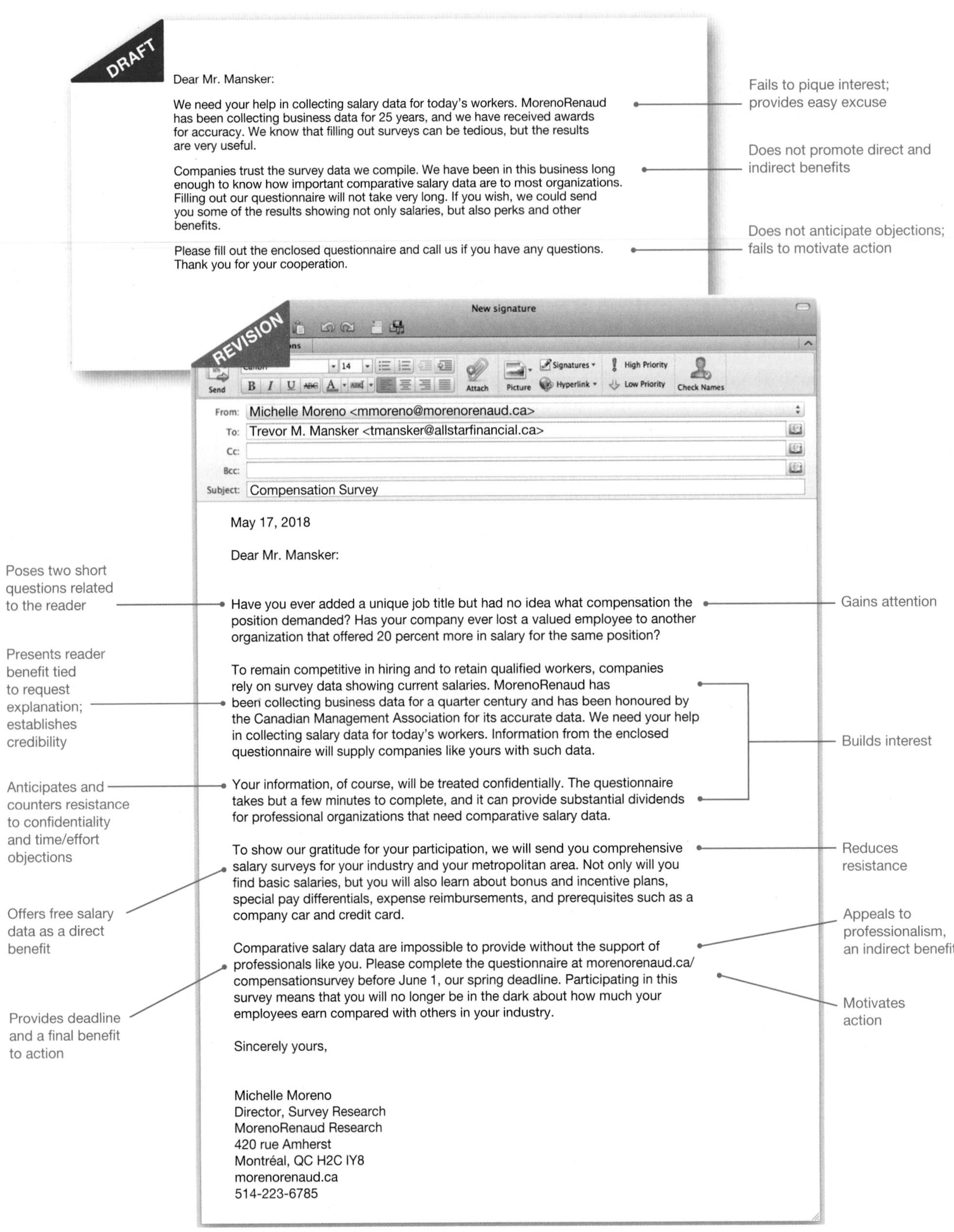
DRAFT
Dear Mr. Mansker:
We need your help in collecting salary data for today's workers. MorenoRenaud has been collecting business data for 25 years, and we have received awards for accuracy. We know that filling out surveys can be tedious, but the results are very useful.
Companies trust the survey data we compile. We have been in this business long enough to know how important comparative salary data are to most organizations. Filling out our questionnaire will not take very long. If you wish, we could send you some of the results showing not only salaries, but also perks and other benefits.
Please fill out the enclosed questionnaire and call us if you have any questions. Thank you for your cooperation.
Fails to pique interest; provides easy excuse
Does not promote direct and indirect benefits
Does not anticipate objections; fails to motivate action
REVISION
New signature
Send
Attach
Picture
Signatures
Hyperlink
High Priority
Low Priority
Check Names
From: Michelle Moreno <mmoreno@morenorenaud.ca>
To: Trevor M. Mansker <tmansker@allstarfinancial.ca>
Cc:
Bcc:
Subject: Compensation Survey
May 17, 2018
Dear Mr. Mansker:
Have you ever added a unique job title but had no idea what compensation the position demanded? Has your company ever lost a valued employee to another organization that offered 20 percent more in salary for the same position?
To remain competitive in hiring and to retain qualified workers, companies rely on survey data showing current salaries. MorenoRenaud has been collecting business data for a quarter century and has been honoured by the Canadian Management Association for its accurate data. We need your help in collecting salary data for today's workers. Information from the enclosed questionnaire will supply companies like yours with such data.
Your information, of course, will be treated confidentially. The questionnaire takes but a few minutes to complete, and it can provide substantial dividends for professional organizations that need comparative salary data.
To show our gratitude for your participation, we will send you comprehensive salary surveys for your industry and your metropolitan area. Not only will you find basic salaries, but you will also learn about bonus and incentive plans, special pay differentials, expense reimbursements, and prerequisites such as a company car and credit card.
Comparative salary data are impossible to provide without the support of professionals like you. Please complete the questionnaire at morenorenaud.ca/compensationsurvey before June 1, our spring deadline. Participating in this survey means that you will no longer be in the dark about how much your employees earn compared with others in your industry.
Sincerely yours,
Michelle Moreno
Director, Survey Research
MorenoRenaud Research
420 rue Amherst
Montréal, QC H2C IY8
morenorenaud.ca
514-223-6785
Poses two short questions related to the reader
Gains attention
Presents reader benefit tied to request explanation; establishes credibility
Builds interest
Anticipates and counters resistance to confidentiality and time/effort objections
Reduces resistance
Offers free salary data as a direct benefit
Appeals to professionalism, an indirect benefit
Provides deadline and a final benefit to action
Motivates action

salary data. For most organizations, salary information is strictly confidential. What can she do to convince strangers to part with such private information?

The hurriedly written first version of the request suffers from many faults. It fails to pique the interest of the reader in the opening. It also provides an easy excuse for Mr. Mansker to refuse (*filling out surveys can be tedious*). In the body, Mr. Mansker doesn't receive any incentive to accept the request. The writing is self-serving and offers few specifics. In addition, the draft does not anticipate objections and fails to suggest counter-arguments. Lastly, the closing does not motivate action by providing a deadline or a final benefit.

In the revised version, Michelle begins her persuasive request by posing two short questions that spotlight the need for salary information. To build interest and establish trust, she mentions that Moreno Renaud has been collecting business data for a quarter century and has received awards from the Canadian Marketing Association. Developing credibility is especially important when persuading strangers to do something. Making a reasonable request tied to benefits is also important. Michelle does this by emphasizing the need for current salary information.

To reduce resistance, Michelle promises confidentiality and explains that the questionnaire takes but a few moments to complete. She offers free salary data as a direct benefit. This data may help the receiver learn how his company's salary scale compares with others in its industry. But Michelle doesn't count on this offer as the only motivator. As an indirect benefit, she appeals to the professionalism of the receiver. She's hoping that the receiver will recognize the value of providing salary data to the entire profession. To motivate action, Michelle closes with a deadline and reminds the reader that his company need not be in the dark about comparative salaries within the industry.

This help request incorporates many of the techniques that are effective in persuasion: establishing credibility, making a reasonable and precise request, tying facts to benefits, and overcoming resistance. These techniques can be summarized in the writing plan below.

WRITING PLAN FOR A PERSUASIVE REQUEST

- **Gain attention** in the opening.
- **Build interest** in the body.
- **Reduce resistance** in the body.
- **Motivate action** in the closing.

Persuasive claim and complaint messages make reasonable requests backed by solid evidence.

6.3 Persuasive Situation: Making Claims and Complaints

Let's say you buy a new car and the transmission repeatedly requires servicing. When you finally get tired of taking it in for repair, you decide to send an email to the car manufacturer's district office, asking that the company install a new transmission in your car. You know that your request will be resisted. You must convince the manufacturer that replacement, not repair, is needed. Routine claim situations, when there are no "grey" areas at all, such as those you encountered in Chapter 5, should be straightforward and direct. Persuasive claims and complaints, on the other hand, are generally more effective when they are indirect.

Use persuasion when you must change attitudes or produce action.

The organization of an effective persuasive claim or complaint message centres on the closing and the persuasion. First, decide what action you want taken to satisfy the claim. Then, decide how you can prove the worth of your claim. Carefully plan the reasoning you will follow in convincing the reader to take the action you request. If the claim is addressed to a business, the most effective appeals are generally to the organization's pride in its products and its services. Refer to its reputation for integrity and your confidence in it. Show why your claim is valid and why the company will be doing the right thing in granting it. Most organizations are sincere in their efforts to showcase quality products and services that gain consumer respect.

The most successful appeals are to a company's pride in its products and services.

Although claim messages often contain an aspect of complaint, try not to be angry. Hostility and emotional threats toward an organization do little to achieve the goal of a claim message. Claims are usually referred to a customer service department. The representative answering the claim probably had nothing to do with the design, production, delivery, or servicing of the product or service. An abusive message may serve only to offend, making it hard for the representative to evaluate the claim rationally.

A writing plan for an indirect persuasive claim or complaint follows the steps below.

WRITING PLAN FOR A CLAIM OR COMPLAINT

- **Gain attention** in the opening by paying the receiver a compliment.
- **Build interest** in the body by explaining and justifying the claim or complaint with convincing reasons and without anger.
- **Reduce resistance** in the body by subtly suggesting the responsibility of the receiver. Appeal to the receiver's sense of fairness or desire for customer satisfaction.
- **Motivate action** in the closing by explaining exactly what action you want taken and when.

Claim messages should avoid negative and emotional words and should not attempt to fix blame.

Observe how the claim email shown in Figure 6.3 illustrates the suggestions above. When Arte International Furnishings in Concord, Ontario, purchased two VoIP systems, it discovered that they would not work without producing an annoying static sound. The company's attempt, via the Internet, to return the VoIP systems has been ignored by the retailer. Despite these difficulties, notice the writer's positive opening, her well-documented claims, and her specific request for action.

6.4 Persuasive Situation: Getting Coworkers and Managers Onside

When it comes to persuasion, the hierarchy at work determines how you write—whether you choose a direct or indirect approach, for example. You may consider what type and amount of evidence to include, depending on whether you wish to persuade your coworkers or your own manager or other managers. The authority of your audience may also help you decide whether to adopt a formal or informal tone.

FIGURE 6.3 | Complex Claim

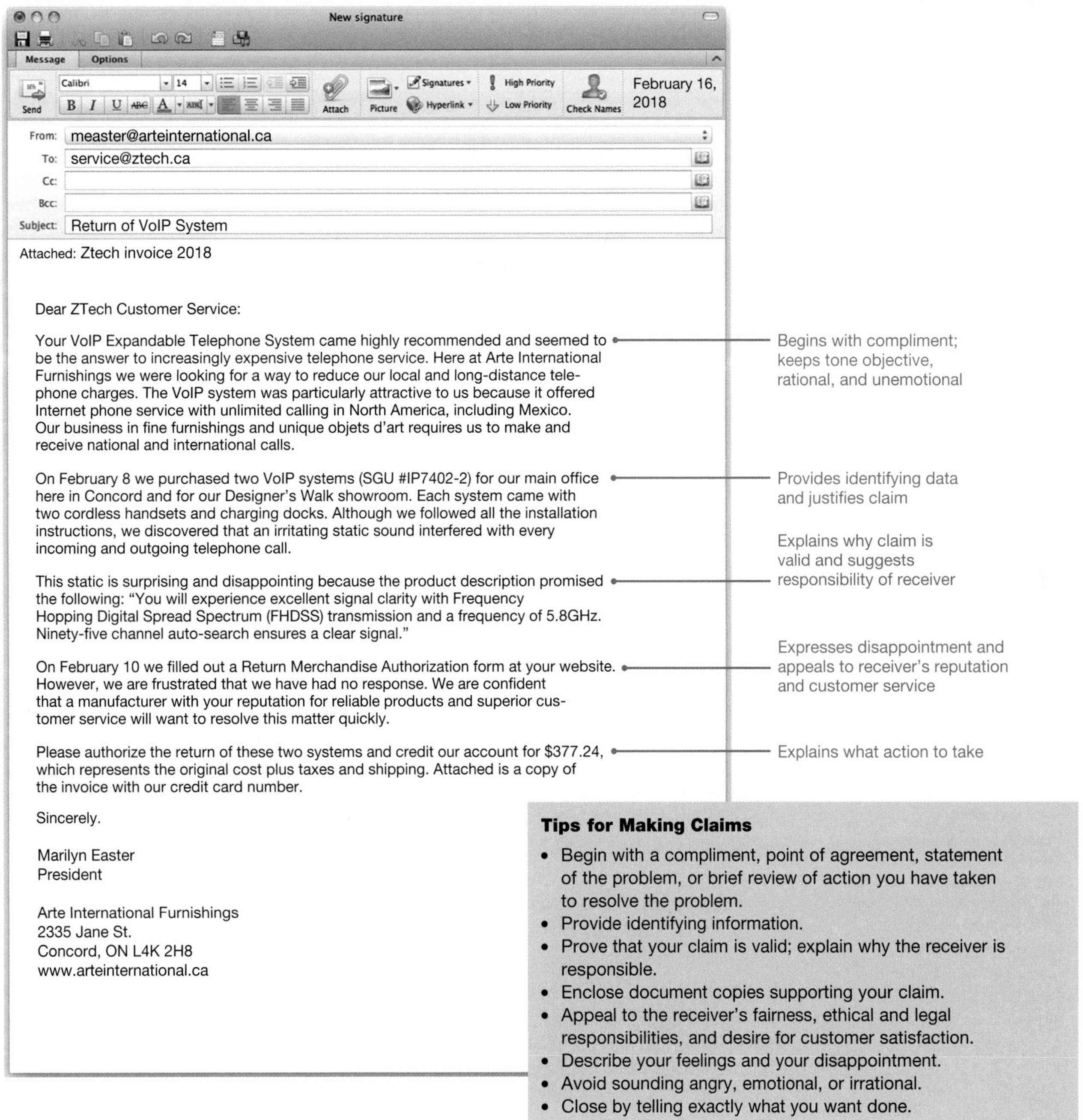

Tips for Making Claims

- Begin with a compliment, point of agreement, statement of the problem, or brief review of action you have taken to resolve the problem.
- Provide identifying information.
- Prove that your claim is valid; explain why the receiver is responsible.
- Enclose document copies supporting your claim.
- Appeal to the receiver's fairness, ethical and legal responsibilities, and desire for customer satisfaction.
- Describe your feelings and your disappointment.
- Avoid sounding angry, emotional, or irrational.
- Close by telling exactly what you want done.

PERSUADING OTHER EMPLOYEES. Instructions or directives moving downward from employees to other employees whom they manage (i.e., direct reports) usually require little persuasion. Employees expect to be directed in how to perform their jobs. These messages (such as information about procedures, equipment, or customer service) follow the direct pattern, with the purpose immediately stated. However, employees are sometimes asked to perform in a capacity outside their work roles or to accept changes that are not in their best interests (such as pay cuts, job transfers, or reduced benefits). Occasionally, superiors need to address sensitive

Internal persuasive messages present honest arguments detailing specific reader or company benefits.

workplace issues such as bullying or diversity programs. Similarly, supervisors may want to create buy-in when introducing a healthier cafeteria menu or mandatory volunteering effort. In these instances, a persuasive message using the indirect pattern may be most effective.

The goal is not to manipulate employees or to deceive them with trickery. Rather, the goal is to present a strong but honest argument, emphasizing points that are important to the receiver or the organization. In business, honesty is not just the best policy—it is the only policy. People see right through puffery and misrepresentation. For this reason, the indirect pattern is effective only when supported by accurate, honest evidence.

PERSUADING YOUR MANAGER. Another form of persuasion within organizations centres on suggestions made by employees to their managers. Convincing management to adopt a procedure or invest in a product or new equipment generally requires skillful communication. Managers are just as resistant to change as others are. Knowing precisely what they're asking for and providing evidence of why the request is necessary are critical factors when employees submit recommendations to their manager. It's also important to be realistic in your requests, recognizing that your manager has other employees whose needs may be different from your own. Equally important when asking something of your manager is to focus on their needs. How can you make your suggestion sound like something your manager also wants or needs?

OFFICE INSIDER

"When you create the impression that you are a person of honesty and integrity, you will have a considerable advantage over someone who is perceived otherwise."

—Paul M. Sandler, litigation lawyer, writing on legal ethos

Office Insider based on Sandler, P. M. cited in Power of persuasion. (n.d.). SourceWatch. Retrieved from http://www.sourcewatch.org/index.php?title=Power_of_persuasion

Obviously, when you set out to persuade someone at work who is above you in the company hierarchy, do so carefully. Use words like *suggest* and *recommend*, and craft sentences using conditional verb tenses such as: *It might be a good idea if...* ; *We might think about doing....* The conditional tense lets you offer suggestions without threatening the person's authority.

In Figure 6.4 you can see a persuasive memo (attached to an email) written by Marketing Assistant Monica Cho, who wants her manager to authorize the purchase of a multi-function colour laser copier. She has researched the prices, features, and maintenance costs of the machines. They often serve as copiers, faxes, scanners, and printers and can cost several thousand dollars. Monica has found an outstanding deal offered by a local office supplier. Because Monica knows that her boss, Samuel Neesen, favours "cold, hard facts," she lists current monthly costs for copying at Copy Quick to increase her chances of gaining approval. Finally, she calculates the amortization of the purchase price and monthly costs of running the new colour copier.

Notice that Monica's memo isn't short. An indirect persuasive request will typically take more space than a direct request because proving a case requires evidence. In the end, Monica chose to send her memo as an email attachment accompanied by a polite, short note because she wanted to keep the document format in Microsoft Word intact. She also felt that the message was too long to paste into an email. Monica's persuasive memo and her email include a subject line that announces the purpose of the message without disclosing the actual request. By delaying the request until she has had a chance to describe the problem and discuss a solution, Monica prevents the reader's premature rejection.

When selling an idea to management, writers often are successful if they make a strong case for saving or earning money.

The strength of this persuasive message, though, is in the clear presentation of comparison figures showing how much money the company can save by purchasing a remanufactured copier. Buying a copier that uses low-cost solid ink instead of expensive laser cartridges is another argument in this machine's favour. Although the organization pattern is not obvious, the memo does follow most of the Writing Plan for a Persuasive Request from earlier in this chapter, by beginning with an attention-getter (a frank description of the problem), building interest (with easy-to-read facts and figures), providing benefits, and reducing resistance. Notice that the conclusion suggests what action is to be taken, makes it easy to respond, and repeats the main benefit to motivate action.

FIGURE 6.4 | Interoffice Persuasive Memo Attached to Email Cover Note

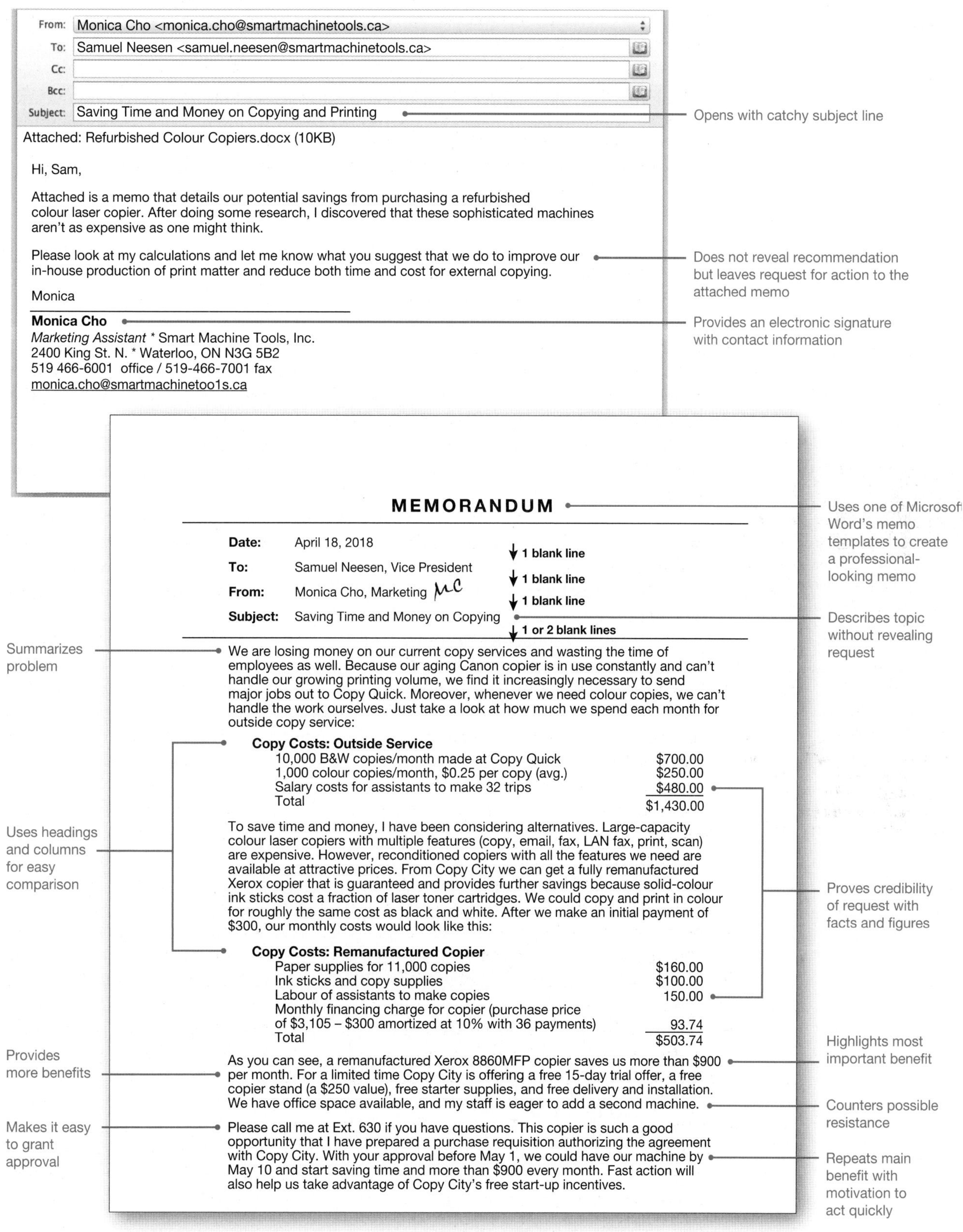
From: Monica Cho <monica.cho@smartmachinetools.ca>

To: Samuel Neesen <samuel.neesen@smartmachinetools.ca>

Cc:

Bcc:

Subject: Saving Time and Money on Copying and Printing

Attached: Refurbished Colour Copiers.docx (10KB)

Hi, Sam,

Attached is a memo that details our potential savings from purchasing a refurbished colour laser copier. After doing some research, I discovered that these sophisticated machines aren't as expensive as one might think.

Please look at my calculations and let me know what you suggest that we do to improve our in-house production of print matter and reduce both time and cost for external copying.

Monica

Monica Cho
Marketing Assistant * Smart Machine Tools, Inc.
2400 King St. N. * Waterloo, ON N3G 5B2
519 466-6001 office / 519-466-7001 fax
monica.cho@smartmachinetoo1s.ca

MEMORANDUM

Date: April 18, 2018

To: Samuel Neesen, Vice President

From: Monica Cho, Marketing MC

Subject: Saving Time and Money on Copying

We are losing money on our current copy services and wasting the time of employees as well. Because our aging Canon copier is in use constantly and can't handle our growing printing volume, we find it increasingly necessary to send major jobs out to Copy Quick. Moreover, whenever we need colour copies, we can't handle the work ourselves. Just take a look at how much we spend each month for outside copy service:

Copy Costs: Outside Service

10,000 B&W copies/month made at Copy Quick	$700.00
1,000 colour copies/month, $0.25 per copy (avg.)	$250.00
Salary costs for assistants to make 32 trips	$480.00
Total	$1,430.00

To save time and money, I have been considering alternatives. Large-capacity colour laser copiers with multiple features (copy, email, fax, LAN fax, print, scan) are expensive. However, reconditioned copiers with all the features we need are available at attractive prices. From Copy City we can get a fully remanufactured Xerox copier that is guaranteed and provides further savings because solid-colour ink sticks cost a fraction of laser toner cartridges. We could copy and print in colour for roughly the same cost as black and white. After we make an initial payment of $300, our monthly costs would look like this:

Copy Costs: Remanufactured Copier

Paper supplies for 11,000 copies	$160.00
Ink sticks and copy supplies	$100.00
Labour of assistants to make copies	150.00
Monthly financing charge for copier (purchase price of $3,105 – $300 amortized at 10% with 36 payments)	93.74
Total	$503.74

As you can see, a remanufactured Xerox 8860MFP copier saves us more than $900 per month. For a limited time Copy City is offering a free 15-day trial offer, a free copier stand (a $250 value), free starter supplies, and free delivery and installation. We have office space available, and my staff is eager to add a second machine.

Please call me at Ext. 630 if you have questions. This copier is such a good opportunity that I have prepared a purchase requisition authorizing the agreement with Copy City. With your approval before May 1, we could have our machine by May 10 and start saving time and more than $900 every month. Fast action will also help us take advantage of Copy City's free start-up incentives.

Opens with catchy subject line
Does not reveal recommendation but leaves request for action to the attached memo
Provides an electronic signature with contact information
1 blank line
1 blank line
1 blank line
1 or 2 blank lines
Uses one of Microsoft Word's memo templates to create a professional-looking memo
Describes topic without revealing request
Summarizes problem
Uses headings and columns for easy comparison
Proves credibility of request with facts and figures
Provides more benefits
Highlights most important benefit
Counters possible resistance
Makes it easy to grant approval
Repeats main benefit with motivation to act quickly

6.5 Persuasive Situation: Sales and Promotional Messages

Sales messages use persuasion to promote specific products and services. The focus in this part of the chapter is on direct-mail sales letters, but the communication strategy you will learn here can be applied to all forms of sales and promotions, including print, online, social, and digital media, as well as traditional copywriting for radio and TV advertisements. Smart companies strive to develop a balanced approach to their overall marketing strategy, including both traditional direct mail as well as social/digital marketing when appropriate.

6.5a Sales Messages

Traditional direct-mail marketing uses snail mail or flyering; new media marketing uses email, social media, and digital media.

Sales letters are generally part of a package that may contain a brochure, price list, illustrations, testimonials, and other persuasive appeals. Professionals who specialize in traditional direct-mail services have made a science of analyzing a market, developing an effective mailing list, studying the product, preparing a sophisticated campaign aimed at a target audience, and motivating the reader to act. You have probably received many direct-mail packages, often called "junk mail."

Learning to write sales letters helps you sell yourself and your ideas as well as become a smarter consumer.

Because sales letters are usually written by marketing communications specialists, you may never write one on the job. Why, then, learn how to write a sales letter? In many ways, every message we draft is a form of sales letter. We sell our ideas, our organizations, and ourselves. When you apply for a job, you are both the seller and the product. Learning the techniques of sales writing will help you be more successful in any communication that requires persuasion and promotion. Furthermore, you will recognize sales strategies, thus enabling you to become a more perceptive consumer of ideas, products, and services.

Your primary goal in writing a sales message is to get someone to devote a few moments of attention to it.[7] You may be promoting a product, a service, an idea, or yourself. In each case the most effective messages will follow a writing plan. This is the same recipe we studied earlier, but the ingredients are different.

The AIRA pattern (attention, interest, resistance, and action) is used in selling because it is highly effective.

WRITING PLAN FOR A SALES MESSAGE: AIRA

Professional marketers and salespeople follow the AIRA pattern (attention, interest, desire, and action) when persuading consumers. In addition to telemarketing and personal selling, this pattern works very well for written messages.

- **Opening:** Gain *attention.* Offer something valuable; promise a benefit to the reader; ask a question; or provide a quotation, fact, product feature, testimonial, startling statement, or personalized action setting.
- **Body:** Build *interest and desire;* reduce *resistance.* Describe central selling points and make rational and emotional appeals. Elicit desire in the reader and reduce resistance. Use testimonials, money-back guarantees, free samples, performance tests, or other techniques.
- **Closing:** Motivate *action.* Offer a gift, promise an incentive, limit the offer, set a deadline, or guarantee satisfaction.

WORKPLACE IN FOCUS

Trying to sell a micro car to Canadians has been a gamble for Daimler AG, manufacturer of the luxurious Mercedes-Benz brand but also maker of the diminutive Smart Fortwo. Prompted by skyrocketing gasoline prices, European and Asian drivers have long embraced small automobiles. But SUV-, truck-, and van-loving Canadians? Although the Smart is well engineered and sells briskly in over 30 countries, its promoters have had to work harder to win over Canadians, especially those not living in large urban centres. *What might rural or suburban Canadian car buyers worry about most when they see an automobile such as the Smart? What strategies might reduce their resistance?*

Courtesy of Dana Loewy

ATTENTION. One of the most critical elements of a sales letter is its opening paragraph, the attention-getter. This opener should be short (one to five lines), honest, relevant, and stimulating. Marketing pros have found that eye-catching typographical arrangements or provocative messages, such as the following, can hook a reader's attention:

- **Offer:** A free trip to Hawaii is just the beginning!
- **Benefit:** Now you can raise your sales income by 50 percent or even more with the proven techniques found in....
- **Open-ended suggestive question:** Do you want your family to be safe?
- **Quotation or proverb:** Necessity is the mother of invention.
- **Compliment:** Life is full of milestones. You have reached one. You deserve....
- **Fact:** A recent *Maclean's* poll says that three quarters of Canadians are not happy with the quality of financial advice they're receiving.
- **Product feature:** Electronic stability control, ABS, and other active and passive safety features explain why the ultra-compact new Smart Fortwo has achieved a four-star crash rating in Quebec.
- **Testimonial:** The most recent J.D. Power survey of "initial quality" shows that BMW ranks at the top of brands with the fewest defects and malfunctions, ahead of Chrysler, Hyundai, Lexus, Porsche, and Toyota.
- **Startling statement:** Let the poor and hungry feed themselves! For just $100 they can.
- **Personalized action setting:** It's 6:30 p.m. and you are working overtime to meet a pressing deadline. Suddenly your copier breaks down. The production of your colour-laser brochures screeches to a halt. How you wish you had purchased the Worry-Free-Anytime service contract from Canon.

Other openings calculated to capture attention might include a solution to a problem, an anecdote, a personalized statement using the receiver's name, or a relevant current event.

INTEREST AND DESIRE. In this phase of your sales message, you should clearly describe the product or service in order to build interest/desire. Think of this part as a promise that the product or service will satisfy the audience's needs. In simple language, emphasize the central selling points that you identified during your prewriting analysis. Those selling points can be developed using rational or emotional appeals.

Build interest by describing the benefits a product or service offers and by making rational or emotional appeals.

Rational appeals focus on making or saving money, increasing efficiency, or making good use of resources.

Rational appeals are associated with reason and intellect. They translate selling points into references to making or saving money, increasing efficiency, or making the best use of resources. In general, rational appeals are appropriate when a product is expensive, long lasting, or important to health, security, and financial success. Emotional appeals relate to status, ego, and sensual feelings. Appealing to the emotions is sometimes effective when a product is inexpensive, short-lived, or nonessential. Many clever sales messages, however, combine emotional and rational strategies for a dual appeal. Consider these examples:

Rational Appeal

Cheery Maids is a one-stop solution: for one low monthly charge, you will receive biweekly visits from a team of our professional, fully-bonded cleaning staff who will clean your house from top to bottom. Enjoy both peace of mind and your time away from work without having to do your own cleaning.

Emotional appeals focus on status, ego, and sensual feelings.

Emotional Appeal

Tired of 9 to 5? Tired of commutes that seem to stretch longer and longer each day? Tired of getting home only to find you need to cook and clean the house because it's such a mess? Let Cheery Maids take part of the "tired" out of your life by providing you with cheerful, competitively priced home-cleaning services.

Dual Appeal

By signing up today with Cheery Maids, you'll receive two free cleanings in the next calendar year. Not only will you be able to leave the "dirty work" to our trained professionals, you'll have money left over to enjoy a couple of relaxing nights out at dinner and a movie with the family—on us!

A physical description of your product is not enough, however. Experienced salespeople know that no matter how well you know your product, no one is persuaded by cold, hard facts alone. In the end, "people buy because of the product benefits."[8] Your job is to translate those cold facts into warm feelings and reader benefits. Let's say a sales letter promotes a hand cream made with Vitamin A and aloe and cocoa butter extracts. Those facts become *Nature's hand helpers—including soothing aloe and cocoa extracts, and firming Vitamin A—form invisible gloves that protect your sensitive skin against the hardships of work, harsh detergents, and constant environmental assaults.*

Dana Fradon/The New Yorker Collection/The Cartoon Bank

REDUCE RESISTANCE. The goal at this stage in the sales message is to overcome resistance. You also try to make the audience want the product or service and to anticipate objections, focusing strongly on reader benefits. Here the promises of the attention and interest sections are covered in great detail. Marketing pros use a number of techniques to overcome resistance.

- **Testimonials:** *I always receive friendly and on-time service when I take my car to a Canadian Tire mechanic for servicing. I just wouldn't go anywhere else!*—Vince McRae, Edmundston, NB. (overcomes the resistance that this is just a marketing campaign with no truth behind it)

- **Names of satisfied users (with permission, of course):** *See the bottom of this message to learn about some of the IT professionals who are already taking advantage of our conference webinar subscription service and are 100% satisfied with the experience.* (overcomes the resistance that the service/product isn't guaranteed to be successful)
- **Money-back guarantee or warranty:** *Not only do we offer free shipping on all online orders over $25, we guarantee everything we sell. If you're not happy, simply use the enclosed postage coupon to return your purchase to us free of charge and receive a full refund.* (overcomes the resistance that the product/service is expensive)
- **Free trial or sample:** *Welcome to the wine store. Would you care for a sample of a wonderful new white wine? Go ahead and enjoy a piece of cheddar and a cracker—they pair nicely with the minerally quality of this Riesling ... I have a coupon for $1 off per bottle if you'd like to take some home....* (overcomes the resistance that you've never tried this product/service)
- **Performance tests, polls, or awards:** *At Luce this week, Chef Ferretti, who has just returned from Washington, D.C., where he won the prestigious North American Chef Competition for best innovative dish, is offering a three-course tasting menu including one-course wine pairing for $89.* (overcomes the resistance that you'd rather stick with what you know)

In addition, you need to anticipate objections and questions the receiver may have. When possible, translate these objections into selling points (*Tax season can be a stressful time and you want to make sure you can trust the person who prepares your income tax returns. For this reason we offer a free 30-minute consultation with one of our tax preparation specialists who will walk you through your return and explain how we arrived at our calculations.*). Be sure, of course, that your claims are accurate and do not stretch the truth.

When price is an obstacle, consider these suggestions:

- Delay mentioning price until after you have created a desire for the product.
- Show the price in small units, such as the price per month or per ten downloads of a magazine subscription service.
- Demonstrate how the reader saves money by, for instance, subscribing for two or three years.
- Compare your prices with those of a competitor.
- If applicable, offer advantageous financing terms.

ACTION. All the effort put into a sales message is wasted if the reader fails to respond. To make it easy for readers to act, you can provide a reply card, a stamped and pre-addressed envelope, a toll-free telephone number, a convenient Web address, or a promise of a follow-up call. Because readers often need an extra push, consider including additional motivators, such as the following:

Techniques for motivating action include offering a gift or incentive, limiting an offer, and guaranteeing satisfaction.

- **Offer a gift:** You will receive a free iPod nano with the purchase of any new car.
- **Promise an incentive:** With every new, paid subscription, we will plant a tree in one of Canada's pollution-busting boreal forests.
- **Limit the offer:** Only the first 100 customers receive free cheques.
- **Set a deadline:** You must act before June 1 to get these low prices.
- **Guarantee satisfaction:** We will return your full payment if you are not entirely satisfied—no questions asked.

The final paragraph of the sales letter carries the call to action. This is where you tell readers what you want done and give them reasons for doing it. Most sales letters also include postscripts because they make for irresistible reading. Even readers who might skim over or bypass paragraphs are drawn to a P.S. Therefore, use a postscript to reveal your strongest motivator, to add a special inducement for a quick response, or to re-emphasize a central selling point.

PUTTING IT ALL TOGETHER. Direct-mail sales letters are the number two preferred marketing medium, right behind email, because they can be personalized, directed to target audiences, and filled with a more complete message than other advertising media.[9] However, direct mail is expensive. That is why the total sales message is crafted so painstakingly.

Figure 6.5 shows a sales letter addressed to a target group of existing bank customers. To sell the new Groceries Plus Mastercard, the letter incorporates all four AIRA components of an effective persuasive message. Notice that the personalized action-setting opener places the reader in a familiar situation (walking into a supermarket) and draws an analogy between the choosing which aisle to go down first and choosing between many credit cards.

FIGURE 6.5 | Persuasive Direct-Mail Sales Letter

FoodCo. Financial ***Life.Easier.***

April 2, 2018

Mr. Tony Stronge
1501 Whitechurch Way
Dartmouth, NS
B3E 48V

Dear Mr. Stronge,

You've probably experienced this situation recently: it's the end of a busy weekend and you still have to do the groceries. When you arrive at the store, it's crowded, people are in a rush, and you're confused – where should I begin? The produce aisle? The frozen aisle? The meat and dairy? Choices can be daunting as well as frustrating, which is why we're here to make your life easier.

The new FoodCo Groceries Plus Mastercard takes making the choice of which credit card to use simple. Which other credit card offers you instantaneous free groceries? Only ours. Watch your free groceries pile up each time you use your card. Don't be frustrated by all the choice that's out there. Pick the card you know you'll find useful – the only one that earns you instant free groceries with each purchase.

Already convinced? Go to www.foodco.ca/groceriesplus to apply immediately. Just for filling out the online application, you'll receive $25 in free groceries!

If you're wondering why you should switch to the Groceries Plus Mastercard, just listen to what one satisfied customer has to say:

You might take trips once a year, and it takes you 30 years to pay off a mortgage, so why tie your credit card to one of these rare occurences? I buy groceries each week (and sometimes more than once a week), which is why I think my Groceries Plus Mastercard makes a lot of sense. Each time I use it, I'm earning money off my next grocery purchase. It makes a lot of sense. – Barb Lyons, Windsor, NS

There are plenty of reasons to switch cards. It's easy and quick to do so online and you can start earning free groceries today.

Sincerely,

Tom Ramanauskas
Director, Consumer Cards

P.S. Apply right now at www.foodco.ca/groceriesplus and receive $25 off your next grocery purchase!

Places reader in a recognizable situational context

Gains attention

Implies analogy with opening situation

Builds interest

Inserts call-out with offer and to re-ignite attention

Creates desire (and reduces resistance) via rational credibility of testimonial

Repeats sales pitch in final sentence

Spotlights free offer in post-script to prompt reply

The writer develops a rational central selling point (a credit card that earns you free groceries is one you'll use happily) and repeats this selling point in all the components of the letter. Notice, too, how a testimonial from a satisfied customer lends support to the sales message, and how the closing pushes for action. Also, see how call-outs (bolded, indented attention-grabbing messages) appear within the body of the letter.

Because the price of the credit card (a $100 yearly fee) is not a selling feature, it is mentioned only on the reply card. This sales letter repeats its strongest motivator—$25 in free groceries for signing up—in the high-impact P.S. line.

Although you want to be persuasive in sales letters, you must guard against overstepping legal and ethical boundaries. Be sure to check out the Communication Workshop in the MindTap to see specific examples of what is legal and what is not.

6.5b Promotional Messages

To make the best use of limited advertising dollars while reaching a great number of potential customers, many businesses are turning to the Internet and to digital marketing campaigns in particular. Much like traditional direct mail, digital marketing can attract new customers, help keep existing ones, encourage future sales, cross-sell, and cut costs. As consumers become more comfortable and secure with online purchases, they will receive more email sales messages.

Email has in fact become the primary channel that consumers use to interact with brands. It is the most used channel for written, personal communication (45 percent), and 77 percent of consumers prefer permission-based marketing through email.[10] One recent estimate suggests that email-only marketing campaigns perform 95 times better than direct mail in terms of return on investment.[11]

In the future, customers will be more likely to receive ads for products and services they actually use and like, and they can always opt out of receiving such marketing emails. An Econsultancy study of 1,400 U.S. consumers found that 42 percent prefer to receive ads by email compared to 3 percent who favoured social networking sites and only 1 percent who preferred Twitter.[12]

SELLING BY EMAIL. If your organization requires an online sales message, try using the following techniques gleaned from the best-performing emails.

Communicate only with those who have given permission! By sending messages only to "opt-in" folks, you greatly increase your "open rate"—those email messages that will be opened. Email users detest spam. However, receivers are surprisingly receptive to offers tailored specifically for them. Remember that today's customer is somebody—not anybody. Marketers must make it easy for the recipient to unsubscribe.

Send only targeted, not "blanket," mailings. Include something special for a select group.

Sales and promotional email often comes with colourful and eye-catching graphics and a minimum of text. To allow for embedded images, sound, and even video, the email is coded in HTML and can be viewed in an email program or an Internet browser on a computer or mobile phone. Software programs make it easy to create e-newsletters for email distribution. Often at the time of purchase or inquiry customers are prompted to provide an email address or create an account and sign up to receive e-newsletters and periodic promotions. See, for example, the newsletter sign up at Live Nation, an online concert-ticket retailer (http://promo.livenation.com/email/setlist).

The principles you have learned to apply to traditional sales messages also work with electronic promotional tools. However, online sales messages are often shorter than direct mail, feature colourful graphics, and occasionally even have sound or video clips. They offer a richer experience to readers, who can click hyperlinks to access content that interests them. When such messages are sent out as ads or periodic e-newsletters, they may not have salutations or closings. Rather, they may resemble Web pages.

Here are a few guidelines that will help you create effective online sales messages:

- **Craft a catchy subject line.** Offer discounts or premiums: *Spring Sale: Buy now and save 20 percent!* Promise solutions to everyday work-related problems. Highlight hot new industry topics. Invite readers to scan a top-ten list of items such as issues, trends, or people.
- **Keep the main information "above the fold."** Email messages should be top heavy. Primary points should appear early in the message so that they capture the reader's attention.
- **Make the message short, conversational, and focused.** Because on-screen text is taxing to read, be brief. Focus on one or two central selling points only.
- **Convey urgency.** Top-performing sales emails state an offer deadline or demonstrate why the state of the industry demands action on the reader's part. Good messages also tie the product to relevant current events.
- **Sprinkle testimonials throughout the copy.** Consumers' own words are the best sales copy. These comments can serve as call-outs or be integrated into the copy.
- **Provide a means for opting out.** It is polite and also a good business tactic (and in many places, a law) to include a statement that tells receivers how to be removed from the sender's mailing database.

USING SOCIAL MEDIA TO CONNECT WITH CUSTOMERS. Besides the static one-directional email sales and promotions channel, businesses are increasingly looking to social media and blogs to send out their persuasive and promotional messages to partner firms and customers. As we have seen, social media are not primarily suited for overt selling; however, tweets and other posts can be used to influence others and to project a professional, positive online presence. These new tools can also be useful internally when communicating with employees.

OFFICE INSIDER

"Facebook is the equivalent to us [of] what TV was for marketers back in the 1960s. It's an integral part of what we do now."

—Davide Grasso, vice president Global Brand Marketing, Nike Inc.

- **Facebook.** Facebook is the Web's dominant social network. Nike's three-minute commercial "Write the Future" was first launched on the company's Facebook site. The video went viral, and over one weekend, the number of Nike's Facebook fans doubled from 1.6 million to 3.1 million. Soft-drink giant Coca-Cola maintains by far the largest presence on Facebook with more than 12 million fans. Coca-Cola has made Facebook a central focus of its marketing plans.

A recent study by public relations giant Burson-Marsteller suggests that social media offer huge research and brand-building opportunities. Media-savvy businesses face a public that wants to be heard. If they listen to and engage with users, companies can positively affect their customers' beliefs as well as counter potentially negative perceptions.[13] Almost 80 percent of major global companies market their brands and communicate with the public on social media sites.[14] Despite concerns after repeated privacy breaches, to proponents of social media, sites such as Facebook promise advertising that is less obtrusive and more tailored to users' needs than traditional, widely distributed ads.

- **Blogs.** In the right hands, blogs can be powerful marketing tools. Information technology giant Hewlett-Packard (HP) invites guest bloggers to contribute to its site as advisers to small businesses, for example. Executives, HP employees, and outside experts discuss a wide range of technology- and company-related topics. Although not overtly pushing a marketing message, ultimately HP wants to generate goodwill; hence, the blogs serve as a public relations tool.[15] Nearly half of the CEOs questioned in one survey said they believe blogs are useful for external public relations, and 59 percent said they find blogs valuable for internal communication.[16] Many companies now use blogs to subtly market their products and develop a brand image.
- **Twitter.** Twitter has become a big part of marketing today. As Tamar Weinberg, author of *The New Community Rules: Marketing on the Social Web*, has shown,

Twitter has been used successfully by both large and small companies as well as organizations in the social sector to increase sales and to perform other functions such as impact-raising and crisis management, as can be seen below in Figure 6.6.[17]

Note that the compact format of a tweet requires extreme conciseness and efficiency. Don't expect the full AIRA strategy to be represented in a 140-character Twitter message. Instead, you may see attention getters and calls for action, both of which must be catchy and intriguing. Regardless, many of the principles of persuasion discussed in this chapter apply even to micromessages.

Clearly, business communicators today—especially those who work in publicity, advertising, marketing, and sales—have to become experts at the relatively new communication genres such as social media, whose interfaces are radically different than that of the traditional letter: more flexible, colourful, touchable, changeable, and so on.

FIGURE 6.6 | Persuasive Tweets

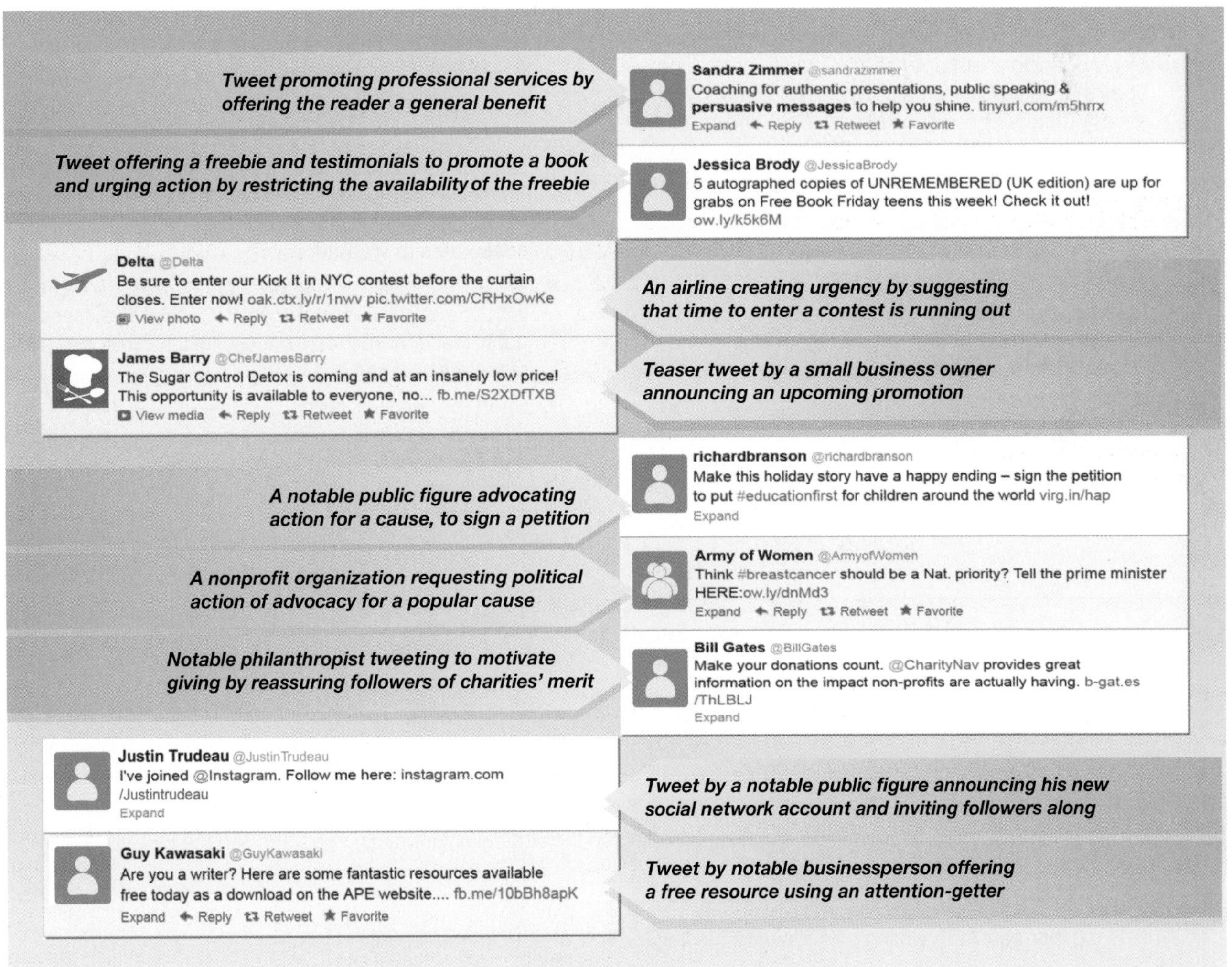

SUMMARY OF LEARNING OBJECTIVES

6.1 Explain digital-age persuasion and the time-proven AIRA persuasive technique.

- Business communicators need to use persuasion when making more than routine demands and facing a skeptical audience.
- Digital-age persuasion techniques are different from those used in earlier periods because persuasive messages have exploded in volume and reach; messages now travel at warp speed; all kinds of organizations are persuaders; and persuasion is subtler and more misleading and has become more complex and impersonal.
- Effective persuasion involves establishing credibility; making specific, reasonable requests; linking facts to benefits; recognizing the power of loss; overcoming resistance; and sharing solutions and compromising.

6.2 Write persuasive messages to request help.

- Convincing a reluctant person requires planning and skill and sometimes a little luck.
- The AIRA writing plan for persuasive requests consists of an opening that captures the reader's attention; a body that establishes credibility, builds interest by using specific details and reduces resistance; and a closing that motivates action while showing courtesy.

6.3 Write persuasive messages to make claims or complaints.

- Complaints and some persuasive claims deliver bad news; some vent anger, yet persuasion is necessary to effect change.
- Persuasive claims and complaints may involve damaged products, billing errors, wrong shipments, warranty problems, limited return policies, or insurance snafus.
- Employing a moderate tone, claim/complaint messages need to be logical and open with praise, a statement of fact or agreement, and a quick review of what was done to resolve the problem.
- In the body, writers highlight what happened and why the claim/complaint is legitimate; they enclose supporting documents such as invoices, shipping orders, warranties, and payments.
- The closing specifies what is to be done (e.g., a refund, replacement, or credit).

6.4 Write persuasive messages to get things done within your organization.

- Today's executives try to achieve buy-in from subordinates instead of forcing them to do things such as volunteer for projects or join programs that require lifestyle changes.
- Messages flowing downward require attention to tone and rely on honest, accurate evidence.
- Messages to management should provide facts, figures, and evidence and make strong dollars-and-cents cases for proposed ideas using a warm, professional tone.

6.5 Write persuasive direct-mail, email, and online messages to sell goods and services.

- Whether delivered by postal mail or by email, marketers design sales messages to encourage consumers to read and act on the message.
- Sales letters are still an important part of multichannel marketing campaigns that can make sales, generate leads, boost retail traffic, solicit donations, and direct consumers to websites.
- Skilled e-marketers create catchy subject lines, start with the most important points, make the message conversational and focused, use testimonials, and allow readers to opt out.
- Short persuasive posts and tweets concisely pitch offers, prompt responses, and draw attention to events and media links. Principles of persuasion apply even to micromessages.

CHAPTER REVIEW

1. List the characteristics of persuasion in the digital age. (Obj. 1)
2. List effective persuasion techniques. (Obj. 1)
3. What do claim/complaint messages typically involve, and how should they be crafted? (Obj. 3)
4. How can you ensure that your claim/complaint message is developed logically? (Obj. 3)
5. How have shifts in authority in digital-age organizations affected the strategies for creating goodwill and the tone of workplace persuasive messages? (Obj. 4)
6. When might persuasion be necessary in messages flowing upward? (Obj. 4)
7. What is the four-part AIRA writing plan for sales messages, and what does the acronym stand for? (Obj. 5)
8. What distinguishes rational, emotional, and dual appeals in persuasion? (Obj. 5)
9. Name the best practices for e-marketers hoping to write effective email and online sales messages. (Obj. 5)
10. Describe the purpose and characteristics of persuasive tweets and other online posts. (Obj. 5)

CRITICAL THINKING

1. *Recline in your first-class seat and snooze, or sip a freshly stirred drink while listening to 12 channels of superb audio.* Of what type of persuasive appeal is this an example? How does it compare to the following: Take one of four daily direct flights to Europe on our modern Airbus aircraft, and enjoy the most legroom of any airline. If we are ever late, you will receive coupons for free trips. (Obj. 5)
2. The word *persuasion* turns some people off. What negative connotations can it have and why? (Objs. 1, 5)
3. What motivating impulse may prompt individuals to agree to requests that do not directly benefit themselves or their organizations? (Obj. 3)
4. If many direct-mail messages are thrown in the garbage, and if email sales messages are often deleted before they're opened, why should we learn how to write them effectively? (Obj. 5)
5. Two students at Cambridge University in England raised more than $40,000 toward their university tuition by wearing business logos painted on their faces for a day.[18] Dunlop the tire-maker, however, went to the extreme by offering a set of free tires to those who would have the company's flying-D logo permanently tattooed somewhere on their bodies. Ninety-eight people complied.[19] Is it ethical for advertisers to resort to such promotions dubbed "skinvertising"? To what degree do you find such messages effective? Would you participate—why or why not? (Objs. 1, 5)

ACTIVITIES AND CASES

6.1 FAVOUR REQUEST: INVITING A SPEAKER (OBJ. 2)

Your Task. Analyze the following poorly written invitation. List its weaknesses and outline a writing strategy. If your instructor directs, revise it.

Dear Dr. Schulz:

Because you're a local Nanaimo author, we thought it might not be too much trouble for you to speak at our Canadian Association of Independent Management banquet May 5. Some of us business students here at Glenbow Valley College admired your book *Beyond Race and Gender,* which appeared last spring and became such a hit across the country. One of our instructors said you were now the country's management guru. What exactly did you mean when you said that Canada is the "Mulligan stew" of the Americas?

Because we have no funds for honoraria, we have to rely on local speakers. Dr. Lester Pierfont and Deputy Mayor Shirley Slye were speakers in the past. Our banquets usually begin at 6:30 with a social hour, followed by dinner at 7:30, and the speaker from 8:30 until 9:00 or 9:15. We can arrange transportation for you and your wife if you need it.

We realize that you must be very busy, but we hope you'll agree. Please let our adviser, Duncan Rankin, have the favour of an early response.

1. List at least five weaknesses.
2. Outline a writing plan for a favour request.

   Opening:

   Body:

   Closing:

6.2 PERSUASIVE SUGGESTION: ASKING FOR TUITION REIMBURSEMENT (OBJ. 2)

Your Task. Analyze the poorly written email in Figure 6.7. List its weaknesses. If your instructor directs, revise it.

1. List at least five weaknesses in this email.
2. Outline a writing plan for this email.

   Opening:

   Body:

   Closing:

FIGURE 6.7 | Tuition Help

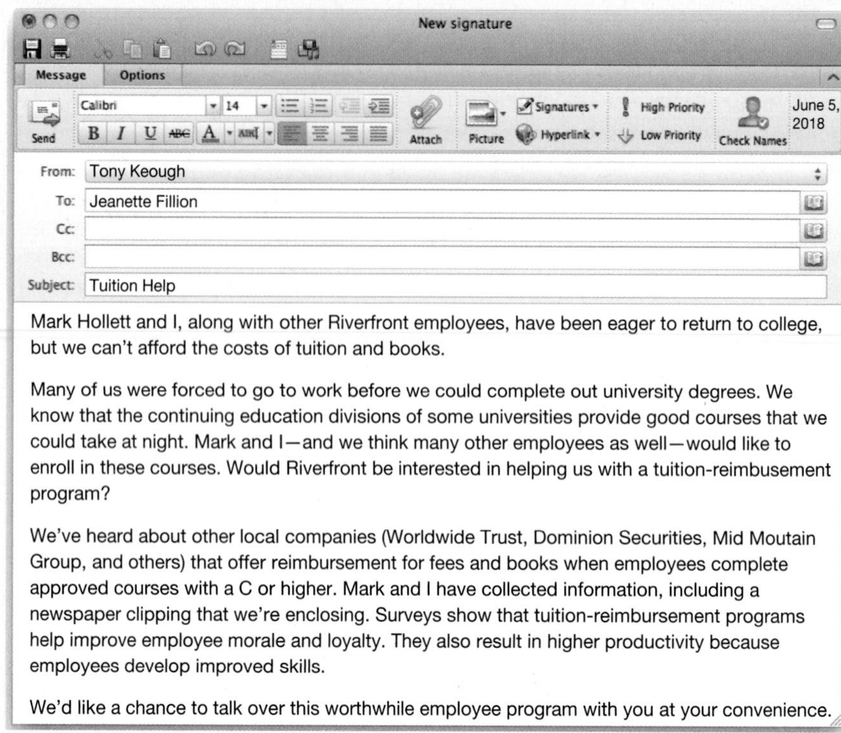

New signature

Message Options

Send Calibri 14 Attach Picture Signatures Hyperlink High Priority Low Priority Check Names June 5, 2018

From: Tony Keough

To: Jeanette Fillion

Cc:

Bcc:

Subject: Tuition Help

Mark Hollett and I, along with other Riverfront employees, have been eager to return to college, but we can't afford the costs of tuition and books.

Many of us were forced to go to work before we could complete out university degrees. We know that the continuing education divisions of some universities provide good courses that we could take at night. Mark and I—and we think many other employees as well—would like to enroll in these courses. Would Riverfront be interested in helping us with a tuition-reimbusement program?

We've heard about other local companies (Worldwide Trust, Dominion Securities, Mid Moutain Group, and others) that offer reimbursement for fees and books when employees complete approved courses with a C or higher. Mark and I have collected information, including a newspaper clipping that we're enclosing. Surveys show that tuition-reimbursement programs help improve employee morale and loyalty. They also result in higher productivity because employees develop improved skills.

We'd like a chance to talk over this worthwhile employee program with you at your convenience.

6.3 SALES LETTER: ANALYZING THE PITCH (OBJ. 5)

Read the following sales letter and analyze its effectiveness by answering the questions listed after the letter.

Dear Friend of the University of Prince Edward Island,

You are part of a special group of alumni—doctors, lawyers, bankers, managers, professors—who have a wide variety of credit cards available to them. For this reason I am inviting you to choose the superior benefits of the UPEI *Platinum Preferred* Visa credit card.

The UPEI Alumni Association has planned, in association with Atlantic Bank, a superior credit card with excellent benefits, personalized customer care, and best of all, no annual fee.

Each purchase made with your UPEI *Platinum Preferred* Visa card leads directly to a contribution to the UPEI Alumni Association. This extra benefit costs nothing, but allows the Association to continue its vital work on campus and in the community.

Yours sincerely,

Margaret Simpson
Director of Alumni Relations
UPEI Alumni Association

1. What technique captures the reader's attention in the opening? Is it effective?
2. What are the central selling points?
3. Does the letter use rational, emotional, or a combination of appeals? Explain.
4. What technique builds interest in the product? Are benefits obvious?
5. How is price handled?
6. Does the letter anticipate reader resistance and offer counter-arguments?
7. What action is the reader to take? How is the action made easy?

Your Task. Revise the above letter, adding any improvements you think necessary based on your answers to the above questions.

MINDTAP

Visit **MindTap** for a variety of videos, additional exercises, activities, and quizzes to support your learning.

Negative Writing Situations

CHAPTER 7

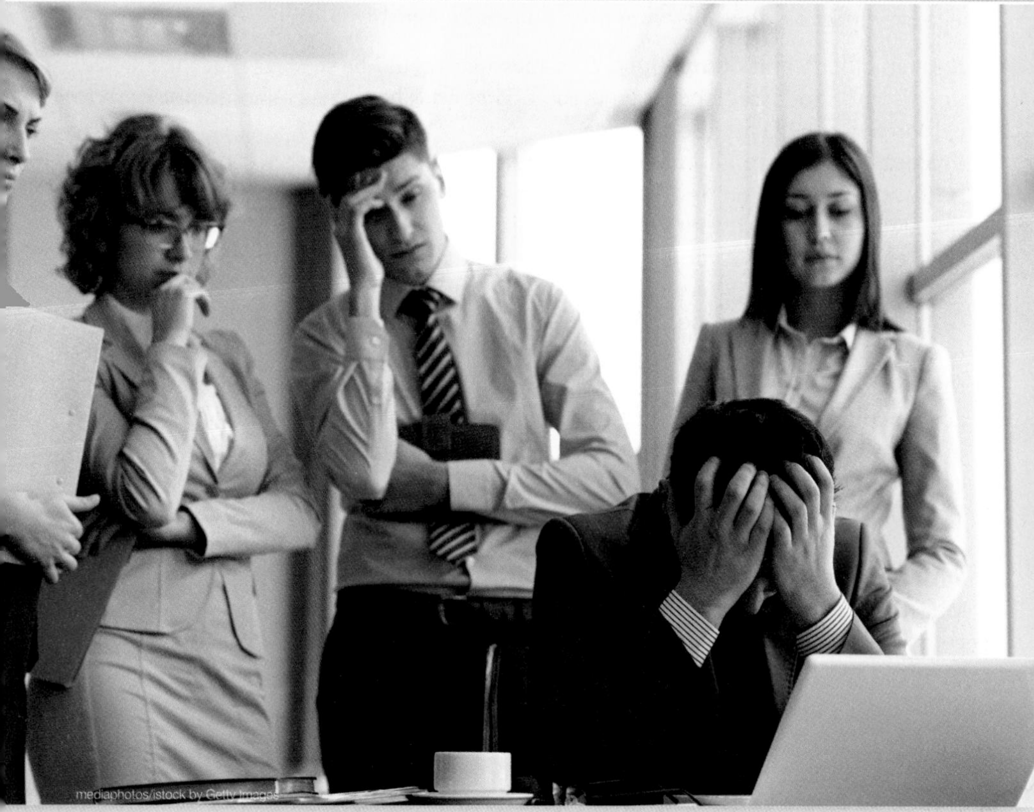
mediaphotos/iStock by Getty Images

OBJECTIVES

After studying this chapter, you should be able to

7.1 Explain the goals of business communicators when conveying negative news.

7.2 Compare the direct and indirect strategies for communicating negative news.

7.3 Describe the components of effective indirect negative messages, including opening with a buffer, apologizing, showing empathy, presenting the reasons, cushioning the bad news, and closing pleasantly.

7.4 Write negative messages for client/customer situations: collections, refusals (e.g., denying requests or claims), and situations when customers are disappointed.

7.5 Write negative messages for internal situations (e.g., employee bad news).

7.1 Your Goals When Communicating Negative News

Even the best-run businesses will sometimes make mistakes. Goods arrive late or are not delivered at all, products fail, service disappoints, billing is mishandled, or customers are misunderstood. You may have to write messages ending business relationships, declining proposals, announcing price increases, refusing requests for donations, terminating employees, turning down invitations, or responding to unhappy customers. You might have to apologize for mistakes in orders, the rudeness of employees, overlooked appointments, pricing errors, faulty accounting, defective products, or jumbled instructions. As a company representative, you may even have to respond to complaints voiced about your organization on Twitter, Facebook, or consumer comment websites.

Every businessperson must occasionally deliver negative news. Because bad news disappoints, irritates, and sometimes angers the receiver, your main goal in such messages is to be thoughtful. The bad feelings associated with disappointing news can generally be reduced if the receiver knows the reasons for the rejection, feels that the news was revealed sensitively, and believes that the matter was treated seriously and fairly.

OFFICE INSIDER

"Despite the fact that we sometimes have to send negative messages at work, it is imperative to turn the situation around and focus on lessons learned and experience gained."

In this chapter you will learn when to use the direct strategy and when to use the indirect strategy to deliver negative news. You will also learn the goals of business communicators when writing negative messages and learn techniques for achieving those goals in several typical situations.

7.1a Top Goals in Communicating Negative News

The sting of bad news can be reduced by giving reasons, communicating sensitively, and treating the receiver fairly.

Delivering bad news is not the easiest writing (or speaking) task you may have, but it can be gratifying if you do it effectively. As a business communicator dealing with a negative situation, the following are your main goals:

- **Explain clearly and completely.** Your message should be so clear that the receiver understands and, we hope, accepts the bad news. The receiver should not have to call or write to clarify the message.
- **Project a professional image.** Your message should project a professional and positive image of you and your organization. Even when irate customers use a threatening tone or overstate their claims, you must use polite language, control your emotions, and respond with clear explanations of why a negative message was necessary.
- **Convey empathy and sensitivity.** Negative news is more easily accepted if it is delivered sensitively. Use language that respects the receiver and attempts to reduce bad feelings. Accepting blame, when appropriate, and apologizing goes far in smoothing over negative messages. But avoid creating legal liability or responsibility for you or your organization (e.g., by making promises you can't keep).
- **Be fair.** Show that the situation or decision was fair, impartial, and rational. Receivers are far more likely to accept negative news if they feel they were treated fairly.
- **Maintain friendly relations.** Make an effort to include statements that show your desire to continue pleasant relations with the receiver. As you learned in Chapter 5, when writing routine adjustment messages, one of your goals is to regain the confidence of customers.

The goals in communicating negative news are explaining clearly, acting professionally, conveying empathy, being fair, maintaining friendly relations, and dealing with the situation in a timely fashion.

These goals are ambitious, and you may not always be successful in achieving them all. With experience, however, you will be able to vary these strategies and adapt them to your organization's specific communication needs.

7.1b The Importance of Timely Responses in Negative Situations

Because of the speed of communication in the workplace today (i.e., most employees have smartphones, are on social media, etc.), bad news—which has always "travelled fast"—now travels even faster and sometimes gets broadcast outside the company to people and organizations that shouldn't really be seeing it. For this reason, timeliness is extremely important when communicating in negative situations.

Whenever possible, negative situations such as firings, restructurings, and company-related crises should be dealt with immediately and personally. As one crisis communications expert argues, "the timeliness of communication is paramount in a crisis,"[1] and existing communication approval systems may need to be stepped around to deliver the message quickly. That said, timeliness is not so vital that you should switch to informal and inappropriate communication channels. For example, texting termination notices (as some managers and owners have begun to do) is a poor communication choice because it indicates that the terminated employee is so unimportant that an informal text was deemed the appropriate way to fire him or her.[2]

7.2 The Choice Between Direct and Indirect Negative News Strategies

In any negative situation, you have a choice between two basic strategies for delivering negative news: direct and indirect. Which approach is best suited for your particular message? To answer this question, you will analyze how your receiver will react to this news as well as the degree of negativity included in the message.

WHEN TO USE THE DIRECT STRATEGY. Not all negative situations at work are crises or involve personal misfortune. In these cases, as a business communicator, you should feel free to use a direct-strategy negative message. The direct strategy, with the bad news appearing first followed by the reasons and a pleasant closing, is effective in situations such as the following:

The direct pattern is appropriate when the bad news is not damaging, when the receiver might overlook the bad news, when the organization expects directness, when the receiver prefers directness, or when firmness is necessary.

- **When the bad news is not damaging.** If the bad news is insignificant (such as a small increase in cost) and doesn't personally affect the receiver, then the direct strategy certainly makes sense.
- **When the receiver may overlook the bad news.** Rate increases, changes in service, new policy requirements—these critical messages may require boldness to ensure attention.
- **When organizations prefer directness.** Some companies expect all internal messages and announcements—even bad news—to be straightforward and presented without frills.
- **When the receiver prefers directness.** If you suspect that the reader prefers that the facts be presented immediately, use the direct pattern.
- **When firmness is necessary.** Messages that must demonstrate determination and strength should not use delaying techniques. For example, the last in a series of collection letters that seek payment of overdue accounts may require a direct opener.

WRITING PLAN FOR A DIRECT-STRATEGY NEGATIVE MESSAGE

- **Bad news** in the opening
- **Reason(s)** for bad news in the body
- **Pleasant closing**

Figure 7.1 is an example of a typical direct-strategy negative message that follows the writing plan above. In this case, a routine notice arrives in your mailbox (or inbox) announcing a price increase in your phone service. Notice that the bad news is communicated in the opening sentence of the message. The reason comes after. Also notice how much shorter this message is than the indirect-style negative messages we will examine later in the chapter.

WHEN TO USE THE INDIRECT STRATEGY. The indirect strategy does not reveal the bad news immediately. This strategy, at least theoretically, enables you to keep the reader's attention until you have been able to explain the reasons for the bad news. Some writing experts suggest that the indirect strategy "ill suits today's skeptical, impatient, even cynical audience."[3] To be sure, in social media, bluntness

FIGURE 7.1 | Direct-Strategy Negative Message

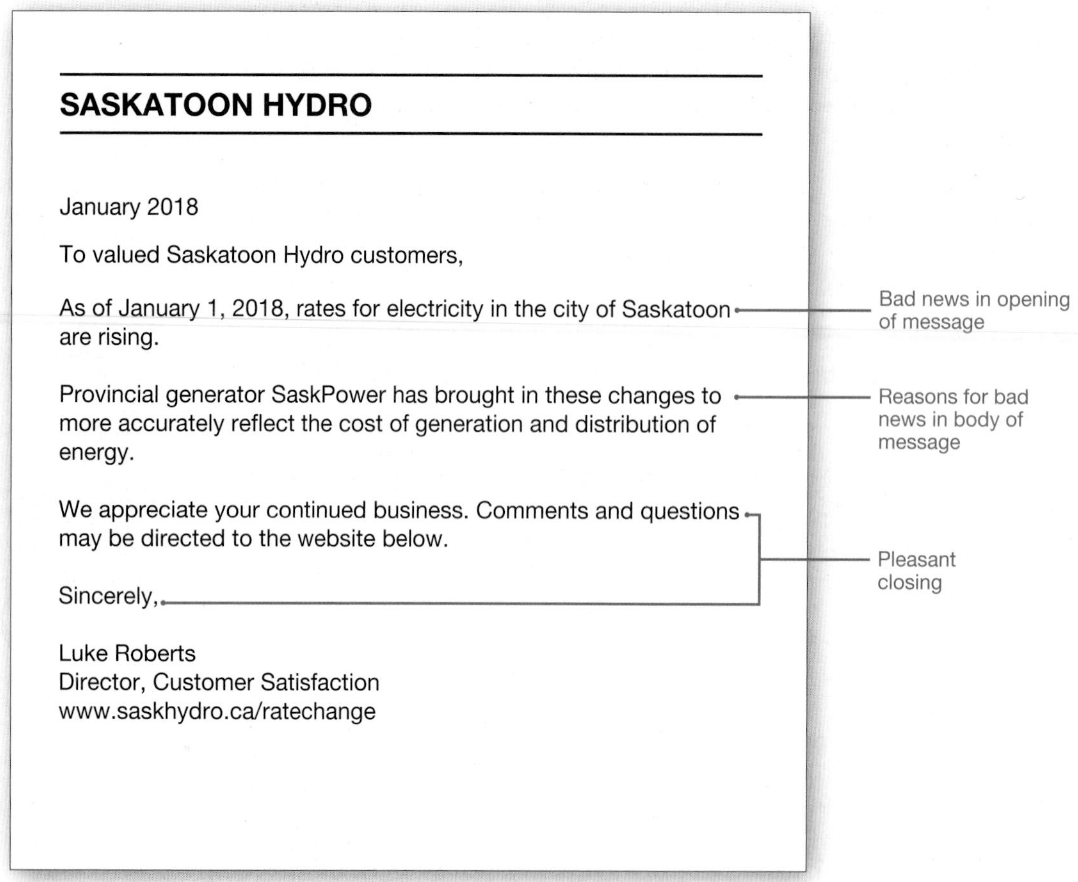
SASKATOON HYDRO

January 2018

To valued Saskatoon Hydro customers,

As of January 1, 2018, rates for electricity in the city of Saskatoon are rising.

Provincial generator SaskPower has brought in these changes to more accurately reflect the cost of generation and distribution of energy.

We appreciate your continued business. Comments and questions may be directed to the website below.

Sincerely,

Luke Roberts
Director, Customer Satisfaction
www.saskhydro.ca/ratechange

seems to dominate public debate. Directness is equated with honesty; indirectness, with deceit. Regardless, many communicators prefer to use the indirect strategy to soften negative news. Whereas good news can be revealed quickly, bad news may be easier to accept when broken gradually. Here are typical instances in which the indirect strategy works well:

- **When the bad news is personally upsetting.** If the negative news involves the receiver personally, such as a layoff notice, the indirect strategy makes sense. Telling an employee that he or she no longer has a job is probably best done in person and by starting indirectly and giving reasons first. When a company has made a mistake that inconveniences or disadvantages a customer, the indirect strategy also makes sense.
- **When the bad news will provoke a hostile reaction.** When your message will irritate or infuriate the recipient, the indirect method may be best. It begins with a buffer and reasons, thus encouraging the reader to finish reading or hearing the message. A blunt announcement may make the receiver stop reading.
- **When the bad news threatens the customer relationship.** If the negative message may damage a customer relationship, the indirect strategy may help salvage the customer bond. Beginning slowly and presenting reasons that explain what

happened can be more helpful than directly announcing bad news or failing to adequately explain the reasons.

- **When the bad news is unexpected.** Readers who are totally surprised by bad news tend to have a more negative reaction than those who expected it. If a company suddenly closes an office or a plant and employees had no inkling of the closure, that bad news would be better received if it were revealed cautiously with reasons first.

The indirect approach does not guarantee that recipients will be pleased, because, after all, bad news is just that—bad. However, many communicators prefer to use it. Figure 7.2 shows how to apply the indirect strategy effectively.

The indirect pattern softens the impact of bad news.

7.3 The Four Components of Effective Indirect Negative Messages

Although you probably won't make receivers happy when delivering negative news, you can reduce resentment by structuring your message sensitively. To do so, indirect negative messages should contain some of or all of these components: buffer, reasons, bad news, and closing. These components are shown in Figure 7.2.

To reduce negative feelings, use a buffer to open sensitive bad-news messages.

7.3a Buffer the Opening

A buffer is a device that reduces shock or pain. To buffer the pain of bad news, begin your message with a neutral but meaningful statement that makes the reader continue reading. The buffer should be relevant and concise. Although it avoids revealing the bad news immediately, it should not convey a false impression that good news follows. It should provide a natural transition to the explanation

FIGURE 7.2 | Four Components of an Indirect-Strategy Negative Message

Buffer	Reasons	Bad News	Closing
Open with a neutral but meaningful statement that does not mention the bad news.	Explain the causes of the bad news before disclosing it.	Reveal the bad news without emphasizing it. Provide an alternative or compromise, if possible.	End with a personalized, forward-looking, pleasant statement. Avoid referring to the bad news.
• Best news • Compliment • Appreciation • Agreement • Facts • Understanding • Apology	• Cautious explanation • Reader or other benefits • Company policy explanation • Positive words • Evidence that matter was considered fairly and seriously	• Embedded placement • Passive voice • Implied refusal • Compromise • Alternative	• Forward look • Information about alternative • Good wishes • Freebies • Resale • Sales promotion

A buffer opens an indirect negative message with a neutral, concise, relevant, and upbeat statement.

A good buffer may include the best news, a compliment, appreciation, facts regarding the problem, a statement indicating understanding, or an apology.

that follows. The individual situation, of course, will help determine what you should put in the buffer. Here are some possibilities for opening indirect negative messages:

- **Best news.** Start with the part of the message that represents the best news. For example, in a website announcement plus in-branch signage that discloses reduced operating hours but increased staffing, you might say *Beginning July 1, we're adding extra staff in our branch locations, and we'll be open to serve you between 9:30 a.m. and 4:30 p.m.*
- **Compliment.** Praise the receiver's accomplishments, organization, or efforts, but do so with honesty and sincerity. For instance, in a letter declining an invitation to speak, you could write *I admire the Canadian Red Cross for its disaster response efforts in Canada and overseas. I am honoured that you asked me to speak Friday, November 5.*
- **Appreciation.** Convey thanks to the reader for doing business, for sending something, for a service or job well done, for showing confidence in your organization, for expressing feelings, or for simply providing feedback. In a letter terminating an employee's contract, you might say *Thank you for your work on the past two seasons of* Riley's Cove. *Your efforts contributed to a wonderful television program enjoyed across Canada.* Avoid thanking the reader, however, for something you are about to refuse.
- **Agreement.** Make a relevant statement with which both sender and receiver can agree. A letter that rejects an application for a credit card might be phrased *Having access to a credit card is an important part of your financial well-being. While we thank you for your recent application for a GoldPlus Visa Card, your application did not meet our criteria for approval. However, we're happy to offer you a Classic Visa Card....*
- **Facts.** Provide objective information that introduces the bad news. For example, in a memo announcing cutbacks in the hours of the employees' cafeteria, you might say *During the past five years the number of employees eating breakfast in our cafeteria has dropped from 32 percent to 12 percent.*
- **Understanding.** Show that you care about the reader. In announcing a product defect, the writer can still manage to express concern for the customer: *We know you expect superior performance from all the products you purchase from OfficeCity. That's why we're writing personally about the Excell printer cartridges you recently ordered.*

CONSIDER APOLOGIZING IN THE BUFFER. You learned about apologies in adjustment situations in Chapter 5. We expand that discussion here because apologies are often part of negative situations. The truth is that sincere apologies work. A study of letters responding to customer complaints revealed that 67 percent carried an apology of some sort.[4] An apology is defined as an "admission of blameworthiness and regret for an undesirable event."[5] Apologies to customers are especially important if you or your company erred. They cost nothing, and they go a long way in soothing hard feelings. Here are some tips on how to apologize effectively in business messages:

- **Apologize sincerely.** People dislike apologies that sound hollow (*We regret that you were inconvenienced* or *We regret that you are disturbed*). Focusing on your regret does not convey sincerity. Explaining what you will do to prevent recurrence of the problem projects sincerity.
- **Accept responsibility.** One CEO was criticized for the following weak apology: *I want our customers to know how much I personally regret any difficulties you may experience as a result of the unauthorized intrusion into our computer systems.* Communication experts faulted this apology because it did not acknowledge responsibility.[6]
- **Use good judgment.** Don't admit blame if it might prompt a lawsuit.

OFFICE INSIDER

When leaders accept blame or apologize, it is "one of the most powerful and resonant gestures in the human arsenal—almost as powerful as a declaration of love. If love means, 'I care about you, and I'm happy about it,' then an apology means, 'I hurt you, and I'm sorry about it.'"

—Marshall Smith, leadership coach and management consultant

Consider these poor and improved apologies:

Poor Apology	Improved Apology
We regret that you are unhappy with the price of frozen yogurt purchased at one of our self-serve scoop shops.	We are genuinely sorry that you were disappointed in the price of frozen yogurt recently purchased at one of our self-serve scoop shops. Your opinion is important to us, and we appreciate your giving us the opportunity to look into the problem you describe.
We apologize if anyone was affected.	I apologize for the frustration our delay caused you. As soon as I received your message, I began looking into the cause of the delay and realized that our delivery tracking system must be improved.

CONSIDER SHOWING EMPATHY IN THE BUFFER. One of the hardest things to do in apologies is to convey sympathy and empathy. As discussed in Chapter 2, *empathy* is the ability to understand and enter into the feelings of another. When ice storms trapped JetBlue Airways passengers on hot planes for hours, then-CEO David Neeleman wrote a letter of apology that sounded as if it came from his heart. He said, "Dear JetBlue Customers: We are sorry and embarrassed. But most of all, we are deeply sorry." Later in his letter he said, "Words cannot express how truly sorry we are for the anxiety, frustration, and inconvenience that you, your family, friends, and colleagues experienced."[7] Neeleman put himself into the shoes of his customers and tried to experience their pain.

Empathy involves understanding and entering into the feelings of someone else.

You can express empathy in various ways:

- **In writing to an unhappy customer:** We did not intentionally delay the shipment, and we sincerely regret the disappointment and frustration you must have suffered.
- **In terminating employees:** It is with great regret that we must take this step. Rest assured that I will be more than happy to write letters of recommendation for anyone who asks.
- **In responding to a complaint:** I am deeply saddened that our service failure disrupted your sale, and we will do everything in our power to....
- **In showing genuine feelings:** You have every right to be disappointed. I am truly sorry that....

"Dear Valued Customer: We're sorry, but company policy forbids apologies. Sincerely yours."

7.3b Present the Reasons for the Negative News

The most important part of an indirect negative message is the section that explains why a negative decision is necessary. Without sound reasons for denying a request or refusing a claim, a message will fail, no matter how cleverly it is organized or written. As part of your planning before writing, you analyzed the problem and decided to refuse a request for specific reasons. Before disclosing the bad news, try to explain those reasons. Providing an explanation reduces feelings of ill will and improves the chances that the reader/listener will accept the bad news.

Bad-news messages should explain reasons before stating the negative news.

WORKPLACE IN FOCUS

Société Générale suffered the worst loss in banking history when a junior employee liquidated more than $7 billion in a fraudulent trading scheme. In a letter to the bank's customers, CEO Daniel Bouton opened immediately with the bad news: "It is my duty to inform you that Société Générale has been a victim of a serious internal fraud committed by an imprudent employee in the Corporate and Investment Banking Division." Bouton went on to reveal a disaster-response plan and assured customers that lost funds would be replaced with emergency funding from the international banking community. *Should the bank have buffered this bad news by revealing it more gradually in the letter?*

Kiev.Victor/Shutterstock.com

- **Explain clearly and cautiously.** If the reasons are not confidential or legally questionable, you can be specific: *Growers supplied us with a limited number of patio roses, and our demand this year was twice that of last year.* In responding to a billing error, explain what happened: *After you informed us of an error on your January bill, we investigated the matter and admit the mistake was ours. Until our new automated system is fully online, we are still subject to human error. Rest assured that your account has been credited, as you will see on your next bill.* In refusing a favour request, explain why the request can't be fulfilled: *On January 17 we have a board of directors meeting that I must attend.* However, in an effort to be the "good guy," don't make dangerous or unrealistic promises: *Although we can't contribute now, we expect increased revenues next year and promise a generous gift then.*

Readers accept bad news more readily if they see that someone benefits.

- **Cite plausible reader benefits.** Readers are more open to bad news if in some way, even indirectly, it may help them. In refusing a customer's request for free hemming of skirts and slacks, a clothing company wrote: "We tested our ability to hem skirts a few years ago. This process proved to be very time-consuming. We have decided not to offer this service because the additional cost would have increased the selling price of our skirts substantially, and we did not want to impose that cost on all our customers."[8] Readers also accept bad news more readily if they recognize that someone or something else benefits, such as other workers or the environment: *Although we would like to consider your application, we prefer to fill managerial positions from within.* Avoid trying to show reader benefits, though, if they appear insincere: *To improve our service to you, we're increasing our brokerage fees.*
- **Explain company policy.** Readers don't like blanket policy statements prohibiting something: *Company policy prevents us from making cash refunds* or *Proposals may be accepted from local companies only* or *Company policy requires us to promote from within.* Instead of hiding behind company policy, gently explain why the policy makes sense: *We prefer to promote from within because it rewards the loyalty of our employees. In addition, we've found that people familiar with our organization make the quickest contribution to our team effort.* By offering explanations you demonstrate that you care about your readers and are treating them as important individuals.
- **Choose positive words.** Because the words you use can affect a reader's response, choose carefully. Remember that the objective of the indirect pattern is to hold the reader's attention until you've had a chance to explain the reasons justifying

the bad news. To keep the reader in a receptive mood, avoid expressions that might cause the reader to tune out. Be sensitive to negative words such as claim, error, failure, fault, impossible, mistaken, misunderstand, never, regret, unwilling, unfortunately, and violate.

- **Show fairness and seriousness.** In explaining reasons, demonstrate to the reader that you take the matter seriously, have investigated carefully, and are making an unbiased decision. Customers are more accepting of disappointing news when they feel that their requests have been heard and that they have been treated fairly. Avoid deflecting responsibility, known as "passing the buck," or blaming others within your organization. Such unprofessional behaviour makes the reader lose faith in you and your company.

7.3c Present the Negative News in a "Cushioned" Way

Although you can't prevent the disappointment that bad news brings, you can reduce the pain somewhat by presenting the news sensitively. Be especially considerate when the reader will suffer personally from the negative news. A number of thoughtful techniques can lessen the impact.

Techniques for cushioning bad news include positioning it strategically, using the passive voice, emphasizing the positive, implying the refusal, and suggesting alternatives or compromises.

- **Position the negative news strategically.** Instead of spotlighting it, enclose the bad news between other sentences, perhaps among your reasons. Try not to let the refusal begin or end a paragraph—the reader's eye will linger on these high-visibility spots. Another technique that reduces shock is putting a painful idea in a subordinate clause: *Although the board did not award you a bonus this year, we are thankful for your enthusiasm and loyalty and highly encourage you to apply once again next year.* Subordinate clauses often begin with words such as *although*, *as*, *because*, *if*, and *since*.
- **Use the passive voice.** Passive-voice verbs enable you to describe an action without connecting the action to a specific person. Whereas the active voice focuses attention on a person (*We don't accept unsolicited proposals*), the passive voice highlights the action (*Unsolicited proposals are not accepted because...*). Use the passive voice for the bad news. In some instances you can combine passive-voice verbs and a subordinate clause: *Although unsolicited proposals are not currently being accepted, we encourage you to try again beginning March 30, after which time our policy may have changed.*
- **Highlight the positive.** As you learned earlier, messages are far more effective when you describe what you can do instead of what you can't do. Rather than *We will no longer accept requests for product changes after June 1*, try a more positive appeal: *We are accepting requests for product changes until June 1.*
- **Imply the refusal.** It's sometimes possible to avoid a direct statement of refusal. Often your reasons and explanations leave no doubt that a request has been denied. Explicit refusals may be unnecessary and at times cruel. In this refusal to contribute to a charity, for example, the writer never actually says no: *Because we will soon be relocating to new offices, all our funds are earmarked for moving costs and furnishings. We hope that next year we'll be able to support your worthwhile charity.* This implied refusal is effective even though the bad news is not stated. The danger of an implied refusal, of course, is that it can be so subtle that the reader misses it. Be certain that you make the bad news clear, thus preventing the need for further correspondence.
- **Suggest a compromise or an alternative.** A refusal is not so harsh—for the sender or the receiver—if a suitable compromise, substitute, or alternative is available. In denying permission to a class to visit a research facility, for instance, this writer softens the bad news by proposing an alternative: *Although class tours of the entire research facility are not given due to safety and security reasons, we do offer tours of parts of the facility during our open house in the fall.* You can further reduce the impact of the bad news by refusing to dwell on it. Present it briefly (or imply it), and move on to your closing.

7.3d Close Pleasantly

Closings to bad-news messages might include a forward look, an alternative, good wishes, special offers, or resale or sales promotional information.

After explaining the negative news sensitively, close the message with a pleasant statement that promotes goodwill. The closing should be personalized and may include a forward look, an alternative, good wishes, special offers, resale information, or an off-the-subject remark.

- **Alternative follow-up.** If an alternative exists, end your letter with follow-through advice. For example, in a letter rejecting a customer's demand for replacement of landscaping plants, you might say *We will be happy to give you a free inspection and consultation. Please call 746-8112 to arrange a date for a visit.* In a message to a prospective homebuyer: *Although the lot you saw last week is now sold, we do have two excellent view lots available at a slightly higher price.* In reacting to an Internet misprint: *Please note that our website contained an unfortunate misprint offering $850-per-night Banff luxury chalets at $85. Although we cannot honour that rate, we are offering a special half-price rate of $425 to those who responded.*
- **Special offers.** When customers complain—primarily about food products or small consumer items—companies often send coupons, samples, or gifts to restore confidence and to promote future business. In response to a customer's complaint about a frozen dinner, you could write *Thank you for your loyalty and for sharing in our efforts to make Green Valley frozen entrées the best they can be. We appreciate your input so much that we'd like to buy you dinner. We've enclosed a coupon to cover the cost of your next entrée.*
- **Good wishes.** A conversation in which someone is fired or downsized might read: *We want you to know your contribution here has been highly valued, and we wish you all the best as you look for rewarding work in a different setting. Please be in touch with your manager about securing a reference.*
- **Forward look.** Anticipate future relations or business. A letter that refuses a contract proposal might read: *Thank you for your bid. We look forward to working with your talented staff when future projects demand your special expertise.*
- **Resale or sales promotion.** When the bad news is not devastating or personal, references to resale information or promotion may be appropriate: *The laptops you ordered are unusually popular because they have more plug-ins for peripheral devices than any other laptop in their price range. To help you locate additional accessories for these computers, we invite you to visit our website at..., where our online catalogue provides a huge selection of peripheral devices such as stereo speakers, printers, personal digital assistants, and digital pagers.*

Avoid endings that sound superficial, insincere, inappropriate, or self-serving. Don't invite further correspondence (*If you have any questions, do not hesitate ...*), and don't refer again to the bad news. Take another look at the elements in Figure 7.2 whenever you need to review writing sensitive negative messages.

7.4 Writing Negative Messages for Customer/Client Situations

You've just learned the ideal components that should be included in direct and indirect negative workplace messages. Now it's time to apply these skills. When faced with a negative situation at work, one that demands you communicate instead of remaining silent, first think about how the receiver will react to your news and then decide whether to use the direct or the indirect strategy. The following are some typical negative-news situations relating to customers and clients.

7.4a Collections

One of the most important processes in business is the collection process. Collection is the steps a company takes to ensure that its unpaid invoices get paid. The first

FIGURE 7.3 | Direct Strategy Collection Letter

FRASER, AHMET, AND GRANDPRE

3017–66 Avenue Northwest, Suite 222
Edmonton, AB T6H 1Y2

August 14, 2018

Tom Przybylski
Unity Ltd.
9 Givins Dr., Unit 5
Edmonton, AB T2A 4X3

Dear Mr. Przybylski:

Re: Invoice No. 443-2010

Outstanding Amount Due: $19,567.87

You are indebted to the firm of Fraser, Ahmet, and Grandpre in the amount of $19,567.87, for services rendered and for which you were invoiced on March 30, 2018. A copy of the outstanding invoice is enclosed for your reference, as is a copy of a reminder letter sent to you on July 2, 2018.

Unless we receive a certified cheque or money order, payable to Fraser, Ahmet, and Grandpre, in the amount of $19,567.87, or unless satisfactory payment arrangements are made within seven (7) business days, we are left no choice but to pursue collection of the amount owing. We are not prepared to continue carrying your accounts receivable and we will take all necessary steps for the recovery of this amount from you.

We do not wish to proceed in this fashion and would appreciate your cooperation instead. We look forward to hearing from you on or before August 21, 2018.

Yours sincerely,

Pat McAfee

Pat McAfee
Office Manager/Collections Clerk

phase in the collection process is usually the sending of a short reminder letter or email that lets clients or customers know their invoice is outstanding. Best practices stipulate that a copy of the outstanding invoice should be attached to this short reminder message, in case the client has misplaced the original.

An understanding of how to write a negative message becomes useful in the second step of the collection process. If the client or customer with the outstanding invoice does not reply in a timely manner to the short reminder message, it is time to write a direct bad-news message demanding payment. Figure 7.3 shows a typical example of such a message, which uses the direct strategy discussed earlier in the chapter: refer to the negative news, then give reasons, then close pleasantly.

The main objective of a collection letter is not only to receive payment, but also to make sure that the goodwill of the client or customer is retained.

According to the website of Credit Guru Inc., a company that offers advice on the collection process, the main features of a well-written collection letter are a reminder of the dates of the invoice, a reminder of the total amount outstanding, a request for immediate payment or payment by a specified date, a request for the payment to be sent by the quickest means (e.g., courier, e-transfer), and finally, a sense of urgency coupled with an unapologetic and nonthreatening tone.[9]

7.4b Refusals and Responses to Criticism

The indirect strategy is appropriate when refusing requests for time, money, information, or action.

As you move forward in your career and become a professional or a representative of an organization, you may receive requests for favours or contributions. When you must refuse these requests, you will first think about how well you know the receiver and how he or she will react to your refusal and decide whether to use the direct or the indirect strategy. You may also have to say *no* to customer claims, deny credit, and manage disappointment, anger, and attempts to tarnish your organization's image. Your goal is always to resolve the situation in a prompt, fair, and tactful manner. Use the indirect strategy and the following writing plan, which was discussed earlier in the chapter:

WRITING PLAN FOR REFUSING REQUESTS OR CLAIMS AND FOR DEALING WITH CRITICISM

- **Buffer:** Start with a neutral statement that both reader and writer can agree on, such as a compliment, an appreciative comment, a quick review of the facts, or an apology. Add a key idea or word that acts as a transition to the reasons.
- **Reasons:** Present valid reasons for the refusal or refutation, avoiding words that create a negative tone. Include resale or sales promotion material if appropriate.
- **Bad news:** Soften the blow by de-emphasizing the bad news, using the passive voice, accentuating the positive, or implying a refusal. Suggest a compromise, alternative, or substitute if possible. The alternative can be part of the bad news or part of the closing.
- **Closing:** Renew good feelings with a positive statement. Avoid referring to the bad news. Include resale or promotion information, if appropriate. Look forward to continued business or relationship.

REFUSING FAVOUR REQUESTS. Requests for favours, money, information, and action may come from charities, friends, or business partners. Many are from people representing commendable causes, and you may wish you could comply. However, resources are usually limited.

Two versions of a request refusal are shown in Figure 7.4. A magazine writer requested salary information for an article, but this information could not be released. The ineffective version begins with needless information that could be implied. The second paragraph creates a harsh tone with such negative words as *sorry, must refuse, violate*, and *liable*. Since the refusal precedes the explanation, the reader probably will not be in a receptive frame of mind to accept the reasons for refusing. Notice, too, that the bad news is emphasized by its placement in a short

FIGURE 7.4 | Refusing an External Favour Request

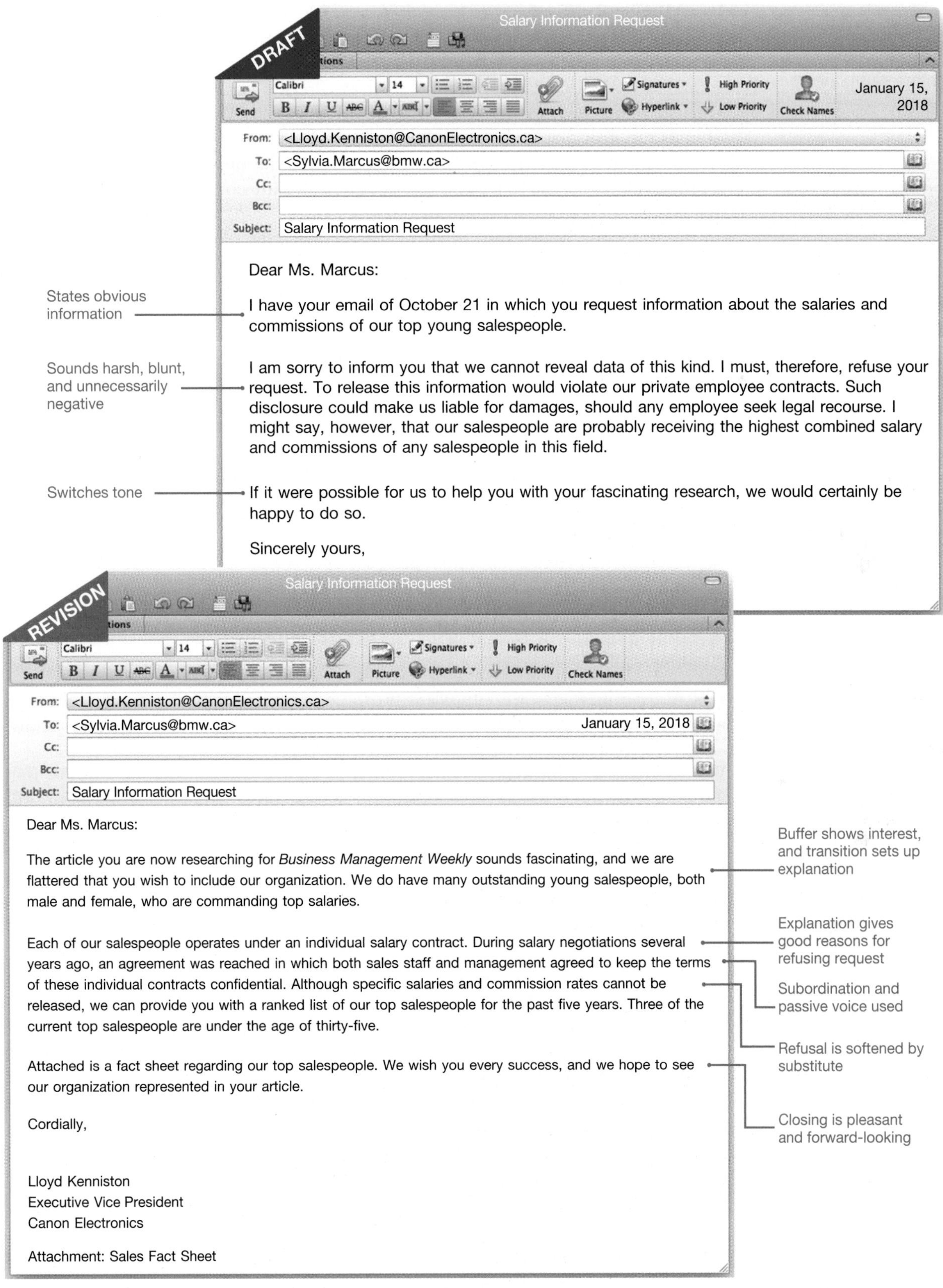
DRAFT
Salary Information Request
January 15, 2018
From: <Lloyd.Kenniston@CanonElectronics.ca>
To: <Sylvia.Marcus@bmw.ca>
Subject: Salary Information Request
Dear Ms. Marcus:
I have your email of October 21 in which you request information about the salaries and commissions of our top young salespeople.
I am sorry to inform you that we cannot reveal data of this kind. I must, therefore, refuse your request. To release this information would violate our private employee contracts. Such disclosure could make us liable for damages, should any employee seek legal recourse. I might say, however, that our salespeople are probably receiving the highest combined salary and commissions of any salespeople in this field.
If it were possible for us to help you with your fascinating research, we would certainly be happy to do so.
Sincerely yours,
States obvious information
Sounds harsh, blunt, and unnecessarily negative
Switches tone
REVISION
Salary Information Request
From: <Lloyd.Kenniston@CanonElectronics.ca>
To: <Sylvia.Marcus@bmw.ca>
January 15, 2018
Subject: Salary Information Request
Dear Ms. Marcus:
The article you are now researching for Business Management Weekly sounds fascinating, and we are flattered that you wish to include our organization. We do have many outstanding young salespeople, both male and female, who are commanding top salaries.
Each of our salespeople operates under an individual salary contract. During salary negotiations several years ago, an agreement was reached in which both sales staff and management agreed to keep the terms of these individual contracts confidential. Although specific salaries and commission rates cannot be released, we can provide you with a ranked list of our top salespeople for the past five years. Three of the current top salespeople are under the age of thirty-five.
Attached is a fact sheet regarding our top salespeople. We wish you every success, and we hope to see our organization represented in your article.
Cordially,
Lloyd Kenniston
Executive Vice President
Canon Electronics
Attachment: Sales Fact Sheet
Buffer shows interest, and transition sets up explanation
Explanation gives good reasons for refusing request
Subordination and passive voice used
Refusal is softened by substitute
Closing is pleasant and forward-looking

sentence at the beginning of a paragraph. It stands out and adds more weight to the rejection already felt by the reader.

Moreover, the refusal explanation is overly graphic, containing references to possible litigation. The tone at this point is threatening and unduly harsh. Then, suddenly, the author throws in a self-serving comment about the high salary and commissions of his salespeople. Instead of offering constructive alternatives, the ineffective version reveals only tiny bits of the desired data. Finally, the closing sounds too insincere and doesn't build goodwill.

In refusing requests, avoid a harsh tone or being too explicit; offer constructive alternatives whenever possible.

In the more effective version of this refusal, the opening reflects the writer's genuine interest in the request. But it does not indicate compliance. The second sentence acts as a transition by introducing the words *salespeople* and *salaries*, repeated in the following paragraph. Reasons for refusing this request are objectively presented in an explanation that precedes the refusal. Notice that the refusal (*Although specific salaries and commission rates cannot be released*) is a subordinate clause in a long sentence in the middle of a paragraph. To further soften the blow, the letter offers an alternative. The cordial closing refers to the alternative, avoids mention of the refusal, and looks to the future.

DEALING WITH DISAPPOINTED CUSTOMERS. Businesses must occasionally respond to disappointed customers. Whenever possible, these problems should be dealt with immediately and personally. Most business professionals strive to control the damage and resolve such problems in the following manner:[10]

- Call or email the individual immediately.
- Describe the problem and apologize.
- Explain why the problem occurred, what they are doing to resolve it, and how they will prevent it from happening again.
- Promote goodwill by following up with a print message that documents the phone call.

Written messages are important (a) to communicate when personal contact is impossible, (b) to establish a record of the incident, (c) to formally confirm follow-up procedures, and (d) to promote good relations.

A bad-news follow-up letter is shown in Figure 7.5. Consultant Jane Moffatt found herself in the embarrassing position of explaining why she had given out the name of her client to a salesperson. The client, Premier Resources International, had hired her firm, Azad Consulting Associates, to help find an appropriate service for outsourcing its payroll functions. Without realizing it, Jane had mentioned to a potential vendor (QuickPay Services, Inc.) that her client was considering hiring an outside service to handle its payroll. An overly eager salesperson from QuickPay Services immediately called on Premier, thus angering the client.

Jane first called her client to explain and apologize. She was careful to control her voice and rate of speaking. She also followed up with the letter shown in Figure 7.5. The letter not only confirms the telephone conversation but also adds the right touch of formality. It sends the nonverbal message that the writer takes the matter seriously and that it is important enough to warrant a hard-copy letter.

Many consumer problems are handled with letters, either written by consumers as complaints or by companies in response. However, email and social networks are also firmly established channels for delivering complaints and negative messages.

RESPONDING TO NEGATIVE ONLINE POSTS OR REVIEWS. Today's impatient, hyperconnected consumers eagerly embrace the idea of delivering their complaints to social networking sites rather than calling customer service departments. Why rely on word of mouth or send a letter to a company about poor service or a defective product when you can jump online and shout your grievance to the entire world? Today's consumers are quick to voice their displeasure with negative posts and reviews via Twitter, Facebook, Yelp, Cruise Critic, and other sites.

FIGURE 7.5 | Follow-Up Message to Disappointed Client

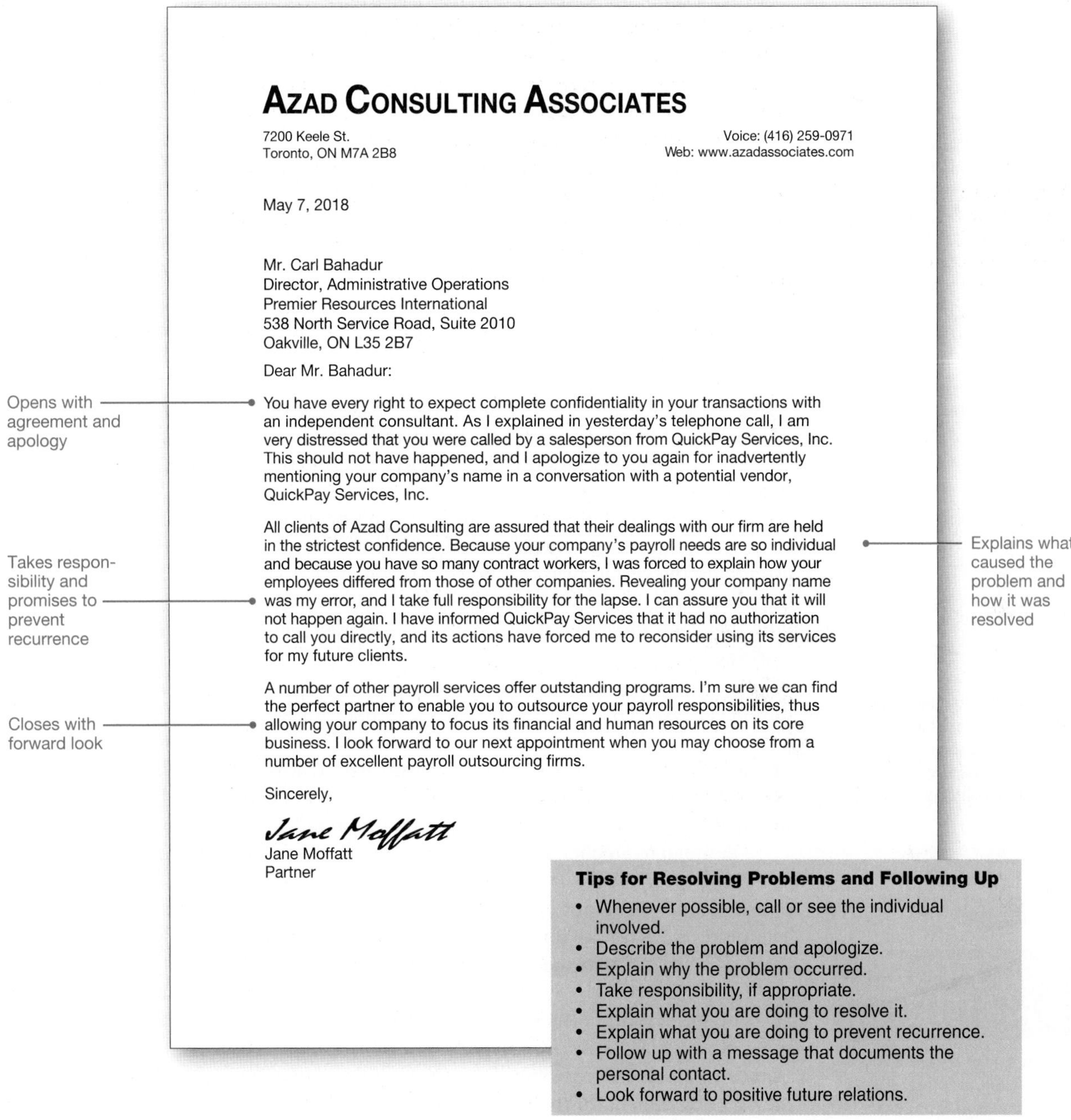

AZAD CONSULTING ASSOCIATES

7200 Keele St.
Toronto, ON M7A 2B8

Voice: (416) 259-0971
Web: www.azadassociates.com

May 7, 2018

Mr. Carl Bahadur
Director, Administrative Operations
Premier Resources International
538 North Service Road, Suite 2010
Oakville, ON L35 2B7

Dear Mr. Bahadur:

You have every right to expect complete confidentiality in your transactions with an independent consultant. As I explained in yesterday's telephone call, I am very distressed that you were called by a salesperson from QuickPay Services, Inc. This should not have happened, and I apologize to you again for inadvertently mentioning your company's name in a conversation with a potential vendor, QuickPay Services, Inc.

All clients of Azad Consulting are assured that their dealings with our firm are held in the strictest confidence. Because your company's payroll needs are so individual and because you have so many contract workers, I was forced to explain how your employees differed from those of other companies. Revealing your company name was my error, and I take full responsibility for the lapse. I can assure you that it will not happen again. I have informed QuickPay Services that it had no authorization to call you directly, and its actions have forced me to reconsider using its services for my future clients.

A number of other payroll services offer outstanding programs. I'm sure we can find the perfect partner to enable you to outsource your payroll responsibilities, thus allowing your company to focus its financial and human resources on its core business. I look forward to our next appointment when you may choose from a number of excellent payroll outsourcing firms.

Sincerely,

Jane Moffatt

Jane Moffatt
Partner

Tips for Resolving Problems and Following Up

- Whenever possible, call or see the individual involved.
- Describe the problem and apologize.
- Explain why the problem occurred.
- Take responsibility, if appropriate.
- Explain what you are doing to resolve it.
- Explain what you are doing to prevent recurrence.
- Follow up with a message that documents the personal contact.
- Look forward to positive future relations.

How can organizations respond to negative posts and reviews online? Experts suggest the following pointers:

- **Verify the situation.** Investigate to learn what happened. If the complaint is legitimate and your organization fouled up, it's best to fess up. Admit the problem—using the same channel as the person who made the complaint—and try to remedy it.
- **Respond quickly and constructively.** Offer to follow up offline; send your contact information. Be polite and helpful.
- **Consider freebies.** Suggest a refund or a discount on future services. Dissatisfied customers often write a second more positive review if they have received a refund.

- **Learn how to improve.** Look upon online comments as opportunities for growth and improvement. See complaining customers as real-time focus groups that can provide valuable insights.
- **Accept the inevitable.** Recognize that nearly every business will experience some negativity, especially on today's readily accessible social media sites. Do what you can to respond constructively, and then move on.

In denying claims, writers use the reasons-before-refusal strategy to set an empathic tone and buffer the bad news.

DENYING CLAIMS. Customers occasionally want something they are not entitled to or something you can't grant. They may misunderstand warranties or make unreasonable demands. Because these customers are often unhappy with a product or service, they are emotionally involved. Writing or saying *no* to emotionally involved receivers will probably be your most challenging communication task. As publisher Malcolm Forbes once observed, "To be agreeable while disagreeing—that's an art."[11]

Although customer claims are often granted, occasionally some must be refused.

Fortunately, the reasons-before-refusal plan helps you be empathic and artful in breaking bad news. Obviously, in denial letters you will need to adopt the proper tone. Don't blame customers, even if they are at fault. Avoid "you" statements that sound preachy (*You would have known that cash refunds are impossible if you had read your contract*). Use neutral, objective language to explain why the claim must be refused. Consider offering resale information to rebuild the customer's confidence in your products or organization.

Messages responding to claims that can't be approved because the customer or employee is mistaken, misinformed, unreasonable, or possibly even dishonest are essentially delivering negative news. As you've learned, the indirect strategy communicates negative news with the least pain. It also allows the sender to explain why the claim must be refused before the reader realizes the bad news and begins resisting.

When refusing customer claims, explain objectively and do not assume that the customer is foolish or dishonest.

In the email shown in Figure 7.6, the writer denies a customer's claim for the difference between the price the customer paid for speakers and the price she saw advertised locally (which would have resulted in a cash refund of $151). While Premier Sound Sales does match any advertised lower price, the price-matching policy applies only to exact models. This claim must be rejected because the advertisement the customer submitted shows a different, older speaker model.

The email to Stephen Dominique opens with a buffer that agrees with a statement in the customer's letter. It repeats the key idea of product confidence as a transition to the second paragraph. Next comes an explanation of the price-matching policy. The writer does not assume that the customer is trying to pull a fast one. Nor does the writer suggest that the customer is a dummy who didn't read or understand the price-matching policy.

OFFICE INSIDER

"As soon as you realize there is a problem, let your client know by phone or, if possible, in person. It's better to let them hear bad news from you than to discover it on their own because it establishes your candour."

The safest path is a neutral explanation of the policy along with precise distinctions between the customer's speakers and the older ones. The writer also gets a chance to resell the customer's speakers and demonstrate what a quality product they are. By the end of the third paragraph, it's evident to the reader that her claim is unjustified.

Notice how most of the components in an effective claim refusal are woven together in this letter: buffer, transition, explanation, and pleasant closing. The only missing part is an alternative, which was impossible in this situation.

7.5 Writing Negative Messages for Internal Situations

Bad news, whether delivered in person or in writing, is usually better received when reasons are given first.

A tactful tone and a reasons-first approach help preserve friendly relations with customers. These same techniques are useful when delivering bad news within organizations. Interpersonal bad news might involve telling the boss that something went wrong or confronting an employee about poor performance. Organizational

FIGURE 7.6 | Refusing a Claim

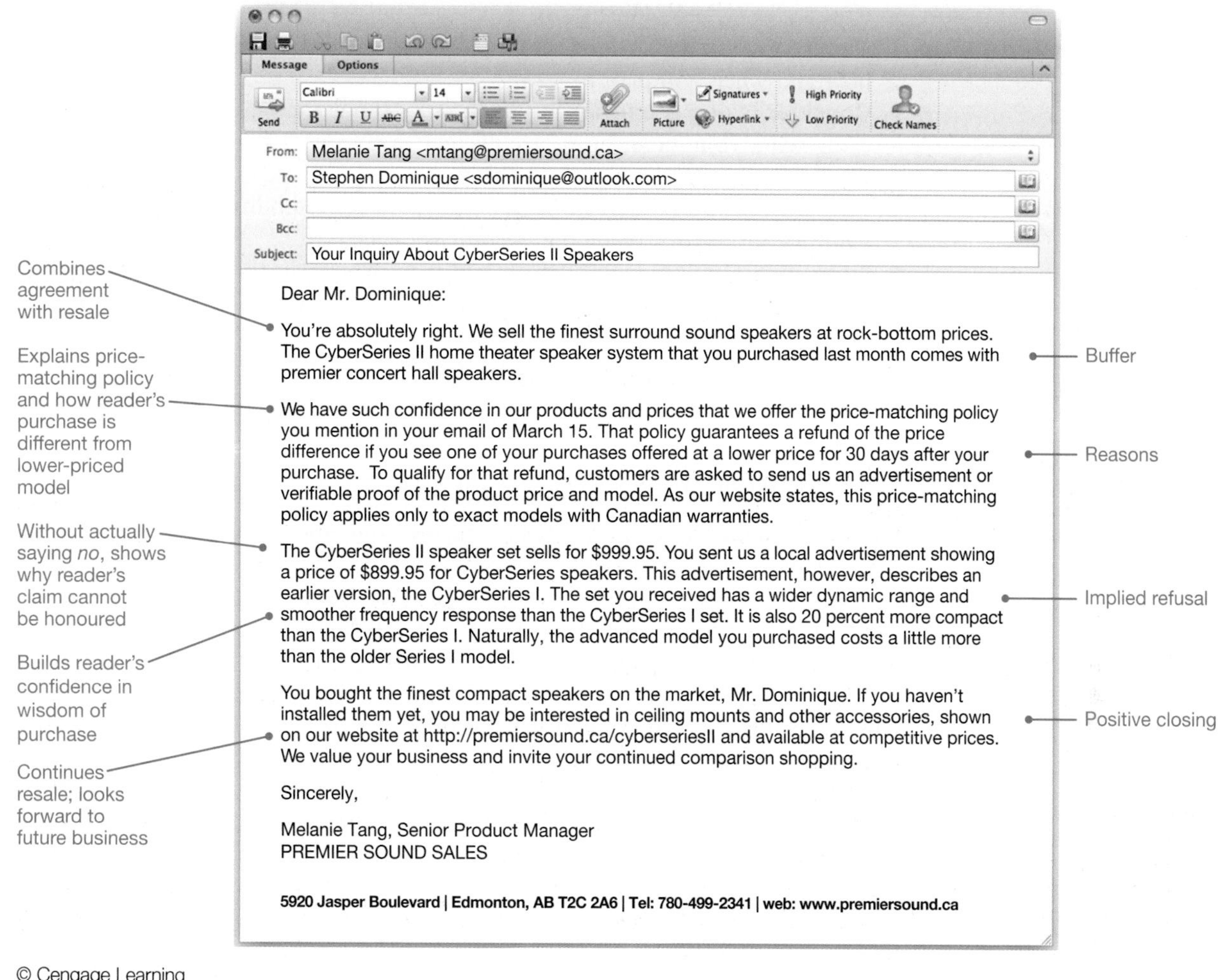

From: Melanie Tang <mtang@premiersound.ca>
To: Stephen Dominique <sdominique@outlook.com>
Cc:
Bcc:
Subject: Your Inquiry About CyberSeries II Speakers
Dear Mr. Dominique:
You're absolutely right. We sell the finest surround sound speakers at rock-bottom prices. The CyberSeries II home theater speaker system that you purchased last month comes with premier concert hall speakers.
We have such confidence in our products and prices that we offer the price-matching policy you mention in your email of March 15. That policy guarantees a refund of the price difference if you see one of your purchases offered at a lower price for 30 days after your purchase. To qualify for that refund, customers are asked to send us an advertisement or verifiable proof of the product price and model. As our website states, this price-matching policy applies only to exact models with Canadian warranties.
The CyberSeries II speaker set sells for $999.95. You sent us a local advertisement showing a price of $899.95 for CyberSeries speakers. This advertisement, however, describes an earlier version, the CyberSeries I. The set you received has a wider dynamic range and smoother frequency response than the CyberSeries I set. It is also 20 percent more compact than the CyberSeries I. Naturally, the advanced model you purchased costs a little more than the older Series I model.
You bought the finest compact speakers on the market, Mr. Dominique. If you haven't installed them yet, you may be interested in ceiling mounts and other accessories, shown on our website at http://premiersound.ca/cyberseriesII and available at competitive prices. We value your business and invite your continued comparison shopping.
Sincerely,
Melanie Tang, Senior Product Manager
PREMIER SOUND SALES
5920 Jasper Boulevard | Edmonton, AB T2C 2A6 | Tel: 780-499-2341 | web: www.premiersound.ca
Combines agreement with resale
Explains price-matching policy and how reader's purchase is different from lower-priced model
Without actually saying *no*, shows why reader's claim cannot be honoured
Builds reader's confidence in wisdom of purchase
Continues resale; looks forward to future business
Buffer
Reasons
Implied refusal
Positive closing

© Cengage Learning

bad news might involve declining profits, lost contracts, harmful lawsuits, public relations controversies, and changes in policy. Generally, bad news is better received when reasons are given first. Within organizations, you may find yourself giving bad news in person or in writing.

7.5a Delivering Bad News in Person

When you have the unhappy responsibility of delivering bad news, decide whether the negative information is newsworthy. For example, trivial, noncriminal mistakes or one-time bad behaviours are best left alone. However, fraudulent travel claims, consistent hostile behaviour, or failing projects must be reported.[12] For example, you might have to tell the boss that the team's computer crashed, losing all its important files. As a team leader or supervisor, you might be required to confront an underperforming employee. If you know that the news will upset the receiver, the reasons-first strategy is most effective. When the bad news involves one person or a small group nearby, you should generally deliver that news in person. Here are pointers on how to do so tactfully, professionally, and safely:[13]

- **Gather all the information.** Cool down and have all the facts before marching in on the boss or confronting someone. Remember that every story has two sides.

OFFICE INSIDER

"Any message beginning with 'you' when talking to a coworker is best avoided—it comes across as shaking your finger at the person, and no one wants to feel like he or she is talking to their mother! Better choices are 'Can we...?' or 'Let's...'"

When you must deliver bad news in person, be sure to gather all the information, prepare, and rehearse.

- **Prepare and rehearse.** Outline what you plan to say so that you are confident, coherent, and dispassionate.
- **Explain: past, present, future.** If you are telling the boss about a problem such as the computer crash, explain what caused the crash, the current situation, and how and when you plan to fix it.
- **Consider taking a partner.** If you fear a "shoot the messenger" reaction, especially from your boss, bring a colleague with you. Each person should have a consistent and credible part in the presentation. If possible, take advantage of your organization's internal resources. To lend credibility to your view, call on auditors, inspectors, or human resources experts.
- **Think about timing.** Don't deliver bad news when someone is already stressed or grumpy. Experts also advise against giving bad news on Friday afternoon when people have the weekend to dwell on it.
- **Be patient with the reaction.** Give the receiver time to vent, think, recover, and act wisely.

7.5b Refusing Workplace Requests

Internal request refusals focus on explanations and praise, maintaining a positive tone, and offering alternatives.

Occasionally, managers must refuse requests from employees. In Figure 7.7 you see the first draft and revision of a message responding to a request from a key specialist, Melvin Arroyo. He wants permission to attend a conference. However, he can't attend the conference because the timing is bad; he must be present at budget planning meetings scheduled for the same two weeks. Normally, this matter would be discussed in person. However, Melvin has been travelling among branch offices, and he just hasn't been in the office recently.

The vice president's first inclination was to send a quick email, as shown in the Figure 7.7 draft, and "tell it like it is." However, the vice president realized that this message was going to hurt and that it had possible danger areas. Moreover, the message misses a chance to give Melvin positive feedback. An improved version of the email starts with a buffer that delivers honest praise (*pleased with the exceptional leadership you have provided and your genuine professional commitment*). By the way, don't be stingy with compliments; they cost you nothing. The buffer also includes the date of the meeting, used strategically to connect the reasons that follow.

The middle paragraph provides reasons for the refusal. Notice that they focus on positive elements: Melvin is the specialist; the company relies on his expertise; and everyone will benefit if he passes up the conference. In this section it becomes obvious that the request will be refused. The writer is not forced to say *No, you may not attend*. Although the refusal is implied, the reader gets the message.

The closing suggests a qualified alternative (*if our workloads permit, we will try to send you then*). It also ends positively with gratitude for Melvin's contributions to the organization and with another compliment (*you're a valuable player*). The improved version focuses on explanations and praise rather than on refusals and apologies. The success of this message depends on sincerity and attention to the entire writing process, not just on using a buffer or scattering a few compliments throughout.

7.5c Announcing Negative News to Employees

In the social media age, damaging information can rarely be contained for long. Executives can almost count on it to be leaked. Corporate officers who fail to communicate effectively and proactively may end up on the defensive, facing an uphill battle to limit the damage. Many of the techniques used to communicate bad news

FIGURE 7.7 | Refusing an Internal Request

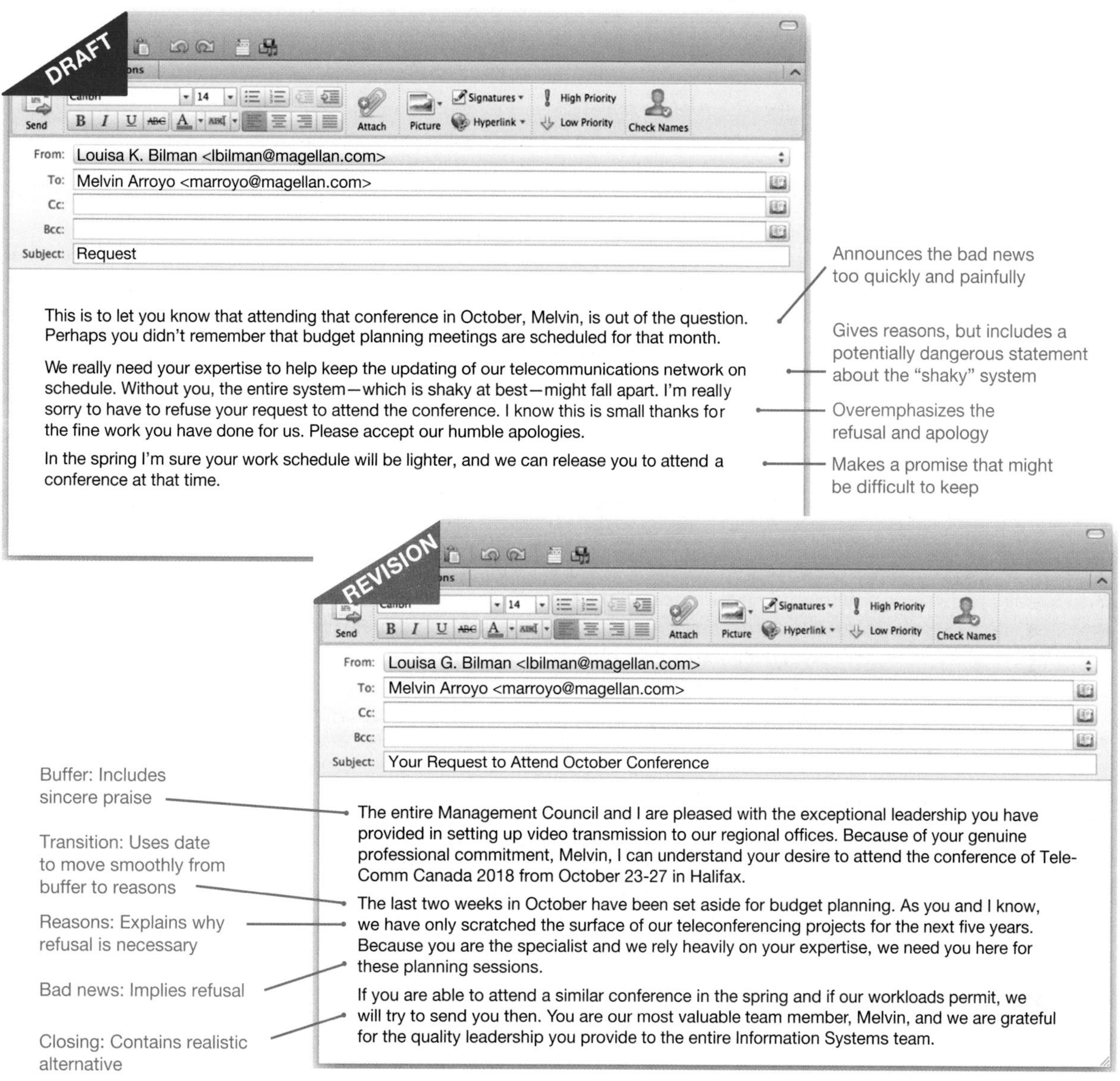

in person are useful when organizations face a crisis or must deliver negative news to their workers and other groups.

DRAFT
From: Louisa K. Bilman <lbilman@magellan.com>
To: Melvin Arroyo <marroyo@magellan.com>
Cc:
Bcc:
Subject: Request
This is to let you know that attending that conference in October, Melvin, is out of the question. Perhaps you didn't remember that budget planning meetings are scheduled for that month.
We really need your expertise to help keep the updating of our telecommunications network on schedule. Without you, the entire system—which is shaky at best—might fall apart. I'm really sorry to have to refuse your request to attend the conference. I know this is small thanks for the fine work you have done for us. Please accept our humble apologies.
In the spring I'm sure your work schedule will be lighter, and we can release you to attend a conference at that time.
Announces the bad news too quickly and painfully
Gives reasons, but includes a potentially dangerous statement about the "shaky" system
Overemphasizes the refusal and apology
Makes a promise that might be difficult to keep
REVISION
From: Louisa G. Bilman <lbilman@magellan.com>
To: Melvin Arroyo <marroyo@magellan.com>
Cc:
Bcc:
Subject: Your Request to Attend October Conference
The entire Management Council and I are pleased with the exceptional leadership you have provided in setting up video transmission to our regional offices. Because of your genuine professional commitment, Melvin, I can understand your desire to attend the conference of Tele-Comm Canada 2018 from October 23-27 in Halifax.
The last two weeks in October have been set aside for budget planning. As you and I know, we have only scratched the surface of our teleconferencing projects for the next five years. Because you are the specialist and we rely heavily on your expertise, we need you here for these planning sessions.
If you are able to attend a similar conference in the spring and if our workloads permit, we will try to send you then. You are our most valuable team member, Melvin, and we are grateful for the quality leadership you provide to the entire Information Systems team.
Buffer: Includes sincere praise
Transition: Uses date to move smoothly from buffer to reasons
Reasons: Explains why refusal is necessary
Bad news: Implies refusal
Closing: Contains realistic alternative

KEEP COMMUNICATION OPEN AND HONEST. Smart organizations in crisis prefer to communicate the news openly to employees and other stakeholders. A crisis might involve serious performance problems, a major relocation, massive layoffs, a management shakeup, or public controversy. Instead of letting rumours distort the truth, managers ought to explain the organization's side of the story honestly and promptly.

WRITING PLAN FOR ANNOUNCING NEGATIVE NEWS TO EMPLOYEES

- **Buffer:** Start with a neutral or positive statement that transitions to the reasons for the bad news. Consider opening with the best news, a compliment, appreciation, agreement, or solid facts. Show understanding.
- **Reasons:** Explain the logic behind the bad news. Provide a rational explanation using positive words and displaying empathy. If possible, mention reader benefits.
- **Bad news:** Position the bad news so that it does not stand out. Be positive, but don't sugar-coat the bad news. Use objective language.
- **Closing:** Provide information about an alternative, if one exists. If appropriate, describe what will happen next. Look forward positively.

CHOOSE THE BEST COMMUNICATION CHANNEL. Morale can be destroyed when employees learn of major events affecting their jobs through the grapevine or from news accounts—rather than from management. When bad news must be delivered to individual employees, management may want to deliver the news personally. With large groups, however, this is generally impossible. Instead, organizations deliver bad news through multiple channels, ranging from hard-copy memos to digital media. Such messages can take the form of intranet posts, emails, videos, webcasts, internal as well as external blogs, and voice mail.

DRAFT A NEGATIVE NEWS INTRANET POST. The draft of the intranet blog post shown in Figure 7.8 announces a substantial increase in the cost of employee health care benefits. However, the message suffers from many problems. It announces jolting news bluntly in the first sentence. Worse, it offers little or no explanation for the steep increase in costs. It also sounds insincere (*We did everything possible…*) and arbitrary. In a final miscue, the writer fails to give credit to the company for absorbing previous health cost increases.

REVISE YOUR INTRANET POST. The revision of this negative news message uses the indirect strategy and improves the tone considerably. Notice that it opens with a relevant, upbeat buffer regarding health care—but says nothing about increasing costs. For a smooth transition, the second paragraph begins with a key idea from the opening (*comprehensive package*). The reasons section discusses rising costs with explanations and figures. The bad news (*you will be paying $119 a month*) is clearly presented but embedded within the paragraph. Throughout, the writer strives to show the fairness of the company's position. The ending, which does not refer to the bad news, emphasizes how much the company is paying and what a wise investment it is.

The entire message demonstrates a kinder, gentler approach than that shown in the first draft. Of prime importance in breaking bad news to employees is providing clear, convincing reasons that explain the decision. Parallel to this internal blog post, the message was also sent by email. In smaller companies in which some workers do not have company email, a hard-copy memo would be posted prominently on bulletin boards and in the lunchroom.

The indirect strategy is unethical only if the writer intends to deceive the reader.

7.5d Keeping the Indirect Strategy Ethical

You may worry that the indirect strategy is unethical or manipulative or contains a lie because the writer deliberately delays the main idea. But consider the alternative.

FIGURE 7.8 | Announcing Negative News to Employees

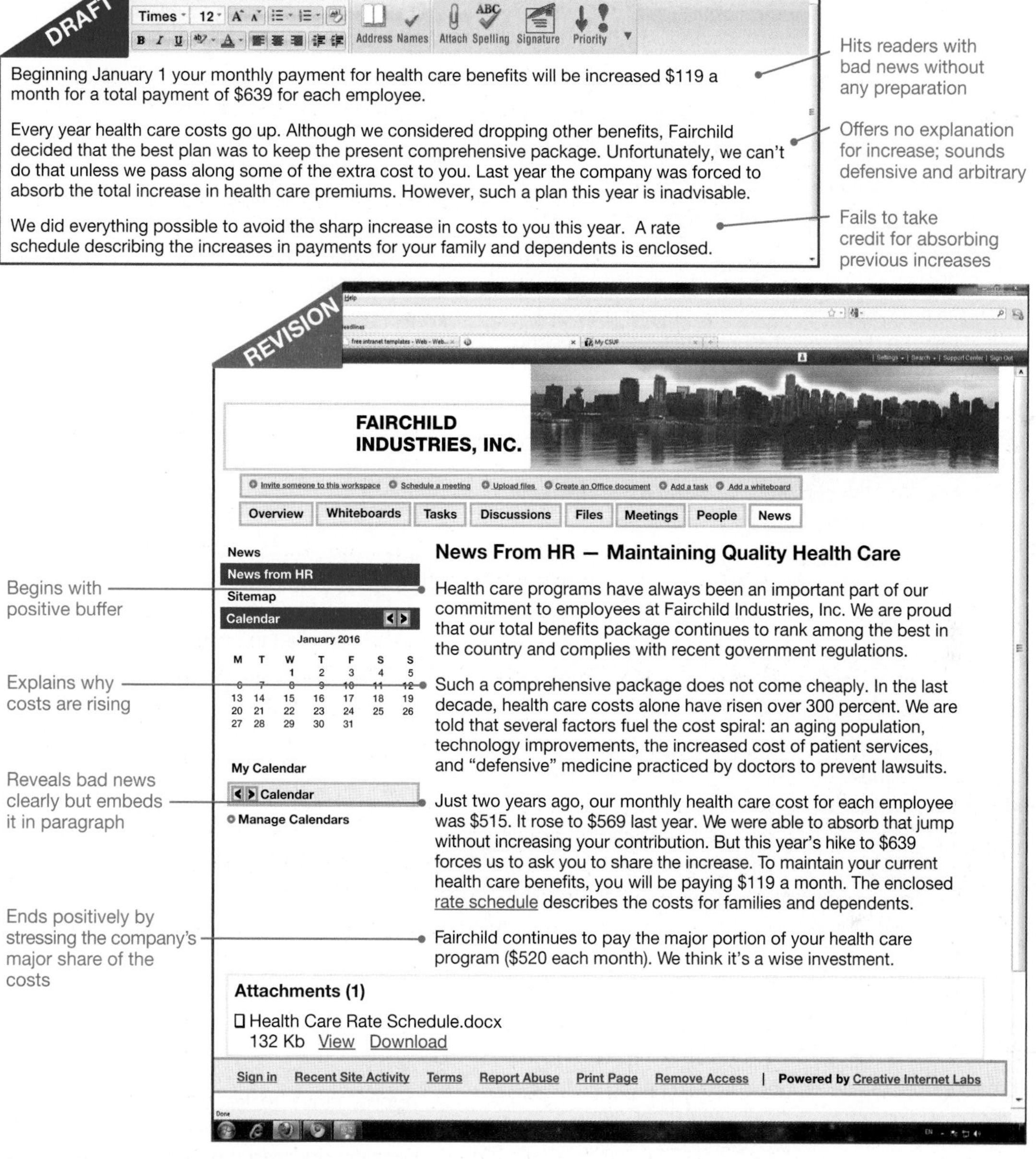

Breaking bad news bluntly can cause pain and hard feelings. By delaying bad news, you soften the blow somewhat, as well as ensure that your reasoning will be read while the receiver is still receptive. Your motives are not to deceive the reader or to hide the news. Rather, your goal is to be a compassionate, yet effective, communicator.

The key to ethical communication lies in the motives of the sender. Unethical communicators intend to deceive. For example, Victoria's Secret, the clothing and lingerie chain, once offered free $10 gift certificates. However, when customers tried to use the certificates, they found that they were required to make a minimum purchase of $50 worth of merchandise.[14] For this misleading, deceptive, and unethical offer, the chain paid a $100,000 fine. Although the indirect strategy provides a setting in which to announce bad news, it should not be used to avoid or misrepresent the truth.

SUMMARY OF LEARNING OBJECTIVES

7.1 Explain the goals of business communicators when conveying negative news.

- Explain clearly and completely while projecting a professional image.
- Convey empathy, sensitivity, and fairness.
- Maintain friendly relations, especially with customers.

7.2 Compare the direct and indirect strategies for communicating negative news.

- Use the direct strategy, with the bad news first, when the news is not damaging, when the receiver may overlook it, when the organization or receiver prefers directness, or when firmness is necessary.
- Use the indirect strategy, with a buffer and explanation preceding the bad news, when the bad news is personally upsetting, when it may provoke a hostile reaction, when it threatens the customer relationship, and when the news is unexpected.
- To avoid being unethical, never use the indirect method to deceive or manipulate the truth.

7.3 Describe the components of effective indirect negative messages, including opening with a buffer, apologizing, showing empathy, presenting the reasons, cushioning the bad news, and closing pleasantly.

- To soften bad news, start with a buffer such as the best news, a compliment, appreciation, agreement, facts, understanding, or an apology.
- If you apologize, do it promptly and sincerely. Accept responsibility but don't admit blame without consulting a superior or company counsel. Strive to project empathy.
- In presenting the reasons for the bad news, explain clearly, cite reader or other benefits if plausible, explain company policy if necessary, choose positive words, and strive to show fairness and serious intent.
- In breaking the bad news, position it and word it strategically by (a) sandwiching it between other sentences, (b) presenting it in a subordinating clause, (c) using passive-voice verbs to depersonalize an action, (d) highlighting whatever is positive, (e) implying the refusal instead of stating it directly, and (f) suggesting a compromise or an alternative.
- To close pleasantly, you could (a) suggest a means of following through on an alternative, (b) offer freebies, (c) extend good wishes, (d) anticipate future business, or (e) offer resale information or a sales promotion.

7.4 Write negative messages for client/customer situations: collections, refusals (e.g., denying requests or claims), and situations when customers are disappointed.

- In rejecting requests for favours, money, information, and action, follow the bad-news strategy: (a) begin with a buffer, (b) present valid reasons, (c) explain the bad news and possibly an alternative, and (d) close with good feelings and a positive statement.
- To deal with disappointed customers in print, (a) call or email the individual immediately; (b) describe the problem and apologize; (c) explain why the problem occurred, what you are doing to resolve it, and how you will prevent it from happening again; and (d) promote goodwill with a follow-up message.
- To handle negative posts and reviews online, (a) verify the situation, (b) respond quickly and constructively, (c) consider giving freebies such as refunds or discounts, (d) learn to improve by considering people who made negative comments as real-time focus groups, and (e) be prepared to accept the inevitable and move on.
- To deny claims, (a) use the reasons-before-refusal plan, (b) don't blame customers (even if they are at fault), (c) use neutral objective language to explain why the claim must be refused, and (d) consider offering resale information to rebuild the customer's confidence in your products or organization.

7.5 Write negative messages for internal situations (e.g., employee bad news).

- To deliver workplace bad news in person, (a) gather all the information; (b) prepare and rehearse; (c) explain the past, present, and future; (d) consider taking a partner; (e) choose the best time to deliver the news; and (f) be patient with the reaction.
- In announcing bad news to employees and to the public, strive to keep the communication open and honest, choose the best communication channel, and consider applying the indirect strategy.
- Be positive, but don't sugar-coat the bad news; use objective language.
- Recognize that the indirect strategy, while it does soften the truth, must, in order to stay ethical, never deny the truth.

CHAPTER REVIEW

1. When denying a claim from an irate customer who is threatening and overstates the claim, why do you want to remain professional and fair? (Obj. 1)
2. What is the primary difference between the direct and the indirect strategies? (Obj. 2)
3. When would you be more inclined to use the direct strategy in delivering negative news? (Obj. 2)
4. What is a buffer? Name five or more techniques to buffer the opening of a negative-news message. (Obj. 3)

5. Why should you apologize to customers if you or your company erred? What is the best way to do it? (Obj. 3)
6. In delivering negative news, what five techniques can be used to cushion that news? (Obj. 3)
7. What is a process used by many business professionals in resolving problems with disappointed customers? (Obj. 4)
8. How can negative online comments be turned into positive growth for an organization? (Obj. 4)
9. How can a subordinate tactfully, professionally, and safely deliver upsetting news personally to a superior? (Obj. 5)
10. What are some channels that large organizations may use to deliver bad news to employees? (Obj. 5)
11. How is the indirect negative news strategy an ethical strategy? (Obj. 5)

CRITICAL THINKING

1. Communication author Dana Bristol-Smith likens delivering bad news to removing a Band-Aid—you can do it slowly or quickly. She thinks that doing so quickly is better, particularly when companies must give bad news to employees.[15] Do you agree or disagree? Why? (Objs. 1, 2)
2. A survey of business professionals revealed that most respondents reported that every effort should be made to resolve business problems in person. Why is this logical? Why is this problematic? (Objs. 1, 2)
3. Respected industry analyst Gartner Research issued a report naming social networking as one of the top ten "disruptive" (innovative, game-changing) influences shaping information technology today.[16] To what degree should organizations fear websites where consumers post negative messages about products and services? What actions can companies take in response to this disruptive influence? (Objs. 3, 4)
4. Does bad news travel faster and farther than good news? Why? What implications would this have for companies responding to unhappy customers? (Obj. 4)
5. Why might it be a bad idea to be blunt and terse toward people with a low income when denying them credit? (Objs. 1, 2)
6. Why is the "reasons" section of a negative news message so important? (Objs. 4, 5)
7. Radio Shack infamously fired 400 of its employees by email a number of years ago. More recently, the CEO of electric-car manufacturer Tesla, Elon Musk, used his blog to announce layoffs. Why would most business communication and management experts frown upon such behaviour? Do you agree or disagree with these experts? (Objs. 1, 4, 5)

ACTIVITIES AND CASES

7.1 REQUEST REFUSAL: PINK DRAGONS SINK APPLICATION (OBJS. 1–4)

Shopify, the Ottawa-based ecommerce company, prides itself on its commitment to employees who receive generous benefits and enjoy a supportive corporate culture. This core value may have contributed to the company's ranking as the top place to work in Canada.[17] The software giant is also known for its community involvement and corporate social responsibility efforts. This is why, like most large companies, Shopify receives many requests for sponsorships of charity events and community projects. True to its innovative spirit, the software company has streamlined the application process by providing an online sponsorship request form at its website.

You work in Corporate Affairs/Community Relations at Shopify and periodically help decide which nonprofits will obtain support. Just yesterday you received an email from the Pink Dragons of Ottawa-Hull, a dragon boat racing team of breast cancer survivors. The ancient Chinese sport has spread around the globe with competitions held not only in Asia but also in many Western countries. Dragon boat racing has gained popularity in North America among breast cancer patients who bond with fellow survivors, engage in healthy competition, and exercise regularly on the water. Synchronicity and technique are more important than brute strength, which is the main reason even recreational paddlers enjoy this fast-growing water sport.

The newly formed survivor team would like Shopify to sponsor a dragon boat festival in Toronto in less than a month, an event potentially drawing at least 20 survivor teams that would compete against each other. Your company is already funding several cancer charities and has a policy of sponsoring many causes. Naturally, no corporate giving program has infinite funds, nor can it green-light every request. Shopify steers clear of religious, political, and sexually explicit events. The team judging the sponsorship entries wants to ensure that each proposal reaches audiences affiliated with Shopify. Most important, applicants must submit their requests at least six weeks before the event.

Your Task. As a junior staff member in Corporate Affairs/Community Relations, write an email to Pink Dragon captain Josephine Rosa (jrosa@pinkdragons.ca) refusing her initial request and explaining the Shopify sponsorship philosophy and submission rules.

7.2 CLAIM DENIAL: LOST IN FLIGHT (OBJS. 1–4)

Air Transat has an unhappy customer. Genna Frymoyer-Morris flew from Montreal to Lisbon. The flight stopped briefly at the Ponta Delgada International Airport in the Azores, where she got off the plane for half an hour. When she returned to her seat, her $500 prescription reading glasses were gone. She asked the flight attendant where the glasses were, and the attendant said they probably were thrown away since the cleaning crew had come in with big bags and tossed everything left on the plane in them.

Ms. Frymoyer-Morris tried to locate the glasses through the airline's lost-and-found service, but she failed. Then she wrote a strong letter to the airline demanding reimbursement for the loss. She felt that it was obvious that she was returning to her seat. The airline, however, knows that a large number of passengers arriving at hubs switch planes for their connecting flights. The airline does not know who is returning. What's more, flight attendants usually announce that the plane is continuing to another city and that passengers who are returning should take their belongings. Cabin cleaning crews speed through planes removing newspapers, magazines, leftover foods, and trash. Airlines feel no responsibility for personal items left in cabins.

Your Task. As a staff member of the customer relations department of Air Transat, deny the customer's claim but retain her goodwill using techniques learned in this chapter. The airline never refunds cash, but it might consider travel vouchers for the value of the glasses. Remember that apologies cost nothing. Write a claim denial to Ms. Genna Frymoyer-Morris, 1805 Rue du Chemin, Mont Tremblant, QC J8E 0A3.

7.3 CUSTOMER NEGATIVE NEWS: COSTLY SUV UPGRADE (OBJ. 4)

Steven Chan, a consultant from Regina, Saskatchewan, was surprised when he picked up his rental car from Budget at the Calgary airport over Easter weekend. He had reserved a full-size car, but the rental agent told him he could upgrade to a Ford Excursion for an additional $25 a day. "She told me it was easy to drive," Mr. Chan reported. "But when I saw it, I realized it was huge—like a tank. You could fit a full-size bed inside."

On his trip Mr. Chan managed to scratch the paint and damage the rear-door step. He didn't worry, though. He thought the damage would be covered because he had charged the rental on his American Express card. He knew that the company offered backup car rental insurance coverage. To his dismay, he discovered that its car rental coverage excluded large SUVs. "I just assumed they'd cover it," he confessed. He wrote to Budget to complain about not being warned that certain credit cards may not cover damage to large SUVs or luxury cars.

Budget agents always encourage renters to sign up for Budget's own "risk product." They don't feel that it is their responsibility to study the policies of customers' insurance carriers and explain what may or may not be covered. Moreover, they try to move customers into their rental cars as quickly as possible and avoid lengthy discussions of insurance coverage. Customers who do not purchase insurance are at risk. Mr. Chan does not make any claim against Budget, but he is upset about being "pitched" to upgrade to the larger SUV, which he didn't really want.[18]

Your Task. As a member of the customer care staff at Budget, respond to Mr. Chan's complaint. Budget obviously is not going to pay for the SUV repairs, but it does want to salvage his goodwill and future business. Offer him a coupon worth two days' free rental of any full-size sedan. Write to Steven Chan, 201–548 Hillsdale Street, Regina, SK S32 0A2.

Visit **MindTap** for a variety of videos, additional exercises, activities, and quizzes to support your learning.

Business Reports and Proposals

UNIT 04

CHAPTER 8
Informal Reports

CHAPTER 9
Proposals and Formal Reports

colinLund/Shutterstock.com

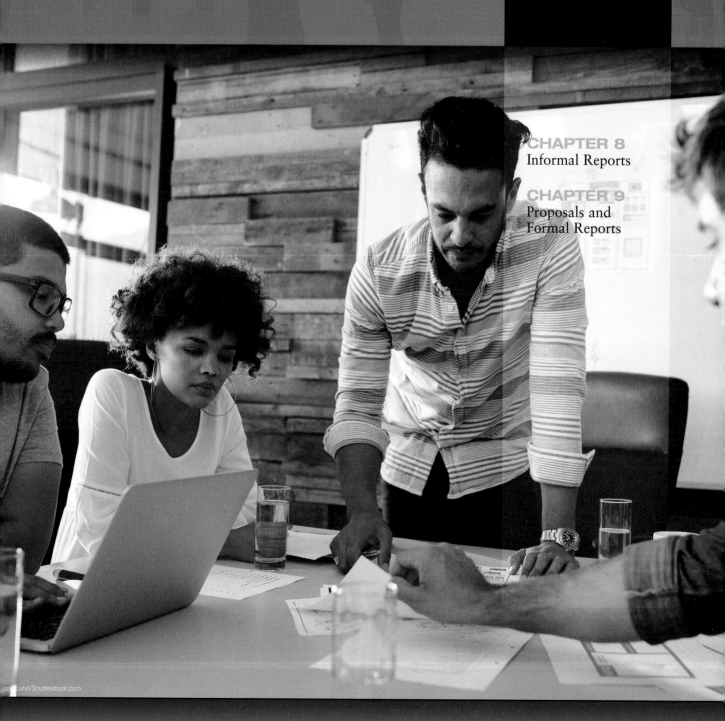

COMMUNICATION TECHNOLOGY IN THE NEWS

Advancing Sustainability Reporting in Canada

Kathrin Bohr, Toronto Sustainability Speaker Series: CSR Reporting, *August 23, 2016*

Two years ago Stakeholder Research Associates (SRA) conducted a study into the state of sustainability reporting in Canada. At that time we found that 42%, or fewer than half of Canadian companies listed on the TSX Composite Index publicly disclosed environmental, social and governance (ESG) information. We recently repeated our research and found that, in 2016, 56% of companies listed on the Index provided some form of ESG disclosure, an increase of 14% compared to 2014. Our research also showed an increase in the number of companies that included ESG information in their annual reports—55% in 2016 compared to 52% in 2014.

At first glance this appears to be a positive trend. However, our review suggests that while the number of companies providing ESG information increased over two years, reporting quality did not. Certainly a number of Canadian companies continue to demonstrate best practices, among them, Teck, Telus, Bombardier, TD for example. But many listed companies short change investors and other stakeholders, offering woefully inadequate public disclosure, providing but a few web pages on a handful of topics that fail to tell a cohesive and complete story of the company's ESG impacts, let alone progress toward measured reduction of those impacts.

Interestingly, we also observed a decrease in the number of companies using the Global Reporting Initiative (GRI) guidelines, with 50% referencing the GRI in 2016, down from 71% two years prior. It's not clear the cause of this drop. It could be the result of "GRI fatigue" following the release of the GRI G4 Guidelines in 2013, which asked reporters to up their "materiality" approach while resetting report goal posts—a fatigue that may well be compounded by the release of new GRI Standards later this year. Another view suggests that listed companies increasingly are understanding the need for and value of ESG disclosure to investors and other stakeholders, and are only now taking first tentative steps on their disclosure journey. Just as it did for Canadian reporters 20 years ago, it is our hope that comprehensive, guidance-based, value-creating reporting framework will follow for this new wave of reporters.

What we know is that sustainability reporting in Canada has plateaued. Yet, our conversations with reporters tell us that there is an appetite for a re-energized community and a desire to realize the full value of ESG disclosure.

Summarize the article you've just read in a two- to three-sentence paragraph. Answer the following questions, either on your own or in a small group. Be prepared to present your answers in a short presentation or in an email to your instructor.

QUESTIONS:

1. How does what you've learned in this article change your perception of business communication?
2. How might what you've learned in this article change your own communication style?
3. Come up with pro and con arguments for the following debate/discussion topic: Large as well as small- and medium-size Canadian companies should be required to publish annual sustainability reports.

Informal Reports

CHAPTER

8

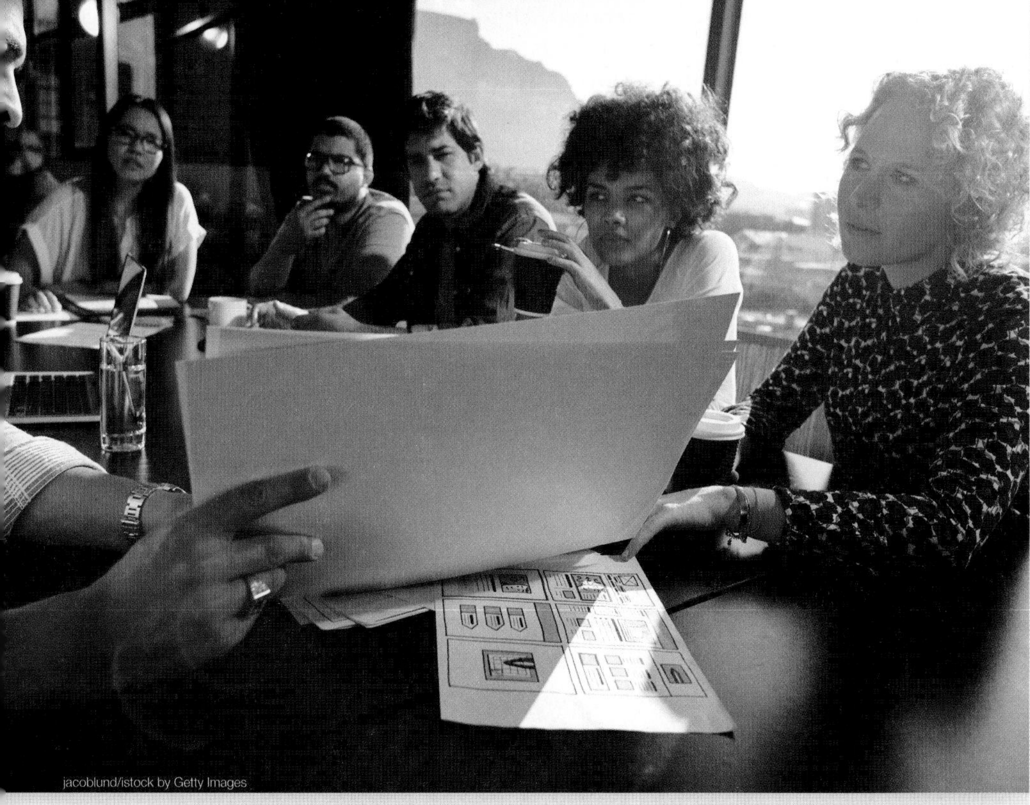

jacoblund/istock by Getty Images

OBJECTIVES

After studying this chapter, you should be able to

8.1 Explain informational and analytical business report functions and organization.

8.2 Describe typical report formats including heading levels.

8.3 Determine the problem to be addressed and the report's purpose.

8.4 Write informal informational reports.

8.5 Write informal analytical reports.

8.1 The Function and Organization of Informal Reports

Good report writers are skilled at simplifying facts so that anyone can understand them. Collecting information and organizing it clearly and simply into meaningful reports are skills that all successful businesspeople today require. In this digital age of information, reports play a significant role in helping decision makers solve problems. You can learn to write and design good reports by examining basic techniques and by analyzing appropriate models.

Because of their abundance and diversity, business reports are difficult to define. They may range from informal email trip reports to formal 200-page financial forecasts. Some reports may be presented orally in front of a group using PowerPoint, while other reports appear as emails, memos, or in template forms. Still others consist primarily of numerical data, such as tax reports or profit-and-loss statements.

Although reports vary in length, content, format, organization, and level of formality, they all have one common purpose: they are organized attempts to answer business questions and solve business problems in writing or in presentation format. Reports are informal when the information included in them deals with routine or recurring events, or when decisions taken based on the report have a relatively

Informal reports are relatively short (under ten pages) and are usually written in memo or letter format. Sometimes, they are attached to emails or presented in the body of the email itself if the context is quite informal.

low financial threshold. Decisions with large budgets attached usually come after a formal report has been researched and presented; you'll look at formal reports in Chapter 9.

8.1a Functions of Reports

Most reports can be classified into two functional categories: information reports and analytical reports.

INFORMATION REPORTS. Reports that present data without analysis or recommendations are primarily informational. Although writers collect and organize facts, they are not expected to analyze the facts (i.e., say what the facts mean) for readers. A trip report describing an employee's visit to a conference, for example, simply presents information. Other reports that present information without analysis could involve routine operations (e.g., an incident report in a fast-food restaurant), compliance with regulations (e.g., a status update on a new government regulation rollout in a bank), or company policies and procedures (e.g., a status update on employee reaction to enforcement of a new company policy in a manufacturing company).

ANALYTICAL REPORTS. Reports that provide analysis and conclusions as well as data are analytical. If requested, writers also supply recommendations. Analysis is the process of breaking down a problem into its parts in order to understand it better and solve it (e.g., each time you write an outline, as shown in Figure 3.2 on page 49, you are analyzing a problem). Analytical reports attempt to provide the insight necessary to persuade readers to act or change their opinions. For example, a recommendation report that compares several potential locations for an employee fitness club might recommend one site, but not until after it has analyzed and discussed the alternatives. This analysis should persuade readers to accept the writer's choice. Similarly, a feasibility report that analyzes the ability of a private chef school to open a satellite campus in a nearby city will either say *yes this can be done* or *no it can't*, but it will also discuss the alternative course of action.

8.1b Report Organization

Like routine, persuasive, or negative messages, reports may be organized using the direct or indirect method. The reader's expectations and the content of a report determine its pattern of development, as shown in Figure 8.1.

DIRECT STRATEGY. When the purpose for writing is presented close to the beginning, the organizational strategy is direct. Information reports are usually arranged directly. They open with an introduction, followed by the facts, which may be listed using headings for greater readability, and a summary.

How you format a report depends on its length, topic, audience, and purpose.

Analytical reports may also be organized directly, especially when readers are supportive or are familiar with the topic. Many busy executives prefer this pattern because it gives them the results of the report immediately. They don't have to spend time wading through the facts, findings, discussion, and analyses to get to the two items they are most interested in—the conclusions and recommendations. You should be aware, though, that unless readers are familiar with the topic, they may find the direct pattern confusing. Some readers prefer the indirect pattern because it seems logical and mirrors the way we solve problems.

INDIRECT STRATEGY. When the conclusions and recommendations, if requested, appear at the end of the report, the organizational pattern is indirect. Such reports usually begin with an introduction or description of the problem, followed by facts and interpretation from the writer. They end with conclusions and recommendations. This pattern is helpful when readers are unfamiliar with the problem. It is

FIGURE 8.1 | Audience Analysis and Report Organization

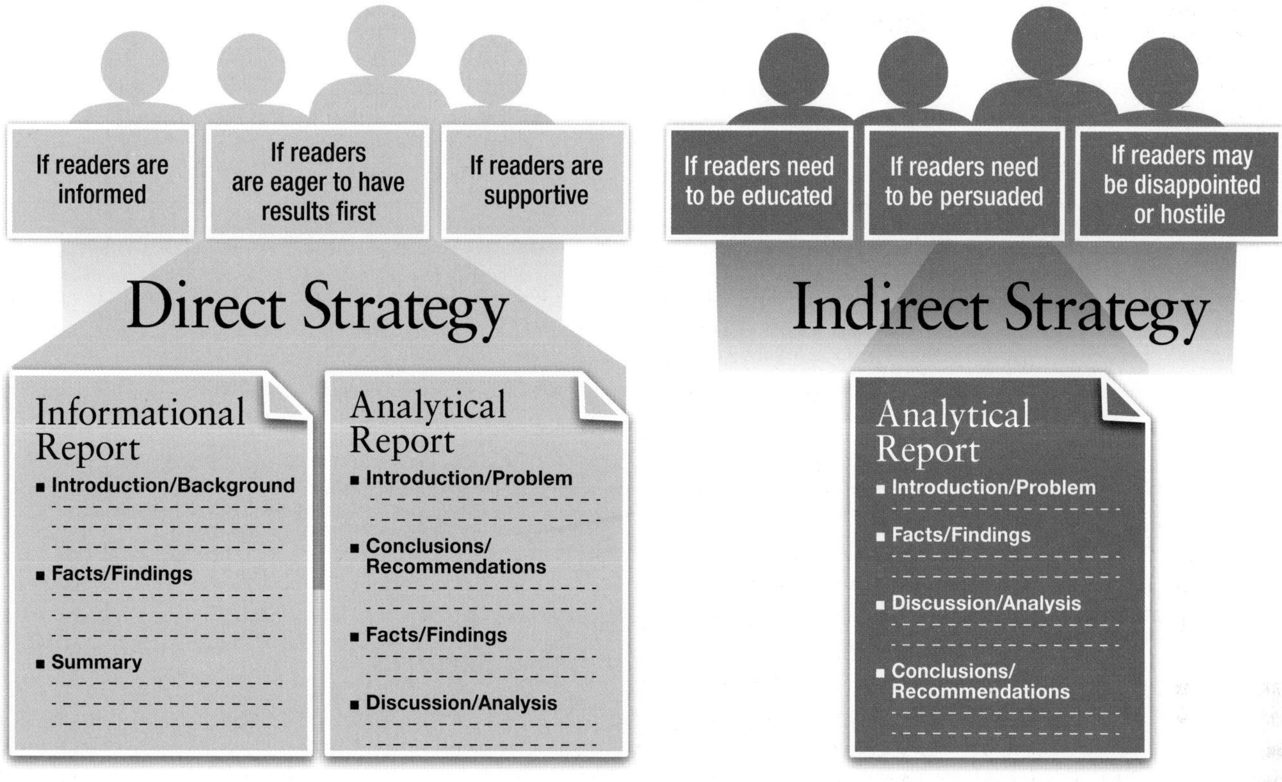

also useful when readers must be persuaded or when they may be disappointed in or hostile toward the report's findings. The writer is more likely to retain the reader's interest by first explaining, justifying, and analyzing the facts and then making recommendations. This pattern also seems most rational to readers because it follows the normal thought process: problem, alternatives (facts), solution.

8.2 Informal Formats and Headings

The design of a report should be visually appealing and professional-looking. The report should include a hierarchy of meaningful headings that highlight major points, allowing readers to see the flow of ideas. Some organizations use templates and reporting software to standardize the look of their reports.

8.2a Typical Report Formats

The format of a report is governed by its length, topic, audience, and purpose. After considering these elements, you will probably choose from among the following seven formats.

ELECTRONIC FORMAT. In today's less formal workplace, informal reports are often sent as emails. The report is either written in the body of the email, or it is attached to the email as a memo, a letter, or a PowerPoint deck. Increasingly, businesses encourage employees to upload reports to the company intranet or sharing software (e.g., Google Docs) or cloud-based storage, especially for team-based writing.

LETTER FORMAT. Use letter format for short (usually eight or fewer pages), informal reports addressed outside an organization. Prepared using a company's letterhead, a letter report, like the one in Figure 8.2, contains a date, inside address, salutation, and complimentary close. Although this format may carry information similar to that found in correspondence, letter reports usually are longer and show more careful organization than most letters. They also include headings.

FIGURE 8.2 | Informational Report: Email Cover With Letter Attachment

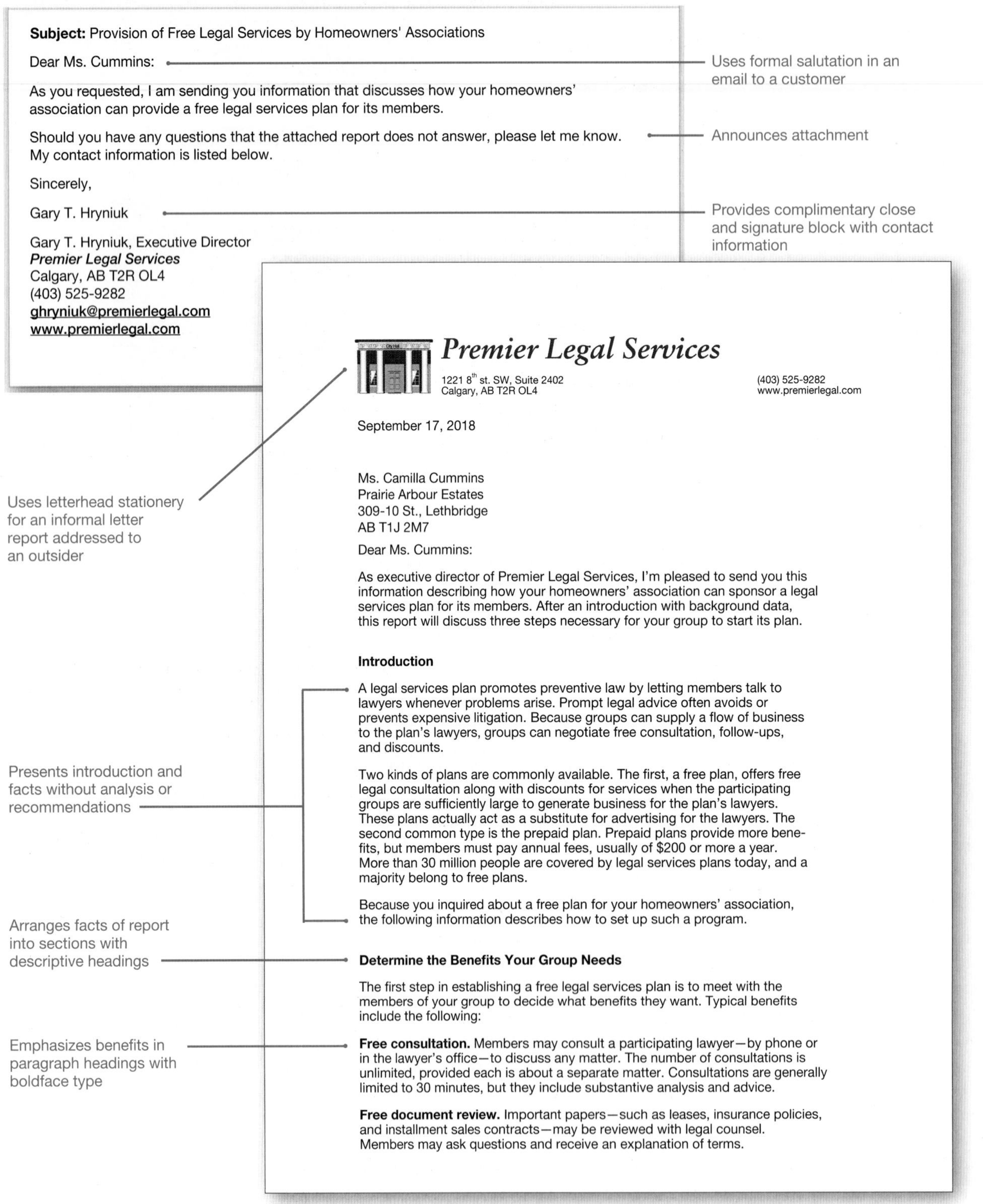

Subject: Provision of Free Legal Services by Homeowners' Associations

Dear Ms. Cummins:

As you requested, I am sending you information that discusses how your homeowners' association can provide a free legal services plan for its members.

Should you have any questions that the attached report does not answer, please let me know. My contact information is listed below.

Sincerely,

Gary T. Hryniuk

Gary T. Hryniuk, Executive Director
Premier Legal Services
Calgary, AB T2R OL4
(403) 525-9282
ghryniuk@premierlegal.com
www.premierlegal.com

Premier Legal Services

1221 8th st. SW, Suite 2402
Calgary, AB T2R OL4

(403) 525-9282
www.premierlegal.com

September 17, 2018

Ms. Camilla Cummins
Prairie Arbour Estates
309-10 St., Lethbridge
AB T1J 2M7

Dear Ms. Cummins:

As executive director of Premier Legal Services, I'm pleased to send you this information describing how your homeowners' association can sponsor a legal services plan for its members. After an introduction with background data, this report will discuss three steps necessary for your group to start its plan.

Introduction

A legal services plan promotes preventive law by letting members talk to lawyers whenever problems arise. Prompt legal advice often avoids or prevents expensive litigation. Because groups can supply a flow of business to the plan's lawyers, groups can negotiate free consultation, follow-ups, and discounts.

Two kinds of plans are commonly available. The first, a free plan, offers free legal consultation along with discounts for services when the participating groups are sufficiently large to generate business for the plan's lawyers. These plans actually act as a substitute for advertising for the lawyers. The second common type is the prepaid plan. Prepaid plans provide more benefits, but members must pay annual fees, usually of $200 or more a year. More than 30 million people are covered by legal services plans today, and a majority belong to free plans.

Because you inquired about a free plan for your homeowners' association, the following information describes how to set up such a program.

Determine the Benefits Your Group Needs

The first step in establishing a free legal services plan is to meet with the members of your group to decide what benefits they want. Typical benefits include the following:

Free consultation. Members may consult a participating lawyer—by phone or in the lawyer's office—to discuss any matter. The number of consultations is unlimited, provided each is about a separate matter. Consultations are generally limited to 30 minutes, but they include substantive analysis and advice.

Free document review. Important papers—such as leases, insurance policies, and installment sales contracts—may be reviewed with legal counsel. Members may ask questions and receive an explanation of terms.

FIGURE 8.2 | *(Continued)*

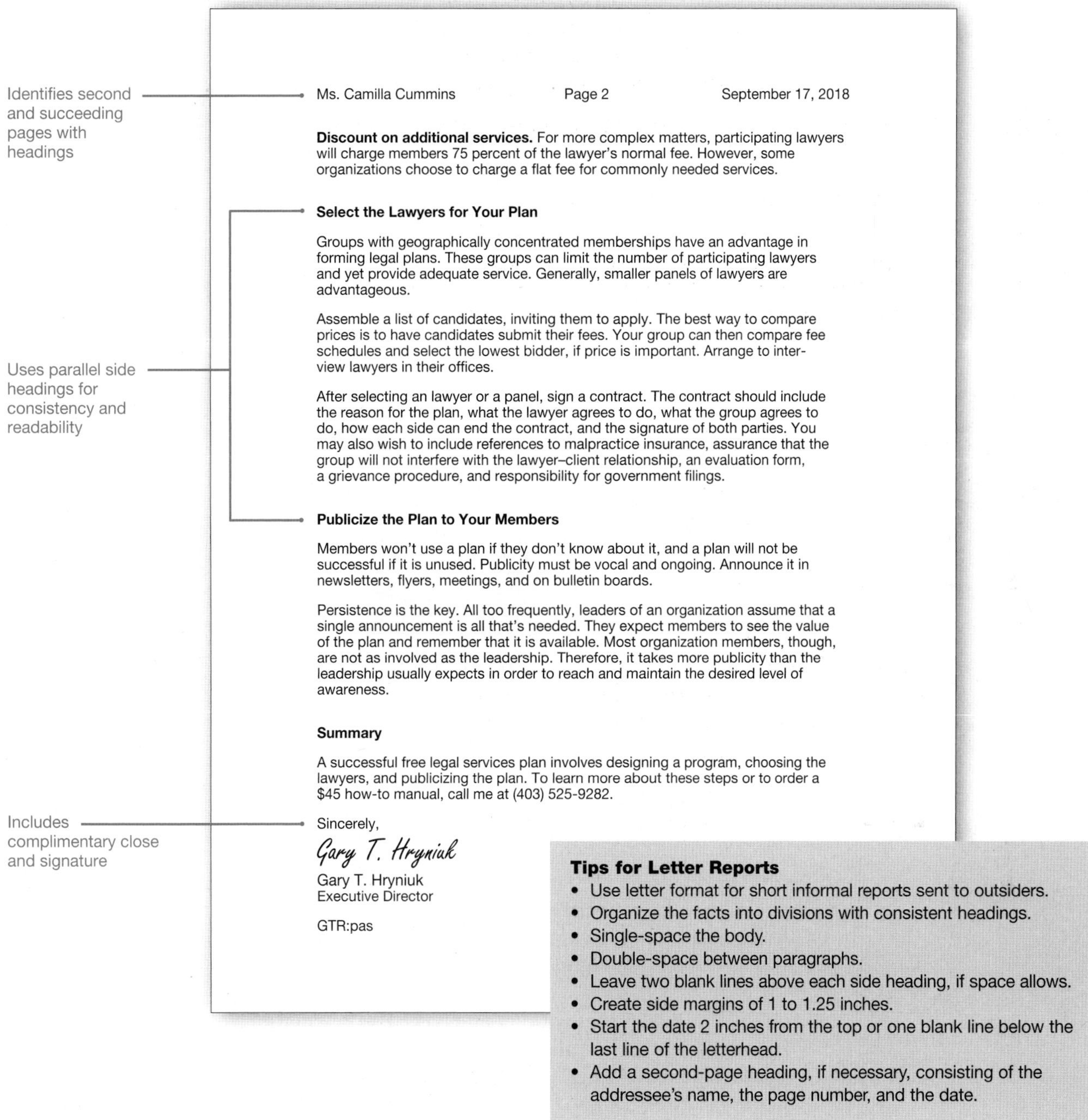

Identifies second and succeeding pages with headings

Uses parallel side headings for consistency and readability

Includes complimentary close and signature

Ms. Camilla Cummins Page 2 September 17, 2018

Discount on additional services. For more complex matters, participating lawyers will charge members 75 percent of the lawyer's normal fee. However, some organizations choose to charge a flat fee for commonly needed services.

Select the Lawyers for Your Plan

Groups with geographically concentrated memberships have an advantage in forming legal plans. These groups can limit the number of participating lawyers and yet provide adequate service. Generally, smaller panels of lawyers are advantageous.

Assemble a list of candidates, inviting them to apply. The best way to compare prices is to have candidates submit their fees. Your group can then compare fee schedules and select the lowest bidder, if price is important. Arrange to interview lawyers in their offices.

After selecting an lawyer or a panel, sign a contract. The contract should include the reason for the plan, what the lawyer agrees to do, what the group agrees to do, how each side can end the contract, and the signature of both parties. You may also wish to include references to malpractice insurance, assurance that the group will not interfere with the lawyer–client relationship, an evaluation form, a grievance procedure, and responsibility for government filings.

Publicize the Plan to Your Members

Members won't use a plan if they don't know about it, and a plan will not be successful if it is unused. Publicity must be vocal and ongoing. Announce it in newsletters, flyers, meetings, and on bulletin boards.

Persistence is the key. All too frequently, leaders of an organization assume that a single announcement is all that's needed. They expect members to see the value of the plan and remember that it is available. Most organization members, though, are not as involved as the leadership. Therefore, it takes more publicity than the leadership usually expects in order to reach and maintain the desired level of awareness.

Summary

A successful free legal services plan involves designing a program, choosing the lawyers, and publicizing the plan. To learn more about these steps or to order a $45 how-to manual, call me at (403) 525-9282.

Sincerely,

Gary T. Hryniuk

Gary T. Hryniuk
Executive Director

GTR:pas

Tips for Letter Reports

- Use letter format for short informal reports sent to outsiders.
- Organize the facts into divisions with consistent headings.
- Single-space the body.
- Double-space between paragraphs.
- Leave two blank lines above each side heading, if space allows.
- Create side margins of 1 to 1.25 inches.
- Start the date 2 inches from the top or one blank line below the last line of the letterhead.
- Add a second-page heading, if necessary, consisting of the addressee's name, the page number, and the date.

MEMO FORMAT. For short informal reports that stay within organizations, memo format is appropriate. Memo reports begin with essential background information, using standard headings: *Date*, *To*, *From*, and *Subject*. Like letter reports, memo reports differ from regular memos in length, use of headings, and deliberate organization. Note that the writer in Figure 8.2 attaches the report to an email message, which introduces the attachment.

DIGITAL SLIDE FORMAT. Because reports are often presented within companies to managers and other employees, it has become quite common today for informal internal reports to be created as slides in PowerPoint or another presentation

FIGURE 8.3 | Informal Report Formatted as Slides

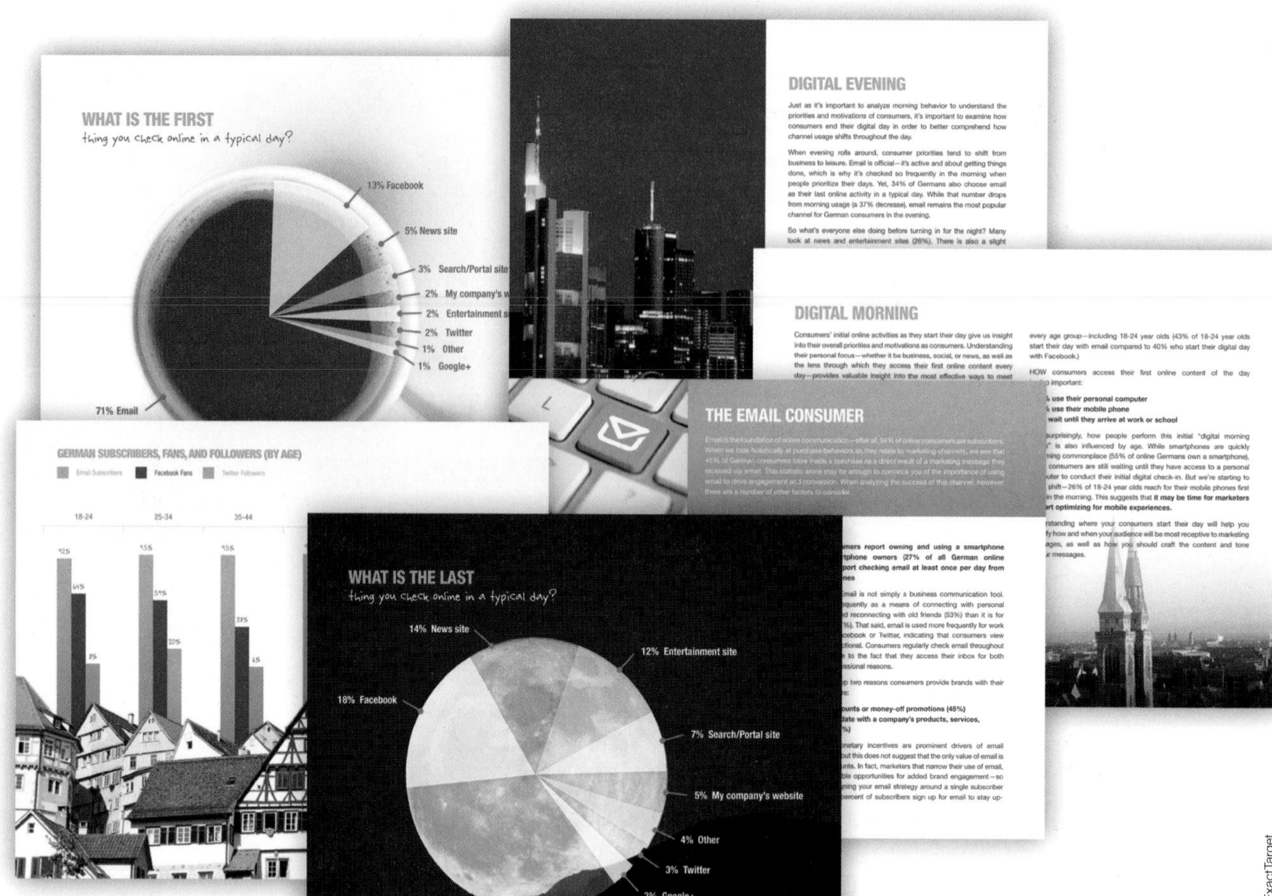

http://www.exacttarget.com/resource-center/digital-marketing/infographics/sff-german-digital-republic

ExactTarget

software. During a presentation, the slides are used to help the presenter discuss the report. The presenter can also choose to email or otherwise distribute the PowerPoint deck before the presentation or afterward. An example of an informal report in slide format is shown in Figure 8.3.

INFOGRAPHICS. Infographics are visual representations of data or information. They display complex information quickly and clearly, and are easier to understand than written text. Infographics are also affordable and easily shared on social media platforms. In fact, a good infographic can go viral when viewers embed and spread the word about it on their social media networks. Infographics can tell compelling stories that help all types of organizations attract and inform consumers, as can be seen in Figure 8.4.

TEMPLATE FORMAT. Templates (either company-produced or available online, for example, from Microsoft Word) are often used for repetitive data, such as monthly sales reports, performance appraisals, merchandise inventories, expense claims, and personnel and financial reports. Standardized headings in these templates save time for the writer. Templates also make similar information easy to locate and ensure that all necessary information is provided.

MANUSCRIPT FORMAT. For longer, more formal reports, use manuscript format. Such reports begin with a title followed by systematically displayed headings and

FIGURE 8.4 | Informal Report Formatted as Infographic

Santé publique Ontario
PARTENAIRES POUR LA SANTÉ

What can you do
to support physical activity in children?

GET O.U.T. AND BE ACTIVE!

Outside in nature
Using community resources
Together as a family

Full infographic and references can be found at:
www.publichealthontario.ca/ParentalSupport

Public Health Ontario

subheadings. You will see examples of proposals and formal reports using manuscript format in Chapter 9.

8.2b Effective Report Headings

Headings assist readers in comprehending the organization of a report. Viewers can see major ideas at a glance. Also, headings provide resting points for the mind and the eye, breaking up large chunks of text into manageable and readable segments.

Report writers may use functional, talking, or combination headings, examples of which are shown in Figure 8.5. To create effective report headings, follow these basic guidelines:

- **Use a clear hierarchy of heading levels.** A hierarchy refers to the level of importance of the headings in a document. Some reports have one level of heading and others may have three. A heading's placement, size, and font should match those of the other headings in the same level. Writers may use varying font styles and sizes, but the hierarchy must be clear to the reader. Remember, too, that reports are easier to follow when they use not more than three heading levels. Figure 8.6 illustrates the hierarchy of report heading levels.
- **Capitalize and emphasize carefully.** A writer might choose to use all capital letters for main titles, such as a report or chapter title. For first- and second-level headings, they follow the traditional rules for headings: capitalize the first letter of main words such as nouns, verbs, adjectives, adverbs, and so on. Do not capitalize articles (*a, an, the*), conjunctions (*and, but, or, nor*), and prepositions with three or fewer letters (*in, to, by, for*) unless they are the first or last words in the heading. Headings generally appear in bold font, as shown in Figure 8.6.
- **Create grammatically equal heading levels.** Create headings that are grammatically equal, or parallel, within the same level. For example, *Developing Product Teams* and *Presenting Plan to Management* are parallel headings; they both

FIGURE 8.5 | Three Heading Types for Reports

Functional Headings	Talking Headings	Combination Headings
• Background • Findings • Personnel • Production Costs	• Lack of Space and Cost Compound Parking Program • Survey Shows Support for Parking Fees	• Introduction: Lack of Parking Reaches Crisis Proportions • Parking Recommendations: Shuttle and New Structures

FIGURE 8.6 | Hierarchy of Headings in Reports

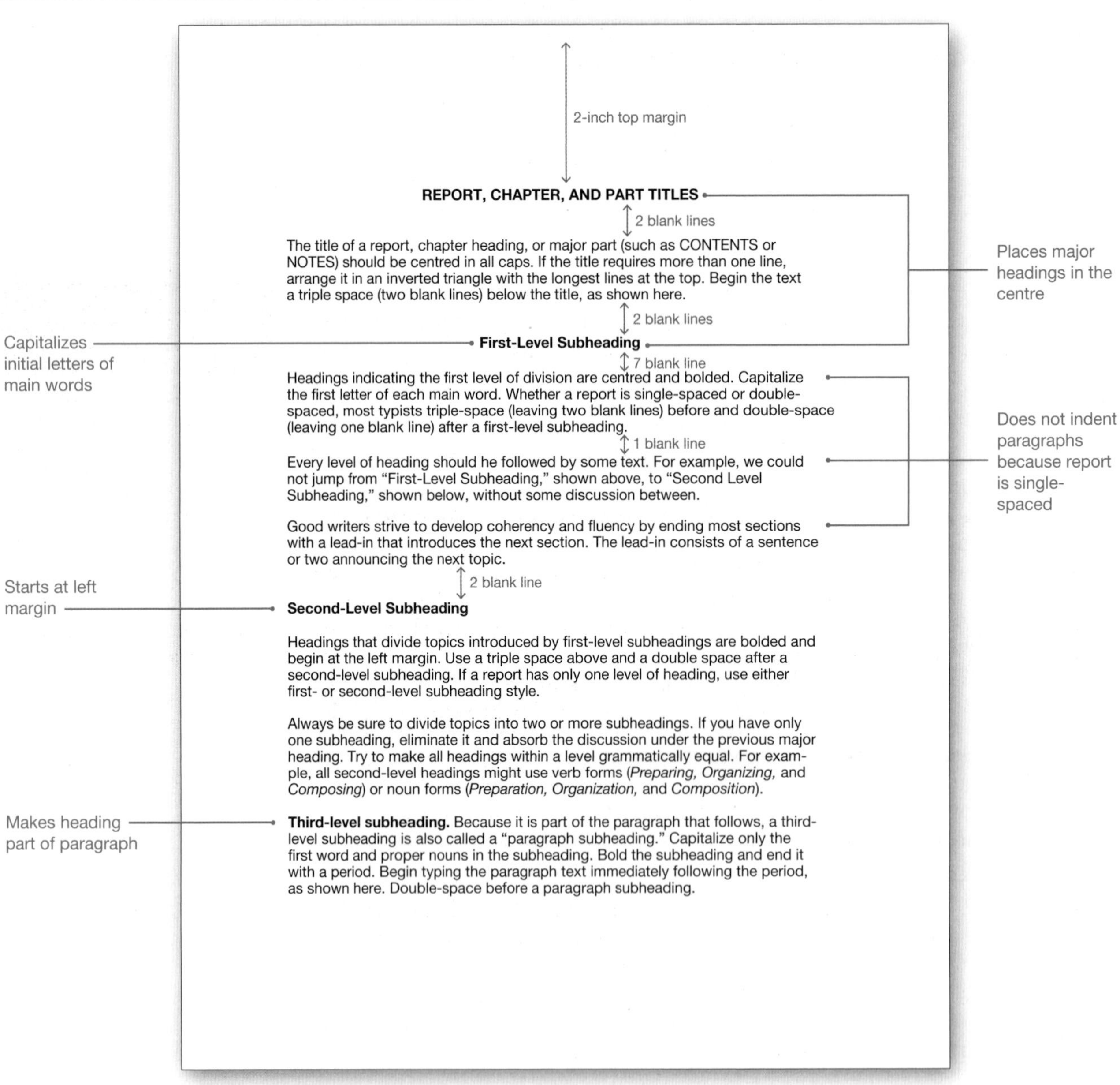

REPORT, CHAPTER, AND PART TITLES

The title of a report, chapter heading, or major part (such as CONTENTS or NOTES) should be centred in all caps. If the title requires more than one line, arrange it in an inverted triangle with the longest lines at the top. Begin the text a triple space (two blank lines) below the title, as shown here.

First-Level Subheading

Headings indicating the first level of division are centred and bolded. Capitalize the first letter of each main word. Whether a report is single-spaced or double-spaced, most typists triple-space (leaving two blank lines) before and double-space (leaving one blank line) after a first-level subheading.

Every level of heading should he followed by some text. For example, we could not jump from "First-Level Subheading," shown above, to "Second Level Subheading," shown below, without some discussion between.

Good writers strive to develop coherency and fluency by ending most sections with a lead-in that introduces the next section. The lead-in consists of a sentence or two announcing the next topic.

Second-Level Subheading

Headings that divide topics introduced by first-level subheadings are bolded and begin at the left margin. Use a triple space above and a double space after a second-level subheading. If a report has only one level of heading, use either first- or second-level subheading style.

Always be sure to divide topics into two or more subheadings. If you have only one subheading, eliminate it and absorb the discussion under the previous major heading. Try to make all headings within a level grammatically equal. For example, all second-level headings might use verb forms (*Preparing, Organizing,* and *Composing*) or noun forms (*Preparation, Organization,* and *Composition*).

Third-level subheading. Because it is part of the paragraph that follows, a third-level subheading is also called a "paragraph subheading." Capitalize only the first word and proper nouns in the subheading. Bold the subheading and end it with a period. Begin typing the paragraph text immediately following the period, as shown here. Double-space before a paragraph subheading.

begin with an action word ending in *-ing*. *Development of Product Teams* and *Presenting Plan to Management* are not parallel headings.

- **For short reports use one or two heading levels.** In a short report, first-level headings might be bold and left-aligned; second-level headings might be bold paragraph headings.
- **Include at least one heading per report page, but don't end the page with a stand-alone heading.** Headings increase the readability and add visual appeal to report pages. Try to use at least one heading per page to break up blocks of text and reveal the content's topic. If a heading at the bottom of a page gets separated from the text that follows, move that heading to the top of the following page.
- **Apply punctuation correctly.** Stand-alone bold headings do not require end punctuation. Paragraph headings, on the other hand, are followed by a period, which separates them from the text that follows.
- **Keep headings short but clear.** One-word headings are emphatic but not always clear. For example, the heading *Project* does not adequately describe the expectations of a summer internship project at an energy company. A better heading would be *(Company name)'s Internship Expectations*. Keep your headings brief (no more than eight words), but make them meaningful. Clarity is more important than brevity.

8.3 Determining the Problem and Purpose in Informal Reports

Simple informal reports might not require much research or data analysis; however, complex reports will. Whatever the case, analyzing the problem your report addresses and its purpose will keep it on target and determine how much data and research is needed. The following guidelines will help you plan your report and gather relevant data.

OFFICE INSIDER

A nonprofit organization polled 120 businesses to find out what type of writing they required of their employees. More than half of the business leaders responded that they "frequently" or "almost always" produce technical reports (59 percent), formal reports (62 percent), and memos and correspondence (70 percent).

8.3a Problem and Purpose Statements

The first step in writing a report is analyzing or determining the problem the report will address. Preparing a written problem statement helps clarify the task. Suppose a pharmaceutical company wants to investigate the problem of high transportation costs for its sales representatives. Some sales reps visit clients using company-leased cars; others drive their own cars and are reimbursed for expenses. The leasing agreements for 12 cars expire in three months. The company wants to investigate the transportation choices and report the findings before the leases are renewed. The following problem statement helps clarify the reason for the report:

> **Problem statement:** The leases on all company cars will expire in three months. We must decide whether to renew them or develop a new policy regarding transportation for sales reps. Expenses and reimbursement paperwork for employee-owned cars are excessive.

A statement of purpose further defines the report's scope. To begin, develop questions that help clarify the purpose: Should the company compare the costs for buying and leasing cars? Should the company gather current data on reimbursement costs for those driving personal cars? Will the report writers evaluate the data and recommend a course of action? Should the sales reps' reactions be considered? Then write a statement of purpose that answers the questions.

Statement of purpose: To recommend a plan that provides sales reps with cars to be used in their calls. The report will compare costs for three plans: outright ownership, leasing, and compensation for employee-owned cars. Data will include the sales reps' reactions to each plan.

Preparing a written purpose statement is a good idea because it limits the scope and keeps the project on target. In writing useful purpose statements, choose action verbs that say what you intend to do: *analyze, choose, investigate, compare, justify, evaluate, explain*, and so on. Notice that the preceding purpose statement uses the action verbs *recommend* and *compare*.

Begin a report by stating the problem to be solved, question to be answered, or task to be completed. Then, draft a statement of purpose. Be able to explain why you are writing the report.

Some reports require only a simple statement of purpose (e.g., to investigate expanded teller hours, to select a manager from among four candidates, to describe the position of accounts supervisor, while others require expanded purpose statements.

8.3b Gather Data

A professional report, even an informal one, is based on solid, accurate, verifiable facts found in primary and secondary research sources. Typical sources for informal reports include company records; surveys, interviews; observation, and secondary research from printed and digital sources like newspaper articles.

The facts for reports are often obtained from company records, observation, surveys, interviews, and secondary research.

COMPANY RECORDS. Many business-related reports begin with an analysis of company files. From them you can observe past performance and methods used to solve previous problems. You can collect pertinent facts that will help determine a course of action. For example, if a telecommunications company is interested in revamping the design of the bills it sends to customers, the project manager assigned to this task would want to gather examples of previous bill designs to ensure that improvements are made and old designs aren't reused.

OBSERVATION. Another logical source of data for many problems lies in personal observation and experience. For example, if you were writing a report on the need for additional computer equipment, you might observe how much the current equipment is being used and for what purpose.

SURVEYS. Primary data from groups of people can be collected most efficiently and economically by conducting surveys. For example, if you were part of a committee investigating the success of a campus-wide recycling program, you might begin by using a questionnaire to survey use of the program by students and faculty. You might also do some informal telephoning to see if departments on campus know about the program and are using it.

INTERVIEWS. Talking with individuals directly concerned with the problem produces excellent primary information. Interviews also allow for one-on-one communication, thus giving you an opportunity to explain your questions and ideas in eliciting the most accurate information. For example, a food company adding a new low-fat organic bar to its nutrition bar line would solicit interview or focus-group feedback before releasing the new product to the market. Questions posed to people paid to taste the sample bar might include "Did you find the bar tasty? Nutritious? Healthy?" and "Did you find the packaging attractive? Easy to open?"

SECONDARY RESEARCH. You will probably be interested in finding examples from other organizations that shed light on the problem identified in your report. For example, an automobile parts manufacturer eager to drum up new business in the hybrid and electric vehicle market could do in-house research or pay for

WORKPLACE IN FOCUS

Because of the Internet, gathering and analyzing survey data for business reports has never been easier. Since launching in 1999, SurveyMonkey has become the world's largest survey company. The firm helps companies and other researchers conduct millions of surveys online daily. SurveyMonkey provides online templates and sound survey methodologies, and business managers simply plug-in the questions they need answered and hit Send. Surveys take place online, with results appearing in real-time, ready for use in business reports.[1] *What are some of the most common uses of surveys in business?*

Dusit/Shutterstock.com

professional research into hybrid and electric vehicle manufacturing. Hundreds of articles on this topic are available electronically through online resources, such as library databases. From a home, office, or library computer, you can obtain access to vast amounts of information provided by governments, newspapers, magazines, and companies from all over the world. Using search engines such as Google and Google Scholar will also yield hundreds of results on any topic.

When doing secondary research on the Internet, an extra step must be taken that isn't necessary when using library databases. You need to verify the accuracy of your sources. Because the Internet is a public space where anyone can post information, you must be able to separate credible, useful information from opinion and noncredible sources. Do this by asking yourself a number of questions, which are discussed in more detail in the Communication Workshop in the MindTap.

8.4 Writing Informal Informational Reports

Informational reports describe periodic, recurring activities (such as monthly sales or weekly customer calls) as well as situational, nonrecurring events (such as trips, conferences, and special projects). Short informational reports may also include summaries of longer publications. Most informational reports have one thing in common: a neutral or receptive audience. The readers of informational reports do not need to be persuaded; they simply need to be informed.

You can expect to write many informational reports as an entry-level or middle-management employee. These reports generally deliver nonsensitive data and are therefore written directly. Although the writing style is usually conversational and informal, the report contents must be clear to all readers.

8.4a Trip, Convention, and Conference Reports

Employees sent on business trips to conventions and conferences typically submit reports to document the events they attended and what they learned. These reports often inform management about business trends, procedures, legal requirements, or other information that would affect their operations and products.

Reports that provide data are informational; reports that draw conclusions and make recommendations are analytical.

When writing a trip or conference report, select the most relevant material and organize it coherently. Generally, it is best not to use chronological sequencing (*in the morning we did X, at lunch we heard Y, and in the afternoon we did Z*). Instead, you should focus on three to five topics in which your reader will be interested. These items become the body of the report. Then simply add an introduction and a closing, and your report is organized. Here is a general outline for trip, conference, and convention reports:

- Begin by identifying the event (name, date, and location) and previewing the topics that were discussed.
- In the body, summarize the main topics that might benefit others in the organization. Use headings and bullets to add readability.
- Close by expressing appreciation, mentioning the value of the trip or event, and offering to share the information.
- Itemize your expenses, if requested, on a separate sheet.

Prakash Kohli was recently authorized to attend an IT conference in Germany. His boss, David Wong, encouraged Prakash to attend and asked him to come back and explain what he learned from the experts. When he returns, Prakash writes the conference report shown in Figure 8.7. He includes information that would most benefit the employees at Future Engine. This is an example of a direct-strategy report.

8.4b Progress, Status, and Milestone Reports

Continuing projects often require progress or status reports to describe their status. When you or your team use project management principles, the report may be called a milestone report. Such reports may be external (telling customers how their projects are advancing) or internal (informing management of the status of activities). Progress reports typically follow this development strategy:

- The purpose and nature of the project
- A complete summary of the work already completed
- A thorough description of work currently in progress, including personnel, methods, and obstacles, as well as attempts to remedy obstacles
- A forecast of future activities in relation to the scheduled completion date, including recommendations and requests

Progress reports tell management whether nonroutine projects are on schedule.

In Figure 8.8 Avrom Gil explains the market research project being done on the impact of a recent industry/consumer show. He begins with a statement summarizing the research project in relation to the expected completion date. He then updates the client with a brief summary of the project's progress. He emphasizes the present status of the project and offers some preliminary data to build interest then concludes by describing the next steps to be taken.

Some business communicators use progress reports to do more than merely report progress. These reports can also be used to offer ideas and suggest possibilities. Let's say you are reporting on the progress of redesigning the company website. You might suggest a different way to handle customer responses. Instead of making an official recommendation, which might be rejected, you can lay the foundation for a change within your progress report. Progress reports can also be used to build the image of a dedicated, conscientious employee.

8.4c Minutes Reports

Minutes reports provide a summary of what happened in a meeting. Traditional minutes, illustrated in Figure 8.9, are written whenever a formal meeting has taken place. If you are the secretary or note taker of a meeting, you'll want to write minutes that do the following:

- Provide the name of the group, as well as the date, time, and place of the meeting.
- Identify the names of attendees and absentees, if appropriate.
- Describe the disposition of previous minutes (not required in informal meetings).

FIGURE 8.7 | Conference Report

Subject: Trip Report from the CeBIT Trade Show

Hi, Dave!

As you requested, I am sending you the attached trip report describing my amazing experiences at the largest IT trade show in the world, the CeBIT.

Thank you for the opportunity. I networked with a lot of people and had an enjoyable time.

Cheers,
Prakash

Prakash Kohli, Developer
Future Engine, Inc.
408.532.3434 Ext. 811
pkohli@future-engine.com
www.future-engine.com

Uses informal form of address

Announces attachment

Uses informal yet professional language

Includes complimentary close and signature block

FUTURE ENGINE, INC.
MEMORANDUM

Date: March 16, 2018

To: David Wong, IT Director

From: Prakash Kohli, Developer PK

Subject: Trip Report from the CeBIT Trade Show in Hannover, Germany

As you know, I attended the huge CeBIT computer show in Hannover on March 4–9. CeBIT runs for six days and attracts almost 500,000 visitors from Germany, Europe, and all over the world to the famed Hannover fairgrounds. It features 27 halls full of technology and people. If you've been to Comdex Las Vegas in the fall, think of a show that is easily five times larger. Let me describe our booth, overall trends, and the contacts I made in Hannover.

Our Booth at the Fair

Our Future Engine booth spanned two floors. The ground floor had a theater with large screen, demonstration stations, and partners showing their products and services. Upstairs we had tables and chairs for business meetings, press interviews, food, and drinks—along with a cooking area and a dishwasher. Because no one has time to get food elsewhere, we ate in the booth.

Hot Tech Trends

The top story at this year's CeBIT was Green IT. The expo management decided to spotlight a range of topics dealing with Green IT, showcasing many approaches in the Green IT Village in Hall 9. The main focus centered on highly energy-efficient solutions and power-saving technologies and their contribution to climate protection. *Green IT* is the big buzzword now and was even dubbed the "Megatrend of this expo" by the organizer. Only the future will tell whether Green IT will be able to spawn attractive new business areas.

Customers and Prospects

CeBIT is a fantastic way to connect with customers and prospects. Sometimes it's a way of meeting people you only knew virtually. In this case, we had three fans of our Internetpakt.com podcast visit us at the booth: Jürgen Schmidt, Karin Richter, and Peter Jahn of MEGAFunk. All three came in our white FE T-Shirts, which could only be rewarded with new black Internetpakt.com T-Shirts. All in all, we made about 600 contacts and have 50 solid leads. The visit was definitely worthwhile and will pay off very soon.

In closing, this was probably one of the best conference experiences I've ever had. Customers and partners like FE; they are excited about our technology, and they want more. Some know us because of our software solutions and were surprised to learn that we sell hardware, too (this is a good sign). All want us to grow and gain in influence.

Check out my CeBIT photo gallery on Flickr for some more impressions of our booth at CeBIT with comments. Thank you for giving me the opportunity to network and to experience one of the biggest trade shows in the business. My itemized expenses and receipts are attached.

Identifies the event

Focuses on three main points

Summarizes key information

Highlights the value of the trip

Shows appreciation and mentions expenses

Tips for Trip Reports

- Use memo format for short informal reports sent within the organization.
- Identify the event (exact date, name, and location) and preview the topics to be discussed.
- Summarize in the body three to five main points that might benefit the reader.
- Itemize your expenses, if requested, on a separate sheet. Mention this in the report.
- Close by expressing appreciation, suggesting action to be taken, or synthesizing the value of the trip or event.

FIGURE 8.8 | Progress Report

Subject: Progress of CanDesign 2018 Research Project

Hi, Lina,

Please find attached the requested progress report.

If you have any questions, please give me a call.

Best,
Avrom

Short, professional message introduces attached progress report.

PROGRESS OF CANDESIGN 2018 RESEARCH PROJECT

To: ltersigni@canevent.ca
From: agil@westwindresearch.ca
Subject: Progress of CanDesign 2018 Research Project

[attachment]

Dear Ms. Tersigni,

Market research on the impact of CanDesign 2018 and implications for CanDesign 2019 has entered the analysis stage (phase 3). We are on schedule, based on our original project plan, and our final report will be available to you after February 27, 2018.

Section describes completed work concisely.

Accomplished so far

We have completed the first two phases of the project. Phase 1 (completed February 5, 2018) involved designing the survey questionnaire. Phase 2 (completed February 19, 2018) involved distributing the questionnaire to two groups: paid attendees of CanDesign 2018 and industry professionals, as well as collecting results. Over 700 completed questionnaires have been received to date (85% of target).

Section discusses current activities.

Current work

My team is analyzing the results of the questionnaire. Early results show high satisfaction levels (~80%) among attendees, but a small drop in satisfaction among industry professionals (~72%) compared with (~75% last year). In addition, a significant number of both attendees and professionals (~25% and ~27%) express dissatisfaction with the show website, especially its navigation design. We will be correlating 2018 results to both 2016 and 2017 results in hopes of showing trends.

Section lists tasks still to be completed.

Still to come

Before submitting our final report, we will need to perform the rest of our analysis and correlations. Also, we are convening two focus groups (as per project plan) to see whether one-on-one contact with attendees and industry professionals confirms the results of the questionnaires.

One unresolved issue is renumeration for focus group attendees. Before we invite attendees, I will need confirmation about what we can offer attendees at our focus groups. I will be in touch later today to speak with you about this.

We are largely on track for the completion of this market research project and look forward to sharing results with you on or after February 27.

Tips for Writing Progress Reports

- Identify the purpose and the nature of the project immediately.
- Supply background information only if the reader must be educated.
- Describe the work completed.
- Discuss the work in progress, including personnel, activities, methods, and locations.
- Identify problems and possible remedies.
- Consider future activities.
- Close by giving the expected date of completion.

FIGURE 8.9 | Minutes Report

Lor-Dan Produce Distribution
Safety Committee
Bi-annual Meeting Minutes
September 14, 2018

Present: A. Faccinelli, T. Loredan, M. Baransky, V. Singh

Absent: B. Fortier

Topics Discussed

1. Strategizing for our next Safe At Work inspection. Ministry of Labour officials will most probably be visiting the warehouse in early 2019 — we want to improve our scores. Should we hold a company-wide meeting, or rely on managers to filter down best practices within specific areas? Should we reach out to competitors who scored higher in 2013 to solicit advice?

2. Complying with Occupational Health and Safety Act provisions on Workplace Harrassment and Violence. We haven't drafted our policy yet, and are behind many of our competitors. Ministry of Labour regularly does blitz inspections looking for compliance in this area. Who should draft policy? Target dates? How do we make sure all Lor-Dan employees know and understand eventual policy?

Decisions

1. Hold company-wide meeting by November 1, 2018, to explain Safe at Work inspections and compliance. Reach out to two competitors by October 15, 2018, for advice on more successful compliance with Ministry inspections.

2. Harrassment and Violence policy should be drafted by subcommittee by October 15, 2018, for draft discussion at above meeting. Publish harassment and violence brochure and posters for distribution to employees and posting in warehouse.

Action Items

1. V. Singh and B. Fortier to organize meeting on or by November 1, 2018.
2. A. Faccinelli to contact competitors for advice by October 15, 2018.
3. T. Loredan, M. Baransky, and one employee to form subcommittee to draft harassment/violence policy by October 15, 2018.
4. Once above policy is finalized, ask C. Coletor (Director, HR) to print and distribute internally (estimated by November 15, 2018).

Next Meeting: March 15, 2019 Room and Agenda TBA

- Record new business, announcements, and reports.
- Include the precise wording of motions; record the vote and action taken.
- Conclude with the name and signature of the person recording the minutes.

Notice in Figure 8.9 that the writer of the minutes summarizes discussions rather than capturing every comment. However, when a decision is made, it is recorded as close to verbatim (i.e., word for word) as possible.

In more formal meetings, before a decision is taken a "motion" must be called and that motion voted on by the majority in the room. A formal minutes report would list these motions (who made it, seconded it, and the fact that it was passed), but few organizations use formal minutes any longer.

Meeting minutes record summaries of old business, new business, announcements, and reports, as well as the precise wording of motions.

8.4d Summary Reports

In today's economy, data is what drives organizations. Data is important because without it, business decisions cannot be made. Because there is a huge amount of data available today on any given topic, people who make decisions don't always

A summary condenses the primary ideas, conclusions, and recommendations of a longer publication.

have the time to read and review data on a particular problem, issue, or topic. Therefore, decision makers need the essential elements of an issue or problem presented in a short, logical, easy-to-understand format that helps them quickly grasp what's vital.

Any time you take what someone else has written or said and reduce it to a concise, accurate, and faithful version of the original—in your own words—you are summarizing. A well-written summary report does three things: it (1) provides all the important points from the original without introducing new material; (2) has a clear structure that often reflects the structure of the original material; and (3) is independent of the original, meaning the reader of the summary can glean all essential information in the original without having to refer to it.

In Figure 8.10, a new vice president of Corporate Social Responsibility asks one of his managers to do research on the state of sustainability reporting in Canada, as the company they work for has been criticized for not producing such a report.

There are four steps to writing an effective summary:

- **Read the material carefully for understanding.** Ideally, you will read the original three times: the first time to understand the topic; the second time to highlight the main points (usually no more than three in an article-length piece); and the third time to see the overall pattern.
- **Lay out the structure of your summary.** Simply write the main points you've underlined or highlighted in a list. For example, the manager summarizing the article found at the beginning of this chapter) has identified two main points and one solution/conclusion. To lay out the structure of her summary, she would write:

  Main point 1: 56% of companies on the TSX report on sustainability.

  Main point 2: However, the quality of reporting is declining, e.g. fewer companies using GRI guidelines.

  Solution/conclusion: While sustainability reporting may have plateaued, there's a need/appetite for increased reporting.

- **Write a first draft.** In this step, you take your list from the step before and convert it into your own words, in amplified full sentences. Our summary writer might draft write something like this:

  As requested, I've researched current opinion on sustainability reporting in Canadian companies.

  One useful article I found was by Kathrin Bohr on the Toronto Sustainability Speaker Series website. In Bohr's article, "Advancing Sustainability Reporting in Canada" (August 23, 2016), she makes the following points...

  She concludes by saying that even though sustainability reporting appears to have plateaued in 2016, there is an appetite among a number of constituencies for increased reporting.

  If you have any questions or would like me to provide more information or complete more research, just let me know.

  Regards,
  Bailey Bingley

- **Proofread and revise.** The final step of writing a summary, like any written document, is to proofread for grammar, spelling, punctuation, and style mistakes and to rewrite where necessary. A proofread and revised final version of this informational summary report appears in Figure 8.10.

FIGURE 8.10 | Summary Report

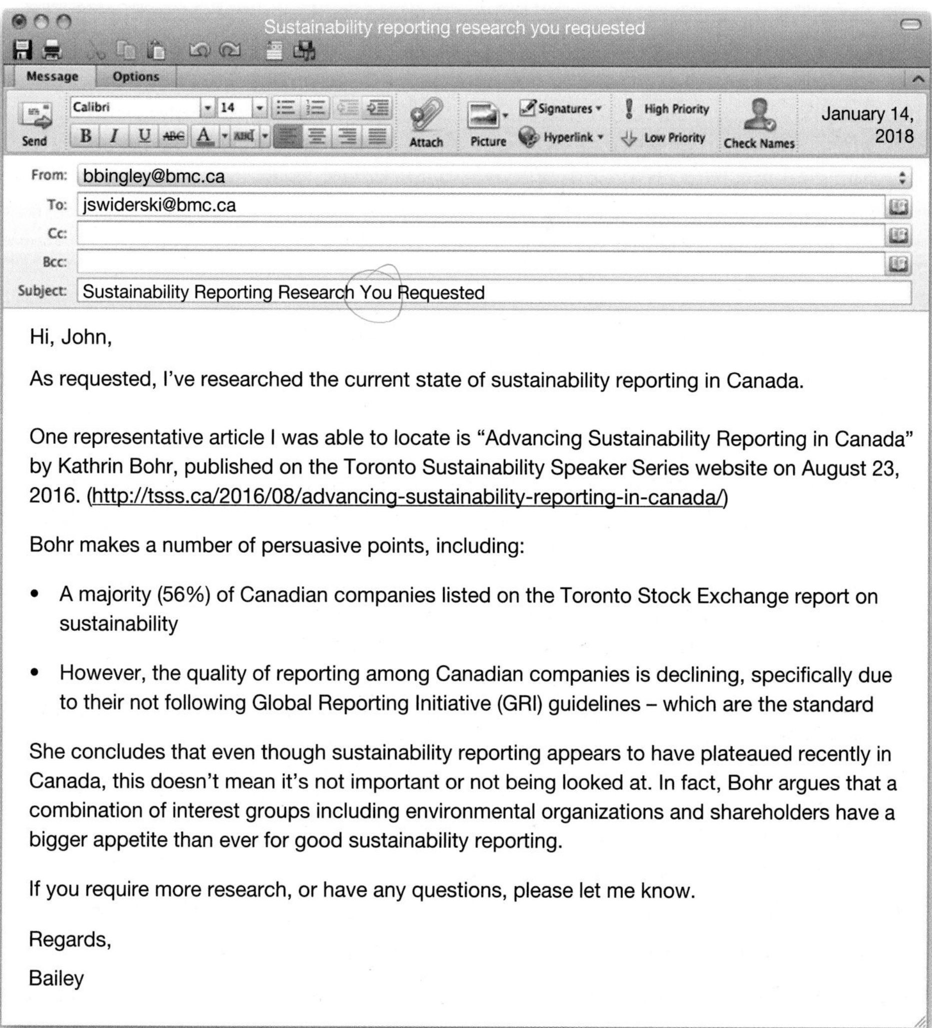
Sustainability reporting research you requested

From: bbingley@bmc.ca
To: jswiderski@bmc.ca
Cc:
Bcc:
Subject: Sustainability Reporting Research You Requested

January 14, 2018

Hi, John,

As requested, I've researched the current state of sustainability reporting in Canada.

One representative article I was able to locate is "Advancing Sustainability Reporting in Canada" by Kathrin Bohr, published on the Toronto Sustainability Speaker Series website on August 23, 2016. (http://tsss.ca/2016/08/advancing-sustainability-reporting-in-canada/)

Bohr makes a number of persuasive points, including:

- A majority (56%) of Canadian companies listed on the Toronto Stock Exchange report on sustainability
- However, the quality of reporting among Canadian companies is declining, specifically due to their not following Global Reporting Initiative (GRI) guidelines – which are the standard

She concludes that even though sustainability reporting appears to have plateaued recently in Canada, this doesn't mean it's not important or not being looked at. In fact, Bohr argues that a combination of interest groups including environmental organizations and shareholders have a bigger appetite than ever for good sustainability reporting.

If you require more research, or have any questions, please let me know.

Regards,

Bailey

8.5 Writing Informal Analytical Reports

Analytical reports involve collecting and analyzing data, evaluating the results, drawing conclusions, and making recommendations.

Analytical reports differ significantly from informational reports. Although both seek to collect and present data clearly, analytical reports also evaluate the data and typically try to persuade the reader to accept the conclusions and act on the recommendations. Informational reports emphasize facts; analytical reports emphasize reasoning and conclusions.

In some situations you may organize analytical reports directly with the conclusions and recommendations near the beginning. Directness is appropriate when the reader has confidence in the writer, based on either experience or credentials. Frontloading the recommendations also works when the topic is routine or familiar and the reader is supportive.

Directness can backfire, though. If you announce the recommendations too quickly, the reader may immediately object to a single idea. You may not have expected that this idea would trigger a negative reaction. Once the reader has an unfavourable mind-set, changing it may be difficult or impossible. A reader may also believe that you have oversimplified or overlooked something significant if you lay out all the recommendations before explaining how you arrived at them. When you must lead the reader through the process of discovering the solution or recommendation, use the indirect strategy: present conclusions and recommendations last.

Most analytical reports answer questions about specific problems and aid in decision making (e.g., *How can we use social media most effectively? Should we close the Moose Jaw plant? How can we improve customer service?*). Analytical reports provide conclusions that help management answer these questions.

8.5a Justification/Recommendation Reports

Justification/recommendation reports analyze a problem, discuss options, and present a recommendation, solution, or action to be taken.

Both managers and employees must occasionally write reports that justify or recommend something, such as buying equipment, changing a procedure, hiring an employee, consolidating departments, or investing funds. Large organizations sometimes prescribe how these reports should be organized; they use forms of templates with conventional headings. At other times, such reports are not standardized. For example, an employee takes it upon himself to write a report suggesting improvements in telephone customer service because he feels strongly about it. When you are free to select an organizational plan yourself, however, let your audience and topic determine your choice of direct or indirect structure.

For non-sensitive topics and recommendations that will be agreeable to readers, you can organize directly according to the following sequence:

- Identify the problem or need briefly in the introduction.
- Announce the recommendation, solution, or action concisely and with action verbs.
- Discuss pros, cons, and costs. Explain more fully the benefits of the recommendation or steps to be taken to solve the problem.
- Conclude with a summary specifying the recommendation and action to be taken.

Lara Brown, an executive assistant at a large petroleum and mining company in Calgary, applied the preceding process in writing the recommendation report shown in Figure 8.11. Her boss, the director of Human Resources, asked her to investigate ways to persuade employees to quit smoking. Lara explained that the company had banned smoking many years ago inside the buildings but never tried very hard to get smokers to actually kick the habit. Lara's job was to gather information about the problem and learn how other companies have helped workers stop smoking. The report would go to her boss, but Lara knew he would pass it along to the management council for approval.

If the report were just for her boss, Lara would put her recommendation right up front because she was sure he would support it. But the management council is another story. The managers need to be persuaded because of the costs involved—and because some of them are smokers. Therefore, Lara put the alternative she favoured last. To gain credibility, Lara footnoted her sources. She had enough material for a ten-page report, but she kept it to two pages to conform to her company's report policy.

INDIRECT STRATEGY. When a reader may oppose a recommendation or when circumstances suggest caution, do not rush to reveal your recommendation. Consider using the following sequence for an indirect approach to your recommendations:

- Refer to the problem in general terms, not to your recommendation, in the subject line.

- Describe the problem or need your recommendation addresses. Use specific examples, supporting statistics, and authoritative quotes to lend credibility to the seriousness of the problem.
- Discuss alternative solutions, beginning with the least likely to succeed.
- Present the most promising alternative (your recommendation) last.
- Show how the advantages of your recommendation outweigh its disadvantages.
- Summarize your recommendation. If appropriate, specify the action it requires.
- Ask for authorization to proceed, if necessary.

Feasibility reports analyze whether a proposal or plan will work.

8.5b Feasibility Reports

Feasibility reports examine the practicality and advisability of following a course of action. They answer this question: Will this plan or proposal work? Feasibility

FIGURE 8.11 | Justification/Recommendation Report

Date: October 11, 2018

To: Gordon McClure, Director, Human Resources

From: Lara Brown, Executive Assistant *LB*

Subject: Smoking Cessation Programs for Employees

At your request, I have examined measures that encourage employees to quit smoking. As company records show, approximately 23 percent of our employees still smoke, despite the antismoking and clean-air policies we adopted in 2017. To collect data for this report, I studied professional and government publications; I also inquired at companies and clinics about stop-smoking programs.

This report presents data describing the significance of the problem, three alternative solutions, and a recommendation based on my investigation.

Significance of Problem: Health Care and Productivity Losses

Employees who smoke are costly to any organization. The following statistics show the effects of smoking for workers and for organizations:

- Absenteeism is 40 to 50 percent greater among smoking employees.
- Accidents are two to three times greater among smokers.
- Bronchitis, lung and heart disease, cancer, and early death are more frequent among smokers (Arhelger, 2016, p. 4).

Although our clean-air policy prohibits smoking in the building, shop, and office, we have done little to encourage employees to stop smoking. Many workers still go outside to smoke at lunch and breaks. Other companies have been far more proactive in their attempts to stop employee smoking. Many companies have found that persuading employees to stop smoking was a decisive factor in reducing their health insurance premiums. Following is a discussion of three common stop-smoking measures tried by other companies, along with a projected cost factor for each (Rindfleisch, 2016, p. 4).

Alternative 1: Literature and Events

The least expensive and easiest stop-smoking measure involves the distribution of literature, such as "The Ten-Step Plan" from Smokefree Enterprises and government pamphlets citing smoking dangers. Some companies have also sponsored events such as the Great Canadian Smoke-Out, a one-day occasion intended to develop group spirit in spurring smokers to quit. "Studies show, however," says one expert, "that literature and company-sponsored events have little permanent effect in helping smokers quit" (Mendel, 2015, p. 108).

Cost: Negligible

Introduces purpose of report, tells method of data collection, and previews organization

Avoids revealing recommendation immediately

Uses headings that combine function and description

Documents data sources for credibility; uses APA style citing author and year in the text

Gordon McClure October 11, 2018 Page 2

Alternative 2: Stop-Smoking Programs Outside the Workplace

Local clinics provide treatment programs in classes at their centers. Here in Calgary we have the Smokers' Treatment Centre, ACC Motivation Centre, and New-Choice Program for Stopping Smoking. These behaviour-modification stop-smoking programs are acknowledged to be more effective than literature distribution or incentive programs. However, studies of companies using off-workplace programs show that many employees fail to attend regularly and do not complete the programs.

Cost: $1,200 per employee, three-month individual program (Your-Choice Program)
$900 per employee, three-month group session

Highlights costs for easy comparison

Alternative 3: Stop-Smoking Programs at the Workplace

Many clinics offer workplace programs with counsellors meeting employees in company conference rooms. These programs have the advantage of keeping a firm's employees together so that they develop a group spirit and exert pressure on each other to succeed. The most successful programs are on company premises and also on company time. Employees participating in such programs had a 72 percent greater success record than employees attending the same stop-smoking program at an outside clinic (Honda, 2015, p. 35). A disadvantage of this arrangement, of course, is lost work time—amounting to about two hours a week for three months.

Arranges alternatives so that most effective is last

Cost: $900 per employee, two hours per week of release time for three months

Conclusions and Recommendation

Summarizes findings and ends with specific recommendation

Smokers require discipline, counselling, and professional assistance to kick the nicotine habit, as explained at the Canadian Cancer Society website ("Guide to Quitting Smoking," 2016). Workplace stop-smoking programs on company time are more effective than literature, incentives, and off-workplace programs. If our goal is to reduce health care costs and lead our employees to healthful lives, we should invest in a workplace stop-smoking program with release time for smokers. Although the program temporarily reduces productivity, we can expect to recapture that loss in lower health care premiums and healthier employees.

Therefore, I recommend that we begin a stop-smoking treatment program on company premises with two hours per week of release time for participants for three months.

Reveals recommendation only after discussing all alternatives

Lists all references in APA Style

Gordon McClure October 11, 2018 Page 3

References

Magazine — Arhelger, Z. (2016, November 5). The end of smoking. *Canadian Business*, pp. 3–8.

Website article — Guide to quitting smoking. (2016, October 17). Retrieved from the Canadian Cancer Society website: http://www.cancer.ca

Journal article, database — Honda, E. M. (2015) Managing anti-smoking campaigns: The case for company programs. *Management Quarterly 32*(2), 29–47. Retrieved from http://search.ebscohost.com/

Book — Mendel, I. A. (2015) *The puff stops here*. Toronto: Science Publications.

Newspaper article — Rindfleisch, T. (2016, December 4). Smoke-free workplaces can help smokers quit, expert says. *Evening Chronicle*, p. 4.

Tips for Memo Reports

- Use memo format for short (eight or fewer pages) informal reports within an organization.
- Create side margins of 1 to 1.25 inches.
- Start the date 2 inches from the top or 1 blank line below the last line of the letterhead.
- Sign your initials on the *From* line.
- Use an informal, conversational style.
- For a receptive audience, put recommendations first.
- For an unreceptive audience, put recommendations last.

reports are typically internal reports written to advise on matters such as consolidating departments, offering a wellness program to employees, or hiring an outside firm to handle a company's accounting or computing operations. These reports may also be written by consultants called in to investigate a problem. The focus in these reports is on the decision: stopping or proceeding with the proposal. Since your role is not to persuade the reader to accept the decision, you'll want to present the decision immediately. In writing feasibility reports, consider this plan:

- Announce your decision immediately.
- Describe the background and problem necessitating the proposal.
- Discuss the benefits of the proposal.
- Describe any problems that may result.
- Calculate the costs associated with the proposal, if appropriate.
- Show the time frame necessary for implementation of the proposal.

Elizabeth Webb, customer service manager for a large insurance company in London, Ontario, wrote the feasibility report shown in Figure 8.12. Because her company had been losing customer service reps (CSRs) after they were trained, she talked with the vice president about the problem. He didn't want her to take time away from her job to investigate what other companies were doing to retain their CSRs. Instead, he suggested that they hire a consultant to investigate. The vice president then wanted to know whether the consultant's plan was feasible. Although Elizabeth's report is only one page long, it provides all the necessary information: background, benefits, problems, costs, and time frame.

8.5c Yardstick Reports

Yardstick reports examine problems with two or more solutions. To determine the best solution, the writer establishes criteria by which to compare the alternatives. The criteria then act as a yardstick against which all the alternatives are measured, as shown in Figure 8.13. The yardstick approach is effective for companies that must establish specifications for equipment purchases and then compare each manufacturer's product with the established specs. The yardstick approach is also effective when exact specifications cannot be established.

For example, a yardstick report might help a company decide on an inexpensive job perk. Perks are nontraditional benefits that appeal to current and future employees. Popular job perks include free food and beverages, flexible scheduling and telecommuting options, and on-site gyms and fitness classes. A yardstick report may help a company decide what job perks make the most sense. If the company wants to encourage long-term wellness, it might consider offering employees discounted fitness club memberships, on-site yoga classes, or ergonomic workstations. The yardstick report would describe and compare the three alternatives in terms of (a) costs, (b) long-term benefits, and (c) expected participation level. After interviewing employees and talking to people whose companies offer similar benefits, report writers would compare the alternatives and recommend the most workable job perk.

The real advantage to yardstick reports is that alternatives can be measured consistently using the same criteria. Writers using a yardstick approach typically do the following:

- Begin by describing the problem or need.
- Explain possible solutions and alternatives.
- Establish criteria for comparing the alternatives; tell how the criteria were selected or developed.
- Discuss and evaluate each alternative in terms of the criteria.
- Draw conclusions and make recommendations.

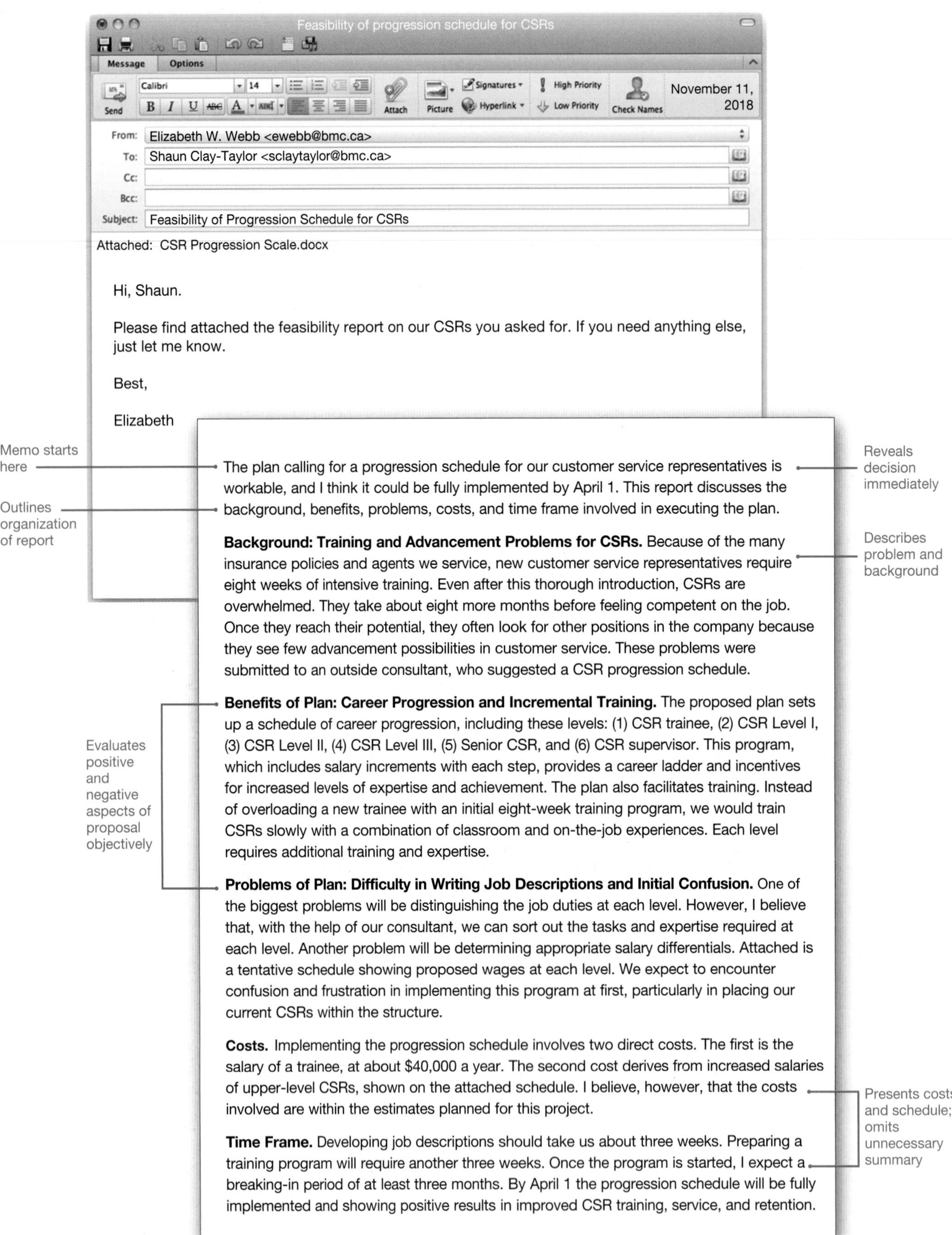

Feasibility of progression schedule for CSRs
Message
Options
Send
Calibri
14
Attach
Picture
Signatures
Hyperlink
High Priority
Low Priority
Check Names
November 11, 2018
From: Elizabeth W. Webb <ewebb@bmc.ca>
To: Shaun Clay-Taylor <sclaytaylor@bmc.ca>
Cc:
Bcc:
Subject: Feasibility of Progression Schedule for CSRs
Attached: CSR Progression Scale.docx
Hi, Shaun.
Please find attached the feasibility report on our CSRs you asked for. If you need anything else, just let me know.
Best,
Elizabeth
Memo starts here
Outlines organization of report
Reveals decision immediately
Describes problem and background
Evaluates positive and negative aspects of proposal objectively
Presents costs and schedule; omits unnecessary summary

The plan calling for a progression schedule for our customer service representatives is workable, and I think it could be fully implemented by April 1. This report discusses the background, benefits, problems, costs, and time frame involved in executing the plan.

Background: Training and Advancement Problems for CSRs. Because of the many insurance policies and agents we service, new customer service representatives require eight weeks of intensive training. Even after this thorough introduction, CSRs are overwhelmed. They take about eight more months before feeling competent on the job. Once they reach their potential, they often look for other positions in the company because they see few advancement possibilities in customer service. These problems were submitted to an outside consultant, who suggested a CSR progression schedule.

Benefits of Plan: Career Progression and Incremental Training. The proposed plan sets up a schedule of career progression, including these levels: (1) CSR trainee, (2) CSR Level I, (3) CSR Level II, (4) CSR Level III, (5) Senior CSR, and (6) CSR supervisor. This program, which includes salary increments with each step, provides a career ladder and incentives for increased levels of expertise and achievement. The plan also facilitates training. Instead of overloading a new trainee with an initial eight-week training program, we would train CSRs slowly with a combination of classroom and on-the-job experiences. Each level requires additional training and expertise.

Problems of Plan: Difficulty in Writing Job Descriptions and Initial Confusion. One of the biggest problems will be distinguishing the job duties at each level. However, I believe that, with the help of our consultant, we can sort out the tasks and expertise required at each level. Another problem will be determining appropriate salary differentials. Attached is a tentative schedule showing proposed wages at each level. We expect to encounter confusion and frustration in implementing this program at first, particularly in placing our current CSRs within the structure.

Costs. Implementing the progression schedule involves two direct costs. The first is the salary of a trainee, at about $40,000 a year. The second cost derives from increased salaries of upper-level CSRs, shown on the attached schedule. I believe, however, that the costs involved are within the estimates planned for this project.

Time Frame. Developing job descriptions should take us about three weeks. Preparing a training program will require another three weeks. Once the program is started, I expect a breaking-in period of at least three months. By April 1 the progression schedule will be fully implemented and showing positive results in improved CSR training, service, and retention.

Maria Rios, benefits administrator for computer manufacturer CompuTech, was called on to write the report in Figure 8.13 comparing outplacement agencies and recommending one to management.

Maria gathered information about three outplacement agencies and wanted to organize it systematically. She chose to evaluate each agency using the following categories: counselling services, administrative and research assistance, reputation, and costs.

Maria shows the results of her research in Table 1 and Table 2. She uses the criteria as headings and discusses how each agency meets, or fails to meet, each criterion. Making a recommendation is easy once Maria creates the tables and compares the agencies.

FIGURE 8.13 | Yardstick Report

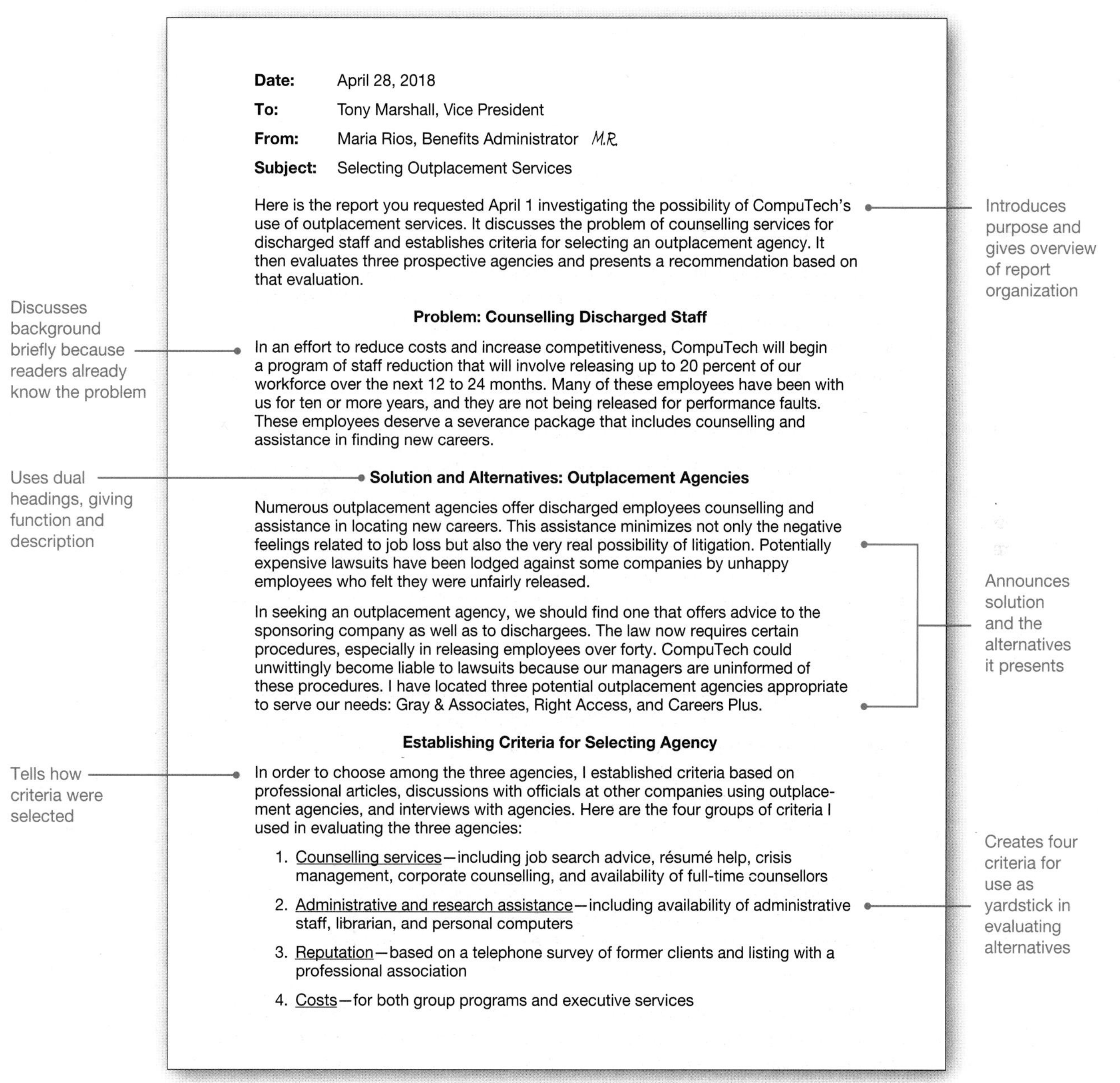

Date: April 28, 2018

To: Tony Marshall, Vice President

From: Maria Rios, Benefits Administrator *M.R.*

Subject: Selecting Outplacement Services

Here is the report you requested April 1 investigating the possibility of CompuTech's use of outplacement services. It discusses the problem of counselling services for discharged staff and establishes criteria for selecting an outplacement agency. It then evaluates three prospective agencies and presents a recommendation based on that evaluation.

Problem: Counselling Discharged Staff

In an effort to reduce costs and increase competitiveness, CompuTech will begin a program of staff reduction that will involve releasing up to 20 percent of our workforce over the next 12 to 24 months. Many of these employees have been with us for ten or more years, and they are not being released for performance faults. These employees deserve a severance package that includes counselling and assistance in finding new careers.

Solution and Alternatives: Outplacement Agencies

Numerous outplacement agencies offer discharged employees counselling and assistance in locating new careers. This assistance minimizes not only the negative feelings related to job loss but also the very real possibility of litigation. Potentially expensive lawsuits have been lodged against some companies by unhappy employees who felt they were unfairly released.

In seeking an outplacement agency, we should find one that offers advice to the sponsoring company as well as to dischargees. The law now requires certain procedures, especially in releasing employees over forty. CompuTech could unwittingly become liable to lawsuits because our managers are uninformed of these procedures. I have located three potential outplacement agencies appropriate to serve our needs: Gray & Associates, Right Access, and Careers Plus.

Establishing Criteria for Selecting Agency

In order to choose among the three agencies, I established criteria based on professional articles, discussions with officials at other companies using outplacement agencies, and interviews with agencies. Here are the four groups of criteria I used in evaluating the three agencies:

1. Counselling services—including job search advice, résumé help, crisis management, corporate counselling, and availability of full-time counsellors
2. Administrative and research assistance—including availability of administrative staff, librarian, and personal computers
3. Reputation—based on a telephone survey of former clients and listing with a professional association
4. Costs—for both group programs and executive services

Introduces purpose and gives overview of report organization
Discusses background briefly because readers already know the problem
Uses dual headings, giving function and description
Announces solution and the alternatives it presents
Tells how criteria were selected
Creates four criteria for use as yardstick in evaluating alternatives

FIGURE 8.13 | *(Continued)*

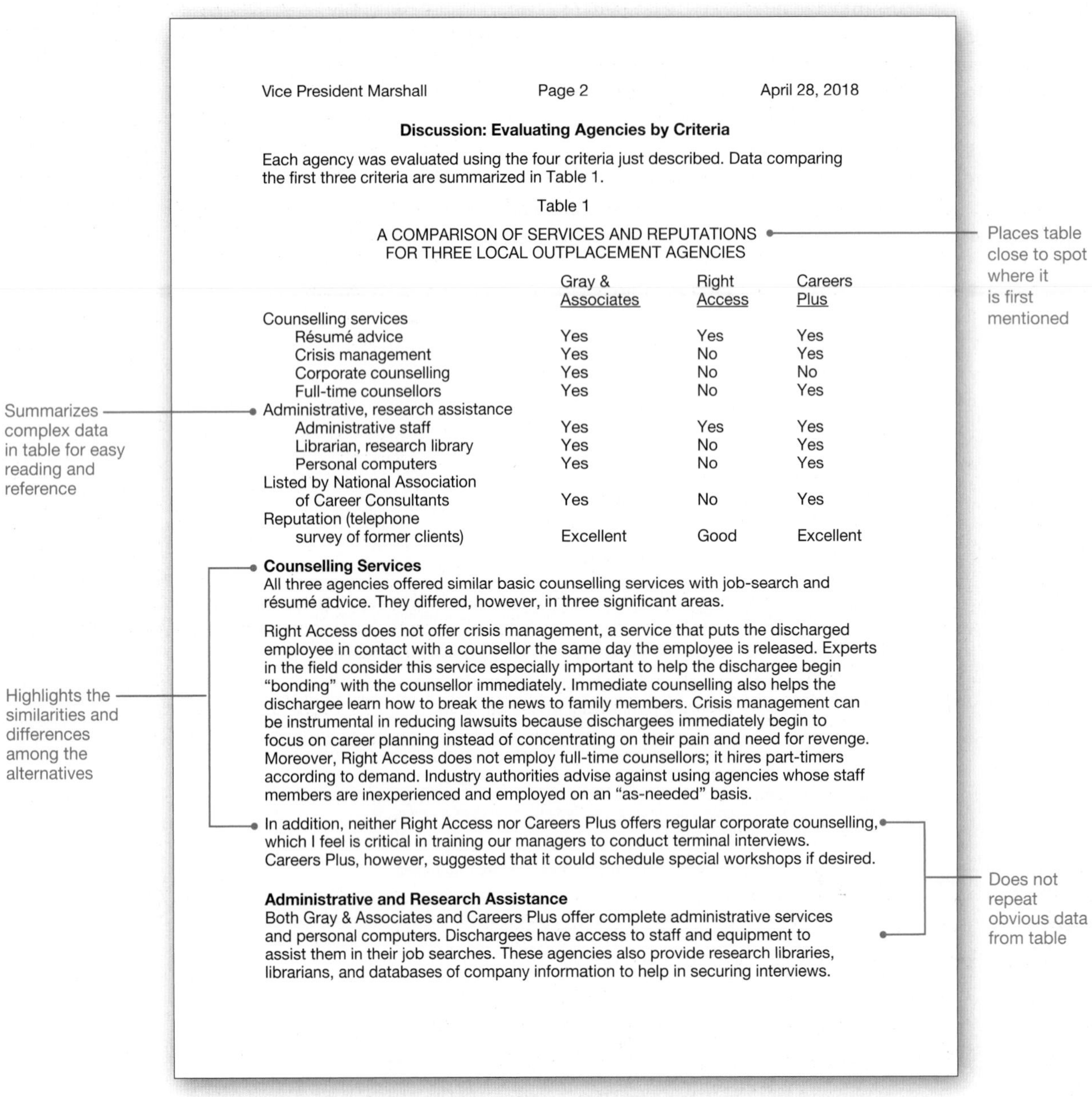

Vice President Marshall — Page 2 — April 28, 2018

Discussion: Evaluating Agencies by Criteria

Each agency was evaluated using the four criteria just described. Data comparing the first three criteria are summarized in Table 1.

Table 1

A COMPARISON OF SERVICES AND REPUTATIONS FOR THREE LOCAL OUTPLACEMENT AGENCIES

	Gray & Associates	Right Access	Careers Plus
Counselling services			
Résumé advice	Yes	Yes	Yes
Crisis management	Yes	No	Yes
Corporate counselling	Yes	No	No
Full-time counsellors	Yes	No	Yes
Administrative, research assistance			
Administrative staff	Yes	Yes	Yes
Librarian, research library	Yes	No	Yes
Personal computers	Yes	No	Yes
Listed by National Association of Career Consultants	Yes	No	Yes
Reputation (telephone survey of former clients)	Excellent	Good	Excellent

Counselling Services

All three agencies offered similar basic counselling services with job-search and résumé advice. They differed, however, in three significant areas.

Right Access does not offer crisis management, a service that puts the discharged employee in contact with a counsellor the same day the employee is released. Experts in the field consider this service especially important to help the dischargee begin "bonding" with the counsellor immediately. Immediate counselling also helps the dischargee learn how to break the news to family members. Crisis management can be instrumental in reducing lawsuits because dischargees immediately begin to focus on career planning instead of concentrating on their pain and need for revenge. Moreover, Right Access does not employ full-time counsellors; it hires part-timers according to demand. Industry authorities advise against using agencies whose staff members are inexperienced and employed on an "as-needed" basis.

In addition, neither Right Access nor Careers Plus offers regular corporate counselling, which I feel is critical in training our managers to conduct terminal interviews. Careers Plus, however, suggested that it could schedule special workshops if desired.

Administrative and Research Assistance

Both Gray & Associates and Careers Plus offer complete administrative services and personal computers. Dischargees have access to staff and equipment to assist them in their job searches. These agencies also provide research libraries, librarians, and databases of company information to help in securing interviews.

Places table close to spot where it is first mentioned
Summarizes complex data in table for easy reading and reference
Highlights the similarities and differences among the alternatives
Does not repeat obvious data from table

SUMMARY OF LEARNING OBJECTIVES

8.1 Explain informational and analytical business report functions and organization.

- Informational reports present data without analysis or recommendations, such as monthly sales reports, status updates, and compliance reports.
- Analytical reports provide data or findings, analyses, and conclusions. Examples include justification, recommendation, feasibility, and yardstick reports.
- Audience reaction and content determine whether a report is organized directly or indirectly.
- Reports organized directly reveal the purpose and conclusions immediately; reports organized indirectly place the conclusions and recommendations last.
- Like other business messages, reports can range from informal to formal, depending on their purpose, audience, and situation.

8.2 Describe typical report formats including heading levels.

- Report formats vary, depending on the report's length, topic, audience, and purpose.
- Common report formats include email, letter, memo, manuscript, and template; digital reports can be created and shared as slide decks and infographics.
- Report headings add visual appeal and readability; they reveal the report's organization and flow of ideas.
- The hierarchy of heading levels should be clear to a reader; headings in the same level should use the same font size and style, placement, and capitalization.

8.3 Determine the problem to be addressed and the report's purpose.

- Clarifying the problem the report will address is the first step in writing a report.
- A purpose statement states the reasons for the report and answers the questions that prompted the report.
- Typical sources of secondary information used in reports are company records, books, journals, magazines, newspapers, and Web resources.
- Typical sources of primary, or firsthand, information used in reports are personal observations, surveys, questionnaires, and interviews with topic experts.

8.4 Write informal informational reports.

- Informational reports provide information about recurring activities (e.g., monthly sales or project updates) as well as one-time events (e.g., trips, conferences, and special projects).
- Trip, convention, and conference reports include a preview of the topics covered, a summary of topics that will benefit the organization, and concluding thoughts about the overall value of the event.
- Progress, or interim, reports include a project description, background information, work completed, work in progress, problems encountered, and future plans.
- Meeting minutes include the names of attendees and absentees, a discussion of old and new business, committee reports, and decisions made.

8.5 Write informal analytical reports.

- Analytical reports, such as justification/recommendation, feasibility, and yardstick reports, evaluate information, draw conclusions, and make recommendations.
- Justification/recommendation reports are organized directly when the reader is supportive and indirectly when the reader needs persuasion to accept the recommendations.
- Feasibility reports are written directly and examine the practicality and advisability of following a course of action.
- Yardstick reports examine problems by using a standard set of criteria to compare several alternatives before recommending a solution.

CHAPTER REVIEW

1. Explain the difference between providing information and providing an analysis of information. (Objs. 1, 4, 5)
2. Why are there two different patterns of organization for informal reports? (Obj. 1)
3. List the main report formats and when each should be used. (Obj. 2)
4. Describe functional and talking headings and give an example of each. (Obj. 2)
5. Define primary and secondary research and give two examples of each. (Obj. 3)
6. What three questions do progress reports typically address? (Obj. 4)
7. What is the purpose of a meeting minutes report? (Obj. 4)
8. What is the difference between a justification/recommendation report and a feasibility report? (Obj. 5)
9. How can a yardstick report be useful to an organization? (Obj. 5)

CRITICAL THINKING

1. Why are most informal reports written using the direct strategy? (Obj. 1)
2. Is there a significant difference between a report that provides information and a regular email or other message that provides information? (Objs. 1, 2)
3. Is it a good idea to always provide analysis when asked to write reports, or are there times when it's okay to present information only? (Objs. 1, 3)
4. What technology trends do you think will affect business reporting and delivery in the future? (Obj. 2)
5. *Providing a summary is both an exercise in information gathering and an analytical task.* Discuss this statement and provide examples to back it up. (Objs. 4, 5)

ACTIVITIES AND CASES

8.1 EVALUATING HEADINGS AND TITLES (OBJ. 2)

Identify the following report headings and titles as "talking" or "functional/descriptive." Discuss the usefulness and effectiveness of each.

1. Background
2. Oil Imports Slow in China
3. Discussion of Findings
4. Rosier Job Outlook: Emerging From the Crisis
5. Recommendation: Return to Stocks Is Paying Off Again
6. Adobe Exceeds Expectations on Creative Suite Sales
7. Best Android Apps for Business: PocketCloud, Ignition, and TouchDown
8. Budget

8.2 CONFERENCE REPORT: LEARNING ABOUT FOOD IN NIAGARA FALLS (OBJS. 3, 4)

You are the General Manager of the Milestones Restaurant in downtown Kingston, ON. Each year, one or two employees from each regional group within the restaurant chain are chosen to attend the annual Restaurants Canada Leadership Conference. This year, your district manager says that you can attend on behalf of the regional group. Excited, you check out the conference sessions online at www.rcshow.com. At the annual conference in downtown Toronto, you take part in three very stimulating sessions that offer all kinds of ideas for improving sales and customer experience at your location in Kingston. These sessions include: "Personalizing the Customer Experience," "Millenials are Massive," and "Artificial Intelligence and Restaurants."

Your Task. The district manager asks you to create a 15-minute presentation with PowerPoint slides in which you can give a "topline" summary of what you learned in your three sessions. Create a conference report using PowerPoint. Use Google to search for information on the three session topics you "took part in." The district manager also asks for a one-page conference report to be emailed to him a week before the presentation.

8.3 TRIP REPORT: SERVICING REPS IN THE FIELD (OBJS. 3, 4)

You are a corporate trainer for a well-known line of makeup and skin care products called Jeneuve. The products are sold across Canada in department stores and drug stores such as Hudson's Bay, Shopper's Drug Mart, and London Drugs. As the corporate trainer, a large part of your job is conducting training seminars across the country, once in the fall and once in the spring. During these training seminars, not only do you train customer service reps in the retail locations about your new products, changes in current products, etc., you also listen to their feedback about what's working and what's not, and take that feedback home to head office in Montreal.

Your Task. During your fall tour through Western Canada, things generally went well as you introduced reps to Jeneuve's new line of products for men including Beard Oil, Beard Balm, and Beard Protector, as well as products for women including Glitter-J tears, Juicy-J lipstick, and Colour-J eyeliner. The reps in large cities like Vancouver and Calgary were more enthusiastic about these new products than the reps in smaller cities like Lethbridge and Kelowna. At the same time, you heard some critical feedback from your large stores in the Greater Toronto Area. One complaint is that Jeneuve does not offer a line of women's cosmetics for women with darker skin tones. As usual after your fall trip, your VP, Sandy Fairchilde, requests a detailed trip report in memo format.

http://www.cosmopolitan.com/style-beauty/beauty/news/a50647/women-of-color-makeup-foundation/

Visit **MindTap** for a variety of videos, additional exercises, activities, and quizzes to support your learning.

CHAPTER 9

Proposals and Formal Reports

Saklakova/istock via Getty Images

OBJECTIVES

After studying this chapter, you should be able to

9.1 Write effective informal business proposals.

9.2 Describe a plan for writing formal reports.

9.3 Collect data for reports effectively from primary and secondary sources.

9.4 Document sources effectively in a report

9.5 Convert report data into meaningful visual aids and graphics.

9.6 Draft and sequence a formal report using standard components.

9.1 Writing Business Proposals

Proposals are persuasive written offers to solve problems, provide services, or sell equipment or other goods. Proposals can mean life or death for a business. Multimillion-dollar aerospace and engineering firms depend on proposals to compete for business. People running smaller businesses—such as electricians, contractors, plumbers, and interior designers—also depend on proposals to sell their services and products.

Proposals are persuasive offers to solve problems, provide services, or sell equipment.

Many organizations, including in the nonprofit sector, earn a sizable portion of their income from proposals (which are often called grants applications in the nonprofit sector).

The ability to write effective proposals is especially important today. In writing proposals, the most important thing to remember is that they constitute a type of sales presentation in which you offer a value proposition, so they must be persuasive, not merely mechanical descriptions of what you can do.

9.1a Types of Proposals

Writers prepare proposals for various reasons, such as asking for funds or promoting products and services to customers. Some proposals are brief; some are lengthy and complex. A proposal recipient could be a manager inside your company or a potential client outside your company. All types of proposals share two significant characteristics: (1) they use easy-to-understand language, and (2) they show the value and benefits of the product or services being recommended. Proposals may be classified as (a) informal or formal, (b) internal or external, and (c) solicited or unsolicited.

Informal proposals may contain an introduction, background information, the plan, staffing requirements, a budget, and an authorization request.

INFORMAL OR FORMAL. Informal proposals are short reports, often formatted as memos or letters. Proposal sections can vary, but an informal proposal might include the following parts: (a) an introduction or description of the problem; (b) pertinent background information or a statement of need; (c) the proposal benefits and schedule for completion; (d) the staffing requirements; (e) a budget analysis; and (f) a conclusion that may include an authorization request. Figure 9.1 shows an informal letter proposal to a Canadian dentist who sought to improve patient satisfaction. The research company submitting the proposal describes the benefits of a patient survey to gather data about the level of patient satisfaction. As you can see, the proposal contains the basic components of an informal proposal.

Formal proposals are more complex and may range from 5 to 200 or more pages. For example, the recently completed train link to Toronto's Pearson Airport from downtown (the Union Pearson Express) was a huge engineering and logistical undertaking. The proposals by AirLINX Transit Partners Inc. to build a station at the airport and three kilometres of track, and by Sumitomo Corporation of Americas to build the train cars,[1] were much longer than the two-page letter proposal in Figure 9.1.

In addition to the six basic parts just described, formal proposals contain some or all of the following additional parts: a copy of the RFP, a letter of transmittal, an abstract and/or executive summary, a title page, a table of contents, figures, and appendixes containing such items as detailed budgets and staffing information. In this book we will not model formal proposals in detail because it's unlikely that a business communicator in an entry-level position would write such a detailed proposal. Formal proposal writing is usually handled either by consultants or by employees with significant experience in this area.

Many organizations, especially those run on a consulting model, depend entirely on proposals to generate their income. Companies such as Microsoft employ staffs of people who do nothing but prepare proposals to compete for new business. For more information about industry standards and resources, visit the website of the Association of Proposal Management Professionals (www.apmp-mapleleaf.org).

INTERNAL OR EXTERNAL. Proposal writers may submit internal proposals to management when they see benefits in changing a company policy, purchasing equipment, or adding new products and services. A company decision maker will review the proposal and accept or reject the idea. Internal proposals may resemble justification and recommendation reports, as discussed in Chapter 8. Most proposals, however, are external and addressed to clients, customers, and stakeholders outside the company. An external sales proposal to a client would show how the company's goods or services would solve a problem or benefit the client.

Another type of external proposal is a grant request, written to obtain funding from an agency that supports the nonprofit sector. For example, Family Services of Greater Vancouver may submit yearly grant applications to United Way of the Lower Mainland for operating or special project expenses around reducing infant mortality.

SOLICITED OR UNSOLICITED. When government organizations or businesses have a specific need, they prepare a *request for proposal* (RFP), a document that specifies their requirements. Government agencies as well as private businesses use RFPs to solicit competitive bids from vendors. RFPs ensure that bids are comparable and that funds are awarded fairly. For example, let's say that the City of Fredericton wants to upgrade the laptops and software in its Human Resources Department. Once it knows exactly what it wants, it prepares a request for proposal (RFP) specifying its requirements. It then publishes the RFP, and companies interested in bidding on the job submit proposals. RFPs were traditionally publicized in newspapers (and known as *tenders*), but today they're published on websites, such as www.merx.com, the best-known Canadian RFP site.

Enterprising companies looking for work or special projects might submit unsolicited proposals. For example, the world-renowned architect who designed the Louvre Museum pyramid in Paris, I. M. Pei, was so intrigued by the mission of the Buck Institute for Research on Aging that he submitted an unsolicited proposal to design the biomedical research facility in Novato, California.[2] Pei's proposal must have impressed the decision makers, because the research facility now features his geometric elements and floating staircases.

Both large and small companies are likely to use RFPs to solicit bids on their projects. This enables them to compare prices from various companies on their projects. Not only do they want a good price from their project bidders, but they also want the legal protection offered by proposals, which are considered legal contracts.

9.1b Components of Informal Proposals

Informal proposals are often presented in letter format (or sometimes in a form, e.g., in a grant application). Sometimes called letter proposals, they contain six parts: introduction, background, proposal or plan, staffing, budget, and authorization request. The informal proposal shown in Figure 9.1 illustrates these six parts, in the context of a proposal addressed to a Calgary dentist who wants to improve patient satisfaction.

INTRODUCTION. The introduction states the reasons for the proposal and highlights the writer's qualifications. To grab attention and be persuasive, the introduction contains a "hook," such as:

- Hinting at extraordinary results with details to be revealed shortly.
- Promising low costs or speedy results.
- Mentioning a remarkable resource (well-known authority, new computer program, well-trained staff) available exclusively to you.
- Identifying a serious problem (worry item) and promising a solution, to be explained later.
- Specifying a key issue or benefit that you feel is the heart of the proposal.[3]

Effective proposal openers capture interest by promising concrete results or resources or by identifying key benefits, issues, or outcomes.

For example, in the proposal shown in Figure 9.1, writer Alex Parsons confidently focuses on a key benefit. She guesses that the potential client, Dr. Atala, will be most interested in receiving a concrete plan for making changes based on her patients' opinions. If this were a more complex (formal) proposal, the introduction would also describe the scope and limitations of the project.

BACKGROUND. The background section identifies the problem and discusses the goals or purposes of the project. The background is also the place to go over some recent history. In other words, briefly summarize what circumstances led to you writing the proposal, whether solicited or unsolicited. For example, in Figure 9.1, the "history" of the situation is alluded to in the sentence *We know that you have been incorporating a total quality management system in your practice.*

In a proposal, your aim is to convince the reader that you understand the problem completely. Thus, if you are responding to an RFP, this means repeating its language. For example, if the RFP asks for the *design of a maintenance program for high-speed mail-sorting equipment*, you would use the same language in explaining the purpose of your proposal. This section might include segments entitled *Basic Requirements, Most Critical Tasks*, and *Most Important Secondary Problems.*

OFFICE INSIDER

"To conquer writer's block in proposal writing, begin with a bulleted list of what the customer is looking for. This list is like a road map; it gets you started and keeps you headed in the right direction."

—Mary Piecewicz, former Hewlett-Packard proposal manager, interview with Mary Ellen Guffey

PLAN. In the plan section, you should discuss your methods for solving the problem. In some proposals this is tricky: you want to disclose enough of your plan to secure the contract without giving away so much information that your services aren't needed. Without specifics about implementation, though, your proposal has little chance, so you must decide how much to reveal. Explain what you propose to do and how it will benefit the reader.

Remember, too, that a proposal is a sales presentation/value proposition. Sell your methods, product, and "deliverables"—items that will be left with the client. In this section some writers specify how the project will be managed and audited, how its progress will be audited, and what milestones along the way will indicate the project is progressing as planned. Most writers also include a schedule of activities or a timetable showing when events take place.

STAFFING. The staffing section describes the credentials and expertise of the project leaders and the company as a whole. A well-written staffing section describes the capabilities of the whole company. Although the example in Figure 9.1 does not

FIGURE 9.1 | Informal "Letter" Proposal

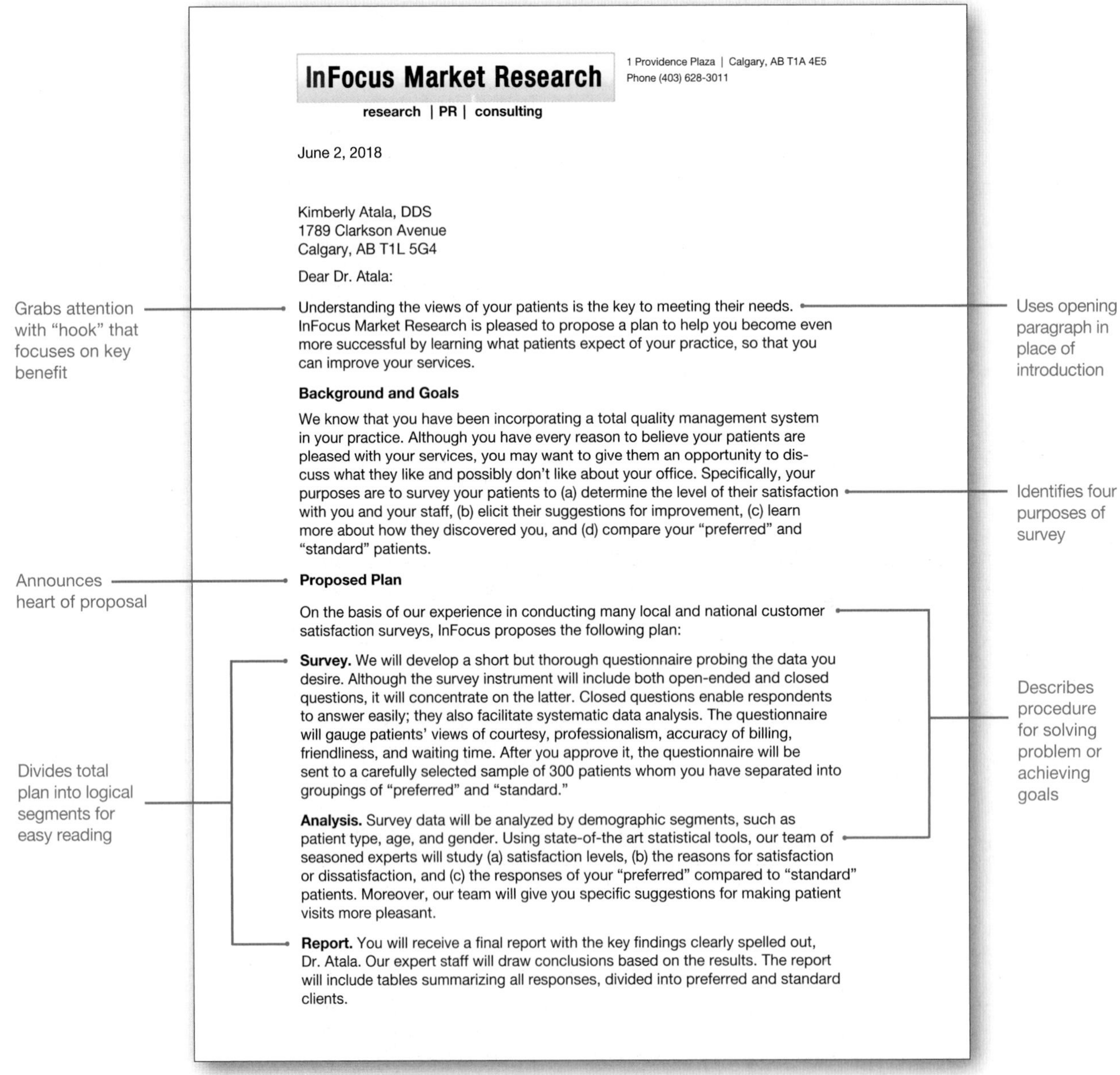

InFocus Market Research
research | PR | consulting

1 Providence Plaza | Calgary, AB T1A 4E5
Phone (403) 628-3011

June 2, 2018

Kimberly Atala, DDS
1789 Clarkson Avenue
Calgary, AB T1L 5G4

Dear Dr. Atala:

Understanding the views of your patients is the key to meeting their needs. InFocus Market Research is pleased to propose a plan to help you become even more successful by learning what patients expect of your practice, so that you can improve your services.

Background and Goals

We know that you have been incorporating a total quality management system in your practice. Although you have every reason to believe your patients are pleased with your services, you may want to give them an opportunity to discuss what they like and possibly don't like about your office. Specifically, your purposes are to survey your patients to (a) determine the level of their satisfaction with you and your staff, (b) elicit their suggestions for improvement, (c) learn more about how they discovered you, and (d) compare your "preferred" and "standard" patients.

Proposed Plan

On the basis of our experience in conducting many local and national customer satisfaction surveys, InFocus proposes the following plan:

Survey. We will develop a short but thorough questionnaire probing the data you desire. Although the survey instrument will include both open-ended and closed questions, it will concentrate on the latter. Closed questions enable respondents to answer easily; they also facilitate systematic data analysis. The questionnaire will gauge patients' views of courtesy, professionalism, accuracy of billing, friendliness, and waiting time. After you approve it, the questionnaire will be sent to a carefully selected sample of 300 patients whom you have separated into groupings of "preferred" and "standard."

Analysis. Survey data will be analyzed by demographic segments, such as patient type, age, and gender. Using state-of-the art statistical tools, our team of seasoned experts will study (a) satisfaction levels, (b) the reasons for satisfaction or dissatisfaction, and (c) the responses of your "preferred" compared to "standard" patients. Moreover, our team will give you specific suggestions for making patient visits more pleasant.

Report. You will receive a final report with the key findings clearly spelled out, Dr. Atala. Our expert staff will draw conclusions based on the results. The report will include tables summarizing all responses, divided into preferred and standard clients.

Grabs attention with "hook" that focuses on key benefit
Uses opening paragraph in place of introduction
Identifies four purposes of survey
Announces heart of proposal
Describes procedure for solving problem or achieving goals
Divides total plan into logical segments for easy reading

FIGURE 9.1 | *(Continued)*

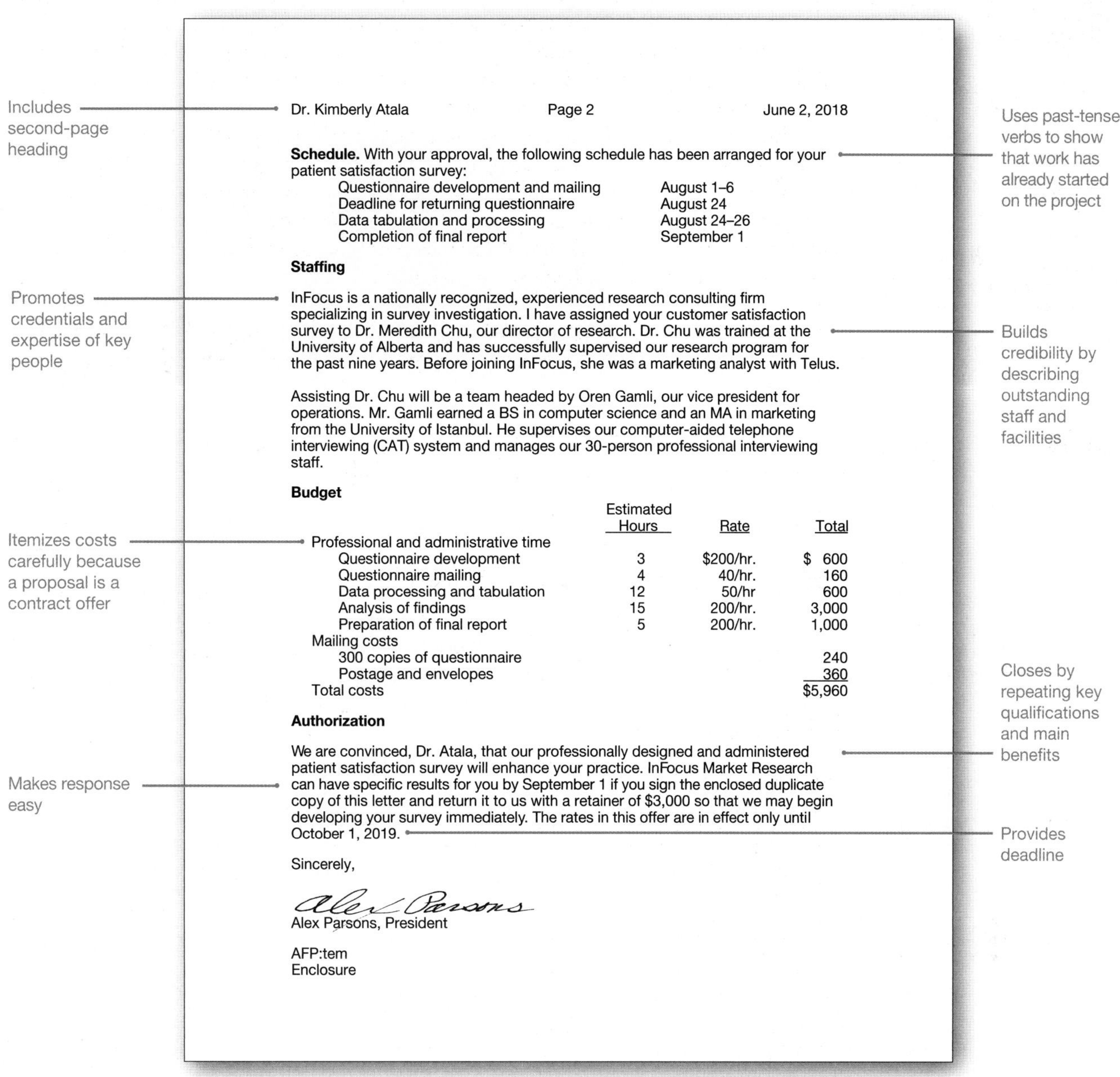

Includes second-page heading
Promotes credentials and expertise of key people
Itemizes costs carefully because a proposal is a contract offer
Makes response easy
Uses past-tense verbs to show that work has already started on the project
Builds credibility by describing outstanding staff and facilities
Closes by repeating key qualifications and main benefits
Provides deadline

Dr. Kimberly Atala   Page 2   June 2, 2018

Schedule. With your approval, the following schedule has been arranged for your patient satisfaction survey:

Questionnaire development and mailing	August 1–6
Deadline for returning questionnaire	August 24
Data tabulation and processing	August 24–26
Completion of final report	September 1

Staffing

InFocus is a nationally recognized, experienced research consulting firm specializing in survey investigation. I have assigned your customer satisfaction survey to Dr. Meredith Chu, our director of research. Dr. Chu was trained at the University of Alberta and has successfully supervised our research program for the past nine years. Before joining InFocus, she was a marketing analyst with Telus.

Assisting Dr. Chu will be a team headed by Oren Gamli, our vice president for operations. Mr. Gamli earned a BS in computer science and an MA in marketing from the University of Istanbul. He supervises our computer-aided telephone interviewing (CAT) system and manages our 30-person professional interviewing staff.

Budget

	Estimated Hours	Rate	Total
Professional and administrative time			
Questionnaire development	3	$200/hr.	$ 600
Questionnaire mailing	4	40/hr.	160
Data processing and tabulation	12	50/hr	600
Analysis of findings	15	200/hr.	3,000
Preparation of final report	5	200/hr.	1,000
Mailing costs			
300 copies of questionnaire			240
Postage and envelopes			360
Total costs			$5,960

Authorization

We are convinced, Dr. Atala, that our professionally designed and administered patient satisfaction survey will enhance your practice. InFocus Market Research can have specific results for you by September 1 if you sign the enclosed duplicate copy of this letter and return it to us with a retainer of $3,000 so that we may begin developing your survey immediately. The rates in this offer are in effect only until October 1, 2019.

Sincerely,

Alex Parsons

Alex Parsons, President

AFP:tem
Enclosure

do so, staffing sections often list other high-profile jobs that have been undertaken by the company as a way of building interest and reducing resistance. For example, before she mentioned Dr. Chu and Mr. Gamli, Parsons could have said, *Among our well-known clients are Husky Energy and the Calgary Board of Education.*

The plan section must give enough information to secure the contract but not so much detail that the services are not needed.

The staffing section may also identify the size and qualifications of the support staff, along with other resources such as computer facilities and special programs for analyzing statistics. In longer proposals, résumés of key people may be provided. The staffing section is a good place to endorse and promote your staff.

BUDGET. The most important item in proposals, many would argue, is the budget, a list of project costs. You need to prepare this section carefully because it represents a contract; you can't raise the price later—even if your costs increase. You can—and should—protect yourself with a deadline for acceptance. In the budget section some

WORKPLACE IN FOCUS

In a move reminiscent of suburban bomb shelters of the Cold War era, urban planners are preparing "lilypad cities" to house survivors if climate disaster fears ever materialize. Should the planet become inundated by rising sea levels, these zero-emission ships could literally bob around the globe as self-sustaining habitats, complete with energy supplied from solar panels and wind turbines. Designed by award-winning Belgian architect Vincent Callebaut, and inspired by the shape of lilypads, the giant floating metropolises are both stylish and loaded with the comforts of modern living. *What types of organizations might submit proposals in the development of lilypad cities and for what types of goods and services?*

Europics/Newscom

writers itemize hours and costs; others present a total sum only. A proposal to install a complex IT system might, for example, contain a detailed line-by-line budget.

Because a proposal is a legal contract, the budget must be researched carefully.

In the proposal shown in Figure 9.1, Parsons felt that she needed to justify the budget for her firm's patient-satisfaction survey, so she itemized the costs. But the budget included for a proposal to conduct a one-day seminar to improve employee communication skills might be a lump sum only. Your analysis of the project and your audience will help you decide what kind of budget to prepare.

Formal proposals respond to big projects and may contain 200 or more pages.

AUTHORIZATION AND CONCLUSION. Informal proposals close with a request for approval or authorization and remind the reader of key benefits and motivate action. It might also include a deadline date beyond which the offer is invalid. Learning to write an authorization statement—which must find a way of saying you want the job without appearing too greedy or needy—is an important persuasive exercise.

9.2 A Plan for Writing Formal Business Reports

A formal report is as a document in which a writer analyzes findings, draws conclusions, and makes recommendations intended to solve a problem and help decision makers.

9.2a Steps in the Report Process

Writing a formal report takes time. It requires planning, research, and organization. Because this is a complex process, writers are most successful when they follow specific steps, as outlined in the following sections.

DETERMINE THE PURPOSE AND SCOPE OF THE REPORT. Formal reports begin with a purpose statement. Preparing a written purpose statement is helpful because it defines the focus of the report and provides a standard that keeps the project on target. Notice the use of action words (*adding, writing,* and *establishing*):

> **Simple purpose statement:** *To recommend adding three positions to our sales team, writing a job description for the sales team leader, and establishing recruitment guidelines for sales team hiring.*

You can determine the scope of the report by defining and limiting the problem or problems that will be researched and analyzed. Consider these questions: How much time do you have to complete the report? How accessible is the data you need? If interviews or surveys are appropriate, how many people should you contact, and what questions should you ask?

ANTICIPATE THE NEEDS OF THE AUDIENCE. Keep in mind that the audience may or may not be familiar with the topic. Your goal is to present key findings that are relevant to your audience. If you were reporting to a targeted audience of human resources managers, the following facts gathered from an employee survey would be considered relevant: *According to the company survey completed by 425 of our 515 employees, 72 percent of employees are currently happy with their health benefits package.* A good report writer considers the needs of the audience every step of the way.

DRAFT A WORK PLAN. A work plan is a tentative plan (sometimes created using software like Excel or MS Project, but it can also be a simple Word document) that guides the investigation. This plan should include a clear problem statement, a purpose statement, and a description of the research methods to be used. A good work plan also involves a tentative outline of the report's major sections and a logical work schedule for completion of major tasks.

CONDUCT RESEARCH USING PRIMARY AND SECONDARY SOURCES. Formal report writers conduct most of their research using *secondary sources*—that is, information that has been previously analyzed and compiled. Books, articles, Web documents, podcasts, correspondence, and annual reports are examples of secondary sources. In contrast, writers may conduct some of their research using primary sources—information and data gathered from firsthand experience. Interviews, observations, surveys, questionnaires, and meetings are examples of primary research. Research methods are discussed in the section "Researching Primary and Secondary Data" later in this chapter.

ORGANIZE, ANALYZE, AND DRAW CONCLUSIONS. Formal report writers should organize their information logically and base their recommendations on solid facts to impress decision makers. They should analyze the findings and make sure they are relevant to the report's purpose.

As you sort through your information, decide what information is substantiated and credible. Give readers only the information they need. Then arrange that information using one of the strategies shown in Figure 9.2.

Conclude the report by summarizing your findings, drawing conclusions, and making recommendations. The way you conclude depends on the purpose of your report and what the reader needs. A well-organized report with conclusions based on solid data will impress management and other decision makers.

DESIGN GRAPHICS TO CLARIFY THE REPORT'S MESSAGE. Presenting quantitative data helps your reader to visually understand information. Trends, comparisons, and cycles are easier to comprehend when they are expressed graphically. These visual elements in reports draw attention, add interest, and often help readers gain information quickly. Visuals include drawings, graphs, maps, charts, photographs, tables, and infographics. This topic is covered in more depth in the section "Convert Your Data Into Meaningful Graphics" later in this chapter.

9.2b Editing Formal Business Reports

The final step in preparing a formal business report involves editing and proofreading. Because the reader is the one who determines the report's success, review

WORKPLACE IN FOCUS

The Conference Board of Canada is a nonpartisan organization that sees itself as "building a better future for Canadians by making our economy and society more dynamic and competitive."[4] As part of this mission, the Board employs researchers and publishes (on its website) their research reports on topics like economic trends, organizational performance, and public policy. These research reports are often quoted in the media. At the Board's "In the News" link, you can find video clips of Conference Board experts discussing the research they've conducted. Similarly, many of the research reports are posted on the organization's site, including one on "Healthy Brains at Work: Employer-Sponsored Mental Health Benefits and Programs." *Why is it important in a free-market society for the Conference Board of Canada to invest in this type of publicly available research reporting?*

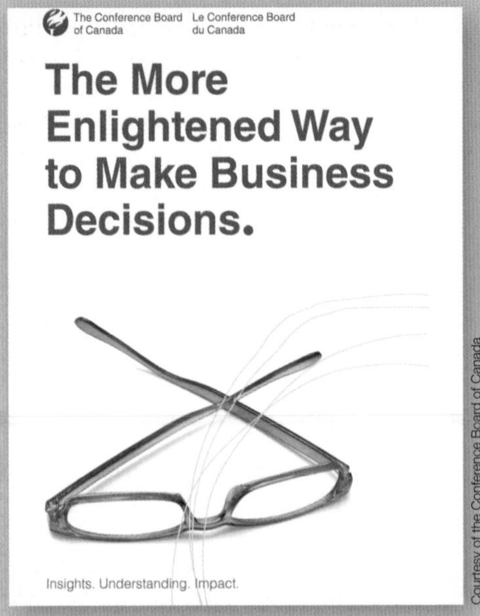

Courtesy of the Conference Board of Canada

FIGURE 9.2 | Strategies for Organizing Report Findings

STRATEGY TYPE	DATA ARRANGEMENT	USEFUL APPLICATION
Chronological	Arrange information in a time sequence to show history or development of topic.	Useful in showing time relationships, such as five-year profit figures or a series of events leading to a problem.
Geographical	Organize information by geographic regions or locations.	Appropriate for topics that are easily divided into locations, such as Atlantic Provinces, Central Canada, etc.
Topic/Function	Arrange by topics or functions. May use a prescribed, conventional format.	Works well for topics with established categories or for recurring reports.
Compare/Contrast	Present problem and show alternative solutions. Use consistent criteria. Show how the solutions are similar and different.	Best used for "before and after" scenarios or when comparing alternatives.
Importance	Arrange from least to most important, lowest to highest priority, or lowest to highest value, etc.	Appropriate when persuading the audience to take a specific action or change a belief.
Simple/Complex	Proceed from simple to more complex concepts or topics.	Useful for technical or abstract topics.
Best Case/Worst Case	Describe the best and the worst possible scenarios.	Useful when dramatic effect is needed to achieve results; helpful when audience is uninterested or uninformed.

the report as if you were the intended audience. Pay particular attention to the following elements:

- **Format.** Look at the report's format and assess the report's visual appeal.
- **Consistency.** Review the report for consistency in margins, page numbers, indents, line spacing, heading parallelism, and font style.
- **Graphics.** Make sure all graphics have meaningful titles, make written information more clear, and are placed in the report near the words that describe them.

- **Heading levels.** Check the heading levels for consistency in font style and placement. Headings and subheadings should be meaningful and help the reader follow the report's logic.
- **Accuracy.** Review the content for accuracy and clarity. Make sure all facts are documented.
- **Mechanics.** Correct all grammar, punctuation, capitalization, and usage errors. These errors will damage your credibility and might cause the reader to mistrust the report's content.

9.3 Researching Primary and Secondary Data

One of the most important steps in the process of writing a report is doing research that will help solve the business problem at hand. A report is only as good as its data, so you'll want to spend considerable time collecting data before you begin writing.

Data fall into two broad categories, primary and secondary. Primary data result from firsthand experience and observation. Secondary data come from reading what others have experienced and observed. Secondary data are easier and less expensive to develop than primary data, which might involve interviewing large groups or sending out questionnaires.

9.3a Locating Secondary Research Sources

Secondary research is where nearly every research project should begin. Often something has already been written about your topic. Reviewing secondary sources can save time and effort and help you avoid costly primary research to develop data that already exist. Most secondary material is available in online databases conveniently located in your school or company library.

Primary data come from firsthand experience and observation; secondary data, from reading articles, books, websites, reports, and statistics

PRINT RESOURCES. We've seen a steady move away from print to electronic data, but some information is still most easily accessible in print.

Although researchers are increasingly turning to electronic data, some data are available only in print.

BOOKS. Although sometimes outdated, depending on how quickly a particular body of knowledge changes, books provide excellent in-depth data and interpretation on many subjects. For example, if you are investigating best practices in website design, you will find numerous books with valuable information in your nearest library. Books are located through online catalogues that can be accessed in the library, on any campus computer, or from home with an Internet connection and valid password. Most library catalogues today enable you to learn not only whether a book is in the library's holdings but also whether it is currently available.

Books provide historical, in-depth data; periodicals provide limited but current coverage.

PERIODICALS. Magazines, newspapers, and journals are called periodicals because of their recurrent or periodic publication. Articles in journals and other periodicals will be extremely useful to you because they are concise, limited in scope, and current, and they can supplement information in books. For example, if you want to understand the latest trends and research in the business communication field, you would browse through recent volumes of the *Journal of Business Communication*. And if you're studying the fluctuating prices of commodities like food and energy, a reputable newspaper's business section would be a good place to start to get oriented to the topic.

RESEARCH DATABASES. As a writer of business reports, you will most likely do much of your secondary research using online research databases. Many researchers turn to databases first because they are fast, focused, and available online. Databases are exactly what they sound like: large collections of information in electronic format. In research databases, the information is almost every article published in

Most researchers today begin by looking in online databases, which are collections of almost every article published in any publication.

Review information online through research databases that are accessible by computer and searchable.

every newspaper, magazine, academic journal, and trade journal—a huge amount of information, by any measure. By using these online resources you can look for the secondary data you require without ever leaving your office or home.

The strength of databases lies in the fact that they are current and field-specific. For example, if you go to the Mohawk College Library website (www.mohawkcollege.ca/student-life/library), you will instantly see the "Search all library collections at once" search form and underneath it a link that says "A–Z Databases." Clicking here, you can see popular databases in your area of study (e.g., Business, Health, Hospitality, Technology) or scroll down through the various databases. If you then click on CBCA Business, for example, you are "in" a database, one that focuses on business-related articles from Canadian sources. Libraries pay for these databases partly through your tuition fees. If in your workplace you do not have access to an institution's databases, your local public library (e.g., Vancouver Public Library) will have databases available for your use (assuming you have a valid library card!).

Learning how to use an online database takes some practice. We suggest you go to your library's site and experiment with online databases. Choose a topic like *trends in business communication* and see what you come up with. Figure 9.3 shows a student doing just this, using the above-mentioned CBCA database. Try to find one current article from a newspaper, a magazine, and a journal. Do you get better results when you use the basic or the advanced search function? Do you get better results by separating the topic into parts, for example, *trends* and *business* and *communication*, or by typing in the whole phrase at once? If you're having trouble, you can always sign up for a free guided seminar at your library, or ask a librarian for help next time you're there.

THE INTERNET. The Internet includes an enormous collection of pages created by people, organizations, and governments around the world. The Internet is interactive, mobile, and user-friendly with multimedia content ranging from digital sound files to vivid images and video files. With trillions of pages of information available on the Internet, chances are that if you have a question, an answer exists online. To a business researcher, the Internet offers a wide range of organizational and commercial information. You can expect to find such items as product and service facts, public relations material, mission statements, staff directories, press releases, current company news, government information, selected article reprints, collaborative

FIGURE 9.3 | Conducting Secondary Research With a Research Database

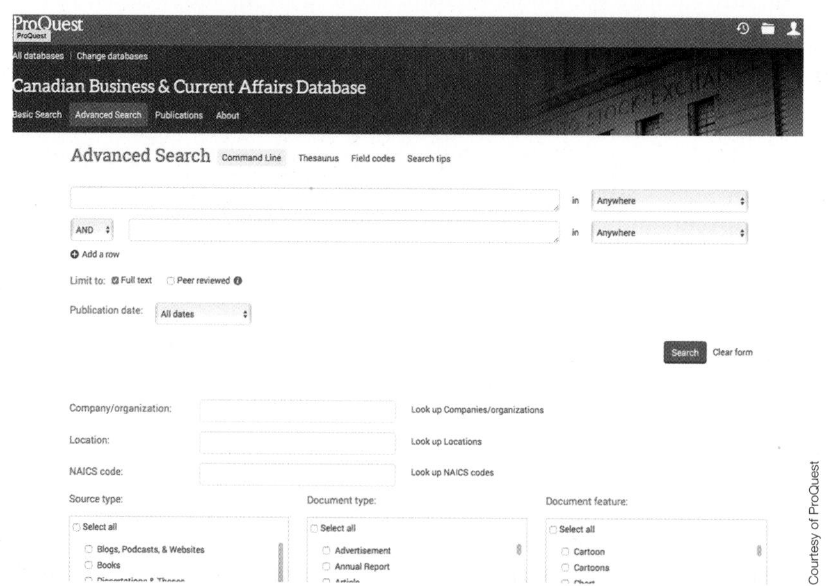

Courtesy of ProQuest

scientific project reports, stock research, financial information, and employment information.

The Internet is unquestionably one of the greatest sources of information now available to anyone needing simple facts quickly and inexpensively. But finding relevant, credible information can be frustrating and time-consuming. The constantly changing contents of the Internet and its lack of organization irritate budding researchers. Moreover, content isn't always reliable. Anyone can publish content without any quality control or guarantee. To succeed in your search for information and answers, you need to understand how to browse the Internet and use search engines. You also need to understand how to evaluate the information you find.

SEARCH TOOLS AND TIPS. A search tool, also called a search engine, is a service that indexes, organizes, and often rates and reviews Web pages. Some search tools rely on people to maintain a catalogue of websites or pages. Others use software to identify key information. They all begin a search based on the keywords that you enter. The most-used search engine at this writing is Google. It has developed a huge following with its ease of use and its "uncanny ability to sort through millions of Web pages and put the sites you really want at the top of its results pages."[5]

A search engine is a service that indexes, organizes, and often rates and reviews Web pages.

INTERNET SEARCH TIPS AND TECHNIQUES. To conduct a thorough search using Google use these tips and techniques:

- **Consider Google Scholar.** If you'd like to find high-quality peer-reviewed sources from academic journals, start with Google Scholar before moving on to the regular Google search engine.
- **Understand case sensitivity.** Generally use lowercase for your searches, unless you are searching for a term that is typically written in upper- and lowercase, such as a person's name.
- **Use nouns as search words and as many as eight words in a query.** The right key words—and more of them—can narrow your search considerably.
- **Use quotation marks.** When searching for a phrase, such as *cost-benefit analysis,* most search engines will retrieve documents having all or some of the terms. This and/or strategy is the default of most search engines. To locate occurrences of a specific phrase, enclose it in quotation marks.
- **Omit articles and prepositions.** Known as "stop words," articles and prepositions don't add value to a search. Instead of *request for proposal*, use *proposal request.*
- **Proofread your search words.** Make sure you are searching for the right thing by proofreading your search words carefully. For example, searching for *sock market* will come up with substantially different results than searching for *stock market.*
- **Save the best.** To keep track of your favourite websites, save them as bookmarks or favourites.
- **Keep trying.** If a search produces no results, check your spelling. Try synonyms and variations on words. Try to be less specific in your search term. If your search produces too many hits, try to be more specific. Think of words that uniquely identify what you are looking for, and use as many relevant keywords as possible.

THE INTERNET AND CREDIBILITY. When searching the Internet, you need to check the credibility and accuracy of the information you find. Anyone can publish online, and credibility is sometimes difficult to determine. Wikis and unmoderated discussion forums are a case in point. The authorship may be unverifiable, and the credibility of the information may be questionable.

To assess the credibility of a Web page, scrutinize what you find using the following criteria:

- **Currency.** What is the date of the Web page? If the information is time sensitive and the site has not been updated recently, the site is probably not reliable.

- **Authority.** Who publishes or sponsors this Web page? Is information about the author or sponsoring organization available on the About Us page? Can the author be contacted? Be skeptical about data and assertions from individuals and organizations whose credentials are not verifiable.
- **Content.** Is the purpose of the page to entertain, inform, convince, or sell? Is the purpose readily apparent? Who is the intended audience, based on content, tone, and style? Evaluate the overall value of the content and see how it compares with other resources on this topic.
- **Accuracy.** Do the facts that are presented seem reliable? Do you find errors in spelling, grammar, or usage? Do you see any evidence of bias? Are references provided? Do the external links work? Errors and missing references should alert you that the data may be questionable.

9.3b Generating Primary Data

Primary data come from firsthand experience.

Although you'll begin a business report by searching for secondary data, you'll need primary data to give a complete, up-to-date, and original picture. If, for example, management wants to discover the cause of increased employee turnover in its Halifax office, it must investigate conditions in Halifax by collecting recent information. Providing answers to business problems often means generating primary data through surveys, interviews, observation, or experimentation.

SURVEYS. Surveys collect data from groups of people. When companies develop new products, for example, they often survey consumers to learn their needs. The advantages of surveys are that they gather data economically and efficiently. Emailed and online surveys reach big groups nearby or at great distances. Moreover, surveys are easy to respond to because they're designed with closed-ended, quantifiable questions. It's easy to pick an answer on a professionally designed survey, thus improving the accuracy of the data.

Surveys also have disadvantages. Most of us rank them as an intrusion on our increasingly important private time, so response rates may be no higher than 10 percent. Furthermore, those who do respond may not represent an accurate sample of the overall population, thus invalidating generalizations for the group. Let's say, for example, that an insurance company sends out a survey questionnaire asking about provisions in a new policy. If only older people respond, the survey data cannot be used to generalize what people in other age groups might think.

A final problem with surveys has to do with truthfulness. Some respondents exaggerate their incomes or distort other facts, thus causing the results to be unreliable. Nevertheless, surveys are still considered the best way to generate data for business and student reports.

Surveys yield efficient and economical primary data for reports.

Best practices in survey design are taught in research methods courses at colleges and universities. The basic rules—explain why the survey is being done, use a limited number of questions (usually fewer than ten), include questions that produce quantifiable answers, and avoid leading/biased/ambiguous questions—should all be adhered to. These days, many students as well as professional researchers use free survey software by companies like SurveyMonkey to create and conduct their surveys. Figure 9.4 shows part of a survey created using SurveyMonkey's free software. You can find more information about survey design at the SurveyMonkey site: www.surveymonkey.com/mp/writing-survey-questions/.

Interviews with experts produce useful report data, especially when little has been written about a topic.

INTERVIEWS. Some of the best report information, particularly on topics about which little has been written, comes from individuals. These individuals are usually experts or veterans in their fields. Consider both in-house and outside experts for business reports. Tapping these sources will call for in-person, email, or telephone interviews. To elicit the most useful data, try the techniques discussed below in Figure 9.5.

FIGURE 9.4 | Sample Survey Created Using SurveyMonkey

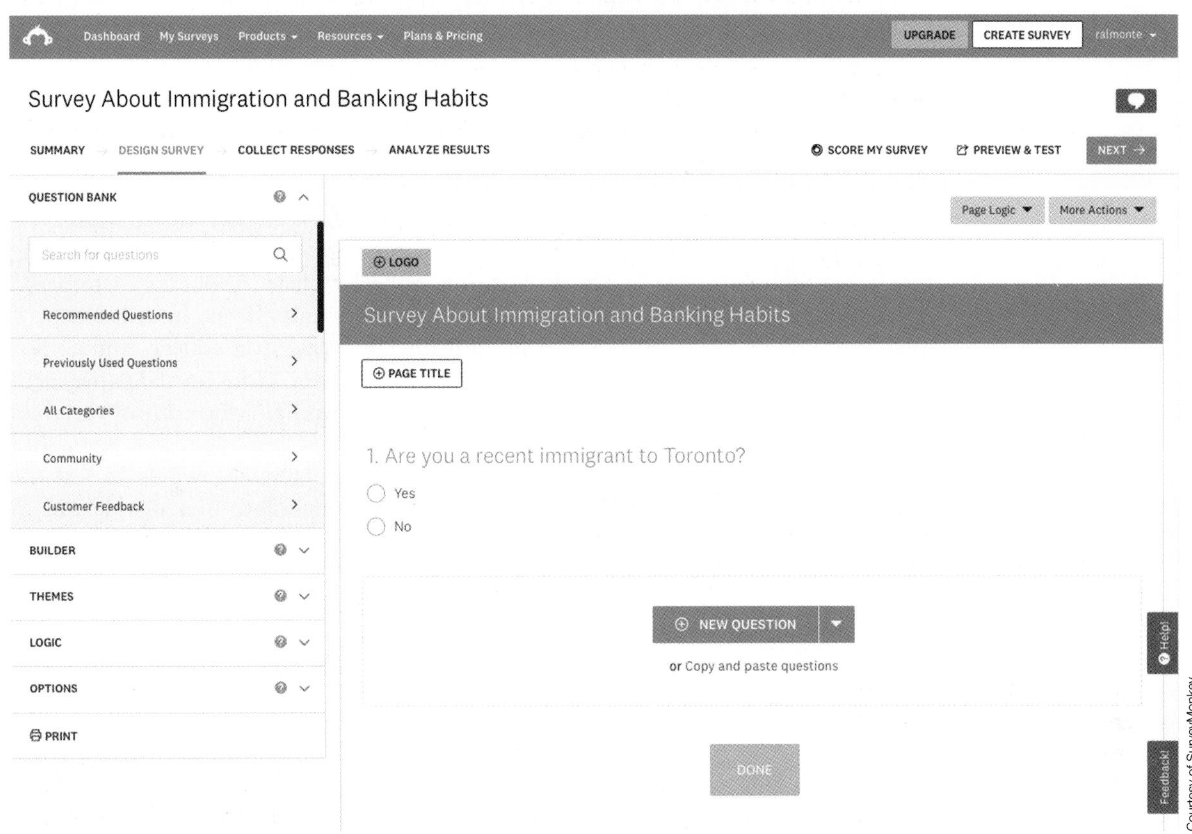

Courtesy of SurveyMonkey

FIGURE 9.5 | How to Schedule and Conduct Interviews

Locate an expert	Interview knowledgeable individuals who are experts in their field.
Prepare for the interview	Read all you can about the topic you will discuss so you can converse intelligently. Learn the name and background of the individual you are interviewing. Be familiar with the terminology of the topic. Let's say you are interviewing a corporate communication expert about the advantages of creating a corporate blog. You ought to be familiar with terms such as *brand management, RSS feeds, traffic*, and *damage control*.
Maintain a profes-sional attitude	Call before the interview to confirm the appointment, and arrive on time. You'll also want to be professional in your dress, language, and behaviour. "If the interview is being conducted via email or Skype, send a reminder message the day before and ensure the recipient receives your interview questions the day before in order to prepare."
Ask objective and open-ended questions	Adopt a courteous, respectful attitude when asking questions. Open-ended questions encourage a variety of responses. Do not debate any issues and do not interrupt. You are there to listen, not to talk.
Watch the time	Tell interviewees in advance how much time you'll need. Watch the clock and keep the interview discussion on track.
End graciously	Conclude graciously with a general question, such as *Is there anything you would like to add?* Express your appreciation, and ask permission to contact the interviewee later if necessary.

OBSERVATION AND EXPERIMENTATION. Some kinds of primary data can be obtained only through firsthand observation and investigation. How long does a typical caller wait before a customer service representative answers the call? How is a new piece of equipment operated? Are complaints of sexual harassment being taken seriously? Observation produces rich data, but that information is especially prone to charges of subjectivity. One can interpret an observation in many ways. Thus, to make observations more objective, try to quantify them.

For example, record customer telephone wait time for 60-minute periods at different times throughout a week. Or compare the number of sexual harassment complaints made with the number of investigations undertaken and the resulting actions.

When you observe, plan ahead. Arrive early enough to introduce yourself and set up whatever equipment you think is necessary. Make sure you have received permissions beforehand, particularly if you are recording. In addition, take notes, not only about the events or actions but also about the settings. Changes in environment often have an effect on actions. Famous for his out-of-the box thinking, Howard Schultz, the executive chairman of Starbucks, is known to hate research, advertising, and customer surveys. Instead of relying on sophisticated marketing research, Schultz visits 25 Starbucks locations a week to learn about his customers.[6]

Experimentation produces data suggesting causes and effects. Informal experimentation might be as simple as a pre-test and post-test in a college course. Did students expand their knowledge as a result of the course? More formal experimentation is undertaken by scientists and professional researchers who control variables to test their effects.

Some of the best report data come from firsthand observation and investigation.

Imagine that Mordens' of Winnipeg Candy Manufacturing wants to test the hypothesis (which is a tentative assumption) that chocolate lifts people out of depression. An experiment testing the hypothesis would separate depressed individuals into two groups: those who ate chocolate (the experimental group) and those who did not (the control group). What effect did chocolate have? Such experiments are not done haphazardly, however. Valid experiments require sophisticated research designs, careful attention to matching the experimental and control groups, and ethical considerations.

9.4 Documenting and Citing Sources in Business Reports

In writing business reports, you will often build on the ideas and words of others. In Western culture, whenever you "borrow" the ideas or words of others, you must give credit to your information sources. This is called *documentation*. You can learn more about common documentation (or citation) styles in Appendix C.

9.4a Documentation Guidelines

Whether you quote or paraphrase another person's words, you must document the source. To use the ideas of others skillfully and ethically, you need to know why, what, and how to document.

WHY DOCUMENT. As a careful business writer and presenter, you should document your data properly for the following reasons:

- **To strengthen your argument.** Including good data from reputable sources will convince readers of your credibility and the logic of your reasoning.
- **To protect yourself.** Acknowledging your sources keeps you honest. It's unethical and illegal to use others' ideas without proper documentation.
- **To instruct the reader/audience.** Citing references enables readers and listeners to pursue a topic further and make use of the information themselves.

WHAT TO DOCUMENT. When you write reports, you are continually dealing with other people's ideas. You are expected to conduct research, synthesize ideas, and build on the work of others. But you are also expected to give proper credit for borrowed material. To avoid plagiarism, give credit whenever you use the following:[7]

- Another person's ideas, opinions, examples, or theory
- Any facts, statistics, graphs, and drawings that are not common knowledge

- Quotations of another person's actual spoken or written words
- Paraphrases of another person's spoken or written words
- Visuals, images, and any kind of electronic media

Information that is common knowledge requires no documentation. For example, the statement *Many businesspeople agree that* Report on Business *is among Canada's top mainstream business sources* would require no citation. Statements that are not common knowledge, however, must be documented. For example, *Alberta is home to seven of Canada's top ten fastest-growing large cities* would require a citation because most people don't know this fact (in this case the information came from a story on Huffingtonpost.ca quoting Statistics Canada's 2011 census). Cite sources for proprietary information such as statistics organized and reported by a newspaper or magazine. You probably use citations to document direct quotations, but you must also cite ideas that you summarize in your own words.

HOW TO PARAPHRASE. In writing reports and using the ideas of others, you will probably rely heavily on *paraphrasing*, which means restating an original passage in your own words and in your own style. To do a good job of paraphrasing, follow these steps:

1. Read the original material carefully to comprehend its full meaning.
2. Write your own version without looking at the original.
3. Avoid repeating the grammatical structure of the original and merely replacing words with synonyms.
4. Reread the original to be sure you covered the main points but did not borrow specific language.

To better understand the difference between plagiarizing and paraphrasing, study the following passages. Notice that the writer of the plagiarized version uses the same grammatical construction as the source and often merely replaces words with synonyms. Even the acceptable version, however, requires a reference to the source author.

Original Source

We have seen, in a short amount of time, the disappearance of a large number of household brands that failed to take sufficient and early heed of the software revolution that is upending traditional brick-and-mortar businesses and creating a globally pervasive digital economy.[8]

Plagiarized Version

Many trusted household name brands disappeared very swiftly because they did not sufficiently and early pay attention to the software revolution that is toppling traditional physical businesses and creating a global digital economy. (Saylor, 2012)

The plagiarized version uses the same sentence structure as the original and makes few changes other than replacing some words.

Effective Paraphrase

Digital technology has allowed a whole new virtual global economy to blossom and very swiftly wiped out some formerly powerful companies that responded too late or inadequately to the disruptive force that has swept the globe. (Saylor, 2012)

The acceptable paraphrase presents ideas from a different perspective and uses a different sentence structure than the original.

HOW TO DOCUMENT. Documentation is achieved through citations. A citation is how you tell your reader from where the idea or phrase or sentence was borrowed. The original reason behind citations (before plagiarism became a big problem) was to allow anyone reading your work to find your sources should he or she wish to do additional research. If someone says to you, "But you didn't cite it!" he or she means you didn't include a proper citation.

For example, in a report that reads

> *Lemire and Gaudreault (2006) estimated that in 2003, Canada's road and highway network had over 50 percent of its useful life behind it, while federal and provincial bridges had passed the halfway mark of their useful lives.*[9]

the APA-style citation is the combination of the lead-in phrase—*Lemire and Gaudreault ... estimated*—and the bracketed date reference—*(2006)*. The basic elements of an APA-style in-text citation are thus the author's name(s) + a verb (e.g., Almonte estimates, says, shows, argues, explains) + the date of publication. There will be times when you don't have these pieces of information.

For more information on such cases, as well as the two main citation methods—footnote/endnote (or Chicago style) and parenthetic (or APA and MLA style)—please read Appendix C. Also study Figures 9.8–9.11 (p. 196) to see how sources are documented there. Besides in-text citations, you will cite each source you've used (primary and secondary) at the end of your report on a page called the "Works Cited" or "References" page. There is a specific format for how this is done, also found in Appendix C.

OFFICE INSIDER

Changing the words of an original source is not sufficient to prevent plagiarism. If you have retained the essential idea of an original source and have not cited it, then no matter how drastically you may have altered its context or presentation, you have still plagiarized.

9.5 Convert Your Data Into Meaningful Graphics

After collecting and interpreting information, you need to consider how best to present it. If your report contains complex numerical data, you should consider graphics such as tables and charts. These graphics clarify your data, create visual interest for the reader, and make your numerical data meaningful. In contrast, readers tend to be bored and confused by text paragraphs packed with complex data and numbers. Use the following points as a general guide to creating effective graphics in a report:

- Clearly identify the contents of the visual aid with meaningful titles and numbering (e.g., *Figure 1: Internet Use at Canadian Companies*).
- Refer the reader to the visual aid by discussing it in the text and mentioning its location and figure number (e.g., *as Figure 1 below shows...*).
- Locate the visual aid close to its reference in the text.
- Strive for vertical placement of visual aids. Readers are disoriented by horizontal pages in reports.
- Give credit to the source if appropriate (e.g., *Source: Statistics Canada*).

Effective graphics clarify numerical data and simplify complex ideas.

The same data can be shown in many forms. For example, a company's quarterly sales can be displayed in a chart, table, or graph. That's why you need to know how to match the appropriate graphic with your objective and how to incorporate it into your report.

9.5a Matching Graphics and Objectives

Tables permit systematic presentation of large amounts of data, while charts enhance visual comparisons.

Before creating successful graphics, you should first decide what data you want to highlight and which graphics are most appropriate to your objectives. Figure 9.6 summarizes appropriate uses for each type of graphic and the sections that follow discuss each type in detail.

9.5b Creating Tables, Charts, and Infographics

The saying "a picture is worth a thousand words" definitely applies in business, where decision-makers are pressed for time and need information in an easy-to-digest format. For this reason, report writers over the past ten years have begun to move away from large amounts of text and towards a more visual style of report

FIGURE 9.6 | Matching Graphics to Objectives

Graphic		Objective
Table		To show exact figures and values
Bar Chart	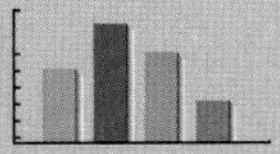	To compare one item with others
Line Chart	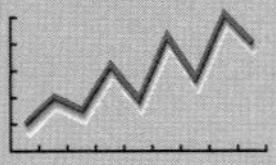	To demonstrate changes in quantitative data over time
Pie Chart	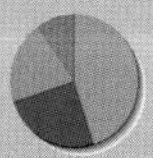	To visualize a whole unit and the proportions of its components
Flow Chart	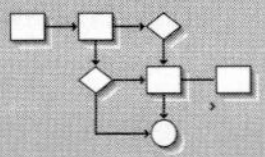	To display a process or procedure
Organization Chart	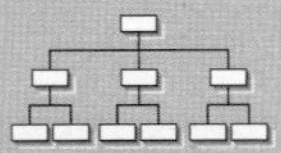	To define a hierarchy of elements
Photograph, Map, Illustration	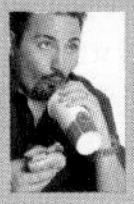	To create authenticity, to spotlight a location, and to show an item in use

Agree	Undecided	Disagree
2.2	5.48	3.3
3.7	6.2	4.75
4.8	22.4	6.58
1.25	3.4	2.44

writing in which tables, charts, and infographics are prominently used to succinctly convey data.

TABLES. Probably the most frequently used visual aid in reports is the table. A table presents quantitative information in a systematic order of columns and rows. Here are tips for designing good tables, one of which is illustrated in Figure 9.7:

- Provide clear heads for the rows and columns.
- Identify the units in which figures are given (percentages, dollars, units per worker-hour, and so forth) in the table title, in the column or row head, with the first item in a column, or in a note at the bottom.
- Arrange items in a logical order (alphabetical, chronological, geographical, highest to lowest) depending on what you need to emphasize.
- Use *N/A* (not available) for missing data.
- Make long tables easier to read by shading alternate lines or by leaving a blank line after groups of five.

BAR CHARTS. Although they lack the precision of tables, bar charts enable you to make emphatic visual comparisons. Bar charts can be used to compare related items, illustrate changes in data over time, and show segments as part of a whole. Figures 9.8 through 9.11 show vertical, horizontal, grouped, and segmented bar charts that highlight income for an entertainment company called MPM. Note how the varied bar charts present information in different ways.

Bar charts enable readers to compare related items, see changes over time, and understand how parts relate to a whole.

FIGURE 9.7 | Table Summarizing Data

FIGURE 1 SATSUNO COMPUTING NUMBER OF TABLETS SOLD, 2018					
Region	1st Qtr.	2nd Qtr.	3rd Qtr.	4th Qtr.	Yearly Totals
Atlantic	13 302	15 003	15 550	16 210	60 065
Central	12 678	11 836	10 689	14 136	49 339
Prairie	10 345	11 934	10 899	12 763	45 941
Pacific	9 345	8 921	9 565	10 256	38 087
Total	45 670	47 694	46 703	53 365	193 432

FIGURE 9.8 | Vertical Bar Chart

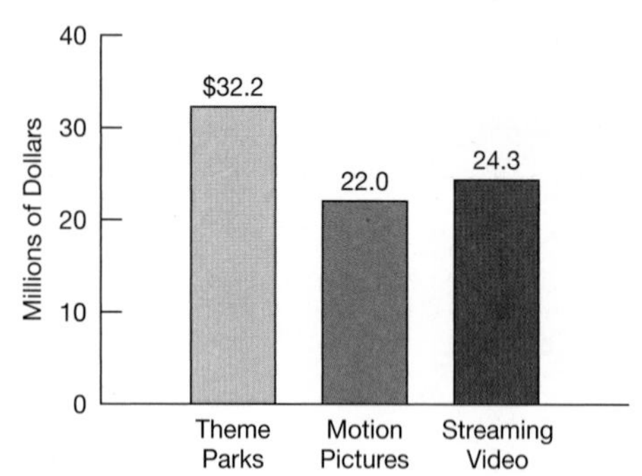

Source: *Industry Profiles* (New York: DataPro, 2017), p. 225.

FIGURE 9.9 | Horizontal Bar Chart

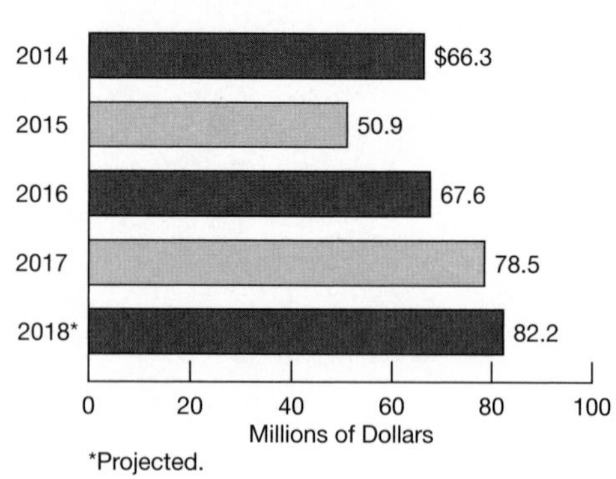

Source: *Industry Profiles* (New York: DataPro, 2017).

FIGURE 9.10 | Grouped Bar Chart

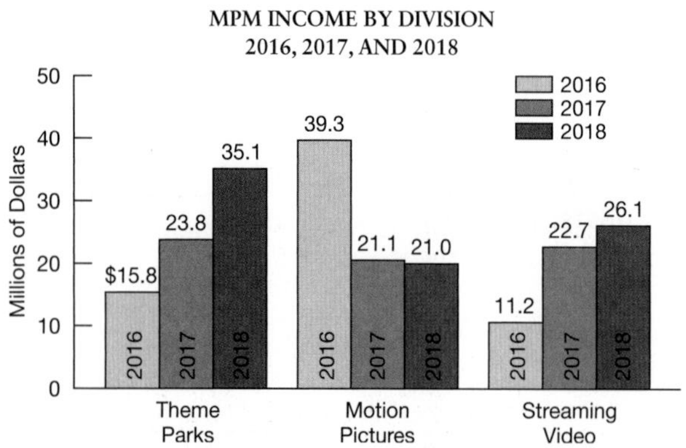

Source: *Industry Profiles* (New York: DataPro, 2017).

FIGURE 9.11 | Segmented 100 Percent Bar Chart

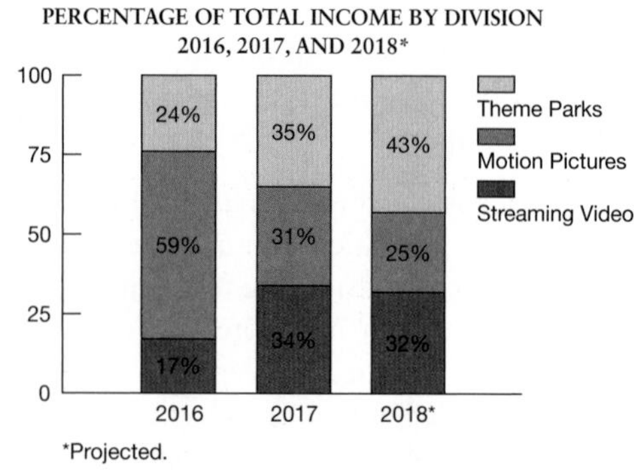

Source: *Industry Profiles* (New York: DataPro, 2017).

Many suggestions for tables also hold true for bar charts. Here are a few additional tips:

- Keep the length of each bar and segment proportional.
- Include a total figure in the middle of a bar or at its end if the figure helps the reader and does not clutter the chart.
- Start dollar or percentage amounts at zero.

LINE CHARTS. The major advantage of line charts is that they show changes over time, thus indicating trends. Figures 9.12 through 9.14 show line charts that reflect revenue trends for the major divisions of MPM. Notice that line charts do not provide precise data. Instead, they give an overview or impression of the data. Experienced report writers use tables to list exact data; they use line charts or bar charts to spotlight important points or trends.

Line charts illustrate trends and changes in data over time.

Simple line charts (Figure 9.12) show just one variable. Multiple line charts combine several variables (Figure 9.13). Segmented line charts (Figure 9.14), also called surface charts, illustrate how the components of a whole change over time.

Here are tips for preparing line charts:

- Begin with a grid divided into squares.
- Arrange the time component (usually years) horizontally across the bottom; arrange values for the other variable vertically.
- Draw small dots at the intersections to indicate each value at a given year.
- Connect the dots and add colour if desired.
- To prepare a segmented (surface) chart, plot the first value (e.g., *streaming video*) across the bottom; add the next item (e.g., *motion picture income*) to the first figures for every increment; for the third item (e.g., *theme park income*) add its value to the total of the first two items. The top line indicates the total of the three values.

FIGURE 9.12 | Simple Line Chart

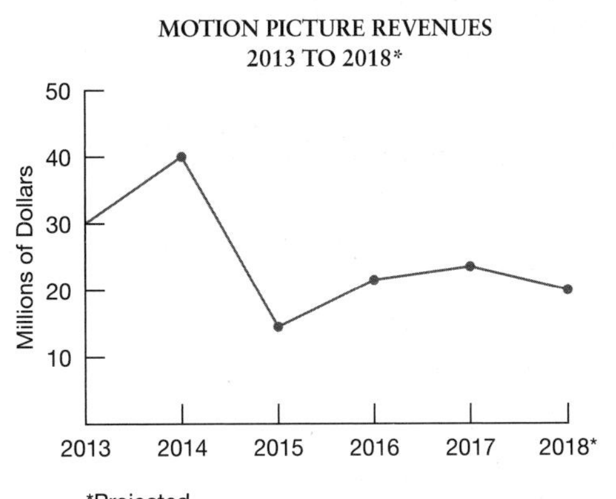

Source: *Industry Profiles* (New York: DataPro, 2017).
© Cengage Learning

FIGURE 9.13 | Multiple Line Chart

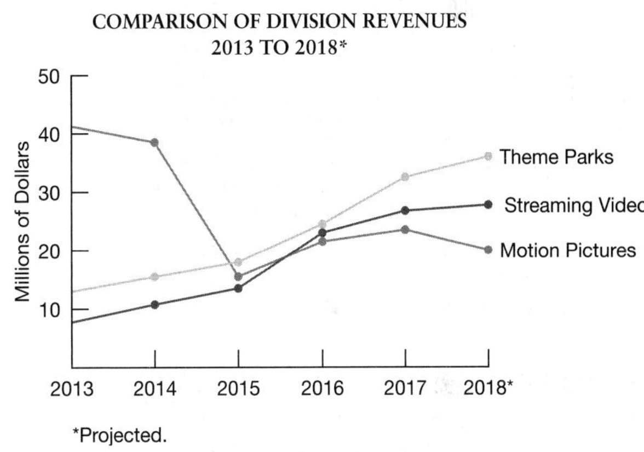

Source: *Industry Profiles* (New York: DataPro, 2017).
© Cengage Learning

FIGURE 9.14 | Segmented Line (Surface) Chart

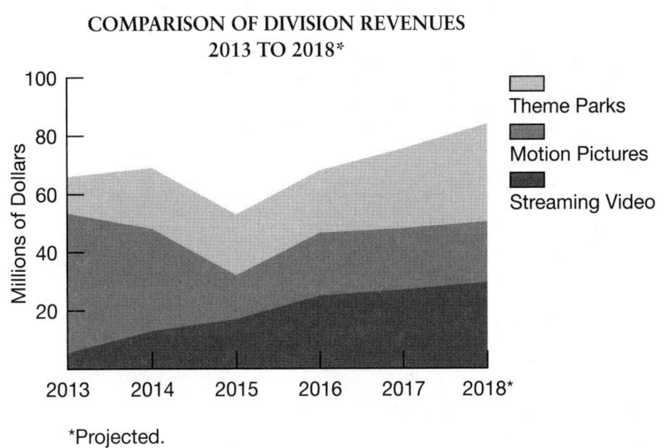

Source: *Industry Profiles* (New York: DataPro, 2017).
© Cengage Learning

FIGURE 9.15 | Pie Chart

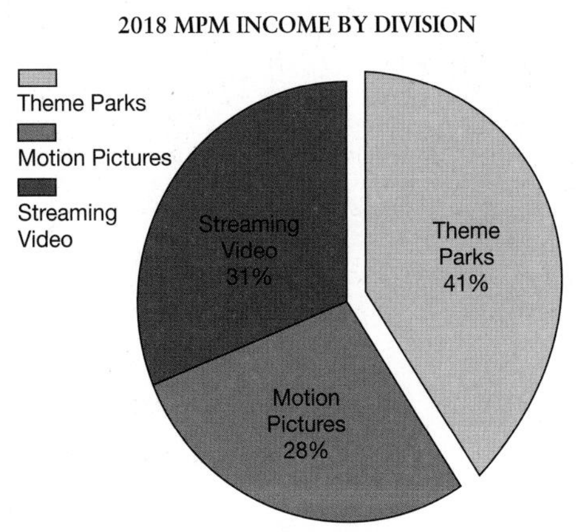

Source: *Industry Profiles* (New York: DataPro, 2017).
© Cengage Learning

Pie charts are most useful in showing the proportion of parts to a whole.

PIE CHARTS. Pie, or circle, charts help readers visualize a whole and the proportion of its components, or wedges. Pie charts, though less flexible than bar or line charts, are useful in showing percentages, as Figure 9.15 illustrates. For the most effective pie charts, follow these suggestions:

- Begin at the 12 o'clock position, drawing the largest wedge first. (Computer software programs don't always observe this advice, but if you're drawing your own charts, you can.)
- Include, if possible, the actual percentage or absolute value for each wedge.
- Use four to eight segments for best results; if necessary, group small portions into one wedge called "Other."
- Distinguish wedges with colour, shading, or cross-hatching.
- Keep all labels horizontal.

Flow charts are useful for clarifying procedures.

FLOW CHARTS. Procedures are simplified and clarified by diagramming them in a flow chart, as shown in Figure 9.16. Whether you need to describe the procedure for handling a customer's purchase order or outline steps in solving a problem, flow charts help the reader visualize the process. Traditional flow charts use the following symbols:

Flow charts use standard symbols to illustrate a process or procedure.

- Ovals to designate the beginning and end of a process
- Diamonds to denote decision points
- Rectangles to represent major activities or steps

ORGANIZATION CHARTS. Many large organizations are so complex that they need charts to show the chain of command, from the boss down to managers and employees. Organization charts like the one in Figure 9.17 provide such information as who reports to whom, how many subordinates work for each manager (the span of control), and what channels of official communication exist. These charts may illustrate a company's structure—for example, by function, customer, or product. They may also be organized by the work being performed in each job or by the hierarchy of decision making.

FIGURE 9.16 | Flow Chart

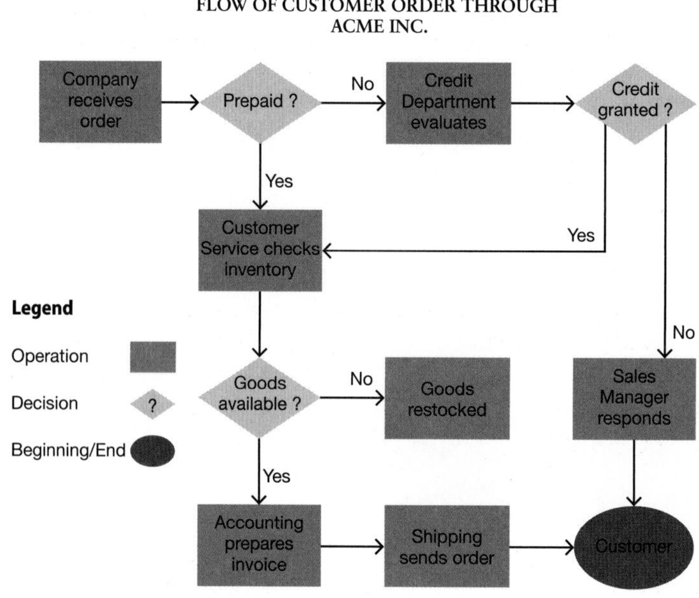

FIGURE 9.17 | Organization Chart

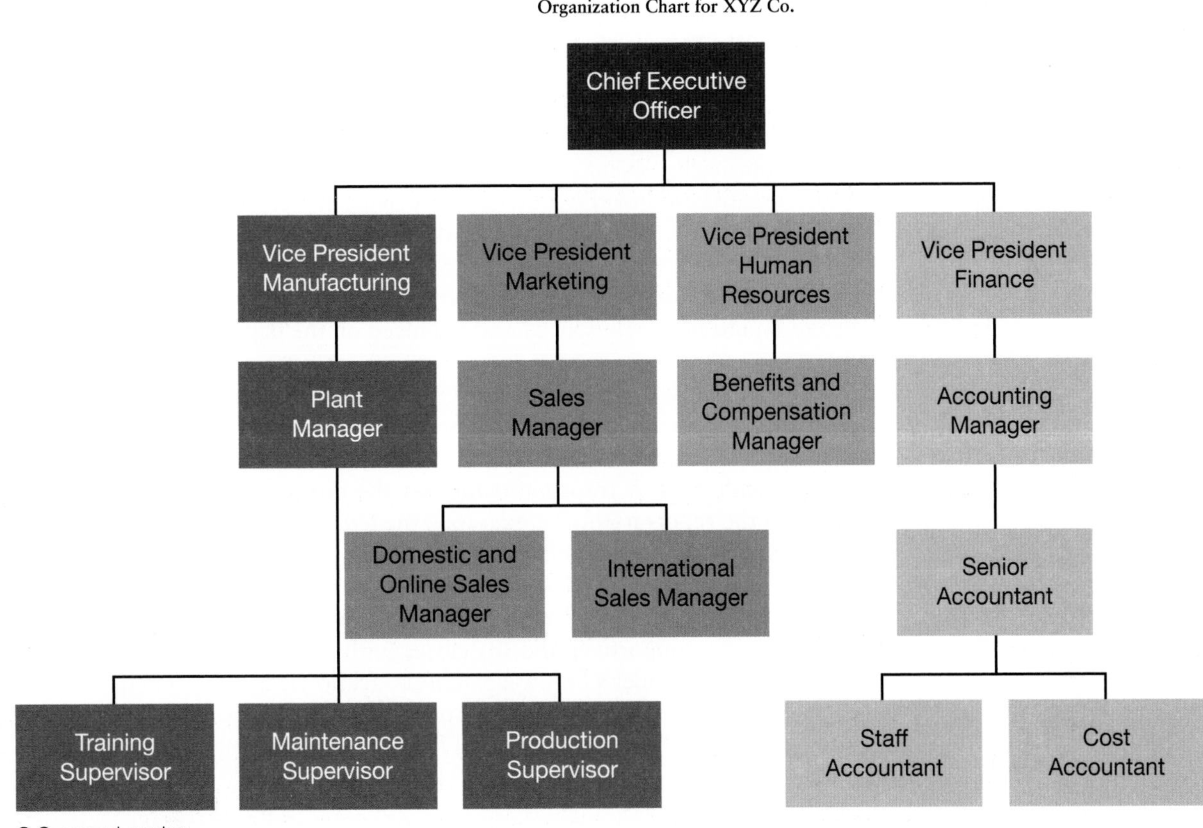

USING SOFTWARE TO PRODUCE GRAPHICS AND INFOGRAPHICS. Designing effective graphics is easy with software. Spreadsheet programs such as Microsoft's Excel as well as presentation graphics programs such as Microsoft's PowerPoint allow anyone to design quality graphics. These graphics can be printed for distribution in meetings or used in slides for presentations.

An *infographic* is a visual representation of complex information in a format that is easy to understand. Compelling infographics tell a story by combining images and graphic elements, such as charts and diagrams. Free software from providers like piktochart.com, venngage.com, and canva.com allows anyone to create professional-looking infographics, like the one you encountered earlier in Chapter 8 (Figure 8.4). Because these data visualizations tend to be long, they are commonly shared in online environments.

9.6 Drafting and Sequencing the Report

Formal business reports containing substantial research, analysis, and recommendations are generally organized into three major parts: (1) front matter, (2) body, and (3) back matter. Following is a description of the order and content of each part. Refer to the model formal report in Figure 9.18 (starting on p. 202) for illustrations of most of these sections.

9.6a Front Matter Contents

Front matter items (everything before the body of a report) and back matter items (everything after the conclusions and recommendations) lengthen formal reports but enhance their professional tone and serve their multiple audiences. Formal reports may be read by many levels of managers, along with technical specialists and financial consultants. Therefore, breaking a long, formal report into small segments—and sometimes repeating the same information in different ways in these segments—makes a report more accessible and easier to understand.

A letter or memo of transmittal formally hands over the report to its recipient. It presents a brief summary of the report, expresses appreciation for the job, and offers to do more work if necessary.

TITLE PAGE. A report title page, as illustrated in the Figure 9.18 model report, begins with the name of the report typed in uppercase letters (no underscore and no quotation marks). Next comes *Prepared for* (or *Submitted to*) and the name, title, and organization of the individual receiving the report. Lower on the page is *Prepared by* (or *Submitted by*) and the author's name plus any necessary identification. The last item on the title page is the date of submission. All items after the title appear in a combination of upper- and lowercase letters. The information on the title page should be evenly spaced and balanced on the page for a professional look.

LETTER OR MEMO OR EMAIL OF TRANSMITTAL. Generally written on organization letterhead (unless being sent via email), a transmittal introduces a formal report. You will recall that letters are sent to external audiences; memos, to internal audiences. A transmittal follows the direct strategy and is usually less formal than the report itself. For example, the letter or memo may use contractions and the first-person pronouns *I* and *we*. The transmittal typically (a) announces the topic of the report and tells how it was authorized; (b) briefly describes the project; (c) highlights the report's findings, conclusions, and recommendations, if the reader is expected to be supportive; and (d) closes with appreciation for the assignment, instructions for the reader's follow-up actions, acknowledgment of help from others, or offers of assistance in answering questions. If a report is going to various readers, a special transmittal should be prepared for each, anticipating how each reader will use the report.

TABLE OF CONTENTS. The table of contents shows the headings in a report and their page numbers. It gives an overview of the report topics and helps readers locate them. You should wait to prepare the table of contents until after you have completed the report. For short reports you should include all headings. For longer reports you might want to list only first- and second-level headings. Leaders (spaced or unspaced dots) help guide the eye from the heading to the page number. Items may be indented in outline form or typed flush with the left margin.

LIST OF FIGURES. For reports with several figures or tables, you should include a list to help readers locate them. This list should appear on the same page as the table of contents, space permitting. For each figure or table, include a title and page number.

EXECUTIVE SUMMARY OR ABSTRACT. The purpose of an executive summary is to present an overview of a longer report to people who may not have time to read the entire document. This time-saving device summarizes the purpose, key points, findings, and conclusions. An executive summary is usually no longer than 10 percent of the original document. Therefore, a twenty-page report might require a two-page executive summary.

9.6b Body Contents

The body of a report includes an introduction, a discussion of findings, and conclusions or recommendations.

The main section of a report is the body. It generally begins with an introduction, includes a discussion of findings, and concludes with a summary and often with recommendations.

INTRODUCTION. Formal reports start with an introduction that sets the scene and announces the subject. Because they contain many parts serving different purposes, the same information may be included in the letter or memo of transmittal, executive summary, and introduction. To avoid sounding repetitious, try to present the information slightly differently in each section.

A good report introduction typically covers the following elements, although not necessarily in this order:

- **Background:** Describe the events leading up to the problem or need.
- **Problem and purpose:** Explain the report topic and specify the problem or need that motivated the report.
- **Significance:** Say why the topic is important. You may wish to quote experts or cite newspapers, journals, books, Web resources, and other secondary sources to establish the importance of the topic.
- **Scope and limitations:** Clarify the boundaries of the report, defining what will be included or excluded.
- **Sources and methods:** Describe your secondary sources (periodicals, books, databases). Also explain how you collected primary data, including survey size, sample design, and statistical programs used.
- **Definitions:** Define any terms you'll use in your findings section that may not be clear to every reader.
- **Organization:** Orient readers by giving them a road map that previews the structure of the report.

FINDINGS. This is the main section of the report and contains numerous headings and subheadings. It is not necessary to use the title *Findings*; many business report writers prefer to begin immediately with the major headings into which the body of the report is divided. Present your findings objectively, avoiding the use of first-person pronouns (*I, we*). Include tables, charts, and graphs to illustrate findings. Analytic and scientific reports may include another section entitled *Implications of Findings*, in which the findings are analyzed and related to the problem. Less formal reports contain the author's analysis of the research findings within the findings section itself. In other words, most business research reports present data and follow the presentation by analyzing what the data means.

CONCLUSIONS AND RECOMMENDATIONS. If the report has been largely informational, it ends with a summary of the data presented. However, the report will usually also analyze its research findings; in that case it should end with conclusions drawn from the analyses. An analytic report frequently poses research questions. The conclusion to such a report reviews the major findings and answers the research questions. If a report seeks to determine a course of action, it may end with conclusions and recommendations. Recommendations regarding a course of action may be placed in a separate section or incorporated with the conclusions. Recommendations should be numbered in order of descending importance (i.e., the most important recommendation first) and should begin with a present-tense verb (e.g., *Purchase, Inform, Reduce*, etc.).

9.6c Back Matter Contents

The back matter of most reports includes a reference section and one or more appendixes. The reference section includes a bibliography of sources, and the appendix contains supplemental information or source documents. In organizing the back matter sections, use standard Arabic numerals to number the pages.

Endnotes, a bibliography, and appendixes may appear after the body of the report.

WORKS CITED, REFERENCES, OR BIBLIOGRAPHY. If you use the MLA referencing format, list all sources of information alphabetically in a section titled *Works Cited*. If you use the APA format, list your sources in a section called *References*. Your listed sources must correspond to in-text citations in the report whenever you are borrowing words or ideas from published and unpublished resources.

9.6d Model Formal Report

Formal business reports generally aim to study problems and recommend solutions. In the formal report shown in Figure 9.18, Brigitte Morceaux, senior research consultant with Petit, Morceaux Industrial Consultants, examined the economic impact of a local industrial park on the city of Winnipeg, resulting in this formal report.

Brigitte's report illustrates many of the points discussed in this chapter. Although it is a good example of a traditional report format and style, it should not be viewed as the only way to present a report. For example, as mentioned earlier in this chapter, some reports today have less text and more graphics than this model report, others are presented via PowerPoint slides.

FIGURE 9.18 | Model Formal Report

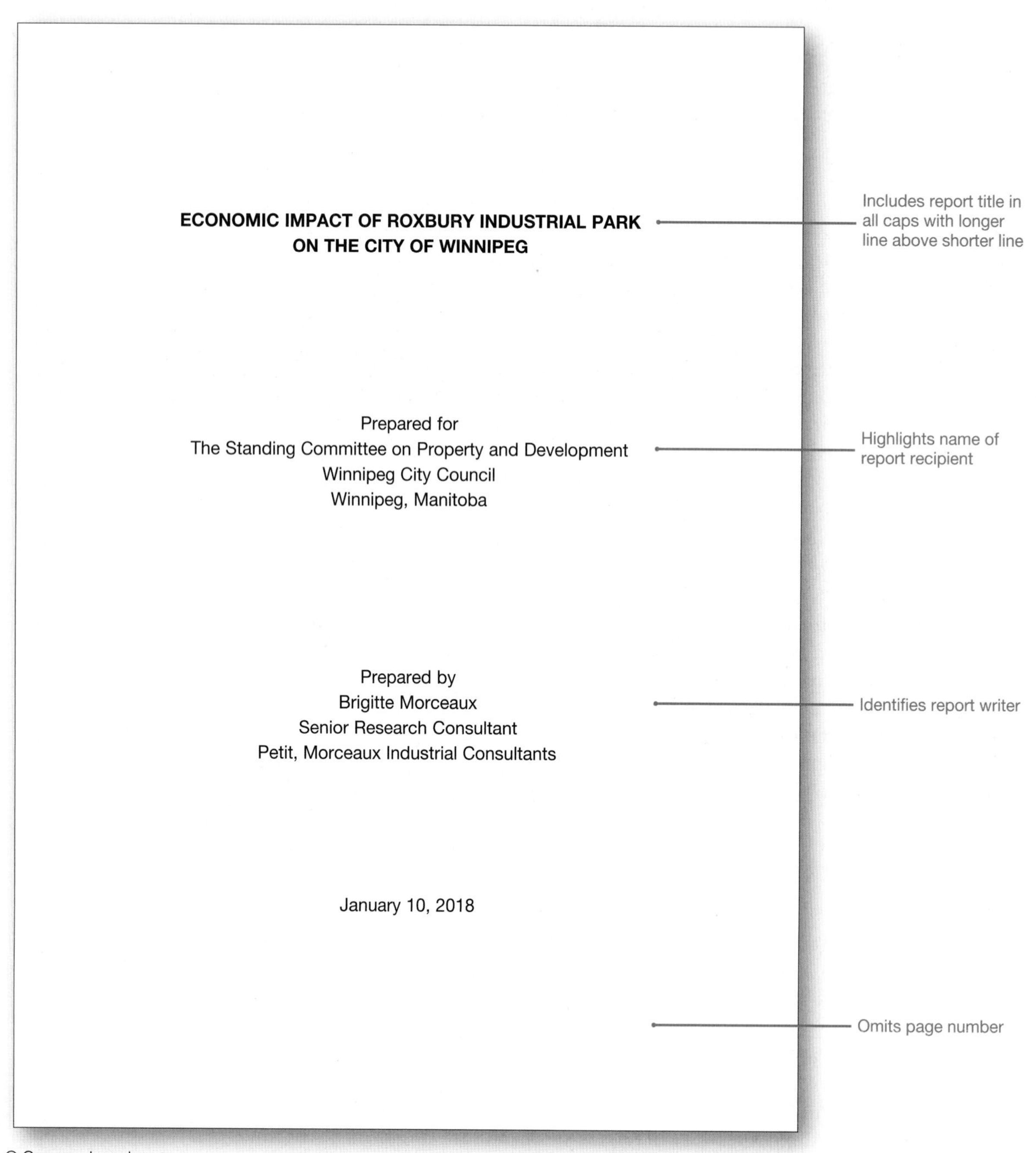
ECONOMIC IMPACT OF ROXBURY INDUSTRIAL PARK ON THE CITY OF WINNIPEG

Prepared for
The Standing Committee on Property and Development
Winnipeg City Council
Winnipeg, Manitoba

Prepared by
Brigitte Morceaux
Senior Research Consultant
Petit, Morceaux Industrial Consultants

January 10, 2018

FIGURE 9.18 | *(Continued)*

Announces report and identifies authorization

Gives broad overview of report purposes

Describes primary and secondary research

Offers to discuss report; expresses appreciation

PETIT, MORCEAUX INDUSTRIAL CONSULTANTS

588 Main Street
Winnipeg, Manitoba R2L 1E6

www.petitmorceaux.com
(204) 549-1101

January 12, 2018

Councillor Richard Moody
Chairperson
Standing Committee on Property and Development
City of Winnipeg
Winnipeg, MB R2L 1E9

Dear Councillor Moody:

The attached report, requested by the Standing Policy Committee on Property and Development in a letter dated May 20, describes the economic impact of Roxbury Industrial Park on the City of Winnipeg. We believe you will find the results of this study useful in evaluating future development of industrial parks within the city limits.

This study was designed to examine economic impact in three areas:

(1) Current and projected tax and other revenues accruing to the city from Roxbury Industrial Park

(2) Current and projected employment generated by the park

(3) Indirect effects on local employment, income, and economic growth

Primary research consisted of interviews with 15 Roxbury Industrial Park tenants and managers, in addition to a 2017 survey of over 5000 RIP employees. Secondary research sources included the Annual Budget of the City of Winnipeg, other government publications, periodicals, books, and online resources. Results of this research, discussed more fully in this report, indicate that Roxbury Industrial Park exerts a significant beneficial influence on the Winnipeg metropolitan economy.

I would be pleased to discuss this report and its conclusions with you at your request. My firm and I thank you for your confidence in selecting our company to prepare this comprehensive report.

Sincerely,

Brigitte Morceaux

Brigitte Morceaux
Senior Research Consultant
bmonceaux@petitmonceaux.com

BM:mef

Attachment

FIGURE 9.18 | *(Continued)*

TABLE OF CONTENTS

LIST OF FIGURES

iii

Uses leaders to guide eye from heading to page number

Indents secondary headings to show levels of outline

Includes tables and figures in one list for simplified numbering

FIGURE 9.18 | *(Continued)*

EXECUTIVE SUMMARY

Opens directly with major research findings

Winnipeg can benefit from the development of industrial parks like the Roxbury Industrial Park. Both direct and indirect economic benefits result, as shown by this in-depth study conducted by Petit, Morceaux Industrial Consultants. The study was authorized by the Standing Committee on Property and Development when Goldman-Lyon & Associates sought City Council's approval for the proposed construction of a G-L industrial park. The City Council requested evidence demonstrating that an existing development could actually benefit the city.

Identifies data sources

Our conclusion that Winnipeg benefits from industrial parks is based on data supplied by a survey of 5000 Roxbury Industrial Park employees, personal interviews with managers and tenants of RIP, City and Provincial documents, and professional literature.

Summarizes organization of report

Analysis of the data revealed benefits in three areas:

(1) Revenues. The City of Winnipeg earned nearly $1 million in tax and other revenues from the Roxbury Industrial Park in 2017. By 2021 this income is expected to reach $1.7 million (in constant 2017 dollars).

(2) Employment. In 2017 RIP businesses employed a total of 7035 workers, who earned an average wage of $28 120. By 2021 RIP businesses are expected to employ directly nearly 15 000 employees who will earn salaries totalling over $450 million.

(3) Indirect benefits. Because of the multiplier effect, by 2021 Roxbury Industrial Park will directly and indirectly generate a total of 38 362 jobs in the Winnipeg area.

Condenses recommendations

On the basis of these findings, it is recommended that development of additional industrial parks be encouraged to stimulate local economic growth.

iv

ECONOMIC IMPACT OF ROXBURY INDUSTRIAL PARK

Shortened report title repeated at beginning of Introduction

PROBLEM

This study was designed to analyze the direct and indirect economic impact of Roxbury Industrial Park on the City of Winnipeg. Specifically, the study seeks answers to these questions:

(1) What current tax and other revenues result directly from this park? What tax and other revenues may be expected in the future?

(2) How many and what kind of jobs are directly attributable to the park? What is the employment picture for the future?

(3) What indirect effects has Roxbury Industrial Park had on local employment, incomes, and economic growth?

Lists three problem questions

BACKGROUND

The Standing Committee on Property and Development commissioned this study of Roxbury Industrial Park at the request of Winnipeg City Council. Before authorizing the development of a proposed Goldman-Lyon industrial park, the City Council requested a study examining the economic effects of an existing park. Members of Council wanted to determine to what extent industrial parks benefit the local community, and they chose Roxbury Industrial Park as an example.

Describes authorization for report and background of study

For those who are unfamiliar with it, Roxbury Industrial Park is a 40-hectare industrial park located in Winnipeg about 2.5 kilometres from the centre of the city. Most of the area lies within a specially designated area known as Redevelopment Project No. 2, which is part of the Winnipeg Capital Region Development Commission's planning area. Planning for the park began in 2014; construction started in 2016.

1

FIGURE 9.18 | *(Continued)*

Provides specifics for data sources

MLA-style (parenthetical) citation

Previews organization of report

Uses topical arrangement

Places figure close to textual reference

The park now contains 14 building complexes with over 25 000 square metres of completed building space. The majority of the buildings are used for office, research and development, marketing and distribution, or manufacturing uses. Approximately 5 hectares of the original area are yet to be developed.

Data for this report came from a 2017 survey of over 5000 Roxbury Industrial Park employees, interviews with 15 RIP tenants and managers, the Annual Budget of the City of Winnipeg, current books, articles, journals, and online resources. Projections for future revenues resulted from analysis of past trends and *Estimates of Revenues for Debt Service Coverage, Redevelopment Project Area 2* (Miller, 2014, pp. 78–79).

DISCUSSION OF FINDINGS

The results of this research indicate that major direct and indirect benefits have accrued to the City of Winnipeg and surrounding municipal areas as a result of the development of Roxbury Industrial Park. The research findings presented here fall into three categories: (a) revenues, (b) employment, and (c) indirect effects.

Revenues

Roxbury Industrial Park contributes a variety of tax and other revenues to the City of Winnipeg. Figure 1 summarizes revenues.

Figure 1

REVENUES RECEIVED BY THE CITY OF WINNIPEG
FROM ROXBURY INDUSTRIAL PARK

Current Revenues and Projections to 2021

	2017	2021
Property taxes	$604 140	$1 035 390
Revenues from licences	126 265	216 396
Business taxes	75 518	129 424
Provincial service receipts	53 768	92 134
Licences and permits	48 331	82 831
Other revenues	64 039	111 987
Total	$972 061	$1 668 162

City of Winnipeg Chief Financial Officer. (2017). 2018 annual financial report. Retrieved from http://www.winnipeg.ca/financials/2018

2

Sales and Use Revenues

As shown in Figure 1, the city's largest source of revenues from RIP is the property tax. Revenues from this source totalled $604 140 in 2017, according to the City of Winnipeg Standing Committee on Finance (City of Winnipeg, 2015, p.103). Property taxes accounted for more than half of the park's total contribution to the City of $972 061.

Continues interpreting figures in table

Other Revenues

Other major sources of City revenues from RIP in 2017 include revenues from licences such as motor vehicle in lieu fees, trailer coach licences ($126 265), business taxes ($75 518), and provincial service receipts ($53 768).

Projections

Total City revenues from RIP will nearly double by 2018, producing an income of $1.7 million. This projection is based on an annual growth rate of 1.4 percent in constant 2017 dollars.

Employment

One of the most important factors to consider in the overall effect of an industrial park is employment. In Roxbury Industrial Park the distribution, number, and wages of people employed will change considerably in the next five years.

Sets stage for next topics to be discussed

Distribution

A total of 7035 employees currently work in various industry groups at Roxbury Industrial Park, as shown below in Figure 2. The largest number of workers (58 percent) is employed in manufacturing and assembly operations. In the next largest category, the computer and electronics industry employs 24 percent of the workers. Some overlap probably exists because electronics assembly could be included in either group. Employees also work in publishing (9 percent), warehousing and storage (5 percent), and other industries (4 percent).

Although the distribution of employees at Roxbury Industrial Park shows a wide range of employment categories, it must be noted that other industrial parks would likely generate an entirely different range of job categories.

3

FIGURE 9.18 | *(Continued)*

Figure 2

EMPLOYMENT DISTRIBUTION OF INDUSTRY GROUPS

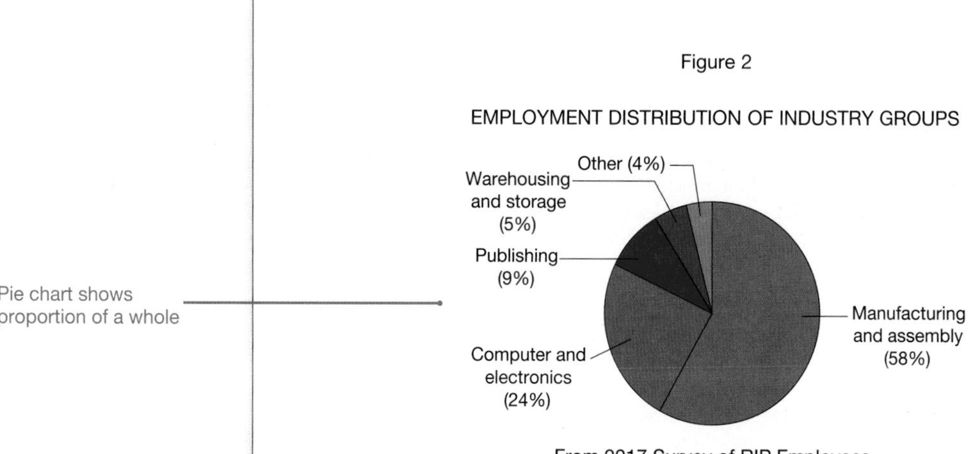

Pie chart shows proportion of a whole

From 2017 Survey of RIP Employees.

Wages

In 2017 employees at RIP earned a total of $278 million in wages, as shown in Figure 3. The average employee in that year earned $58 120. The highest average wages were paid to employees in white-collar fields, such as computer and electronics ($46 800) and publishing ($40 300). Average wages for workers in blue-collar fields ranged from $37 400 in manufacturing and assembly to $34 200 in warehousing and storage.

Figure 3

AVERAGE ANNUAL WAGES BY INDUSTRIAL GROUP

Roxbury Industrial Park, 2017

Industry Group	Employees	Annual Wages	Total
Manufacturing and assembly	4 073	$37 400	$152 330 200
Computer and electronics	1 657	46 800	77 547 600
Publishing	672	40 300	27 081 600
Warehousing and storage	370	34 200	12 654 000
Other	263	31 900	8 389 700
	7 035	$58 120	$278 003 100

Table condenses complex data into readable and understandable form

From 2017 Survey of RIP employees.

4

Projections

By 2021 Roxbury Industrial Park is expected to more than double its number of employees, bringing the total to over 15 000 workers. The total payroll in 2018 will also more than double, producing over $450 million (using constant 2017 dollars) in salaries to RIP employees. These projections are based on an 8 percent growth rate, along with anticipated increased employment as the park reaches its capacity (Miller, 2014, pp.78–79).

Clarifies information and explains what it means in relation to original research questions

Future development in the park will influence employment and payrolls. As Ivan Novak, RIP project manager, stated in an interview, much of the remaining five hectares is planned for medium-rise office buildings, garden offices, and other structures for commercial, professional, and personal services (September 2017). Average wages for employees are expected to increase because of an anticipated shift to higher-paying white-collar jobs. Industrial parks often follow a similar pattern of evolution (Badri 38–45). Like many industrial parks, RIP evolved from a warehousing centre into a manufacturing complex.

CONCLUSIONS AND RECOMMENDATIONS

Summarizes conclusions and recommendations

Analysis of tax revenues, employment data, personal interviews, and professional literature leads to the following conclusions and recommendations about the economic impact of Roxbury Industrial Park on the City of Winnipeg:

1. Property tax and other revenues produced nearly $1 million in income to the City of Winnipeg in 2017. By 2018 revenues are expected to produce $1.7 million in city income.
2. RIP currently employs 7035 employees, the majority of whom are working in manufacturing and assembly. The average employee in 2017 earned $38 120.
3. By 2021 RIP is expected to employ more than 15 000 workers producing a total payroll of over $450 million.
4. Employment trends indicate that by 2021 more RIP employees will be engaged in higher-paying white-collar positions.

On the basis of these findings, we recommend that the City Council of Winnipeg authorize the development of additional industrial parks to stimulate local economic growth.

5

FIGURE 9.18 | *(Continued)*

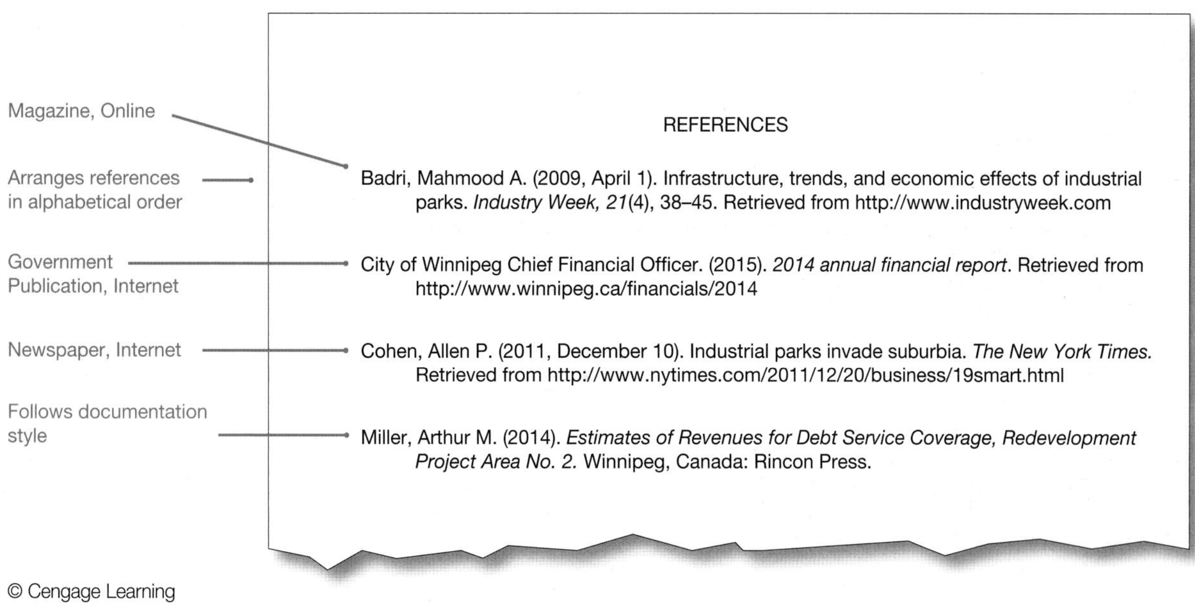

Magazine, Online
Arranges references in alphabetical order
Government Publication, Internet
Newspaper, Internet
Follows documentation style
REFERENCES
Badri, Mahmood A. (2009, April 1). Infrastructure, trends, and economic effects of industrial parks. *Industry Week, 21*(4), 38–45. Retrieved from http://www.industryweek.com
City of Winnipeg Chief Financial Officer. (2015). *2014 annual financial report*. Retrieved from http://www.winnipeg.ca/financials/2014
Cohen, Allen P. (2011, December 10). Industrial parks invade suburbia. *The New York Times*. Retrieved from http://www.nytimes.com/2011/12/20/business/19smart.html
Miller, Arthur M. (2014). *Estimates of Revenues for Debt Service Coverage, Redevelopment Project Area No. 2.* Winnipeg, Canada: Rincon Press.

© Cengage Learning

SUMMARY OF LEARNING OBJECTIVES

9.1 Write effective informal business proposals.

- Proposals are written offers that solve problems, provide services, or sell products.
- Proposals may be solicited (requested by an organization) or unsolicited (written to offer a service, request funding, or solve a problem).
- Components of informal proposals often include an introduction; a background and purpose statement; a proposal, plan, and schedule; staffing requirements; a budget showing project costs; and a conclusion.
- Formal proposals often include additional components, such as a letter of transmittal, a title page, a table of contents, and an appendix.

9.2 Describe a plan for writing formal reports.

- Writers begin formal reports with a statement of purpose that defines the focus of the report.
- Report writers focus on their readers' needs and wants in order to present relevant findings.
- Researchers gather information from primary sources (firsthand observation, interviews, and surveys) and secondary sources (books, articles, journals, and the Web).
- Writers proofread and edit formal reports by reviewing the format, spacing and font consistency, graphics placement, heading levels, data accuracy, and mechanics.

9.3 Collect data for reports effectively from primary and secondary sources.

- Writers gather most of their research from secondary sources by reading what others have published in books, scholarly journals, magazines, and Web documents.
- Web researchers find the information they want by using search operators and advanced search features to filter the results.
- Good writers assess the credibility of each Web resource by evaluating its currency (last update), author or sponsoring organization, content, purpose, and accuracy.
- Report writers gather data from primary sources by distributing surveys, conducting interviews, and collecting data from firsthand observation.

9.4 Document sources effectively in a report

- Documenting sources means giving credit to information sources to avoid plagiarism.
- Copyright refers to "the right to copy"; under fair use, individuals have limited use of copyrighted material without requiring permission.
- Writers should assume that all intellectual property (words, charts, photos, music, and media) is copyrighted and protected whether or not it has a copyright notice.
- Common citation formats include the American Psychological Association (APA), the Modern Language Association (MLA), and the Chicago Manual of Style (CMS).

9.5 Convert report data into meaningful visual aids and graphics.

- Graphics clarify data, add visual interest, and make complex data easy to understand; they should be placed close to where they are referenced.

- Tables show quantitative information in systematic tables and rows; they require meaningful titles, bold column headings, and a logical data arrangement (alphabetical, chronological, etc.)
- Bar charts and line charts show visual comparisons using horizontal or vertical bars or lines of varying lengths; pie charts show a whole and the proportion of its components; flowcharts diagram processes and procedures.
- Infographics, popular in online environments, combine images and graphic elements to illustrate information in an easy-to-understand format.

9.6 Draft and sequence a formal report using standard components.

- Front matter components of formal reports often include the following: title page, letter or memo of transmittal, table of contents, list of figures, and executive summary.
- Body components of formal reports include the introduction, the body, and the conclusions and recommendations.
- The body is the principal section of a formal report and discusses, analyzes, interprets, and evaluates the research findings before drawing conclusions.
- Back matter components of a formal report include a bibliography, which may be a works-cited or reference page, and any appendixes.

CHAPTER REVIEW

1. Who uses requests for proposals (RFPs) and why? (Obj. 1)
2. What are the principal parts and functions of an informal proposal? (Obj. 1)
3. Why is the budget section of a proposal especially important? (Obj. 1)
4. What is the first step in writing a formal report? (Obj. 2)
5. Why do formal report writers include visuals and graphics in reports? (Obj. 5)
6. List three sources of secondary report information, and be prepared to discuss how valuable each might be in writing a formal report about updating your company's travel policy. (Obj. 3)
7. Define these terms: *browser*, *URL*, *search tool*. (Obj. 3)
8. Explain plagiarism and how to avoid it. (Obj. 4)
9. What are the elements of a successful APA citation? (Obj. 4)
10. Pie charts are most helpful in showing what? (Obj. 5)
11. Line graphs are most effective in showing what? (Obj. 5)
12. List three reasons for documenting data in a business report. (Obj. 4)
13. What are some patterns you can use to organize your report's findings? (Obj.2)

CRITICAL THINKING

1. In what ways is a proposal similar to a sales message? (Obj. 1)
2. Why is proposal writing an important function in many businesses? (Obj. 1)
3. To what degree is information obtained on the Web as reliable as information obtained from journals, newspapers, and magazines? Explain. (Obj. 3)
4. Should all reports be written so that they follow the sequence of investigation—that is, description of the initial problem, analysis of issues, data collection, data analysis, and conclusions? Why or why not? (Objs. 4, 6)
5. Are primary or secondary data more likely to be useful in a business report? Why? (Obj. 3)
6. Why is plagiarism a serious issue in the business world? Discuss. (Obj. 4)
7. Do graphic elements enhance a report or do they simply make its presentation more lively? (Obj. 5)

ACTIVITIES AND CASES

9.1 INFORMAL PROPOSAL: PROPOSING A BUSINESS WRITING WORKSHOP (OBJ. 1)

Whether emailing status updates to team members, writing a Web article, preparing meeting agendas, or corresponding with potential customers, employees must write concise, coherent, clear, error-free documents and messages. As the founder of Business Writing Solutions, you offer one- and two-day business writing workshops for businesses and organizations.

Your website features writing tips, workshop descriptions, and your contact information. These workshops are presented on-site in corporate training rooms.

You received an email inquiry from Human Resources Director Janet Somerfield, who is considering a one-day, on-site business writing workshop for employees in her midsized advertising agency. Janet is looking at several seminar companies who offer writing training. She asks about pricing, optimal class size, and course content. She also wants to know whether you can offer feedback on writing samples. Because Janet is considering other training options, you decide to respond with an informal proposal. Your goal is to meet her needs and win the contract.

Decide where it is appropriate to mention the following advantages of improving writing skills in business environments:

- Excellent writing skills help build trusting relationships, improve one's professional image, and add to the credibility of an organization.
- Business associates appreciate clarity, conciseness, and results-focused messages.
- Better writing skills help employees advance their careers, which in turn improves retention.

The one-day workshop is offered in two four-hour blocks in the client's training room. The course includes the following topics: (a) writing results-oriented email messages; (b) structuring routine, persuasive, and negative news messages; (c) reviewing the most common grammar errors; and (d) designing documents for readability. You will also offer feedback on brief writing samples furnished by the participants. Employees who attend the workshop will earn a certificate of completion.

The cost of the writing workshop is $175 per person. If 15 employees participate, the cost would be $2,625. The cost includes workbooks and writing supplies for each participant.

Your Task. Write an informal letter proposal promoting a one-day business writing workshop to Janet Somerfield, Director, Human Resources, The Buzz Agency, 211 Preston Avenue North, Saskatoon, SK S7N 4V2, jsomerfield@buzzagency.ca.

9.2 INFORMAL PROPOSAL: STUDENT VIEWS CONSULTING INC. (OBJ. 1)

Imagine you are in your last semester of college or university. As part of your business program, there is a course you can take called "Consulting Business Simulation." This course allows students to simulate running a consulting business for a semester. You enrol in the course, and on the first day of class the instructor says, "There's only one requirement in this course, and it's worth 100 percent of your grade. You will design, conduct, and write a research proposal and project of your choice for this institution. You won't get paid for it, but you'll have gained a lot of experience that will look good on your résumé." You choose to work with two other students and you call yourselves Student Views Consulting Inc. You decide to tackle the problem of poor customer service at your institution.

Your Task. Write a proposal to the Director of Student Services at your college or university. Propose that your consulting firm carry out a detailed study on current student satisfaction at your institution, which you understand has been problematic lately. For example, there have been questions about how effectively telephone, email, and in-person queries are being handled in various college departments and offices. Also, how the service level at your institution compares to that of competing institutions in the same area has been questioned. Describe the background of this problem and draft a schedule of the work to be done. Cost out this research realistically. When it comes to describing the prior work of Student Views Consulting Inc., make up a realistic list of prior work. Format this proposal as a letter to the Director of Student Services.

9.3 FORMAL BUSINESS REPORT: GATHERING PRIMARY AND SECONDARY INTERCULTURAL DATA (OBJS. 3, 4, 5)

You work for auto parts manufacturer Linamar, a Canadian corporation with numerous overseas offices and manufacturing plants. As part of a "revisioning" of Linamar's international operations, the VP Strategy has asked you to collect information for a report focused on an Asian, Latin American, European, or African country where English is not regularly spoken. Ensure that the country you have selected is represented by a student in your class—you'll need to interview someone from that country.

Your Task. In teams, collect information about your target country from research databases, the Internet, and other sources. Then invite an international student from your target country to be interviewed by your group. As you conduct primary and secondary research, investigate the topics listed in Figure 9.19. Confirm what you learn in your secondary research by talking with your interviewee. When you complete your research, write a report for the VP Strategy at Linamar. Assume that Linamar plans to expand its operations abroad. Your report should advise the company's executives of the social customs, family life, societal attitudes, religious preferences and beliefs, education, and values of the target country. Remember that your company's interests are business oriented; do not dwell on tourist information. Compile your results and write the report.

FIGURE 9.19 | Intercultural Interview Topics and Questions

Social Customs

- How do people react to strangers? Are they friendly? Reserved? Cautious? Suspicious?
- What is the typical greeting for friends? Family members and close friends? Business associates? Elderly people or relatives?
- What are appropriate topics of conversation in business settings? What topics should be avoided?
- What customs are associated with exchanging business cards?
- What are the hours of a typical workday?
- What are the attitudes toward personal space and touching?
- Is gift-giving appropriate when invited to someone's home? If so, what gifts are appropriate?
- What facial expressions or gestures are considered offensive? Is direct eye contact appropriate?
- What is the attitude toward punctuality in social situations? In business situations?
- What gestures indicate agreement? Disagreement? Frustration? Excitement?

Family Life

- What is a typical family unit? Do family units include extended family members?
- How do family life and family size differ in urban and rural settings?
- Do women and men have typical roles in families?
- Do women work outside of the home? In what occupations?
- Are children required by law to attend school? Do families value education?

Housing, Clothing, and Food

- How does housing differ in urban and rural areas? How does housing differ among various socioeconomic groups?
- What special occasions require traditional or ceremonial clothing?
- What types of clothing are considered inappropriate or in poor taste?
- What is appropriate business attire for men? For women?
- What are the typical eating times, and what foods are customary?
- What types of places, food, and drink are appropriate for business entertainment? Where is the seat of honour at a round table? At a rectangular table?

Class Structure

- Into what classes is society organized?
- Do racial, religious, or economic factors determine social status?
- Are there any minority groups? What is their social standing?

Political Patterns

- Are there any immediate threats or signs of political unrest in this country?
- How is political power manifested?
- What media channels are used for expressing political opinions?
- Is it appropriate to talk about politics in social situations?

Religious Preferences and Beliefs

- Are certain religious groups predominant?
- Do religious beliefs influence daily activities?
- Which places, objects, or animals are considered sacred?
- How do religious holidays affect business activities?

Economic Norms

- What are the country's principal exports and products?
- Are workers organized in unions?
- Are businesses owned by individuals, by large public corporations, or by the government?
- How is status shown in an organization? Private office? Floor level? Furnishings?
- Do business associates normally socialize before conducting business?

Value Systems

- Is competitiveness or cooperation more prized?
- Is politeness more important than honesty?
- To what extent is bribery accepted as a way of life?
- Do women own or manage businesses? If so, how are they treated?
- How do people perceive Americans? What behaviours exhibited by Americans are considered offensive?
- What was the hardest adjustment after coming to America?

Visit **MindTap** for a variety of videos, additional exercises, activities, and quizzes to support your learning.

Professionalism and Speaking Skills

UNIT 05

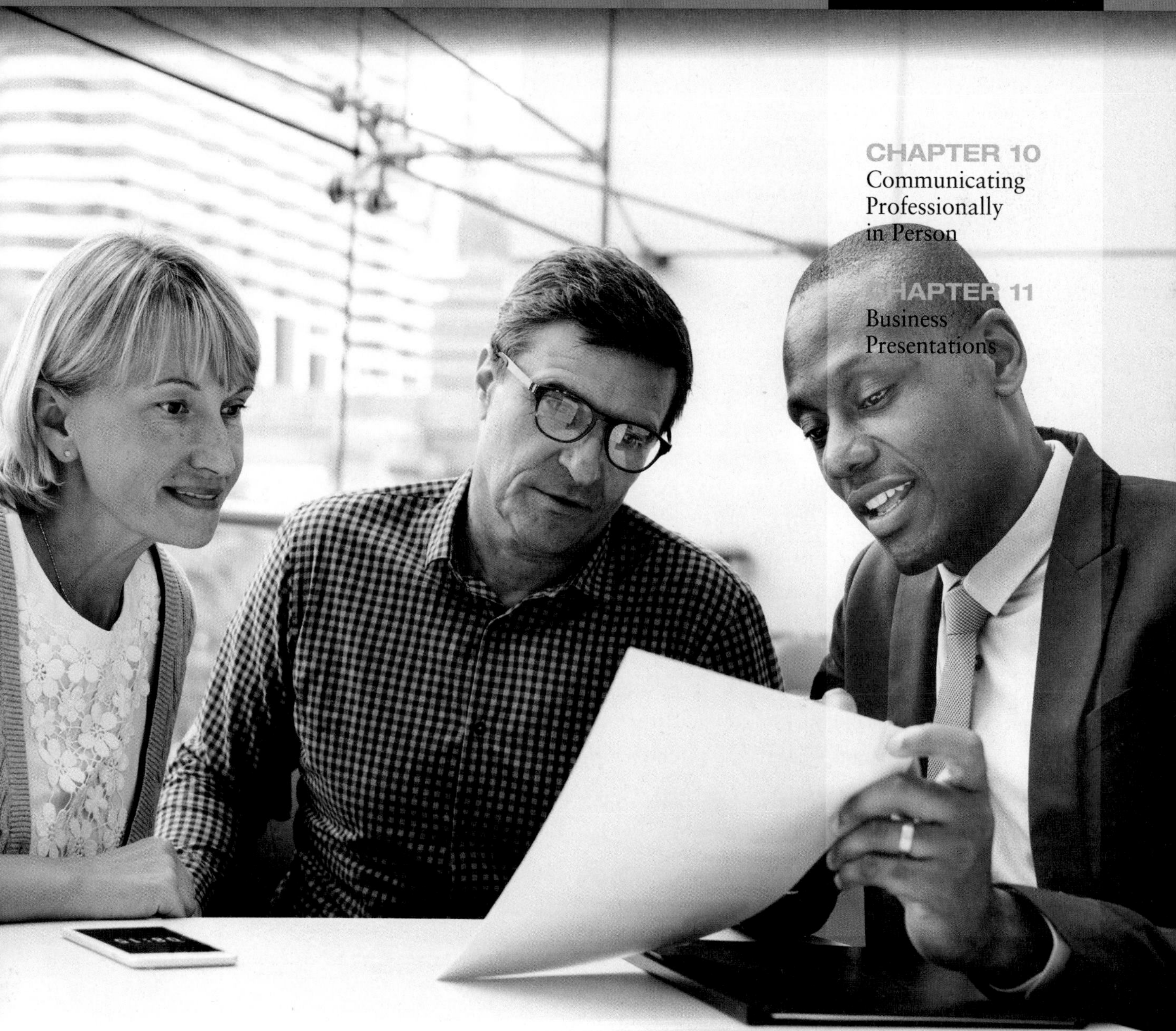

Rawpixel.com/Shutterstock.com

COMMUNICATION TECHNOLOGY IN THE NEWS

Public servants need "civility policy" to deal with harassment, disrespect and conflicts at work, association says

Kathryn May, National Post, *June 22, 2015*

OTTAWA—Nastiness is on the rise in Canada's public service and the federal government should consider a "civility" policy to help stop harassment, disrespect and interpersonal conflicts on the job, says the association representing federal executives.

Civility has emerged as a big issue with the Association of Professional Executives of the Public Service of Canada (APEX), whose own in-house studies flagged how a growing number of employees and executives are targets of "uncivil words and actions," said APEX chief executive officer Lisanne Lacroix.

Lacroix said incivility can poison a workplace and is related to the growing number of mental-health claims over the past decade, which can take public servants off the job for prolonged periods.

APEX has commissioned studies into the health and work of executives. It is also working on a compendium of "best practices" for the joint union-management task force that's studying what's making the public service an unhealthy workplace. APEX has a seat on that task force; its first report is expected in September.

"Our health and work survey showed incivility is on the rise and engagement has dropped, too, so we have to look at these issues and see what can be done and how to reverse the trend," Lacroix said.

APEX urged former Privy Council clerk Wayne Wouters to make mandatory the Mental Health Commission of Canada's national psychological standard for a healthy workplace for all departments.

His successor, Janice Charette, has since made mental health one of her top priorities.

APEX also runs a confidential counselling service for executives, and last year's report showed harassment and bad relationships with superiors were among the leading reasons executives sought help. It urged the Treasury Board then to consider a civility policy—along with a guide on how to deal with uncivil behaviour—as a companion to its harassment prevention policy.

At the same time, APEX commissioned its own "white paper" on the science and research into civility to help give executives some ideas on how to make the workplace "more respectful."

The paper, written by leadership consultant Craig Dowden, concludes the public service is not alone. He says studies indicate incivility has doubled in North America over the past decade, with half of all employees saying they were treated rudely at least once a week at work.

That trend is mirrored in the 2014 public service employees' survey, which found 20 percent of public servants said they were harassed and 63 percent said people in positions of authority were the culprits. Among executives, 11 percent said they were harassed and 63 percent laid the blame on those with authority over them, with 26 percent fingering people who worked for them.

Similarly, APEX's health survey of executives found 22 percent are "verbally abused" by superiors over the course of a year. About 10 percent characterized the workplace as disrespectful, citing discourteous behaviour such as not sharing credit, breaking promises, getting angry, telling lies, blaming and making negative comments.

The health report noted the proportion of executives who reported harassment and incivility was consistent across the ranks.

Dowden describes incivility as rude, insensitive and disrespectful behaviour or comments that can make a workplace toxic.

Last year's public service survey was the first to distinguish types of harassment.

The most common types reported were offensive remarks, unfair treatment and being excluded or ignored. Sexual harassment, a comment or gesture, was reported by nine per cent of those who felt harassed, and 2 percent said they faced "physical violence."

Research suggests incivility in the workplace is caused by various factors—all of which the public service faces in spades. They include pressures associated with downsizing; constant budget restraint; the push to reengineer; the drive to boost productivity; and top-down autocratic management.

Dowden said what makes incivility so insidious is that it is "seemingly inconsequential" and becomes "normalized" and accepted as part of the workplace culture.

Indeed, the public service executives who report harassment say they didn't complain because they didn't think it would make a difference, they feared reprisals, or they were unsure incidents even warranted a complaint.

Dowden said research shows the most common incivility complaints are: cellphones always on; talking behind someone's back; doubting someone's judgment; paying scant attention to opinions; taking credit for other people's work.

Others include: not taking responsibility and blaming someone else; checking email or texting during meetings; using email rather than facing someone when delivering a difficult message; never saying please or thank you; not listening; and talking down to someone.

Research suggests that a tense supervisory relationship has physical consequences as well.

An uncivil boss can increase blood pressure, which can lead to heart disease, stroke or kidney failure. A study published in Occupation and Environmental Medicine found those who spend years with a toxic boss are 30 percent more likely to develop heart disease regardless of the workload, education, social class, income or supervisory status.

Summarize the article you've just read in a two- or three-sentence paragraph. Answer the following questions, either on your own or in a small group. Be prepared to present your answers in a short presentation or in an email to your instructor.

QUESTIONS:

1. How does what you've learned in this article change your perception of business communication?
2. How might what you've learned in this article change your own communication style?
3. Come up with pro and con arguments for the following debate/discussion topic: Employees should be able to handle rude or unprofessional language from coworkers and managers—that's partly what they're paid to do.

CHAPTER

10

Communicating Professionally in Person

OBJECTIVES

After studying this chapter, you should be able to

10.1 Apply professionalism skills in the workplace such as etiquette and an ethical attitude.

10.2 Use your voice effectively in conversations including when offering and receiving constructive criticism.

10.3 Demonstrate professional telephone skills and voice mail etiquette.

10.4 Understand the importance of teamwork and contribute positively to team performance.

10.5 Plan and participate in productive meetings.

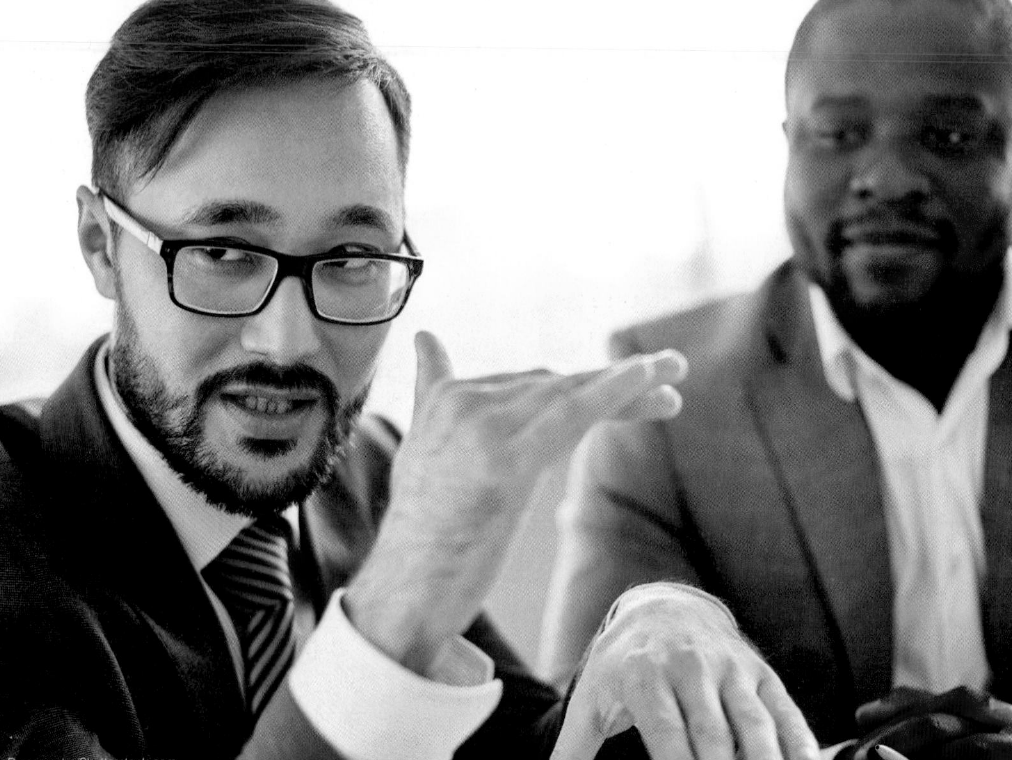

Pressmaster/Shutterstock.com

10.1 Understanding Professionalism, Business Etiquette, and Ethical Behaviour

Whether we call it *professionalism, business etiquette, ethical conduct, social intelligence,* or *soft skills*, we are referring to a whole range of desirable workplace behaviours.

You probably know that being professional is important. When you search for definitions, however, you will find a wide range of meanings. Related terms and synonyms, such as *business etiquette, soft skills, social* or *emotional intelligence, polish*, and *civility*, may add to the confusion. However, they all have one thing in common: they describe desirable workplace behaviour. Businesses desire a workforce that gets along, makes customers feel welcome, and delivers positive results that enhance profits and boost their image. As a new business professional, you have a stake in acquiring skills that will make you a strong job applicant and a valuable, successful employee.

In this section you will learn which professional characteristics are most valued in workplace relationships. Next you will be asked to consider the link between professional and ethical behaviour on the job. Finally, by knowing what recruiters want, you will have the power to shape yourself into the kind of professional they are looking to hire.

10.1a Defining Professional Behaviour

Smooth relations in the workplace and with business partners or the public are crucial for the bottom line. Unfortunately, as the unit-opening article shows, problematic behaviours like rudeness and bullying are a widespread phenomenon today, demonstrated in professional settings among employees, between managers and their employees, and between clients and employees.

As a result, some businesses have established protocol procedures or policies to encourage civility. What exactly are the correct behaviours that make up such procedures and policies? Below is a list that attempts to define professional behaviour you should engage in that can foster positive workplace relations:

CIVILITY. Management consultant Patricia M. Buhler defines rising incivility at work as "behaviour that is considered disrespectful and inconsiderate of others."[1] For an example of a policy encouraging civility, view Royal Bank of Canada's employee code of conduct (www.rbc.com/governance/_assets-custom/pdf/RBCCodeOfConduct.pdf). RBC is very clear about unprofessional and disrespectful behaviour, which when reported becomes the subject of disciplinary action. Most large organizations have similar enforceable policies.

POLISH. You may hear businesspeople refer to someone as being *polished* or displaying polish when dealing with others. In her book with the telling title *Buff and Polish: A Practical Guide to Enhance Your Professional Image and Communication Style*, Kathryn J. Volin focuses on nonverbal techniques and etiquette guidelines that are linked to career success. For example, she addresses making first impressions, shaking hands, improving one's voice quality, listening, and presentation skills.

BUSINESS AND DINING ETIQUETTE. Proper business attire, dining etiquette, and other aspects of your professional presentation can make or break your interview, as you will see in Chapter 13. Even a seemingly harmless act such as sharing a business meal can have a huge impact on your career. In the words of one executive, "Eating is not an executive skill ... but it is especially hard to imagine why anyone negotiating a rise to the top would consider it possible to skip mastering the very simple requirements.... [W]hat else did they skip learning?"[2] This means that you will be judged on more than your college-bred expertise. You will need to hone your etiquette skills as a well-rounded future business professional.

SOCIAL INTELLIGENCE. Occasionally you may encounter the expression *social intelligence*. In the words of one of its modern proponents, it is "the ability to get along well with others and to get them to cooperate with you."[3] Social intelligence points to a deep understanding of culture and life that helps us negotiate interpersonal and social situations. This type of intelligence can be much harder to acquire than simple etiquette. Social intelligence requires us to interact well, be perceptive, show sensitivity toward others, and grasp a situation quickly and accurately.

SOFT SKILLS. Perhaps the most common term for important interpersonal habits is *soft skills*, as opposed to *hard skills*, a term for the technical knowledge in your field. Soft skills are a whole cluster of personal qualities, habits, attitudes (e.g., optimism and friendliness), communication skills, and social graces. Employers want managers and employees who are comfortable with diverse coworkers, who can listen actively to customers and colleagues, who can make eye contact, who display good workplace manners, and who possess a host of other interpersonal skills. *Dress for Success* guru John T. Molloy says that 99 out of 100 executives view social skills as prerequisites to success, whether over cocktails, during dinner, or in

OFFICE INSIDER

"Civility on the job creates an atmosphere of respect and appreciation that ultimately translates to a better reputation and, hence, to better business."

—Ronald M. Bosrock, founder and director of The Global Institute, a research centre

WORKPLACE IN FOCUS

From meetings and interviews to company parties and golf outings, nearly all workplace-related activities involve etiquette. Take Your Dog to Work Day, the ever-popular morale booster held each June 21, has a unique set of guidelines to help maximize fun. Some etiquette gurus say pets must be well-behaved, housebroken, and free of fleas to participate in the four-legged festivity. *Canadian Business* magazine reports that "creating a dog-free zone and policies around appropriate doggie behaviour has quelled" any resistance among workers who don't appreciate dogs in the office.[5] *Why is it important to follow proper business etiquette?*

Ryan McVay/Thinkstock

the boardroom.[4] These skills are immensely important not only to being hired but also to being promoted.

All attempts to explain proper behaviour at work are aimed at identifying traits that make someone a good employee and a compatible coworker. You will want to achieve a positive image on the job and to maintain a solid reputation. For the sake of simplicity, in the discussion that follows, the terms *professionalism*, *business etiquette*, and *soft skills* will be used largely synonymously.

10.1b The Relationship Between Ethics and Professional Behaviour

The wide definition of professionalism also encompasses another crucial quality in a businessperson: *ethics* or *integrity*. Perhaps you subscribe to a negative view of business after learning about companies such as the U.S.'s Enron or Canada's Livent. The collapse of these businesses, along with fraud charges against their executives, has reinforced the cynical perception of business as unethical and greedy. However, for every company that captures the limelight for misconduct, hundreds or even thousands of others operate honestly and serve their customers and the public well. The overwhelming majority of businesses wish to recruit ethical and polished graduates.

Ethics is the study of right and wrong behaviour, from both a theoretical point of view (normative ethics) and a practical point of view (applied ethics). Each day of our lives, we face decisions about how to act: should I give change to someone asking for it on the street, smile at a customer and maintain composure even after he has been slightly rude to me, etc.

At base, all ethical theories whether duty-based (do what's right in all cases), consequentialist-based (do what will make the most people happy), or social contract–based (do what's right because you live in a community and part of this means taking other people's needs into consideration) have one goal in mind: in your interactions with others, you must not always think about things from your own point of view. Exercise empathy as often as you can—don't just do what's right for you, but as often as possible do what's right for the other person or people.

Clearly, there's a direct relationship between an ethical person and a professional person. Professionalism is essentially a type of applied ethics: it's applied because the respectful, pro-social behaviours are happening in a real-world setting, in this case in a business workplace. In effect, professionalism is made up of appearance aspects like dressing and sounding appropriate at work, as well as social aspects like treating the people around you with respect and consideration.

Business etiquette is closely related to everyday ethical behaviour.

Figure 10.1 summarizes the many components of professional workplace behaviour[6] and identifies six main dimensions that will ease your entry into the world of work. Follow these guidelines to ensure your success on the job and increase the likelihood of promotion.

In the workplace we are judged to a great extent on our soft skills and professionalism.

10.1c Professionalism Gives You an Edge

Professional polish is increasingly valuable in our digital economy and will set you apart in competition with others. Hiring managers expect you to have technical expertise in your field. A good résumé and interview may get you in the door. However, soft skills and professional polish will ensure your long-term success. Advancement and promotions will depend on your grasp of workplace etiquette and the ability to communicate with your boss, coworkers, and customers. You will also earn recognition on the job if you prove yourself as an effective and contributing team member—and as a well-rounded professional overall.

Even in highly technical fields such as accounting and finance, employers are looking for professionalism and soft skills. Based on a survey of international accounting executives, *CA Magazine* concluded that "the future is bright for the next generation of accounting and finance professionals provided they are armed

OFFICE INSIDER

"Unprofessional conduct around the office will eventually overflow into official duties. Few of us have mastered the rare art of maintaining multiple personalities."

—Douglas Chismar, liberal arts program director at Ringling College of Art and Design

FIGURE 10.1 | The Six Dimensions of Professional Behaviour

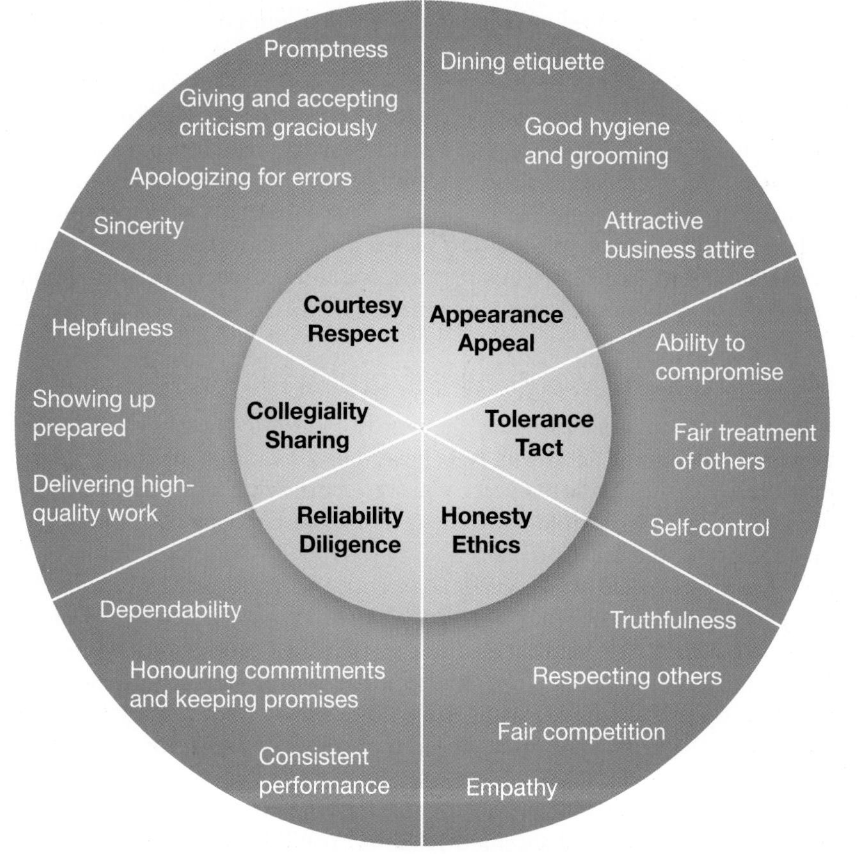

© Cengage Learning

with such soft skills as the ability to communicate, deal with change, and work in a team setting."[7] A survey of chief financial officers revealed that a majority believed that communication skills carry a greater importance today than in the past.[8] Increasingly, finance professionals must be able to interact with the entire organization and explain terms without using financial jargon.

Employment advertisements frequently mention team, communication, and people skills.

Employers want team players who can work together productively. If you look at current online or newspaper want ads, chances are you will find requirements such as the following examples:

- Proven team skills to help deliver on-time, on-budget results
- Strong verbal and written communication skills as well as excellent presentation skills
- Excellent interpersonal, organizational, and teamwork skills
- Interpersonal and team skills plus well-developed communication skills
- Good people skills and superior teamwork abilities

In addition, most hiring managers are looking for new hires who show enthusiasm, are eager to learn, volunteer to tackle even difficult tasks, and exhibit a positive attitude. You will not be hired to warm a seat.

10.2 Successful Face-to-Face Workplace Communication

One-dimensional communication technologies cannot replace the richness or effectiveness of face-to-face communication.

Because technology provides many communication channels, you may think that face-to-face communication is no longer essential or even important in business and professional transactions. You've already learned that email is now the preferred communication channel. Yet despite their popularity and acceptance, new communication technologies can't replace the richness or effectiveness of face-to-face communication.[9] Imagine that you want to tell your boss how you solved a problem. Would you settle for a one-dimensional email when you could step into her office and explain quickly in person?

Face-to-face conversation has many advantages. It allows you to be persuasive and expressive because you can use your voice and body language to make a point. You are less likely to be misunderstood because you can read feedback instantly and make needed adjustments. In conflict resolution, you can reach a solution more efficiently and cooperate to create greater levels of mutual benefit when communicating face to face.[10] Moreover, people want to see each other to satisfy a deep human need for social interaction. For numerous reasons, communicating in person remains the most effective of all communication channels.

10.2a Using Your Voice as a Communication Tool

Like an actor, you can change your voice to make it a more powerful communication tool.

It's been said that language provides the words, but your voice is the "music" that makes words meaningful.[11] You may believe that a beautiful or powerful voice is unattainable. After all, this is the voice you were born with, and it can't be changed. Actually, the voice is a flexible instrument. For example, two of Canada's leading theatre companies, the Stratford and Shaw Festivals in Ontario, both have speech coaches on staff to teach actors various accents and voice techniques. Celebrities, business executives, and everyday people consult voice and speech therapists to help them shake bad habits or help them speak so that they can be understood and not sound less intelligent than they are. Rather than consulting a high-paid specialist, you can pick up useful tips for using your voice most effectively by learning how to control such elements as pronunciation, tone, pitch, volume, rate, and emphasis.

Proper pronunciation means saying words correctly and clearly with the accepted sounds and accented syllables.

PRONUNCIATION. Pronunciation involves saying words correctly and clearly with the accepted sounds and accented syllables. You'll be at a distinct advantage in your job if, through training and practice, you learn to pronounce words correctly.

At work you want to sound intelligent, educated, and competent. If you mispronounce words or slur phrases together, you risk being misunderstood as well as giving a poor impression of yourself. How can you improve your pronunciation skills? The best way is to listen carefully to educated people, read aloud from well-written newspapers like the *Globe and Mail* and the *National Post,* and listen to audio files from online dictionaries.

TONE. The tone of your voice sends a nonverbal message to listeners. It identifies your personality and your mood. Some voices sound enthusiastic and friendly, conveying the impression of an upbeat person who is happy to be with the listener. But voices can also sound controlling, patronizing, slow-witted, angry, or childish. This doesn't mean that the speaker necessarily has that attribute. It may mean that the speaker is merely carrying on a family tradition or pattern learned in childhood. To check your voice tone, record your voice and listen to it critically. Is it projecting a positive quality about you?

PITCH. Effective speakers use a relaxed, controlled, well-pitched voice to attract listeners to their message. Pitch refers to sound vibration frequency; that is, it indicates the highness or lowness of a sound. Most speakers and listeners tend to prefer a variety of pitch patterns. Voices are most attractive when they rise and fall in conversational tones. Flat, monotone voices are considered boring and ineffectual.

VOLUME AND RATE. Volume indicates the degree of loudness or the intensity of sound. Just as you adjust the volume on your MP3 player or television, you should adjust the volume of your speaking to the occasion and your listeners. When speaking face to face, you generally know whether you are speaking too loudly or softly by looking at your listeners. To judge what volume to use, listen carefully to the other person's voice. Use it as a guide for adjusting your voice. Rate refers to the pace of your speech. If you speak too slowly, listeners are bored and their attention wanders. If you speak too quickly, listeners can't understand you. If you're the kind of speaker who speeds up when talking in front of a group of people, monitor the nonverbal signs of your listeners and adjust your rate as needed.

Speaking in a moderately low-pitched voice at about 125 words a minute makes you sound pleasing and professional.

EMPHASIS. By emphasizing or stressing certain words, you can change the meaning you are expressing. For example, read these sentences aloud, emphasizing the italicized words:

> *Matt* said the hard drive failed again. (Matt knows what happened.)
>
> Matt *said* the hard drive failed again. (But he may be wrong.)
>
> Matt said the hard drive failed *again*? (Did he really say that?)

As you can see, emphasis affects the meaning of the words and the thought expressed. To make your message interesting and natural, use emphasis appropriately. You can raise your volume to sound authoritative and raise your pitch to sound disbelieving. Lowering your volume and pitch makes you sound professional or reasonable.

Some speakers today are prone to "uptalk." This is a habit of using a rising inflection at the end of a sentence that makes statements sound like questions. Uptalk is increasingly found in the workplace, with negative results. When statements sound like questions, speakers seem tentative, lacking conviction and authority. On the job, managers afflicted by uptalk may have difficulty convincing staff members to follow directions because their voice inflection implies that other valid options are available. If you want to sound confident and competent, avoid uptalk.

"Uptalk," in which sentences sound like questions, makes speakers seem weak and tentative.

10.2b Making Workplace Conversation Matter

In the workplace, conversations may involve giving and taking instructions, providing feedback, exchanging ideas on products and services, participating in performance appraisals, or engaging in small talk about such things as families and sports. Face-to-face conversation helps people work together harmoniously and feel that they are part of the larger organization. There are several ways to create positive workplace conversations, starting with using correct names and titles.

USE CORRECT NAMES AND TITLES. Although the world seems increasingly informal, it's still wise to use titles and last names when addressing professional adults (*Mrs. Smith*, *Mr. Rivera*). In some organizations senior staff members will speak to junior employees on a first-name basis, but the reverse may not be encouraged. Probably the safest plan is to ask your superiors how they want to be addressed. Customers and others outside the organization should always be addressed by title and last name.

When you meet strangers, do you have trouble remembering their names? You can improve your memory considerably if you associate the person with an object, place, colour, animal, job, adjective, or some other memory hook. For example, *computer pro Kevin, Miami Kim, silver-haired Mr. Lee, bulldog Chris, bookkeeper Lynn, traveller Ms. Janis.* The person's name will also be more deeply embedded in your memory if you use it immediately after being introduced, in subsequent conversation, and when you part.

You will be most effective in workplace conversations if you use correct names and titles, choose appropriate topics, avoid negative and judgmental remarks, and give sincere and specific praise.

CHOOSE APPROPRIATE TOPICS. In some workplace activities, such as social gatherings or interviews, you will be expected to engage in small talk. Be sure to stay away from controversial topics with someone you don't know very well. Avoid politics, religion, or current events items that might start heated arguments until you know the person better. Reading newspapers and listening to radio and TV shows discussing current events will help you to initiate appropriate conversations. Make a mental note of items that you can use in conversation, taking care to remember where you saw or heard the news item so that you can report accurately and authoritatively. Try not to be defensive or annoyed if others present information that upsets you.

AVOID NEGATIVE REMARKS. Workplace conversations are not the place to complain about your colleagues, your friends, the organization, or your job. No one enjoys listening to whiners. And your criticism of others may come back to haunt you. A snipe at your boss or a complaint about a fellow worker may reach him or her, sometimes embellished or distorted with meanings you did not intend. Be careful about publicizing negative judgments. Remember, some people love to repeat statements that will stir up trouble or set off internal workplace wars. It's best not to give them the ammunition.

LISTEN TO LEARN. In conversations with colleagues, subordinates, and customers, train yourself to expect to learn something from what you are hearing. Being attentive is not only instructive but also courteous. Beyond displaying good manners, you'll probably find that your conversation partner has information that you don't have. Being receptive and listening with an open mind means not interrupting or prejudging. Let's say you very much want to be able to work at home for part of your workweek. You try to explain your ideas to your boss, but he cuts you off shortly after you start. He says, "It's out of the question; we need you here every day." Suppose instead he says, "I have strong reservations about your telecommuting, but maybe you'll change my mind," and he settles in to listen to your presentation. Even if your boss decides against your request, you will feel that your ideas were heard and respected.

GIVE SINCERE AND SPECIFIC PRAISE. Probably nothing promotes positive workplace relationships better than sincere and specific praise. Whether the compliments and appreciation are travelling upward to management or horizontally to colleagues, everyone responds well to recognition. Organizations run more smoothly and morale is higher when people feel appreciated. In your workplace conversations, look for ways to recognize good work and good people. Try to be specific. Instead of "You did a good job in leading that meeting," try something more specific, such as "Your leadership skills certainly kept that meeting focused and productive."

10.2c Responding Professionally to Workplace Criticism

When being criticized, you probably will feel that you are being attacked. You can't just sit back and relax. Your heart beats faster, your temperature increases, your face reddens, and you respond with the classic "fight or flight" syndrome. You feel that you want to instantly retaliate or escape from the attacker. But focusing on your feelings distracts you from hearing the content of what is being said, and it prevents you from responding professionally. Some or all of the following suggestions will guide you in reacting positively to criticism so that you can benefit from it:

- **Listen without interrupting.** Even though you might want to protest, make yourself hear the speaker out.
- **Determine the speaker's intent.** Unskilled communicators may throw "verbal bricks" with unintended negative-sounding expressions. If you think the intent is positive, focus on what is being said rather than reacting to poorly chosen words.
- **Acknowledge what you are hearing.** Respond with a pause, a nod, or a neutral statement such as "I understand you have a concern." This buys you time. Do not disagree, counterattack, or blame, which may escalate the situation and harden the speaker's position.
- **Paraphrase what was said.** In your own words, restate objectively what you are hearing; for example, "So what you're saying is...."
- **Ask for more information if necessary.** Clarify what is being said. Stay focused on the main idea rather than interjecting side issues.
- **Agree—if the comments are accurate.** If an apology is in order, give it. Explain what you plan to do differently. If the criticism is on target, the sooner you agree, the more likely you will engender respect from the other person.
- **Disagree respectfully and constructively—if you feel the comments are unfair.** After hearing the criticism, you might say, "May I tell you my perspective?" Or you could try to solve the problem by saying, "How can we improve this situation in a way you believe we can both accept?" If the other person continues to criticize, say "I want to find a way to resolve your concern. When do you want to talk about it next?"
- **Look for a middle position.** Search for a middle position or a compromise. Be genial even if you don't like the person or the situation.

If you feel you are being criticized unfairly, disagree respectfully and constructively; look for a middle position.

Conflict is a normal part of every workplace, but it is not always negative. When managed properly, conflict can improve decision making, clarify values, increase group cohesiveness, stimulate creativity, decrease tensions, and reduce dissatisfaction. Unresolved conflict, however, can destroy productivity and seriously reduce morale.

10.2d Offering Constructive Criticism at Work

No one likes to receive criticism, and most of us don't like to give it either. But cooperative endeavours in the workplace demand feedback and evaluation. How are we doing on a project? What went well? What failed? How can we improve our efforts? Today's workplace often involves team projects. As a team member, you will be called on to judge the work of others. In addition to working on teams, you can also expect to become a supervisor or manager one day. As such, you will need to evaluate your direct reports. Good employees seek good feedback from their supervisors. They want and need timely, detailed observations about their work to reinforce what they do well and help them overcome weak spots. But making that feedback palatable and constructive is not always easy. Depending on your situation, you may find some or all of the following suggestions helpful when you must deliver constructive criticism:

Offering constructive criticism is easier if you plan what you will say, focus on improvement, offer to help, be specific, discuss the behaviour and not the person, speak privately face to face, and avoid anger.

- **Mentally outline your conversation.** Think carefully about what you want to accomplish and what you will say. Find the right words at the right time and in the right setting.
- **Generally, use face-to-face communication.** Most constructive criticism is better delivered in person rather than in emails or memos. Personal feedback offers an opportunity for the listener to ask questions and give explanations. Occasionally, however, complex situations may require a different strategy. You might prefer to write out your opinions and deliver them by telephone or in writing. A written document enables you to organize your thoughts, include all the details, and be sure of keeping your cool. Remember, though, that written documents create permanent records—for better or worse.
- **Focus on improvement.** Instead of attacking, use language that offers alternative behaviour. Use phrases such as "Next time, it would great if you could…."
- **Offer to help.** Criticism is accepted more readily if you volunteer to help in eliminating or solving the problem.
- **Be specific.** Instead of a vague assertion such as "Your work is often late," be more specific: "The specs on the Riverside job were due Thursday at 5 p.m., and you didn't hand them in until Friday." Explain how the person's performance jeopardized the entire project.
- **Avoid broad generalizations.** Don't use words such as *should, never, always*, and other encompassing expressions. They may cause the listener to shut down and become defensive.
- **Discuss the behaviour, not the person.** Instead of "You seem to think you can come to work any time you want," focus on the behaviour: "Coming to work late means that someone else has to fill in until you arrive."
- **Use the word *we* rather than *you*.** "We need to meet project deadlines," is better than saying "You need to meet project deadlines." Emphasize organizational expectations rather than personal ones. Avoid sounding accusatory.
- **Encourage two-way communication.** Even if well-planned, criticism is still hard to deliver. It may surprise or hurt the feelings of the employee. Consider ending your message with, "It can be hard to hear this type of feedback. If you'd like to share your thoughts, I'm listening."
- **Avoid anger, sarcasm, and a raised voice.** Criticism is rarely constructive when tempers flare. Plan in advance what you will say and deliver it in low, controlled, and sincere tones.
- **Keep it private.** Offer praise in public; offer criticism in private. "Setting an example" through public criticism is never a wise management policy.

10.3 Phone and Voice Mail Etiquette

You can make productive phone calls by planning an agenda, identifying the purpose, being courteous and cheerful, and avoiding rambling.

Despite the heavy reliance on email, the telephone is still an extremely important piece of equipment in offices. In a survey of business professionals, 83 percent said that email is "critical/very important" to their productivity and success; 81 percent named the phone as "critical/very important." Both are indispensable communication tools today.[12] As a business communicator, you can be more productive, efficient, and professional by following some simple suggestions.

10.3a Making Professional Phone Calls

Before making a phone call, decide whether the intended call is necessary. Could you find the information yourself? If you wait a while, will the problem resolve itself? Perhaps your message could be delivered more efficiently through some other channel. One company found that phone interruptions consumed about 18 percent of staff members' workdays. Another study found that two thirds of all calls were less important than the work they interrupted. If a phone call must be made, use the following suggestions to make it fully professional.

- **Plan a mini-agenda.** Have you ever been embarrassed when you had to make a second phone call because you forgot an important item the first time? Before placing a call, jot down notes regarding all the topics you need to discuss. Following an agenda guarantees not only a complete call but also a quick one. You'll be less likely to wander from the business at hand while rummaging through your mind trying to remember everything.
- **Use a three-point introduction.** When placing a call, immediately (1) name the person you are calling, (2) identify yourself and your affiliation, and (3) give a brief explanation of your reason for calling. For example: "May I speak to Pieter Kortenaar? This is Hillary Dahl at Evergreen, and I'm seeking information about Sinzer's impact measurement software." This kind of introduction enables the receiving individual to respond immediately without asking further questions.
- **Be brisk if you are rushed.** For business calls when your time is limited, avoid questions such as "How are you?" Instead, say, "Lisa, I knew you'd be the only one who could answer these two questions for me." Another efficient strategy is to set a "contract" with the caller: "Hi, Lisa, I have only ten minutes, but I really wanted to get back to you."
- **Be cheerful and accurate.** Let your voice show the same kind of animation that you radiate when you greet people in person. In your mind try to envision the individual answering the phone. A smile can certainly affect the tone of your voice, so smile at that person. Moreover, be accurate about what you say. "Hang on a second; I'll be right back" is rarely true. Better to say, "It may take me two or three minutes to get that information. Would you prefer to hold or have me call you back?"
- **Bring it to a close.** The responsibility for ending a call lies with the caller. This is sometimes difficult to do if the other person rambles on. You may need to use suggestive closing language, such as "I've certainly enjoyed talking with you," "I've learned what I needed to know, and now I can proceed with my work," "Thanks for your help," or "I must go now, but may I call you again in the future if I need...?"
- **Avoid phone tag.** If you call someone who's not in, ask when it would be best for you to call again. State that you will call at a specific time—and do it. If you ask a person to call you, give a time when you can be reached—and then be sure you are in at that time.
- **Leave complete voice mail messages.** Remember that there's no rush when you leave a voice mail message. Always enunciate clearly. And be sure to provide a complete message, including your name, telephone number, and the time and date of your call. Explain your purpose so that the receiver can be ready with the required information when returning your call.

10.3b Receiving Phone Calls Professionally

With a little forethought, you can project a professional image and make your phone a productive, efficient work tool. Developing good phone manners also reflects well on you and on your organization. Try following the following phone etiquette guidelines for receiving calls professionally:

- **Identify yourself immediately.** In answering your phone or someone else's, provide your name, title or affiliation, and, possibly, a greeting. For example, "Pieter Kortenaar, Sinzer Software. How may I help you?" Force yourself to speak clearly and slowly. Remember that the caller may be unfamiliar with what you are saying and will fail to recognize slurred syllables.

You can improve your telephone reception skills by identifying yourself, being responsive and helpful, and taking accurate messages.

- **Be responsive and helpful.** If you are in a support role, be sympathetic to callers' needs. Instead of "I don't know," try "That's a good question; let me investigate." Instead of "We can't do that," try "That's a tough one; let's see what we can do." Avoid "no" at the beginning of a sentence. It sounds especially abrasive and displeasing because it suggests total rejection.
- **Be cautious when answering calls for others.** Be courteous and helpful, but don't give out confidential information. Better to say "She's away from her desk" or "He's out of the office" than to report a colleague's exact whereabouts.
- **Take messages carefully.** Few things are as frustrating as receiving a potentially important phone message that is illegible. Repeat the spelling of names and verify telephone numbers. Write messages legibly and record their time and date. Promise to give the messages to intended recipients, but don't guarantee return calls.
- **Explain what you're doing when transferring calls.** Give a reason for transferring, and identify the extension to which you are directing the call in case the caller is disconnected.

10.3c Using Smartphones for Business

Smartphones are important workplace communication tools, but they must be used without offending others.

Today's smartphones are sophisticated mobile devices. They enable you to conduct business from virtually anywhere at any time. The smartphone has become an essential part of communication in the workplace and in our personal lives. The Canadian Radio and Telecommunications Commission reported in 2015 that while most Canadians still own landlines, there is a "slow and steady shift away from this technology in favour of wireless services."[13]

Today's smartphones can do much more than making and receiving calls. High-end smartphones function much like mini tablet computers. They can be used to store contact information, make to-do lists, keep track of appointments and important dates, send and receive email, send and receive text and multimedia messages, search the Web, get news and stock quotes from the Internet, take pictures and videos, synchronize with Outlook and other software applications, and many other functions. Whether businesspeople opt for BlackBerrys, Android phones, or the popular iPhone, thousands of applications ("apps") enable them to stay connected, informed, and entertained on the go.

Because so many people depend on their smartphones and cellphones, it is important to understand proper use and etiquette. How are these mobile devices best used? When is it acceptable to take calls? Where should calls be made? Most of us have experienced thoughtless and rude cellphone behaviour. Researchers say that the rampant use of technological devices has worsened workplace incivility, while employers say that the use of cellphones has worsened workplace productivity. To avoid offending, smart business communicators practise cellphone etiquette, as outlined in Figure 10.2. They are careful about location, time, and volume in relation to their cellphone calls.

Avoid taking cellphone calls when you are talking with someone else, and avoid "cell yell."

LOCATION. Use good judgment in placing or accepting cellphone calls. Some places are dangerous or inappropriate for cellphone use. Turn off your cellphone in your vehicle and when entering a conference room, interview, theatre, place of worship, or any other place where it could be distracting or disruptive to others. Taking a call in a crowded room or bar makes it difficult to hear and reflects poorly on you as a professional. A bad connection also makes a bad impression. Static or dropped signals create frustration and miscommunication. Don't sacrifice professionalism for the sake of a garbled phone call. It's smarter to turn off your phone in an area where the signal is weak and when you are likely to have interference. Use voice mail and return the call when conditions are better.

TIME. Often what you are doing is more important than whatever may come over the airwaves to you on your phone. For example, when you are having an important discussion with a business partner, customer, or manager, it is rude to allow yourself to be interrupted by an incoming call. It's also poor manners to practise multitasking while on the phone. What's more, it's dangerous. Although you might be able to read and print out emails, deal with a customer at the counter, and talk on your wireless phone simultaneously, it's impolite and risky. If a phone call is important enough to accept, then it's important enough to stop what you are doing and attend to the conversation.

VOLUME. Many people raise their voices when using their cellphones. "Cell yell" results, much to the annoyance of anyone nearby. Raising your voice is unnecessary since most phones have excellent microphones that can pick up even a whisper. If the connection is bad, louder volume will not improve the sound quality. As in face-to-face conversations, a low, modulated voice sounds professional and projects the proper image.

FIGURE 10.2 | Professional Cellphone Use

Show courtesy

- Don't force others to hear your business.
- Don't make or receive calls in public places, such as post offices, banks, retail stores, trains, and buses.
- Don't allow your phone to ring in theatres, restaurants, museums, classrooms, and meetings.
- Apologize for occasional cellphone blunders.

Keep it down

- Speak in low, conversational tones. Cellphone microphones are sensitive, making it unnecessary to raise your voice.
- Choose a professional ringtone and set it on low or vibrate.

Step outside

- If a call is urgent, step outside to avoid being disruptive.
- Make full use of caller ID to screen incoming calls. Let voice mail take routine calls.

Drive now, talk and text later

- Talking while driving increases accidents almost fourfold, about the same as driving intoxicated.
- Texting while driving is even more dangerous. Don't do it!

10.3d Making the Most of Voice Mail

Because phone calls can be disruptive, many businesspeople are making extensive use of voice mail to intercept and screen incoming calls. Voice mail's popularity results from the many functions it serves, the most important of which is message storage. Because as many as half of all business calls require no discussion or feedback, the messaging capabilities of voice mail can mean huge savings for businesses. Incoming information is delivered without interrupting potential receivers and without all the niceties that most two-way conversations require. Stripped of superfluous chit-chat, voice mail messages allow communicators to focus on essentials. Voice mail also eliminates telephone tag, inaccurate message taking, and time-zone barriers.

However, voice mail should not be overused. Individuals who screen all incoming calls cause irritation, resentment, and needless phone tag. Both receivers and callers can use etiquette guidelines to make voice mail work most effectively for them.

RECEIVING VOICE MAIL MESSAGES. Your voice mail should project professionalism and should provide an efficient mechanism for your callers to leave messages for you. Here are some voice mail etiquette tips to follow:

- **Don't overuse voice mail.** Don't use voice mail to avoid taking phone calls. It is better to answer calls yourself than to let voice mail messages build up.
- **Set the number of rings appropriately.** Set your voice mail to ring as few times as possible before picking up. This shows respect for your callers' time.
- **Prepare a professional, concise, friendly greeting.** Make your mechanical greeting sound warm and inviting, both in tone and content. Your greeting should be in your own voice, not a computer-generated one. Identify yourself and your organization so that callers know they have reached the right number. Thank the caller and briefly explain that you are unavailable. Invite the caller to

leave a message or, if appropriate, call back. Here's a typical voice mail greeting: *Hello, this is Pieter Kortenaar at Sinzer Software, and I appreciate your call. You have reached my voice mailbox because I'm either working with customers or talking on another line at the moment. Please leave your name, number, and reason for calling so that I can be prepared when I return your call.* Give callers an idea of when you will be available, such as *I'll be back at 2:30* or *I'll be out of my office until Wednesday, May 20.* If you screen your calls as a time-management technique, try this message: *I'm not near my phone right now, but I should be able to return calls after 3:30.*

- **Test your message.** Call your number and assess your message. Does it sound inviting? Sincere? Professional? Understandable? Are you pleased with your tone? If not, re-record your message until it conveys the professional image you want.
- **Change your message.** Update your message regularly, especially if you travel for your job.
- **Respond to messages promptly.** Check your messages regularly, and try to return all voice mail messages within one business day.
- **Plan for vacations and other extended absences.** If you will not be picking up voice mail messages for an extended period, let callers know how they can reach someone else if needed.

LEAVING VOICE MAIL MESSAGES. When leaving a voice mail message, you should follow these tips:

- **Be prepared to leave a message.** Before calling someone, be prepared for voice mail. Decide what you are going to say and what information you are going to include in your message. If necessary, write your message down before calling.
- **Leave a concise, thorough message.** When leaving a message, always identify yourself using your complete name and affiliation. Mention the date and time you called and a brief explanation of your reason for calling. Always leave a complete phone number, including the area code, even if you think the receiver already has it. Tell the receiver the best time to return your call. Don't ramble.
- **Use a professional and courteous tone.** When leaving a message, make sure that your tone is professional, enthusiastic, and respectful. Smile when leaving a message to add warmth to your voice.
- **Speak slowly and clearly.** You want to make sure that your receiver will be able to understand your message. Speak slowly and pronounce your words carefully, especially when providing your phone number. The receiver should be able to write information down without having to replay your message.
- **Be careful with confidential information.** Don't leave confidential or private information in a voice mail message. Remember that anyone could gain access to this information.
- **Don't make assumptions.** If you don't receive a call back within a day or two after leaving a message, don't get angry or frustrated. Assume that the message wasn't delivered or that it couldn't be understood. Call back and leave another message, or send the person an email.

10.4 Adding Value in Professional Teams

Organizations are forming teams for better decisions, faster response, increased productivity, greater buy-in, less resistance to change, improved morale, and reduced risks.

As we discussed in Chapter 1, the workplace and economy are changing. One significant recent change is the emphasis on teamwork. You might find yourself a part of a work team, project team, customer support team, supplier team, design team, planning team, functional team, cross-functional team, or some other group. All of these teams are being formed to accomplish specific goals, and your career success will depend on your ability to function well in a team-driven professional environment.

10.4a The Importance of Teams in the Workplace

Businesses are constantly looking for ways to do jobs in better ways at lower costs. They are forming teams for the following reasons:

- **Better decisions.** Decisions are generally more accurate and effective because group and team members contribute different expertise and perspectives.
- **Faster response.** When action is necessary to respond to competition or to solve a problem, small groups and teams can act rapidly.
- **Increased productivity.** Because they are often closer to the action and to the customer, team members can see opportunities for improving efficiency.
- **Greater buy-in.** Decisions arrived at jointly are usually better received because members are committed to the solution and are more willing to support it.
- **Less resistance to change.** People who have input into decisions are less hostile, less aggressive, and less resistant to change.
- **Improved employee morale.** Personal satisfaction and job morale increase when teams are successful.
- **Reduced risks.** Responsibility for a decision is diffused, thus carrying less risk for any individual.

To connect with distant team members across borders and time zones, many organizations are creating *virtual teams*. These are groups of people who work interdependently with a shared purpose across space, time, and organization boundaries using technology.[14]

Virtual teams are groups of people who work interdependently with a shared purpose across space, time, and organization boundaries using technology.

Virtual teams may be local or global. Many workers today complete their tasks from remote locations, thus creating local virtual teams. Hyundai Motors exemplifies virtual teaming at the global level. For its vehicles, Hyundai completes engineering in Korea, research in Tokyo and Germany, styling in California, engine calibration and testing in Michigan, and heat testing in the California desert.[15] Members of its virtual teams coordinate their work and complete their tasks across time and geographic zones. Work is increasingly viewed as what you do rather than a place you go.

10.4b Positive and Negative Team Behaviour

Team members who are committed to achieving the group's purpose contribute by displaying positive behaviour. How can you be a professional team member? The most effective groups have members who are willing to establish rules and abide by those rules. Effective team members are able to analyze tasks and define problems so that they can work toward solutions. They offer information and try out their ideas on the group to stimulate discussion. They show interest in others' ideas by listening actively. Helpful team members also seek to involve silent members. They help to resolve differences, and they encourage a warm, supportive climate by praising and agreeing with others. When they sense that agreement is near, they review significant points and move the group toward its goal by synthesizing points of understanding.

Professional team members follow team rules, analyze tasks, define problems, share information, listen actively to others, and try to involve quiet team members.

Not all groups, however, have members who contribute positively. Negative behaviour is shown by those who constantly put down the ideas and suggestions of others. They insult, criticize, and aggress against others. They waste the group's time with unnecessary recounting of personal achievements or irrelevant topics. The team joker distracts the group with excessive joke telling, inappropriate comments, and disruptive antics. Also disturbing are team members who withdraw and refuse to be drawn out. They have nothing to say, either for or against ideas being considered. To be a productive and welcome member of a group, be prepared to perform the positive tasks described in Figure 10.3. Avoid the negative behaviours.

Negative team behaviour includes insulting, criticizing, aggressing against others, wasting time, and refusing to participate.

FIGURE 10.3 | Positive and Negative Team Behaviours

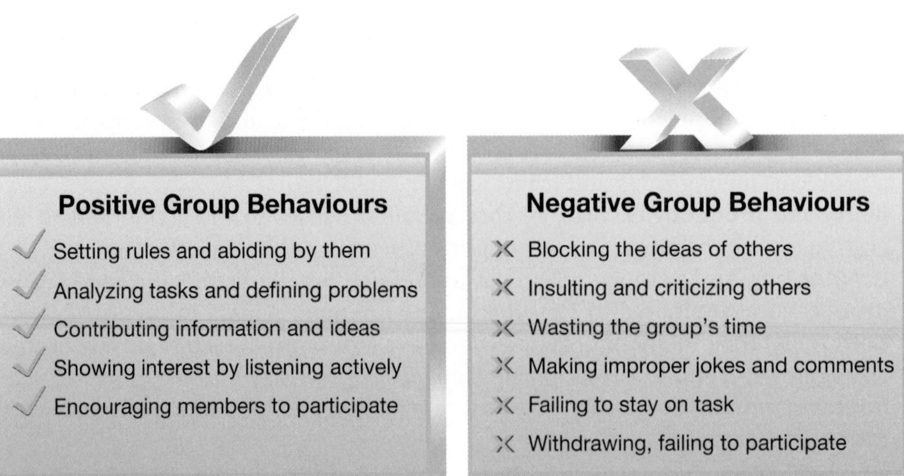

Positive Group Behaviours
Setting rules and abiding by them
Analyzing tasks and defining problems
Contributing information and ideas
Showing interest by listening actively
Encouraging members to participate
Negative Group Behaviours
Blocking the ideas of others
Insulting and criticizing others
Wasting the group's time
Making improper jokes and comments
Failing to stay on task
Withdrawing, failing to participate

10.4c Characteristics of Successful Teams

It's been said that as an acronym TEAM means "Together, Everyone Achieves More."[16] Yet, many teams do not work well together. In fact, some teams can actually increase frustration, lower productivity, and create employee dissatisfaction. Experts who have studied team functioning and decisions have discovered that effective teams share some or all of the following characteristics.

BE SMALL AND DIVERSE. Teams may range from two to twenty-five members, although four or five is optimum for many projects. Larger groups have trouble interacting constructively, much less agreeing on actions.[17] For the most creative decisions, teams generally have male and female members who differ in age, ethnicity, social background, training, and experience. Members should bring complementary skills to a team. The key business advantage of diversity is the ability to view a project and its context from multiple perspectives. Many of us tend to think that everyone in the world is like us because we know only our own experience.[18] Teams with members from a variety of ethnicities and cultures can look at projects beyond the limited view of one culture. Many organizations are finding that diverse teams can produce innovative solutions with broader applications than homogeneous teams can.

Small, diverse teams often produce more creative solutions with broader applications than homogeneous teams do.

AGREE ON PURPOSE. An effective team begins with a purpose. When the Great Lakes Coast Guard faced the task of keeping commerce moving when the lakes and rivers froze, it brought all the stakeholders together to discuss the mission. The Canadian Coast Guard, the U.S. Coast Guard, and the shipping industry formed a partnership to clear and flush ice from the Great Lakes and connecting rivers during winter months. Agreeing on the purpose was the first step in developing a concerted team effort. Preseason planning and daily phone conferences cemented the mission and gained buy-in from all stakeholders.[19]

OFFICE INSIDER

"Teamwork is the ability to work together toward a common vision—to direct individual accomplishments toward organizational objectives. It is the fuel that allows common people to attain uncommon results."

—Andrew Carnegie

AGREE ON PROCEDURES. The best teams develop procedures to guide them. They set up intermediate goals with deadlines. They assign roles and tasks, requiring all members to contribute equivalent amounts of real work. They decide how they will reach decisions using one of the strategies discussed earlier. Procedures are continually evaluated to ensure movement toward the attainment of the team's goals.

FIGURE 10.4 | Six Steps for Dealing With Conflict

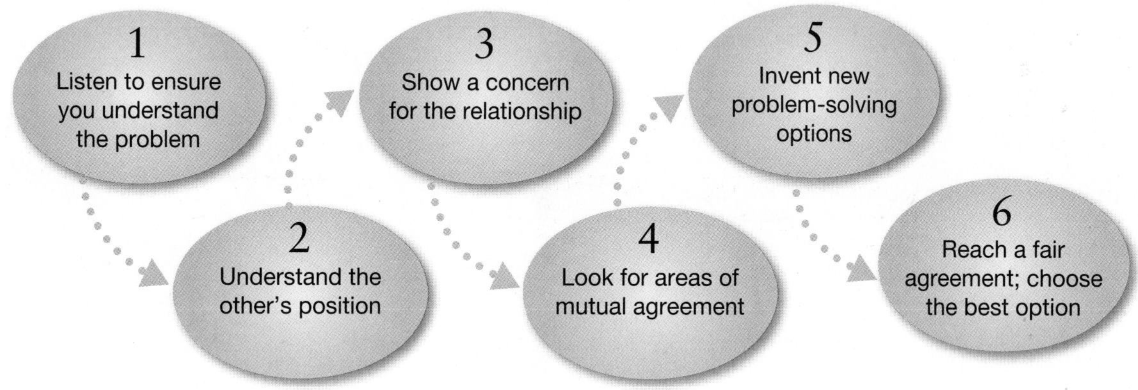

CONFRONT CONFLICT. Poorly functioning teams avoid conflict, preferring sulking, gossiping, or backstabbing. A better plan is to acknowledge conflict and address the root of the problem openly using the plan shown in Figure 10.4. Although it may feel emotionally risky, direct confrontation saves time and enhances team commitment in the long run. To be constructive, however, confrontation must be task-oriented, not person-oriented. An open airing of differences, in which all team members have a chance to speak their minds, should centre on the strengths and weaknesses of the different positions and ideas—not on personalities. After hearing all sides, team members must negotiate a fair settlement, no matter how long it takes.

COMMUNICATE EFFECTIVELY. The best teams exchange information and contribute ideas freely in an informal environment. Team members speak clearly and concisely, avoiding generalities. They encourage feedback. Listeners become actively involved, read body language, and ask clarifying questions before responding. Tactful, constructive disagreement is encouraged. Although a team's task is taken seriously, successful teams are able to inject humour into their interactions.

> **Effective teams exchange information freely and collaborate rather than compete.**

COLLABORATE RATHER THAN COMPETE. Effective team members are genuinely interested in achieving team goals instead of receiving individual recognition. They contribute ideas and feedback unselfishly. They monitor team progress, including what is going right, what is going wrong, and what to do about it. They celebrate individual and team accomplishments.

SHARE LEADERSHIP. Effective teams often have no formal leader. Instead, leadership rotates to those with the appropriate expertise as the team evolves and moves from one phase to another. Many teams operate under a democratic approach. This approach can achieve buy-in to team decisions, boost morale, and create fewer hurt feelings and less resentment. But in times of crisis, a strong team member may need to step up as leader.

ACCEPTANCE OF ETHICAL RESPONSIBILITIES. Team members have a number of specific responsibilities to each other, as shown in Figure 10.5. As a whole, teams have a responsibility to represent the organization's view and respect its privileged information. They should not discuss with outsiders any sensitive issues without permission. In addition, teams have a broader obligation to avoid advocating actions that would endanger members of society at large.

The skills that make you a valuable and ethical team player will serve you well when you run or participate in professional meetings.

FIGURE 10.5 | Ethical Responsibilities of Team Members and Leaders

When people form a group or a team to achieve a purpose, they agree to give up some of their individual sovereignty for the good of the group. They become interdependent and assume responsibilities to one another and to the group. Here are important ethical responsibilities for members to follow:

- **Determine to do your best.** When you commit to the group process, you are obligated to offer your skills freely. Don't hold back, perhaps fearing that you will be repeatedly targeted because you have skills to offer. If the group project is worth doing, it is worth your best effort.
- **Decide to behave with the group's good in mind.** You may find it necessary to set aside your personal goals in favour of the group's goals. Decide to keep an open mind and to listen to evidence and arguments objectively. Strive to evaluate information carefully, even though it may contradict your own views or thwart your personal agendas.
- **Make a commitment to fair play.** Group problem solving is a cooperative, not a competitive, event. Decide that you cannot grind your private axe at the expense of the group project.
- **Expect to give and receive a fair hearing.** When you speak, others should give you a fair hearing. You have a right to expect them to listen carefully, provide you with candid feedback, strive to understand what you say, and treat your ideas seriously. Listeners do not have to agree with you, of course. However, all speakers have a right to a fair hearing.

Rawpixel.com/Shutterstock.com

- **Be willing to take on a participant/analyst role.** As a group member, it is your responsibility to pay attention, evaluate what is happening, analyze what you learn, and help make decisions.
- **As a leader, be ready to model appropriate team behaviour.** It is a leader's responsibility to coach team members in skills and teamwork, to acknowledge achievement and effort, to share knowledge, and to periodically remind members of the team's missions and goals.

10.5 Conducting Professional Business Meetings

Business meetings consist of three or more people who assemble to pool information, solicit feedback, clarify policy, seek consensus, and solve problems. However, as growing numbers of employees work at distant locations, meetings have changed. Workers cannot always meet face-to-face. To be able to exchange information effectively and efficiently, you will need to know how to plan and participate in face-to-face as well as *virtual meetings*.

Because you can expect to attend many workplace meetings, learn to make them efficient, satisfying, and productive.

As you prepare to join the workforce, expect to attend meetings—lots of them! Estimates suggest that workers on average spend four hours a week in meetings and consider more than half of that time as wasted.[20] One business reporter called meetings "the black holes of the workday"[21]; another complained that "long-winded colleagues consume all available oxygen, killing good ideas by asphyxiation."[22] However, if meetings are well run, workers actually desire more, not fewer, of them.[23]

Call meetings only when necessary, and invite only key people.

Moreover, meetings can be career-critical. Instead of treating them as thieves of your valuable time, try to see meetings as golden opportunities to demonstrate your leadership, communication, and problem-solving skills. To help you make the most of these opportunities, this section outlines best practices for running and contributing to successful meetings.

10.5a Preparing for Meetings

A face-to-face meeting provides the richest communication environment. Yet such meetings are also costly, draining the productivity of all participants. If you are in charge of a meeting, determine your purpose, decide how and where to meet, choose the participants, invite them using a digital calendar, and organize an agenda.

DETERMINE THE PURPOSE OF THE MEETING. No meeting should be called unless the topic is important, can't wait, and requires an exchange of ideas. If the flow of information is strictly one way and no immediate feedback will result, then don't schedule a meeting. For example, if people are merely being advised or informed, send an email or memo instead. Remember, the real expense of a meeting is the lost productivity of all the people attending. To decide whether the purpose of the meeting is valid, it's a good idea to consult the key people who will be attending. Ask them what outcomes are desired and how to achieve those goals. This consultation also sets a collaborative tone and encourages full participation.

DECIDE HOW AND WHERE TO MEET. Once you are sure that a meeting is necessary, you must decide whether to meet face-to-face or virtually. If you decide to meet in person, reserve a conference room. If you decide to meet virtually, select the appropriate media and make any necessary arrangements for your voice conference, videoconference, or Web conference. These communication technologies are discussed in Chapter 1.

SELECT PARTICIPANTS. The number of meeting participants is determined by the purpose of the meeting, as shown in Figure 10.6. If the meeting purpose is motivational, such as an employee awards ceremony for Bombardier, then the number of participants is unlimited. But to make decisions, according to studies at 3M Corporation, the best number is five or fewer participants.[24] Ideally, those attending should be people who will make the decision and people with information necessary to make the decision. Also attending should be people who will be responsible for implementing the decision and representatives of groups who will benefit from the decision.

Problem-solving meetings should involve five or fewer people.

USE DIGITAL CALENDARS TO SCHEDULE MEETINGS. Finding a time when everyone can meet is difficult. Fortunately, digital calendars make the task quicker and more efficient. Popular programs are Google Calendar, Apple Calendar, and the business favourite, Outlook Calendar, shown in Figure 10.7. Online calendars and mobile apps enable users to make appointments, schedule meetings, and keep track of daily activities. To schedule meetings, you enter a new meeting request and add the names of attendees. You select a date, enter a start and end time, and list the meeting subject and location. Then the meeting request goes to each attendee. Later you check the attendee availability tab to see a list of all meeting attendees. As the meeting time approaches, the program automatically sends reminders to attendees.

DISTRIBUTE AN AGENDA. At least one day in advance of a meeting, email an agenda of topics to be discussed. Also include any reports or materials that

FIGURE 10.6 | Meeting Purpose and Number of Participants

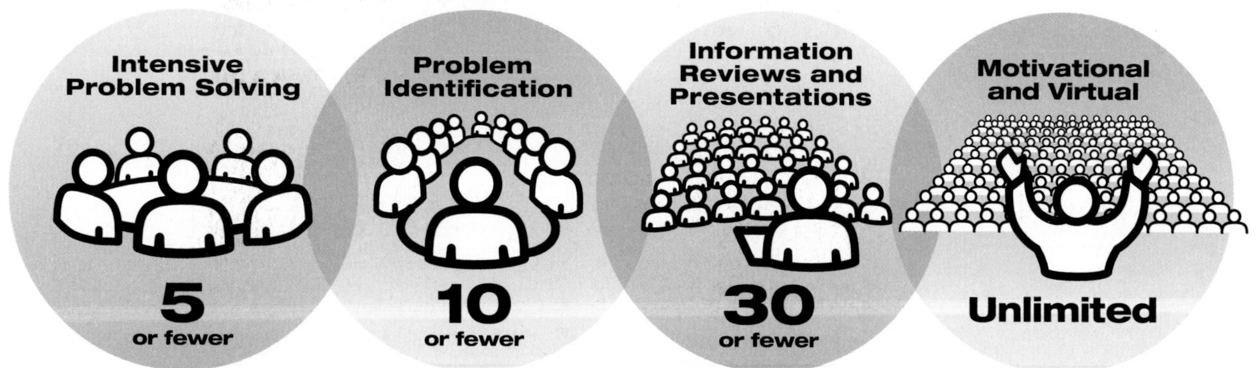

FIGURE 10.7 | Using Calendar Programs

Before a meeting, pass out a meeting agenda showing topics to be discussed and other information.

participants should read in advance. For continuing groups, you might also include a copy of the minutes of the previous meeting. To keep meetings productive, limit the number of agenda items. Remember, the narrower the focus, the greater the chances for success. A good agenda, as illustrated in Figure 10.8, covers the following information:

- Date and place of meeting
- Start time and end time
- Brief description of each topic, in order of priority, including the names of individuals who are responsible for performing some action
- Proposed allotment of time for each topic
- Any pre-meeting preparation expected of participants

FIGURE 10.8 | Typical Meeting Agenda

AGENDA
mAPP Dev™
Sales Department Meeting
November 15, 2018
9:30 a.m.–10:30 a.m.
Corporate Meeting Room

1. Sales update
   - Danny (10 mins.)
2. What's new and hot in the market
   - Monika (10 mins.)
3. Sales training tip of the week: Report on Mobile + WebDevCon 2018
   - Sasha (10 mins.)
4. Other updates: hires, products, etc.
   - Danny (5 mins.)
5. Morale boost: what's going well, where do we want to be, hero of the week
   - Danny + All (20 mins.)

10.5b Managing the Meeting

Whether you are the meeting leader or a participant, it is important to act professionally during the meeting. Meetings can be more efficient and productive if leaders and participants recognize how to get the meeting started, establish ground rules, move the meeting along, and handle conflict.

GET STARTED AND ESTABLISH GROUND RULES. To avoid wasting time and irritating attendees, always start meetings on time—even if some participants are missing. Waiting for latecomers causes resentment and sets a bad precedent. For the same reasons, don't give a quick recap to anyone who arrives late. At the appointed time, open the meeting with a three- to five-minute introduction that includes the following:

Start meetings on time and open with a brief introduction.

- Goal and length of the meeting
- Background of topics or problems
- Possible solutions and constraints
- Tentative agenda
- Ground rules to be followed

A typical set of ground rules might include communicating openly, being supportive, listening carefully, silencing phones, participating fully, confronting conflict frankly, and following the agenda. The next step is to assign one participant to take minutes and one to act as a recorder. The recorder uses a computer and projector or stands at a flipchart or whiteboard to list the main ideas being discussed and agreements reached.

MOVE THE MEETING ALONG. After the preliminaries, the leader should say as little as possible. Remember that the purpose of a meeting is to exchange views, not to hear one person, even the leader, do all the talking. If the group has one member who monopolizes, the leader might say, "Thanks for that perspective, Kurt, but please hold your next point while we hear how Ann would respond to that." This technique also encourages quieter participants to speak up.

To avoid allowing digressions to sidetrack the group, try generating a "parking lot" list. This is a list of important but divergent issues that should be discussed at a later time. Another way to handle digressions is to say, "Folks, we are getting off track here. Forgive me for pressing on, but I need to bring us back to the central issue of...."[25] It's important to adhere to the agenda and the time schedule. Equally important, when the group seems to have reached a consensus, is to summarize the group's position and check to see whether everyone agrees.

Keep the meeting moving by avoiding issues that sidetrack the group.

HANDLE CONFLICT. Conflict is natural and even desirable in workplaces, but it can cause awkwardness and uneasiness. In meetings, conflict typically develops when people feel unheard or misunderstood. If two people are in conflict, the best approach is to encourage each to make a complete case while group members give their full attention. Let each one question the other. Then, the leader should summarize what was said, and the group should offer comments. The group may modify a recommendation or suggest alternatives before reaching consensus on a direction to follow.

When a conflict develops between two members, allow each to make a complete case before the group.

10.5c Ending With a Plan and Following Up

End the meeting at the agreed time or earlier if possible. The leader should summarize what has been decided, who is going to do what, and by what time. It may be necessary to ask people to volunteer to take responsibility for completing action items agreed to in the meeting. No one should leave the meeting without a full understanding of what was accomplished. One effective technique that encourages

Email Meeting Minutes

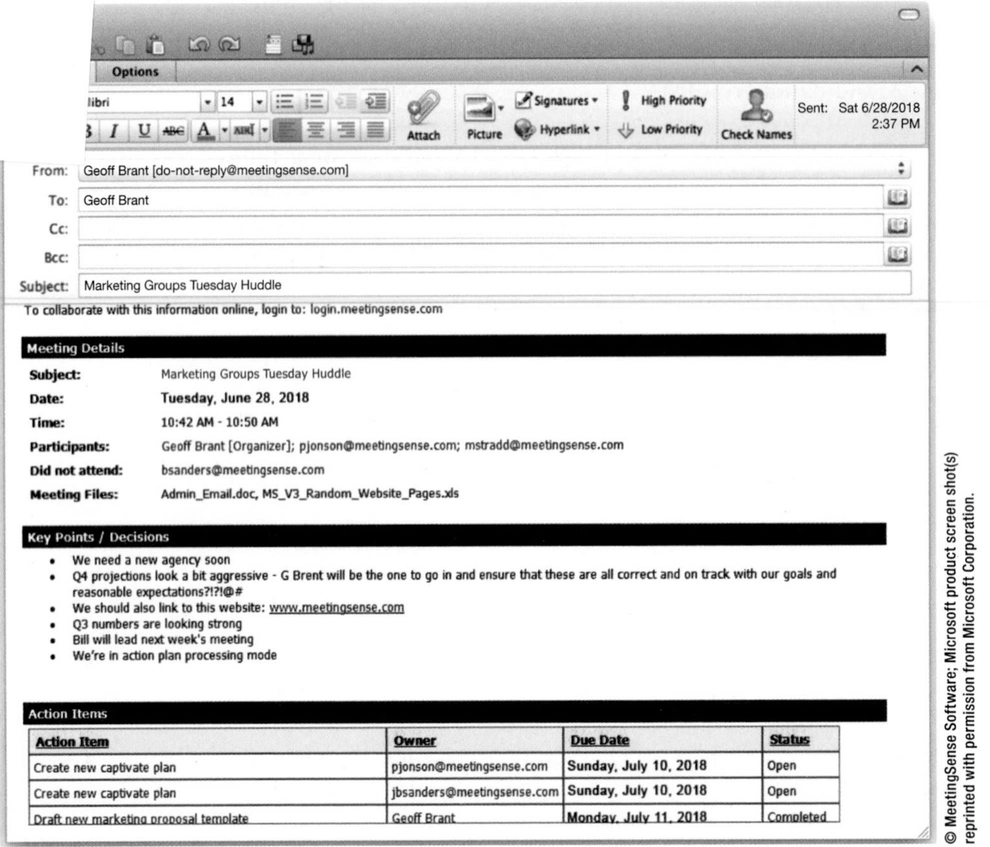

Sent: Sat 6/28/2018 2:37 PM

From: Geoff Brant [do-not-reply@meetingsense.com]
To: Geoff Brant
Cc:
Bcc:
Subject: Marketing Groups Tuesday Huddle

To collaborate with this information online, login to: login.meetingsense.com

Meeting Details

Subject: Marketing Groups Tuesday Huddle
Date: Tuesday, June 28, 2018
Time: 10:42 AM - 10:50 AM
Participants: Geoff Brant [Organizer]; pjonson@meetingsense.com; mstradd@meetingsense.com
Did not attend: bsanders@meetingsense.com
Meeting Files: Admin_Email.doc, MS_V3_Random_Website_Pages.xls

Key Points / Decisions

- We need a new agency soon
- Q4 projections look a bit aggressive - G Brent will be the one to go in and ensure that these are all correct and on track with our goals and reasonable expectations?!?!@#
- We should also link to this website: www.meetingsense.com
- Q3 numbers are looking strong
- Bill will lead next week's meeting
- We're in action plan processing mode

Action Items

Action Item	Owner	Due Date	Status
Create new captivate plan	pjonson@meetingsense.com	Sunday, July 10, 2018	Open
Create new captivate plan	jbsanders@meetingsense.com	Sunday, July 10, 2018	Open
Draft new marketing proposal template	Geoff Brant	Monday, July 11, 2018	Completed

Meeting proceedings are efficiently recorded in a summary distribution template that provides subject, date, time, participant names, absentee names, meeting documents and files, key point, decisions, and action items.

full participation is "once around the table." All attendees are asked to summarize briefly their interpretation of what was decided and what happens next. Of course, this closure technique works best with smaller groups. The leader should conclude by asking the group to set a time for the next meeting. The leader should also assure the group that a report will follow and thank participants for attending.

End the meeting with a summary of accomplishments and a review of action items; follow up by reminding participants of their assigned tasks.

If minutes were taken, they should be distributed within a couple of days after the meeting. Figure 10.9 shows a minutes report generated using a meeting management program (there are also apps that produce similar reports). The key elements to include are important points, decisions, and action items. It is up to the leader to see that what was decided at the meeting is accomplished. The leader may need to call or email people to remind them of their assignments and also to offer help if necessary.

10.5d Preparing for Virtual Meetings

Virtual meetings are real-time gatherings of dispersed participants who connect using communication technology. As travel costs rise and companies slash budgets, many organizations are cutting back on meetings that require travel.[26] Instead, they may meet in audioconferences using telephones or in videoconferences using the Internet.

Saving travel costs and reducing employee fatigue are significant reasons for the digital displacement of business travel. Darryl Draper, a Subaru customer service training manager, estimates that when she travelled nine months out of the year, she reached about 100 people every six months at a cost of $300 a person.

Thanks to virtual technology, she now reaches 2,500 people every six months at a cost of 75 cents a person.[27]

The following best practices recommended by experienced meeting facilitators will help you address pre-meeting issues such as technology glitches, scheduling across time zones, and language challenges.[28]

DEAL WITH TECHNOLOGY. To conduct successful virtual meetings or teleconferences, select the most appropriate technology. Be sure that everyone is able to participate fully using that technology. If someone can't see what is happening on screen, the entire meeting can be disrupted and delayed. Some participants may need coaching before the session begins. Figure 10.10 depicts a virtual design meeting and explains how Web conferencing works.

Before the meeting distribute any materials that will be shared. If documents will be edited or marked during the meeting, find out whether participants know how to use the online editing tools. To avoid panic at the last minute, encourage participants to log in 15 minutes early. Some programs require downloads and installations that can cause immense frustration and disruptions if not done in advance.

RESPECT THE NEEDS OF DISPERSED PARTICIPANTS. When setting the time of the meeting, use Coordinated Universal Time (UTC) so that group members in different time zones are not confused. Be particularly mindful of how the meeting schedule affects others. Avoid spanning a lunch hour, holding someone overtime, or making someone arrive extra early. However, virtual meetings across multiple time zones may inevitably disadvantage some participants. To be fair to all group members, rotate your meeting time so that everyone shares the burden of an inconvenient time.[29] Always follow up in writing.

FIGURE 10.10 | Understanding Web Conferencing

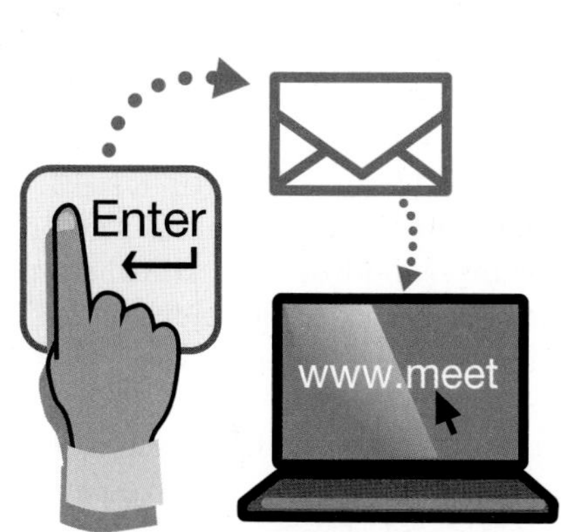

1. Email Contact
Alan T., president of Sportster Marketing, an athletic gear company in Kitchener, ON, sends an email to Meghan R., chief designer at NexxtDesign in Toronto, ON, to discuss a new sports watch. The email includes meeting date and time and a link to launch the session.

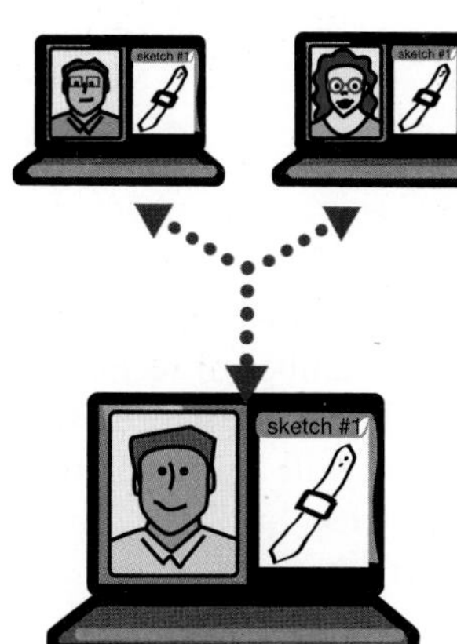

2. Virtual Meeting
When the Web conference begins, participants see live video of each other's faces on their screens. They look at photos of sports watches, share ideas, sketch designs on a shared "virtual whiteboard," and review contract terms.

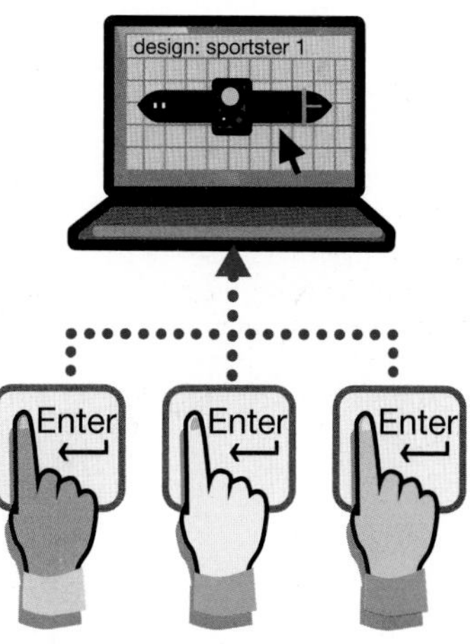

3. Design Collaboration
NexxtDesign artists and Sportster Marketing managers use peer-to-peer software that allows them to share spaces on each other's computers. The software enables them to take turns modifying the designs, and it also tracks all the changes.

10.5e Interacting Professionally in Virtual Meetings

Although the same good meeting management techniques discussed for face-to-face meetings prevail, additional skills and practices are important in virtual meetings. To achieve the best results during virtual meetings, create ground rules, anticipate limited media richness, manage turn-taking, and humanize the interaction with remote members.

ESTABLISH GROUND RULES FOR VIRTUAL MEETINGS. Before beginning, explain how questions may be asked and answered. Many meeting programs allow participants to "raise their hands" with an icon on a side panel of the computer screen. Then they can type in their question for the leader and others to see. Unless the meeting involves people who know each other well, participants in audio conferences should always say their names before beginning to comment.

One of the biggest problems of virtual meetings is background noise from participants' offices or homes. You might hear dogs barking, telephones ringing, and toilets flushing. Meeting planners disagree on whether to require participants to put their phones on mute. Although the mute button reduces noise, it also prevents immediate participation and tends to deaden the conference. Remind the group to silence all electronic alerts and alarms.

As a personal ground rule, don't multitask—and that includes texting and checking email—during virtual meetings. Giving your full attention is critical.

ANTICIPATE THE LIMITATIONS OF VIRTUAL TECHNOLOGY. Collaborating successfully in virtual meetings requires that you learn to manage limitations. Audioconferences in particular lack the richness that nonverbal cues provide during in-person meetings. Therefore, any small infraction or miscue can be blown out of proportion; words and tone can be easily misinterpreted. For example, when individuals meet face to face, they usually can recognize blank looks when people do not understand something being discussed. However, in virtual meetings participants and presenters cannot always see each other.

As a result, when presenting ideas at a virtual meeting, you should be as precise as possible. Give examples and use simple language. Recap and summarize often. Confirm your understanding of what is being discussed. If you are a presenter, project an upbeat, enthusiastic, and strong voice. Without eye contact and nonverbal cues, the best way to keep the attention of the audience is through a powerful voice.

MANAGE TURN-TAKING AND OTHER MEETING PROCEDURES. To encourage participation and avoid traffic jams with everyone talking at once, experts suggest a number of techniques. Participants soon lose interest if the leader is the only one talking. Therefore, encourage dialogue by asking questions of specific people. Often you will learn not only what the person is thinking but also what other participants feel but have not stated.

To elicit participation, go through the list of participants inviting each to speak for 30 seconds without interruption. If individuals have nothing to say, they may pass when their names are called. Leaders should avoid asking vague and leading questions such as *Does everyone agree*? Remote attendees cannot answer easily without drowning out each other's responses.

SUMMARY OF LEARNING OBJECTIVES

10.1 Apply professionalism skills in the workplace such as etiquette and an ethical attitude.

- Professionalism, good business etiquette, developed soft skills, social intelligence, polish, and civility are desirable workplace behaviours that are complemented by a positive online presence.
- Employers most want employees who can prioritize their work, work in teams, and exhibit a positive attitude in addition to displaying good workplace manners and other interpersonal skills.
- Professionalism means having integrity and being ethical; experts believe that no sharp distinction between ethics and etiquette exists. We should always treat others with respect.
- Practising business etiquette on the job and online can put you ahead of others who lack polish.

10.2 Use your voice effectively in conversations including when offering and receiving constructive criticism.

- In-person communication is the richest communication channel; use your voice effectively by honing your pronunciation, voice quality, pitch, volume and rate, and emphasis.
- To excel in face-to-face conversations, use correct names and titles, choose appropriate topics, be positive, listen to learn, give sincere praise, and act professionally in social situations.
- When receiving criticism, avoid interrupting, paraphrase what you are hearing, agree if the criticism is accurate, disagree respectfully, look for compromise, and learn from criticism.
- When criticizing, plan your remarks, do it in person, focus on improvement, offer help, be specific, use the word *we*, encourage two-way communication, stay calm, and keep it private.

10.3 Demonstrate professional telephone skills and voice mail etiquette.

- When calling, follow an agenda, use a three-point introduction, be brisk, try to sound cheerful, be professional and courteous, avoid phone tag, and leave complete voice mail messages.
- When answering, be courteous, identify yourself, be helpful, be cautious when answering calls for others, be respectful when putting people on hold, and explain why you are transferring calls.
- Practise smartphone etiquette by being considerate, observing quiet areas, using your indoor voice, taking only urgent calls, not calling or texting while driving, and choosing a professional ring tone.
- Prepare a friendly voice mail greeting and respond to messages promptly; as a caller, plan your message, be concise, watch your tone, speak slowly, and don't leave sensitive information.

10.4 Understand the importance of teamwork and contribute positively to team performance.

- Teams are popular because they lead to better decisions, faster responses, increased productivity, greater buy-in, less resistance, improved morale, and reduced risks.
- Virtual teams are collaborations among remote coworkers connecting with technology.
- Positive group behaviours include establishing and following rules, resolving differences, being supportive, praising others, and summarizing points of understanding.
- Negative behaviours include having contempt for others, wasting the team's time, and withdrawing.
- Successful teams are small and diverse, agree on a purpose and procedures, confront conflict, communicate well, don't compete but collaborate, are ethical, and share leadership.

10.5 Plan and participate in productive meetings.

- Before a meeting businesspeople determine its purpose and location, choose participants, use a digital calendar, and distribute an agenda.
- Experienced meeting leaders move the meeting along and confront any conflict; they end the meeting on time, make sure everyone is heard, and distribute meeting minutes promptly.
- Virtual meetings save travel costs but require attention to communication technology and to the needs of dispersed participants regarding issues such as different time zones and language barriers.
- Virtual meetings demand specific procedures to handle questions, noise, lack of media richness, and turn-taking.

CHAPTER REVIEW

1. Is incivility common in the workplace? What might be its costs? (Obj. 1)
2. Define the five traits and skills listed in the chapter that demonstrate professionalism. (Obj. 1)
3. Explain the advantages of face-to-face conversation over other communication channels. (Obj. 2)
4. Why is voice an important communication tool, and how can businesspeople use it effectively? (Obj. 2)

5. How can you ensure that your telephone calls on the job are productive? Provide at least six suggestions. (Obj. 3)
6. List at least five tips for receiving telephone calls professionally. (Obj. 3)
7. What are some of the reasons for the popularity of workplace teams? List at least five. (Obj. 4)
8. What is the best approach to address conflict in meetings? (Obj. 5)
9. What techniques can make virtual meetings as effective as face-to-face meetings? (Obj. 5)

CRITICAL THINKING

1. How can we square the empathy needed for ethical professionalism with the individualistic, sometimes greedy, nature of private enterprise (e.g., profit, advancement, etc.)? (Obj. 1)
2. Is face-to-face communication always preferable to one-dimensional channels of communication such as email? Why or why not? (Objs. 1, 2)
3. In what ways can conflict be a positive force in the workplace? (Objs. 2, 4, 5)
4. Commentators often predict that new communications media will destroy old ones. Do you think email, smartphones, and messaging/texting will replace phone calls? Why or why not? (Obj. 3)
5. Why do so many people hate voice mail when it is an efficient system for recording messages? (Obj. 3)
6. What's the right course of action when you're the only person on a team doing any actual work? (Obj. 4)
7. How can business meetings help you advance your career? (Obj. 5)

ACTIVITIES AND CASES

10.1 RESEARCHING PROFESSIONAL WORKPLACE SKILLS AND PRESENTING ANNOTATED SOURCES (OBJ. 1)

You have seen that many definitions for *professionalism* exist. Recently, an opportunity to practise your research skills has arisen when your boss was invited to make a presentation to a group of human relations officers. He asked you and a small group of fellow interns to help him find articles about professionalism, soft skills, social intelligence, and other interpersonal qualities.

Your Task. As a team, divide your research in such a way that each intern is responsible for one or two search terms, depending on the size of your group. Look for articles with definitions of *professionalism, business etiquette, civility, business ethics, social skills, soft skills*, and *social intelligence*. Find at least three useful articles for each search term. If you get bogged down in your research, consult with a business librarian on campus or report to your instructor. After compiling your findings, present your annotated works-cited list as a team in an informational memo report to your boss, Ted Rollins.

10.2 INVESTIGATING SOFT SKILLS: EMPLOYER WISH LIST (OBJ. 1)

What soft skills do employers request when they list job openings in your field?

Your Task. Individually or in teams, check the listings at an online job board such as Monster, Workopolis, CareerBuilder, or Charity Village. Follow the instructions to search job categories and locations. Also check college resources and local newspaper listings of job openings. Find five or more listings in your field. Print or otherwise save the results of your search. Examine the skills requested. How often do the ads mention communication, teamwork, and computer skills? What tasks do the ads mention? Discuss your findings with your team members. Then prepare a list of the most frequently requested soft skills. Your instructor may ask you to submit your findings and/or report to the class. If you are not satisfied with the job selection at any job board, choose ads posted on websites of companies you admire or on LinkedIn.

10.3 SOFT SKILLS: PERSONAL STRENGTHS INVENTORY (OBJ. 1)

When hiring future workers, employers look for hard skills, which are those we learn, such as mastery of software applications or accountancy procedures, as well as soft skills. Soft skills are personal characteristics, strengths, and other assets a person possesses.
Studies have divided soft skills into four categories:

Thinking and problem solving

Oral and written communication

Personal qualities and work ethic

Interpersonal and teamwork

Your Task. Using the preceding categories to guide you, identify your own soft skills, paying attention to attributes you think a potential employer would value. Prepare a list of at least four items for each of the four categories. For example, as evidence of problem solving, you might list a specific workplace or student problem you recognized and solved. You will want to weave these words and phrases into cover letters and résumés, which are covered in Chapter 12.

Visit **MindTap** for a variety of videos, additional exercises, activities, and quizzes to support your learning.

CHAPTER 11

Business Presentations

OBJECTIVES

After studying this chapter, you should be able to

11.1 Differentiate between major presentation types and answer two preparatory questions.

11.2 Organize the presentation effectively and build audience rapport.

11.3 Compare the main types of presentation aid.

11.4 Design effective visual presentations.

11.5 Deploy effective delivery techniques in presentations.

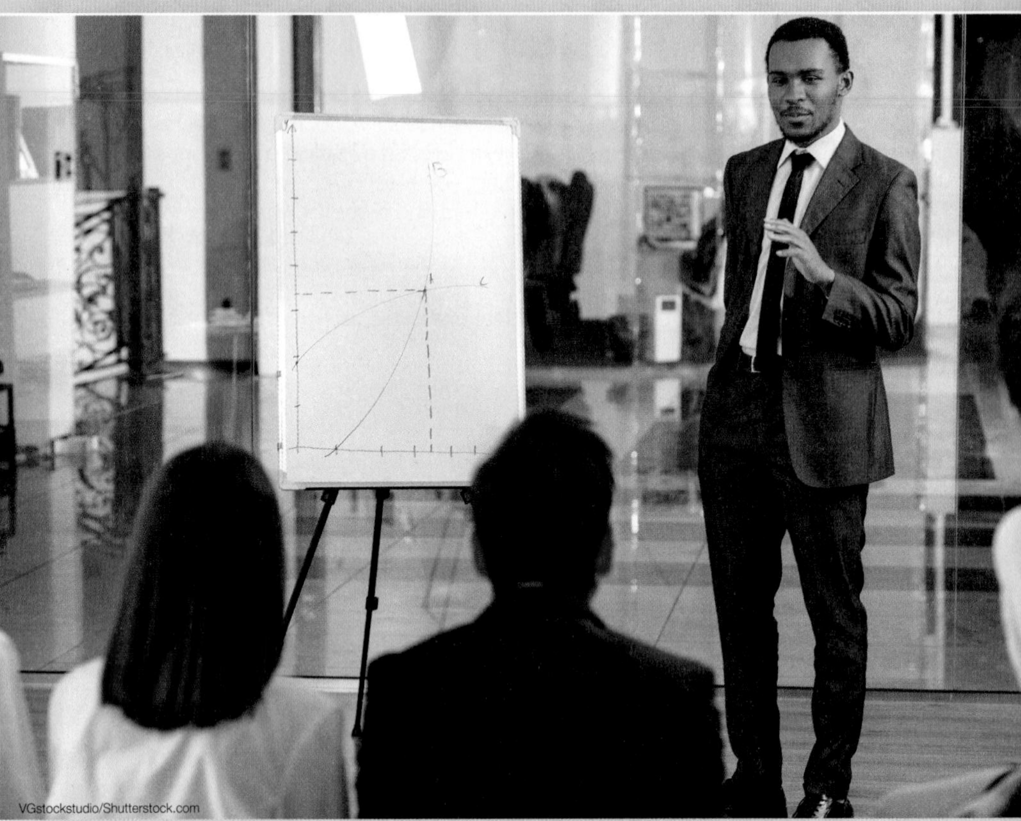
VGstockstudio/Shutterstock.com

11.1 Types of Business Presentation and Preparation

Organizations are interested in hiring people with good presentation skills. Why? The business world is changing. As you have seen, technical skills aren't enough to guarantee success. You also need to be able to communicate ideas effectively in presentations to customers, vendors, members of your team, and management.

11.1a Speaking Skills and Your Career

Speaking skills are useful at every career stage. A study conducted by business communication researchers found that the number one competency hiring managers look for in new employees is strong oral communication skills, including presentation skills.[1] You might, for example, have to make a sales pitch before customers or speak to a professional gathering. You might need to describe your company's expansion plans to your banker, or you might need to persuade management to support your proposed marketing strategy. Speaking skills rank very high on recruiters' wish lists. As reported in another study, between 82 and 95 percent of executives consider oral communication skills very important for college and university graduates.[2]

11.1b Understanding Presentation Types

A common part of a business professional's life is giving presentations. Some presentations are informative, whereas others are persuasive. Some are face to face; others, virtual. Some are performed before big audiences, whereas others are given to smaller groups. Some presentations are elaborate; others are simple. Figure 11.1 shows a sampling of business presentations you may encounter in your career.

OFFICE INSIDER

"Presentation skills are a primary differentiator among you and your peers. Master your presentation skills, and become the master of your career options."

—Andrew Dlugan, communication coach, public speaker

11.1c Preparing for a Presentation

In getting ready for a presentation, you may feel a lot of anxiety. For many people fear of speaking before a group is almost as great as the fear of pain. We get butterflies in our stomachs just thinking about it. For any presentation, you can reduce your fears and lay the foundation for a professional performance by focusing on five areas: preparation, organization, audience rapport, visual aids, and delivery. Preparation involves answering two important questions.

WHAT IS MY PURPOSE? The most important part of your preparation is deciding on your purpose. Do you need to sell a group insurance policy to a prospective client? Do you need to persuade management to increase the marketing budget? Do you need to inform customer service reps of three important ways to prevent miscommunication? Whether it's informing or persuading, by the end of your presentation, what do you want your listeners to remember or do?

Preparing for a presentation means identifying your purpose and knowing the audience.

Erick Rosan, a finance manager at AutoFleet, a car brokerage company, faced such questions as he planned a talk for a class in business communication. His business communication professor had invited him back to school as a guest speaker.

FIGURE 11.1 | Types of Business Presentations

- Overview or summary of an issue, proposal, or problem
- Delivery of information, discussion of questions, collection of feedback

- Oral equivalent of business reports and proposals
- Informational or persuasive oral account, simple or elaborate

- Online, prerecorded audio clip delivered over the Web
- Opportunity to launch products, introduce and train employees, and sell products and services

- Collaboration facilitated by technology (telepresence or Web)
- Real-time meeting online with remote colleagues

- Web-based presentation, lecture, workshop, or seminar
- Digital transmission with or without video to train employees, interact with customers, and promote products

He was asked to talk about what happened after he graduated, how he uses the skills he gained in college in his current job, and what a "day in the life" of his job entails. (You can see the outline for his talk in Figure 11.4, p. 249.) Because Eric obviously knows so much about this topic, he finds it difficult to extract a specific purpose statement for his presentation. After much thought he narrows his purpose to this: *To inform current business students about the realities of the post-college job market using my job as an example.* His entire presentation focuses on ensuring that the class members understand and remember three principal ideas.

WHO IS MY AUDIENCE? A second key element in preparation is analyzing your audience, anticipating its reactions, and adapting accordingly. Understanding four basic audience types, summarized in Figure 11.2, helps you decide how to organize your presentation. A friendly audience, for example, will respond to humour and personal experiences. A neutral audience requires an even, controlled delivery style. An uninterested audience that is forced to attend calls for brevity and a mix of humour, colourful visuals, and startling statistics. A hostile audience can be won over by a calm delivery style, objective data, and expert opinions.

Audience analysis issues include size, age, gender, experience, attitude, and expectations.

Other elements, such as age, education, experience, and size of audience will affect your style and message content. Erick's analysis tells him that while students are "forced" to attend, they will also probably be friendly and eager because he'll be sharing information they may not be getting regularly from their professors. He decides he'll use some humour, but also maintain an even, professional tone. Answer the following questions to help you determine your organizational pattern, delivery style, and supporting material for any presentation.

- How will this topic appeal to this audience?
- How can I relate this information to their needs?
- How can I earn respect so that they accept my message?
- What would be most effective in making my point? Facts? Statistics? Personal experiences? Expert opinion? Humour? Cartoons? Graphic illustrations? Demonstrations? Case histories? Analogies?
- How can I ensure that this audience remembers my main points?

FIGURE 11.2 | Succeeding With Four Audience Types

AUDIENCE MEMBERS	ORGANIZATIONAL PATTERN	DELIVERY STYLE	SUPPORTING MATERIAL
Friendly			
They like you and your topic.	Use any pattern. Try something new. Involve the audience.	Be warm, pleasant, and open. Use lots of eye contact and smiles.	Include humour, personal examples, and experiences.
Neutral			
They are calm, rational; their minds are made up, but they think they are objective.	Present both sides of the issue. Use pro/con or problem/solution patterns. Save time for audience questions.	Be controlled. Do nothing showy. Use confident, small gestures.	Use facts, statistics, expert opinion, and comparison and contrast. Avoid humour, personal stories, and flashy visuals.
Uninterested			
They have short attention spans; they may be there against their will.	Be brief—no more than three points. Avoid topical and pro/con patterns that seem lengthy to the audience.	Be dynamic and entertaining. Move around. Use large gestures.	Use humour, cartoons, colourful visuals, powerful quotations, and startling statistics.
	Avoid darkening the room, standing motionless, passing out handouts, using boring visuals, or expecting the audience to participate.		
Hostile			
They want to take charge or ridicule the speaker; they may be defensive, emotional.	Organize using a noncontroversial pattern, such as a topical, chronological, or geographical strategy.	Be calm and controlled. Speak evenly and slowly.	Include objective data and expert opinion. Avoid anecdotes and humour.
	Avoid a question-and-answer period, if possible; otherwise, use a moderator or accept only written questions.		

11.2 Organizing Presentations for Impact and Rapport

Once you have determined your purpose and analyzed the audience, you're ready to collect information and organize it logically. Good organization and conscious repetition are the two most powerful keys to audience comprehension and retention. In fact, many speech experts recommend the following repetitive, but effective, plan:

Step 1: Tell them what you're going to say.
Step 2: Say it.
Step 3: Tell them what you've just said.

In other words, repeat your main points in the introduction, body, and conclusion of your presentation. Although it sounds boring, this strategy works surprisingly well. This is because in an increasingly wired and mobile and distracting world, people may have trouble concentrating in face-to-face situations and need to be reminded of important points more than once.[3] Let's examine how to construct the three parts of an effective presentation: introduction, body, conclusion.

Good organization and intentional repetition help your audience understand and retain what you say.

11.2a Capture Attention in the Introduction

How many times have you heard a speaker begin with *It's a pleasure to be here.* Or *I'm honoured to be asked to speak.* Boring openings such as these get speakers off to a dull start. Avoid such banalities by striving to accomplish three goals in the introduction to your presentation:

- Capture listeners' attention and get them involved.
- Identify yourself and establish your credibility.
- Preview your main points.

If you're able to appeal to listeners and involve them in your presentation right from the start, you're more likely to hold their attention until the finish. Consider some of the same techniques that you used to open sales messages: a question, a startling fact, a joke, a story, or a quotation. Some speakers achieve involvement by opening with a question or command that requires audience members to raise their hands or stand up. You'll find additional techniques for gaining and keeping audience attention in Figure 11.3.

Attention-grabbing openers include questions, startling facts, jokes, anecdotes, and quotations.

To establish your credibility, you should describe your position, knowledge, or experience—whatever qualifies you to speak. Try as well to connect with your audience by revealing something of yourself. Erick Rosan, for example, plans to talk a bit about his former extracurricular activities at the beginning of his upcoming presentation at his old college, as seen in Figure 11.4. Similarly, a consultant addressing office workers might reminisce about how he started as a temporary worker; a CEO might tell a funny story in which the joke is on herself.

After capturing attention and establishing yourself, you'll want to preview the main points of your topic, perhaps with a visual aid. You may wish to put off actually writing your introduction until after you have organized the rest of the presentation and crystallized your principal ideas.

Take a look at Erick Rosan's introduction, shown in Figure 11.4, to see how he integrated all the elements necessary for a good opening.

11.2b Organize the Body of the Presentation

The biggest problem with most oral presentations is a failure to focus on a few main ideas. The body of your short presentation (20 or fewer minutes) should include a limited number of main points, say, two to four. Develop each main point with adequate, but not excessive, explanation and details. Too many details can obscure

The best presentations focus on a few key ideas.

FIGURE 11.3 | Gaining and Keeping Audience Attention

Experienced speakers know how to capture the attention of an audience and how to maintain that attention during a presentation. You can spruce up your presentations by trying these ten proven techniques.	
A promise	Begin with a realistic promise that keeps the audience expectant (e.g., By the end of this presentation, you will know how you can increase your sales by 50 percent!).
Drama	Open by telling an emotionally moving story or by describing a serious problem that involves the audience. Throughout your talk include other dramatic elements, such as a long pause after a key statement. Change your vocal tone or pitch. Professionals use high-intensity emotions such as anger, joy, sadness, and excitement.
Eye contact	As you begin, command attention by surveying the entire audience to take in all listeners. Give yourself two to five seconds to linger on individuals to avoid fleeting, unconvincing eye contact. Don't just sweep the room and the crowd.
Movement	Leave the lectern area whenever possible. Walk around the conference table or down the aisles of your audience. Try to move toward your audience, especially at the beginning and end of your talk.
Questions	Keep listeners active and involved with rhetorical questions. Ask for a show of hands to get each listener thinking. The response will also give you a quick gauge of audience attention.
Demonstrations	Include a member of the audience in a demonstration (e.g., I'm going to show you exactly how to implement our four-step customer courtesy process, but I need a volunteer from the audience to help me).
Samples/props	If you are promoting a product, consider using items to toss out to the audience or to award as prizes to volunteer participants. You can also pass around product samples or promotional literature. Be careful, though, to maintain control.
Visuals	Give your audience something to look at besides yourself. Use a variety of visual aids in a single session. Also consider writing the concerns expressed by your audience on a flipchart or on the board as you go along.
Dress	Enhance your credibility with your audience by dressing professionally for your presentation. Professional attire will help you look more competent and qualified, which will make your audience more likely to listen to you and take you seriously.
Self-interest	Review your entire presentation to ensure that it meets the critical What's-in-it-for-me audience test. Remember that people are most interested in things that benefit them.

Organize the body by time, geography, function, importance, or some other method that is logical to the receiver.

the main message, so keep your presentation simple and logical. Remember, listeners have no pages to leaf back through should they become confused.

When Erick Rosan began planning his presentation, he realized that he could talk for quite a while on his topic. He also knew that listeners are not good at separating major and minor points. So, instead of submerging his listeners in a sea of information, he sorted out a few principal ideas. First, college students, worried about where they might work after graduating, need concrete advice about how to become employable workers. Second, students need to be reassured that all the hard work they're currently doing (e.g., assignments, exams, research, etc.) is going to be useful in their jobs. Third, students need to understand what a day in the life of a professional is like: how it differs from that of a student or part-time worker (an experience most students already have).

FIGURE 11.4 | Presentation Outline

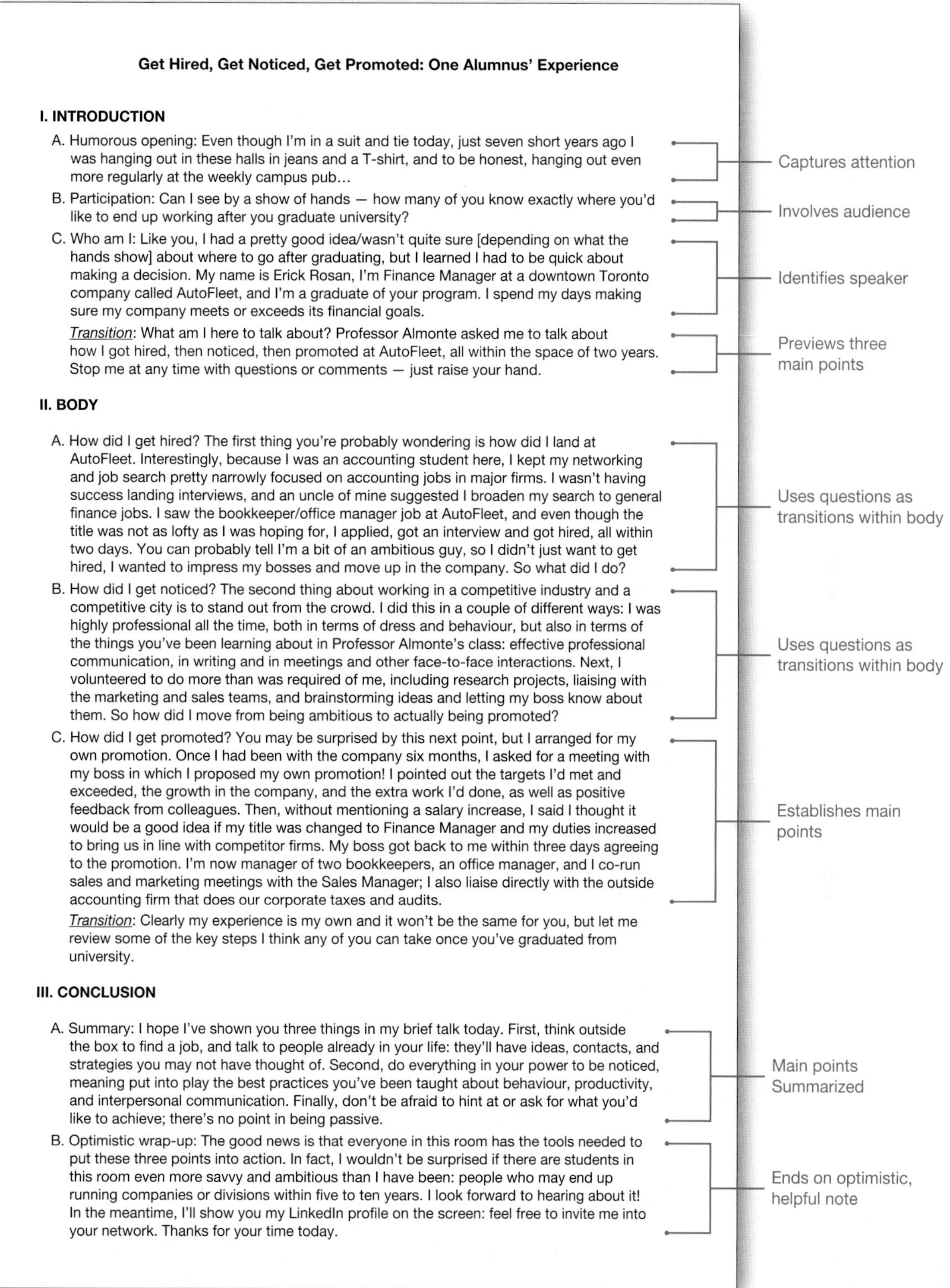

Get Hired, Get Noticed, Get Promoted: One Alumnus' Experience

I. INTRODUCTION

A. Humorous opening: Even though I'm in a suit and tie today, just seven short years ago I was hanging out in these halls in jeans and a T-shirt, and to be honest, hanging out even more regularly at the weekly campus pub…

B. Participation: Can I see by a show of hands — how many of you know exactly where you'd like to end up working after you graduate university?

C. Who am I: Like you, I had a pretty good idea/wasn't quite sure [depending on what the hands show] about where to go after graduating, but I learned I had to be quick about making a decision. My name is Erick Rosan, I'm Finance Manager at a downtown Toronto company called AutoFleet, and I'm a graduate of your program. I spend my days making sure my company meets or exceeds its financial goals.

Transition: What am I here to talk about? Professor Almonte asked me to talk about how I got hired, then noticed, then promoted at AutoFleet, all within the space of two years. Stop me at any time with questions or comments — just raise your hand.

II. BODY

A. How did I get hired? The first thing you're probably wondering is how did I land at AutoFleet. Interestingly, because I was an accounting student here, I kept my networking and job search pretty narrowly focused on accounting jobs in major firms. I wasn't having success landing interviews, and an uncle of mine suggested I broaden my search to general finance jobs. I saw the bookkeeper/office manager job at AutoFleet, and even though the title was not as lofty as I was hoping for, I applied, got an interview and got hired, all within two days. You can probably tell I'm a bit of an ambitious guy, so I didn't just want to get hired, I wanted to impress my bosses and move up in the company. So what did I do?

B. How did I get noticed? The second thing about working in a competitive industry and a competitive city is to stand out from the crowd. I did this in a couple of different ways: I was highly professional all the time, both in terms of dress and behaviour, but also in terms of the things you've been learning about in Professor Almonte's class: effective professional communication, in writing and in meetings and other face-to-face interactions. Next, I volunteered to do more than was required of me, including research projects, liaising with the marketing and sales teams, and brainstorming ideas and letting my boss know about them. So how did I move from being ambitious to actually being promoted?

C. How did I get promoted? You may be surprised by this next point, but I arranged for my own promotion. Once I had been with the company six months, I asked for a meeting with my boss in which I proposed my own promotion! I pointed out the targets I'd met and exceeded, the growth in the company, and the extra work I'd done, as well as positive feedback from colleagues. Then, without mentioning a salary increase, I said I thought it would be a good idea if my title was changed to Finance Manager and my duties increased to bring us in line with competitor firms. My boss got back to me within three days agreeing to the promotion. I'm now manager of two bookkeepers, an office manager, and I co-run sales and marketing meetings with the Sales Manager; I also liaise directly with the outside accounting firm that does our corporate taxes and audits.

Transition: Clearly my experience is my own and it won't be the same for you, but let me review some of the key steps I think any of you can take once you've graduated from university.

III. CONCLUSION

A. Summary: I hope I've shown you three things in my brief talk today. First, think outside the box to find a job, and talk to people already in your life: they'll have ideas, contacts, and strategies you may not have thought of. Second, do everything in your power to be noticed, meaning put into play the best practices you've been taught about behaviour, productivity, and interpersonal communication. Finally, don't be afraid to hint at or ask for what you'd like to achieve; there's no point in being passive.

B. Optimistic wrap-up: The good news is that everyone in this room has the tools needed to put these three points into action. In fact, I wouldn't be surprised if there are students in this room even more savvy and ambitious than I have been: people who may end up running companies or divisions within five to ten years. I look forward to hearing about it! In the meantime, I'll show you my LinkedIn profile on the screen: feel free to invite me into your network. Thanks for your time today.

These would become his main points, but Erick wanted to streamline them further so that his student audience would be sure to remember them. He summarized the three points as follows: *get hired, get noticed, get promoted.* As you can see in Figure 11.4, Erick prepared a sentence outline showing these three main ideas. Each is supported by examples and explanations.

How to organize and sequence main ideas may not be immediately obvious when you begin working on a presentation. In Chapter 9 you studied a number of patterns for organizing written reports. Those patterns, and a few new ones, are equally appropriate for presentations:

- **Chronology.** A presentation describing the history of a problem, organized from the first sign of trouble to the present. We could argue that Erick Rosan's presentation is chronological: first get hired, then get noticed, and finally get promoted.
- **Geography/space.** A presentation about the changing diversity of the workforce, organized by regions in the country (Atlantic, Prairie, and so forth).
- **Topic/function/conventional grouping.** A report discussing mishandled airline baggage, organized by names of airlines. We could also argue that Erick's presentation is topical: topic 1 is getting hired, topic 2 is getting noticed, and topic 3 is getting promoted.
- **Comparison/contrast (pro/con).** A report comparing organic farming methods with those of modern industrial farming.
- **Journalism pattern.** A report describing how identity thieves can ruin your good name, organized by *who, what, when, where, why,* and *how*.
- **Value/size.** A report describing fluctuations in housing costs, organized by prices of homes.
- **Importance.** A report describing five reasons that a company should move its headquarters to a specific city, organized from the most important reason to the least important (using some criteria to judge importance, of course). Erick's presentation can also be seen as being organized this way; he leaves what he judges to be the most important topic (getting promoted) for last.
- **Problem/solution.** A company faces a problem such as declining sales. A solution such as reducing the staff is offered.
- **Simple/complex.** A report explaining genetic modification of plants, organized from simple seed production to complex gene introduction.
- **Best case/worst case.** A report analyzing whether two companies should merge, organized by the best-case result (improved market share, profitability, good employee morale) as opposed to the worst-case result (devalued stock, lost market share, poor employee morale).

When organizing presentations, prepare a little more material than you think you will actually need. Savvy speakers always have something useful in reserve (such as an extra handout or idea)—just in case they finish early.

11.2c Summarize in the Conclusion

Effective presentations conclude with a summary of main points and a graceful exit from the stage/front of the room.

Nervous speakers often rush to wrap up their presentations because they can't wait to flee the stage. But they forget that listeners will remember the conclusion more than any part of a speech. That's why you should spend some time to include an effective conclusion, even in a short presentation. Strive to achieve three goals:

1. Summarize the main themes of the presentation.
2. Leave the audience with a specific/memorable take-away.
3. Include a statement that allows you to leave the podium gracefully.

Some speakers end limply with comments such as *I guess that's about all I have to say*. This leaves bewildered audience members wondering whether they should have bothered listening at all. Skilled speakers alert the audience that they are finishing. They use phrases such as *In conclusion, As I end this presentation*, or *It's time for me to stop, so let me repeat....* Then they proceed immediately to the conclusion. Audiences become justly irritated with a speaker who announces the conclusion but then digresses with one more story or talks on for ten more minutes.

A concluding summary should review major points and focus on what you want the listeners to do, think, or remember. You might say, *In bringing my presentation to a close, I'll briefly repeat my main idea...*; or *In summary, my major purpose has been to...*; or *In support of my purpose, I have presented three major points. They are (a) ..., (b) ..., and (c) ....* Notice how Erick Rosan, in the planned conclusion shown in Figure 11.4, summarizes his three main points and provides a final focus to his audience.

If you are promoting a recommendation, you might end as follows: In conclusion, I recommend that we consider Moncton as the most appropriate home for our new customer service call centre. I make this recommendation using the criteria I've outlined, namely (a) there is an experienced, bilingual workforce available in Moncton, (b) the city is home to other call centres, fostering resource synergies, and (c) Moncton offers the most attractive tax and other municipal and provincial incentives among the cities we've considered.

In your conclusion you can also use an anecdote, an inspiring quotation, or a statement that ties in the attention-capturing opener and offers a new insight. Whatever strategy you choose, be sure to include a memorable take-away that indicates you are finished. For example, This concludes my presentation. After investigating three qualified Canadian cities in detail, we are convinced that Moncton suits our customer service needs best. Your authorization of my recommendation will enable us to move forward quickly with this important infrastructure and productivity goal. Thank you.

11.2d Build Audience Rapport

Good speakers know how to build audience rapport. Rapport is the bond formed with an audience; speakers with good rapport entertain as well as inform. How do they do it? Based on observations of successful and unsuccessful speakers, we can see that the good ones use a number of verbal and nonverbal techniques to connect with the audience. Some of their helpful techniques include providing effective imagery, supplying verbal signposts such as transitions and repetition, and using body language strategically.

EFFECTIVE IMAGERY. You'll lose your audience quickly if your talk is filled with abstractions, generalities, and dry facts. To enliven your presentation and enhance comprehension, try using some of these techniques:

Use analogies, metaphors, similes, personal anecdotes, personalized statistics, and worst- and best-case scenarios instead of dry facts.

- **Analogies.** A comparison of similar traits between dissimilar things can be effective in explaining and drawing connections. For example, *Good customer service can be compared to hosting a good dinner party: people should leave the customer service interaction happier than when they arrived, wanting to come back again.* Or, *Downsizing and restructuring are similar to an overweight person dieting, changing habits, and exercising: painful but necessary.*
- **Metaphors.** A comparison between otherwise dissimilar things without using the words *like* or *as* results in a metaphor. For example, *Those new drill sergeants in Accounting won't let me submit expense claims late, even by five minutes!* or *My desk is a garbage dump.*
- **Similes.** A comparison that includes the words *like* or *as* is a simile. For example, *Building a business team is like building a sports team—you want people not only with the right abilities, but also with the willingness to work together.* Or, *Change management can be about as difficult as converting people to a new religion!*
- **Personal anecdotes.** Nothing connects you faster or better with your audience than a good personal story. In a talk about email best practices, you could reveal your own blunders that became painful learning experiences. In a talk to potential "angel" investors, the creator of a new app could talk about the cool factor of seeing an app he previously developed being used widely by young people.

- **Personalized statistics.** Although often misused, statistics stay with people—particularly when they relate directly to the audience. A speaker discussing job retraining might say, *If this is a typical workplace, I can safely say that half of the people in this room won't be here within three years—that's the rate of job change these days.* If possible, simplify and personalize facts. For example, *The sales of Creemore Springs Brewery totalled 5 million cases last year. That's a full case of Creemore for every man, woman, and child in the Greater Toronto Area.*
- **Worst- and best-case scenarios.** Hearing the worst that could happen can be effective in driving home a point. For example, *I don't want to sound alarmist, but if we don't listen more closely to consumers in terms of what products they want, we could be the next tech company to land in the graveyard of has-beens.*
- **Examples.** Finally, remember that an audience likes to hear specifics. If you're giving a presentation on interpersonal communication, for example, instead of just saying, *Rudeness in the workplace is a growing problem*, it's always better to say something like *Rudeness in the workplace is a growing problem. For example, we've heard from some of our clients that our customer service representatives are using an inappropriate tone of voice.*

Knowledgeable speakers provide verbal signposts to indicate when they are previewing, summarizing, or switching directions.

VERBAL SIGNPOSTS. Presenters should remember that listeners, unlike readers of a report, cannot control the rate of presentation or flip back through pages to review main points. As a result, listeners get lost easily. Knowledgeable speakers help the audience recognize the organization and main points in an oral message with verbal signposts. They keep listeners on track by including helpful previews, summaries, and transitions, such as these:

- Preview
  The next segment of my talk presents three reasons for...
  I'll pass things off to Alia, who'll consider the causes of...
- Switch directions
  So far we've talked solely about...; now let's move to...
  I've argued that ... and..., but an alternate view holds that...
- Summarize
  Let me review with you the major problems I've just discussed.
  You can see, then, that the most significant factors are...

You can further improve any presentation by including appropriate transitional expressions such as *first, second, next, then, therefore, moreover, on the other hand, on the contrary, and in conclusion.* These expressions lend emphasis and tell listeners where you are headed. Notice in Erick Rosan's outline, in Figure 11.4, that his specific transition questions and other elements are designed to help listeners recognize each new principal point.

The way you look, how you move, and how you speak affect the success of your presentation.

NONVERBAL MESSAGES. Although what you say is most important, the nonverbal messages you send can also have a potent effect on how well your message is received. How you look, how you move, and how you speak can make or break your presentation. The following suggestions focus on nonverbal tips to ensure that your verbal message is well received.

- **Look professional.** Like it or not, you will be judged by your appearance. For everything but small, in-house presentations, be sure you dress professionally. The rule of thumb is that you should dress at least as well as the best-dressed person in the company.
- **Animate your body.** Be enthusiastic and let your body show it. Emphasize ideas with your hands to enhance points about size, number, and direction. Use a variety of gestures, but try not to consciously plan them in advance.
- **Punctuate your words.** You can keep your audience interested by varying your tone, volume, pitch, and pace. Use pauses before and after important points. Allow the audience to take in your ideas.

- **Get out from behind the podium/table/desk.** Avoid being planted behind the furniture. Movement makes you look natural and comfortable. You might pick a few places in the room to walk to. Even if you must stay close to your visual aids, make a point of leaving them occasionally so that the audience can see your whole body.
- **Vary your facial expression.** Begin with a smile, but change your expressions to correspond with the thoughts you are voicing. You can shake your head to show disagreement, roll your eyes to show disdain, look heavenward for guidance, or wrinkle your brow to show concern or dismay. To see how speakers convey meaning without words, mute the sound on your TV and watch the facial expressions of any well-known talk-show host.

11.3 Types of Presentation Aids

Visual aids clarify points, improve comprehension, and aid retention.

Before you give a business presentation, consider this wise proverb: "Tell me, I forget. Show me, I remember. Involve me, I understand." Your goals as a speaker are to make listeners understand, remember, and act on your ideas. To get them interested and involved, include effective visual aids. Some experts say that we acquire 85 percent of all our knowledge visually. Therefore, an oral presentation that incorporates visual aids is far more likely to be understood and retained than one lacking visual enhancement.

Good visual aids have many purposes. They emphasize and clarify main points, thus improving comprehension and retention. They increase audience interest, and they make the presenter appear more professional, better prepared, and more persuasive. Furthermore, research published in the journal *Information & Management*, shows that the use of visual aids during presentations leads to "a strong improvement in comprehension and retention."[4] Visual aids are particularly helpful for inexperienced speakers because the audience concentrates on the aid rather than on the speaker. Good visuals also serve to jog the memory of a speaker, thus improving self-confidence, poise, and delivery.

11.3a Types of Visual Aids

Fortunately for today's presenters, many forms of visual media are available to enhance a presentation. Figure 11.5 describes a number of visual aids and compares their degree of formality and other considerations. Some of the most popular visual aids are PowerPoint or Prezi slides, infographics, a flipchart/blackboard/whiteboard/smartboard, and handouts.

SLIDES. With today's excellent software programs—such as PowerPoint and Prezi—you can create dynamic, colourful presentations with your laptop or tablet. The output from these programs is shown on a computer monitor, a TV monitor, or, in professional and academic settings, on a screen. With a little expertise and advanced equipment, you can create a slide presentation that includes professional sound, videos, and hyperlinks, as described in the discussion of slide presentations below. Slides can also be uploaded to a website or turned into podcasts to be broadcast live over the Internet. PowerPoint slides are linear whereas Prezi slides have a nonlinear, 3D interface that lends them an almost movie-like quality.

INFOGRAPHICS. Infographics are a new way of visually displaying information. They take what's best about traditional graphics (i.e., graphs, charts, logos, icons) and meld it with what's best about cartoons and animations (i.e., faces, bodies, stick figures) to produce a new type of visual information. Almost any type of information or data set can be turned into an infographic, using software that is available free of charge on the Internet. Popular sites include Piktochart (www.piktochart.com) and Venngage (www.venngage.com). Infographics are usually added to a PowerPoint or Prezi slide presentation, but they can also be printed out as a handout. An example of an infographic is found later in the chapter as part of Figure 11.5.

FIGURE 11.5 | Pros and Cons of Presentation Visual Aids

AID	PROS	CONS
PowerPoint or Prezi slides Sebastien Decoret/123 RF	Create professional appearance with many colour, art, graphic, and font options. Easy to use and transport via removable storage media, Web download, or email attachment. Inexpensive to update. Cinematic zoomable quality with Prezi slides	Present potential incompatibility issues. Require costly projection equipment and practice for smooth delivery. Tempt user to include razzle-dazzle features that may fail to add value. Distract viewers during zooming or transitions.
Infographic Antun Hirsman/Shutterstock.com	Appealing visualization of data.	Oversimplication of complex ideas/concepts.
Flipcharts or boards Antun Hirsman/Shutterstock.com	Provide inexpensive option available at most sites. Easy to create, modify or customize on the spot, record comments from the audience, combine with more high-tech visuals in the same presentation, create instant digital record of what happened during presentation.	Require graphics talent. Difficult for larger audiences to see. Prepared flipcharts are cumbersome to transport and easily worn with use. Smartboards take significant practice to master.
Handouts or speaker's notes By Grimgram/Shutterstock.com	Encourage audience participation. Easy to maintain and update. Enhance recall because audience keeps reference material.	Increase risk of unauthorized duplication of speaker's material. Can be difficult to transport. May cause speaker to lose audience's attention.
Video brux/Shutterstock.com	Gives an accurate representation of the content; strong indication of forethought and preparation.	Creates potential for compatibility issues related to computer video formats. Expensive to create and update.
Props robuart/Shutterstock.com	Offer a realistic reinforcement of message content. Increase audience participation with close observation.	Lead to extra work and expense in transporting and replacing worn objects. Limited use with larger audiences.

FLIPCHART/WHITEBOARD/BLACKBOARD/SMARTBOARD. Even though it may seem old-fashioned, effective use of a blackboard and chalk, a whiteboard and dry-erase markers, or a paper flipchart and magic markers is one of the best ways to teach a relatively small audience something so that it sticks in people's minds. If you think about it, the reason for this effectiveness is clear. Instead of just using your voice and assuming people will listen, understand, and take notes, writing down major headings, important concepts, new vocabulary words, and so on, gives the audience a double dose of information: orally through your voice and visually from your writing on the board. Another reason using these boards is effective? It makes you dynamic. You are *doing* something besides just talking.

Smartboards are now found in many classrooms and workplace meetings rooms—they take things one step further by allowing presenters to bring up and create new resources on-site. For example, a presenter can access a website on the smartboard and physically touch the screen to go to web links; "save" what's on the board and have it immediately translate into a file; or write on the board with a special stylus and save what's been written into a digital file.

HANDOUTS. You can enhance presentations by distributing pictures, outlines, brochures, articles, charts, summaries, or other supplements. Speakers who use slides often prepare a set of their slides (called a "deck") along with notes to hand out to viewers, with mixed results. Often, the audience doesn't pay attention to the speaker but noisily flips through the printed-out pages of the slides. Timing the distribution of any handout is tricky. If given out during a presentation, your handouts tend to distract the audience, causing you to lose control. Thus, it's probably best to discuss most handouts during the presentation but delay distributing them until after you finish.

11.4 Designing Effective Presentations

Some presenters prefer to create their visuals first and then develop the narrative around their visuals. Others prepare their content first and then create the visual component. The risk associated with the first approach is that you may be tempted to spend too much time making your visuals look good and not enough time preparing your content. Remember that great-looking slides never compensate for thin content.

Slide presentations are economical, flexible, professional, and easy to prepare.

11.4a Analyze the Situation and Purpose

Critics say that PowerPoint is too regimented and produces "bullet-pointed morons."

Making the best content and design choices for your visual presentation depends on your analysis of the presentation situation and its purpose. Will your visuals be used during a live presentation? Will they be part of a self-running presentation such as in a store kiosk? Will they be saved on a server so that those with Internet access can watch the presentation at their convenience? Will they be sent to a client—as an attachment instead of a hard-copy report? Are you converting slide shows into video podcasts using a program like Jing or Camtasia for viewing on the Internet via a laptop, tablet, or smartphone?

If you are emailing the presentation or posting it online as a self-contained file, the slides will typically feature more text than if they were delivered orally. If, on the other hand, you are creating slides for a live presentation, your analysis will include answering questions such as these: *Should I prepare speaker's notes pages for my own use during the presentation? Should I distribute hard copies of my slides to my audience?*

11.4b Anticipate Your Audience

Think about how you can design your visuals to get the most positive response from your audience. Audiences respond, for example, to the colours you use. Because the messages that colours convey can vary from culture to culture, colours must be chosen carefully. In the Western world, blue and white are the colours of credibility,

FIGURE 11.6 | SlideRocket Presentation

http://www.sliderocket.com/product/

SlideRocket is a cloud-based presentation software. Like PowerPoint, it allows users to create slides, but it takes the emphasis off bullet points. Instead, SlideRocket offers numerous tools to help users create visually rich slides: stock photos, flash animation, 2D and 3D transitional effects, tables, and charts.

WORKPLACE IN FOCUS

Although videoconferencing, Web seminars (or webinars), and other virtual-meeting platforms can make business presentations more stimulating and cost-effective, failure to manage these tools may lead to embarrassing career blunders. In one instance, a business executive delivering a virtual presentation became flummoxed when the words "I love you, Teddy Bear" appeared unexpectedly on the computer screen. The instant message, which a love interest had transmitted during the meeting, was visible to all attendees, earning the executive the nickname Teddy Bear. *What precautions should communicators take to ensure the smooth delivery of presentations with Internet content?*

© Stockbyte/Getty Images

transparency, tranquility, conservatism, and trust. Therefore, they are the background colour of choice for many business presentations. Green relates to interaction, growth, money, and stability. It can work well as a background or an accent colour. Purple can be used as a background or accent colour. It conveys spirituality, aspirations, or humour.[5] As for slide text, adjust the colour so it provides high contrast and is readable. Black or blue, for example, usually work well on a white background.

Just as you anticipate audience members' reactions to colour, you can usually anticipate their reactions to special effects. Using animation and sound effects—flying objects, swirling text, and the like—only because they are available is not a good idea. This is a concern especially in Prezi, because zooming in and out of frames is at the core of this software.[6] Special effects may distract your audience, drawing attention away from your main points. Add animation features only if doing so helps to convey your message or adds interest to the content. When your audience members leave, they should be commenting on the ideas you conveyed—not the cool swivels and sound effects.

11.4c Adapt Text and Colour Selections

Follow the 6-×-6 rule and select background and text colours based on the lightness of the room.

Adapt the amount of text on your slide to how your audience will use the slides. As a general guideline, most graphic designers encourage the 6-×-6 rule: "Six bullets per screen, max; six words per bullet, max."[7] You may find, however, that breaking this rule is sometimes necessary, particularly when your users will be viewing the presentation on their own with no speaker assistance.

Adjust colours based on where the presentation will be given. Use light text on a dark background for presentations in darkened rooms. Use dark text on a light background for presentations in lighted rooms. Avoid using a dark font on a dark background, such as red text on a dark blue background. In the same way, avoid using a light font on a light background, such as white text on a pale blue background. Dark on dark or light on light results in low contrast, making the slides difficult to read.

11.4d Organize Your Visuals

When you prepare slides or infographics, you'll likely translate the major headings in your outline into titles for slides or headings for infographics sections. So you'll have an introduction slide, body slides, and a conclusion slide. In each of these five or so slides, you'll then paste from Word or write bullet points under each slide title using short phrases. In Chapter 4 you learned to improve readability by using graphic highlighting techniques, including bullets, numbers, and headings. In preparing a slide presentation, you will put those techniques into practice.

11.4e Design Your Visuals

All presentation and infographic software requires you to (a) select or create a template that will serve as the background for your presentation and (b) add content (i.e., text, images, or links) that best conveys your message. In both PowerPoint and Prezi, as well as infographic software like Piktochart, you can use one of the templates provided with the software (see examples in Figure 11.7), download templates from the Internet, or create a template from scratch.

Most business communicators (unless they are in creative fields like design, advertising, or performing arts) usually choose existing templates because they are designed by professionals who know how to combine harmonious colours, borders, bullet styles, and fonts for pleasing visual effects. If you prefer, you can alter existing templates so they better suit your needs. Adding a corporate logo, adjusting the colour

Overused templates and clip art produce visual clichés that may bore audiences.

FIGURE 11.7 | Selecting Design Templates in PowerPoint and Prezi

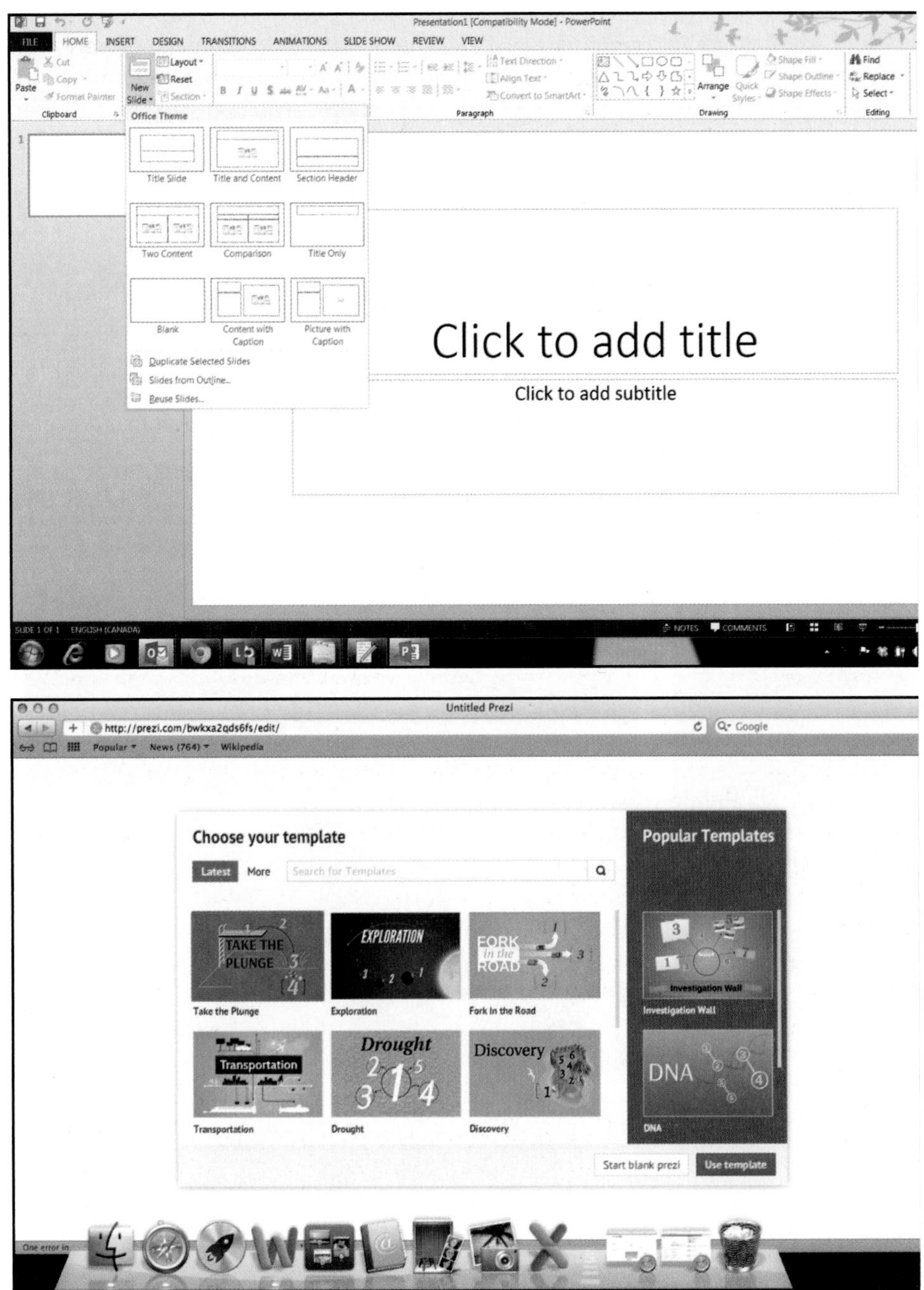

scheme to better match the colours used on your organization's website, and selecting a different font are just some of the ways you can customize existing templates.

Be careful, though, of what one expert labels "visual clichés."[8] Overused templates and even clip art that come with slide software can weary viewers who have seen them repeatedly in presentations. Instead of using a standard template, search for "PowerPoint template" in Google. You will see hundreds of template options available as free downloads. Unless your employer requires that presentations all have the same look, your audience may appreciate fresh templates that complement the purpose of your presentation and provide visual variety. That said, there's an argument to be made for consistency of slide appearance; for example, consistency connotes professionalism.

As Figure 11.8 shows, you should experiment with graphic elements that will enhance your presentation by making your visuals more appealing and memorable. One of the simplest but most effective lessons to learn is to try to avoid long, boring bulleted lists like the one in the left-hand slide of Figure 11.8.

If you look more closely at Figure 11.8, you will notice that the listed items on the first slide are not parallel. The second and sixth bullet points express the same thought, that shopping online is convenient and easy for customers. Some bullet points are too long. The bullets on the improved slide (right-hand side) are short, well within the 6-×-6 rule, although they are complete sentences and easy to read (due to the use of the bullets). The photograph in the revised slide also adds interest and helps illustrate the point.

Another effective and simple lesson about using slides is illustrated in Figure 11.9. The figure shows the same "reasons for online selling" from Figure 11.8, but has used a spoke diagram to add variety to the presentation. This spoke diagram is just one of many diagram possibilities available in PowerPoint's Chart and SmartArt galleries. Similar diagram options exist in Prezi and in infographic software. You can also animate each item in the diagram. As a best practice, try occasionally (e.g., once per presentation) to convert pure text and bullet points to diagrams, charts, and other images to add punch to your slide show. You will keep your audiences interested and help them retain the information you are presenting.

Numeric information is more easily grasped in charts or graphs than in a listing of numbers. In most programs, you can also animate your graphs and charts.

FIGURE 11.8 | Revising Slides for Greater Impact

The slide on the left contains bullet points that are not parallel and that overlap meaning. The second and sixth bullet points say the same thing. Moreover, some bullet points are too long. After revision, the slide on the right has a more convincing title illustrating the "you" view. The bullet points are shorter, and each begins with a verb for parallelism. The photo adds interest. Note that the revised slide features a more lively and readable colour scheme, starting with the title.

FIGURE 11.9 | Converting a Bulleted Slide Into a Diagram

Revised With a SmartArt Graphic

SmartArt Graphics Options

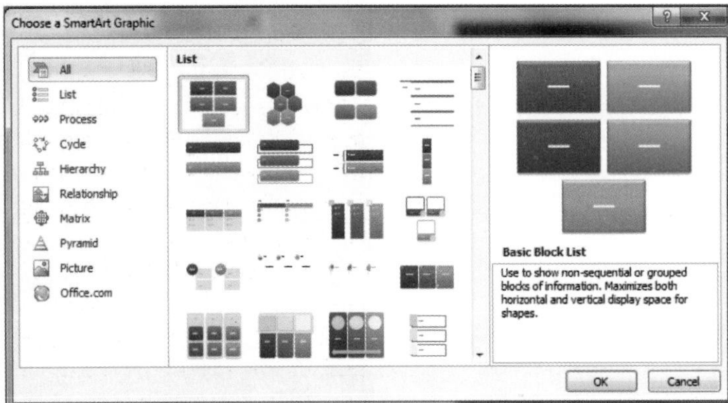

The same content that appears in the Figure 11.8 slides takes on a totally different look when arranged as spokes radiating from a central idea. Add a 3D effect and a muted background image to the middle shape, for example, and you depart from the usual boring template look. When presenting this slide, you can animate each item and control when it is revealed, further enlivening your presentation. PowerPoint provides SmartArt graphics with many choices of diagrams and shapes for arranging information.

Say, for instance, you have four columns in a bar chart. You can control when each column appears to your audience by determining in what order and how each column appears on the screen. The idea is to use animation strategically to introduce elements of the presentation simultaneously as they are mentioned in your spoken remarks, as a way of adding suspense to your presentation. Figure 11.10 shows how a chart can be used in PowerPoint to illustrate the concept of selling online, which is being discussed in a presentation.

Use animation to introduce elements of a presentation as they unfold in your spoken remarks.

Remember that not every point or thought requires a visual. In fact, it is smart to switch off the slides occasionally and direct the focus to yourself. Darkening the screen while you discuss a point, tell a story, give an example, or involve the audience will add variety to your presentation.

Create a slide only if the slide accomplishes at least one of the following purposes:

- Generates interest in what you are saying and helps the audience follow your ideas
- Highlights points you want your audience to remember
- Introduces or reviews your key points
- Provides a transition from one major point to the next
- Illustrates and simplifies complex ideas

In a later section of this chapter, you will find specific steps to follow as you create your presentation.

11.4f Revise, Proofread, and Evaluate Your Slide Show

Before giving the presentation, you should build in time to focus on making your presentation as clear and concise as possible. In other words, just as you revise written messages, you also need to revise visual messages. For example, if you are listing items in a slide, be sure that all items use parallel grammatical form. If you created your own slide template, be sure all slides have the same background colour. If you quickly created the presentation from scratch, make sure the slides are in the right order so they don't confuse your audience. If you haven't yet proofread the slides, do so to make sure there are no spelling, punctuation, grammar, or style errors.

Nothing is as embarrassing as projecting errors on a huge screen in front of your audience. Also check for consistency in how you capitalize and punctuate throughout the presentation. Finally, do a quick scan to ensure that basic slide best practices, such as number of bullet points per slide and length of sentence per bullet, are appropriate, so as not to overwhelm your audience.

FIGURE 11.10 | Using a Bar Chart to Illustrate a Concept

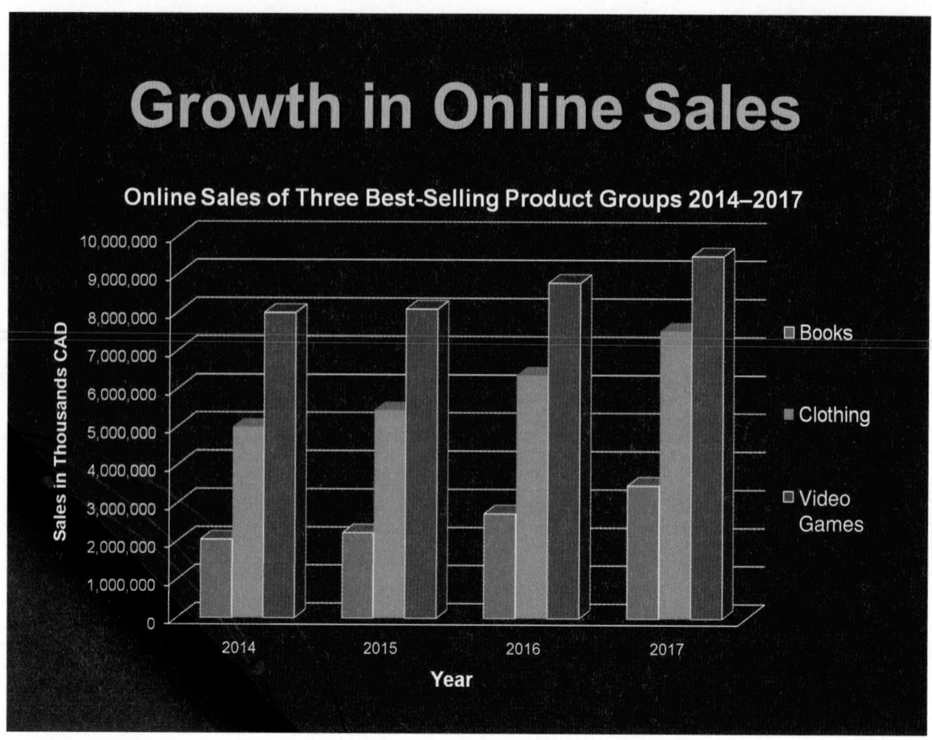

This slide was created using PowerPoint's Insert Chart function. The information presented here is more exciting and easier to comprehend than if it had been presented in a bulleted list.

Figure 11.11 shows how to revise a typical slide to improve it for conciseness, parallelism, and other features. Look closely at the design tips described in the first slide and determine which suggestions were not followed. Then compare it with the revised slide.

Notice that both slides in Figure 11.11 feature a blue background. This calming colour is the colour of choice for many business presentations (though white is just as popular an option for its elegance and ease of reading). However, the background swirls on the first slide are distracting. In addition, the uppercase white font is hard to read and contributes to making the image look busy. Inserting a transparent overlay and choosing a dark font to mute the distracting waves create a cleaner-looking slide.

As a last step before presenting, critically evaluate your slide show. Consider whether you have done all you can to use the tools PowerPoint or Prezi provide to communicate your message in a visually appealing way. In addition, test your slides on the equipment and in the room you will be using during your presentation. Do the colours you selected work in this new setting? Are the font styles and sizes readable from the back of the room?

11.4g Use Slides Effectively in Front of an Audience

A fabulous slide show can be ruined if you are unfamiliar with the equipment.

It's worth remembering that many promising presentations have been sabotaged by technology glitches or by the presenter's unfamiliarity with the equipment. Fabulous slides are of value only if you can manage the technology expertly. The late Apple CEO Steve Jobs was famous for his ability to wow his audiences during his keynote addresses. A journalist described his approach as follows: "Jobs unveils Apple's latest products as if he were a particularly hip and plugged-in friend showing off inventions in your living room. Truth is, the sense of informality comes only after gruelling hours of practice."[9] At one of his rehearsals, for example, Jobs spent more than four hours on stage practising and reviewing every technical and performance aspect of his product launch.

FIGURE 11.11 | Designing More Effective Slides

Before Revision

Reasons for Selling Online

- Your online business can grow globally.
- Customer convenience.
- You can conduct your business 24/7.
- No need for renting a retail store or hiring employees.
- Reduce inquiries by providing policies and a privacy statement.
- Customers can buy quickly and easily.

After Revision

The slide on the left is difficult to read and understand because it violates many slide-making rules. How many violations can you detect? The slide on the right illustrates an improved version of the same information. Which slide do you think viewers would rather read?

PRACTISE AND PREPARE. Allow plenty of time before your presentation to set up and test your equipment.[10] Confirm that the places you plan to stand are not in the line of the projected image. Audience members don't appreciate having part of the slide displayed on your body. Make sure that all video or Web links are working, that the sound level is appropriate (if audio is part of the slides), and that you know how to operate all features the first time you try. No matter how much time you put into pre-show setup and testing, you still have no guarantee that all will go smoothly. Therefore, you should always bring backups of your presentation. Handouts of your presentation provide a good substitute. Transferring your presentation to a USB flash drive that can run from any available laptop might prove useful as well.

> To keep your audience interested, maintain eye contact, don't read from your slides, consider using a radio remote and a laser pointer, and turn off an image when it has been discussed.

KEEP YOUR AUDIENCE ENGAGED. In addition to using the technology to enhance and enrich your message, here are additional tips for performing like a professional and keeping the audience engaged:

- Know your material so that you are free to look at your audience with only the occasional gaze at the screen, but not at your notes. Maintain genuine eye contact to connect with individuals in the room.
- As you show new elements on a slide or frame, allow the audience time to absorb the information. Then paraphrase and elaborate on what the listeners have seen. Don't insult your audience's intelligence by reading verbatim from a slide or frame.
- Leave the lights as bright as you can. Make sure the audience can see your face and eyes.
- Don't leave a slide on the screen when you are no longer discussing it. In PowerPoint, in Slide Show, View Show mode, strike *B* on the keyboard to turn off the screen image by blackening it (or press *W* to turn the screen white). Hit the key again to turn the screen back on.

Some presenters allow their slides or frames to steal their thunder. One expert urges speakers to "use their PowerPresence in preference to their PowerPoint."[11] In developing visuals, don't expect them to carry the show.

You can avoid being upstaged by not relying totally on your visuals. Help the audience see your points by using other techniques. For example, drawing a diagram on a whiteboard or flipchart can be more engaging than showing slide after slide of static drawings. Demonstrating or displaying real objects or props is a welcome relief from slides. Remember that slides should be used only to help your audience

> Slides should be used to help audiences understand a message—you are still the main attraction!

FIGURE 11.12 | Giving Powerful Slide Presentations in Eight Steps

We have now discussed many suggestions for designing effective slide presentations, but you may still be wondering how to put it all together. Here is a step-by-step process for creating a powerful multimedia presentation:

Start with the text	• Choose a simple but effective template. • Express your ideas using clear, concise wording—one idea per slide. • Ensure each slide has no more than three to five lines of text.
Select background and fonts	• Choose a simple but professional font, such as Arial or Times New Roman. • Choose a point size between 24 and 36, with titles larger than the text font. • Ensure the background colour is professional and easy to read (e.g., white or very light colours).
Choose images that help communicate your message	• Introduce images such as clip art, photographs, or maps to complement your text. • If copying images from the Internet, ensure a source line is included, such as "Source: Google Images."
Create graphics	• Use your software's built-in tools to create graphs or infographics. • Possible graphics include flow chart, pie chart, bar chart, etc. • Ensure graphics are understandable even by someone with no knowledge of your presentation material. Keep it simple!
Add special effects	• Use your software's built-in tools to create effects like zooming, fading, wiping, animation, or audio. • Use these effects only if they will make the presentation more persuasive.
Create hyperlinks to approximate the Web-browsing experience	• Paste appropriate Internet links into your presentation. • Ensure the links are used sparingly—otherwise you'll dilute the persuasiveness of the presentation.
Engage your audience by asking for interaction	• Consider integrating audience response tools into your presentation. • Free tools include Kahoot (for quizzes) and Socrative (for giving feedback).
Post your presentation to the Internet	• Consider posting your presentation to YouTube or your company's intranet. • Free software like Jing allows you to record your presentation as a video with your voice recorded over it.

Learn to simplify complex information in visually appealing graphics.

Internet options for slide presentations range from posting slides online to conducting a live Web conference with slides, narration, and speaker control.

understand the message and to add interest. You are still the main attraction! If in doubt, review the eight steps in Figure 11.12.

11.5 Polishing Your Delivery and Following Up

Once you've organized your presentation and prepared visuals, you're ready to practise delivering it. Here are suggestions for selecting a delivery method, along with specific techniques to use before, during, and after your presentation.

11.5a Consider Your Delivery Method

Inexperienced speakers often feel that they must memorize an entire presentation to be effective. Unless you're a professional performer, however, you will sound wooden and unnatural; and forgetting your place can be embarrassing. Therefore, memorizing an entire oral presentation is not recommended. However, memorizing significant parts—the introduction, the conclusion, and perhaps a meaningful quotation—can be dramatic and impressive.

If memorizing won't work, is reading your presentation the best plan? Definitely not. Reading to an audience is boring and ineffective. Because reading suggests that you don't know your topic well, the audience loses confidence in your expertise. Reading also prevents you from maintaining eye contact. You can't see audience reactions; consequently, you can't benefit from feedback.

Neither the memorizing nor the reading method creates convincing presentations. The best plan, by far, is a "cue-card" method. As Erick Rosan, the guest speaker from earlier in this chapter did, plan your presentation carefully and talk from cue cards containing key sentences and major ideas. One of Erick's cue cards is shown below in Figure 11.13. By preparing and then practising with cue cards, you can talk to your audience in a conversational manner. Your cards should include neither entire paragraphs nor single words. Instead, they should contain phrases that help you introduce each major idea. Cue cards will keep you on track and prompt your memory, but only if you have rehearsed the presentation thoroughly.

11.5b Consider Delivery Techniques

The best method for delivering your presentation is speaking from carefully prepared note cards.

Nearly everyone experiences some degree of stage fright when speaking before a group. But you can capitalize on the adrenaline that is coursing through your body by converting it to excitement and enthusiasm for your performance. People who don't prepare suffer the most anxiety and give the worst performances. You can learn to give effective presentations by focusing on four areas: preparation, organization, visual aids, and delivery.

Stage fright is both natural and controllable.

Being afraid is quite natural and results from actual physiological changes occurring in your body. Faced with a frightening situation, your body responds with the fight-or-flight response, discussed more fully in Figure 11.14. You can learn to control and reduce stage fright, as well as to incorporate techniques for effective speaking, by using the following strategies and techniques before, during, and after your presentation.

Thorough preparation, extensive rehearsal, and stress-reduction techniques can lessen stage fright.

BEFORE YOUR PRESENTATION

- **Prepare thoroughly.** One of the most effective strategies for reducing stage fright is knowing your subject thoroughly. Research your topic diligently and prepare a careful sentence outline. Those who try to "wing it" usually suffer the worst butterflies—and make the worst presentations.
- **Rehearse repeatedly.** When you rehearse, practise your entire presentation, not just the first half. Place your outline sentences on separate cards. You may also wish to include transitional sentences to help you move to the next topic. Use these cards as you practise, and include your visual aids in your rehearsal. Rehearse alone or before friends and family. Also try rehearsing on audio- or videotape so that you can evaluate your effectiveness.

FIGURE 11.13 | Sample Cue Card for Presentation

A. How did I get hired at AutoFleet?

- Looked at accounting jobs
- Talked to uncle; broadened search
- Applied, was interviewed, and hired at AutoFleet
- Wanted to impress boss

So what did I do?...

FIGURE 11.14 | How to Conquer Stage Fright

Ever get nervous before giving a speech? Everyone does! And it is not all in your head, either. When you face something threatening or challenging, your body reacts in what psychologists call the fight-or-flight response. This physical reflex provides your body with increased energy to deal with threatening situations. It also creates those sensations—dry mouth, sweaty hands, increased heart rate, and stomach butterflies—that we associate with stage fright. The fight-or-flight response arouses your body for action—in this case, making a presentation.

Because everyone feels some form of apprehension before speaking, it is impossible to eliminate the physiological symptoms altogether. However, you can reduce their effects with the following techniques:

Breathe deeply	Use deep breathing to ease your fight-or-flight symptoms. Inhale to a count of ten, hold this breath to a count of ten, and exhale to a count of ten. Concentrate on your counting and your breathing; both activities reduce your stress.
Convert your fear	Don't view your sweaty palms and dry mouth as evidence of fear. Interpret them as symptoms of exuberance, excitement, and enthusiasm to share your ideas.
Know your topic and come prepared	Feel confident about your topic. Select a topic that you know well and that is relevant to your audience. Test your equipment and arrive with time to spare.
Use positive self-talk	Remind yourself that you know your topic and are prepared. Tell yourself that the audience is on your side—because it is! Moreover, most speakers appear to be more confident than they feel. Make this apparent confidence work for you.
Take a sip of water	Drink some water to alleviate your dry mouth and constricted voice box, especially if you are talking for more than 15 minutes.
Shift the spotlight to your visuals	At least some of the time the audience will be focusing on your slides, transparencies, handouts, or whatever you have prepared—and not totally on you.
Ignore any stumbles	Don't apologize or confess your nervousness. If you keep going, the audience will forget any mistakes quickly.
Don't admit you are nervous	Never tell your audience that you are nervous. They will probably never notice!
Feel proud when you finish	You will be surprised at how good you feel when you finish. Take pride in what you have accomplished, and your audience will reward you with applause and congratulations. Your body, of course, will call off the fight-or-flight response and return to normal!

- **Time yourself.** Most audiences tend to get restless during longer talks. Thus, try to complete your presentation in no more than 20 minutes. Set a timer during your rehearsal to measure your speaking time.
- **Request a lectern.** Every beginning speaker needs the security of a high desk or lectern from which to deliver a presentation. It serves as a note holder and a convenient place to rest wandering hands and arms.
- **Check the room.** Before you talk, make sure that a lectern has been provided. If you are using sound equipment or a projector, be certain it is operational. Check electrical outlets and the position of the viewing screen. Ensure that the seating arrangement is appropriate to your needs.
- **Greet members of the audience.** Try to make contact with a few members of the audience when you enter the room, while you are waiting to be introduced,

or when you walk to the podium. Your body language should convey friendliness, confidence, and enjoyment.

- **Practise stress reduction.** If you feel tension and fear while you are waiting your turn to speak, use stress-reduction techniques, such as deep breathing. Additional techniques to help you conquer stage fright are presented in Figure 11.14.

DURING YOUR PRESENTATION

- **Begin with a pause.** When you first approach the audience, take a moment to adjust your notes and make yourself comfortable. Establish your control of the situation.
- **Present your first few sentences from memory.** By memorizing your opening, you can immediately establish rapport with the audience through eye contact. You'll also sound confident and knowledgeable.
- **Maintain eye contact.** If the size of the audience overwhelms you, pick out two individuals on the right and two on the left. Talk directly to these people.
- **Control your voice and vocabulary.** This means speaking in moderated tones but loudly enough to be heard. Eliminate verbal static, such as *ah, er, you know,* and *um*. Silence is preferable to meaningless fillers when you are thinking of your next idea.
- **Put the brakes on.** Many novice speakers talk too rapidly, displaying their nervousness and making it difficult for audience members to understand their ideas. Slow down and listen to what you are saying.
- **Move naturally.** You can use the lectern to hold your notes so that you are free to move about casually and naturally. Avoid fidgeting with your notes, your clothing, or items in your pockets. Learn to use your body to express a point. See the infographic in Figure 11.15 for a summary of what not to do with your body in presentations.
- **Use visual aids effectively.** Discuss and interpret each visual aid for the audience. Move aside as you describe it so that it can be seen fully. Use a pointer if necessary.
- **Avoid digressions.** Stick to your outline and notes. Don't suddenly include clever little anecdotes or digressions that occur to you on the spot. If it's not part of your rehearsed material, leave it out so that you can finish on time. Remember, too, that your audience may not be as enthralled with your topic as you are.
- **Summarize your main points.** Conclude your presentation by reiterating your main points or by emphasizing what you want the audience to think or do. Once you have announced your conclusion, proceed to it directly.

Eye contact, a moderate tone of voice, and natural movements enhance a presentation.

AFTER YOUR PRESENTATION

- **Distribute handouts.** If you prepared handouts with data the audience will need, pass them out when you finish.
- **Encourage questions.** If the situation permits a question-and-answer period, announce it at the beginning of your presentation. Then, when you finish, ask for questions. Set a time limit for questions and answers.
- **Repeat questions.** Although the speaker may hear the question, audience members often do not. Begin each answer with a repetition of the question. This also gives you thinking time. Then, direct your answer to the entire audience.
- **Reinforce your main points.** You can use your answers to restate your primary ideas (*I'm glad you brought that up because it gives me a chance to elaborate on...*). In answering questions, avoid becoming defensive or debating the questioner.
- **Keep control.** Don't allow one individual to take over. Keep the entire audience involved.
- **Avoid "Yes, but" answers.** The word "but" immediately cancels any preceding message. Try replacing it with "and." For example, *Yes, X has been tried. And Y works even better because...*

The time to answer questions, distribute handouts, and reiterate main points is after a presentation.

FIGURE 11.15 | Top Body Language Presentation Errors

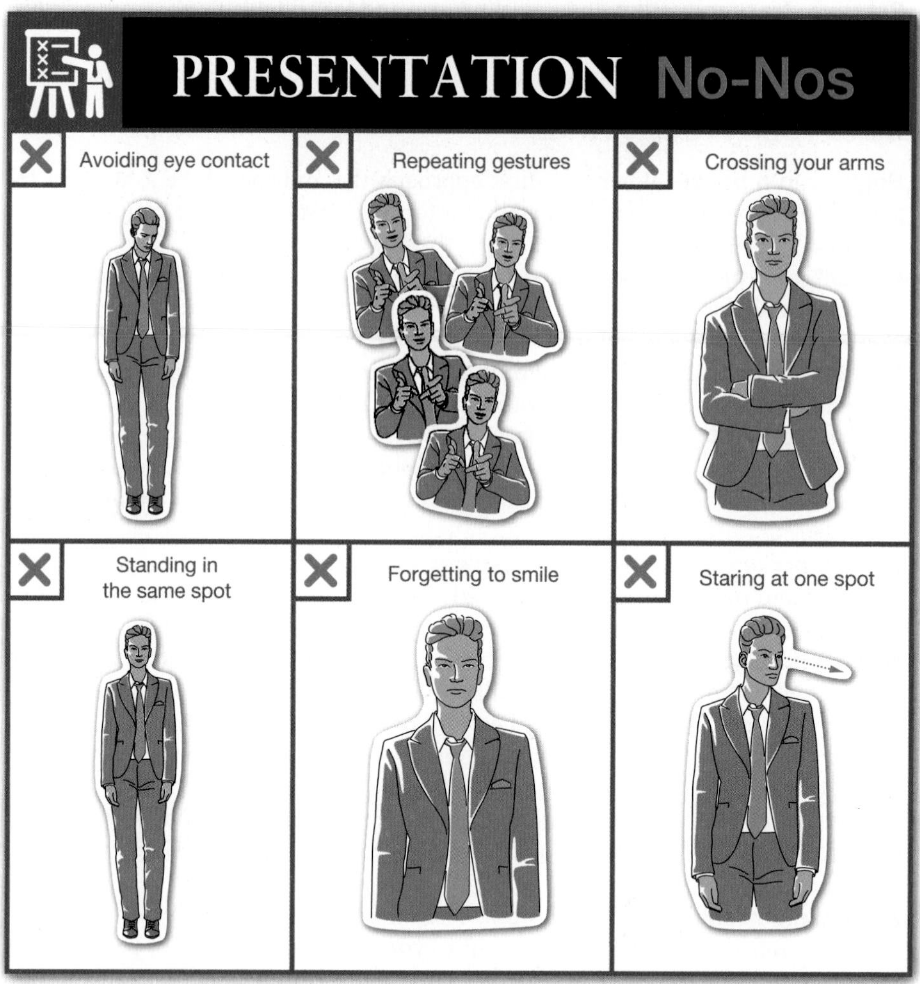

- **End with a summary and appreciation.** To signal the end of the session before you take the last question, say something like *We have time for just one more question.* As you answer the last question, try to work it into a summary of your main points. Then, express appreciation to the audience for the opportunity to talk with them.

SUMMARY OF LEARNING OBJECTIVES

11.1 Differentiate between major presentation types and answer two preparatory questions.

- Excellent presentation skills are sought by employers and will benefit you at any career stage.
- Presentation types include briefings, reports, podcasts, and webinars; they can be informative or persuasive, face-to-face or virtual, and complex or simple.
- Savvy speakers know what they want to accomplish and are able to adjust to friendly, neutral, uninterested, as well as hostile audiences.

11.2 Organize the presentation effectively and build audience rapport.

- In the opening, capture the audience's attention, introduce yourself and establish your credibility, and preview your talk.
- Organize the body using chronology, space, function, comparison/contrast, a journalistic pattern, value/size, importance, problem/solution, simple/complex, or best case/worst case.
- In the conclusion, summarize the main topics of your talk, leave the audience with a memorable take-away, and end with a statement that provides a graceful exit.

- Build rapport by using effective imagery, verbal signposts, and positive nonverbal messages.

11.3 Compare the main types of presentation aid.

- Your audience is more likely to retain your talk if you use well-prepared visual aids.
- Good visuals emphasize and clarify main points, increase audience interest, prove you are professional, illustrate your message better than words alone, and serve to jog your memory.
- Common types of visual aids are multimedia slides, zoom presentations, videos, handouts, flipcharts and whiteboards, as well as props.
- In good hands PowerPoint is helpful, but you should focus on using more images and less text.

11.4 Design effective visual presentations.

- The purpose and the audience determine the slide design, which includes colour, images, and special effects.
- Building a presentation involves organizing and composing slide content, avoiding overused templates, and revising, proofreading, and evaluating the final product.
- The eight steps to creating impressive multimedia slides are as follows: start with the text, select a template, choose images, create graphics, add special effects, create hyperlinks, engage your audience with interaction, and consider posting online.

11.5 Deploy effective delivery techniques in presentations.

- When delivering a business presentation, don't memorize your talk or read from notes; rather, speak extemporaneously and use notes only when you're not using presentation software.
- Before your presentation prepare and rehearse, time yourself, dress professionally, request a lectern, check the room, greet members of the audience, and practise stress reduction.
- During the presentation deliver your first sentence from memory, maintain eye contact, control your voice, show enthusiasm, slow down, move naturally, use visual aids skillfully, and stay on topic.
- After the presentation distribute handouts, encourage and repeat questions, reinforce your main points, avoid *Yes, but* answers, and end with a summary and appreciation.

CHAPTER REVIEW

1. List and describe five types of presentations a business professional might make. (Obj. 1)
2. The age, gender, education level, experience, and size of the audience will affect your presentation style and message. List at least five questions you should answer to determine your organizational pattern, delivery style, and supporting material. (Obj. 1)
3. Which effective three-step organizational plan do many speech experts recommend, and why does it work well for oral presentations despite its redundancy? (Obj. 2)
4. What three goals should you accomplish in the introduction to your presentation? (Obj. 2)
5. Name at least eight techniques that can help you gain and keep audience attention. (Obj. 2)
6. List high-tech and low-tech visual aids that you can use when speaking to an audience. Which two are the most popular? (Obj. 3)
7. What is the 6-×-6 rule, and what might prompt a presentation slide creator to break it? (Obj. 4)
8. Which delivery method is best for persuasive business presentations? Explain why. (Obj. 5)
9. How can speakers overcome stage fright? Name at least six helpful techniques. (Obj. 5)

CRITICAL THINKING

1. Why is repetition always a good idea in writing, but an excellent idea when presenting? (Objs. 1, 2)
2. Which of the visual aid options you learned about in this chapter is the most effective? Is using the same visual aid as everyone else necessarily the best choice in a presentation? (Obj. 4)
3. If PowerPoint, Prezi, and the use of infographics are so effective, why are people critical of their use in presentations? (Objs. 3,4)
4. How can speakers prevent visuals from overtaking the presentation? (Objs. 3,4)
5. To what degree do you think stage fright is real, as opposed to an excuse we make because of our discomfort? (Obj. 5)

ACTIVITIES AND CASES

11.1 IT'S ALL ABOUT THE AUDIENCE (OBJ. 2)

As we saw at the beginning of this chapter, it's vital to think about your audience before developing a presentation. Depending on the type of audience, certain elements of your presentation will be emphasized, while others will be downplayed or eliminated altogether.

Your Task. Choose one of the presentation topics below and one of the audience sets below. Spend 15 minutes brainstorming what each presentation will look like; then, in front of a partner, a group, or the entire class, deliver a short improvised presentation in two different ways. Once you're done, see if your partner/group/class can figure out what you've done differently and why you chose to do so.

Topics	**Audience sets**
Surviving your first year of college/university	a) Your institution's board of governors b) Your institution's orientation day
The pros and cons of a particular piece of technology	a) A prospective customer b) Your parents
Your recent work experience	a) Your best friend b) A prospective employer
Choose a topic of your own with your instructor's permission	a) A formal audience b) An informal audience

11.2 FOLLOW YOUR FAVOURITE ENTREPRENEUR OR TYCOON (OBJS. 2–5)

An important part of business today is using social media to enhance a brand. In this activity you'll research and present on how well-known business people use Twitter to enhance their own brands.

Your Task. If you don't already have a Twitter account, go to http://twitter.com and sign up so that you can follow businesspeople and examine the topics they like to tweet about. In the Search window on top of the page, enter the name of the businessperson whose tweets you wish to follow. Arlene Dickinson, Richard Branson, Michele Romanow, Suze Orman, Guy Kawasaki, Kevin O'Leary, and other well-known businesspeople are avid Twitter users. Over the course of a few days, read the tweets of your favourite expert. After a while, you should be able to discern certain trends and areas of interest. Note whether and how your subject responds to queries from followers. What are his or her favourite topics? Report your findings to the class using notes or PowerPoint. If you find particularly intriguing tweets and links, share them with the class.

11.3 HOW MUCH SPEAKING CAN YOU EXPECT IN YOUR FIELD? (OBJS. 2, 4, 5)

It's common for job postings to ask for candidates with "excellent communication skills." Clearly, these ads mean oral as well as written communication.

Your Task. Interview one or two individuals in your professional field. How is oral communication important in this profession? Does the need for oral skills change as one advances? What suggestions can these people make to newcomers to the field for developing proficient oral communication skills? Discuss your findings with your class in a brief presentation. Try to use one visual aid you've not used before (e.g., Prezi, infographic, etc).

Visit **MindTap** for a variety of videos, additional exercises, activities, and quizzes to support your learning.

Communicating for Employment

UNIT 06

JPM/Getty Images

COMMUNICATION TECHNOLOGY IN THE NEWS

Forget the resumé: Online profiles the tool of young job seekers. High school students learning to build professional digital profiles instead of relying on the traditional paper resumé.

Don't bother polishing that resumé.

In the digital age, it's dead, says high school teacher and filmmaker Anthony Perrotta, who instead encourages his students to "brand" themselves with professional-looking Twitter, YouTube and blog accounts—though not Facebook because, as his teens tell him, "that's for moms and dads now."

"We live in a culture of the hyperlink," said Perrotta, who teaches at Chaminade College School, an all-boys school in the Toronto Catholic board.

"I can tell you I made movies, but if you go to my website, you can see my work … a viable digital footprint shows what you know and what you've done. On a résumé, anyone can say anything."

Perrotta is speaking on the subject at Reading for the Love of It, a national language arts conference in February, showing teachers how their students' work can be shared online. And for this generation, that's a key to getting them more engaged in what they're doing in class.

"There are a lot of teachers doing great digital work, but my thing is 'where does it live?'" he said. "Great things are happening, but what's the next step?"

Whether the résumé is obsolete is still up for debate in the business world—with many companies relying on it for job applicants—but experts do believe it is on the way out.

"We are used to the 50-year-old tools of business cards and résumés. For the next evolution of jobs, who looks at a boring, two-page résumé? You have to present a portfolio of something written or something cool you've done," said Professor Beatrix Dart of the University of Toronto, adding LinkedIn has "become the online résumé in the professional community."

"If you think about trends in the industry and in the economy to be more tech-based, the next generation will be more tech-focused and even things like business cards are pretty old-fashioned these days. If you go to a conference, you don't exchange business cards, you slip over your v-card, your electronic one. That's becoming more the norm as we speak.

"But it's a few more years until the paper résumé will be dead," added Dart, who teaches at U of T's Rotman School of Management.

At Ryerson University's Career Centre, director Caroline Konrad said they're telling students "the résumé is not the be-all and end-all it might have been 10 years ago. It's another tool in the tool box."

The résumé is generally still a requirement and "needs to be sharp," but because they all look the same "having an online presence is a necessary step."

Students are also encouraged to use social media, "even just to follow companies and leaders on Twitter so they are up-to-date on what's going on."

For Perrotta's business students, social media gives them a chance to show "what you want the world to know about you," while building connections through comments on blogs or responses via Twitter. Some of the boys' work has been noticed: After creating high-quality posters advertising the latest Star Wars movie, they got some local media attention that led to Disney Canada offering them a few passes to the Canadian premiere of the blockbuster movie.

Getting recognition online is appealing to youth, who spend most of their lives online, he said.

"They need to know their voice and their work—it's beyond marks. Good marks are important, but they don't mean you have good skills."

Grade 9 student Gemner Sandoval said he'll use his blog to write about world issues, his faith, music and photography, while Vincent Pham plans to post about his desire to become a priest. Tweeting and blogging show they are active, engaged citizens, they say.

"It is better to have an online presence," added Daniel Mobilio, 14. "If people search you on the Internet, you don't want them to get a bad impression of you."

Justin Alvarado has a personal Twitter account to share sports news and photos, and started a professional one "to allow me to express what I can really do. It gives you a better reputation with companies. It shows you can advertise yourself; it shows independence and responsibility too."

Using social media also allows his relatives, who live in Ecuador, to see his work. "Even if I'm not discovered by a big company," he said, "it's the exposure to my family that really hits it home."

Summarize the article you've just read in a two- or three-sentence paragraph. Answer the following questions, either on your own or in a small group. Be prepared to present your answers in a short presentation or in an email to your instructor.

QUESTIONS:

1. How does what you've learned in this article change your perception of business communication?
2. How might what you've learned in this article change your own communication style or strategy?
3. Come up with pro and con arguments for the following debate/discussion topic: Young people without a persuasive Internet presence are less likely to be hired.

CHAPTER

12

The Job Search, Résumés, and Cover Letters

OBJECTIVES

After studying this chapter, you should be able to

12.1 Prepare for employment by identifying your interests and market requirements.

12.2 Use traditional and digital job search techniques in the open and hidden markets.

12.3 Organize and format persuasive chronological and functional résumés.

12.4 Use social media, video, and infographic résumés as alternatives to traditional résumés.

12.5 Write a persuasive cover letter to accompany your résumé.

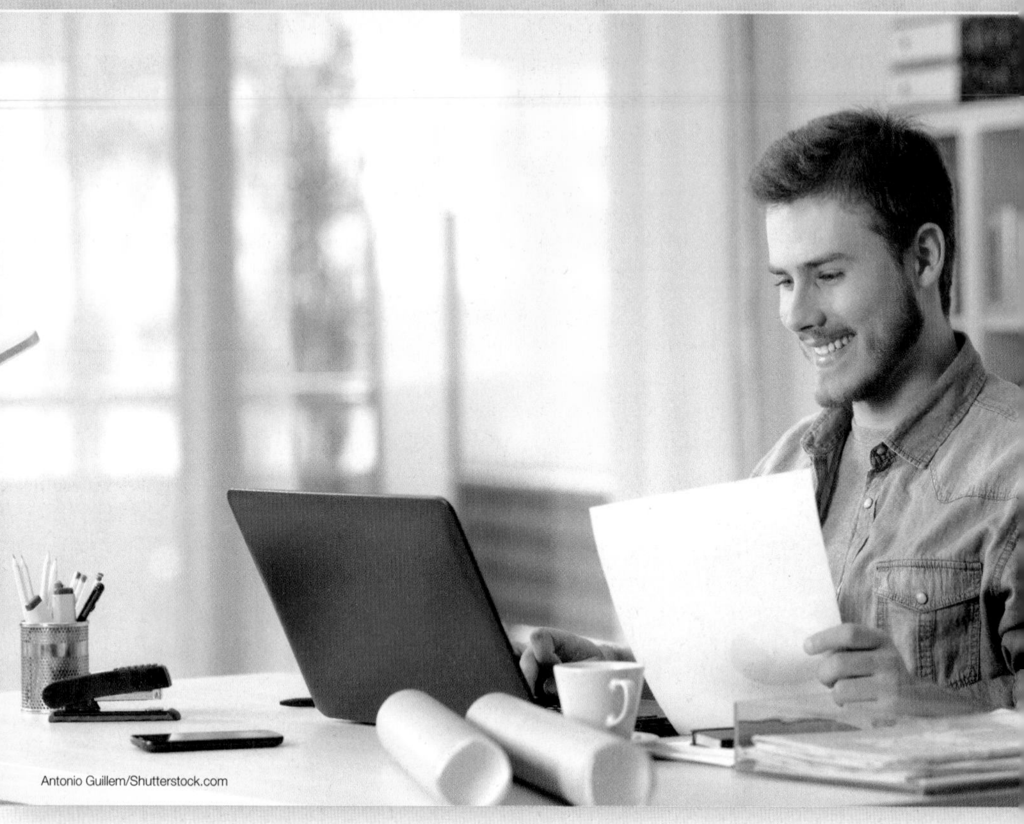

Antonio Guillem/Shutterstock.com

12.1 Preparing for Employment

Whether you are applying for your first permanent position, competing for promotion, or changing careers, you'll be more successful if you understand employment communication and how to promote yourself with a winning résumé and related digital tools.

Employers today are most interested in how a candidate will add value to their organizations. That's why successful candidates customize their résumés to highlight their qualifications for each opening. In addition, career paths are no longer linear; most new hires will not start in a job and steadily rise through the ranks. Jobs are more short-lived and people are constantly relearning and retraining.

The résumé is still important, but it may not be the document that introduces the job seeker these days. Instead, the résumé may come only after the candidate has established a real-world relationship. Although we sometimes hear that the "print résumé is dead," the truth is that every job hunter needs one. Whether offered online or in print, your résumé should always be available and current.

It's natural to think that the first step in finding a job is to write a résumé. However, the employment communication process actually begins long before you are ready to prepare your résumé. Regardless of the kind of employment you seek, you must invest time and effort in getting ready. Your best plan for landing the job of your dreams involves following the steps outlined in Figure 12.1.

FIGURE 12.1 | Job Searching in the Digital Age

Analyze Yourself

- Identify your interests and goals.
- Assess your qualifications.
- Explore career opportunities.

Develop a Job-Search Strategy

- Search the open job market.
- Pursue the hidden job market.
- Cultivate your online presence.
- Build your personal brand.
- Network, network, network!

Create a Customized Résumé

- Choose a résumé style.
- Organize your info concisely.
- Tailor your résumé to each position.
- Optimize for digital technology.

Know the Hiring Process

- Submit a résumé, application, or e-portfolio.
- Undergo screening and hiring interviews.
- Accept an offer or reevaluate your progress.

12.1a Identify Your Interests

Begin by looking inside yourself to analyze what you like and dislike so that you can make good employment choices. Career counsellors at your college or university can help you with this process or you can do a self-examination online. For guidance in choosing a field that eventually proves to be satisfying, answer the following questions. You can use your responses to match the description of opportunities you come across in your job search. If a number of your responses appear in a particular job description, there's a good chance it might be a good fit for you.

Finding a satisfying career means learning about oneself, the job market, and the employment process.

- Do I enjoy working with people, data, or things?
- How important is it to be my own boss?
- How important are salary, benefits, and job stability?
- What type of working conditions, colleagues, and job stimulation am I looking for?
- Would I rather work for a large or small company?
- Must I work in a specific city, geographical area, or climate?
- Am I looking for security, travel opportunities, money, power, or prestige?
- How would I describe the perfect job, boss, and coworkers?

Analyzing your likes and dislikes helps you make wise employment decisions.

Answering specific questions can help you choose a career.

12.1b Assess Your Qualifications

In addition to your interests, assess your qualifications. Employers today want to know what assets you have to offer them. Your responses to the following questions will target your thinking as well as prepare a foundation for your résumé. As you'll see later in this chapter, there is room in a résumé to include answers to most of the questions below. Remember that employers seek more than empty assurances; they will want proof of your qualifications.

Assessing your skills and experience prepares you to write a persuasive résumé.

- What technology skills can I offer? (Name specific software programs and tools.)
- What other hard skills have I acquired in school, on the job, or through activities? How can I demonstrate these skills?
- Do I work well with people? What proof can I offer? (Consider extracurricular activities, clubs, and jobs.)
- Am I a leader, self-starter, or manager? What evidence can I offer?
- Do I speak, write, or understand another language?

- Do I learn quickly? Am I creative? How can I demonstrate these characteristics?
- Do I communicate well in speech and in writing? How can I verify these talents?

12.1c Explore Career Opportunities

Today's job market is vastly different from that of a decade or two ago. As a result of job trends and personal choices, the average Canadian can expect to change careers at least three times and change jobs at least seven times in a lifetime. As a student, you may not have yet settled on your first career choice; or you may be embarking on a second or perhaps third career. Although you may be changing jobs in the future, you still need to train for a specific career area now. When choosing an area, you'll make the best decisions if you can match your interests and qualifications with the requirements of specific careers. But where can you find career information? Here are some suggestions:

Career information can be obtained at school career centres and libraries, from the Internet, in classified ads, and from professional organizations.

- **Visit your campus career centre.** Most centres will have literature on job search techniques, workshops on résumé and cover-letter writing, information about local job fairs, and Internet connections that allow you to investigate any field you may be interested in.
- **Search the Internet.** Many job search sites (e.g., Workopolis, Monster, and Charity Village) offer career planning information and resources. For example, Charity Village's "Tools & Resources" page includes links such as "Career Assessment Questionnaire" and "Practice Interview Questions." A sample job site list of opportunities is shown in Figure 12.2.
- **Use your library.** Consult the latest edition of the Index of Occupational Titles and the Canadian government's National Occupational Classification (http://noc.esdc.gc.ca/English/home.aspx) for information about career duties, qualifications, salaries, and employment trends.

Summer and part-time jobs and internships are good opportunities to learn about different careers.

- **Take a summer job, internship, or part-time position in your field.** Nothing is better than trying out a career by actually working in it or in a similar area. Many companies offer internships, or may be open to you creating your own internship via networking. They may also offer temporary jobs to begin training students and to develop relationships with them (e.g., Walmart hires thousands of holiday-season workers—a possible entry to a retail management career). These relationships sometimes blossom into permanent positions.
- **Volunteer with a nonprofit organization.** Many colleges and universities encourage service learning opportunities. In volunteering their services to nonprofit organizations in their city or town, students gain valuable experience. Nonprofits, in turn, appreciate the expertise and fresh ideas that students bring and are often happy to provide free training.
- **Interview someone in your chosen field.** People are usually flattered when asked to describe their careers. Once you've settled on your intended career or sector, use LinkedIn and Google to find names of leaders within organizations. Then, send a polite email or voice mail in which you request an informational interview. In the interview, politely inquire about needed skills, required courses, financial and other rewards, benefits, working conditions, future trends, and entry requirements.
- **Monitor job ads.** Early in your postsecondary education career, begin monitoring company websites for job listings. Check job availability, qualifications sought, duties, and salary range. Don't wait until you're about to graduate to see how the job market looks.
- **Join professional organizations in your field.** Organizations like the Canadian Marketing Association (CMA) and the Human Resources Professionals Association (HRPA) are fantastic places to find out about your intended career. Frequently, these organizations offer student membership status and reduced rates for conferences and workshops. You'll get inside information on issues, career news, and possible jobs, as well as the opportunity to meet people who are working in the field you've identified as your future goal.

FIGURE 12.2 | Typical Job Site

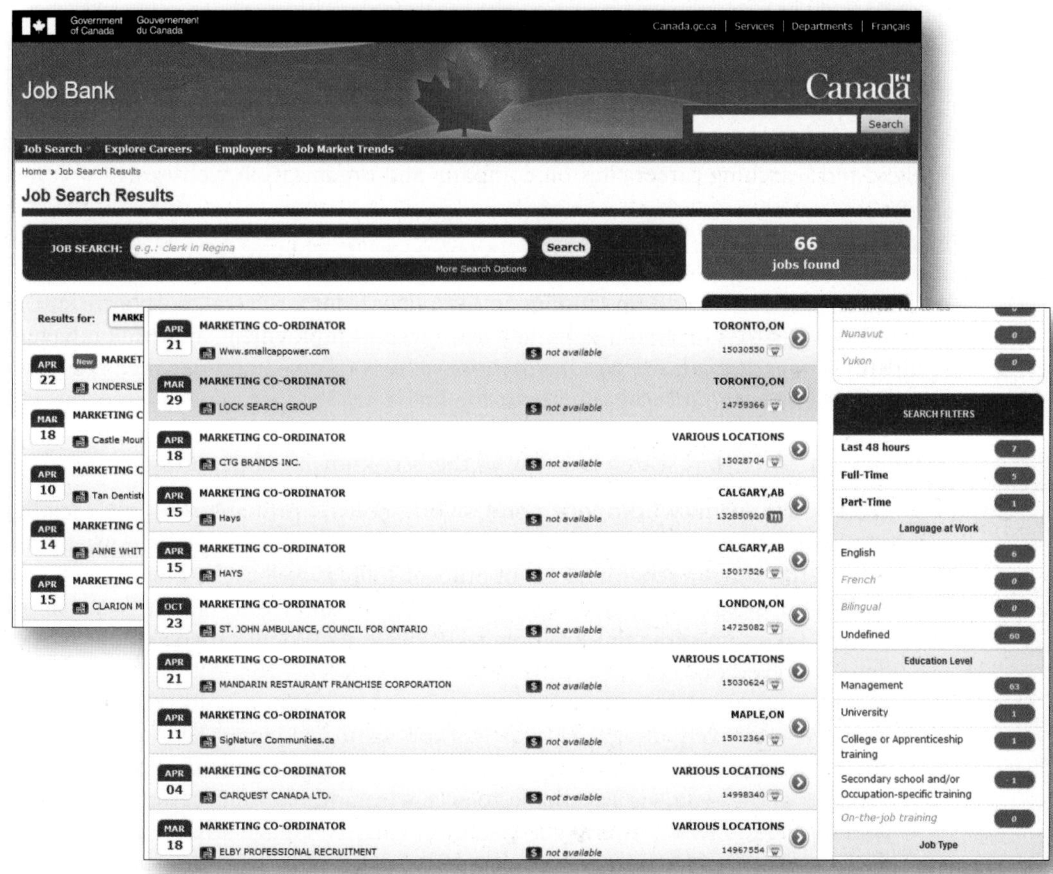

Source: Government of Canada Job Bank search results
URL: http://www.jobbank.gc.ca/job_search_results.do;jsessionid=70B1BC28180A2852A768194992CF7B49.imnav2?searchstring=Canada&button.submit=Search
Employment and Social Development Canada, 2014. Reproduced with the permission of the Minister of Employment and Social Development Canada, 2014.

12.2 Searching for Jobs in the Open and Hidden Markets

Another significant change in the workplace involves the way we find jobs. Prior to the early 2000s, a job seeker browsed the local newspaper's classified ads, found a likely sounding job listing, prepared a résumé on paper, and sent it out by mail (and later by fax). Today, searching for a job online has become a common, but not always fruitful, approach. With all the publicity given to Internet employment sites, you might think that online job searching has totally replaced traditional methods. Not so!

Although websites such as Workopolis and Monster list millions of jobs, actually landing a job is much harder than just clicking a mouse. In addition, these job sites are facing competition from social networking sites such as LinkedIn and Facebook.[1]

Job sites list many jobs, but finding a job online requires more work than simply clicking a mouse.

Both recruiters and job seekers complain about employment sites. Corporate recruiters say that the big sites can bring a flood of candidates, many of whom are not suited for the listed jobs. Workplace experts estimate that the average large corporation can be inundated with up to 2,000 résumés a day.[2] Job candidates grumble that listings are frequently out of date and fail to produce leads. Some career advisers call these sites "black holes"[3] into which résumés vanish without a trace. Some applicants worry about the privacy of information posted at big sites.

All that said, experts in source of hire (i.e., the study of where and how new hires come about) say that although internal referrals are still the greatest source of hires at about 25 percent, employment sites account for just under 20 percent.[4] Clearly, a successful job search will come about through a combination of networking with people who already work inside companies, searching employment sites, and searching career sites on company and organization websites.

12.2a Use Leading "Open Market" Employment Sites

Whether or not you end up landing an interview from a referral, corporate site, or employment site, you should definitely learn to use employment sites (if you haven't already!) to gather job search information, such as résumé, interviewing, and salary tips. These sites can inform you about the kinds of jobs that are available, the skill sets required, and the current vocabulary of both job searching and the area you're looking in. Start your search at a few of the best-known online job sites:

- **Workopolis (www.workopolis.com).** Workopolis is probably Canada's leading employment site. It includes thousands of jobs in all major industries. A useful feature on this site is a separate area for Student Jobs, as well as the blog-style "Latest News and Advice" area that offers timely advice and stories about issues in job search. Take some time to learn how to navigate Workopolis if you've not already done so—everyone else has!
- **Monster (www.monster.ca).** Monster is similar to Workopolis, but its website is not as effectively designed. Like Workopolis it includes thousands of jobs in all major industries. A differentiator between Monster and Workopolis is that Monster allows you, via Facebook, to access instant, real-time career counselling.
- **Charity Village (www.charityvillage.com).** Charity Village advertises jobs solely in the nonprofit sector. Sometimes overlooked by students and graduates, this site offers a wealth of opportunities in traditional business areas such as accounting, finance, customer service, and marketing.
- **Other employment sites.** If you Google "Canadian employment sites," you'll get a number of interesting hits. For example, Indeed and Eluta have simple interfaces. You may also try a more specific search in Google, such as "Hospitality Jobs Canada." The first hit is Hcareers (www.hcareers.ca), a reputable employment site exclusively targeted to jobs in the hospitality, tourism, and leisure industry. From this site you can also link to job boards in the public service, federally and provincially.

12.2b Go Beyond the Big Employment Sites

Job prospects may be more promising at the websites of corporations, professional associations, employers' organizations, niche fields, and, most recently, professional networking sites.

As the source-of-hire study cited above shows, savvy candidates also know how to use the Internet to search for jobs at sites such as the following:

- **Company sites.** Next to internal referrals, probably the best way to find a job online is at a company's own website. Usually jobs are found at a link with the name "Employment" or "Careers" or "Work for us." One poll found that 70 percent of job seekers felt they were more likely to obtain an interview if they posted their résumés on company sites. In addition to finding a more direct route to decision makers, job seekers thought that they could keep their job searches more private at corporate websites than at big job board sites.[5]
- **Association websites.** Online job listings have proved to be the single most popular feature of many professional organizations such as the Canadian Apparel Federation. If you go to the association's website at www.apparel.ca you'll see that one of the six squares on the home page is the job board. Clicking on this link takes you to a job board with positions in apparel (clothing) companies across the country. Even if you have no interest in a career in apparel, why not try a search

FIGURE 12.3 | Three Leading "Open Market" Employment Sites

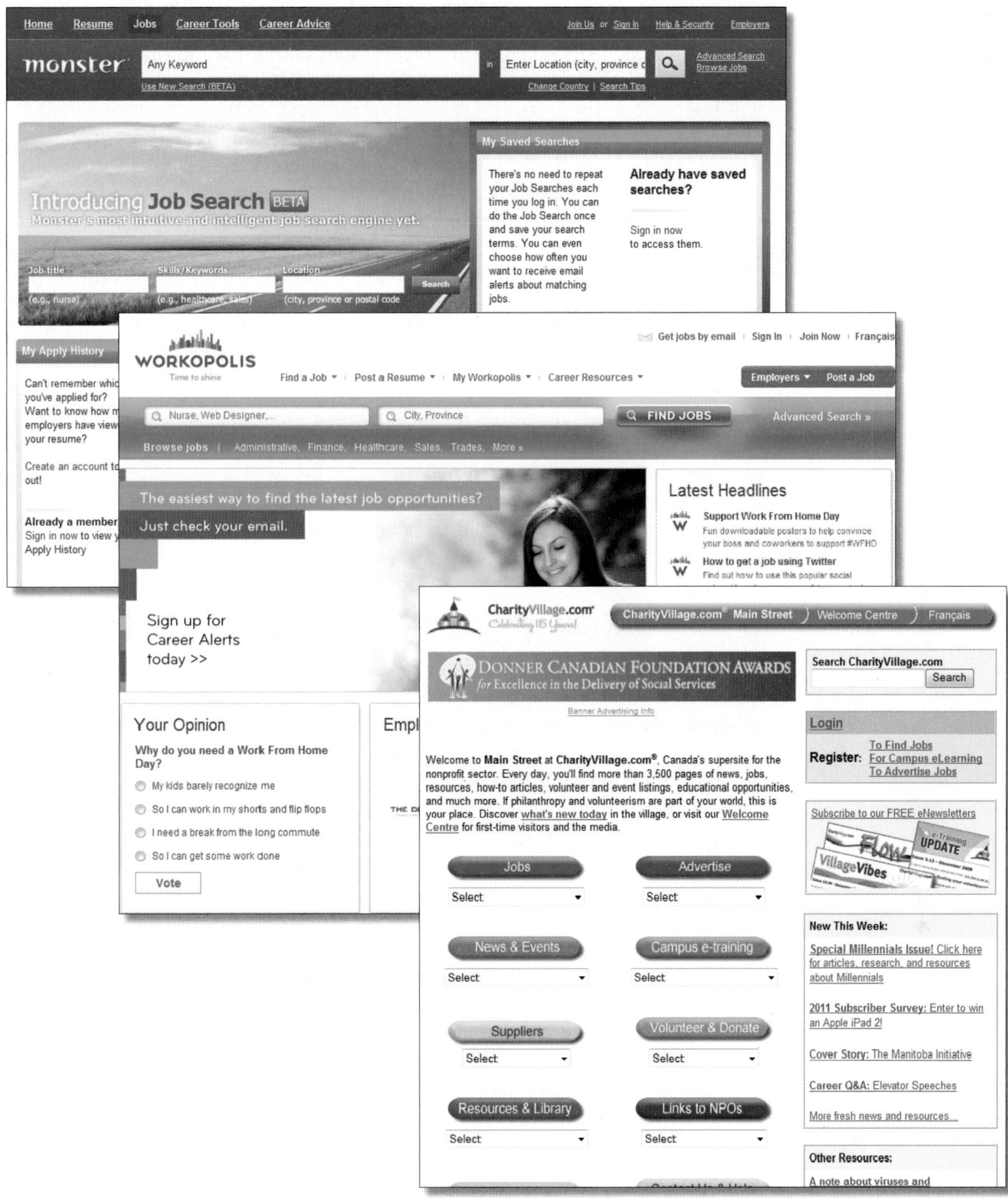

for your geographical area and see what jobs exist? You may be surprised. To find a list of several trade associations in Canada, go to the Government of Canada's site on this topic, at www.ic.gc.ca/eic/site/ccc_bt-rec_ec.nsf/eng/h_00001.html. You can also enter a job category plus the words "association" and "Canada" and see what comes up, for example "film editor" and "association." Sometimes job boards at association sites are open only to fee-paying members, and you'll have to decide whether it's a good idea to join your target association, perhaps as a student member.

12.2c Use LinkedIn and Other Social Networking Sites

LinkedIn continues to dominate the world of job searching and recruiting. In a recent poll of 1,843 staffing professionals, 97 percent said they used LinkedIn as a recruiting tool.[6] At LinkedIn, job seekers can search for job openings directly, and they can also follow companies for the latest news and current job openings. (You will learn more about using LinkedIn in the next section on networking.) Beyond LinkedIn, other social networking sites such as Facebook and Twitter also advertise job openings and recruit potential employees. Because organizations may post open jobs to their Facebook or Twitter pages prior to advertising them elsewhere, you might gain a head start on submitting an application by following them on these sites.

When posting job-search information online, it's natural to want to put your best foot forward and openly share information that will get you a job. The challenge is striking a balance between supplying enough information and protecting your privacy.

A traditional job search campaign might include checking classified ads and announcements in professional publications, contacting companies, and developing a network of contacts.

Thousands of employment sites listing millions of jobs now flood the Internet. The sobering reality, however, is that landing a job still depends largely on personal contacts. Stanford University sociologist Mark Granovetter found that 70 percent of jobs are discovered through networking.[7] Job-search consultant Debra Feldman concurs: "More important than what you know is who knows what you know. Make sure you are on the radar of people who have access to the kind of job leads you want."[8]

12.2d Network to Find "Hidden Market" Opportunities

The most successful job candidates try to transform themselves from unknown into known quantities through networking. More jobs today are found through referrals and person-to-person contacts than through any other method. That's because people trust what they know. Therefore, your goal is to become known to a large network of people, and this means going beyond close friends.

BUILD A PERSONAL NETWORK. Building a personal network involves meeting people you don't yet know and talking to them about your respective fields or industries so that you can gain information and locate possible job vacancies. Not only are many jobs never advertised, but some positions aren't even contemplated until the right person appears. One recent college grad underwent three interviews for a position, but the company hired someone else. After being turned down, the grad explained why he thought he was perfect for this company but perhaps in a different role. Apparently, the hiring manager agreed and decided to create a new job (in social media) because of the skills, personality, and perseverance of this determined young grad. Networking pays off, but it requires dedication. Here are three steps that will help you establish your own network:

- **Step 1. Develop a contact list.** Make a list of anyone who would be willing to talk with you about finding a job, including teachers, coworkers, former teachers and employers, neighbours, family members and their friends. Even if you haven't talked with people in years, reach out to them in person or online. Consider asking your campus career centre for alumni willing to talk with students. Also dig into your social networking circles, which we will discuss shortly.
- **Step 2. Make contacts in person and online.** Call the people on your list or connect online. To set up a meeting in person, say, *Hi,_________. I'm looking for a job and I wonder if you could help me out. Could I come over to talk about it?* During your visit be friendly, well-organized, polite, and interested in what your contact has to say. Provide a copy of your résumé, and try to keep the conversation centred on your job search. Your goal is to get two or more

referrals. In pinpointing your request, ask, *Do you know of anyone who might have an opening for a person with my skills?* If the person does not, ask, *Do you know of anyone else who might know of someone who would?*

- **Step 3. Follow up on your referrals.** Call or contact the people on your list. You might say something like, *Hello. I'm Stacy Rivera, a friend of Jason Tilden. He suggested that I ask you for help. I'm looking for a position as a marketing trainee, and he thought you might be willing to spare a few minutes and steer me in the right direction.* Don't ask for a job. During your referral interview, ask how the individual got started in this line of work, what he or she likes best (or least) about the work, what career paths exist in the field, and what problems must be overcome by a newcomer. Most important, ask how a person with your background and skills might get started in the field. Send an informal thank-you note to anyone who helps you in your job search, and stay in touch with the most promising people. Ask whether you could stay in contact every three weeks or so during your job search.

USE SOCIAL MEDIA TO NETWORK. Job searchers have a powerful new tool at their disposal: social media networks. These networks not only keep you in touch with friends but also function beautifully in a job search. If you just send out your résumé blindly, chances are good that not much will happen. However, if you have a referral, your chances of getting a job multiply. Today's expansion of online networks results in an additional path to developing coveted referrals.

If you are looking for a job, LinkedIn is the top social media site for you to use. LinkedIn is where you can let recruiters know of your talents and where you begin your professional networking, as illustrated in Figure 12.4. For hiring managers to find your LinkedIn profile, however, you may need to customize your URL, which is the address of your page. To drive your name to the top of a Google search, advises career coach Susan Adams, scroll down to the LinkedIn "public profile" on your profile page, and edit the URL. Try your first and last name and then your last name and first name, and then add a middle initial, if necessary. Test a variety of combinations with punctuation and spacing until the combination leads directly to your profile.[9]

In writing your LinkedIn career summary, use keywords and phrases that might appear in job descriptions. Include quantifiable achievements and specifics that reveal your skills. You can borrow most of this from your résumé. In the Work Experience and Education fields, include all of your experience, not just your current position. For the Recommendations section, encourage instructors and employers to recommend you. Having more recommendations in your profile makes you look more credible, trustworthy, and reliable.

One of the best ways to use LinkedIn is to search for a company in which you are interested. Try to find company employees who are connected to other people you know. Then use that contact as a referral when you apply. You can also send an email to everyone in your LinkedIn network asking for help or for people they could put you in touch with. Don't be afraid to ask an online contact for advice on getting started in a career and for suggestions to help a newcomer break into that career. Another excellent way to use a contact is to ask that person to look at your résumé and help you tweak it. Like Facebook, LinkedIn has status updates, and it's a good idea to update yours regularly so that your connections know what is happening in your career search.

Employers often use social media sites to check the online presence of a candidate. In fact, one report claimed that 91 percent of recruiters check Facebook, Twitter, and LinkedIn to filter out applicants.[10] Make sure your social networking accounts represent you professionally. You can make it easy for your potential employer to learn more about you by including an informative bio in your Twitter or Facebook profile that has a link to your LinkedIn profile. You can also make yourself more discoverable by posting thoughtful blog posts and tweets on topics related to your career goal.

12.2e Building a Personal Brand

A large part of your job-search strategy involves seeing yourself as a brand. You may be thinking, *Who me? A brand?* Yes, absolutely! Even college grads should seriously consider branding because finding a job today is tough. Before you get into the thick of the job hunt, focus on developing your brand so that you know what you want to emphasize.

Personal branding involves deciding what makes you special and desirable in the job market. What is your unique selling point? What special skill set makes you stand out among all job applicants? What would your instructors or employers say is your greatest strength? Think about your intended audience. What are you promoting about yourself?

Try to come up with a tagline that describes what you do and who you are. Ask yourself questions such as these: Do you follow through with every promise? Are you a fast learner? Hardworking? What can you take credit for? It's OK to shed a little modesty and strut your stuff. However, do keep your tagline simple, short, and truthful so that it's easy to remember. See Figure 12.4 for some sample taglines appropriate for new grads.

Once you have a tagline, prepare a professional-looking business card with your name and tagline. Include an easy-to-remember email address such as *firstname .lastname@domain.com.*

Now that you have your tagline and business card, work on an elevator speech. This is a pitch that you can give in 30 seconds or less describing who you are and what you can offer, in case you bump into someone who's in a position to hire or recommend you. Tweak your speech for your audience, and practise until you can say it naturally.

FIGURE 12.4 | Branding Yourself to Land a Job

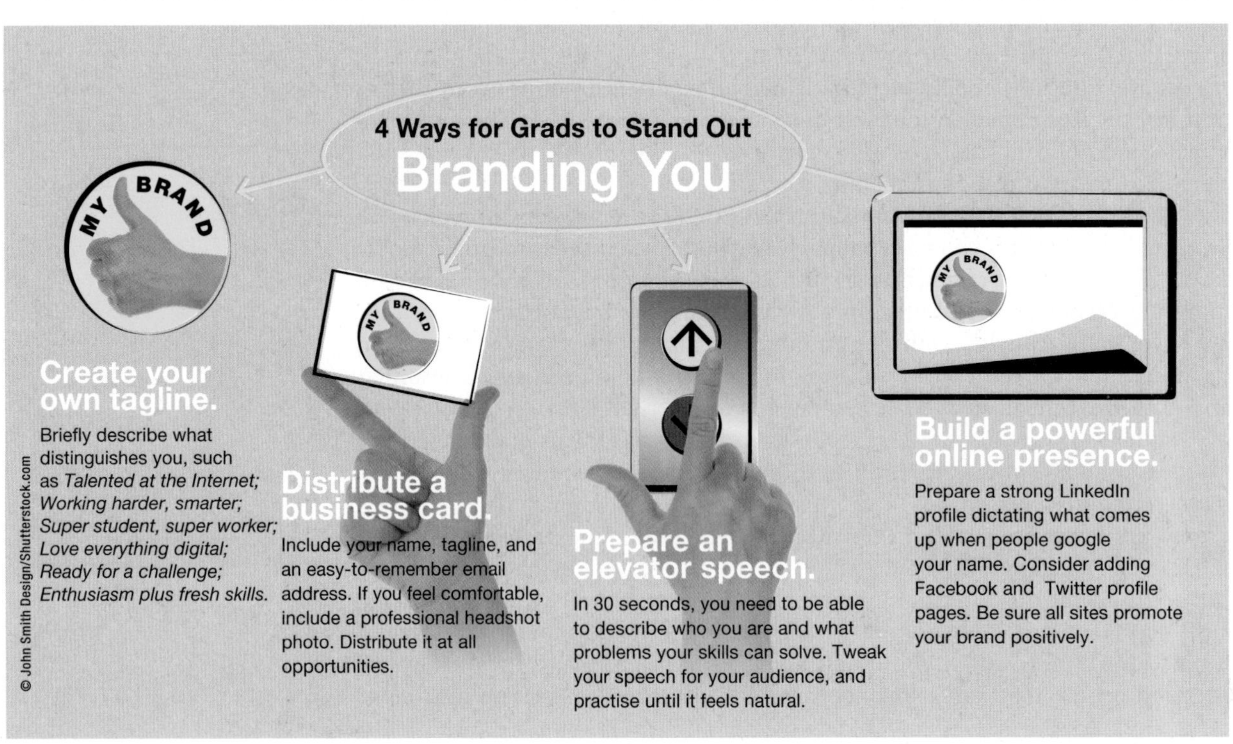

12.3 Creating Persuasive Résumés

After reviewing employment ads, you can begin writing a persuasive résumé. This document does more than merely list your qualifications; it packages your assets into a convincing advertisement that sells you for a specific job. The goal of a persuasive résumé is to get an interview. Even if you are not in the job market at this moment, preparing a résumé has advantages. Having a current résumé makes you look well-organized and professional should an unexpected employment opportunity arise. Moreover, preparing a résumé early can help you recognize weak areas and give you time to bolster your credentials.

12.3a Choose a Résumé Style

Your qualifications and career goal will help you choose between two basic résumé styles: chronological or functional.

CHRONOLOGICAL. Most popular with recruiters is the chronological résumé, shown in Figure 12.8 (p. 287). It lists work history job by job, starting with the most recent position (i.e., starting in the present and working back to older jobs). Recruiters are familiar with the chronological résumé, and as many as three quarters of them prefer to see a candidate's résumé in this format.[11] The chronological style works well for candidates who have experience in their field of employment and for those who show steady career growth. It's also the most honest form: it clearly shows what your work experience includes. Some students or new Canadians who lack extensive local experience may want to try the functional format, which is described below.

Chronological résumés focus on past employment; functional résumés focus on skills.

FUNCTIONAL. The functional résumé, shown in Figure 12.9 (p. 288), focuses attention on a candidate's skills rather than on past employment. Like a chronological résumé, the functional résumé begins with the candidate's name, address, telephone number, job objective, and education. Instead of listing jobs, though, the functional résumé lists skills and accomplishments, such as *Supervisory and Management Skills* or *Retail and Customer Service Experience*. This résumé style highlights accomplishments and can de-emphasize a negative or negligible employment history. People who have changed jobs frequently or who have gaps in their employment history may prefer the functional résumé. Be aware, though, that online employment sites may insist on chronological format. In addition, some recruiters may be suspicious of functional résumés, thinking the candidate is hiding something.

Although the functional résumé of Kevin Touhy shown in Figure 12.9 (p. 288) concentrates on skills, it does include a short employment section because he recognizes that recruiters expect it. Notice that Kevin breaks his skills into three categories. An easier method is to make one large list, perhaps with a title such as *Areas of Accomplishment, Summary of Qualifications,* or *Areas of Expertise and Ability.*

12.3b Decide on Length

Conventional wisdom has always held that recruiters prefer one-page résumés. A controlled study of 570 recruiters, however, revealed that while they *claimed* they preferred one-page résumés, they actually *chose* to interview the applicants with two-page résumés.[12] Recruiters who are serious about candidates often prefer a fuller picture with the kind of details that can be provided in a two-page résumé. On the other hand, recruiters are extremely busy, and concise résumés help speed up their work.

Recruiters often choose to interview candidates with longer résumés.

Perhaps the best advice is to make your résumé as long as needed to sell your skills to recruiters and hiring managers. Individuals with more experience will naturally have longer résumés. Those with fewer than ten years of experience, those making a major career change, and those who have had only one or two employers

The parts of a résumé should be arranged with the most important qualifications first.

will likely have a one-page résumé. Finally, some senior-level managers and executives with a lengthy history of major accomplishments might have a résumé that is three pages or longer.[13] A recent survey by a global staffing firm found that 61 percent of hiring managers now prefer to receive two-page résumés from experienced candidates for management jobs; 31 percent stated that they would accept three pages. Even applicants for low-level staff jobs may opt for two pages, 44 percent of recruiters said.[14]

12.3c Organize Your Information Under Headings

A résumé emphasizes skills and achievements aimed at a particular job or company. It shows a candidate's most important qualifications first, and it de-emphasizes any weaknesses. In organizing your information, try to create as few headings as possible; more than six generally looks cluttered. No two résumés are ever exactly alike, but job applicants usually include information under all or some of these headings: career objective; summary of qualifications; education; experience; capabilities and skills; awards and activities; personal information; and references. Besides these headings, a résumé always begins with a main heading.

MAIN HEADING. Keep the main heading of your résumé as uncluttered as possible. (Don't include the word *résumé* or *CV*; it's like putting the word *email* in the subject line of an email; i.e., it's redundant.) Begin with your name, add your middle initial for a professional look, and format it so that it stands out on the page. Following your name, list your contact information, including your complete address, area code and phone number (voice mail enabled), and email address. Some candidates now add links to their LinkedIn page or to a video résumé they've posted on a site like YouTube. If you do this, make sure these links lead to professional-looking and professional-sounding sites.

The recorded message at the phone number you list should be in your voice, mention your full name, and be concise and professional (e.g., "Thanks for your call. You've reached Casey Jepson. Please leave a message after the beep. I'll reply shortly."). If you are expecting an important recruiting call on your cellphone, pick up only when you are in a quiet environment and can concentrate.

Career objectives are most appropriate for specific, targeted positions, but they may limit a broader job search.

Make sure your email address sounds professional instead of something like *1foxylady@yahoo.com* or *hotdaddy@gmail.com*. Also be sure that you are using a personal email address. Putting your work email address on your résumé announces to prospective employers that you are using your current employer's resources to look for another job. See Figure 12.8 (p. 287) for an example of an effective main heading.

CAREER OBJECTIVE. Career objectives make the recruiter's life easier by quickly classifying the résumé. But such declarations may also disqualify a candidate if the stated objective doesn't match a company's job description.[15] A well-written objective customized for the job opening can add value to a résumé.

Your objective should focus on the employer's needs. Therefore, it should be written from the employer's perspective, not your own. Focus on how you can contribute to the organization, not on what the organization can do for you.

> Ineffective: *To obtain a meaningful and rewarding position that enables me to learn more about the graphic design field and allows for advancement.*

> Effective: *Position with advertising firm designing websites, publications, logos, and promotional displays for clients, where creativity, software knowledge, and proven communication skills can be used to build client base and expand operations.*

Also be careful that your career objective doesn't downplay your talents. For example, some consultants warn against using the words *entry level* in your objective, as they emphasize lack of experience or show poor self-confidence. Finally, your objective should be concise. Try to limit your objective to no more than two or three lines. Avoid using complete sentences and the pronoun "I." A good example of a career objective can be found in Figure 12.9 (p. 288).

If you choose to omit the career objective, be sure to discuss your objectives and goals in your cover letter. Savvy job seekers are also incorporating their objectives into a summary of qualifications, which is discussed next.

A summary of qualifications section presents your most impressive accomplishments and qualifications in one concise bulleted list.

SUMMARY OF QUALIFICATIONS. "The biggest change in résumés over the last decade has been a switch from an objective to a summary at the top," says career expert Wendy Enelow.[16] Recruiters are busy, and smart job seekers add a summary of qualifications to their résumés to save the time of recruiters and hiring managers. Once a job is advertised, a hiring manager may get hundreds or even thousands of résumés in response. A summary at the top of your résumé makes it easier to read and ensures that a recruiter, who may be skimming résumés quickly, does not overlook your most impressive qualifications. A well-written summary motivates the recruiter to read further.

A summary of qualifications will include three to eight bulleted statements that prove you are the ideal candidate for the position. When formulating these statements, consider your experience in the field, your education, your unique skills, awards you have won, certifications, and any other accomplishments that you want to highlight. Include quantifiable accomplishments wherever possible (e.g., *Over five years' experience in...*). Target the most important qualifications an employer will be looking for in the person hired for this position. Examples of summaries of qualifications appear in Figures 12.8 (p. 287) and 12.9 (p. 288).

The education section shows degrees and grades but does not list all courses a job applicant has taken.

EDUCATION. The next component in a chronological résumé is your education—if it is more noteworthy than your work experience. In this section you should include the name and location of schools, dates of attendance, major fields of study, and certifications received (e.g., diplomas, degrees). Once you have attended college, you don't need to list high-school information on your résumé.

Although some hiring managers may think that applicants are hiding something if they omit a poor record of grades, others suggest leaving out a poor GPA. Instead, they advise that students try to excel in internships, show extracurricular leadership, and target smaller, lesser-known companies to offset low grades.

Refer to courses only if you can relate them to the position sought. When relevant, include certificates earned, seminars attended, workshops completed, and honours earned. If your education is incomplete, include such statements as *BBA degree expected May 2018*. Title this section *Education, Academic Preparation,* or *Professional Training*. If you are preparing a functional résumé, you will probably put the education section below your skills summaries, as Kevin Touhy has done in Figure 12.9 (p. 288).

The work experience section of a résumé should list specifics and quantify achievements.

WORK EXPERIENCE OR EMPLOYMENT HISTORY. If your work experience is significant and relevant to the position sought, this information should appear before your education information. List your most recent employment first and work backwards, including only those jobs that you think will help you win the targeted position. A job application form may demand a full employment history, but your résumé may be selective. Be aware, though, that time gaps in your employment history will probably be questioned in the interview. For each position show the following:

- Employer's name, city/town, and province
- Dates of employment (month and year)
- Most important job title
- Significant duties, activities, accomplishments, and promotions

Describe your employment achievements concisely but concretely to make what résumé consultants call a strong "value proposition." Avoid generalities by striving to be more specific.

Ineffective: *Worked with customers.*

Effective: *Served 40 or more retail customers a day; Successfully resolved problems about custom stationery orders; or Acted as intermediary among customers, printers, and suppliers.*

Whenever possible, quantify your accomplishments instead of making them sound vague.

Ineffective: *Did equipment study*; or *Was successful in sales.*

Effective: *Conducted study of equipment needs of 100 small businesses in Hamilton, ON; or Personally generated orders for sales of $90,000 annually.*

Professional recruiters routinely report that if they don't spot quantifiable results in the first 10 seconds of reading your résumé, they will move on to the next one.

Your employment achievements and job duties will be easier to read if you place them in a bulleted list. Don't try to list every single thing you have done on the job; instead, customize your information so that it relates to the target job. Ensure your list of job duties shows what you have to contribute and how you are qualified for the position you are applying for. Don't make your bullet points complete sentences, and avoid using personal pronouns (*I, me, my*) in them. If you have performed a lot of the same duties for multiple employers, you don't have to repeat them.

In addition to technical skills, employers seek individuals with developed soft skills. This means you will want to select work experiences and achievements that illustrate your initiative, dependability, responsibility, problem solving, flexibility, creativity, leadership, and interpersonal communication strengths. One soft skill employers repeatedly ask for is people who can work together in teams.

Ineffective: *Worked effectively in teams.*

Effective: *Collaborated with interdepartmental five-person team to develop ten-page handbook for temporary workers.*

Statements describing your work experience can be made forceful and persuasive by using action verbs, such as those listed in Figure 12.5 and illustrated in Figure 12.6.

FIGURE 12.5 | Action Verbs to Strengthen a Résumé

COMMUNICATION SKILLS	TEAMWORK, SUPERVISION SKILLS	MANAGEMENT, LEADERSHIP SKILLS	RESEARCH SKILLS	CLERICAL, DETAIL SKILLS	CREATIVE SKILLS
clarified	advised	analyzed	assessed	activated	acted
collaborated	coordinated	authorized	collected	approved	conceptualized
explained	demonstrated	coordinated	critiqued	classified	designed
interpreted	developed	directed	diagnosed	edited	fashioned
integrated	evaluated	headed	formulated	generated	founded
persuaded	expedited	implemented	gathered	maintained	illustrated
promoted	facilitated	improved	interpreted	monitored	integrated
resolved	guided	increased	investigated	proofread	invented
summarized	motivated	organized	reviewed	recorded	originated
translated	set goals	scheduled	studied	streamlined	revitalized
wrote	trained	strengthened	systematized	updated	shaped

© Cengage Learning

FIGURE 12.6 | Action Verbs to Quantify Achievements

Identified weaknesses in internships and **researched** five alternate programs

Reduced delivery delays by an average of three days per order

Streamlined filing system, reducing 400-item backlog to zero

Organized holiday awards program for 1,200 attendees and 140 workers

Designed customer feedback form for company website

Represented 2,500 students on committee involving university policies and procedures

Calculated shipping charges for overseas deliveries and **recommended** most economical rates

Managed 24-station computer network linking data in three departments

Distributed and **explained** voter registration forms to over 500 prospective voters

Praised by top management for enthusiastic teamwork and achievement

Secured national recognition from Tree Canada for tree project

CAPABILITIES AND SKILLS. Recruiters want to know specifically what you can do for their companies. Therefore, list your skills, including your abilities with any special Internet, mobile app, software, office equipment, and communication technology tools.

Emphasize the skills and aptitudes that prove you are qualified for a specific position.

Ineffective: *Have payroll experience.*

Effective: *Proficient/competent/experienced in preparing federal, provincial, and local payroll tax returns as well as franchise and personal property tax returns.*

If you can speak a foreign language or use sign language, include it on your résumé. Describe proficiencies you have acquired through training and experience.

Ineffective: *Trained in computer graphics.*

Effective: *Certified in Adobe Photoshop and Illustrator and Web design through an intensive 350-hour classroom program.*

You will also want to highlight exceptional aptitudes, such as working well under stress, learning computer programs quickly, and interacting with customers. If possible, provide details and evidence that back up your assertions; for example, *Led Conflict Resolution workshop through staff development department on 10 occasions for over 200 employees.* For recent graduates, this section can be used to give recruiters evidence of your potential. Instead of *Capabilities*, the section might be called *Skills and Abilities.*

Those job hunters preparing a functional résumé will place more focus on skills than on any other section. A well-written functional résumé groups skills into categories such as *Accounting/Finance Skills, Management/Leadership Skills, Communication/Teamwork Skills*, and *Computer/Technology Skills*. Each skills category includes a bulleted list of achievements and experience that demonstrate the skill, including specific quantifiable amounts (e.g., *20 seminars*) whenever possible. These skills categories should be placed at the beginning of the résumé where they will be highlighted, followed by education and work experience. The action verbs shown in Figures 12.5 and 12.6 can also be used when constructing a functional résumé.

Awards, honours, and activities are appropriate for the résumé.

AWARDS, HONOURS, AND ACTIVITIES. If you have three or more awards or honours, highlight them by listing them under a separate heading. If not, put them with *Activities* or in the *Education* or *Work Experience* section if appropriate. Include awards, scholarships (financial and other), fellowships, dean's list, sports or other team affiliations, and so on.

Ineffective: *Recipient of King Scholarship*

Effective: *Recipient of King Scholarship given by Macdonald College to outstanding graduates who combine academic excellence and extracurricular activities.*

It's also appropriate to include school, community, volunteer, and professional activities. Employers are interested in evidence that you are a well-rounded person. This section provides an opportunity to demonstrate leadership and soft skills. Strive to use specific action statements.

Omit personal data not related to job qualifications.

Ineffective: *Treasurer of business club*

Effective: *Collected dues, kept financial records, and paid bills while serving as treasurer of 35-member business management club.*

PERSONAL DATA. Résumés omit personal data, such as birthdate, marital status, or national origin. Such information doesn't relate to occupational qualifications, and recruiters are legally barred from asking for such information. Some job seekers do, however, include hobbies or interests (such as skiing or photography) that might grab the recruiter's attention or serve as conversation starters. You could also indicate your willingness to travel or to relocate, since many companies will be interested.

REFERENCES. Recruiters prefer that you bring to the interview a list of individuals willing to discuss your qualifications. Therefore, you should prepare a separate list, such as that in Figure 12.7, when you begin your job search. Ask three of your professors, your current employer or previous employers, colleagues, or other

FIGURE 12.7 | Sample Reference List

Casey J. Jepson
201–1300 John A. Macdonald Blvd.
Kingston, ON K3E 4A5

Home: (613) 555-1926 Cell: (613) 555-8876 Email: cjepson78@gmail.com

Mr. Jeff Schmitz
Branch Manager, TD Canada Trust
940 Sydenham Rd.
Kingston, ON K1A 2H0
(613) 555-1172
jschmitz@tdcanadatrust.ca

Mr. Sandra Ostheimer
Communication Professor
St. Lawrence College
12 Portsmouth Rd.
Kingston, ON K2B 4R4
(613) 555-8009
sostheim@stlawrence.ca

Ms. Susan Winder
Manager, Sears
855 Gardiners Rd.
Kingston, ON K7K 6P8
(613) 555-4335

professional contacts whether they would be willing to answer inquiries regarding your qualifications for employment. Be sure to provide them with an opportunity to refuse. No reference at all is better than a negative one.

Do not include personal references, such as friends, family, or neighbours, because recruiters will rarely consult them. One final note: most recruiters see little reason to include the statement *References available upon request* at the end of your résumé. It is unnecessary and takes up precious space.

In Figures 12.8 and 12.9, you will find models corresponding to the two main résumé types. Notice as you study the models that the chronological résumé (Figure 12.8) is for a current student with only one type of experience; the functional résumé (Figure 12.9) is for a recent graduate with largely unrelated work experience; and the third combination-style résumé (Figure 12.10) is for a graduate with significant related experience following her postsecondary education. Use the appropriate model to help you organize the content and format of your own persuasive résumé.

References are unnecessary for the résumé, but they should be available for the interview.

FIGURE 12.8 | Chronological Résumé: Current Student

Casey J. Jepson
201–1300 John A. Macdonald Blvd.
Kingston, ON K3E 4A5

Phone: 613–555-8876
Email: cjepson82@gmail.com
http://www.youtube.com/watch?v=a2L8DHECtNj

Includes URL of a video résumé posted on YouTube

SUMMARY OF QUALIFICATIONS

- Over two years' experience in customer service positions in major organizations
- Excellent customer service skills including oral communication, listening, and written communication
- Proven teamwork and interpersonal skills including leadership, cooperation, and on-time delivery
- Mastery of computer skills (MOS certification)
- Strengths in research, proofreading, coaching, and math

EXPERIENCE

Customer Service Representative, Co-op placement
St. Lawrence College, Kingston, ON
September 2015 - present

- Provide friendly, helpful senrice via face-to-face, phone, email, and messaging channels at a large urban college
- File weekly incident/outlier reports
- Work effectively in team of 15–20 co-op students and fulltime CSRs

Front Desk Representative, part-time
TD Canada Trust, Kingston, ON
May 2013-June 2014

- Provide friendly, helpful face–to–face senrice at busy urban bank branch
- Replace lost and stolen credit and debit cards for clients
- Liaise with branch manager and tellers to increase branch profitability

Customer Associate, part-time
Sears, Kingston, ON
May 2012–June 2012; December 2012

- Manage busy cash desk in women's clothing department
- Provide friendly, helpful face–to–face answers to customer queries

EDUCATION

St. Lawrence College, Kingston, ON
Major: Retail Management Advanced Diploma
Graduation expected June 2016
Current average: A-

ACTIVITIES AND AWARDS

- Member of St. Lawrence Enactus team
- Nominated for SLC Ambassador Award (recognizes outstanding students for excellence in and out of classroom)
- Volunteer leader at annual student orientation (2014 & 2015)

FIGURE 12.9 | Functional Résumé: Recent College Graduate With Unrelated Part-Time Experience

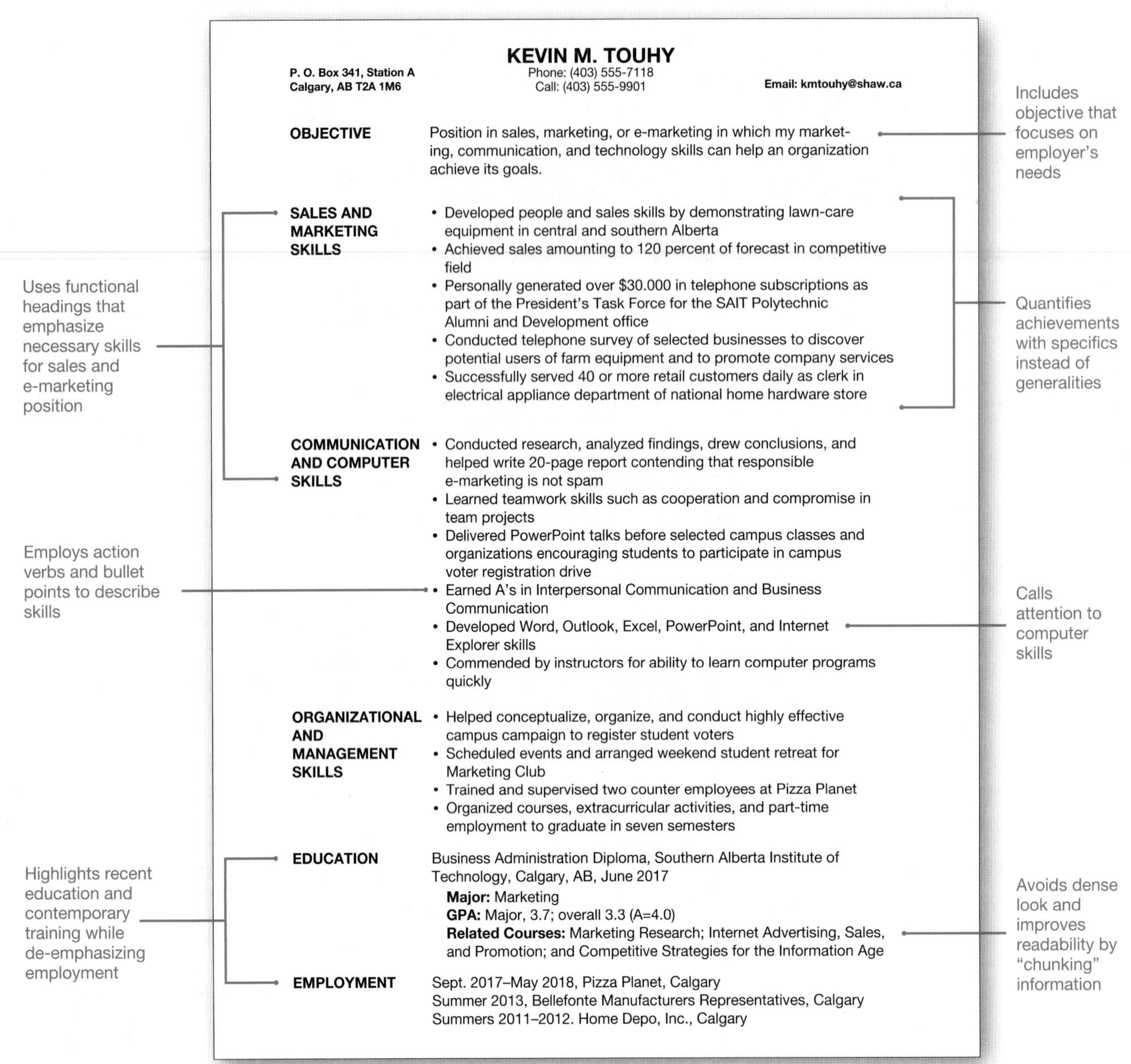
KEVIN M. TOUHY

P. O. Box 341, Station A
Calgary, AB T2A 1M6

Phone: (403) 555-7118
Call: (403) 555-9901

Email: kmtouhy@shaw.ca

OBJECTIVE Position in sales, marketing, or e-marketing in which my marketing, communication, and technology skills can help an organization achieve its goals.

SALES AND MARKETING SKILLS

- Developed people and sales skills by demonstrating lawn-care equipment in central and southern Alberta
- Achieved sales amounting to 120 percent of forecast in competitive field
- Personally generated over $30.000 in telephone subscriptions as part of the President's Task Force for the SAIT Polytechnic Alumni and Development office
- Conducted telephone survey of selected businesses to discover potential users of farm equipment and to promote company services
- Successfully served 40 or more retail customers daily as clerk in electrical appliance department of national home hardware store

COMMUNICATION AND COMPUTER SKILLS

- Conducted research, analyzed findings, drew conclusions, and helped write 20-page report contending that responsible e-marketing is not spam
- Learned teamwork skills such as cooperation and compromise in team projects
- Delivered PowerPoint talks before selected campus classes and organizations encouraging students to participate in campus voter registration drive
- Earned A's in Interpersonal Communication and Business Communication
- Developed Word, Outlook, Excel, PowerPoint, and Internet Explorer skills
- Commended by instructors for ability to learn computer programs quickly

ORGANIZATIONAL AND MANAGEMENT SKILLS

- Helped conceptualize, organize, and conduct highly effective campus campaign to register student voters
- Scheduled events and arranged weekend student retreat for Marketing Club
- Trained and supervised two counter employees at Pizza Planet
- Organized courses, extracurricular activities, and part-time employment to graduate in seven semesters

EDUCATION Business Administration Diploma, Southern Alberta Institute of Technology, Calgary, AB, June 2017
Major: Marketing
GPA: Major, 3.7; overall 3.3 (A=4.0)
Related Courses: Marketing Research; Internet Advertising, Sales, and Promotion; and Competitive Strategies for the Information Age

EMPLOYMENT Sept. 2017–May 2018, Pizza Planet, Calgary
Summer 2013, Bellefonte Manufacturers Representatives, Calgary
Summers 2011–2012. Home Depo, Inc., Calgary

Includes objective that focuses on employer's needs
Uses functional headings that emphasize necessary skills for sales and e-marketing position
Quantifies achievements with specifics instead of generalities
Employs action verbs and bullet points to describe skills
Calls attention to computer skills
Highlights recent education and contemporary training while de-emphasizing employment
Avoids dense look and improves readability by "chunking" information

Recent graduate Kevin Touhy chose this functional format to de-emphasize his meagre work experience and emphasize his potential in sales and marketing. This version of his résumé is more generic than one targeted for a specific position. Nevertheless, it emphasizes his strong points with specific achievements and includes an employment section to satisfy recruiters. The functional format presents ability-focused topics. It illustrates what the job seeker can do for the employer instead of narrating a history of previous jobs. Although recruiters prefer chronological résumés, the functional format is a good choice for new graduates, career changers, and those with employment gaps.

12.3d Online Résumé Reading Patterns

With increasing numbers of résumés being read online, it's wise for job applicants to know what researchers have found about how people read online text. Eye-tracking research reveals that people read text-based pages online in an F-shaped pattern.[17] That is, they read horizontally from the top of the page, concentrating on the top third and then focusing on the left side as they read downward. This roughly corresponds to the shape of a capital F. Smart applicants will arrange the most important information in the top section of the résumé. Additional significant information should appear at the beginning of each group down the left side.

FIGURE 12.10 | Combination Résumé: University Graduate With Substantial Experience

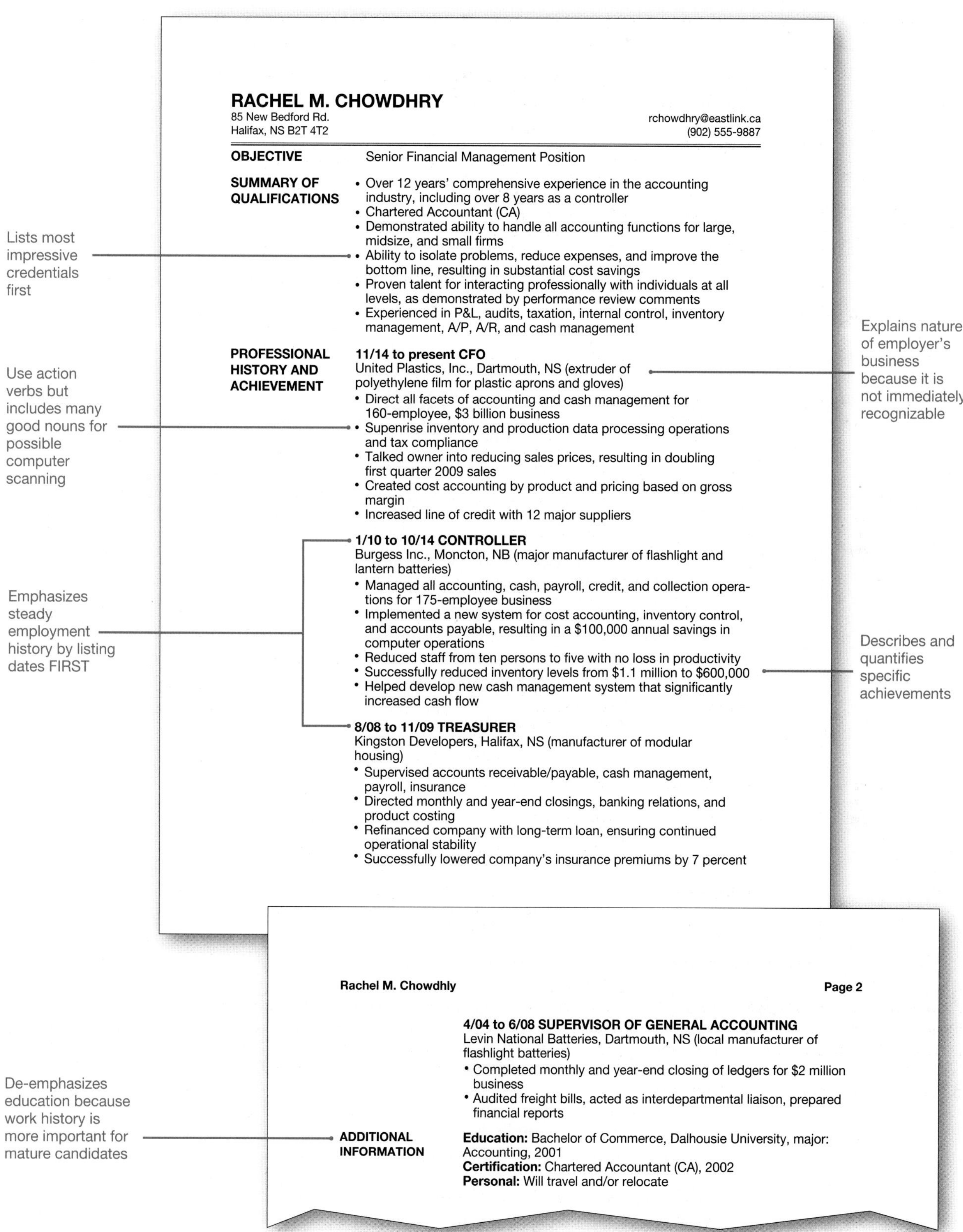

Lists most impressive credentials first
Use action verbs but includes many good nouns for possible computer scanning
Emphasizes steady employment history by listing dates FIRST
Explains nature of employer's business because it is not immediately recognizable
Describes and quantifies specific achievements
De-emphasizes education because work history is more important for mature candidates
RACHEL M. CHOWDHRY
85 New Bedford Rd.
Halifax, NS B2T 4T2
rchowdhry@eastlink.ca
(902) 555-9887
OBJECTIVE
Senior Financial Management Position
SUMMARY OF QUALIFICATIONS
• Over 12 years' comprehensive experience in the accounting industry, including over 8 years as a controller
• Chartered Accountant (CA)
• Demonstrated ability to handle all accounting functions for large, midsize, and small firms
• Ability to isolate problems, reduce expenses, and improve the bottom line, resulting in substantial cost savings
• Proven talent for interacting professionally with individuals at all levels, as demonstrated by performance review comments
• Experienced in P&L, audits, taxation, internal control, inventory management, A/P, A/R, and cash management
PROFESSIONAL HISTORY AND ACHIEVEMENT
11/14 to present CFO
United Plastics, Inc., Dartmouth, NS (extruder of polyethylene film for plastic aprons and gloves)
• Direct all facets of accounting and cash management for 160-employee, $3 billion business
• Supenrise inventory and production data processing operations and tax compliance
• Talked owner into reducing sales prices, resulting in doubling first quarter 2009 sales
• Created cost accounting by product and pricing based on gross margin
• Increased line of credit with 12 major suppliers
1/10 to 10/14 CONTROLLER
Burgess Inc., Moncton, NB (major manufacturer of flashlight and lantern batteries)
• Managed all accounting, cash, payroll, credit, and collection operations for 175-employee business
• Implemented a new system for cost accounting, inventory control, and accounts payable, resulting in a $100,000 annual savings in computer operations
• Reduced staff from ten persons to five with no loss in productivity
• Successfully reduced inventory levels from $1.1 million to $600,000
• Helped develop new cash management system that significantly increased cash flow
8/08 to 11/09 TREASURER
Kingston Developers, Halifax, NS (manufacturer of modular housing)
• Supervised accounts receivable/payable, cash management, payroll, insurance
• Directed monthly and year-end closings, banking relations, and product costing
• Refinanced company with long-term loan, ensuring continued operational stability
• Successfully lowered company's insurance premiums by 7 percent
Rachel M. Chowdhly
Page 2
4/04 to 6/08 SUPERVISOR OF GENERAL ACCOUNTING
Levin National Batteries, Dartmouth, NS (local manufacturer of flashlight batteries)
• Completed monthly and year-end closing of ledgers for $2 million business
• Audited freight bills, acted as interdepartmental liaison, prepared financial reports
ADDITIONAL INFORMATION
Education: Bachelor of Commerce, Dalhousie University, major: Accounting, 2001
Certification: Chartered Accountant (CA), 2002
Personal: Will travel and/or relocate

Because Rachel has many years of experience and seeks executive-level employment, she highlighted her experience by placing it before her education. Her summary of qualifications highlighted her most impressive experience and skills. This chronological two-page résumé shows the steady progression of her career to executive positions, a movement that impresses and reassures recruiters.

12.3e Polish Your Résumé and Keep It Honest

As you continue to work on your résumé, look for ways to improve it. For example, consider consolidating headings. By condensing your information into as few headings as possible, you will produce a clean, professional-looking document. Ask yourself what graphic highlighting techniques you can use to improve readability: capitalization, underlining, indenting, and bulleting. Experiment with headings and styles to achieve a pleasing, easy-to-read message. Moreover, look for ways to eliminate wordiness. For example, instead of *Supervised two employees who worked at the counter,* try *Supervised two counter employees.*

A résumé is expected to showcase a candidate's strengths and minimize weaknesses. For this reason, recruiters expect a certain degree of self-promotion. Some résumé writers, however, step over the line that separates honest self-marketing from deceptive half-truths and flat-out lies. Distorting facts on a résumé is unethical; lying may be illegal. Most important, either practice can destroy a career. In the Communication Workshop in the MindTap, learn more about how to keep your résumé honest and the consequences of fudging the facts.

12.3f Proofread Your Résumé

After revising your résumé, you must proofread, proofread, and proofread again for spelling, grammar, mechanics, content, and format. Then have a knowledgeable friend or relative proofread it yet again. This is one document that must be perfect. Because the job market is so competitive, one typo, misspelled word, or grammatical error could eliminate you from consideration.

By now you may be thinking that you'd like to hire someone to write your résumé. Don't! First, you know yourself better than anyone else could know you. Second, you will end up with either a generic or a one-time résumé. A generic résumé in today's highly competitive job market will lose out to a customized résumé nine times out of ten. Equally useless is a one-time résumé aimed at a single job. What if you don't get that job? Because you will need to revise your résumé many times as you seek a variety of jobs, be prepared to write (and rewrite) it yourself.

12.4 Increasing Your Chances With Digital Tools

Just as digital media have changed the way candidates seek jobs, they have also changed the way employers select qualified candidates. For example, the first reader of your résumé may very well be applicant tracking system software (ATS). Estimates suggest that as many as 90 percent of large companies use these systems.[18] Applicant tracking systems are favoured not only by large companies but also by job boards such as Monster to screen candidates and filter applications. You can expect to be seeing more of them with their restrictive forms and emphasis on keywords. Savvy candidates will learn to "game" the system by playing according to the ATS rules.

12.4a Get Your Résumé Selected: Maximize Keyword Hits

Job seekers can increase the probability of their résumés being selected by ATS through the words they choose. The following techniques, in addition to those cited earlier, can boost the chances of having your résumé selected:

- **Include specific keywords or keyword phrases.** Carefully study ads and job descriptions for the position you want. Describe your experience, education, and qualifications in terms associated with the job advertisement or job description for this position.
- **Focus on nouns.** Although action verbs will make your résumé appeal to a recruiter, ATS will often be looking for nouns in three categories: (a) a job title, position, or role (e.g., *accountant, Web developer, team leader*); (b) a technical

WORKPLACE IN FOCUS

A scandal in Canada's largest board of education has shone the spotlight on people who are willing to fudge the facts of their résumé. Chris Spence, ex-director of the Toronto District School Board, decided to resign once it was revealed that he had been plagiarizing (i.e., pretending the writing of other authors was his own) in an article he had written for the *Toronto Star*, in a blog he maintained after joining the school board, and most damagingly—and still the subject of an investigation by the university—in his PhD dissertation. Spence's fall from grace was documented daily in the media and he apologized publicly in a press conference as part of his resignation. *Is the temptation to take credit for work and experiences that you have not actually done worth the potential embarrassment and consequences?*

© Copyright *The Globe and Mail* Inc.

skill or specialization (e.g., *Javascript, e-newsletter editor*); and (c) a certification, a tool used, or specific experience (e.g., *Certified Financial Analyst, experience with WordPress*).[19]

- **Use variations of the job title.** ATS may seek a slightly different job title from what you list. To be safe, include variations and abbreviations (e.g., *occupational therapist, certified occupational therapist*, or COTA). If you don't have experience in your targeted area, use the job title you seek in your objective.
- **Concentrate on the skills section.** A majority of keywords sought by employees relate to specialized or technical skill requirements. Therefore, be sure the skills section of your résumé is loaded with nouns that describe your skills and qualifications.
- **Skip a keyword summary.** Avoid grouping nouns in a keyword summary because recruiters may perceive them to be manipulative.[20]

Study résumé models for ideas on improving your format.

OFFICE INSIDER

It sounds basic, but make sure that your résumé is free of typos and other errors. When applying by email, there is more of a tendency to rush and make careless mistakes. For many employers, this shows a lack of attention to detail and is an easy way to eliminate someone from consideration.

12.4b Expand Your Résumé's Appeal: Add Video

Another way of bolstering your traditional résumé and cover letter is to upload a video that profiles you and your skills to a site like YouTube or Vimeo. These video-sharing sites allow you to broadcast yourself and are incredibly powerful tools—a well-produced video résumé may open doors and secure an interview where other techniques have failed.[21] They allow candidates to demonstrate their public speaking, interpersonal, and technical skills more impressively than they can in traditional print résumés. Both employers and applicants can save recruitment and travel costs by using video résumés. Instead of flying distant candidates to interviews, organizations can see them digitally.

However, some recruiters are skeptical about video résumés because they fear that such applications will take more time to view than paper-based résumés do. Moreover, a lack of professionalism when creating video résumés can lead to embarrassment.

People who blog and write about video résumés suggest incorporating a number of best practices. These practices include ensuring excellent video quality; taking advantage of multiple authentic locations (your desk, outside a store you once worked at, etc.); using professional language; offering something unique from a traditional résumé; editing the sound and lighting so that there are no distractions;

and limiting video length to between three and five minutes.[22] Also, if you're satisfied with your video résumé, we suggest that you include a link to it in the heading of your traditional résumé, under your email address.

12.4c Translate Into Pictures: The Infographic Résumé

A hot trend in business is the infographic résumé. It uses colourful charts, graphics, and timelines to illustrate a candidate's work history and experience. No one could deny that an infographic résumé really stands out. "Anyone looking at it," says blogger Randy Krum, "is 650% more likely to remember it days later."[23] James Coleman, a graduating senior from the University of Saskatchewan, created an infographic résumé that secured a job. Shown in Figure 12.11, James's résumé uses a time line to track his experience and education. Colourful bubbles indicate his digital skills.

Most of us, however, are not talented enough to create professional-looking infographics. To the rescue are many companies that now offer infographic apps. Vizualize.me turns a user's LinkedIn profile information into a beautiful Web-based infographic, while Kinzaa.com lets you create a slick visual infographic-style résumé.

Will a dazzling infographic get you a job? Among hiring managers, the consensus is that infographic résumés help candidates set themselves apart, but such visual displays may not be appropriate for every kind of job.[24] In more traditional fields such as accounting and financial services, hiring managers want to see a standard print-based résumé. One hiring manager pointed out that traditional résumés evolved this way for a reason: they make comparison, evaluation, and selection easier for employers.[25]

FIGURE 12.11 | Infographics: A Novel Way to Show Education, Experience, and Skills

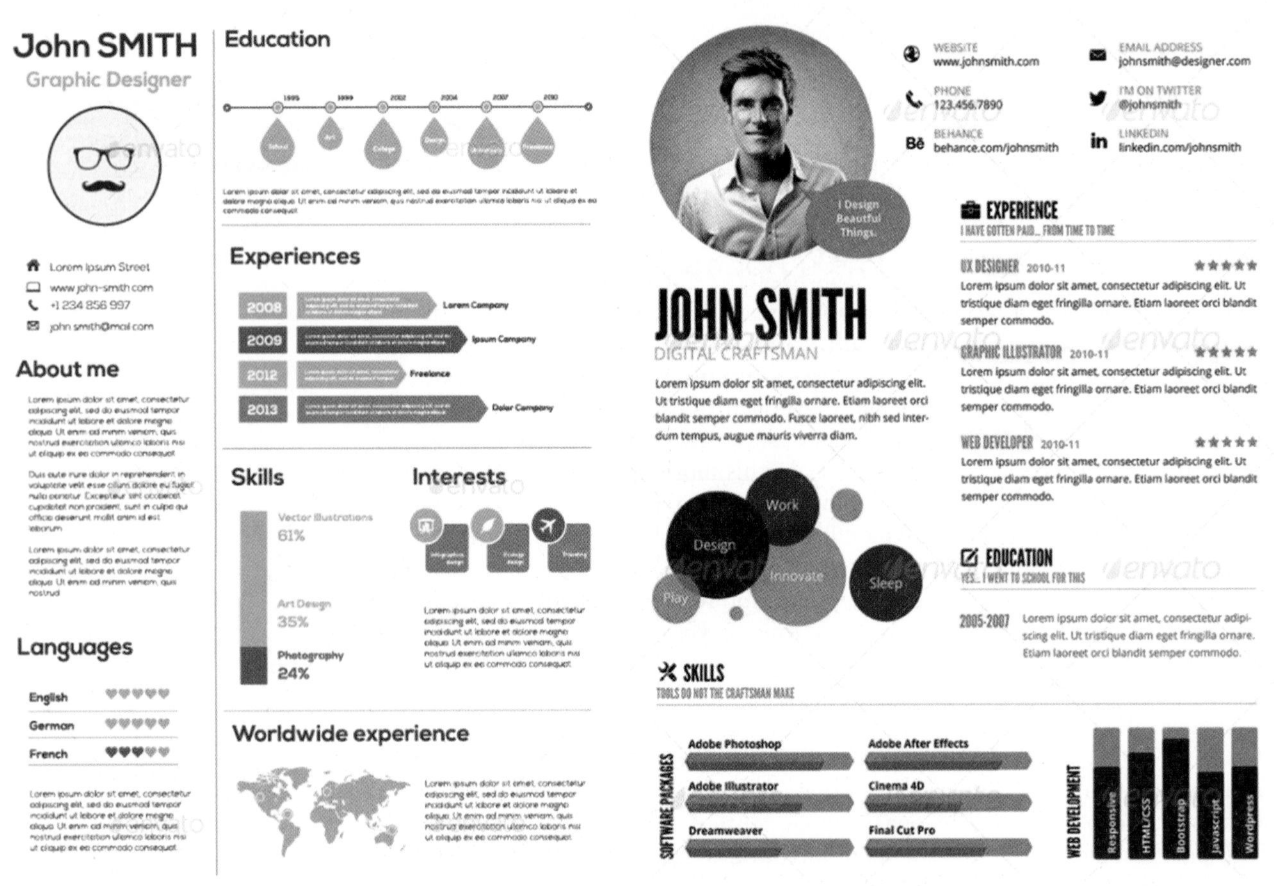

12.4d Submitting Your Résumé

Send or post your résumé in the format the employer requests.

If you are responding to a job posting on a company website or a job board, be sure to read the listing carefully to make sure you know how the employer wants you to submit your résumé. Not following the prospective employer's instructions can eliminate you from consideration before your résumé is even reviewed. Employers will probably ask you to submit your résumé in one of the following ways:

- **Word document.** Recruiters will probably ask applicants to attach their résumés as Word documents to an email. Alternatively, you may be asked to upload your Word file directly onto the recruiter's site.
- **PDF document.** For the sake of safety, many hiring managers prefer PDF (portable document format) files. A PDF résumé will look exactly like the original and cannot be easily altered. Save your Word résumé file as a PDF file (check for PDF under Format when you click Save As) and keep it in the same folder as your Word version.
- **Company database.** Some organizations prefer that you complete an online form with your résumé information. This enables them to plug your data into their formats for rapid searching. You might be asked paste your résumé into the form. In this case, save a separate version of the résumé as "Plain Text" before pasting it.
- **Fax.** In rare cases, you may be asked to fax your résumé. When doing so, use at least a 12-point font to improve readability. Thinner fonts—such as Times, Palatino, New Century Schoolbook, Arial, and Bookman—are clearer than thicker ones. Avoid underlines, which may look broken or choppy when faxed.

Whichever method you use to submit your résumé, don't send it on its own. In almost all cases a résumé is accompanied by a persuasive cover letter, which is discussed in the next section.

12.5 Persuasive Cover Letters

Cover letters introduce résumés, relate writer strengths to reader benefits, and help obtain an interview.

To accompany your résumé, you'll send a persuasive cover letter. The cover letter introduces the résumé, highlights ways your strengths will benefit the reader, and helps obtain an interview by personalizing you. In many ways your cover letter is a sales letter; it sells your talents and tries to beat the competition. It will, therefore include many of the techniques you learned for sales letters in Chapter 6.

Human resources professionals disagree on how long to make cover letters. Many prefer short letters with no more than four paragraphs; instead of concentrating on the letter, these readers focus on the résumé. Others desire longer letters that supply more information, thus giving them a better opportunity to evaluate a candidate's qualifications and gauge his or her personality. They argue that hiring and training new employees is expensive and time-consuming; extra data can guide them in making the best choice the first time. Use your judgment; if you feel, for example, that you need space to explain in more detail what you can do for a prospective employer, do so.

Regardless of its length, a cover letter should have three primary parts: (1) an opening that gets attention, (2) a body that builds interest and reduces resistance by explaining why you're the right candidate for the role, and (3) a closing that motivates action.

12.5a Gain Attention in the Opening

The opening in a cover letter gets attention by addressing the receiver by name.

The first step in gaining the interest of your reader is addressing that individual by name. Rather than sending your letter to the "Human Resources Department," try to obtain the name of the appropriate individual. Make it a rule to call the organization for the correct spelling and the complete address. This personal touch distinguishes your letter and demonstrates your serious interest.

How you open your cover letter depends largely on whether your résumé is for a position that is solicited or unsolicited. If an employment position has been announced and applicants are being solicited, you can use a direct approach. If you do not know whether a position is open and you are prospecting for a job, use an indirect approach. Whether direct or indirect, the opening should attract the attention of the reader. Strive for openings that are more imaginative than *I would like to apply for....* Instead, you could say *I'm pleased to submit my application for the X position, to which I am able to bring significant related experience.*

Openings for solicited jobs refer to the source of the information, the job title, and qualifications for the position.

OPENINGS FOR SOLICITED JOBS. Here are some of the best techniques to open a letter of application for a job that has been announced:

- **Refer to the name of an employee in the company.** Remember that employers always hope to hire known quantities rather than complete strangers:

  Mitchell Sims, a member of your Customer Service Department, told me that DataTech is seeking an experienced customer service representative. The attached summary of my qualifications demonstrates my preparation for this position.

  At the suggestion of Ms. Claudette Guertin of your Human Resources Department, I submit my qualifications for the position of personnel assistant.

- **Refer to the source of your information precisely.** If you are answering an advertisement, include the exact position advertised and the name and date of the publication. For large organizations it's also wise to mention the section of the newspaper where the ad appeared:

  Your listing on Workopolis for a junior accountant (competition 15-003) greatly appeals to me. With my accounting training and computer experience, I believe I could serve the City of Richmond well.

  The September 10 issue of the *National Post* reports that you are seeking a mature, organized, and reliable administrative assistant (position 15-A54) with excellent communication skills.

  Susan Butler, placement director at Carleton University, told me that Open Text Corporation has an opening for a technical writer with knowledge of Web design and graphics.

- **Refer to the job title and describe how your qualifications fit the requirements.** Human Resources directors are looking for a match between an applicant's credentials and the job needs:

  Will an honours graduate with a degree in recreation studies and two years of part-time experience organizing social activities for a retirement community qualify for your position of activity director?

  Because of my specialized training in accounting at Simon Fraser University, I feel confident that I have the qualifications you described in your advertisement for an accountant trainee.

OPENINGS FOR UNSOLICITED JOBS. If you are unsure whether a position actually exists, you may wish to use a more persuasive opening. Since your goal is to convince this person to read on, try one of the following techniques:

Openings for unsolicited jobs show interest in and knowledge of the company, as well as spotlighting reader benefits.

- **Demonstrate interest in and knowledge of the reader's business.** Show the Human Resources director that you have done your research and that this organization is more than a mere name to you.

  Since the Canadian Automobile Association is organizing a new IT team for its recently established group insurance division, could you use the services of a well-trained Business Intelligence graduate who seeks to become a professional underwriter?

- **Show how your special talents and background will benefit the company.** Human Resources directors need to be convinced that you can do something for them.

  Could your rapidly expanding publications division use the services of an editorial assistant who offers exceptional language skills, an honours degree from Brandon University, and two years' experience in producing a school literary publication?

In applying for an advertised job, Kendra Hawkins wrote the solicited cover letter shown in Figure 12.12. Notice that her opening identifies the position and the job board completely so that the reader knows exactly what advertisement Kendra refers to. Using features of Microsoft Word, Kendra designed her own letterhead that uses her name and looks professionally printed.

The body of a cover letter should build interest, reduce resistance, and discuss relevant personal traits.

FIGURE 12.12 | Solicited Cover Letter

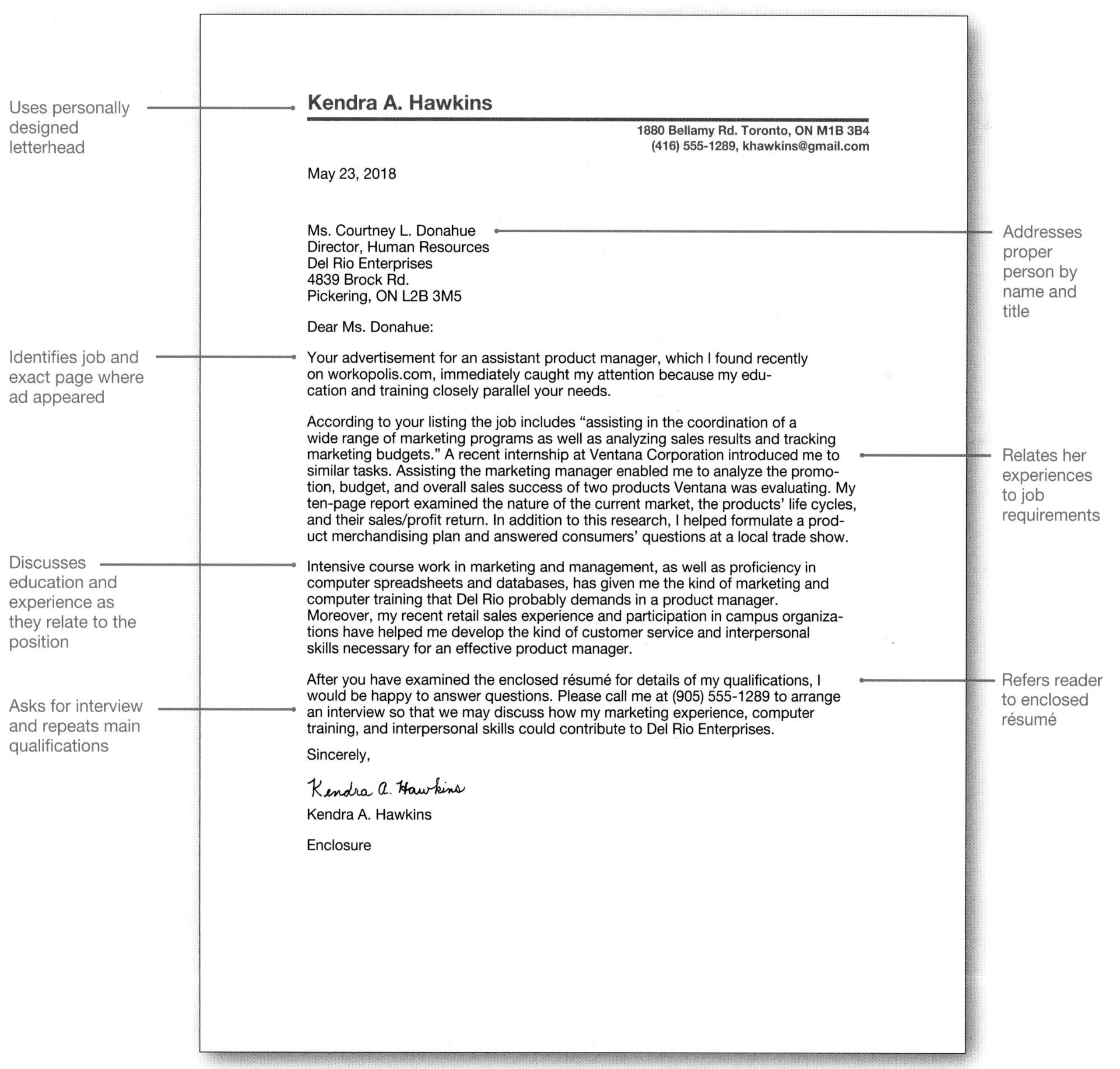

Kendra A. Hawkins

1880 Bellamy Rd. Toronto, ON M1B 3B4
(416) 555-1289, khawkins@gmail.com

May 23, 2018

Ms. Courtney L. Donahue
Director, Human Resources
Del Rio Enterprises
4839 Brock Rd.
Pickering, ON L2B 3M5

Dear Ms. Donahue:

Your advertisement for an assistant product manager, which I found recently on workopolis.com, immediately caught my attention because my education and training closely parallel your needs.

According to your listing the job includes "assisting in the coordination of a wide range of marketing programs as well as analyzing sales results and tracking marketing budgets." A recent internship at Ventana Corporation introduced me to similar tasks. Assisting the marketing manager enabled me to analyze the promotion, budget, and overall sales success of two products Ventana was evaluating. My ten-page report examined the nature of the current market, the products' life cycles, and their sales/profit return. In addition to this research, I helped formulate a product merchandising plan and answered consumers' questions at a local trade show.

Intensive course work in marketing and management, as well as proficiency in computer spreadsheets and databases, has given me the kind of marketing and computer training that Del Rio probably demands in a product manager. Moreover, my recent retail sales experience and participation in campus organizations have helped me develop the kind of customer service and interpersonal skills necessary for an effective product manager.

After you have examined the enclosed résumé for details of my qualifications, I would be happy to answer questions. Please call me at (905) 555-1289 to arrange an interview so that we may discuss how my marketing experience, computer training, and interpersonal skills could contribute to Del Rio Enterprises.

Sincerely,

Kendra A. Hawkins

Kendra A. Hawkins

Enclosure

Uses personally designed letterhead
Addresses proper person by name and title
Identifies job and exact page where ad appeared
Relates her experiences to job requirements
Discusses education and experience as they relate to the position
Refers reader to enclosed résumé
Asks for interview and repeats main qualifications

More challenging are unsolicited letters of application, such as Donald Vinton's, shown in Figure 12.13. Because he's writing a cover letter where no advertised job exists, he is essentially hoping to create a job. For this reason his opening must grab the reader's attention immediately. To do this, he capitalizes on company information appearing in an online news story. Donald purposely keeps his application letter short and to the point because he anticipates that a busy executive will be unwilling to read a long, detailed letter. Donald's unsolicited letter "prospects" for a job. Some job candidates feel that such letters may be even more productive than efforts to secure advertised jobs, since "prospecting" candidates face less competition. Donald's letter uses a standard return address format, placing his name, street, city, province, and postal code above the date.

Spotlighting reader benefits means matching your personal strengths to an employer's needs.

12.5b Build Interest in the Body

Once you have captured the attention of the reader, you can use the body of the letter to build interest and reduce resistance. Keep in mind that your résumé emphasizes what you have done in the past; your cover letter stresses what you can do in the future for the employer.

Your first goal is to relate your letter to a specific position. If you are responding to a listing, you'll want to explain how your preparation and experience fill the stated requirements. If you are prospecting for a job, you may not know the exact

FIGURE 12.13 | Unsolicited Cover Letter

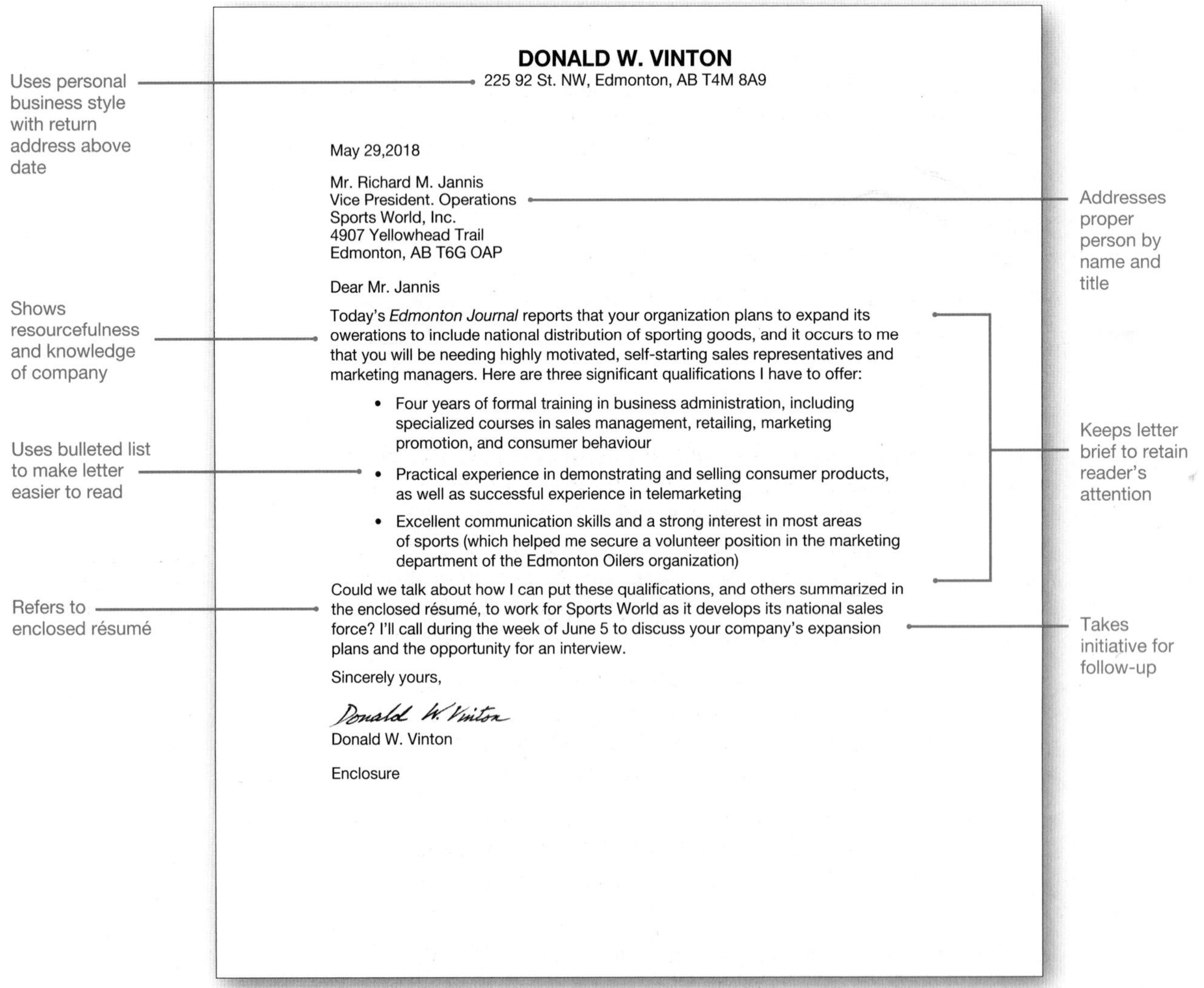

DONALD W. VINTON
225 92 St. NW, Edmonton, AB T4M 8A9

May 29,2018

Mr. Richard M. Jannis
Vice President. Operations
Sports World, Inc.
4907 Yellowhead Trail
Edmonton, AB T6G OAP

Dear Mr. Jannis

Today's *Edmonton Journal* reports that your organization plans to expand its owerations to include national distribution of sporting goods, and it occurs to me that you will be needing highly motivated, self-starting sales representatives and marketing managers. Here are three significant qualifications I have to offer:

- Four years of formal training in business administration, including specialized courses in sales management, retailing, marketing promotion, and consumer behaviour
- Practical experience in demonstrating and selling consumer products, as well as successful experience in telemarketing
- Excellent communication skills and a strong interest in most areas of sports (which helped me secure a volunteer position in the marketing department of the Edmonton Oilers organization)

Could we talk about how I can put these qualifications, and others summarized in the enclosed résumé, to work for Sports World as it develops its national sales force? I'll call during the week of June 5 to discuss your company's expansion plans and the opportunity for an interview.

Sincerely yours,

Donald W. Vinton

Donald W. Vinton

Enclosure

requirements. Your employment research and knowledge of your field, however, should give you a reasonably good idea of what is expected for this position.

It's also important to emphasize reader benefits. In other words, you should describe your strong points in relation to the needs of the employer. In one employment survey many human resources professionals expressed the same view: "I want you to tell me what you can do for my organization. This is much more important to me than telling me what courses you took in college or what 'duties' you performed on your previous jobs."[26] Instead of simply saying what you've done—*I have completed courses in business communication, report writing, and technical writing*—say how what you've done will be useful in the position for which you're applying:

> Courses in business communication, report writing, and technical writing have helped me develop the research and writing skills required of your technical writers.

Choose your strongest qualifications and show how they fit the targeted job. And remember, students with little experience are better off spotlighting their education and its practical applications, as these candidates did:

> Because you're looking for an architect's apprentice with proven ability, I've submitted a drawing of mine that won second place in the Algonquin College drafting contest last year.

> Successfully transcribing over 100 letters and memos in my college transcription class gave me experience in converting the spoken word into the written word, an exacting communication skill demanded of your legal assistants.

In the body of your letter, you'll also want to discuss relevant personal traits. Employers are looking for candidates who, among other things, are team players, take responsibility, show initiative, and learn easily. Finally, in this section or the next, you should refer the reader to your résumé. Do so directly or as part of another statement, as shown here:

> Please refer to the attached résumé for additional information regarding my education and experience.

> As you will notice from my résumé, I am graduating in June with a bachelor's degree in business administration.

12.5c Motivate Action in the Closing

After presenting your case, you should conclude with a spur to action. This is where you ask for an interview. However, never directly ask for the job. To do so would be presumptuous and naive. In indirectly requesting an interview, suggest reader benefits or review your strongest points. Be sincere and appreciative. Remember to make it easy for the reader to agree by supplying your phone number, email address, and the best times to call you. And keep in mind that some human resources managers prefer that you take the initiative to call them. Here are possible endings:

The closing of a cover letter should include a request for an interview.

> I hope this brief description of my qualifications and the additional information on my résumé indicate to you my genuine desire to put my skills in accounting to work for you. Please call me at (416) 488-2291 before 10 a.m. or after 3 p.m. to arrange an interview.

> To add a hard-working, experienced strategic communications practitioner to your team, please call me at (604) 492-1433 to arrange an interview. I can meet with you at any time convenient to your schedule.

> Next week, after you have examined the attached résumé, I will call you to discuss the possibility of arranging an interview.

12.5d Avoid "I" Dominance

As you revise your cover letter, notice how many sentences begin with "I." Although it's impossible to talk about yourself without using "I," you can reduce the number of sentences beginning with this pronoun by using two techniques. First, place "I" in the middle of sentences instead of dominating the opening. Instead of *I was the top salesperson in my department*, try *While working in X department, I did Y and Z*, or *Among 15 coworkers, I received top ratings from my managers*. Incorporating "I" into the middle of sentences considerably reduces its domination.

A second technique for avoiding "I" dominance involves making activities and outcomes, not yourself, the subjects of sentences. For example, rather than *I took classes in business communication and data mining*, say *Classes in business communication and data mining prepared me to....* Instead of *I enjoyed helping customers*, say *Helping customers taught me to be patient under stress.*

12.5e Send Your Cover Letter by Email

Serious job candidates send a professional cover letter even if the résumé is submitted by email, by fax, or through online channels.

More than 90 percent of résumés at Fortune 500 companies arrive by email or are submitted through the corporate website.[27] Some applicants make the mistake of not including cover letters with their résumés when they submit them by email. An application submitted electronically should contain two separate files: a cover letter file and a résumé file. An application that arrives without a cover letter makes the receiver wonder what it is and why it was sent. Recruiters want you to introduce yourself, and they also are eager to see some evidence that you can write. Some candidates either skip the cover letter or think they can get by with one-line email cover notes such as this: *Please see attached résumé, and thanks for your consideration.*

A cover letter should look professional and suggest quality.

If you are serious about landing the job, take the time to prepare a professional cover letter. As illustrated in Figure 12.14, an electronic application should include a brief cover note, plus the two files mentioned above, as attachments.

FIGURE 12.14 | Job Application Sent Electronically

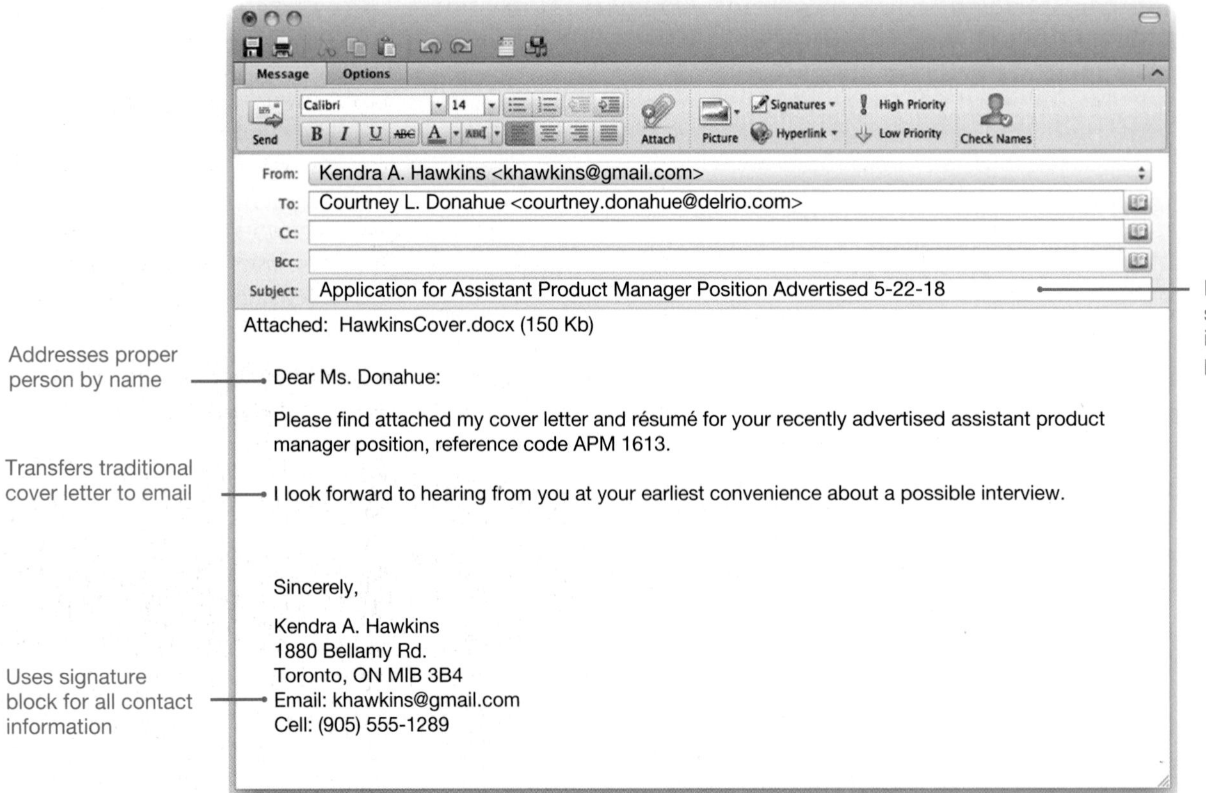

SUMMARY OF LEARNING OBJECTIVES

12.1 Prepare for employment by identifying your interests and market requirements.

- Searching for a job in this digital age has dramatically changed. Search engines, job boards, and social networks have all become indispensable tools in hunting for a job.
- Emphasis today is on what the employer wants, not what the candidate wants.

  Begin the job-search process by learning about yourself, your field of interest, and your qualifications. How do your skills match what employers seek?
- Search the Web, visit a campus career centre, take a summer job, interview someone in your field, volunteer, or join professional organizations.
- Identify job availability, the skills and qualifications required, duties, and salaries.

12.2 Use traditional and digital job search techniques in the open and hidden markets.

- The primary sources of jobs today are networking (46 percent); Internet job boards and company websites (25 percent); and agencies (14 percent).
- In searching the open job market—that is, jobs that are listed and advertised—study the big job boards, such as CareerBuilder, Monster, and Charity Village.
- To find a job with a specific company, go directly to that company's website and check its openings and possibilities.
- Nearly all serious candidates today post profiles on LinkedIn.
- For jobs in specialized fields, search some of the many niche sites, such as Accountemps for temporary accounting positions or Dice for technology positions.
- Estimates suggest that as many as 80 percent of jobs are in the hidden job market—that is, never advertised. Successful job candidates find jobs in the hidden job market through networking.
- An effective networking procedure involves (a) developing a contact list, (b) reaching out to these contacts in person and online in search of referrals, and (c) following up on referrals.
- Because electronic media and digital tools continue to change our lives, you should use social media networks—especially LinkedIn—to extend your networking efforts.
- Effective networking strategies include building a personal brand, preparing a professional business card with a tagline, composing a 30-second elevator speech that describes what you can offer, and developing a strong online presence.

12.3 Organize and format persuasive chronological and functional résumés.

- Because of intense competition, you must customize your résumés for every position you seek.
- Chronological résumés, which list work and education by dates, rank highest with recruiters. Functional résumés, which highlight skills instead of jobs, may be helpful for people with little experience, those changing careers, and those with negative employment histories.
- In preparing a résumé, organize your skills and achievements to aim at a particular job or company.
- Study models to effectively arrange the résumé main heading and the optional career objective, summary of qualifications, education, work experience, capabilities, awards, and activities sections.
- The most effective résumés include action verbs to appeal to human readers and job-specific nouns that become keywords selected by applicant tracking systems.
- As you complete your résumé, look for ways to strengthen it by polishing, proofreading, and checking for honesty and accuracy.

12.4 Use social media, video, and infographic résumés as alternatives to traditional résumés.

- To increase the probability of having your résumé selected by an automated tracking system, include specific keywords, especially nouns that name job titles, technical skills, and tools used or specific experience.
- Consider preparing a career e-portfolio to showcase your qualifications. This collection of digital files can feature your talents, accomplishments, and technical skills. It may include examples of academic performance, photographs, multimedia files, and other items beyond what can be shown in a résumé.
- A video résumé enables you to present your experience, qualifications, and interests in video form.
- A hot trend among creative candidates is the infographic résumé, which provides charts, graphics, and timelines to illustrate a candidate's work history and experience.
- Most candidates, however, should start with a basic print-based résumé from which they can make a plain-text résumé stripped of formatting to be embedded within email messages and submitted online.

12.5 Write a persuasive cover letter to accompany your résumé.

- Although cover messages are questioned by some in today's digital world, recruiters and hiring managers overwhelmingly favour them.
- Cover messages help recruiters make decisions, and they enable candidates to set themselves apart from others.
- In the opening of a cover message, gain attention by addressing the receiver by name and identifying the job. You might also identify the person who referred you.
- In the body of the message, build interest by stressing your strengths in relation to the stated requirements. Explain what you can do for the targeted company.

- In the body or closing, refer to your résumé, request an interview, and make it easy for the receiver to respond.
- If you are submitting your cover message by email, shorten it a bit and include your complete contact information in the signature block.

CHAPTER REVIEW

1. When preparing to search for a job, what should you do before writing a résumé? (Obj. 1)
2. What are the current trends in sources of new jobs? Which sources are trending upward and which are trending downward? (Obj. 2)
3. Although one may not actually find a job on the Internet, how can the big job boards be helpful to job hunters? (Obj. 2)
4. What is the hidden job market, and how can candidates find jobs in it? (Obj. 2)
5. In searching for a job, how can you build a personal brand, and why is it important to do so? (Obj. 2)
6. What is a customized résumé and why should you have one? (Obj. 3)
7. How do chronological and functional résumés differ, and what are the advantages and disadvantages of each? (Obj. 3)
8. What is an ATS, and how does it affect the way you prepare a résumé? (Obj. 4)
9. How can you maximize the keyword hits in your résumé? What three categories are most important? (Obj. 4)
10. What are the three parts of a cover message, and what does each part contain? (Obj. 5)

CRITICAL THINKING

1. How has the concept of the job changed, and how will this affect your employment search? (Obj. 1)
2. To what degree is a social media profile (e.g., on LinkedIn or Facebook) a replacement for the traditional cover letter/résumé package? (Obj. 2)
3. How is a résumé different from a job application form? (Obj. 3)
4. If a combination résumé combines the chronological and functional types, why isn't a combination résumé the style everyone uses? (Obj. 3)
5. Some job candidates think that applying for unsolicited jobs can be more fruitful than applying for advertised openings. Discuss the advantages and disadvantages of letters that "prospect" for jobs. (Obj. 2)
6. **Ethical Issue:** At work, fellow employee Karl confesses that he did not complete the degree he claims on his résumé. You have never liked Karl, but he does satisfactory work. You are both competing for the same promotion. You are considering writing an anonymous note to the boss telling him to verify Karl's degree. Use Google or your library database to research Canadian guidelines for whistle-blowing at work. Based on your research, do you think your plan is a good one? (Objs. 1, 2)
7. A cover letter is a persuasive letter, but do you really want to reduce a potential employer's resistance? Why might this be dangerous? (Obj. 5)

ACTIVITIES AND CASES

12.1 INTERESTS AND QUALIFICATIONS INVENTORY (OBJ. 1)

It's often surprising what kind of information you can find out about your fellow classmates in a classroom setting. Imagine you are conducting a study for your college's co-op office or student association. The co-op office or student association wants to know the future career interests and aspirations of the college's students as well as their current qualifications.

Your Task. Choose three people in your class (preferably classmates you don't know very well) and interview them. Ask them the questions listed on page 273 under "Identify Your Interests" and then the questions on pages 273–274 under "Assess Your Qualifications." Develop a profile of each of your interviewees, and email this profile to your instructor. Your instructor may choose to share the "inventory" with you in a later class. How might you use this inventory for future networking purposes?

12.2 EVALUATING YOUR QUALIFICATIONS (OBJ. 1)

Your Task. Prepare four worksheets that inventory your own qualifications in the areas of employment; education; capabilities and skills; and honours and activities. Use active verbs when appropriate.

a. *Employment.* Begin with your most recent job or internship. For each position list the following information: employer; job title; dates of employment; and three to five duties, activities, or accomplishments. Emphasize activities related to your job goal. Strive to quantify your achievements.
b. *Education.* List degrees, certificates, diplomas, and training accomplishments. Include courses, seminars, or skills that are relevant to your job goal. Calculate your GPA in your major.
c. *Capabilities and skills.* List all capabilities and skills that recommend you for the job you seek. Use words such as *skilled, competent, trained, experienced*, and *ability to*. Also list five or more qualities or interpersonal skills necessary for a successful individual in your chosen field. Write action statements demonstrating that you possess some of these qualities. Empty assurances aren't good enough; try to show evidence (*Developed teamwork skills by working with a committee of eight to produce a...*).
d. *Awards, honours, and activities.* Explain any awards so that the reader will understand them. List school, community, and professional activities that suggest you are a well-rounded individual or possess traits relevant to your target job.

12.3 CHOOSING A CAREER PATH (OBJ. 1)

Your Task. Visit your school library, local library, or employment centre. Select an appropriate resource such as Human Resources and Skills Development Canada's *National Occupational Classification* (www5.hrsdc.gc.ca/NOC/English/NOC/2011/Welcome.aspx) to find a description for a position for which you could apply in two to five years. Photocopy or print the pages from the resource you chose that describe employment in the area in which you are interested. Were you able to find the job that interests you? If not, where else can you find information on this job?

Visit **MindTap** for a variety of videos, additional exercises, activities, and quizzes to support your learning.

CHAPTER

13

Interviews and Follow-Up

OBJECTIVES

After studying this chapter, you should be able to

13.1 Explain the purposes and types of job interviews.

13.2 Describe what to do before an interview to make an impressive initial contact.

13.3 Describe what to do during an interview to create a favourable impression.

13.4 Describe what to do immediately after an interview to maintain the positive impression you've created.

13.5 Prepare other employment-related documents.

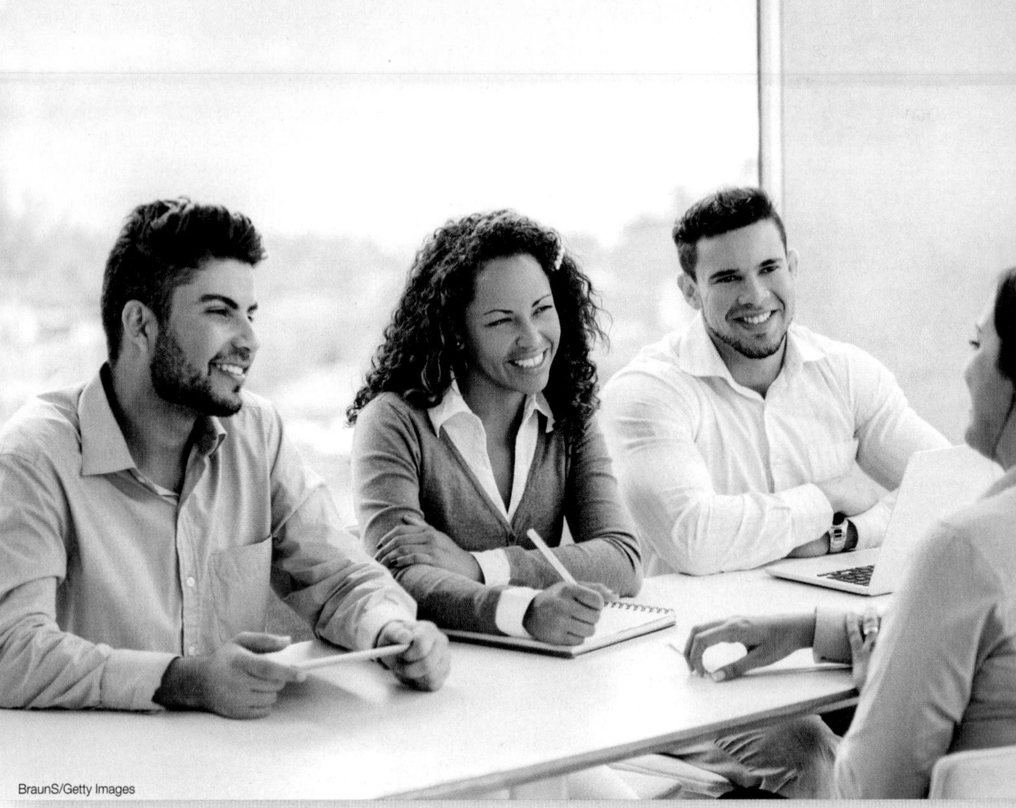

BraunS/Getty Images

13.1 Purposes and Types of Employment Interviews

Whether you are completing your education and searching for your first full-time position or in the workforce and striving to change jobs, a job interview can be life changing. Because employment is a major part of everyone's life, job interviews take on enormous importance.

Most people consider job interviews to be extremely stressful. However, the more you learn about the process and the more prepared you are, the less stress you will feel. Also, a job interview is a two-way street. It's not just about being judged by the employer. You, the candidate, will be using the job interview to evaluate the employer and find out if you really want to work for this organization.

Clearly, job interviews are intimidating for most of us. No one enjoys being judged and possibly rejected. Should you expect to be nervous about an upcoming job interview? Of course. Everyone is uneasy about being scrutinized and questioned. But think of how much more nervous you would be if you had no idea what to expect in the interview and were unprepared.

Yes, you can expect to be nervous. But you can also expect to succeed in an interview when you know what's coming and when you prepare thoroughly. Remember, it's often the degree of preparation as well as the appearance of confidence that determines who gets the job.

13.1a Purposes of Employment Interviews

An interview is your opportunity to (a) convince the employer of your potential, (b) learn more about the job and the company, and (c) expand on the information in your résumé. This is the time for you to gather information about whether you would fit into the company culture. You should also be thinking about whether this job suits your career goals.

From the employer's perspective, the interview is an opportunity to (a) assess your abilities in relation to the requirements for the position; (b) discuss your training, experience, knowledge, and abilities in more detail; (c) see what drives and motivates you; and (d) decide whether you would fit into the organization.

13.1b Types of Employment Interviews

Job applicants generally face two interviews: screening interviews and hiring/placement interviews, as shown in Figure 13.1. You must succeed in the first to proceed to the second. Once you make it to the hiring/placement interview, you will find a variety of interview styles, including one-on-one, panel, group, sequential, stress, and online interviews. You will be better prepared if you know what to expect in each type of interview.

SCREENING INTERVIEWS. Screening interviews eliminate candidates who fail to meet minimum "hard skill" as opposed to "soft skill" requirements. Companies use screening interviews to save time and money by weeding out lesser-qualified candidates before scheduling face-to-face interviews. Although some screening interviews are conducted during job fairs or on college campuses, many screening interviews take place on the telephone, and some take place online.[1]

Today, screening interviews are often completed using specialized software. Companies like Self Management Group sell simulation software to organizations in various sectors, such as banking and retail. According to the sales pitch for these products, they can help these companies "make better hiring decisions and select candidates who are more likely to stay, perform, and deliver results."[2] In essence, the screening software experience is like taking a test in an online course or when applying for a driver's licence. During a screening interview, the interviewer will probably ask you to provide details about the education and experience listed on your résumé; therefore, you must be prepared to promote your qualifications. Remember that the person conducting the screening interview is trying to determine whether you should move on to the next step in the interview process.

A screening interview may be as short as five minutes. Even though it may be short, don't treat it casually. If you don't perform well, it may be your last interview with that organization. You can use the tips that follow in this chapter to succeed during the screening process.

Screening interviews are intended to eliminate those who fail to meet minimum requirements.

HIRING/PLACEMENT INTERVIEWS. The most promising candidates selected from screening interviews will be invited to hiring/placement interviews. Hiring managers want to learn whether candidates are motivated, qualified, and a good fit for the position. Their goal is to learn how the candidate would fit into their organization. Conducted in depth, hiring/placement interviews may take many forms.

In hiring/placement interviews, recruiters try to learn how the candidate might fit into their organization.

ONE-ON-ONE INTERVIEWS. This is the most common interview type. You can expect to sit down with a company representative (or two) and talk about the job and your qualifications. If the representative is the hiring manager, questions will be specific and job-related. If the representative is from the human resources department, the questions will probably be more general.

FIGURE 13.1 | The Job Interview Process

1. Know the interviewing sequence.
Expect a telephone screening interview.
If you are successful, next comes the hiring interview.
Be prepared to answer questions in a one-on-one, panel, group, or video interview.
2. Research the target company.
Study the company's history, mission, goals, size, and management structure.
Know its strengths and weaknesses.
Try to connect with someone in the company.
3. Prepare thoroughly.
Rehearse detailed but brief success stories.
Practise stories that illustrate dealing with a crisis, handling tough situations, juggling priorities, and working on a team.
Clean up your online presence.
4. Look sharp, be sharp.
Suit up! Dress professionally to feel confident.
Be ready for questions that gauge your interest, explore your experience, and reveal your skills.
Practise using the STAR method to answer behavioral questions.
5. End positively.
Summarize your strongest qualifications.
Show enthusiasm; say that you want the job!
Ask what happens next.
6. Follow up.
Send a note thanking the interviewer.
Contact your references.
Check in with the interviewer if you hear nothing after five days.

PANEL INTERVIEWS. Panel interviews are typically conducted by people who will be your supervisors and colleagues. Usually seated around a table, interviewers may take turns asking questions. Panel interviews are advantageous because they save time and show you how the staff works together. For these interviews, you can prepare basic biographical information about each panel member. When answering questions, maintain eye contact with the questioner as well as with the other team members. Try to take notes during the interview so that you can remember each person's questions and what was important to that individual.[3]

GROUP INTERVIEWS. Group interviews occur when a company interviews several candidates for the same position at the same time. Some employers use this technique to measure leadership skills and communication styles. During a group interview, stay focused on the interviewer and treat the other candidates with respect. Even if you are nervous, try to remain calm, take your time when responding, and express yourself clearly. The key during a group interview is to make yourself stand out from the other candidates in a positive way.[4]

SEQUENTIAL INTERVIEWS. In a sequential interview, you meet individually with two or more interviewers over the course of several hours or days. For example, you may meet separately with human resources representatives, your hiring manager, and potential future supervisors and colleagues in your division or department. You must listen carefully and respond positively to all interviewers. Promote your qualifications to each one; don't assume that any interviewer knows what was said in a previous interview. Keep your responses fresh, even when repeating yourself many times over. Subsequent interviews also tend to be more in-depth than first interviews, which means that you need to be even more prepared and know even more about the company.

STRESS INTERVIEWS. This interview type, rarely used, tests your reactions in difficult situations. In a stress interview, you may, for example, be forced to wait a long time before being greeted by the interviewer, or you may be given a test with an impossible time limit, or you may be treated rudely (all on purpose, of course).

Hiring interview types include one-on-one, panel, group, sequential, stress, and online.

If asked rapid-fire questions from many directions, take the time to slow things down. For example, *I would be happy to answer your question, Ms. X, but allow me to finish responding to Mr. Z.* If greeted with silence, another stress technique, you might say *Would you like me to begin the interview? Let me tell you about myself.* Or ask a question such as *Can you give me more information about the position?* The best way to handle stress interview situations is to remain calm and give carefully considered answers.

ONLINE, VIDEO, AND VIRTUAL INTERVIEWS. Many companies today use technology to interview job candidates from a distance. Although conference call interviews have a long tradition, today's savvy companies such as Zappos.com use webcams and videoconferencing software to conduct interviews. If an applicant doesn't have a webcam, Zappos sends one with a return label.[5]

Using Skype and a webcam saves job applicants and companies time and money, especially when applicants are not in the same geographic location as the company. Even though your interview may be online, conducted with videoconferencing software and a webcam, don't take it any less seriously than a face-to-face interview.

While it's technically possible to interview online via videoconferencing, a study finds that this channel is not favourably viewed by employers or candidates.

Despite the technical ability to conduct interviews online through videoconferencing, there is evidence that, although flexible and time-saving, these types of interviews are not viewed in as positive a light (by both employers and candidates) as traditional, in-person interviews.[6]

13.2 Before the Interview

Being active in the job market means that you must be prepared to be contacted by potential employers. As discussed earlier, employers use screening interviews to narrow the list of candidates. If you do well in the screening interview, you will be invited to an in-person or online meeting. Below are tips for how to prepare yourself before an interview.

After submitting a résumé, you may be contacted by phone by potential employers for a screening interview.

13.2a Use Professional Phone Techniques

Even with the popularity of email, many employers still contact job applicants by phone to set up interviews. Employers can judge how well applicants communicate by hearing their voices and expressions and tone over the phone. Therefore, once you are actively looking for a job, remember that any time the phone rings it could be a potential employer. Don't make the mistake of letting an unprofessional voice mail message or an unfriendly-sounding roommate ruin your chances. Here's how you can avoid such problems:

- Make sure that your voice mail instructions are concise and professional, with no distracting background sounds. If your home voice mail instructions are for your entire family, consider offering only your personal cellphone number on your résumé. The instructions should be in your own voice and include your full name for clarity.
- Tell anyone who might answer your phone about your job search. Explain to them the importance of acting professionally and taking complete messages. Family members or roommates can affect the first impression an employer has of you.
- Don't answer your cellphone unless you are in a quiet enough location to have a conversation with a prospective employer. It is hard to pay close attention when you are in a noisy restaurant or on a crowded bus. That said, if you do answer the phone in a noisy situation and find an employer on the other end, say hello politely, identify yourself, apologize for the noise, and ask whether the employer wants to continue the conversation or have you call back shortly.

13.2b Make the First Conversation Impressive

Sounding flustered, unprepared, or unprofessional when an employer calls may ruin a job seeker's chances with that company.

Whether you answer the phone directly or return an employer's call, make sure you are prepared for the conversation. Remember that this is the first time the employer has heard your voice. How you conduct yourself on the phone will create a lasting impression. To make that first impression a positive one, follow these tips:

- Keep a list near or in your phones of the positions for which you have applied.
- Treat any call from an employer just like an interview. Use a professional tone and appropriate language. Be polite and enthusiastic, and sell your qualifications.
- If caught off guard by the call, ask whether you can call back in a few minutes. Organize your materials and yourself.
- Have a copy of your résumé available so that you can answer any questions that come up. Also have your list of references, a calendar, and a notepad handy. If you're talking on a smartphone, you'll be able to access a calendar and notepad on the phone itself.
- Be prepared to undergo a screening interview. As discussed earlier, this might occur during the first phone call.
- Take notes during the phone conversation. Obtain accurate directions, and verify the spelling of your interviewer's name. If you will be interviewed by more than one person, get all of their names.
- Before you hang up, reconfirm the date and time of your interview. You could say something like *I look forward to meeting with you next Wednesday at 2 p.m.*

13.2c Research the Target Company

Once you've scheduled an in-person or online interview, start preparing for it. One of the most important steps in effective interviewing is gathering detailed information about a prospective employer. Never enter an interview cold. Recruiters are impressed by candidates who have done their homework.

Before your interview, take time to research the target company and learn about its goals, customers, competitors, reputation, branding, and so forth.

Search the potential employer's website, news sites, trade journals, and industry directories. Don't forget to Google the interviewer.[7] Learn all you can about the company's history, mission and goals, size, geographic locations, number of employees, customers, competitors, culture, management structure, reputation in the community, financial condition, strengths and weaknesses, and future plans, as well as the names of its leaders. Also, learn what you can about the industry in which the company operates. Visit the library and explore your campus career centre to find additional information about the target company and its field, service, or product.

Analyze the company's advertising. One candidate, a marketing major, spent a great deal of time poring over brochures from an aerospace contractor. During his initial interview, he shocked and impressed the recruiter with his knowledge of the company's guidance systems. The candidate had, in fact, relieved the interviewer of his least-favourite task—explaining the company's complicated technology.

Talking with company employees is always a good idea, if you can manage it. They are probably the best source of inside information. Try to speak to someone who is currently employed there, but not working in the immediate area where you wish to be hired. You may be able to find this person by using LinkedIn. Remember, however, that asking favours of someone who doesn't know you is a risky proposition and is best handled with complete transparency.

Researching an organization enlightens candidates and impresses recruiters.

Finally, you may also want to connect with the company through social media. "Like" the company on Facebook and comment shrewdly on the organization's status updates and other posts. You may hear about vacancies before they are advertised. If you follow the company and its key people on Twitter, you may draw some positive attention to yourself and perhaps even hear about up-to-the-minute job openings. If you know the interviewers' names, look up their profiles on LinkedIn but don't try to connect with them before actually meeting them. You may find more in-depth information about these individuals on LinkedIn than on Facebook.[8]

The best source of inside information is company employees.

In learning about a company, you may uncover information that convinces you that this is not the company for you. It's always better to learn about negatives early in the process. More likely, though, the information you collect will help you tailor your interview responses to the organization's needs. You know how flattered you feel when an employer knows about you and your background. That feeling works both ways. Employers are pleased when job candidates take an interest in them. Be ready to put in plenty of effort in investigating a target employer because this effort really pays off at interview time.

In addition, one of the best things a job seeker can do is to get into the habit of reading the newspaper regularly. The best place to go for current information on Canadian companies is the business sections of the two national newspapers: *nationalpost.com* and *theglobeandmail.com*. Your local city or town newspaper will occasionally profile local businesses.

13.2d Prepare and Practise

After you've learned about the target organization, study the job description. As mentioned earlier, successful job candidates never go into interviews cold. They prepare success stories and practise answers to typical questions. They also plan their responses to any problem areas on their résumés. As part of their preparation before the interview, they decide what to wear, and they gather the items they plan to take with them, such as a portfolio of projects completed.

REHEARSE SUCCESS STORIES. To feel confident and be able to sell your qualifications, prepare and practise success stories. These are specific examples of your educational and work-related experience that demonstrate your qualifications and achievements. Look over the job description and your résumé to determine what skills, training, personal characteristics, and experience you want to emphasize during the interview. Then prepare a success story for each one. Quantify whenever possible, for example, by mentioning dollars saved or percentage of sales increased. Your success stories should be detailed but brief. Think of them as 30-second sound bites.

Practise telling your stories until they fluently roll off your tongue and sound natural. Then in the interview be certain to find places to insert them. Tell stories about (a) dealing with a crisis, (b) handling a tough interpersonal situation, (c) successfully juggling many priorities, (d) changing course to deal with changed circumstances, (e) learning from a mistake, (f) working on a team, and (g) going above and beyond expectations.[9]

Practise success stories that emphasize your most strategic skills, areas of knowledge, strongest personality traits, and key accomplishments.

PRACTISE ANSWERS TO POSSIBLE QUESTIONS. Imagine the kinds of questions you may be asked and work out sample answers. Although you can't anticipate precise questions, you can expect to be asked about your education, skills, experience, and availability. Practise answering some typical interview questions aloud, either in a mirror, with a friend, while driving in your car, or before going to bed. Keep practising until you have the best responses down pat. Consider recording a practice session to see and hear how you answer questions. Do you look and sound enthusiastic?

CLEAN UP DIGITAL DIRT. A study showed that 45 percent of employers screen candidates using Google and social networking sites such as Facebook, LinkedIn, MySpace, and Twitter.[10] Even more important, 70 percent of recruiters have found something online that caused them not to hire a candidate.[11] The top reasons cited for not considering an applicant after an online search were that the candidate (a) posted provocative or inappropriate photographs or information; (b) posted content about drinking or doing drugs; (c) talked negatively about current or previous employers, colleagues, or clients; (d) exhibited poor communication skills; (e) made discriminatory comments; (f) lied about qualifications; or (g) revealed a current or previous employer's confidential information.[12]

For example, the president of a small consulting company was about to hire a summer intern when he discovered the student's Facebook page. The candidate described his interests as "smokin' blunts [cigars hollowed out and stuffed with marijuana], shooting people and obsessive sex."[13] The executive quickly lost interest in this candidate. Even if the student was merely posturing, it showed poor judgment. Teasing photographs and provocative comments about drinking, drug use, and sexual exploits make students look immature and unprofessional. Follow these steps to clean up your online presence:

- **Remove questionable content.** Delete incriminating, provocative, or distasteful photos, content, and links that could make you look unprofessional to potential employers.
- **Stay positive.** Don't complain about things in your professional or personal life online. Even negative reviews you have written on sites such as Amazon.com can turn employers off.
- **Be selective about who is on your list of friends.** You don't want to miss out on an opportunity because you seem to associate with negative, immature, or unprofessional people. Your best bet is to make your personal social media pages private.
- **Avoid joining groups or pages that may be viewed negatively.** Remember that online searches can turn up your online activities, including group memberships, blog postings, and so on. If you think any activity you are involved in might show poor judgment, remove yourself immediately.
- **Don't discuss your job search if you are still employed.** Employees can find themselves in trouble with their current employers by writing status updates or sending tweets about their job search.
- **Set up a professional social media page or create your own personal website.** Use Facebook, LinkedIn, or other social networking sites to create a professional page. Many employers actually find information during their online searches that convinces them to hire candidates. Make sure your professional page demonstrates creativity, strong communication skills, and well-roundedness.[14]

Make sure everything posted about you online is professional and positive.

EXPECT TO EXPLAIN PROBLEM AREAS ON YOUR RÉSUMÉ. Interviewers are certain to question you about problem areas on your résumé. If you have little or no experience, you might emphasize your recent training and up-to-date skills. If you have gaps in your résumé, be prepared to answer questions about them positively and truthfully. If you were fired from a job, accept some responsibility for what happened and explain what you gained from the experience. Don't criticize a previous employer, and don't hide the real reasons. If you received low grades for one term, explain why and point to your improved grades in subsequent terms.

DECIDE HOW TO DRESS. What you wear to a job interview still matters. Even if some employees in the organization dress casually, you should look qualified, competent, and successful. When in doubt, a business suit is a good idea as it will probably be expected. Avoid loud colours; strive for a coordinated, natural appearance. Favourite colours for interviews are grey and dark blue. Don't overdo jewellery, and make sure that what you do wear is clean, pressed, odour-free, and lint-free. Shoes should be polished and scuff-free, and they should be "dress" shoes, not casual running shoes.

To summarize, ensure that what you wear projects professionalism and shows your respect for the interview situation.

GATHER ITEMS TO BRING. Decide what you should bring with you to the interview, and get everything ready the night before. You should plan to bring copies of your résumé, your references list, a pad of paper and pen, money for parking or for public transit, and samples of your work, if appropriate. If you deem the workplace to be tech savvy, bring along your smartphone or tablet if you own one, just in case. Place everything in a businesslike bag, briefcase or folder to add a final professional touch to your look.

13.2e Get to Your Interview

Allow ample time to arrive unflustered, and be congenial to everyone who greets you.

The big day has arrived! Ideally you are fully prepared for your interview. Now you need to make sure that everything goes smoothly. That means arriving on time and handling that fear you are likely to feel.

On the morning of your interview, give yourself plenty of time to groom and dress. Then give yourself ample time to get to the employer's office. If something unexpected happens that will to cause you to be late, such as an accident or transit issue, call the interviewer right away to explain what is happening. On the way to the interview, don't smoke, don't eat anything messy or smelly, and don't load up on perfume or cologne. Arrive at the interview five or ten minutes early.

When you enter the office, be courteous to everyone. Remember that you are being judged not only by the interviewer but by the receptionist and anyone else who sees you before and after the interview. They will notice how you sit, what you read, and how you look. Introduce yourself to the receptionist if there is one, and to whomever else you may bump into, and wait to be invited to sit.

Greet the interviewer confidently, and don't be afraid to initiate a handshake. Doing so exhibits professionalism and confidence. Extend your hand, look the interviewer directly in the eye, smile pleasantly, and say, *I'm pleased to meet you, Mr. Thomas. I'm Constance Ferraro.* A firm but not crushing handshake sends a nonverbal message of poise and assurance. Once introductions have taken place, wait for the interviewer to offer you a chair. Make small talk with upbeat comments, such as *This is a beautiful headquarters* or *I'm very impressed with the facilities you have here.* Don't immediately begin rummaging in your briefcase, bag, or folder for your résumé. Being at ease and unrushed suggest that you are self-confident.

Fight fear by practising, preparing thoroughly, breathing deeply, and knowing that you are in charge for part of the interview.

13.2f Fight Fear

Expect to be nervous before and during the interview: it's natural! Other than public speaking, employment interviews are some of the most anxiety-inducing events in people's lives. One of the best ways to overcome fear is to know what happens in a typical interview. You can further reduce your fears by following these suggestions:

- **Practise interviewing.** Try to get as much interviewing practice as you can—especially with real companies. The more times you experience the interview situation, the less nervous you will be. If offered, campus mock interviews also provide excellent practice, and the interviewers will offer tips for improvement.
- **Prepare thoroughly.** Research the company. Know how you will answer the most frequently asked questions. Be ready with success stories. Rehearse your closing statement. One of the best ways to reduce butterflies is to know that you have done all you can to be ready for the interview.
- **Understand the process.** Find out ahead of time how the interview will be structured. Will you be meeting with an individual, or will you be interviewed by a panel? Is this the first of a series of interviews? Don't be afraid to ask about these details before the interview so that an unfamiliar situation won't catch you off guard.
- **Dress professionally.** If you know you look sharp, you will feel more confident.
- **Breathe deeply.** Take deep breaths, particularly if you feel anxious while waiting for the interviewer. Deep breathing makes you concentrate on something other than the interview and also provides much-needed oxygen.
- **Know that you are not alone.** Everyone feels some level of anxiety during a job interview. Interviewers expect some nervousness, and a skilled interviewer will try to put you at ease.
- **Remember that an interview is a two-way street.** The interviewer isn't the only one who is gleaning information. You have come to learn about the job and the company. In fact, during some parts of the interview, you will be in charge. This should give you courage.

13.3 During the Interview

During the interview you will be answering questions and asking some of your own. Your behaviour, body language, and other nonverbal cues will also be on display. The interviewer will be trying to learn more about you, and you should learn more about the job and the organization. Although you may be asked some unique questions, many interviewers ask standard, time-proven questions, which means that you can prepare your answers ahead of time.

13.3a Send Positive Nonverbal Messages and Act Professionally

Send positive nonverbal messages by arriving on time, being courteous, dressing professionally, greeting the interviewer confidently, controlling your body movements, making eye contact, listening attentively, and smiling.

You have already sent nonverbal messages to your interviewer by arriving on time, being courteous, dressing professionally, and greeting the receptionist confidently.

Continue to send positive nonverbal messages throughout the interview. Remember that what comes out of your mouth and what is written on your résumé are not the only messages an interviewer receives from you. Here are suggestions that will help you send the right nonverbal messages during interviews:

- **Control your body movements.** Keep your hands, arms, and elbows to yourself. Don't lean on a desk. Keep your feet on the floor. Don't cross your arms in front of you. Keep your hands out of your pockets.
- **Exhibit good posture.** Sit erect, leaning forward slightly. Don't slouch in your chair; at the same time, don't look too stiff and uncomfortable. Good posture demonstrates confidence and interest.
- **Practise appropriate eye contact.** A direct eye gaze, at least in North America, suggests interest and trustworthiness. If you are being interviewed by a panel, remember to maintain eye contact with all interviewers.

WORKPLACE IN FOCUS

As the old saying goes, "You never get a second chance to make a first impression." Until recently, image consultants differed on how much time individuals have to put their best face forward. But a study conducted by two psychologists has concluded that it takes only one-tenth of a second to form judgments about the key character traits of others. In practical terms, this means employers will make inferences about one's likableness, competence, trustworthiness, and aggressiveness in the blink of an eye. *What should job candidates do to make a good first impression during an interview?*

StockLite/Shutterstock.com

- **Use gestures effectively.** Nod to show agreement and interest. Gestures should be used as needed, but don't overdo it.
- **Smile enough to convey a positive attitude.** Have a friend give you honest feedback on whether you generally smile too much or not enough.
- **Listen attentively.** Show the interviewer you are interested and attentive by listening carefully to the questions being asked. This will also help you answer questions appropriately.
- **Turn off your devices.** Avoid the embarrassment of allowing your phone to ring, or even to buzz, during an interview. Turn phones off completely; don't just switch them to vibrate.
- **Don't chew gum.** Chewing gum during an interview is distracting and unprofessional.
- **Sound enthusiastic and interested—but sincere.** The tone of your voice has an enormous effect on the words you say. Avoid sounding bored, frustrated, or sarcastic during an interview. Employers want employees who are enthusiastic and interested.
- **Avoid "empty" words.** Filling your answers with verbal pauses such as *um*, *uh*, *like*, and *basically* communicates that you are not prepared. Also avoid annoying distractions such as clearing your throat repeatedly or sighing deeply.

Above all, remember that employers want to hire people who have confidence in their own abilities. To put yourself into an employer's shoes, so to speak, think of the interview from his or her point of view, as explained in Figure 13.1. Then, let your body language, posture, dress, and vocal tone prove that you are self-assured.

13.3b Answer Typical Questions Confidently

The way you answer questions can be almost as important as what you say. Use the interviewer's name and title from time to time when you answer: *Ms. Lyon, I would be pleased to tell you about….* People like to hear their own names. But be sure you are pronouncing the name correctly. Avoid answering questions with a simple *yes or no*; elaborate on your answers to better promote yourself and your assets. Keep answers positive; try not to criticize anything or anyone.

How you answer questions can be as important as the answers themselves.

Occasionally it may be necessary to clarify vague questions. Some interviewers are inexperienced in the role. You may have to ask your own question to understand what was asked: *By … do you mean…?*

Consider closing some of your responses with *Does that answer your question?* or *Would you like me to elaborate on any particular experience?*

Stay focused on the skills and traits that employers seek; don't reveal weaknesses.

Always aim your answers at the key characteristics interviewers seek: expertise and competence, motivation, interpersonal skills, decision-making skills, enthusiasm

FIGURE 13.2 | Interview Actions to Avoid

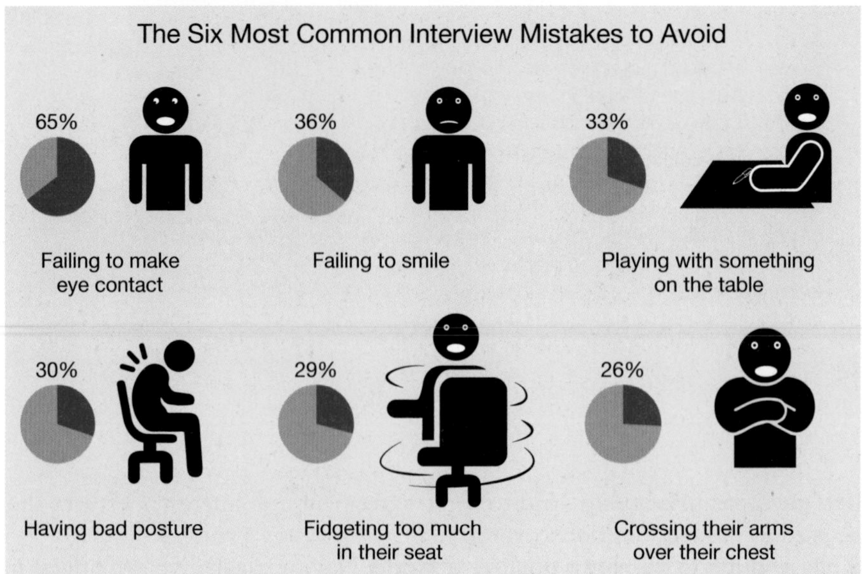

A survey of hiring managers showed that between 26% and 65% of potential employees commit these errors during interviews.
Data courtesy of CareerBuilder

for the job, and a pleasing personality. And remember to stay focused on your strengths. Don't reveal weaknesses, even if you think they make you look human. You won't be hired for your weaknesses, only for your strengths.

Enunciate clearly: remember, that you will be judged by how well you communicate. Avoid slurred words such as *gonna* and *y'know*, as well as slangy expressions such as *yeah*, *like*, and *whatever*. Also eliminate verbal static (*ah, and, um*). As you practise for the interview, a good idea is to record answers to expected interview questions. Is your speech filled with verbal static?

You can't expect to be perfect in an employment interview. No one is. But you can increase your chances of success by avoiding the behaviours described in Figure 13.2.

Prepare for get-acquainted questions by practising a short formula response.

The following section presents questions that are often asked during employment interviews. To get you thinking about how to respond, we've provided an answer or discussion for the first question in each group. As you read the remaining questions in each group, think about how you could respond most effectively.

OFFICE INSIDER

"Occasionally you bump into a talented and competent candidate ... who's so lacking in humility and realness that you can't take a chance. This young man had a lot of the right stuff, but when he started telling us that he had never made a mistake in his life and didn't expect to, we knew we'd heard enough."

—Jack and Suzy Welch, management consultants and authors

QUESTIONS TO GET ACQUAINTED. After introductions, recruiters generally start the interviewing with personal questions that put the candidate at ease. They are also striving to gain a picture of the candidate to see if he or she will fit into the organization's culture.

1. Tell me about yourself.

   Experts agree that you must keep this answer short (one to two minutes, tops) but on target. Try practising this formula: "My name is ______. I have completed a ______ degree with a major in ______. Recently I worked for ______ as a ______. Before that I worked for ______ as a ______. My strengths are ______ (interpersonal) and ______ (technical)." Try rehearsing your response in 30-second segments devoted to your education, your work experience, and your qualities/skills. Some candidates end with "Now that I've told you about myself, can you tell me a little more about the position?"

2. What are your greatest strengths?
3. Do you prefer to work by yourself or with others? Why?
4. What was your major in college, and why did you choose it?
5. What are some things you do in your spare time?

Recruiters want to know how interested you are in this organization and in this specific position.

QUESTIONS TO GAUGE YOUR INTEREST. Interviewers want to understand your motivation for applying for a position. Although they realize you are probably interviewing for other positions, they still want to know why you are interested in this particular position with this organization. These types of questions help them determine your level of interest.

1. Why do you want to work for (*name of company*)?

   Questions like this illustrate why you must research an organization thoroughly before the interview. The answer to this question must prove that you understand the company and its culture. This is the perfect place to bring up the company research you did before the interview. Show what you know about the company, and discuss why you would like to become a part of this organization. Describe your desire to work for this organization not only from your perspective but also from its point of view. What do you have to offer?

2. Why are you interested in this position?
3. What do you know about our company?
4. Why do you want to work in the ______ industry?
5. What interests you about our products (services)?

QUESTIONS ABOUT YOUR EXPERIENCE AND ACCOMPLISHMENTS. After questions about your background and education, the interview generally becomes more specific, with questions about your experience and accomplishments.

Employers will hire a candidate with less experience and fewer accomplishments if he or she can demonstrate the skills required.

1. Why should we hire you when we have applicants with more experience or better credentials?

   In answering this question, remember that employers often hire people who present themselves well instead of others with better credentials. Emphasize your personal strengths that could be an advantage with this employer. Are you a hard worker? How can you demonstrate it? Have you had recent training? Some people have had more years of experience but actually have less knowledge because they have done the same thing over and over. Stress your experience using new technologies and equipment. Be sure to mention any software you can use effectively. Emphasize that you are open to new ideas and learn quickly.

2. Describe the most rewarding experience of your career so far.
3. How have your education and professional experiences prepared you for this position?
4. What were your major accomplishments in each of your past jobs?
5. What was a typical workday like?
6. What job functions did you enjoy most? Least? Why?
7. Tell me about your computer skills.
8. Who was the toughest boss you ever worked for and why?
9. What were your major achievements in college?
10. Why did you leave your last position? OR: Why are you leaving your current position?

When asked about the future, show ambition and interest in succeeding with this company.

QUESTIONS ABOUT THE FUTURE. Questions that look into the future tend to stump some candidates, especially those who have not prepared adequately. Some of these questions give you a chance to discuss your personal future goals, while others require you to think on your feet and explain how you would respond in hypothetical situations.

1. Where do you expect to be five (or ten) years from now?

   Formulate a realistic plan with respect to your present age and situation. The important thing is to be prepared for this question. Show an interest in the current job and in making a contribution to the organization. Talk about the levels of responsibility you would like to achieve. One employment counsellor suggests showing ambition but not committing to a specific job title. Suggest that you hope to learn enough to have progressed to a position in which you will continue to grow. Keep your answer focused on educational and professional goals, not personal goals.

Strive to convert discussion of your weaknesses to topics that show your strengths.

2. If you got this position, what would you do to be sure you fit in?
3. This is a large (or small) organization. Do you think you would like that environment?
4. Do you plan to continue your education?
5. What do you predict for the future of the ______ industry?
6. How do you think you can contribute to this company?
7. What would you most like to accomplish if you get this position?
8. How do you keep current with what is happening in your profession?

CHALLENGING QUESTIONS. The following questions may make you uncomfortable, but the important thing to remember is to answer truthfully without dwelling on your weaknesses. As quickly as possible, convert any negative response into a discussion of your strengths.

1. What are your greatest weaknesses?

   It's amazing how many candidates knock themselves out of the competition by answering this question poorly. Actually, you have many choices. You can present a strength as a weakness (*Some people complain that I'm a workaholic or too attentive to details*). You can mention a corrected weakness (*I found that I really needed to learn about the Internet, so I took a course*). You can cite an unrelated skill (*I really need to brush up on my French*). You can cite a learning objective (*One of my long-term goals is to learn more about international management. Does your company have any plans to expand overseas?*). Another possibility is to reaffirm your qualifications (*I have no weaknesses that affect my ability to do this job*). Be careful that your answer doesn't sound like a cliché (*I tend to be a perfectionist*) and instead shows careful analysis of your abilities.

2. What type of people do you have little patience for?
3. If you could live your life over, what would you change and why?
4. How would your former (or current) supervisor describe you as an employee?
5. What do you want the most from your job?
6. What is your grade point average, and does it accurately reflect your abilities?
7. Who in your life has influenced you the most and why?
8. What are you reading right now?
9. Describe your ideal work environment.
10. Is the customer always right?
11. How do you define success?

SITUATIONAL QUESTIONS. Questions related to situations help employers test your thought processes and logical thinking. When using situational questions, interviewers describe a hypothetical situation and ask how you would handle it.

Situational questions differ based on the type of position for which you are interviewing. Knowledge of the position and the company culture will help you respond favourably to these questions. Even if the situation sounds negative, keep your response positive. Here are just a few examples:

1. You receive a call from an irate customer who complains about the service she received last night at your restaurant. She is demanding her money back. How would you handle the situation?

   When answering situational questions, it's always a good idea to tie your answer to a real experience from your past. You could say, for example, that you experienced a similar situation in one of your retail positions, and then explain the similarity. Tell the interviewer that you learned to first agree with the complaining customer in order to validate her complaint. Your next step would be to remedy the complaint, which does not necessarily mean giving the complaining customer what she is asking for. For example, in this case, based on restaurant policy, you could say politely that while you cannot refund her money, you can offer a two-for-one coupon valid for a year and a promise that service will be exemplary next time.

2. If you were aware that a coworker was falsifying data, what would you do?
3. Your manager has just told you that she is dissatisfied with your work, but you think it is acceptable. How would you resolve the conflict?
4. Your manager has told you to do something a certain way, and you think that way is wrong and that you know a far better way to complete the task. What would you do?
5. Assume that you are hired for this position. You soon learn that one of the staff is extremely resentful because she applied for your position and was turned down. As a result, she is being unhelpful and obstructive. How would you handle the situation?
6. A colleague has told you in confidence that she suspects another colleague of stealing. What would your actions be?
7. You have noticed that communication between upper management and entry-level employees is eroding. How would you solve this problem?

Employers find that situational and behavioural interview questions give them useful information about job candidates.

BEHAVIOURAL QUESTIONS. Instead of traditional interview questions, you may be asked to tell stories. The interviewer may say, *Describe a time when ...* or *Tell me about a situation in which....* To respond effectively, learn to use the storytelling or STAR technique. Ask yourself, what the Situation or Task was, what Action you took, and what the Results were.[15] Practise using this method, illustrated in Figure 13.3, to recall specific examples of your skills and accomplishments. To be fully prepared, develop a coherent and articulate STAR narrative for every bullet point on your résumé. When answering behavioural questions, describe only educational and work-related situations or tasks, and try to keep them as current as possible. Here are a few examples of behavioural questions:

1. Tell me about a time when you solved a difficult problem.

   Tell a concise story explaining the situation or task, what you did, and the result. For example, When I was at Ace Products, we continually had a problem of excessive back orders. After analyzing the situation, I discovered that orders went through many unnecessary steps. I suggested that we eliminate much of the paperwork. As a result, we reduced back orders by 30 percent. Go on to emphasize what you learned and how you can apply that learning to this job. Practise your success stories in advance so that you will be ready.

2. Describe a situation in which you were able to use persuasion to successfully convince someone to see things your way.

FIGURE 13.3 | STAR Technique for Answering Behavioural Interview Questions

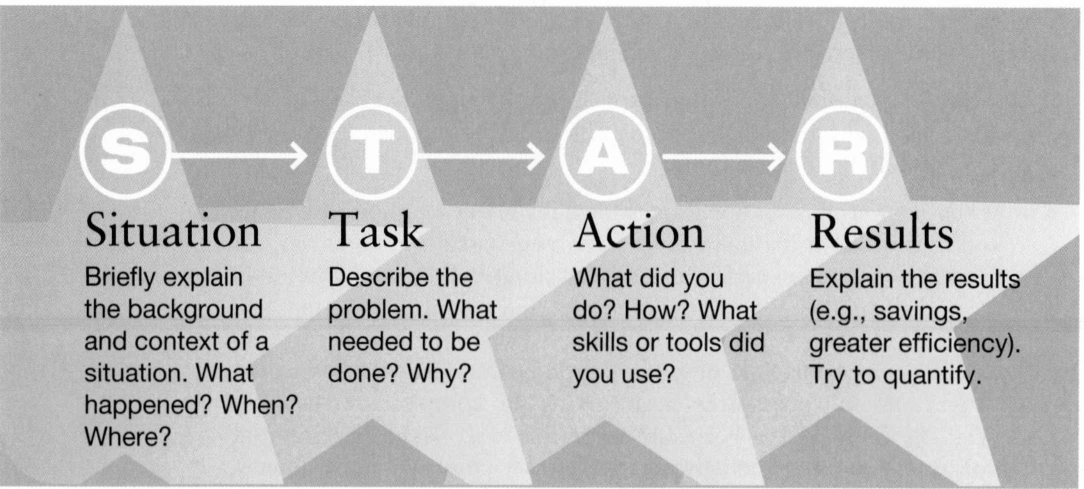

You may respond to an illegal question by asking tactfully how it relates to the responsibilities of the position.

3. Describe a time when you had to analyze information and make a recommendation.
4. Describe a time that you worked successfully as part of a team.
5. Tell me about a time you dealt with confidential information.
6. Give me an example of a time when you were under stress to meet a deadline.
7. Tell me about a time when you had to go above and beyond the call of duty in order to get a job done.
8. Tell me about a time you were able to successfully deal with another person even when that person may not have personally liked you (or vice versa).
9. Give me an example of an occasion when you showed initiative and took the lead.
10. Tell me about a recent situation in which you had to deal with an upset customer or coworker.

ILLEGAL AND INAPPROPRIATE QUESTIONS. Because human rights legislation protects job applicants from discrimination, interviewers may not ask questions such as those in the following list. Nevertheless, you may face an inexperienced or unscrupulous interviewer who does ask some of these questions. How should you react? If you find the question harmless and if you want the job, go ahead and answer. If you think that answering would damage your chance to be hired, try to deflect the question tactfully with a response such as *Could you tell me how my marital status relates to the responsibilities of this position?* Or you could use the opportunity to further emphasize your strengths. An older worker responding to a question about age might mention experience, fitness, knowledge, maturity, stability, or extensive business contacts. You might also wish to reconsider working for an organization that sanctions such procedures.

Here are some illegal or inappropriate questions that you may or may not want to answer:

1. Are you married, divorced, separated, single, or living common-law?
2. Is your spouse subject to transfer in his/her job? Tell me about your spouse's job.
3. What is your corrected vision? (But it is legal to ask about quality of vision if visual acuity is directly related to safety or some other factor of the job.)
4. Do you have any disabilities? Do you drink or take drugs? Have you ever received psychiatric care or been hospitalized for emotional problems? Have you ever received workers' compensation? (But it is legal to ask if you have any

condition that could affect your ability to do the job or if you have any condition that should be considered during selection.)

5. Have you ever been arrested? Have you ever been convicted of a crime? Do you have a criminal record? (But if bonding is a requirement of the job, it is legal to ask if you are eligible.)
6. How old are you? What is your date of birth? Can I see your birth certificate? (But it is legal to ask *Are you eligible to work under Canadian laws pertaining to age restrictions?*)
7. In what other countries do you have a current address? (But it is legal to ask *What is your current address, and how long have you lived there?*)
8. What is your maiden name? (But it is legal to ask *What is your full name?*)
9. What is your religion? How often do you attend religious services? Would you work on a specific religious holiday? Can you provide a reference from a clergyperson or religious leader?
10. Do you have children? What are your childcare arrangements? (But it is legal to ask *Can you work the required hours?* and *Are you available for overtime?*)
11. Where were you born? Were you born in Canada? Can you provide proof of citizenship? (But it is legal to ask *Are you legally entitled to work in Canada?*)
12. Were you involved in military service in another country? (But it is legal to ask about Canadian military service.)
13. What is your first language? Where did you receive your language training? (But it is legal to ask if you understand, read, write, and/or speak the language[s] required for the job.)
14. How much do you weigh? How tall are you?
15. What is your sexual orientation?
16. Are you under medical care? Who is your family doctor? Are you receiving therapy or counselling? (But it is legal to make offers of employment conditional on successful completion of a medical exam that is relevant to that job.)

13.3c Ask Your Own Questions

At some point in the interview, you will be asked if you have any questions. The worst thing you can say is no. Instead, ask questions that will help you gain information and will impress the interviewer with your thoughtfulness and interest in the position. Remember that the interview is an opportunity for you to see how you would fit with the company. Use this opportunity to find out whether this job is right for you. Be aware that you don't have to wait for the interviewer to ask you for questions. You can ask your own questions throughout the interview to learn more about the company and position. Here are some questions you might ask:

Your questions should impress the interviewer but also draw out valuable information about the job.

1. What will my duties be (if not already discussed)?
2. Tell me what it's like working here in terms of the people, management practices, workloads, expected performance, and rewards.
3. What training programs are available from this organization? What specific training will be given for this position?
4. Who would be my immediate supervisor?
5. What is the organizational structure, and where does this position fit in?
6. Is travel required in this position?
7. How is job performance evaluated?
8. Assuming my work is excellent, where do you see me in five years?
9. How long do employees generally stay with this organization?
10. What are the major challenges for a person in this position?
11. What do you see in the future for this organization?
12. What do employees say they like best about working for this organization?
13. May I have a tour of the facilities?
14. When do you expect to make a decision?

Do not ask about salary or benefits, especially during the first interview. It is best to let the interviewer bring those topics up first.

13.3d End Positively

After you've asked your questions, the interviewer will signal the end of the interview, usually by standing up or by expressing appreciation that you came. If not addressed earlier, you should at this time find out what action will follow. Demonstrate your interest in the position by asking when it will be filled or what the next step will be. Too many candidates leave the interview without knowing their status or when they will hear from the recruiter. Don't be afraid to say that you want the job!

Before you leave, summarize your strongest qualifications, show enthusiasm for obtaining this position, and thank the interviewer for a constructive interview and for considering you for the position. Ask the interviewer for a business card, which will provide the information you need to write a thank-you letter, which is discussed below. Shake the interviewer's hand with confidence, and acknowledge anyone else you see on the way out. Be sure to thank the receptionist if there is one. Leaving the interview gracefully and enthusiastically will leave a lasting impression on those responsible for making the final hiring decision.

13.4 After the Interview

End the interview by thanking the interviewer, reviewing your strengths for this position, and asking what action will follow.

A follow-up thank-you message shows your good manners and your enthusiasm for the job.

After leaving the interview, immediately write down key points that were discussed, the names of people you spoke with, and other details in case you are called back for a second interview. Write down key points that were discussed and the names of people you spoke with. Ask yourself what went really well and what could have been improved. Note your strengths and weaknesses during the interview so that you can work to improve in future interviews. Next, write down your follow-up plans. To whom should you send thank-you messages? Will you contact the employer by phone? If so, when? Then be sure to follow up on those plans, beginning with writing a thank-you message and contacting your references.

13.4a Thank Your Interviewer

After a job interview you should always send a thank-you message, also called a follow-up message. This courtesy sets you apart from other applicants, some of whom will not bother. Your message also reminds the interviewer of your visit as well as suggesting your good manners and genuine enthusiasm for the job.

Follow-up messages are most effective if sent immediately after the interview. Experts believe that a thoughtful follow-up note carries as much weight as the cover letter does. Almost nine out of ten senior executives admit that in their evaluation of a job candidate they are swayed by a written thank you.[16] In your thank-you message refer to the date of the interview, the exact job title for which you were interviewed, and the specific topics discussed. Don't get carried away after a successful interview and send a poorly planned thank-you email that reads like a text message or sounds too chummy. Smart interviewees don't ruin their chances by communicating with recruiters in hasty text messages.

In addition to being respectful when following up after an interview, try to avoid worn-out phrases, such as *Thank you for taking the time to interview me.* There are better ways of expressing the same idea. Try *Today's interview was enjoyable; thank you for the opportunity.* Be careful, too, about overusing *I*, especially to begin sentences. Most important, show that you really want the job and that you are qualified for it. Notice how the thank-you email in Figure 13.4 conveys both enthusiasm and confidence.

If you have been interviewed by more than one person, send a separate message to the two most important people in the room (e.g., hiring manager; human resources recruiter). These days most follow-up messages are sent by email, so make sure to get the correct addresses before you leave the interview. One job candidate summarizes her method for sending follow-up emails in this way: thank the employer for the interview opportunity, very briefly summarize what was discussed during the face-to-face interview, and add a bit of information you didn't get to mention during the interview.[17]

13.4b Contact Your References

Once you've thanked your interviewer, it's time to alert your references that they may be contacted by the employer. You might also have to request a letter of recommendation to be sent to the employer by a certain date. As discussed earlier, you should already have asked permission to use these individuals as references, and you should have supplied them with a copy of your résumé and information about the types of positions you are seeking.

FIGURE 13.4 | Interview Follow-Up Email

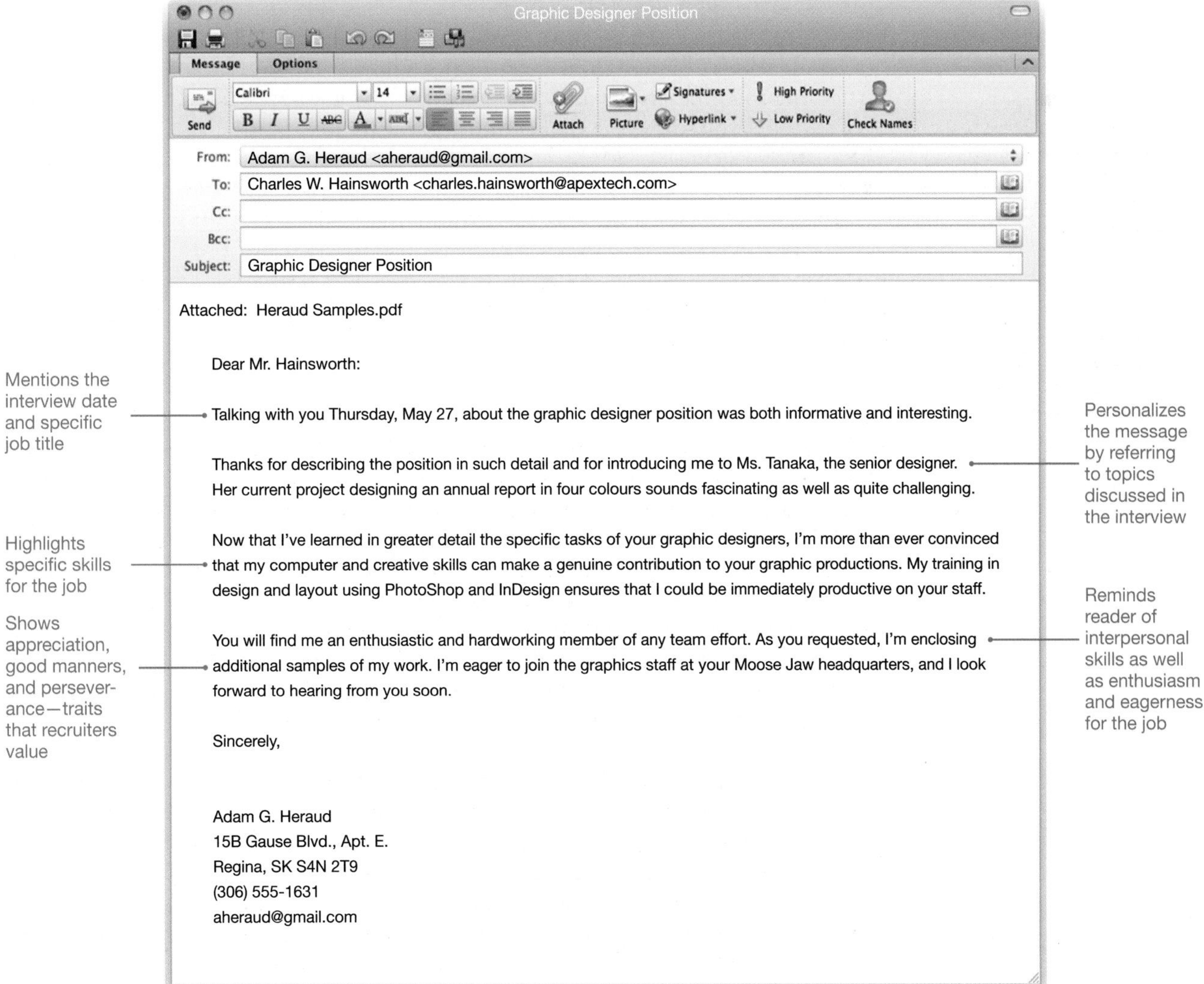

In a reference request message, explain immediately why you are writing. Identify the target position and company.

Specify the job requirements so that the recommender knows what to stress.

To provide the best possible recommendation, your references need information. What position have you applied for and with what company? What should they stress to the prospective employer? Let's say you are applying for a specific job that requires a letter of recommendation. Professor Orenstein has already agreed to be a reference for you. To get the best letter of recommendation from Professor Orenstein, help her out. Send her an email telling her about the position, its requirements, and the recommendation deadline. Attach a copy of your résumé. You might remind her of a positive experience with you that she could use in the recommendation. Remember that recommenders need evidence to support generalizations, as the student has provided in the following request:

> Dear Professor Orenstein:
>
> Recently I interviewed for the position of administrative assistant in the Human Resources Department of Host International. Because you kindly agreed to help me, I'd like to ask you to be available by phone to provide a recommendation to Host.
>
> The position calls for good organizational, interpersonal, and writing skills, as well as computer experience. To help you review my skills and training, I enclose my résumé. As you may recall, I earned an A in your business communication class last fall; and you commended my research report for its clarity and organization.
>
> You can expect to hear from James Jenkins at Host International (jjenkins@hinternational.com) before July 1. He said he'd call in the morning before 10 a.m. I'm grateful for your support, and I promise to let you know the results of my job search.

13.4c Follow Up

If you don't hear from the interviewer within five days, consider following up. The standard advice to job candidates is to call to follow up a few days after the interview. However, some experts suggest that cold calling a hiring manager is fraught with risk. You may be putting a busy recruiter on the spot and forcing him or her to search for your application. In addition, remember that you are not the only candidate; multiply your phone call by the 200 applicants whom some hiring managers interview.[18] Therefore, you don't want to be a pest. Sending an email to find out how the decision process is going may be best because such a message is much less intrusive.

However, if you believe it is safe to follow up by phone, or if the recruiter suggested it, practise saying something like, *I'm wondering what else I can do to convince you that I'm the right person for this job*, or *I'm calling to find out the status of your search for the ___________ position*. When following up, it's important to sound professional and courteous. Sounding desperate, angry, or frustrated because you have not been contacted can ruin your chances. The following follow-up email would impress the interviewer:

> Dear Ms. Kahn:
>
> I enjoyed my interview with you last Thursday for the receptionist position. You should know that I'm very interested in this opportunity with Coastal Enterprises. Because you mentioned that you might have an answer this week, I'm eager to know how your decision process is coming along. I look forward to hearing from you.
>
> Sincerely,

Depending on the response you get to your first follow-up request, you may have to follow up additional times. Keep in mind, though, that some employers won't tell you about their hiring decision unless you are the one hired. Don't harass the interviewer, and don't force a decision. If you don't hear back from an employer within several weeks after following up, it is best to assume that you didn't get the job and to continue with your job search.

A follow-up message inquires courteously and does not sound angry or desperate.

13.5 Other Employment Documents

Although the résumé and cover letter are your major tasks, other important documents and messages are often required during the employment process. Because each of these tasks reveals something about you and your communication skills, you will want to put your best foot forward. These documents often subtly influence company officials to offer a job.

13.5a Application Form

Some organizations require job candidates to fill out job application forms instead of, or in addition to, submitting résumés. This practice lets them gather and store standardized data about each applicant. Whether the application is on paper or online, follow the directions carefully and provide accurate information. The following suggestions can help you be prepared:

- Put your résumé on your smartphone. If you don't have a smartphone, carry a card that has some basic information written on it, such as graduation dates; beginning and ending dates of all employment; salary history; full names, titles, and present work addresses of former supervisors; full addresses and phone numbers of current and previous employers; and full names, occupational titles, occupational addresses, and telephone numbers of persons who have agreed to serve as references.
- Look over all the questions before starting.
- Fill out the form neatly, using blue or black ink. Career counsellors recommend printing your responses.
- Answer all questions honestly. Write *Not applicable* or *N/A* if appropriate.
- Use accurate spelling, grammar, and punctuation.
- If asked for the position desired, give a specific job title or type of position. Don't say, *Anything* or *Open*. These answers will make you look unfocused; moreover, they make it difficult for employers to know what you are qualified for or interested in.
- Be prepared for a salary question. Unless you know what comparable employees are earning in the company, the best strategy is to suggest a salary range or to write *Negotiable* or *Open*. See the Communication Workshop in the MindTap for tips on dealing with money matters while interviewing.
- Be prepared to explain the reasons for leaving previous positions. Use positive or neutral phrases such as *Relocation, Seasonal, To accept a position with more responsibility, Temporary position, To continue education,* or *Career change*. Avoid words or phrases such as *Fired, Quit, Didn't get along with supervisor,* or *Pregnancy*.
- Look over the application before submitting to make sure it is complete and that you have followed all instructions. Sign and date the application.

13.5b Application or Résumé Follow-Up Message

If your résumé or application generates no response within a reasonable time, you may decide to send a short follow-up email such as the following. Doing so (a) jogs the memory of the human resources staff, (b) demonstrates your serious interest, and (c) allows you to emphasize your qualifications or to add new information.

Open follow-up messages by reminding the reader of your interest.

Review your strengths or add new qualifications in follow-up messages.

Dear Ms. Lavecchia:

Please know I am still interested in becoming an administrative support specialist with Quad, Inc.

Since submitting my application [or résumé] in May, I have completed my degree and have been employed as a summer replacement for office workers in several downtown offices. This experience has honed my communication and project management skills. It has also introduced me to a wide range of office procedures.

Please keep my application in your active file and let me know when I may put my formal training, technical skills, and practical experience to work for you.

Sincerely,

13.5c Rejection Follow-Up Message

Refer to specifics of your interview in your follow-up message.

In follow-up messages take the initiative by saying when you will call for an update.

Confirm your acceptance of the position with enthusiasm.

If you didn't get the job and you think it was perfect for you, don't give up. Employment specialists encourage applicants to respond to a rejection. The candidate who was offered the position may decline, or other positions may open up. In a rejection follow-up email, it is okay to admit you are disappointed. Be sure to add, however, that you are still interested and will contact the company again in a month in case a job opens up. Then follow through for a couple of months—but don't overdo it. You should be professional and persistent, but not a pest. Here's an example of an effective rejection follow-up message:

Dear Mr. O'Neal:

Although I'm disappointed that someone else was selected for your accounting position, I appreciate your promptness and courtesy in notifying me.

Because I firmly believe that I have the technical and interpersonal skills needed to work in your fast-paced environment, I hope you will keep my résumé in your active file. My desire to become a productive member of Deloitte staff remains strong.

I enjoyed our interview, and I especially appreciate the time you and Ms. Goldstein spent describing your company's presence in international markets. To enhance my qualifications, I have enrolled in a CFA program.

If you have an opening for which I am qualified, please reach me at (519) 555-3901. In the meantime, I will call you in a month to discuss employment possibilities.

Sincerely,

13.5d Job Acceptance and Rejection Messages

Job acceptance messages should review salary and benefits details.

You will eventually be offered a position you want. Although you will likely accept the position over the phone, it is a good idea to follow up with an acceptance email to confirm the details and to formalize the acceptance. Your acceptance message might look like this:

Dear Ms. Madhumali:

Include the specific starting date before closing job acceptance messages.

It was a pleasure talking with you earlier today. As I mentioned, I am delighted to accept the position of Web designer with Innovative Creations, Inc., in your Richmond office. I look forward to becoming part of the IC team and to starting work on a variety of exciting and innovative projects.

As we agreed, my starting salary will be $76,000, with a benefits package including health and life insurance, retirement plan, stock options, and three weeks of vacation per year.

I look forward to starting my position with Innovative Creations on September 15, 2019. Before that date I will send you the completed tax and insurance forms you need. Thanks again for everything, Ms. Madhumali.

Sincerely,

If you must turn down a job offer, show your professionalism by writing a sincere email. This message should thank the employer for the job offer and explain briefly that you are turning it down. Taking the time to extend this courtesy could help you in the future if this employer has a position you really want. Here's an example of a job rejection message:

In a job rejection message thank the employer for the job offer and decline the offer without giving specifics. Express gratitude and best wishes for the future.

Dear Mr. Opperman:

Thank you very much for offering me the position of sales representative with Bendall Pharmaceuticals. It was a difficult decision to make, but I have accepted a position with another company.

I appreciate your taking the time to interview me, and I wish Bendall much success in the future.

Sincerely,

13.5e Resignation Letter

After you have been in a position for a period of time, you may find it necessary to leave. Perhaps you have been offered a better position, or maybe you have decided to return to school full-time. Whatever the reason, you should leave your position gracefully and tactfully. Although you will likely discuss your resignation in person with your supervisor, it is a good idea to document your resignation by writing a formal letter. Some resignation letters are brief, while others contain great detail. Remember that many resignation letters are placed in human resources files; therefore, it should be formatted and written using the professional business letter-writing techniques you learned earlier. Here is an example of the body of a basic letter of resignation:

Confirm the exact date of resignation in your letter. Remind employer of your contributions.

In your resignation letter offer assistance to prepare for your resignation. End with thanks and a forward-looking statement.

Dear Ms. Patrick:

This letter serves as formal notice of my resignation from Allied Corporation, effective Friday, August 15. I have enjoyed working as your office assistant for the past two years, and I am grateful for everything I have learned during my employment with Allied.

Please let me know what I can do over the next two weeks to help you prepare for my departure. I would be happy to help with finding and training my replacement.

Thanks again for providing such a positive employment experience.

Sincerely,

Although this employee gave a standard two-week notice, a longer notice may be necessary. The higher and more responsible your position (and depending on the contract you might have signed), the longer the notice you must give your employer.

Writing job acceptance, job rejection, and resignation messages requires effort. That effort is worth it because you are building bridges that later may carry you to even better jobs in the future.

SUMMARY OF LEARNING OBJECTIVES

13.1 Explain the purposes and types of job interviews.

- An interviewer wants to (a) find out whether your skills are right for the job, (b) discuss your abilities in detail, (c) probe for motivation, and (d) see whether you would fit into the organization.
- An interviewee has a chance to (a) show potential, (b) learn about the job and company, and (c) elaborate on the information in the résumé.
- Screening interviews help companies weed out lesser-qualified candidates before scheduling face-to-face hiring/placement interviews with the most promising applicants.
- Hiring interviews include one-on-one, panel, group, sequential, stress, and online or virtual interviews.

13.2 Describe what to do before an interview to make an impressive initial contact.

- Aim to make a good first impression on the phone by being polite and enthusiastic, recording a professional voice mail greeting, and alerting any housemates that a potential employer may call.
- Research the company on the Web, analyze its advertising and media presence, and try to locate insider information; then prepare by rehearsing success stories and cleaning up any digital dirt.
- Allow plenty of time for travelling to the interview; greet the interviewer politely and be pleasant.
- Fight fear by preparing thoroughly and dressing professionally; remember to breathe.

13.3 Describe what to do during an interview to create a favourable impression.

- Be aware of your body language, exhibit good posture, maintain eye contact, use gestures effectively, listen, smile, turn off your cell phone, don't chew gum, use proper speech, and be confident.
- Aim your answers at the key characteristics interviewers seek; focus on your strengths.
- Expect questions designed to get acquainted, gauge your interest, determine your accomplishments, probe for future plans, and challenge you; anticipate situational, behavioural, and inappropriate questions.
- Demonstrate interest by asking your own questions; end positively and say goodbye graciously.

13.4 Describe what to do immediately after an interview to maintain the positive impression you've created.

- Send a thank-you note, email, or letter immediately after the interview to each interviewer, but do not text message; reiterate your interest and qualifications, but avoid overused phrases.
- Alert your references to expect recruiter calls, and give them the appropriate information so they can support generalizations about you with specific evidence.
- A few days after the interview, follow up by email or by calling the recruiter, if you believe it's safe, but don't be a pest. If you call, be professional and courteous.

13.5 Prepare other employment-related documents.

- Follow-up messages reveal a lot about you and your communication skills; prepare each with care.
- To fill out application forms neatly and accurately, carry records summarizing your vital statistics.
- In an application or résumé follow-up message, remind the recruiter of your application, demonstrate serious interest, and emphasize your qualifications.
- Even if you didn't get the job, write a follow-up email or letter; be persistent yet not annoying.
- When accepting a job, follow up in writing to confirm what was discussed; when declining an offer, be professional and sincere. Thank the interviewer and courteously turn down the position.
- If you decide to resign, write a graceful and tactful formal letter to document your decision.

CHAPTER REVIEW

1. Name the main purposes of interviews—for job candidates as well as for employers. (Obj. 1)
2. If you have sent out your résumé to many companies, what information should you keep handy and why? (Obj. 2)
3. Briefly describe the types of hiring/placement interviews you may encounter. (Obj. 1)
4. How can you address problem areas on your résumé such as lack of experience, getting fired, or earning low grades? (Obj. 3)
5. Name at least six interviewing behaviours you can exhibit that send positive nonverbal messages. (Obj. 3)
6. What is your greatest fear of what you might do or what might happen to you during an employment interview? How can you overcome your fears? (Obj. 3)
7. Should you be candid with an interviewer when asked about your weaknesses? (Obj. 3)
8. How can you clarify vague questions from recruiters? (Obj. 3)
9. How should you respond to questions you believe to be illegal? (Obj. 3)
10. List the steps you should take immediately following your job interview.(Obj. 4)
11. Explain the various kinds of follow-up employment messages. (Obj. 5)

CRITICAL THINKING

1. Online multiple-choice questionnaires are a hot trend in recruiting. Employers can ask how applicants would handle tricky situations, how happy they are, and how much they may have stolen from previous employers. Multiple-choice format makes it tricky for applicants to know whether to be truthful or to say what the prospective employer wants to hear. What's wrong with this type of "screening" activity? (Obj. 1)
2. Is it normal to be nervous about an employment interview? What can be done to overcome this fear? (Obj. 2)
3. What can you do to improve the first impression you make at an interview? (Obj. 2)
4. In employment interviews, do you think that behavioural questions (such as *Tell me about a business problem you have had and how you solved it*) are more effective than traditional questions (such as *Tell me what you are good at and why*)? (Obj. 3)
5. If you are asked an illegal interview question, why is it important to first assess the intentions of the interviewer? (Obj. 3)
6. Why is it important to ask one's own questions of the interviewer? (Obj. 3)
7. Why is it a smart strategy to thank an interviewer, to follow up, and even to send a rejection follow-up message? Are any risks associated with this strategy? (Obj. 4)

ACTIVITIES AND CASES

13.1 RESEARCHING AN ORGANIZATION (OBJ. 2)

Often graduates find employment through co-op placements or through family networks. However, it's equally possible to find employment by researching organizations with which you've had no contact.

Your Task. Select an organization where you would like to be employed. Assume you've been selected for an interview. Using resources described in this chapter, locate information about the organization's leaders and their business philosophy. Find out about the organization's accomplishments, setbacks, finances, products, customers, competition, and advertising. Prepare a summary report documenting your findings.

13.2 LEARNING WHAT JOBS ARE REALLY ABOUT THROUGH BLOGS, FACEBOOK, AND TWITTER (OBJ. 2)

Blogs and social media have become important tools in the employment search process. By accessing blogs and social media, job seekers can learn more about a company's culture and day-to-day activities.

Your Task. Using the Web, locate a blog that is maintained by an employee of a company where you would like to work. Monitor the blog for at least a week. Also, access the company's Facebook page and monitor its Twitter feeds for at least a week. Prepare a short report that summarizes what you learned about the company through reading the blog postings, status updates, and tweets. Include a statement of whether this information would be valuable during your job search.

13.3 BUILDING INTERVIEW SKILLS (OBJ. 2)

Successful interviews require diligent preparation and repeated practice. To be prepared, you need to know what skills are required for your targeted position. In addition to software and communication skills, employers generally want to know whether a candidate works well with a team, accepts responsibility, solves problems, is efficient, meets deadlines, shows leadership, saves time and money, and is a hard worker.

Your Task. Consider a position for which you are eligible now or one for which you will be eligible when you complete your education. Identify the skills and traits necessary for this position. If you prepared a résumé in Chapter 12, be sure that it addresses these targeted areas. Now prepare interview worksheets listing at least ten skills (both technical and other skills) or traits a recruiter will want to discuss in an interview for your targeted position, and provide examples of how you are proficient at these skills.

Visit **MindTap** for a variety of videos, additional exercises, activities, and quizzes to support your learning.

A Guide to Document Formats

Business communicators produce documents and messages that have standardized formats. Becoming familiar with these formats is important because documents and messages actually say two things about the writer. Meaning is conveyed by the words chosen to express the writer's ideas. A sense of trust and credibility is conveyed by the appearance of a document and its adherence to recognized formats.

To ensure that what you write and send out speaks favourably about you and your organization, you'll want to give special attention to the appearance and formatting of your emails, letters, envelopes, memos, and fax cover sheets. While we don't cover texts, social media posts, and instant messages in this appendix, as you learned earlier, these short messages should have a professional tone when sent at work, meaning they should not contain slang or other inappropriate language, they should be short and to the point, and they should deal with one issue at a time.

EMAILS

Email has been around now for about 20 years; as a result, certain formatting and usage norms have developed. The following suggestions, illustrated in Figure A.1 and also in Figure 5.2 on page 88, can guide you in setting up the parts of an email. Always check, however, with your organization so that you can observe its practices.

TO LINE. Type the receiver's email address after To. If replying to an email, your software will fill in the address once you click on Reply. If responding to someone you once were in touch with, you can either click Reply in an old saved email from that person, or type in the address once again.

CC AND BCC. Insert the email address of anyone who is to receive a copy of the message. Cc stands for *carbon copy* or *courtesy copy*. Don't be tempted, though, to send needless copies just because it's so easy. Some organizations develop an internal style in which anyone cc'd on an original email should be cc'd on the response. Other organizations ask employees to only cc when it's necessary. Check with your manager or experienced coworker.

Bcc stands for *blind carbon copy*. Some writers use bcc to send a copy of the message without the addressee's knowledge. Writers also use the bcc line for mailing lists. When a message is being sent to a number of people and their email addresses should not be revealed, the bcc line works well to conceal the names and addresses of all receivers.

SUBJECT. Identify the subject of the email with a brief but descriptive summary of the topic. Be sure to include enough information to be clear and compelling. Capitalize the initial letters of principal words.

SALUTATION. Include a brief greeting, if you like. Some writers use a salutation such as *Dear Selina* followed by a comma or a colon. Others are more informal with *Hi, Selina!* or *Good morning* or *Greetings*. Some writers simulate a salutation by including the name of the receiver in an abbreviated first line, as shown in Figure A.1. Others writers treat an email like a memo and skip the salutation

FIGURE A.1 | Effective Email

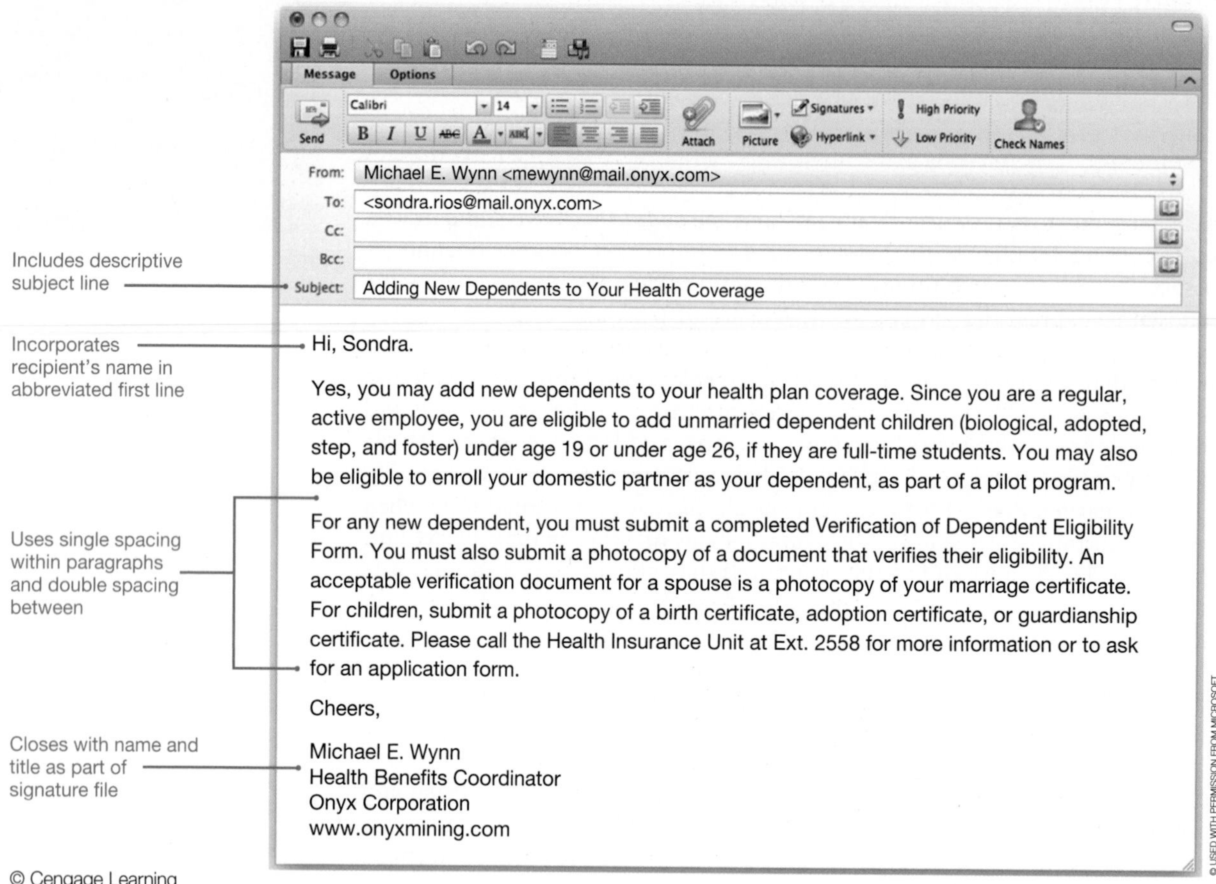

entirely or include only a brief salutation consisting of the recipient's name, such as *Dave*.

MESSAGE. Cover just one topic in your email, and try to keep your total message under one screen in length. Single space and be sure to use both upper- and lowercase letters. Double space between paragraphs, and use graphic highlighting (bullets, numbering) whenever you are listing three or more items.

CLOSING. Conclude your emails with a short expression such as *Cheers* or *Best wishes* or *Regards* followed by your name. If the recipient is unlikely to know you, it's not a bad idea to include your title and organization. In order not to have to type all this information with every email sent out, most professional email users prepare an email signature that includes name, title, and department/company name, and that can also be embellished with an electronic business card, hyperlink (e.g., to the company's website), and a picture. Use restraint, however, because email signatures take up precious space. Writers of email sent within organizations may omit a closing and even skip their names at the ends of messages because receivers will recognize them from their identification in the opening lines.

LETTERS

Business communicators write business letters primarily to correspond with people outside the organization. Letters may go to customers, vendors, other businesses, and the government, as discussed earlier in this book. The following information will help you format your letters following conventional guidelines.

Letter Parts

Professional-looking business letters are arranged in a conventional sequence with standard parts. Following is a discussion of how to use these letter parts properly. Figure A.2 illustrates the parts in a block-style letter.

LETTERHEAD. Most business organizations use 8.5-by-11-inch paper (215.9 by 279.4 millimetres) printed with a letterhead displaying their official name, street address, website address, email address, and telephone and fax numbers. The letterhead may also include a logo and an advertising tag line such as *Ebank: A new way to bank.*

DATELINE. On letterhead paper you should place the date two blank lines below the last line of the letterhead or 5 centimetres from the top edge of the paper (line 13). On plain paper, place the date immediately below your return address. Since the date goes on line 13, start the return address an appropriate number of lines above it. The most common dateline format is as follows: *June 9, 2018*. Don't use *th* (or *rd*) when the date is written this way. For European or military correspondence, use the following dateline format: *9 June 2018*. Notice that no commas are used.

ADDRESSEE AND DELIVERY NOTATIONS. Delivery notations such as *FAX TRANSMISSION, FEDERAL EXPRESS, MESSENGER DELIVERY, CONFIDENTIAL*, or *CERTIFIED MAIL* are typed in all capital letters two blank lines above the inside address.

INSIDE ADDRESS. Type the inside address—that is, the address of the organization or person receiving the letter—single-spaced, starting at the left margin. The number of lines between the dateline and the inside address depends on the size of the letter body, the type size (point or pitch size), and the length of the typing lines. Generally, two to ten lines is appropriate.

Be careful to duplicate the exact wording and spelling of the recipient's name and address on your documents. Usually you can copy this information from the letterhead of the correspondence you are answering. If, for example, you are responding to *Jackson & Perkins Company*, don't address your letter to *Jackson and Perkins Corp.*

Always be sure to include a courtesy title such as *Mr., Ms., Mrs., Dr.*, or *Professor* before a person's name in the inside address—for both the letter and the envelope. Although many women in business today favour *Ms.*, you'll want to use whatever title the addressee prefers.

In general, avoid abbreviations (such as *Ave.* or *Co.*) unless they appear in the printed letterhead of the document being answered.

ATTENTION LINE. An attention line allows you to send your message officially to an organization but to direct it to a specific individual, officer, or department. However, if you know an individual's complete name, it's always better to use it as the first line of the inside address and avoid an attention line. Here are two common formats for attention lines:

MultiMedia Enterprises
931 Calkins Avenue
Toronto, ON M3W 1E6

Attention Marketing Director

MultiMedia Enterprises
Attention: Marketing Director
931 Calkins Road
Toronto, ON M3W 1E6

Attention lines may be typed in all caps or with upper- and lowercase letters. The colon following *Attention* is optional. Notice that an attention line may be placed two lines below the address block or printed as the second line of the inside address. You'll want to use the latter format if you're composing on a word processor, because the address block may be copied to the envelope and the attention line will not interfere with the last-line placement of the postal code. (Mail can be sorted more easily if the postal code appears in the last line of a typed address.)

FIGURE A.2 | Block and Modified Block Letter Styles

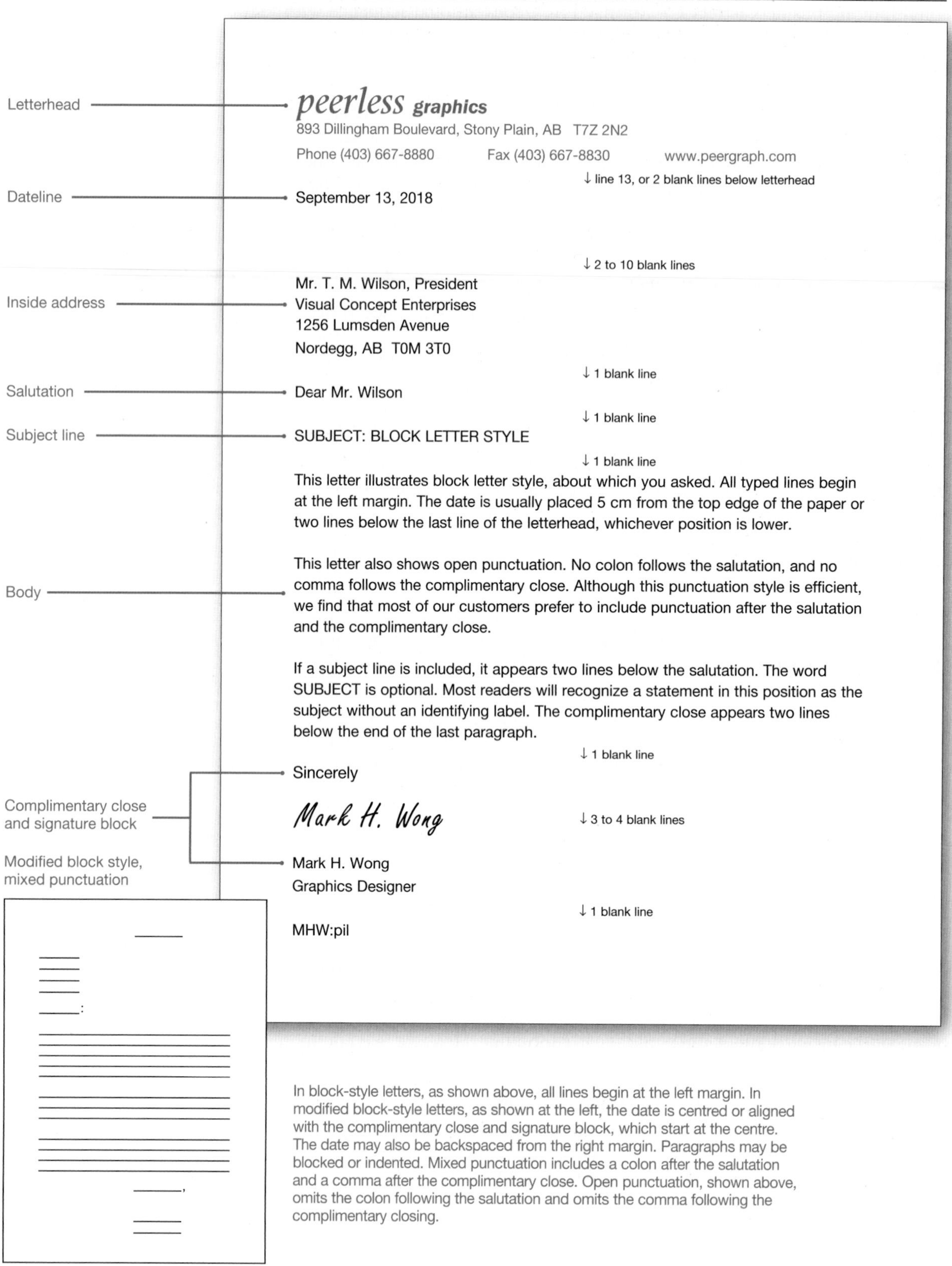

peerless graphics
893 Dillingham Boulevard, Stony Plain, AB T7Z 2N2
Phone (403) 667-8880 Fax (403) 667-8830 www.peergraph.com

September 13, 2018

Mr. T. M. Wilson, President
Visual Concept Enterprises
1256 Lumsden Avenue
Nordegg, AB T0M 3T0

Dear Mr. Wilson

SUBJECT: BLOCK LETTER STYLE

This letter illustrates block letter style, about which you asked. All typed lines begin at the left margin. The date is usually placed 5 cm from the top edge of the paper or two lines below the last line of the letterhead, whichever position is lower.

This letter also shows open punctuation. No colon follows the salutation, and no comma follows the complimentary close. Although this punctuation style is efficient, we find that most of our customers prefer to include punctuation after the salutation and the complimentary close.

If a subject line is included, it appears two lines below the salutation. The word SUBJECT is optional. Most readers will recognize a statement in this position as the subject without an identifying label. The complimentary close appears two lines below the end of the last paragraph.

Sincerely

Mark H. Wong

Mark H. Wong
Graphics Designer

MHW:pil

In block-style letters, as shown above, all lines begin at the left margin. In modified block-style letters, as shown at the left, the date is centred or aligned with the complimentary close and signature block, which start at the centre. The date may also be backspaced from the right margin. Paragraphs may be blocked or indented. Mixed punctuation includes a colon after the salutation and a comma after the complimentary close. Open punctuation, shown above, omits the colon following the salutation and omits the comma following the complimentary closing.

SALUTATION. Place the letter greeting, or salutation, two lines below the last line of the inside address or the attention line (if used). If the letter is addressed to an individual, use that person's courtesy title and last name (*Dear Mr. Lanham*).

Even if you are on a first-name basis (*Dear Leslie*), be sure to add a colon (not a comma or a semicolon) after the salutation, unless you are using open punctuation. Do not use an individual's full name in the salutation (not *Dear Mr. Leslie Lanham*) unless you are unsure of gender (*Dear Leslie Lanham*).

SUBJECT AND REFERENCE LINES. Although traditionally the subject line is placed one blank line below the salutation, many businesses actually place it above the salutation. Use whatever style your organization prefers. Reference lines often show policy or file numbers; they generally appear two lines above the salutation.

BODY. Most business letters and memos are single-spaced, with double line spacing between paragraphs. Very short messages may be double-spaced with indented paragraphs.

COMPLIMENTARY CLOSE. Typed two lines below the last line of the letter, the complimentary close may be formal (*Yours truly*) or informal (*Sincerely* or *Respectfully*). The simplified letter style omits a complimentary close.

SIGNATURE BLOCK. In most letter styles, the writer's typed name and optional identification appear three to four blank lines below the complimentary close. The combination of name, title, and organization information should be arranged to achieve a balanced look. The name and title may appear on the same line or on separate lines, depending on the length of each. Use commas to separate categories within the same line, but not to conclude a line.

Sincerely,

Jeremy M. Wood

Jeremy M. Wood, Manager
Technical Sales and Services

Respectfully,

Casandra Baker-Murillo

Casandra Baker-Murillo
Executive Vice President

Some organizations include their names in the signature block. In such cases the organization name appears in all caps two lines below the complimentary close, as shown here:

Sincerely,
LITTON COMPUTER SERVICES

Shelina A. Simpson

Ms. Shelina A. Simpson
Executive Assistant

REFERENCE INITIALS. If used, the initials of the typist and writer are typed two lines below the writer's name and title. Generally, the writer's initials are capitalized and the typist's are lowercased, but this format varies.

ENCLOSURE NOTATION. When an enclosure or attachment accompanies a document, a notation to that effect appears two lines below the reference initials. This notation reminds the typist to insert the enclosure in the envelope, and it reminds the recipient to look for the enclosure or attachment. The notation may be spelled out (*Enclosure, Attachment*), or it may be abbreviated (*Enc., Att.*). It may indicate the number of enclosures or attachments, and it may also identify a specific enclosure (*Enclosure: Form 1099*).

COPY NOTATION. If you make copies of correspondence for other individuals, you may use cc to indicate carbon copy, pc to indicate photocopy, or merely c for any kind of copy. A colon following the initial(s) is optional.

SECOND-PAGE HEADING. When a letter extends beyond one page, use plain paper of the same quality and colour as the first page. Identify the second and succeeding pages with a heading consisting of the name of the addressee, the page number, and the date. Use either of the following two formats:

Ms. Rachel Ruiz 2 May 3, 2012

Ms. Rachel Ruiz
Page 2
May 3, 2012

Both headings appear on line 7, followed by two blank lines to separate them from the continuing text. Avoid using a second page if you have only one line or the complimentary close and signature block to fill that page.

PLAIN-PAPER RETURN ADDRESS. If you prepare a personal or business letter on plain paper, place your address immediately above the date. Do not include your name; you will type (and sign) your name at the end of your letter. If your return address contains two lines, begin typing it on line 11 so that the date appears on line 13. Avoid abbreviations other than the two-letter province/territory abbreviation.

580 East Leffels Street
Dartmouth, NS B6R 2F3
December 14, 2012

Ms. Ellen Siemens
Retail Credit Department
Union National Bank
1220 Dunsfield Boulevard
Halifax, NS B4L 2E2

Dear Ms. Siemens:

For letters prepared in the block style, type the return address at the left margin. For modified block-style letters, start the return address at the centre to align with the complimentary close.

Letter and Punctuation Styles

Business letters are generally prepared in either block or modified block style, and they generally use mixed punctuation.

BLOCK STYLE. In the block style, shown in Figure A.2, all lines begin at the left margin. This style is a favourite because it is easy to format.

MODIFIED BLOCK STYLE. The modified block style differs from block style in that the date and closing lines appear in the centre, as shown at the bottom of Figure A.2. The date may be (1) centred, (2) begun at the centre of the page (to align with the closing lines), or (3) backspaced from the right margin. The signature block—including the complimentary close, writer's name and title, or organization identification—begins at the centre. The first line of each paragraph may begin at the left margin or may be indented five or ten spaces. All other lines begin at the left margin.

Most businesses today use mixed punctuation, shown with the modified block-style letter at the bottom left of Figure A.2. This style requires a colon after the salutation and a comma after the complimentary close. Even when the salutation is a first name, the colon is appropriate.

ENVELOPES

An envelope should be of the same quality and colour of stationery as the letter it carries. Because the envelope introduces your message and makes the first impression, you need to be especially careful in addressing it. Moreover, how you fold the letter is important.

RETURN ADDRESS. The return address is usually printed in the upper left corner of an envelope, as shown in Figure A.3. In large companies some form of identification (the writer's initials, name, or location) may be typed or handwritten above the company name and return address. This identification helps return the letter to the sender in case of nondelivery.

On an envelope without a printed return address, single space the return address in the upper left corner. Beginning on line 3 on the fourth space (approximately 12 millimetres or 0.5 inch) from the left edge, type the writer's name, title, company, and mailing address.

MAILING ADDRESS. On legal-sized No. 10 envelopes (10.5 by 24 centimetres), begin the address on line 13 about 11.5 centimetres from the left edge, as shown in Figure A.3. For small envelopes (7.5 by 15 centimetres), begin typing on line 12 about 6.2 centimetres from the left edge.

Canada Post recommends that addresses be typed in all caps without any punctuation. This postal service style, shown in the small envelope in Figure A.3, was

FIGURE A.3 | Envelope Formats

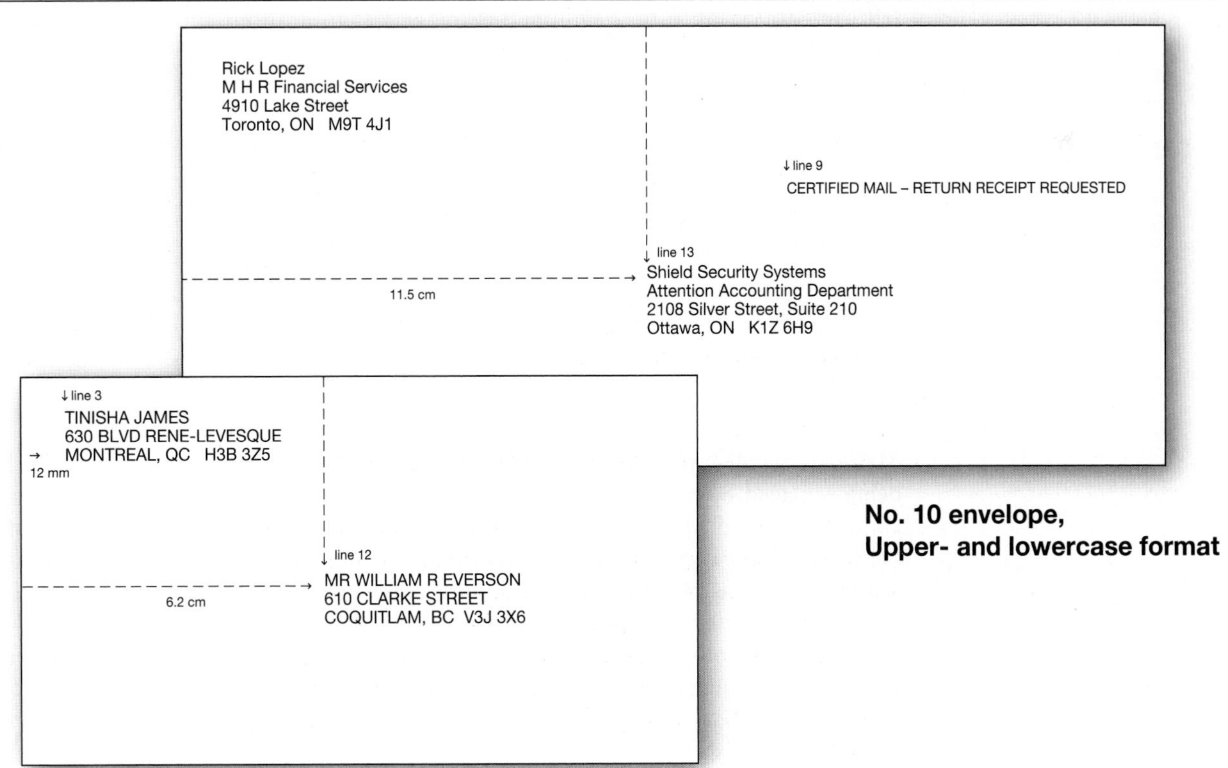

No. 10 envelope, Upper- and lowercase format

No. 6¾ envelope, uppercase format

originally developed to facilitate scanning by optical character readers (OCRs). Today's OCRs, however, are so sophisticated that they scan upper- and lowercase letters easily. Many companies today prefer to use the same format for the envelope as for the inside address. If the same format is used, writers can take advantage of word processing programs to copy the inside address to the envelope, thus saving keystrokes and reducing errors. Having the same format on both the inside address and the envelope also looks more professional and consistent. For these reasons you may choose to use the familiar upper- and lowercase combination format. But you will want to check with your organization to learn its preference.

In addressing your envelopes for delivery in North America, use the two-letter province, territory, and state abbreviations.

FOLDING. The way a letter is folded and inserted into an envelope sends an additional credibility signal about a writer's professionalism and carefulness. Your goal in following the procedures shown here is to produce the least number of creases that may distract readers.

For traditional business letter envelopes, begin with the letter face up. Fold slightly less than one third of the sheet toward the top, as shown in the diagram. Then fold down the top third to within 6 to 7 millimetres of the bottom fold. Insert the letter into the envelope with the last fold toward the bottom of the envelope.

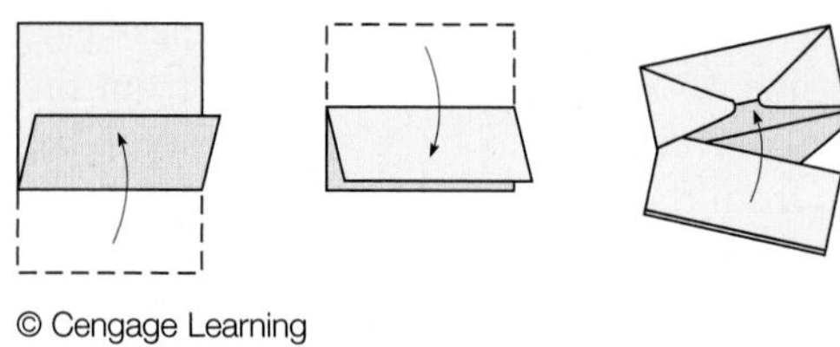

© Cengage Learning

For smaller personal note envelopes, begin by folding the bottom up to within 6 to 7 millimetres of the top edge. Then fold the right third over to the left. Fold the left third to within 6 to 7 millimetres of the last fold. Insert the last fold into the envelope first.

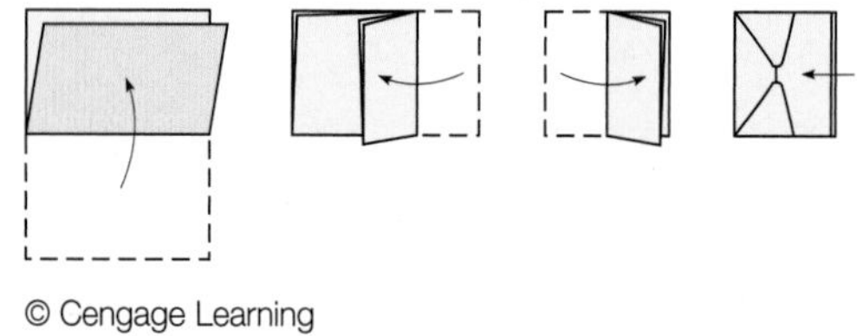

© Cengage Learning

MEMOS

Memos are still important business documents where they are used, but they are being replaced by mass emails in many organizations. For example, in the past if a company wanted to announce an important policy change to its employees, it would send out a hard-copy memo to each employee's mailbox (or desk or workstation). Today, it's increasingly rare to receive hard-copy memos. Nevertheless, you may still find it necessary to create a memo on occasion.

The easiest route is to choose a memo template in Microsoft Word, but if you'd like to design your own memo, follow these instructions:

- Open a Word document and begin typing 3 centimetres from the top of the page.
- Right and left margins may be set at 1.5 inches (4 centimetres).
- Include an optional company name and the word MEMO or MEMORANDUM as a heading. Leave two blank spaces after this heading.

- Create four subheadings on the left side of the page, each separated by one blank line: DATE, TO, FROM, and SUBJECT. The information that comes after each of these subheadings should be stated as clearly and succinctly as possible.
- After the SUBJECT subheading, leave one or two blank lines and begin typing the content of your memo. Single space between lines and double space between paragraphs.
- Do not include a closing salutation or signature. This is one of the major differences between, on the one hand, emails and letters, and on the other, faxes and memos. Because you've included the FROM subheading at the top, you don't need to repeat your name again at the end of a memo or fax.

FAX COVER SHEET

Documents transmitted by fax are usually introduced by a cover sheet, such as that shown in Figure A.4. As with memos, the format can vary considerably, but most important items are incorporated into Microsoft Word's fax templates. Important items in a fax cover sheet are (1) the name and fax number of the receiver, (2) the name and fax number of the sender, (3) the number of pages being sent, and (4) the name, telephone number, and email address of the person to notify in case of unsatisfactory transmission.

When the document being transmitted requires little explanation, you may prefer to attach an adhesive note (such as a Post-it fax transmittal form) to your document instead of a full cover sheet. These notes carry essentially the same information as shown in our printed fax cover sheet. They are perfectly acceptable in most business organizations and can save paper and transmission costs.

FIGURE A.4 | Fax Cover Sheet

FAX TRANSMISSION

DATE: ____________________

TO: ____________________ **FAX NUMBER:** ____________________

____

____

FROM: ____________________ **FAX NUMBER:** ____________________

____

____

NUMBER OF PAGES TRANSMITTED INCLUDING THIS COVER SHEET: ___

MESSAGE:

If any part of this fax transmission is missing or not clearly received, please contact:

NAME: ____________________

PHONE: ____________________

EMAIL: ____________________

APPENDIX

B

Correction Abbreviations and Proofreading Marks

When marking your hard-copy assignments, your instructor may use the following symbols or abbreviations to indicate writing areas for improvement. You may also see them in the workplace when proofreading written documents.

The abbreviations refer to style issues discussed in Appendix D or in the Grammar/Mechanics Handbook at the end of this book. The symbols are proofreading marks used by professional editors (although their usage is diminishing due to the acceptance of electronic tools such as Microsoft Word's Track Changes feature and Adobe's Comment feature). Knowing this information is valuable because part of your career may involve reviewing documents for others.

CORRECTION ABBREVIATIONS

For an explanation of the errors covered by the 11 abbreviations below, consult Chapter 4, the Grammar/Mechanics Handbook, or Appendix D.

ART An article has been used incorrectly or is missing.

AWK Your sentence is awkwardly written (see also PREC below).

PA A pronoun does not agree with its antecedent (the noun it replaces).

PREC Your sentence is imprecise.

PUNCT A punctuation mark has been used incorrectly or is missing.

RO Your sentence has two or more independent clauses without a conjunction or semicolon, or it uses a comma to join the clauses.

SF Your sentence is actually a fragment of a sentence; either a subject or a verb is missing.

SV The subject and verb in your sentence do not agree.

WORDY Your sentence includes repetition or redundancy.

VPR A pronoun in your sentence is vague.

VT One of your verbs is in the wrong tense, or you have shifted its tense unnecessarily.

PROOFREADING MARKS

Proofreading Mark	Draft Copy	Final Copy
Align horizontally	TO: Rick Munoz	TO: Rick Munoz
Align vertically	166.32 132.45	166.32 132.45
Capitalize	Coca-cola runs on android	Coca-Cola runs on Android
Close up space	meeting at 3 p. m.	meeting at 3 p.m.
Centre	Recommendations	Recommendations
Delete	in my final judgement	in my judgment
Insert apostrophe	our companys product	our company's product
Insert comma	you will of course	you will, of course,
Insert semicolon	value therefore, we feel	value; therefore, we feel
Insert hyphen	tax free income	tax-free income
Insert period	Ms Holly Hines	Ms. Holly Hines
Insert quotation mark	shareholders receive a bonus	shareholders receive a "bonus"
Insert space	downloadapps	download apps
Lowercase (remove capitals)	the Vice-President HUMAN RESOURCES	the vice-president Human Resources
Move to left	I. Labour costs	I. Labour costs
Move to right	A. Findings of study	A. Findings of study
Spell out	aimed at 2 depts	aimed at two departments
Start new paragraph	Keep the screen height at eye level.	Keep the screen height at eye level.
Stet (don't delete)	officials talked openly	officials talked openly
Transpose	accounts recievable	accounts receivable
Use boldface	Conclusions	**Conclusions**
Use italics	The Perfect Résumé	*The Perfect Résumé*
Start new line	Globex, 23 Acorn Lane	Globex 23 Acorn Lane
Run lines together	Invoice No. 122059	Invoice No. 122059

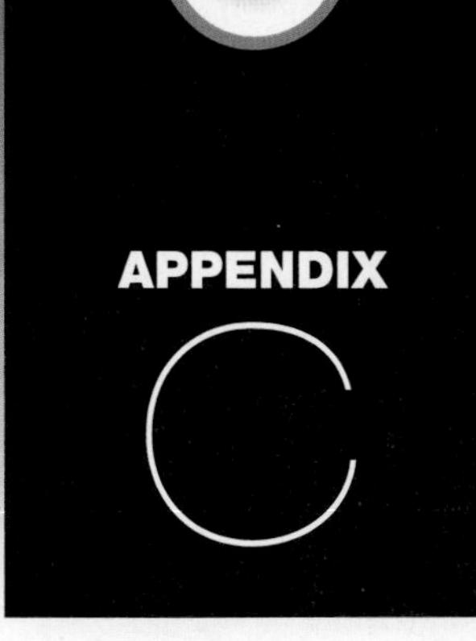

Documentation Formats

Careful writers have many reasons to make sure they properly document any data appearing in reports or messages. Citing sources strengthens a writer's argument, as you learned earlier in this book. Acknowledging sources also shields writers from charges of plagiarism and the loss of reputation that may follow. Moreover, clear references help readers pursue further research. Fortunately, word processing software has taken much of the pain out of documenting data, particularly for footnotes and endnotes.

SOURCE NOTES AND CONTENT NOTES

Before we discuss specific documentation formats, you should know the difference between source notes and content notes. Source notes (also called in-text citations) identify quotations, paraphrased passages, and author references. They lead readers to the sources of cited information, and they must follow a consistent format. Content notes, on the other hand, allow writers to add comments, explain information not directly related to the text, or refer readers to other sections of a report.

TWO DOCUMENTATION METHODS FOR SOURCE NOTES

For years researchers have struggled to develop the perfect documentation system—one that is efficient for the writer and crystal clear to the reader. Most of these systems can be grouped into two methods: the footnote/endnote method and the parenthetic method.

Footnote/Endnote Method

Writers using footnotes or endnotes insert a small superscript (raised) figure into the text close to the place where a reference is mentioned. This number leads the reader to a footnote at the bottom of the page or to an endnote at the end of the document. Footnotes or endnotes contain a complete description of the source document. In this book we have used the endnote method. We chose this style because it is least disruptive to the text.

In referring to a previously mentioned footnote, cite the page number along with the author's last name or a shortened form of the title if no author is given. The Latin forms *ibid., op. cit.,* and *et al.* are rarely seen in business reports today. A portion of a business report using the endnote method for source citation is found in Figure C.1. Figure C.1 demonstrates the endnote method for source citation, given in the traditional style suggested in *The Chicago Manual of Style*, 17th ed. (Chicago: The University of Chicago Press, 2017). Most of the individual citation formats in this book are presented in American Psychological Association (APA) style, and you'll find a comparison of these two citation styles below.

Parenthetic Method

Many academic writers prefer to use a parenthetic style to cite references. In this method a reference to the author appears in parentheses close to the place where it is mentioned in the text. Some parenthetic styles show the author's last name and

FIGURE C.1 | Portion of Report Page Showing *Chicago Manual of Style* Endnote Method

These changes are introducing challenges to companies operating both in Canada and abroad. Obviously, all of these employees need specific business and technology skills, but they also need to be aware of, and be sensitive to, the cultures in which they are living and working.[1] The Bank of Montreal has targeted several of these areas in which to enhance services. Chinese-Canadian business has increased 400 percent in the last five years.[2]

Women are increasing their role as both customer and worker. By the year 2011 women are expected to compose 48 percent of the labour force in Canada, as compared with 27 percent in 1961.[3] However, women hold only about 20 percent of the top management positions in organizations in the industrialized world.[4]

Companies that focus on diversity are improving their bottom line. Recently, Federal Express was named in the *Financial Post* as one the 100 best companies to work for in Canada. Canadian Pacific Forest Products received recognition for ensuring that selection committees had diverse membership, for their development of antiharassment policies, and for other diversity initiatives.[5]

Notes

1. Brenda Lynn, "Diversity in the Workplace: Why We Should Care," *CMA Management Accounting Magazine* 70, no. 5 (June 2010): 9–12.
2. Richard Sommer, "Firms Gain Competitive Strength from Diversity (Says Report by Conference Board of Canada)," *Financial Post,* May 9, 2011, 31.
3. British Columbia, Ministry of Education, Skills, and Training, *The Impact of Demographic Change* (Victoria: Ministry of Education, Skills, and Training, 2012), 35.
4. R. J. Burke and C. A. McKeen, "Do Women at the Top Make a Difference? Gender Proportions and the Experiences of Managerial and Professional Women," *Human Relations* 49, no. 8 (2012): 1093–1104.
5. British Columbia, 36.

date of publication (e.g., *Cook 2000*), while others show the author's last name and page cited (e.g., *Cook 24*). One of the best-known parenthetic systems is the Modern Language Association (MLA) format. The long report shown in Chapter 9 illustrates this format. Below we'll discuss both MLA and American Psychological Association (APA) formats.

Which Method for Business?

Students frequently ask, "What documentation system is most used in business?" While we can't know which style is used in all businesses, anecdotal evidence shows that MLA format is considered more appropriate for humanities subjects, and that for business (both academic and real-world), the APA format, in which the year of publication is mentioned along with the author name, is becoming more generally accepted and expected.

APA STYLE—AMERICAN PSYCHOLOGICAL ASSOCIATION

Popular in the social and physical sciences, and increasingly the standard in business writing, the American Psychological Association (APA) documentation style uses parenthetic citations. That is, each author reference is shown in parentheses when cited in the text. Following are selected features of the APA style. For more information see the *Publication Manual of the American Psychological Association,* 6th ed. (Washington, DC: American Psychological Association, 2010).

In-Text Citation

In-text citations consist of the author's last name, year of publication, and pertinent page number(s). These items appear in parentheses, usually at the end of a clause or end of a sentence in which material is cited. This parenthetic citation, as shown in the following illustration, directs readers to a reference list at the end of the report where complete bibliographic information is recorded.

> The strategy of chicken king Don Tyson was to expand aggressively into other "center-of-the-plate" proteins, such as pork, fish, and turkey (Berss, 2010, p. 64).

One of the paragraphs from the report in Figure C.1, with the citation style changed from Chicago to APA, would look like this:

> These changes are introducing challenges to companies operating both in Canada and abroad. Obviously, as Brenda Lynn (2010) argues, all of these employees need specific business and technology skills, but they also need to be aware of, and be sensitive to, the cultures in which they are living and working. The Bank of Montreal has targeted several of these areas in which to enhance services. Chinese-Canadian business has increased 400 percent in the last five years (Sommer, 2011).

Bibliography

All reference sources are alphabetized in a bibliography entitled "References." Below are selected guidelines summarizing important elements of the APA bibliographic format:

- Include authors' names with the last name first followed by initials, such as: **Smith, M. A.** First and middle names are not used.
- Show the date of publication in parentheses, such as: **Smith, M. A. (2011).**
- Italicize the titles of books and use "sentence-style" (sometimes called *down style*) capitalization. This means that only the first word of a title, proper nouns, and the first word after an internal colon are capitalized. Book titles are followed by the place of publication and publisher's name, such as: **Smith, M. A. (2011).** ***Communication for managers.*** **Elmsford, NY: Pergamon Press.**
- Type the titles of magazine and journal articles without italics or quotation marks. Use sentence-style capitalization for article titles. However, italicize the names of magazines and journals and capitalize the initial letters of all important words. Also italicize the volume number, such as: **Oliveira, T., & Dhillon, G. (2015). From adoption to routinization of B2B e-commerce: Understanding patterns across Europe.** ***Journal of Global Information Management, 23*****(1), 24–43.** ["23(1), 24–43" indicates volume 23, issue 1, pages 24 to 43.]
- Many publications now contain a digital object identifier (DOI), an alphanumeric string that makes them easier to find online. If a DOI is shown, include it instead of a URL.
- Do not include personal communications (such as interviews, telephone conversations, email, and messages from nonarchived discussion groups and online forums) in the reference list, since they are not retrievable.

Electronic References

When print information is available, APA suggests placing it first followed by online information. For example, a newspaper article: **Schellhardt, T. D. (2009, March 4). In a factory schedule, where does religion fit in? *The Wall Street Journal*, pp. B1, B12. Retrieved from http://interactive.wsj.com.** For additional discussion and examples, visit the APA website (http://www.apastyle.org/apa-style-help.aspx).

Figure C.2 shows the format of an APA References List.

FIGURE C.2 | Model APA Bibliography of Sample References

	References
Online annual report	Air Canada. (2014). *2014 annual report*. Retrieved from http://www.aircanada.com/en/about/investor/index.html#reports
Magazine article	Berss, M. (2010, October 24). Protein man. *Forbes, 154,* 64–66.
Journal article with volume and issue numbers and DOI	Gill, A., & Biger, N. (2012). Barriers to small business growth in Canada. *Journal of Small Business and Enterprise Development, 19*(4), 656–668. https://doi.org/10.1108/14626001211277451
Newspaper article, no author	Globalization often means that the fast track leads overseas. (2012, June 16). *The Financial Post,* p. A10.
Magazine article in online research database	Jahl, A. (2013, November 24). PowerPoint of no return. *Canadian Business*, 14–15. Retrieved from CBCA database, George Brown College Library.
Newspaper article, one author	Lancaster, H. (2012, February 7). When taking a tip from a job network, proceed with caution. *The Wall Street Journal,* p. B1.
Website, no author, no publication date	Lasswell's model. (n.d.). Retrieved December 11, 2017, from http://communicationtheory.org/lasswells-model/.
Online newspaper article	Markoff, J. (2009, June 5). Voluntary rules proposed to help ensure privacy for Internet users. *The New York Times*. Retrieved from http://www.nytimes.com
Online magazine article	Murphy, H. L. (2008, August 31). Saturn's orbit still high with consumers. *Marketing News Online*. Retrieved from http://www.ama.org/pubs/mn/0818n1.htm
Brochure	Pinkerton Investigation Services. (2008). *The employer's guide to investigation services* (3rd ed.) [Brochure]. Atlanta, GA: Pinkerton Information Center.
Book, two authors	Rose, R. C., & Garrett, E. M. (2008). *How to make a buck and still be a decent human being.* New York, NY: HarperCollins.
Government publication	Statistics Canada. (2005). *A portrait of persons with disabilities: Target groups project*. Ottawa, ON: Department of Industry, Science and Technology.

MLA STYLE—MODERN LANGUAGE ASSOCIATION

The MLA citation style uses parenthetic author references in the text. These in-text citations guide the reader to a bibliography called "Works Cited." Following are selected characteristics of the MLA style. For more information, consult The Modern Language Association of America, *MLA Handbook for Writers of Research Papers,* 8th ed. (New York: The Modern Language Association of America, 2016).

In-Text Citations

Within the text the author's last name and relevant page reference appear in parentheses, such as "(Chartrand 310)." In-text citations should be placed close to the reference they cite. Notice that no separating comma appears. If the author's name is mentioned in the text, cite only the page number in parentheses. If you don't know the author's name (e.g., when quoting from a website or blog), use the title of the website section or blog entry you took the information from in your in-text citation. Your goal is to avoid interrupting the flow of your writing. Thus, you should strive to place the parenthetical reference where a pause would naturally occur, but as near as possible to the material documented. Note the following examples:

Author's Name in Text

> Peters also notes that stress could be a contributing factor in the health problems reported thus far (135).

Author's Name Unknown

> One website goes so far as to claim that new communication technologies such as BlackBerrys and multipurpose cell phones will soon make in-person conversations "a thing of the past" ("Talking Not Cool").

Author's Name in Reference

> The study was first published in 1958 (Peters 127–35).

Authors' Names in Text

> Others, like Bergstrom and Voorhees (243–51), support a competing theory.

Authors' Names in Reference

> Others support a competing theory (e.g., Bergstrom and Voorhees 243–51).

When citing an entire work—whether a print source, a nonprint source such as a film, a television program, or a Web source that has no pagination or any other reference numbers—MLA style recommends that you include in the text, rather than in a parenthetical reference, the name of the person or organization that begins the corresponding entry in the works-cited list.

Electronic Source With Author

> William J. Kennedy's *Bits and Bytes* discusses new computer technologies in the context of the digital telecommunications revolution. (In the

"Works Cited" list, the reader would find a complete reference under the author's name.)

Electronic Source Without Author

More companies today are using data mining to unlock hidden value in their data. The data mining program "TargetSource," described at the Tener Solutions Group website, helps organizations predict consumer behaviour. (In the "Works Cited" list, the reader would find a complete reference under "Tener Solutions Group," the organization that owns the website.)

Works Cited List

In-text citations lead the reader to complete bibliographical citations in the "Works Cited." This alphabetical listing may contain all works consulted or only those mentioned in the text. Check with your instructor or editor to learn what method is preferred. Below are selected guidelines summarizing important elements of the MLA format for "Works Cited," as shown in Figure C.3.

HANGING INDENTED STYLE. Indent the second and succeeding line for each item. MLA format suggests double-spacing for the entire paper, including the works-cited list. However, Figure C.3 is single-spaced to represent preferred business usage.

BOOK AND WEBSITE TITLES. Italicize the titles of books and use "headline style" for capitalization. This means that the initial letters of all main words are capitalized:

Lewe, Glenda, and Carol D. MacLeod. *Step Into the World of Workplace Learning: A Collection of Authentic Workplace Materials.* Nelson Thomson Learning, 2011.

"ACE Aviation to Take Minority Stake in Merged U.S. Airline." *CBC,* 19 May 2015, www.cbc.ca.

MAGAZINE TITLES. For the titles of magazine articles, include the date of publication but omit volume and issue numbers:

Lee, Mary M. "Investing in International Relationships." *Business Monthly* 18 Feb. 2010, pp. 25–27.

JOURNAL ARTICLES. For journal articles, follow the same format as for magazine articles except include the volume number, issue number, and the year of publication:

Collier, Roger. "Morals, Medicine, and Geography." *Canadian Medical Association Journal*, vol. 179, no. 10, 2014, pp. 996–98.

ITALICS AND UNDERSCORING. MLA style now recommends italicizing book, magazine, and journal titles (instead of underscoring).

Electronic References

The objective in citing sources, whether print publications or electronic publications, is to provide enough information so that your reader can locate your sources.

FIGURE C.3 | Model MLA Bibliography of Sample References

Works Cited

Air Canada. *2014 Annual Report*, 10 Feb. 2015, www.aircanada.com/en/about/investor/documents/2014_ar.pdf.	Online annual report
Beresford, Marcia. "The Shift in Profit." *Maclean's,* 24 Oct. 2011, pp. 25–26.	Magazine article
"Clementine@work." *SPSS*, 15 May 2014, www.spss.com/customer/clem_stories. Accessed 7 Sept. 2014.	Company website, no author
Gill, Amarjit, and Nahum Biger. "Barriers to Small Business Growth in Canada." *Journal of Small Business and Enterprise Development,* vol. 19, no. 4, 2012, pp. 656–668. doi.org/10.1108/14626001211277451.	Journal article with volume and issue numbers and DOI
"Globalization Often Means That the Fast Track Leads Overseas." *The Globe and Mail*, 16 June 2012, p. A10.	Newspaper article, no author
Harris, Rebecca. "It's All About Value for Today's Consumers (Study)." *Marketing,* 20 Oct. 2015, www.marketingmag.ca/consumer/its-all-about-value-for-todays-consumers-study-159542.	Online magazine article
The Impact of Demographic Change. British Columbia Ministry of Education, Skills and Training, 2012.	Government publication (organization is both author and publisher)
Jahl, Andrew. "PowerPoint of No Return." *Canadian Business*, 24 Nov. 2013. *ProQuest,* ezproxy.library.yorku.ca/login?url=http://search.proquest.com.ezproxy.library.yorku.ca/docview/221427923?accountid=15182.	Online research database magazine article, where *ProQuest* is the research database
Lancaster, Hal. "When Taking a Tip From a Job Network, Proceed With Caution." *The Wall Street Journal*, 7 Feb. 2012, p. B1.	Newspaper article, one author
"Lasswell's Model." *Communication Theory*, communicationtheory.org/lasswells-model/. Accessed 11 Dec. 2017.	Website, no author, no date
Pinnacle Security Services. *What Employers Should Know About Employees.* 2nd ed., Pinnacle Information Centre, 2012.	Brochure
Rivers, John. Interview by Susan Smith. 16 May 2015.	Interview
Rose, Richard C., and Echo Montgomery Garrett. *How to Make a Buck and Still Be a Decent Human Being*. HarperCollins Publishers, 2008.	Book, two authors
Wingrove, Josh. "How New Laws Are About to Change Your Privacy." *The Globe and Mail,* 9 June 2014, www.theglobeandmail.com/news/politics/how-new-laws-are-about-to-change-your-privacy/article19054653/.	Online newspaper article

The eighth edition of the *MLA Handbook* makes the following recommendations for citing Web publications:

- Give the same information for electronic sources as you would if you were citing a print publication (e.g., author name, title, page number).
- Give all relevant dates. Because electronic sources can change or move, cite the date the document was produced (if available; if not, omit it) as well as the date you accessed the information. The date of access is helpful because multiple versions of an electronic work may be available, and any version may vary from previous or future versions.

- Include the electronic address or universal resource locator (URL). It should appear immediately after the publication date, followed by a period, and should be the complete address, if possible (exclude "http://"), and be followed by a period. If the URL needs to be divided at the end of a line, do so only after the double slashes or a single slash. Never add a hyphen (or allow your word processor to add one) to mark a break in the address.
- If the publisher has assigned a digital object identifier (DOI) to the publication, cite it instead of the URL.
- Download or print (for future reference) any Web material you use, as online resources frequently move or even disappear.

Article in an Online Journal

Chrisman, Laura, and Laurence Phillips. "Postcolonial Studies and the British Academy." *Jouvert*, vol. 3, no. 3, 1999, english.chass.ncsu.edu/jouvert/index.htm.

Brown, Ronnie R. "Photographs That Should Have Been Taken." *Room of One's Own*, vol. 18, no. 3, Summer 1995, roommagazine.com.

Article in an Online Newspaper or on a Newswire

These sites change very frequently—in some cases daily—so it is a good idea to download or record citation information (and URL, if needed) immediately.

Scarth, Deborah. "Many Top University Students Use Tutors to Keep an Edge." *The Globe and Mail*, 4 June 2000. theglobeandmail.com.

"Canada's Unemployment Rate Dips." Canadian Broadcasting Corporation, 4 June 2000. CBCnews.ca.

Article in an Online Magazine

Campbell, Colin. "Making Bad Times Good." *Maclean's,* 26 Feb. 2009, macleans.ca.

Professional or Personal Website

List the publication information in the following order: the name of the creator of the site, the title of the site (italicized), a version number (for example, edition, posting date, volume or issue number), publisher or sponsor of the site (the name of the organization affiliated with the site), the date of publication (day, month, year, as available; if citing an entire website, cite a range of dates—scroll down and check the bottom of the screen; if no date is available, omit it), the electronic address, and the date you accessed the information. If some of this information is unavailable, cite whatever is available.

Canadian Tire Corporation Limited. *Investor Relations*. 1997–2017, investors.canadiantire.ca.

Ellison, Sara. *Sara's Home Page*. U of Victoria, orca.phys.uvic.ca/~sara/. Accessed 29 July 2015.

Online Book

Many books are now available electronically, either independently or as part of a scholarly project. Some have appeared previously in print, while others exist only on the Web. Follow the general recommendations for citing books in print, but include the additional information required for electronic citations, as outlined below.

If a book that you are citing has appeared in print, it may be important to include the print version of the publication information (e.g., if the book was scanned as part of an online database). In that case, give the name of the author first, if it is available; if not, give the name of the editor, translator, or compiler, followed by a comma and then the appropriate descriptive label (*editor, translator,* or *compiler*). Next give the title of the work (italicized if the work is independent; in quotation marks if the work is part of a larger work); the name of the editor, translator, or compiler (if relevant); the edition or version used; followed by the publication information for the printed version (name of the publisher and year of publication). Then add the following information: the title of the website or database (italicized), the URL, and the date you accessed the information.

If the book you are citing has not been previously published, follow the instructions above regarding the name of the author, editor, translator, or compiler, and the title of the work. Follow that information with the title of the website (italicized); the edition or version used; the publisher or sponsor of the website (if available; if not, omit it); the date of publication (day, month, year, if available; if not, omit it); the URL; and the date you accessed the information (if needed).

Montgomery, Lucy Maud. *Anne of Green Gables*. 1908. *The Literature Network*, www.online-literature.com.

Dewey, John. *Democracy and Education*. Macmillan, 1916. *Wikisource*, 20 Mar. 2016, 06:23 a.m., en.wikisource.org/wiki/Democracy_and_Education. Accessed 22 Nov. 2016.

Other Nonprint Sources

The citations for other nonprint sources will follow the recommendations for print versions, with some additional required information. If you are citing an online posting, you may need to include the URL, as it could otherwise be difficult for your reader to find the posting.

Television/Radio Episode

"Sears Saga." *The National*, narrated by Peter Mansbridge, CBC, 4 June 2014.

Television/Radio Episode Found Online

"CRA to Review Disability Tax Credit Applications." *The National*, CBC, 8 Dec. 2017, www.cbc.ca/news/thenational/cra-to-review-disability-tax-credit-applications-1.4441165?autoplay=true.

Email Communication

Pen Canada. "Your Inquiries to PEN." Received by author, 3 July 2016.

Online Posting

Matus, Roger. "Another University Sends False Admission Emails." *Robert Matus's Death by Email*, InBoxer Inc., 6 Apr. 2009, inboxer.typepad.com/deathbyemail/. Accessed 7 April 2014.

Material From an Online Research Database

Online services such as ProQuest and LexisNexis provide a variety of databases that your college library will have. Give the name of the service (in italics) before the URL and the date you accessed the information (if necessary).

Golden, Anne. "Do Our Foreign Investment Laws Still Have Legs?" *The Globe and Mail*, 1 Dec. 2004, p. A23. *CBCA Current Affairs*, www.proquest.com/libraries/academic/databases/cbca.html.

Podcast

"Cartoonist Lynda Barry on reclaiming the art of child's play." *Writers and Company*, hosted by Eleanor Wachtel, CBC, 29 May 2016, www.cbc.ca/radio/writersandcompany/cartoonist-lynda-barry-on-reclaiming-the-art-of-child-s-play-1.4262131.

Tweet

Include the full text of the tweet in place of a title, and provide the time of posting in addition to the date.

@JustinTrudeau. "Today, we pause to remember the Canadians who've served our country and stood on guard for us: http://bit.ly/2htdEyq." Twitter, 11 Nov. 2017, 5:21 a.m., twitter.com/JustinTrudeau/status/929338309024694272.

APPENDIX D

Style in Writing

Careful writers work hard over time to develop an effective style. While all business writers should be able to write simple declarative sentences (*The stock market is down today*) or even more complex sentences (*The stock market is down today, despite the higher employment numbers*), more experienced writers recognize certain "tricks of the trade" that lend their writing an even more professional, persuasive tone. Some of these tricks are discussed below. Try incorporating them into your work as you progress through your course and your future career.

EMPHASIS

When you are talking with someone, you can emphasize your main ideas by saying them loudly or by repeating them slowly. You could pound the table if you wanted to show real emphasis. Another way you can signal the relative importance of an idea is by raising your eyebrows, shaking your head, or whispering. But when you write, you must rely on other means to tell your readers which ideas are more important than others. Emphasis in writing can be achieved in two ways: mechanically and stylistically.

Emphasis Through Mechanics

To emphasize an idea, a writer may use any of the following devices:

Underlining — Underlining draws the eye to a word.

Italics and boldface — Use *italics* or **boldface** for special meaning and emphasis.

Font changes — Changing from a large font to a smaller font or to a different font adds interest and emphasis.

All caps — Printing words in ALL CAPS is like shouting them.

Dashes — Dashes—if used sparingly—can be effective in capturing attention.

Tabulation — Listing items vertically makes them stand out:

1. First item
2. Second item
3. Third item

You can emphasize an idea mechanically by using underlining, italics, boldface, font changes, all caps, dashes, and tabulation.

You can emphasize ideas stylistically by using vivid words, labelling the main idea, and positioning the main idea strategically.

Other means of achieving mechanical emphasis include the arrangement of space, colour, lines, boxes, columns, titles, headings, and subheadings. Today's software and colour printers provide a wide choice of capabilities for emphasizing ideas.

Emphasis Through Style

Although mechanical means are occasionally appropriate, a good writer more often achieves emphasis stylistically. That is, the writer chooses words carefully and constructs sentences skillfully to emphasize main ideas and de-emphasize minor or negative ideas. Here are four suggestions for emphasizing ideas stylistically:

USE VIVID WORDS. Vivid words are emphatic because the reader can picture ideas clearly.

General One business uses personal selling techniques.

Vivid Avon uses face-to-face selling techniques.

General A customer said that he wanted the contract returned soon.

Vivid Mr. LeClerc insisted that the contract be returned by July 1.

LABEL THE MAIN IDEA. If an idea is significant, tell the reader.

Unlabelled Explore the possibility of leasing a site, but also hire a consultant.

Labelled Explore the possibility of leasing a site, but most important, hire a consultant.

PLACE THE IMPORTANT IDEA FIRST OR LAST IN THE SENTENCE. Ideas have less competition from surrounding words when they appear first or last in a sentence. Observe how the concept of productivity is emphasized in the first and second examples:

Emphatic Productivity is more likely to be increased when profit-sharing plans are linked to individual performance rather than to group performance.

Emphatic Profit-sharing plans linked to individual performance rather than to group performance are more effective in increasing productivity.

Unemphatic Profit-sharing plans are more effective in increasing productivity when they are linked to individual performance rather than to group performance.

PLACE THE IMPORTANT IDEA IN A SIMPLE SENTENCE OR IN AN INDEPENDENT CLAUSE. Don't dilute the effect of the idea by making it share the spotlight with other words and clauses.

Emphatic You are the first trainee we have hired for this program. (Use a simple sentence for emphasis.)

Emphatic Although we considered many candidates, you are the first trainee we have hired for this program. (Independent clause contains main idea.)

Unemphatic Although you are the first trainee we have hired for this program, we had many candidates and expect to expand the program in the future. (Main idea is lost in a dependent clause.)

When to De-Emphasize

You can de-emphasize ideas through word choice and placement.

To de-emphasize something, such as bad news, try one of the following stylistic devices:

USE GENERAL WORDS.

Vivid Our records indicate that you were recently fired.

General Our records indicate that your employment status has changed recently.

PLACE THE BAD NEWS IN A DEPENDENT CLAUSE CONNECTED TO AN INDEPENDENT CLAUSE WITH SOMETHING POSITIVE. In sentences with dependent clauses, the main emphasis is always on the independent clause.

Emphasizes bad news We cannot issue you credit at this time, but we do have a plan that will allow you to fill your immediate needs on a cash basis.

De-emphasizes bad news We have a plan that will allow you to fill your immediate needs on a cash basis since we cannot issue credit at this time.

Active-voice sentences are direct and easy to understand.

ACTIVE AND PASSIVE VOICE

In sentences with active-voice verbs, the subject is the doer of the action. In passive-voice sentences, the subject is acted upon.

Active verb Mr. Wong completed the tax return before the April 30 deadline. (The subject, *Mr. Wong*, is the doer of the action.)

Passive verb The tax return was completed before the April 30 deadline. (The subject, *tax return*, is acted upon.)

In the first sentence, the active-voice verb emphasizes Mr. Wong. In the second sentence, the passive-voice verb emphasizes the tax return. In sentences with passive-voice verbs, the doer of the action may be revealed or left unknown. In business writing, and in personal interactions, some situations demand tact and sensitivity. Instead of using a direct approach with active verbs, we may prefer the indirectness that passive verbs allow. Rather than making a blunt announcement with an active verb (*Gunnar made a major error in the estimate*), we can soften the sentence with a passive construction (*A major error was made in the estimate*).

Although active-voice verbs are preferred in business writing, passive-voice verbs perform useful functions.

Here's a summary of the best use of active- and passive-voice verbs:

- **Use the active voice for most business writing.** It clearly tells what the action is and who is performing that action.
- **Use the passive voice to emphasize an action or the recipient of the action.** *You have been selected to represent us.*
- **Use the passive voice to de-emphasize negative news.** *Your watch has not been repaired.*
- **Use the passive voice to conceal the doer of an action.** *A major error was made in the estimate.*

How can you tell if a verb is active or passive? Identify the subject of the sentence and decide whether the subject is doing the acting or being acted upon. For example, in the sentence *An appointment was made for January 1*, the subject is *appointment*. The subject is being acted upon; therefore, the verb (was made) is passive. Another clue in identifying passive-voice verbs is that they generally include a "to be" helping verb, such as *is, are, was, were, being*, or *been*.

PARALLELISM

Parallelism is a writing technique that creates balanced writing. Sentences written so that their parts are balanced or parallel are easy to read and understand. To achieve parallel construction, use similar structures to express similar ideas. For example, the words *computing, coding, recording*, and *storing* are parallel because they all end in "ing." To express the list as *computing, coding, recording, and storage* is disturbing because the last item is not what the reader expects. Try to match nouns with nouns, verbs with verbs, and clauses with clauses. Avoid mixing active-voice verbs with passive-voice verbs. Your goal is to keep the wording balanced in expressing similar ideas.

Balanced wording helps the reader anticipate and comprehend your meaning.

Lacks parallelism The market for industrial goods includes manufacturers, contractors, wholesalers, and those concerned with the retail function.

Revision The market for industrial goods includes manufacturers, contractors, wholesalers, and retailers. (Parallel construction matches nouns.)

Lacks parallelism Our primary goals are to increase productivity, reduce costs, and the improvement of product quality.

Revision Our primary goals are to increase productivity, reduce costs, and improve product quality. (Parallel construction matches verbs.)

Lacks parallelism We are scheduled to meet in Toronto on January 5, we are meeting in Montreal on the 15th of March, and in Burlington on June 3.

Revision We are scheduled to meet in Toronto on January 5, in Montreal on March 15, and in Burlington on June 3. (Parallel construction matches phrases.)

Lacks parallelism Mrs. Chorney audits all accounts lettered A through L; accounts lettered M through Z are audited by Mr. Faheem.

Revision Mrs. Chorney audits all accounts lettered A through L; Mr. Faheem audits accounts lettered M through Z. (Parallel construction matches active-voice verbs in balanced clauses.)

In presenting lists of data, whether printed horizontally or tabulated vertically, be certain to express all the items in parallel form.

PARALLELISM IN VERTICAL LIST. Three primary objectives of advertising are as follows:

1. Increase the frequency of product use.
2. Introduce complementary products.
3. Enhance the corporate image.

UNITY

Unified sentences contain thoughts that are related to only one main idea. The following sentence lacks unity because the first clause has little or no relationship to the second clause:

Unified sentences contain only related ideas.

Lacks unity Our insurance plan is available in all provinces, and you may name anyone as a beneficiary for your coverage.

Revision Our insurance plan is available in all provinces. What's more, you may name anyone as a beneficiary for your coverage.

The ideas in a sentence are better expressed by separating the two dissimilar clauses and adding a connecting phrase. Three writing faults that destroy sentence unity are imprecise writing, mixed constructions, and misplaced modifiers.

Imprecise sentences often should be broken into two sentences.

Imprecise Writing

Sentences that twist or turn unexpectedly away from the main thought are examples of imprecise writing. Such confusing writing may result when too many thoughts are included in one sentence or when one thought does not relate to another. To rectify an imprecise sentence, revise it so that the reader understands the relationship between the thoughts. If that is impossible, move the unrelated thoughts to a new sentence.

Imprecise writing I appreciate the time you spent with me last week, and I have purchased a computer and software that generate graphics.

Revision I appreciate the time you spent with me last week. As a result of your advice, I have purchased a computer and software that generate graphics.

Imprecise writing The stockholders of a corporation elect a board of directors, although the chief executive officer is appointed by the board and the CEO is not directly responsible to the stockholders.

Revision The stockholders of a corporation elect a board of directors, who in turn appoint the chief executive officer. The CEO is not directly responsible to the stockholders.

Mixed Constructions

Writers who fuse two different grammatical constructions destroy sentence unity and meaning.

Mixed constructions confuse readers.

Mixed construction The reason I am late is because my car battery is dead.

Revision The reason I am late is that my car battery is dead. (The construction introduced by the reason is should be a noun clause beginning with that, not an adverbial clause beginning with because.)

Mixed construction When the stock market index rose five points was our signal to sell.

Revision When the stock market index rose five points, we were prepared to sell. Or: Our signal to sell was an increase of five points in the stock market index.

Dangling and Misplaced Modifiers

For clarity, modifiers must be close to the words they describe or limit. A modifier dangles when the word or phrase it describes is missing from the sentence. A modifier is misplaced when the word or phrase it describes is not close enough for the relationship to be clear. The solution is to position the modifier closer to the word(s) it describes or limits, or to introduce the word that's missing, often a person or place. Introductory verbal phrases are particularly dangerous; be sure to follow them immediately with the words they logically describe or modify.

Modifiers must be close to the words they describe or limit.

Dangling modifier To win the lottery, a ticket must be purchased. (Purchased by whom? The verbal phrase must be followed by a subject.)

Revision To win the lottery, you must purchase a ticket.

Dangling modifier Driving through Tetrahedron Plateau, the ocean suddenly came into view. (Is the ocean driving through Tetrahedron Plateau?)

Revision Driving through Tetrahedron Plateau, we saw the ocean suddenly come into view.

Try this trick for detecting and remedying dangling modifiers. Ask the question "Who or what?" after any introductory phrase. The words immediately following should tell the reader who or what is performing the action. Try the test on the previous danglers.

Misplaced modifier Seeing his error too late, the envelope was immediately resealed by Adrian. (Did the envelope see the error?)

Revision Seeing his error too late, Adrian immediately resealed the envelope.

Misplaced modifier A wart appeared on my left hand that I want removed. (Is the left hand to be removed?)

Revision I want to remove the wart that appeared on my left hand.

Misplaced modifier The busy human resources director interviewed only candidates who had excellent computer skills in the morning. (Were the candidates skilled only in the morning?)

Revision In the morning the busy human resources director interviewed only candidates who had excellent computer skills.

PARAGRAPH COHERENCE

Three ways to create paragraph coherence are (1) repetition of key ideas, (2) use of pronouns, and (3) use of transitional expressions.

A paragraph is a group of sentences with a controlling idea, usually stated first. Paragraphs package similar ideas into meaningful groups for readers. Effective paragraphs are coherent; that is, they hold together. But coherence does not happen accidentally. It is achieved through effective organization and (1) repetition of key ideas, (2) use of pronouns, and (3) use of transitional expressions.

REPETITION OF KEY IDEAS OR KEY WORDS. Repeating a word or key thought from a preceding sentence helps guide a reader from one thought to the next. This redundancy is necessary to build cohesiveness into writing.

Effective repetition Quality problems in production are often the result of inferior raw materials. Some companies have strong programs for ensuring the quality of incoming production materials and supplies.

The second sentence of the preceding paragraph repeats the key idea of quality. Moreover, the words incoming production materials and supplies refer to the raw materials mentioned in the preceding sentence. Good writers find similar words to describe the same idea, thus using repetition to clarify a topic for the reader.

Pronouns with clear antecedents can improve coherence.

USE OF PRONOUNS. Pronouns such as *this*, *that, they, these*, and *those* promote coherence by connecting the thoughts in one sentence to the thoughts in a previous sentence. To make sure that the pronoun reference is clear, consider joining the pronoun with the word to which it refers, thus making the pronoun into an adjective.

PRONOUN REPETITION. Xerox has a four-point program to assist suppliers. This program includes written specifications for production materials and components.

Be very careful, though, in using pronouns. A pronoun without a clear antecedent can be annoying. That's because the reader doesn't know precisely to what the pronoun refers.

FAULTY PRONOUN USE. When company profits increased, employees were given either a cash payment or company stock. This became a real incentive to employees. (Is *This* the cash or the stock or both?)

REVISION. When company profits increased, employees were given either a cash payment or company stock. This profit-sharing plan became a real incentive to employees.

Transitional expressions build paragraph coherence.

USE OF TRANSITIONAL EXPRESSIONS. One of the most effective ways to achieve paragraph coherence is through the use of transitional expressions. These expressions act as road signs: they indicate where the message is headed and they help the reader anticipate what is coming. Here are some of the most effective transitional expressions. They are grouped according to use.

Time Association	Contrast	Illustration
before, after	although	for example
first, second	but	in this way
meanwhile	however	
next	instead	
until	nevertheless	
when, whenever	on the other hand	
Cause, Effect	**Additional Idea**	
consequently	furthermore	
for this reason	in addition	
hence	likewise	
therefore	moreover	

PARAGRAPH LENGTH

The most readable paragraphs contain eight or fewer printed lines.

Although no rule regulates the length of paragraphs, business writers recognize the value of short paragraphs. Paragraphs with eight or fewer printed lines look inviting and readable. Long, solid chunks of print appear formidable. If a topic can't be covered in eight or fewer printed lines (not sentences), consider breaking it into smaller segments.

WRITING IMPROVEMENT EXERCISES

EMPHASIS. For each of the following sentences, circle (a) or (b). Be prepared to justify your choice.

1. Which is more emphatic?
   a. We need a faster, more efficient distribution system.
   b. We need a better distribution system.
2. Which is more emphatic?
   a. Increased advertising would improve sales.
   b. Adding $50,000 in advertising would double our sales.
3. Which is more emphatic?
   a. The committee was powerless to act.
   b. The committee was unable to take action.
4. Which sentence puts more emphasis on product loyalty?
   a. Product loyalty is the primary motivation for advertising.
   b. The primary motivation for advertising is loyalty to the product, although other purposes are also served.
5. Which sentence places more emphasis on the seminar?
   a. An executive training seminar that starts June 1 will include four candidates.
   b. Four candidates will be able to participate in an executive training seminar that we feel will provide a valuable learning experience.

ACTIVE-VOICE VERBS. Business writing is more forceful if it uses active-voice verbs. Revise the following sentences so that the verbs are in the active voice. Put the emphasis on the doer of the action. Add subjects if necessary.

Example The computers were powered up each day at 7 a.m.

Revision Kamal powered up the computers each day at 7 a.m.

1. Initial figures for the bid were submitted before the June 1 deadline.
2. New spices and cooking techniques were tried by South St. Burger to improve its hamburgers.

PASSIVE-VOICE VERBS. When indirectness or tact is required, use passive-voice verbs. Revise the following sentences so that they are in the passive voice.

Example Sade did not submit the accounting statement on time.

Revision The accounting statement was not submitted on time.

1. Andreas made a computational error in the report.
2. We cannot ship your order for 10 monitors until June 15.
3. The government first issued a warning regarding the use of this pesticide over 15 months ago.

PARALLELISM. Revise the following sentences so that their parts are balanced.

1. (Hint: Match verbs.) Some of our priorities include linking employee compensation to performance, keeping administrative costs down, the expansion of computer use, and the improvement of performance review skills of supervisors.
2. (Hint: Match active voice of verbs.) Yin Huang, of the Red River office, will now supervise our Western Division; and the Eastern Division will be supervised by our Ottawa office manager, David Ali.
3. (Hint: Match nouns.) Word processing software is used extensively in the fields of health care, by lawyers, by secretaries in insurance firms, for scripts in the entertainment industry, and in the banking field.
4. If you have decided to cancel our service, please cut your credit card in half, and the card pieces should be returned to us.

SENTENCE UNITY. The following sentences lack unity. Rewrite, correcting the identified fault.

Example (Dangling modifier) By advertising extensively, all the open jobs were filled quickly.

Revision By advertising extensively, we were able to fill all the open jobs quickly.

1. (Dangling modifier) To open a money market account, a deposit of $3,000 is required.
2. (Mixed construction) The reason why Ms. Rutulis is unable to travel extensively is because she has family responsibilities.
3. (Misplaced modifier) Identification passes must be worn at all times in offices and production facilities showing the employee's picture.

COHERENCE. Revise the following paragraphs to improve coherence. Be aware that the transitional expressions and key words selected depend largely on the emphasis desired. Many possible revisions exist.

Example Computer style checkers rank somewhere between artificial intelligence and artificial ignorance. Style checkers are like clever children: smart but not wise. Business writers should be cautious. They should be aware of the usefulness of style checkers. They should know their limitations.

Revision Computer style checkers rank somewhere between artificial intelligence and artificial ignorance. For example, they are like clever children: smart but not wise. For this reason, business writers should be cautious. Although they should be aware of the usefulness of these software programs, business writers should also know their limitations.

1. Our computerized file includes all customer data. It provides space for name, address, and other vital information. It has an area for comments. The area for comments comes in handy. It requires more time and careful keyboarding, though.
2. No one likes to turn out poor products. We began highlighting recurring problems. Employees make a special effort to be more careful in doing their work right the first time. It doesn't have to be returned to them for corrections.

GRAMMAR/MECHANICS HANDBOOK

INTRODUCTION

Because many students need a quick review of basic grammar and mechanics, we provide a number of resources in condensed form. The Grammar/Mechanics Handbook, which offers you a rapid, systematic review, consists of four parts:

- **Grammar/Mechanics Diagnostic Test.** This 65-point pre-test helps you assess your strengths and weaknesses in eight areas of grammar and mechanics. Your instructor may later give you a post-test to assess your improvement.
- **Grammar/Mechanics Profile.** The G/M Profile enables you to pinpoint specific areas in which you need remedial instruction or review.
- **Grammar/Mechanics Review.** Provided here is a concise review of basic principles of grammar, punctuation, capitalization, and number style. The review also provides reinforcement and quiz exercises that help you interact with the principles of grammar and test your comprehension. The guidelines not only provide a study guide for review but will also serve as a reference manual throughout the course. The grammar review can be used for classroom-centred instruction or for self-guided learning.
- **Confusing Words and Frequently Misspelled Words.** A list of selected confusing words, along with a list of 160 frequently misspelled words, completes the Grammar/Mechanics Handbook.

The first step in your systematic review of grammar and mechanics involves completing the following diagnostic pre-test.

GRAMMAR/MECHANICS DIAGNOSTIC PRE-TEST

Name____

This diagnostic pre-test is intended to reveal your strengths and weaknesses in using the following:

plural nouns	adjectives	punctuation
possessive nouns	adverbs	capitalization style
pronouns	prepositions	number style
verbs	conjunctions	

The pre-test is organized into sections corresponding to the preceding categories. In Sections A through H, each sentence is either correct or has one error related to the category under which it is listed. If a sentence is correct, write *C*. If it has an error, underline the error and write the correct form in the space provided. When you finish, check your answers with your instructor and fill out the Grammar/Mechanics Profile at the end of the test.

A. Plural Nouns

companies **Example** Large companys hire numerous CPAs and accountants.

__________ 1. All job candidates are asked whether they can work on Saturday's.

__________ 2. Two students discussed the pro's and con's of using laptops and cellphones in their classes.

__________ 3. Both of Jeff's sister-in-laws worked as secretaries at different facilities.

__________ 4. Neither the Parvezes nor the Harris's knew about the changes in beneficiaries.

__________ 5. Since the early 2000s, most judicial systems and lawyers have invested in packages that detect computer viruses.

B. Possessive Nouns

__________ 6. We sincerely hope that the jurys judgment reflects the stories of all the witnesses.

__________ 7. In a little over two months time, the analysts finished their reports.

__________ 8. Ms. Porters staff is responsible for all accounts receivable for customers purchasing electronics parts.

__________ 9. At the next stockholders meeting, we will discuss benefits for employees and dividends for shareholders.

__________ 10. For the past 90 days, employees in the sales department have complained about Mr. Navetta smoking.

C. Pronouns

<u>me</u> **Example** Whom did you ask to replace Francisco and <u>I</u>?

__________ 11. The chief and myself were quite willing to send copies to whoever requested them.

__________ 12. Much of the project assigned to Samantha and I had to be reassigned to Matt and them.

__________ 13. Although it's CPU was noisy, the computer worked for Jeremy and me.

__________ 14. Just between you and me, only you and I know that she will be transferred.

__________ 15. My friend and I applied at Loblaw because of their excellent benefits.

D. Verb Agreement

<u>has</u> **Example** The list of payments <u>have</u> to be approved by the boss.

__________ 16. This cellphone and its calling plan costs much less than I expected.

__________ 17. A description of the property, together with several other legal documents, were submitted by my lawyer.

__________ 18. There are a wide range of proposals for reducing email overload.

__________ 19. Neither the manager nor the employees in the office think the solution is fair.

__________ 20. Because of the holiday, our committee were unable to meet.

E. Verb Mood, Voice, and Tense

__________ 21. If I was in charge, I would certainly change things.

__________ 22. To make a copy, first open the disk drive door and then you insert the disk.

__________ 23. If I could chose any city, I would select Hong Kong.

__________ 24. Those contracts have laid on his desk for more than two weeks.

________ 25. The auditors have went over these accounts carefully, and they have found no discrepancies.

F. Adjectives and Adverbs

________ 26. Until we have a more clearer picture of what is legal, we will proceed cautiously.

________ 27. Britney thought she had done good in her job interview.

________ 28. A recently appointed official was in charge of monitoring peer to peer file-sharing systems.

________ 29. Robert only has two days before he must submit his end-of-the-year report.

________ 30. The architects submitted their drawings in a last-minute attempt to beat the deadline.

G. Prepositions and Conjunctions

________ 31. Can you tell me where the meeting is scheduled at?

________ 32. It seems like we have been taking this pre-test forever.

________ 33. Our investigation shows that cellphones may be cheaper then landlines.

________ 34. My courses this semester are totally different than last semester's.

________ 35. Do you know where this shipment is going to?

H. Commas

For each of the following sentences, insert any necessary commas. Count the number of commas that you added. Write that number in the space provided. All punctuation must be correct to receive credit for the sentence. If a sentence requires no punctuation, write C.

1 **Example** Because of developments in theory and computer applications^management is becoming more of a science.

________ 36. For example management determines how orders assignments and responsibilities are delegated to employees.

________ 37. Your order Ms. Lee will be sent from Niagara Falls Ontario on July 3.

________ 38. When you need service on any of your equipment we will be happy to help you Mr. Lemieux.

________ 39. Michelle Wong who is the project manager at TeleCom suggested that I call you.

________ 40. You have purchased from us often and your payments in the past have always been prompt.

I. Commas and Semicolons 1

Add commas and semicolons to the following sentences. In the space provided, write the number of punctuation marks that you added.

________ 41. The salesperson turned in his report however he did not indicate the time period it covered.

________ 42. Interest payments on bonds are tax deductible dividend payments are not.

________ 43. We are opening a branch office in Brandon and hope to be able to serve all your needs from that office by the middle of January.

______ 44. As suggested by the committee we must first secure adequate funding then we may consider expansion.

______ 45. When you begin to research a report consider many sources of information namely think about using the Internet, books, periodicals, government publications, and databases.

J. Commas and Semicolons 2

______ 46. After our chief had the printer repaired it jammed again within the first week although we treated it carefully.

______ 47. Our experienced courteous staff has been trained to anticipate your every need.

______ 48. In view of the new law that went into effect on April 1 our current liability insurance must be increased therefore we need to adjust our budget.

______ 49. As stipulated in our contract your agency will develop a social media program and supervise our media budget.

______ 50. As you know Ms. Okui we aim for long-term business relationships not quick profits.

K. Other Punctuation

Each of the following sentences may require colons, question marks, quotation marks, periods, parentheses, and underscores, as well as commas and semicolons. Add the appropriate punctuation to each sentence. Then in the space provided, write the total number of marks that you added or changed.

2 **Example** Fully recharging your digital camera's battery (see page 6 of the instruction manual) takes only 90 minutes.

______ 51. The following members of the department volunteered to help on Saturday Kim Carlos Dan and Sylvia.

______ 52. Mr Phillips, Miss Reed, and Mrs. Garcia usually arrived at the office by 8:30 a m.

______ 53. We recommend that you use hearing protectors see the warning on page 8 when using this electric drill.

______ 54. Did the CEO really say "All employees may take Friday off

______ 55. We are trying to locate an edition of *Canadian Business* that carried an article titled Who Is Reading Your Email

L. Capitalization

For each of the following sentences, underline any letter that should be capitalized. In the space provided, write the number of words you marked.

4 **Example** vice president kumar devised a procedure for expediting purchase orders from area 4 warehouses.

______ 56. although english was his native language, he also spoke spanish and could read french.

______ 57. on a trip to the east coast, uncle henry visited peggy's cove.

______ 58. karen enrolled in classes in history, german, and sociology.

______ 59. the business manager and the vice president each received a new dell computer.

______ 60. james lee, the president of kendrick, inc., will speak at our conference in the spring.

M. Number Style

Decide whether the numbers in the following sentences should be written as words or as figures. Each sentence either is correct or has one error. If it is correct, write C. If it has an error, underline it and write the correct form in the space provided.

five **Example** The bank had 5 branches in three suburbs.

________ 61. More than 3,000,000 people have visited the Parliament Buildings in the past five years.

________ 62. Of the 28 viewer comments we received regarding our online commercial, only three were negative.

________ 63. We set aside forty dollars for petty cash, but by December 1 our fund was depleted.

________ 64. The meeting is scheduled for May fifth at 3 p.m.

________ 65. In the past five years, nearly fifteen percent of the population changed residences at least once.

GRAMMAR/MECHANICS PROFILE

In the spaces at the right, place a check mark to indicate the number of correct answers you had in each category of the Grammar/Mechanics Diagnostic Pre-test.

		NUMBER CORRECT*				
		5	4	3	2	1
1–5	Plural Nouns	___	___	___	___	___
6–10	Possessive Nouns	___	___	___	___	___
11–15	Pronouns	___	___	___	___	___
16–20	Verb Agreement	___	___	___	___	___
21–25	Verb Mood, Voice, and Tense	___	___	___	___	___
26–30	Adjectives and Adverbs	___	___	___	___	___
31–35	Prepositions and Conjunctions	___	___	___	___	___
36–40	Commas	___	___	___	___	___
41–45	Commas and Semicolons 1	___	___	___	___	___
46–50	Commas and Semicolons 2	___	___	___	___	___
51–55	Other Punctuation	___	___	___	___	___
56–60	Capitalization	___	___	___	___	___
61–65	Number Style	___	___	___	___	___

***Note:** 5 = have excellent skills; 4 = need light review; 3 = need careful review; 2 = need to study rules; 1 = need serious study and follow-up reinforcement.

GRAMMAR/MECHANICS REVIEW

Parts of Speech (1.01)

1.01 Functions. English has eight parts of speech. Knowing the functions of the parts of speech helps writers better understand how words are used and how sentences are formed.

a. **Nouns.** Name persons, places, things, qualities, concepts, and activities (e.g., *Kevin, Lethbridge, computer, joy, work, banking*)

b. **Pronouns.** Substitute for nouns (e.g., *he, she, it, they*)

c. **Verbs.** Show the action of a subject or join the subject to words that describe it (e.g., *walk, heard, is, was jumping*)

d. **Adjectives.** Describe or limit nouns and pronouns and often answer the questions *what kind? how many?* and *which one?* (e.g., *red* car, *ten* items, *good* manager)

e. **Adverbs.** Describe or limit verbs, adjectives, or other adverbs and frequently answer the questions *when? how? where?* or *to what extent*? (e.g., *tomorrow, rapidly, here, very*)

f. **Prepositions.** Join nouns or pronouns to other words in sentences (e.g., desk *in* the office, ticket *for* me, letter *to* you)

g. **Conjunctions.** Connect words or groups of words (e.g., you *and* I, Mark *or* Jill)

h. **Interjections.** Express strong feelings (e.g., *Wow! Oh!*)

Nouns (1.02–1.06)

Nouns name persons, places, things, qualities, concepts, and activities. Nouns may be classified into a number of categories.

1.02 Concrete and Abstract. Concrete nouns name specific objects that can be seen, heard, felt, tasted, or smelled. Examples of concrete nouns are *telephone, dollar, IBM*, and *tangerine*. Abstract nouns name generalized ideas such as qualities or concepts that are not easily pictured. *Emotion, power*, and *tension* are typical examples of abstract nouns.

Business writing is most effective when concrete words predominate. It is clearer to write *We need 16-pound copy paper* than to write *We need office supplies.* Chapter 4 provides practice in developing skill in the use of concrete words.

1.03 Proper and Common. Proper nouns name specific persons, places, or things and are always capitalized (*Lululemon Athletica, Kamloops, Jennifer*). All other nouns are common nouns and begin with lowercase letters (*company, city, student*). Rules for capitalization are presented in Sections 3.01–3.16.

1.04 Singular and Plural. Singular nouns name one item; plural nouns name more than one. From a practical view, writers seldom have difficulty with singular nouns. They may need help, however, with the formation and spelling of plural nouns.

1.05 Guidelines for Forming Noun Plurals

a. Add *s* to most nouns *(chair, chairs; mortgage, mortgages; Monday, Mondays).*

b. Add *es* to nouns ending in *s, x, z, ch,* or *sh (bench, benches; boss, bosses; box, boxes; Parvez, Parvezes).*

c. Change the spelling in irregular noun plurals *(man, men; foot, feet; mouse, mice; child, children).*

d. Add *s* to nouns that end in *y* when *y* is preceded by a vowel (*journey, journeys; valley, valleys*).

e. Drop the *y* and add *ies* to nouns ending in *y* when *y* is preceded by a consonant (*company, companies; city, cities; secretary, secretaries*).

f. Add *s* to the principal word in most compound expressions *(editors in chief, fathers-in-law, bills of lading, runners-up).*

g. Add *s* to most numerals, letters of the alphabet, words referred to as words, degrees, and abbreviations (*5s, 2000s, Bs, ands, CPAs, lbs.*).

h. Add *'s* only to clarify letters of the alphabet that might be misread, such as *A's, I's, M's, U's, i's,* and *p's* and *q's*. An expression like *c.o.d.s* requires no apostrophe because it would not easily be misread.

1.06 Collective Nouns. Nouns such as *staff, faculty, committee, group,* and *herd* refer to a collection of people, animals, or objects. Collective nouns may be considered singular or plural depending on their action. See Section 1.10i for a discussion of collective nouns and their agreement with verbs.

Review Exercise A—Nouns

In the space provided for each item, write *a* or *b* to complete the following statements accurately. When you finish, compare your responses with those provided. Answers are provided for odd-numbered items. Your instructor has the remaining answers. For each item on which you need review, consult the numbered principle shown in parentheses.

________ 1. Two of the contest (a) *runner-ups,* (b) *runners-up* protested the judges' choice.

________ 2. Please write to the (a) *Davis's,* (b) *Davises* about the missing contract.

________ 3. That accounting firm employs two (a) *secretaries,* (b) *secretarys* for five CPAs.

________ 4. The home was constructed with numerous (a) *chimneys,* (b) *chimnies.*

________ 5. We asked the (a) *Parvez's,* (b) *Parvezes* to contribute to the fund-raising drive.

________ 6. The stock market is experiencing abnormal (a) *ups and downs,* (b) *up's and down's.*

________ 7. This office is unusually quiet on (a) *Sundays,* (b) *Sunday's.*

________ 8. Two major (a) *countries,* (b) *countrys* will participate in arms negotiations.

________ 9. The (a) *board of directors,* (b) *boards of directors* of all the major companies participated in the surveys.

________ 10. In shipping we are careful to include all (a) *bill of sales,* (b) *bills of sale.*

---

1. b (1.05f) 3. a (1.05e) 5. b (1.05b) 7. a (1.05a) 9. b (1.05f) (Only odd-numbered answers are provided. Consult your instructor for the others.)

GRAMMAR/MECHANICS CHECKUP—1

Nouns

Review Sections 1.01–1.06. Then study each of the following statements. Underline any mistakes and write a correction in the space provided. Record the appropriate Handbook section and letter that illustrates the principle involved. If a sentence is correct, write C. When you finish, compare your responses with those provided on page 417. If your answers differ, carefully study again the principles shown in parentheses.

Companies (1.05e) **Example** Two surveys revealed that many <u>companys</u> will move to the new industrial park.

________ 1. Counter business is higher on Saturday's, but telephone business is greater on Sundays.

________ 2. Some of the citys in Kevin's report offer excellent opportunities.

________ 3. Frozen chickens and turkies are kept in the company's lockers.

________ 4. Only the Nashs and the Lopezes brought their entire families.

________ 5. In the 1980s profits grew rapidly; in the 1990's investments lagged.

________ 6. Both editor in chiefs instituted strict proofreading policies.

________ 7. My monitor makes it difficult to distinguish between *o's* and *a's*.

________ 8. Both runner-ups complained about the winner's behaviour.

Pronouns (1.07–1.09)

Pronouns substitute for nouns. They are classified by case.

1.07 Case. Pronouns function in three cases, as shown in the following chart.

Nominative Case	**Objective Case**	**Possessive Case**
(Used for subjects of verbs and subject complements)	*(Used for objects of prepositions and objects of verbs)*	*(Used to show possession)*
I	me	my, mine
we	us	our, ours
you	you	your, yours
he	him	his
she	her	her, hers
it	it	its
they	them	their, theirs
who, whoever	whom, whomever	whose

1.08 Guidelines for Selecting Pronoun Case

a. Pronouns that serve as subjects of verbs must be in the nominative case:

> *He* and *I* (not *Him* and *me*) decided to apply for the jobs.

b. Pronouns that follow linking verbs (such as *am, is, are, was, were, be, being, been*) and rename the words to which they refer must be in the nominative case.

> It must have been *she* (not *her*) who placed the order. (The nominative-case pronoun *she* follows the linking verb been and renames *it*.)
>
> If it was *he* (not *him*) who called, I have his number. (The nominative-case pronoun *he* follows the linking verb *was* and renames *it*.)

c. Pronouns that serve as objects of verbs or objects of prepositions must be in the objective case:

> Mr. Andrews asked *them* to complete the proposal. (The pronoun *them* is the object of the verb *asked*.)
>
> All computer printouts are sent to *him*. (The pronoun *him* is the object of the preposition *to*.)

Just between you and *me*, profits are falling. (The pronoun *me* is one of the objects of the preposition *between*.)

d. Pronouns that show ownership must be in the possessive case. Possessive pronouns (such as *hers, yours, ours, theirs*, and *its*) require no apostrophes:

I bought a cheap cellphone, but *yours* (not *your's*) is expensive.

All parts of the machine, including *its* (not *it's*) motor, were examined.

The house and *its* (not *it's*) contents will be auctioned.

Don't confuse possessive pronouns and contractions. Contractions are shortened forms of subject–verb phrases (such as *it's* for *it is*, *there's* for *there is*, and *they're* for *they are*).

e. When a pronoun appears in combination with a noun or another pronoun, ignore the extra noun or pronoun and its conjunction. In this way pronoun case becomes more obvious:

The manager promoted Jeff and *me* (not I). (Ignore *Jeff and*.)

f. In statements of comparison, mentally finish the comparative by adding the implied missing words:

Next year I hope to earn as much as *she*. (The verb *earns* is implied here: . . . *as much as she earns*.)

g. Pronouns must be in the same case as the words they replace or rename. When pronouns are used with appositives, ignore the appositive:

A new contract was signed by *us* (not *we*) employees. (Temporarily ignore the appositive *employees* in selecting the pronoun.)

We (not us) citizens have formed our own organization. (Temporarily ignore the appositive *citizens* in selecting the pronoun.)

h. Pronouns ending in *self* should be used only when they refer to previously mentioned nouns or pronouns:

The CEO *himself* answered the telephone.

Robert and *I* (not *myself*) are in charge of the campaign.

i. Use objective-case pronouns as objects of the prepositions *between, but, like*, and *except*:

Everyone but John and *him* (not *he*) qualified for the bonus.

Employees like Miss Gillis and *her* (not *she*) are hard to replace.

j. Use *who* or *whoever* for nominative-case constructions and *whom* or *whomever* for objective-case constructions. In making the correct choice, it's sometimes helpful to substitute *he* for *who* or *whoever* and *him* for *whom* or *whomever*:

For *whom* was this book ordered? (*This book was ordered for him/whom?*)

Who did you say would drop by? (*Who/He ... would drop by?*)

Deliver the package to *whoever* opens the door. (In this sentence the clause *whoever* opens the door functions as the object of the preposition *to*. Within the clause itself, *whoever* is the subject of the verb *opens*. Again, substitution of he might be helpful: *He/Whoever opens the door*.)

1.09 Guidelines for Making Pronouns Agree With Their Antecedents. Pronouns must agree with the words to which they refer (their antecedents) in gender and in number.

a. Use masculine pronouns to refer to masculine antecedents, feminine pronouns to refer to feminine antecedents, and neuter pronouns to refer to antecedents without gender:

The man opened *his* office door. (Masculine gender applies.)

A woman sat at *her* desk. (Feminine gender applies.)

This computer and *its* programs fit our needs. (Neuter gender applies.)

b. Use singular pronouns to refer to singular antecedents:

Common gender pronouns (such as *him* or *his*) traditionally have been used when the gender of the antecedent is unknown. Sensitive writers today, however, prefer to recast such constructions to avoid gender-biased pronouns. Study these examples for bias-free pronouns:

Each student must submit *a* report on Monday.

All students must submit *their* reports on Monday.

Each student must submit *his or her* report on Monday. (This alternative is least acceptable since it is wordy and calls attention to itself.)

c. Use singular pronouns to refer to singular indefinite subjects and plural pronouns for plural indefinite subjects. Words such as *anyone, something,* and *anybody* are considered indefinite because they refer to no specific person or object. Some indefinite pronouns are always singular; others are always plural.

Always Singular		**Always Plural**	
anybody	either	nobody	both
anyone	everyone	no one	few
anything	everything	somebody	many
each	neither	someone	several

Somebody in the group of touring women left *her* (not *their*) purse in the museum.

Either of the companies has the right to exercise *its* (*not their*) option to sell stock.

d. Use singular pronouns to refer to collective nouns and organization names:

The engineering staff is moving *its* (not *their*) facilities on Friday. (The singular pronoun its agrees with the collective noun *staff* because the members of *staff* function as a single unit.)

Jones, Cohen, & Chavez, Inc., *has* (not *have*) cancelled *its* (not *their*) contract with us. (The singular pronoun its agrees with *Jones, Cohen, & Chavez, Inc.*, because the members of the organization are operating as a single unit.)

e. Use a plural pronoun to refer to two antecedents joined by *and*, whether the antecedents are singular or plural:

Our company president and our vice president will be submitting *their* expenses shortly.

f. Ignore intervening phrases—introduced by expressions such as *together with*, *as well as*, and *in addition to*—that separate a pronoun from its antecedent:

> One of our managers, along with several salespeople, is planning *his* retirement. (If you wish to emphasize both subjects equally, join them with *and*: One of our managers *and* several salespeople are planning *their* retirements.)

g. When antecedents are joined by *or* or *nor*, make the pronoun agree with the antecedent closest to it.

> Neither Jackie nor Kim wanted *her* (not *their*) desk moved.

Review Exercise B—Pronouns

In the space provided for each item, write *a, b,* or *c* to complete the statement accurately. When you finish, compare your responses with those provided. For each item on which you need review, consult the numbered principle shown in parentheses.

_____ 1. Send email copies of the policy to the manager or (a) *me*, (b) *myself*.

_____ 2. Much preparation for the seminar was made by Mrs. Cho and (a) *I*, (b) *me* before the brochures were sent out.

_____ 3. A number of inquiries were addressed to Jeff and (a) *I*, (b) *me*, (c) *myself*.

_____ 4. When you visit Western Financial, inquire about (a) *its*, (b) *their* GICs.

_____ 5. Apparently one of the applicants forgot to sign (a) *her*, (b) *their* application.

_____ 6. I've never known any man who could work as fast as (a) *him*, (b) *he*.

_____ 7. Give the supplies to (a) *whoever*, (b) *whomever* ordered them.

_____ 8. When he finally found a job, Dante, along with many other recent graduates, described (a) *his*, (b) *their* experience in an employment blog.

_____ 9. Any woman who becomes a charter member of this organization will be able to have (a) *her*, (b) *their* name inscribed on a commemorative plaque.

_____ 10. Everyone has completed the reports except Debbie and (a) *he*, (b) *him*.

---

1. a (1.08h) 3. b (1.08c, 1.08e) 5. a (1.09b) 7. a (1.08j) 9. a (1.09b)

GRAMMAR/MECHANICS CHECKUP—2

Pronouns

Review Sections 1.07–1.09. Then study each of the following statements. In the space provided, write the word that completes the statement correctly and the number of the Handbook principle illustrated. When you finish, compare your responses with those provided on page 417 again. If your responses differ, carefully study again the principles in parentheses.

its (1.09d) **Example** The Recreation and Benefits Committee will be submitting (its, their) report soon.

_____ 1. I was expecting the manager to call. Was it (he, him) who left the message?

________ 2. A serious disagreement between management and (he, him) caused his resignation.

________ 3. It looks as if (her's, hers) is the only report that cites electronic sources.

________ 4. My friend and (I, me, myself) were also asked to work on Saturday.

________ 5. Give the budget figures to (whoever, whomever) asked for them.

________ 6. Everyone except the broker and (I, me, myself) claimed a share of the commission.

________ 7. No one knows that problem better than (he, him, himself).

________ 8. Investment brochures and information were sent to (we, us) shareholders.

CUMULATIVE EDITING QUIZ 1

Use proofreading marks (see Appendix B) to correct errors in the following sentences. All errors must be corrected to receive credit for the sentence. Check with your instructor for the answers.

Example **Max and ~~her~~ she started ~~there~~ their own company in early 2000s.**

1. Neither the citys nor the countys would take responsibility for there budget overruns.
2. Can we keep this matter just between you and I?
3. Only a few secretarys took the day off, despite the storm.
4. Our staff committee gave their recommendation to the president and I as soon as they finished deliberating.
5. Theres really no excuse for we citizens to have no voice in the matter.
6. The manager and myself will deliver supplies to whomever ordered them.
7. Many basketball and hockey star's earn huge salarys.
8. Are you sure that this apartment is their's?
9. Each student must submit their report on Monday.
10. Both the network administrator and myself are concerned about the increase in personal Web use and it's tendency to slow productivity.

Verbs (1.10–1.15)

Verbs show the action of a subject or join the subject to words that describe it.

1.10 Guidelines for Agreement With Subjects. One of the most troublesome areas in English is subject–verb agreement. Consider the following guidelines for making verbs agree with subjects.

a. A singular subject requires a singular verb:

> The stock market *opens* at 10 a.m. (The singular verb *opens* agrees with the singular subject *market.*)
>
> He *doesn't* (not *don't*) work on Saturday.

b. A plural subject requires a plural verb:

> On the packing slip several items *seem* (not *seems*) to be missing.

c. A verb agrees with its subject regardless of prepositional phrases that may intervene:

This list of management objectives *is* extensive. (The singular verb *is* agrees with the singular subject *list.*)

Every one of the letters *shows* (not *show*) proper form.

d. A verb agrees with its subject regardless of intervening phrases introduced by *as well as, in addition to, such as, including, together with,* and similar expressions:

An important memo, together with several contracts, *is* missing. (The singular verb *is* agrees with the singular subject *memo.*)

The president as well as several other top-level executives *approves* of our proposal. (The singular verb *approves* agrees with the subject *president.*)

e. A verb agrees with its subject regardless of the location of the subject:

Here *is* one of the contracts about which you asked. (The verb *is* agrees with its subject *one,* even though it precedes *one.* The adverb *here* cannot function as a subject.)

There *are* many problems yet to be resolved. (The verb *are* agrees with the subject *problems.* The word *there* does not function as a subject.)

In the next office *are* several printers. (In this inverted sentence, the verb *are* must agree with the subject *printers.*)

f. Subjects joined by *and* require a plural verb:

Analyzing the reader and organizing a strategy *are* the first steps in message writing. (The plural verb *are* agrees with the two subjects, *analyzing* and *organizing.*)

The tone and the wording of the message *were* persuasive. (The plural verb *were* agrees with the two subjects, *tone* and *wording.*)

g. Subjects joined by *or* or *nor* may require singular or plural verbs. Make the verb agree with the closer subject:

Neither the memo nor the report *is* ready. (The singular verb *is* agrees with *report,* the closer of the two subjects.)

h. The following indefinite pronouns are singular and require singular verbs: anyone, anybody, anything, each, either, every, everyone, everybody, everything, many a, neither, nobody, nothing, someone, somebody, and something:

Either of the alternatives that you present *is* acceptable. (The verb *is* agrees with the singular subject *either.*)

i. Collective nouns may take singular or plural verbs, depending on whether the members of the group are operating as a unit or individually:

Our management team *is* united in its goal.

The faculty *are* sharply divided on the tuition issue. (Although acceptable, this sentence sounds better recast: The faculty *members* are sharply divided on the tuition issue.)

j. Organization names and titles of publications, although they may appear to be plural, are singular and require singular verbs.

Bergeron, Anderson, and Horne, Inc., *has* (not *have*) hired a marketing consultant.

Thousands of Investment Tips is (not *are*) again on the bestseller list.

1.11 Voice. Voice is that property of verbs that shows whether the subject of the verb acts or is acted upon. Active-voice verbs direct action from the subject toward the object of the verb. Passive-voice verbs direct action toward the subject.

Active voice:	Our employees *send* many emails.
Passive voice:	Many emails *are sent* by our employees.

Business writers generally prefer active-voice verbs because they are specific and forceful. However, passive-voice constructions can help a writer be tactful. Chapter 3 presents strategies for effective use of active- and passive-voice verbs.

1.12 Mood. Three verb moods express the attitude or thought of the speaker or writer toward a subject: (a) the **indicative** mood expresses a fact; (b) the **imperative** mood expresses a command; and (c) the **subjunctive** mood expresses a doubt, a conjecture, or a suggestion.

Indicative:	I am looking for a job.
Imperative:	Begin your job search by networking.
Subjunctive:	I wish I were working.

Of the three, the subjunctive mood creates the most problems for majority of speakers and writers. The most common use of subjunctive mood occurs in clauses including *if* or *wish*. In such clauses substitute the subjunctive verb *were* for the indicative verb *was:*

If he *were* (not *was*) in my position, he would understand.

Mr. Simon acts as if he *were* (not *was*) the boss.

I wish I *were* (not *was*) able to ship your order.

The subjunctive mood can maintain goodwill while conveying negative information. The sentence *I wish I were able to ship your order* sounds more pleasing to a customer than *I cannot ship your order*. However, for all practical purposes, both sentences convey the same negative message.

1.13 Tense. Verbs show the time of an action by their tense. Speakers and writers can use six tenses to show the time of sentence action; for example:

Present tense:	I *work*; he *works*.
Past tense:	I *worked*; she *worked*.
Future tense:	I *will work*; he *will work*.
Present perfect tense:	I *have worked*; he *has worked*.
Past perfect tense:	I *had worked*; she *had worked*.
Future perfect tense:	I *will have worked*; he *will have worked*.

1.14 Guidelines for Verb Tense

a. Use present tense for statements that, although introduced by past-tense verbs, continue to be true:

What did you say his name *is*? (Use the present tense *is* if his name has not changed.)

b. Avoid unnecessary shifts in verb tenses:

The manager *saw* (not *sees*) a great deal of work yet to be completed and *remained* to do it herself.

Although unnecessary shifts in verb tense are to be avoided, not all the verbs within one sentence have to be in the same tense; for example:

> She *said* (past tense) that she *likes* (present tense) to work late.

1.15 Irregular Verbs. Irregular verbs cause difficulty for some writers and speakers. Unlike regular verbs, irregular verbs do not form the past tense and past participle by adding *-ed* to the present form. Here is a partial list of selected troublesome irregular verbs. Consult a dictionary if you are in doubt about a verb form.

Troublesome Irregular Verbs

Present	Past	Past Participle (*always use helping verbs*)
begin	began	begun
break	broke	broken
choose	chose	chosen
come	came	come
drink	drank	drunk
go	went	gone
lay (to place)	laid	laid
lie (to rest)	lay	lain
ring	rang	rung
see	saw	seen
write	wrote	written

a. Use only past-tense verbs to express past tense. Notice that no helping verbs are used to indicate simple past tense:

> The auditors *went* (not *have went*) over our books carefully.
>
> He *came* (not *come*) to see us yesterday.

b. Use past-participle forms for actions completed before the present time. Notice that past-participle forms require helping verbs:

> Steve *had gone* (not *had went*) before we called. (The past participle *gone* is used with the helping verb *had*.)

c. Avoid inconsistent shifts in subject, voice, and mood. Pay particular attention to this problem area because undesirable shifts are often characteristic of student writing.

Inconsistent: When Mrs. Thobani read the report, the error was found. (The first clause is in the active voice; the second, passive.)

Improved: When Mrs. Thobani read the report, she found the error. (Both clauses are in the active voice.)

Inconsistent: The clerk should first conduct an inventory. Then supplies should be requisitioned. (The first sentence is in the active voice; the second, passive.)

Improved: The clerk should first conduct an inventory. Then he or she should requisition supplies. (Both sentences are in the active voice.)

Inconsistent: All workers must wear security badges, and you must also sign a daily time card. (This sentence contains an inconsistent shift in subject from *all workers* in the first clause to *you* in the second clause.)

Improved: All workers must wear security badges, and they must also sign a daily time card.

Inconsistent: Begin the transaction by opening an account; then you enter the customer's name. (This sentence contains an inconsistent shift from the imperative mood in the first clause to the indicative mood in the second clause.)

Improved: Begin the transaction by opening an account; then enter the customer's name. (Both clauses are now in the imperative mood.)

Review Exercise C—Verbs

In the space provided for each item, write *a* or *b* to complete the statement accurately. When you finish, compare your responses with those provided. For each item on which you need review, consult the numbered principle shown in parentheses.

_______ 1. Our directory of customer names and addresses (a) *was* (b) *were* out-of-date.

_______ 2. Improved communication technologies and increased global competition (a) *is,* (b) *are* changing the world of business.

_______ 3. Yesterday Mrs. Phillips (a) *choose,* (b) *chose* a new office on the second floor.

_______ 4. Our management team and our lawyer (a) *is,* (b) *are* researching the privacy issue.

_______ 5. If you had (a) *saw,* (b) *seen* the rough draft, you would better appreciate the final copy.

_______ 6. Although we have (a) *began,* (b) *begun* to replace outmoded equipment, the pace is slow.

_______ 7. Changing attitudes and increased job opportunities (a) *is,* (b) *are* resulting in increased numbers of working women.

_______ 8. If I (a) *was,* (b) *were* you, I would ask for a raise.

_______ 9. The hydraulic equipment that you ordered (a) *is,* (b) *are* packed and will be shipped Friday.

_______ 10. Either of the proposed laws (a) *is,* (b) *are* going to affect our business negatively.

---

1. a (1.10c) 3. b (1.15a) 5. b (1.15b) 7. b (1.10f) 9. a (1.10a)

Review Exercise D—Verbs

In the following sentence pairs, choose the one that illustrates consistency in use of subject, voice, and mood. Write *a* or *b* in the space provided. When you finish, compare your responses with those provided. For each item on which you need review, consult the numbered principle shown in parentheses.

_______ 1. (a) You need more than a knowledge of technology; one also must be able to interact well with people.

(b) You need more than a knowledge of technology; you also must be able to interact well with people.

_______ 2. (a) Tim and Jon were eager to continue, but Bob wanted to quit.

(b) Tim and Jon were eager to continue, but Bob wants to quit.

_______ 3. (a) The salesperson should consult the price list; then you can give an accurate quote to a customer.

(b) The salesperson should consult the price list; then he or she can give an accurate quote to a customer.

______ 4. (a) Read all the instructions first; then you install the printer program.

(b) Read all the instructions first, and then install the printer program.

______ 5. (a) She was an enthusiastic manager who always had a smile for everyone.

(b) She was an enthusiastic manager who always has a smile for everyone.

1. b (1.15c) 3. b (1.15c) 5. a (1.14b)

GRAMMAR/MECHANICS CHECKUP—3

Verbs

Review Sections 1.10–1.15. Then study each of the following statements. Underline any verbs that are used incorrectly. In the space provided, write the correct form (or C if correct) and the number of the Handbook principle illustrated. When you finish, compare your responses with those provided on page 417. If your responses differ, carefully study again the principles in parentheses.

was (1.10c) **Example** Our inventory of raw materials were presented as collateral for a short-term loan.

______ 1. Located across town is a research institute and our product-testing facility.

______ 2. Can you tell me whether a current list with all customers' names and addresses have been sent to marketing?

______ 3. The credit union, along with 20 other large national banks, offer a variety of savings plans.

______ 4. Locating a bank and selecting a savings/chequing plan often require considerable research and study.

______ 5. If Mr. Tutchone had chose the Maximizer Plus savings plan, his money would have earned maximum interest.

______ 6. Nadia acts as if she was the manager.

______ 7. One of the reasons that our Nunavut sales branches have been so costly are the high cost of living.

In the space provided, write the letter of the sentence that illustrates consistency in subject, voice, and mood.

______ 8. (a) If you will read the instructions, the answer can be found.

(b) If you will read the instructions, you will find the answer.

CUMULATIVE EDITING QUIZ 2

Use proofreading marks (see Appendix B) to correct errors in the following sentences. All errors must be corrected to receive credit for the sentence. Check with your instructor for the answers.

1. The production cost and the markup of each item is important in calculating the sale price.
2. Sheila acts as if she was the manager, but we know she is not.

3. The committee are reconsidering their decision in view of recent health care legislation.
4. My all-in-one computer and it's lightweight keyboard is attractive but difficult to use.
5. Waiting in the outer office is a job applicant and a sales representative who you told to stop by.
6. Each applicant could have submitted his application online if he had went to our website.
7. One of the reasons she applied are that she seen the salarys posted at our website.
8. Either of the options that you may chose are acceptable to Jake and myself.
9. Although there anger and frustration is understandable, both editor in chiefs decided to apologize and reprint the article.
10. The Lopez'es, about who the article was written, accepted the apology graciously.

Adjectives and Adverbs (1.16–1.17)

Adjectives describe or limit nouns and pronouns. They often answer the questions *what kind? how many?* or *which one?* Adverbs describe or limit verbs, adjectives, or other adverbs. They often answer the questions *when? how? where?* or *to what extent?*

1.16 Forms. Most adjectives and adverbs have three forms, or degrees: *positive*, *comparative*, and *superlative*.

	Positive	**Comparative**	**Superlative**
Adjective:	clear	clearer	clearest
Adverb:	clearly	more clearly	most clearly

Some adjectives and adverbs have irregular forms:

	Positive	**Comparative**	**Superlative**
Adjective:	good	better	best
	bad	worse	worst
Adverb:	well	better	best

Adjectives and adverbs composed of two or more syllables are usually compared by the use of *more* and *most*; for example:

The Payroll Department is *more efficient* than the Shipping Department.

Payroll is the *most efficient* department in our organization.

1.17 Guidelines for Use

a. Use the comparative degree of the adjective or adverb to compare two persons or things; use the superlative degree to compare three or more:

Of the two plans, which is *better* (not *best*)?

Of all the plans, we like this one *best* (not *better*).

b. Do not create a double comparative or superlative by using *-er* with *more* or *-est* with *most*:

His explanation couldn't have been *clearer* (not *more clearer*).

c. A linking verb (*is, are, look, seem, feel, sound, appear,* and so forth) may introduce a word that describes the verb's subject. In this case be certain to use an adjective, not an adverb:

The characters on the monitor look *bright* (not *brightly*). (Use the adjective *bright* because it follows the linking verb *look* and modifies the noun *characters.*)

The company's letter made the customer feel *bad* (not *badly*). (The adjective *bad* follows the linking verb *feel* and describes the noun *customer.*)

d. Use adverbs, not adjectives, to describe or limit the action of verbs:

The business is running *smoothly* (not *smooth*). (Use the adverb *smoothly* to describe the action of the verb *is running. Smoothly* explains how the business is running.)

Don't take his remark *personally* (not *personal*). (The adverb *personally* describes the action of the verb *take.*)

Drishti said she did *well* (not *good*) on the test. (Use the adverb *well* to tell how she did.)

e. Two or more adjectives that are joined to create a compound modifier before a noun should be hyphenated:

The *four-year-old* child was tired.

Our agency is planning a *coast-to-coast* campaign.

Hyphenate a compound modifier following a noun only if your dictionary shows the hyphen(s):

Our speaker is very *well-known.* (Include the hyphen because most dictionaries do.)

The tired child was four years old. (Omit the hyphens because the expression follows the word it describes, *child,* and because dictionaries do not indicate hyphens.)

f. Keep adjectives and adverbs close to the words they modify:

She asked for a *cup of hot coffee* (not a *hot cup of coffee*).

Patty *had only two days* of vacation left (not *only had two days*).

Students may sit *in the first five rows* (not *in five first rows*).

He *has saved almost* enough money for the trip (not *has almost saved*).

g. Don't confuse *there* with the possessive pronoun *their* or the contraction *they're:*

Put the documents *there.* (The adverb *there* means "at that place or at that point.")

There are two reasons for the change. (The pronoun *there* is used as function word to introduce a sentence or a clause.)

We already have *their* specifications. (The possessive pronoun *their* shows ownership.)

They're coming to inspect today. (The contraction *they're* is a shortened form of *they are.*)

Review Exercise E—Adjectives and Adverbs

In the space provided for each item, write *a, b,* or *c* to complete the statement accurately. If two sentences are shown, select *a* or *b* to indicate the one expressed more effectively. When you finish, compare your responses with those provided. For each item on which you need review, consult the numbered principle shown in parentheses.

_________ 1. After the interview, Yoshi looked (a) *calm,* (b) *calmly.*

_________ 2. Because we appointed a new manager, the advertising campaign is running (a) *smooth*, (b) *smoothly*.

_________ 3. Darren completed the employment test (a) *satisfactorily*, (b) *satisfactory*.

_________ 4. Which is the (a) *more*, (b) *most* dependable of the two cars?

_________ 5. Of all the copiers we tested, this one is the (a) *easier,* (b) *easiest* to operate.

_________ 6. (a) We only thought that it would take two hours for the test.
(b) We thought that it would take only two hours for the test.

_________ 7. (a) The committee decided to retain the last ten tickets.
(b) The committee decided to retain the ten last tickets.

_________ 8. The time passed (a) *quicker*, (b) *more quickly* than we expected.

_________ 9. Today the financial news is (a) *worse*, (b) *worst* than yesterday.

_________ 10. You must check the document (a) *page by page*, (b) *page-by-page.*

---

1. a (1.17c) 3. a (1.17d) 5. b (1.17a) 7. a (1.17f) 9. a (1.17a)

GRAMMAR/MECHANICS CHECKUP—4

Adjectives and Adverbs

Review Sections 1.16 and 1.17. Then study each of the following statements. Underline any inappropriate forms. In the space provided, write the correct form (or *C* if correct) and the number of the Handbook principle illustrated. You may need to consult your dictionary for current practice regarding some compound adjectives. When you finish, compare your responses with those provided on page 417. If your answers differ, carefully study again the principles in parentheses.

live-and-let-live (1.17e) Example He was one of those individuals with a live and let live attitude.

_________ 1. Most of our long time customers have credit card accounts.

_________ 2. The Internet supplied the answer so quick that we were all amazed.

_________ 3. He only had $5 in his pocket.

_________ 4. Although the car was four years old, it was in good condition.

_________ 5. Of the two colours, which is best for a Web background?

_________ 6. Channel 12 presents up to the minute news broadcasts.

_________ 7. The conclusion drawn from the statistics couldn't have been more clearer.

_________ 8. If you feel badly about the transaction, contact your portfolio manager.

Prepositions (1.18)

Prepositions are connecting words that join nouns or pronouns to other words in a sentence. The words *about, at, from, in,* and *to* are examples of prepositions.

1.18 Guidelines for Use

a. Include necessary prepositions:

What type *of* software do you need (not *What type software*)?

I graduated *from* high school two years ago (not *I graduated high school*).

b. Omit unnecessary prepositions:

Where is the meeting? (Not *Where is the meeting at?*)

Both printers work well. (Not *Both of the printers...*)

Where are you going? (Not *Where are you going to?*)

c. Avoid the overuse of prepositional phrases.

Weak: We have received your application for credit at our branch in the Windsor area.

Improved: We have received your Windsor credit application.

d. Repeat the preposition before the second of two related elements:

Applicants use the résumé effectively by summarizing their most important experiences and *by* relating their education to the jobs sought.

e. Include the second preposition when two prepositions modify a single object:

George's appreciation *of* and aptitude *for* computers led to a promising career.

Conjunctions (1.19)

Conjunctions connect words, phrases, and clauses. They act as signals, indicating when a thought is being added, contrasted, or altered. Coordinating conjunctions (such as *and, or, but*) and other words that act as connectors (such as *however, therefore, when, as*) tell the reader or listener what direction a thought is heading. They are like road signs signalling what's ahead.

1.19 Guidelines for Use

a. Use coordinating conjunctions to connect only sentence elements that are parallel or balanced.

Weak: His report was correct and written in a concise manner.

Improved: His report was correct and concise.

Weak: Management has the capacity to increase fraud, or reduction can be achieved through the policies it adopts.

Improved: Management has the capacity to increase or reduce fraud through the policies it adopts.

b. Do not use the word *like* as a conjunction:

It seems as *if* (not *like*) this day will never end.

c. Avoid using *when* or *where* inappropriately. A common writing fault occurs in sentences with clauses introduced by *is when* and *is where*. Written English ordinarily requires a noun (or a group of words functioning as a noun) following the linking verb is. Instead of acting as conjunctions in these constructions, the words *where* and *when* function as adverbs, creating faulty grammatical equations (adverbs cannot complete equations set up by linking verbs). To avoid the problem, revise the sentence, eliminating *is when* or *is where*.

Weak: A bullish market is when prices are rising in the stock market.

Improved: A bullish market is created when prices are rising in the stock market.

Weak: A flow chart is when you make a diagram showing the step-by-step progression of a procedure.

Improved: A flow chart is a diagram showing the step-by-step progression of a procedure.

Weak: A podcast is where a pre-recorded audio program is posted to a Website.

Improved: A podcast is a pre-recorded audio program posted to a website.

A similar faulty construction occurs in the expression *I hate when*. English requires nouns, noun clauses, or pronouns to act as objects of verbs, not adverbs.

Weak: I hate when we're asked to work overtime.

Improved: I hate it when we're asked to work overtime.

Improved: I hate being asked to work overtime.

d. Don't confuse the adverb *then* with the conjunction *than*. *Then* means "at that time"; *than* indicates the second element in a comparison:

We would rather remodel *than* (not *then*) move.

First, the equipment is turned on; *then* (not *than*) the program is loaded.

Review Exercise F—Prepositions and Conjunctions

In the space provided for each item, write *a* or *b* to indicate the sentence that is expressed more effectively. When you finish, compare your responses with those provided. For each item on which you need review, consult the numbered principle shown in parentheses.

_______ 1. (a) The chief forgot to tell everyone where today's meeting is.
(b) The chief forgot to tell everyone where today's meeting is at.

_______ 2. (a) Josh Samuels graduated college last June.
(b) Josh Samuels graduated from college last June.

_______ 3. (a) Both employees enjoyed setting their own hours.
(b) Both of the employees enjoyed setting their own hours.

_______ 4. (a) What style of typeface should we use?
(b) What style typeface should we use?

_______ 5. (a) Mediation in a labour dispute occurs when a neutral person helps union and management reach an agreement.
(b) Mediation in a labour dispute is where a neutral person helps union and management reach an agreement.

_______ 6. (a) We expect to finish up the work soon.
(b) We expect to finish the work soon.

_______ 7. (a) Your client may respond by email or a telephone call may be made.
(b) Your client may respond by email or by telephone.

_______ 8. (a) Sara exhibited both an awareness of and talent for developing innovations.

(b) Sara exhibited both an awareness and talent for developing innovations.

_______ 9. (a) An ombudsman is an individual hired by management to investigate and resolve employee complaints.

(b) An ombudsman is when management hires an individual to investigate and resolve employee complaints.

_______ 10. (a) By including accurate data and by writing clearly, you will produce effective messages.

(b) By including accurate data and writing clearly, you will produce effective messages.

---

1. a (1.18b) 3. a (1.18b) 5. a (1.19c) 7. b (1.19a) 9. a (1.19c)

GRAMMAR/MECHANICS CHECKUP—5

Prepositions and Conjunctions

Review Sections 1.18 and 1.19. Then study each of the following statements. Write *a* or *b* to indicate the sentence in which the idea is expressed more effectively. Also record the number of the Handbook principle illustrated. When you finish, compare your responses with those provided on page 417. If your answers differ, carefully study again the principles shown in parentheses.

b (1.18a) **Example** (a) Raoul will graduate college this spring.

(b) Raoul will graduate from college this spring.

_______ 1. (a) DataTech enjoyed greater profits this year then it expected.

(b) DataTech enjoyed greater profits this year than it expected.

_______ 2. (a) Dr. Simon has a great interest and appreciation for the study of robotics.

(b) Dr. Simon has a great interest in and appreciation for the study of robotics.

_______ 3. (a) Gross profit is where you compute the difference between total sales and the cost of goods sold.

(b) Gross profit is computed by finding the difference between total sales and the cost of goods sold.

_______ 4. (a) We advertise to increase the frequency of product use, to introduce complementary products, and to enhance our corporate image.

(b) We advertise to have our products used more often, when we have complementary products to introduce, and we are interested in making our corporation look better to the public.

_______ 5. (a) What type printer do you prefer?

(b) What type of printer do you prefer?

_______ 6. (a) The sale of our Halifax office last year should improve this year's profits.

(b) The sale of our office in Halifax during last year should improve the profits for this year.

_______ 7. (a) Do you know where the meeting is at?

(b) Do you know where the meeting is?

_______ 8. (a) They printed the newsletter on yellow paper like we asked them to do.

(b) They printed the newsletter on yellow paper as we asked them to do.

CUMULATIVE EDITING QUIZ 3

Use proofreading marks (see Appendix B) to correct errors in the following sentences. All errors must be corrected to receive credit for the sentence. Check with your instructor for the answers.

1. Her new tablet is definitely more faster then her previous tablet.
2. Max said that he felt badly that he missed his appointment with you and myself.
3. Neither the managers nor the union are happy at how slow the talks are progressing.
4. Just between you and I, we have learned not to take the boss's criticism personal.
5. After completing a case by case search, the consultant promised to send his report to Carlos and I.
6. If you was me, which of the two job offers do you think is best?
7. Did your team members tell you where there meeting is at?
8. Jason felt that he had done good on the three hour certification exam.
9. It seems like our step by step instructions could have been more clearer.
10. I hate when I'm expected to finish up by myself.

PUNCTUATION REVIEW

Commas 1 (2.01–2.04)

2.01 Series. Commas are used to separate three or more equal elements (words, phrases, or short clauses) in a series. To ensure separation of the last two elements, careful writers always use a comma before the conjunction in a series:

Business letters usually contain a dateline, address, salutation, body, and closing. (This series contains words.)

The job of an ombudsman is to examine employee complaints, resolve disagreements between management and employees, and ensure fair treatment. (This series contains phrases.)

Interns complete basic office tasks, marketing coordinators manage author events, and editors proofread completed projects. (This series contains short clauses.)

2.02 Direct Address. Commas are used to set off the names of individuals being addressed:

Your inquiry, *Mrs. Johnson,* has been referred to me.

We genuinely hope that we may serve you, *Mr. Zhou.*

2.03 Parenthetical Expressions. Skilled writers use parenthetical words, phrases, and clauses to guide the reader from one thought to the next. When these expressions interrupt the flow of a sentence and are unnecessary for its grammatical completeness, they should be set off with commas. Examples of commonly used parenthetical expressions follow:

all things considered	however	needless to say
as a matter of fact	in addition	nevertheless
as a result	incidentally	no doubt
as a rule	in fact	of course
at the same time	in my opinion	on the contrary
consequently	in the first place	on the other hand
for example	in the meantime	therefore
furthermore	moreover	under the circumstances

As a matter of fact, I wrote to you just yesterday. (Phrase used at the beginning of a sentence.)

We will, *in the meantime,* send you a replacement order. (Phrase used in the middle of a sentence.)

Your satisfaction is our first concern, *needless to say.* (Phrase used at the end of a sentence.)

Do not use commas if the expression is necessary for the completeness of the sentence:

Kimberly had *no doubt* that she would finish the report. (Omit commas because the expression is necessary for the completeness of the sentence.)

2.04 Dates, Addresses, and Geographical Items. When dates, addresses, and geographical items contain more than one element, the second and succeeding elements are normally set off by commas.

a. Dates:

The conference was held February 2 at our home office. (No comma is needed for one element.)

The conference was held February 2, 2018, at our home office. (Two commas set off the second element.)

The conference was held Tuesday, February 2, 2018, at our home office. (Commas set off the second and third elements.)

In February 2018 the conference was held. (This alternate style omitting commas is acceptable if only the month and year are written.)

b. Addresses:

The letter addressed to Jim W. Ellman, 600 Ellerby Trail, Calgary, AB T4E 8N9, should be sent today. (Commas are used between all elements except the province and postal code, which in this special instance act as a single unit.)

c. Geographical items:

She moved from Whitehorse, Yukon, to Toronto, Ontario. (Commas set off the province/territory unless it appears at the end of the sentence, in which case only one comma is used.)

In separating cities from provinces/territories and days from years, many writers remember the initial comma but forget the final one, as in the examples that follow:

The package from Sydney, Nova Scotia{,} was lost.

We opened June 1, 2009{,} and have grown steadily since.

Review Exercise G—Commas 1

Insert necessary commas in the following sentences. In the space provided, write the number of commas that you add. Write *C* if no commas are needed. When you finish, compare your responses with those provided. For each item on which you need review, consult the numbered principle shown in parentheses.

________ 1. As a rule we do not provide complimentary tickets.

________ 2. I have no doubt that your calculations are correct.

________ 3. Every accredited TV newscaster radio broadcaster and blogger had access to the media room.

________ 4. The employees who are eligible for promotions are Terry Evelyn Vicki Rosanna and Steve.

________ 5. Many of our customers include architects engineers attorneys and others who are interested in database management programs.

________ 6. The new book explains how to choose appropriate legal protection for ideas trade secrets copyrights patents and restrictive covenants.

________ 7. You may however prefer to be in touch directly with the manufacturer in China.

________ 8. The rally has been scheduled for Monday January 12 in the campus stadium.

________ 9. Goodstone Tire & Rubber for example recalled 400,000 steel-belted radial tires because some tires failed their rigorous tests.

________ 10. In the meantime thank you for whatever assistance you are able to furnish.

---

1. (1) rule, (2.03) 3. (2) newscaster, radio broadcaster, (2.01) 5. (3) architects, engineers, attorneys, (2.01) 7. (2) may, however, 9. (2) Rubber, for example, (2.03)

GRAMMAR/MECHANICS CHECKUP—6

Commas 1

Review Sections 2.01–2.04. Then study each of the following statements and insert necessary commas. In the space provided, write the number of commas that you add; write *0* if no commas are needed. Also record the number of the Handbook principle illustrated. When you finish, compare your responses with those on page 417. If your answers differ, carefully study again the principles shown in parentheses.

2 (2.01) **Example** In this class students learn to write clear and concise business letters, memos, and reports.

________ 1. We do not as a rule allow employees to take time off for dental appointments.

________ 2. You may be sure Ms. Schwartz that your car will be ready by 4 p.m.

________ 3. Anyone who is reliable conscientious and honest should be very successful.

________ 4. We are relocating our distribution centre from Calgary Alberta to La Salle Quebec.

________ 5. The last meeting recorded in the minutes was on February 4 2011 in Windsor.

________ 6. The package mailed to Ms. Leslie Holmes 3430 Larkspur Lane Regina Saskatchewan S5L 2E2 arrived three weeks after it was mailed.

______ 7. Eric was assigned three jobs: checking supplies replacing inventories and distributing delivered goods.

______ 8. We will work diligently to retain your business Mr. Fuhai.

Commas 2 (2.05–2.09)

2.05 Independent Clauses. An independent clause is a group of words that has a subject and a verb and that could stand as a complete sentence. When two such clauses are joined by *and, or, nor*, or *but*, use a comma before the conjunction:

> We can ship your merchandise July 12, but we must have your payment first.

> Net income before taxes is calculated, and this total is then combined with income from operations.

Notice that each independent clause in the preceding two examples could stand alone as a complete sentence. Do not use a comma unless each group of words is a complete thought (i.e., has its own subject and verb).

> Our accountant calculates net income before taxes *and* then combines that figure with income from operations. (No comma is needed because no subject follows *and.*)

2.06 Dependent Clauses. Dependent clauses do not make sense by themselves; for their meaning they depend on independent clauses.

a. **Introductory clauses.** When a dependent clause precedes an independent clause, it is followed by a comma. Such clauses are often introduced by *when, if,* and *as*:

> *When your request came*, we responded immediately.

> *As I mentioned earlier*, Clementine James is the manager.

b. **Terminal clauses.** If a dependent clause falls at the end of a sentence, use a comma only if the dependent clause is an afterthought:

> We have rescheduled the meeting for October 23, *if this date meets with your approval.* (Comma used because dependent clause is an afterthought.)

> We responded immediately *when we received your request.* (No comma is needed.)

c. **Essential versus nonessential clauses.** If a dependent clause provides information that is unneeded for the grammatical completeness of a sentence, use commas to set it off. In determining whether such a clause is essential or nonessential, ask yourself whether the reader needs the information contained in the clause to identify the word it explains:

> Our district sales manager, *who just returned from a trip to the Northern Ontario District*, prepared this report. (This construction assumes that there is only one district sales manager. Because the sales manager is clearly identified, the dependent clause is not essential and requires commas.)

> The salesperson *who just returned from a trip to the Northern Ontario District* prepared this report. (The dependent clause in this sentence is necessary to identify which salesperson prepared the report. Therefore, use no commas.)

> The position of assistant sales manager, *which we discussed with you last week*, is still open. (Careful writers use which to introduce nonessential clauses. Commas are also necessary.)

The position *that we discussed with you last week* is still open. (Careful writers use *that* to introduce essential clauses. No commas are used.)

2.07 Phrases. A phrase is a group of related words that lacks both a subject and a verb. A phrase that precedes a main clause is followed by a comma if the phrase contains a verb form or has five or more words:

Beginning November 1, Worldwide Savings will offer two new combination chequing/savings plans. (A comma follows this introductory phrase because the phrase contains the verb form *beginning.*)

To promote our plan, we will conduct an extensive social media advertising campaign. (A comma follows this introductory phrase because the phrase contains the verb form *to promote.*)

In a period of only one year, we were able to improve our market share by 30 percent. (A comma follows the introductory phrase—actually two prepositional phrases—because its total length exceeds five words.)

In 2014 our organization installed a multiuser system that could transfer programs easily. (No comma needed after the short introductory phrase.)

2.08 Two or More Adjectives. Use a comma to separate two or more adjectives that equally describe a noun. A good way to test the need for a comma is this: Mentally insert the word *and* between the adjectives. If the resulting phrase sounds natural, a comma is used to show the omission of *and*:

We're looking for a *versatile, error-free* operating system. (Use a comma to separate *versatile* and *error-free* because they independently describe *operating system. And* has been omitted.)

Our *experienced, courteous* staff is ready to serve you. (Use a comma to separate *experienced* and *courteous* because they independently describe *staff. And* has been omitted.)

It was difficult to refuse the *sincere young* caller. (No commas are needed between *sincere* and *young* because *and* has not been omitted.)

2.09 Appositives. Words that rename or explain preceding nouns or pronouns are called *appositives*. An appositive that provides information not essential to the identification of the word it describes should be set off by commas:

James Wilson, *the project director for Sperling's,* worked with our architect. (The appositive, *the project director for Sperling's,* adds nonessential information. Commas set it off.)

Review Exercise H—Commas 2

Insert only necessary commas in the following sentences. In the space provided, indicate the number of commas that you add for each sentence. If a sentence requires no commas, write *C*. When you finish, compare your responses with those provided. For each item on which you need review, consult the numbered principle shown in parentheses.

________ 1. A corporation must register in the province in which it does business and it must operate within the laws of that province.

________ 2. If you will study the cost analysis you will see that our company offers the best system at the lowest price.

_____ 3. The salesperson who amasses the greatest number of sales points will win a bonus trip to Montreal.

_____ 4. On the basis of these findings I recommend that we retain Jane Rada as our counsel.

_____ 5. The bright young student who worked for us last summer will be able to return this summer.

_____ 6. We will be able to process your application when you return the completed form.

_____ 7. Knowing that you wanted this merchandise immediately I took the liberty of sending it by FedEx.

_____ 8. A tax credit for energy-saving homes will expire at the end of the year but Ottawa might extend it if pressure groups prevail.

_____ 9. For the benefit of employees recently hired we are offering a two-hour seminar regarding employee benefit programs.

_____ 10. The meeting has been rescheduled for September 30 if this date meets with your approval.

---

1. (1) business, (2.05) 3. C (2.06c) 5. C (2.08) 7. (1) immediately, (2.07) 9. (1) hired, (2.07)

GRAMMAR/MECHANICS CHECKUP—7

Commas 2

Review Sections 2.05–2.09. Then study each of the following statements and insert necessary commas. In the space provided, write the number of commas that you add; write *0* if no commas are needed. Also record the number of the Handbook principle(s) illustrated. When you finish, compare your responses with those provided on page 417. If your answers differ, carefully study again the principles shown in parentheses.

<u>1 (2.06a)</u> **Example** When businesses encounter financial problems, they often reduce their administrative staffs.

_____ 1. As stated in the warranty this printer is guaranteed for one year.

_____ 2. Today's profits come from products currently on the market and tomorrow's profits come from products currently on the drawing boards.

_____ 3. One large automobile manufacturer which must remain nameless recognizes that buyer perception is behind the success of any new product.

_____ 4. The imaginative promising agency opened its offices April 22 in Cambridge.

_____ 5. Ian Sims our sales manager in the North Bay area will present the new sales campaign at the June meeting.

_____ 6. To motivate prospective buyers we are offering a cash rebate of $25.

Review of Commas 1 and 2

_____ 7. When you receive the application please fill it out and return it before Monday January 3.

_____ 8. On the other hand we are very interested in hiring hard-working conscientious individuals.

Commas 3 (2.10–2.15)

2.10 Degrees and Abbreviations. Degrees following individuals' names are set off by commas. Abbreviations such as *Jr.* and *Sr.* are also set off by commas unless the individual referred to prefers to omit the commas:

Anne G. Turner, *MBA*, joined the firm.

Michael Migliano, *Jr.*, and Michael Migliano, *Sr.*, work as a team.

Anthony A. Gensler *Jr.* wrote the report. (The individual referred to prefers to omit commas.)

The abbreviations *Inc.* and *Ltd.* are set off by commas only if a company's legal name has a comma just before this kind of abbreviation. To determine a company's practice, consult its stationery or a directory listing:

Firestone and Blythe, *Inc.*, is based in Waterloo. (Notice that two commas are used.)

Computers *Inc.* is extending its franchise system. (The company's legal name does not include a comma before *Inc.*)

2.11 Omitted Words. A comma is used to show the omission of words that are understood:

On Monday we received 15 applications; on Friday, only 3. (Comma shows the omission of *we received.*)

2.12 Contrasting Statements. Commas are used to set off contrasting or opposing expressions. These expressions are often introduced by such words as *not, never, but*, and *yet*:

The prime minister suggested cutbacks, *not* layoffs, to ease the crisis.

Our budget for the year is reduced, *yet* adequate.

The greater the effort, the greater the reward.

If increased emphasis is desired, use dashes instead of commas, as in *Only the sum of $100—not $1,000—was paid on this account.*

2.13 Clarity. Commas are used to separate words repeated for emphasis. Commas are also used to separate words that may be misread if not separated:

The building is a long, long way from completion.

Whatever is, is right.

No matter what, you know we support you.

2.14 Quotations and Appended Questions

a. A comma is used to separate a short quotation from the rest of a sentence. If the quotation is divided into two parts, two commas are used:

The manager asked, "Shouldn't the managers control the specialists?"

"Perhaps the specialists," replied Tim, "have unique information."

b. A comma is used to separate a question appended (added) to a statement:

You will confirm the shipment, won't you?

2.15 Comma Overuse. Do not use commas needlessly. For example, commas should not be inserted merely because you might drop your voice if you were speaking the sentence:

> One of the reasons for expanding our East Coast operations is{,} that we anticipate increased sales in that area. (Do not insert a needless comma before a clause.)
>
> I am looking for an article entitled{,} "State-of-the-Art Communications." (Do not insert a needless comma after the word *entitled*.)
>
> Customers may purchase many food and nonfood items in convenience stores *such as*{,} 7-Eleven and Couche-Tard. (Do not insert a needless comma after *such as*.)
>
> We have{,} at this time{,} an adequate supply of parts. (Do not insert needless commas around prepositional phrases.)

Review Exercise I—Commas 3

Insert only necessary commas in the following sentences. Remove unnecessary commas with the delete sign (☡). In the space provided, indicate the number of commas inserted or deleted in each sentence. If a sentence requires no changes, write C. When you finish, compare your responses with those provided. For each item on which you need review, consult the numbered principle shown in parentheses.

_______ 1. We expected Anna Wisniowska not Tyler Rosen to conduct the audit.

_______ 2. "We simply must have" said Brian "a bigger budget to start this project."

_______ 3. You returned the merchandise last month didn't you?

_______ 4. The better our advertising and recruiting the stronger our personnel pool will be.

_______ 5. "On the contrary" said Kamal Stevens "we will continue our present marketing strategies."

_______ 6. What we need is more not fewer suggestions for improvement.

_______ 7. "Canada is now entering" said Minister Saunders "the Age of Innovation."

_______ 8. The talk by D. A. Spindler PhD was particularly difficult to follow because of his technical and abstract vocabulary.

_______ 9. We are very fortunate to have, at our disposal, the services of excellent professionals.

_______ 10. Emily Sandoval was named legislative counsel; Sam Freeman executive adviser.

---

1. (2) Wisniowska, Rosen, (2.12) 3. (1) month, (2.14b) 5. (2) contrary," Stevens, (2.14a) 7. (2) entering," Saunders, (2.14a) 9. (2) have at our disposal (2.15)

GRAMMAR/MECHANICS CHECKUP—8

Commas 3

Review Sections 2.10–2.15. Then study each of the following statements and insert necessary commas. In the space provided, write the number of commas that you add; write *0* if no commas are needed. Also record the number of the Handbook principle(s) illustrated. When you finish, compare your responses with those provided on page 417. If your answers differ, carefully study again the principles shown in parentheses.

<u>2 (2.12)</u> **Example** It was Lucia Bosano, not Melinda, Ho who was given the Kirkland account.

________ 1. "The choice of a good name" said President Etienne "cannot be overestimated."

________ 2. Hanna H. Cox PhD and Katherine Meridian MBA were hired as consultants.

________ 3. The bigger the investment the greater the profit.

Review Commas 1, 2, 3

________ 4. We think however that you should reexamine your website and that you should consider redesigning its navigation system.

________ 5. Our convention will attract more participants if it is held in a resort location such as Collingwood the Laurentians or Banff.

________ 6. A recent study of productivity that was conducted by authoritative researchers revealed that Canadian workers are more productive than workers in Europe or Japan.

________ 7. The report concluded that Canada's secret productivity weapon was not bigger companies more robots or even brainier managers.

________ 8. As a matter of fact the report said that Canada's productivity resulted from the rigours of unprotected hands-off competition.

CUMULATIVE EDITING QUIZ 4

Use proofreading marks (see Appendix B) to correct errors and omissions in the following sentences. All errors must be corrected to receive credit for the sentence. Check with your instructor for the answers.

1. Emails must be written clear and concise, to ensure that receivers comprehend the message quick.
2. Our next sales campaign of course must target key decision makers.
3. In the meantime our online sales messages must include more then facts testimonials and guarantees.
4. The Small Business Administration which provide disaster loans are establishing additional offices in High River Calgary and Lethbridge.
5. Because we rely on email we have reduced our use of faxes, and voice messages.
6. In business time is money.
7. "The first product to use a bar code" said Alice Beasley "was Wrigley's gum."
8. In 1912, the Model 41 Touring went into production in Sam McLaughlin's plant in Oshawa Ontario.
9. As Professor Payne predicted the resourceful well trained graduate was hired quick.
10. The company's liability insurance in view of the laws that went into effect January 1 need to be increased.

Semicolons (2.16)

2.16 Independent Clauses, Series, Introductory Expressions

a. **Independent clauses with conjunctive adverbs.** Use a semicolon before a conjunctive adverb that separates two independent clauses. Some of the most common conjunctive adverbs are *therefore, consequently, however,* and *moreover:*

> Business messages should sound conversational; *therefore,* writers often use familiar words and contractions.
>
> The bank closes its doors at 5 p.m.; *however,* the ATM is open 24 hours a day.

Notice that the word following a semicolon is *not* capitalized (unless, of course, that word is a proper noun).

b. **Independent clauses without conjunctive adverbs.** Use a semicolon to separate closely related independent clauses when no conjunctive adverb is used:

> RRSPs are taxed upon redemption; TFSAs are not.
>
> Ambient lighting fills the room; task lighting illuminates each workstation.

Use a semicolon in *compound* sentences, not in *complex* sentences:

> After one week the paper feeder jammed; we tried different kinds of paper. (Use a semicolon in a compound sentence.)
>
> After one week the paper feeder jammed, although we tried different kinds of paper. (Use a comma in a complex sentence. Do not use a semicolon after *jammed.*)

The semicolon is very effective for joining two closely related thoughts. Don't use it, however, unless the ideas are truly related.

c. **Independent clauses with other commas.** Normally, a comma precedes *and, or,* and *but* when those conjunctions join independent clauses. However, if either clause contains commas, the writer may elect to change the comma preceding the conjunction to a semicolon to ensure correct reading:

> Our primary concern is financing; and we have discovered, as you warned us, that capital sources are quite scarce.

d. **Series with internal commas.** Use semicolons to separate items in a series when one or more of the items contains internal commas:

> Delegates from Charlottetown, Prince Edward Island; Moncton, New Brunswick; and Truro, Nova Scotia, attended the conference.
>
> The speakers were Kevin Lang, manager, Riko Enterprises; Henry Holtz, vice president, Trendex, Inc.; and Margaret Woo, personnel director, West Coast Productions.

e. **Introductory expressions.** Use a semicolon when an introductory expression such as *namely, for instance, that is,* or *for example* introduces a list following an independent clause:

> Switching to computerized billing are several local companies; namely, Ryson Electronics, Miller Vending Services, and Black Home Heating.
>
> The author of a report should consider many sources; for example, books, periodicals, databases, and newspapers.

Colons (2.17–2.19)

2.17 Listed Items

a. **With colon.** Use a colon after a complete thought that introduces a formal list of items. A formal list is often preceded by such words and phrases as *these, thus, the following,* and *as follows.* A colon is also used when words and phrases like these are implied but not stated:

> Additional costs in selling a house involve *the following:* title examination fee, title insurance costs, and closing fee. (Use a colon when a complete thought introduces a formal list.)

> Collective bargaining focuses on several key issues: cost-of-living adjustments, fringe benefits, job security, and work hours. (The introduction of the list is implied in the preceding clause.)

b. **Without colon.** Do not use a colon when the list immediately follows a *to be* verb or a preposition:

> The employees who should receive the preliminary plan are James Sears, Monica Spears, and Rose Lopretti. (No colon is used after the verb *are.*)

> We expect to consider equipment for Accounting, Legal Services, and Payroll. (No colon is used after the preposition *for.*)

2.18 Quotations. Use a colon to introduce long one-sentence quotations and quotations of two or more sentences:

> Our consultant said: "This system can support up to 32 users. It can be used for decision support, computer-aided design, and software development operations at the same time."

2.19 Salutations. Use a colon after the salutation of a business letter:

> Dear Mrs. Seaman:
>
> Dear Jamie:

Review Exercise J—Semicolons, Colons

In the following sentences, add semicolons, colons, and necessary commas. For each sentence indicate the number of punctuation marks that you add. If a sentence requires no punctuation, write C. When you finish, compare your responses with those provided. For each item on which you need review, consult the numbered principle shown in parentheses.

________ 1. Technological advances make full-motion video viewable on small screens consequently mobile phone makers and carriers are rolling out new services and phones.

________ 2. The sedan version of the automobile is available in these colours Olympic red metallic silver and Aztec gold.

________ 3. The individuals who should receive copies of this announcement are Jeff Wong Alicia Green and Kim Doogan.

________ 4. Many of our potential customers are in Southern Ontario therefore our promotional effort will be strongest in that area.

________ 5. Three dates have been reserved for initial interviews January 15 February 1 and February 12.

_______ 6. Several staff members are near the top of their salary ranges we must reclassify their jobs.

_______ 7. If you apply for an Advantage Express card today we will waive the annual fee moreover you will earn 10,000 bonus miles and reward points for every $1 you spend on purchases.

_______ 8. Monthly reports are missing from the Legal Department Human Resources Department and Engineering Department.

_______ 9. The convention committee is considering Victoria British Columbia Whistler British Columbia and Canmore Alberta.

_______ 10. Sherry first asked about salary next she inquired about benefits.

1. (2) screens; consequently, (2.16a) 3. (2) Wong, Alicia Green, (2.01, 2.17b) 5. (3) interviews: January 15, February 1, (2.01, 2.17a) 7. (3) today, fee; moreover, (2.06a, 2.16a) 9. (5) Victoria, British Columbia; Whistler, British Columbia; Canmore, (2.16d)

GRAMMAR/MECHANICS CHECKUP—9

Semicolons and Colons

Review Sections 2.16–2.19. Then study each of the following statements. Insert any necessary punctuation. Use the delete symbol to omit unnecessary punctuation. In the space provided, indicate the number of changes you made and record the number of the Handbook principle(s) illustrated. (When you replace one punctuation mark with another, count it as one change.) If you make no changes, write *0*. This exercise concentrates on semicolon and colon use, but you will also be responsible for correct comma use. When you finish, compare your responses with those shown on page 417. If your responses differ, carefully study again the specific principles shown in parentheses.

2 (2.16a) **Example** The job of Mr. Wellworth is to make sure that his company has enough cash to meet its obligations; moreover, he is responsible for locating credit when needed.

_______ 1. We must negotiate short-term financing during the following months September October and November.

_______ 2. Although some firms rarely, if ever, need to borrow short-term money many businesses find that they require significant credit to pay for current production and sales costs.

_______ 3. A grocery store probably requires no short-term credit, a greeting card manufacturer however typically would need considerable short-term credit.

_______ 4. The prime interest rate is set by the Bank of Canada and this rate goes up or down as the cost of money to the bank itself fluctuates.

_______ 5. Most banks are in business to lend money to commercial customers for example retailers service companies manufacturers and construction firms.

_______ 6. When Avionics, Inc., was refused by Federal Business Development Bank its financial managers submitted applications to the following Worldwide Investments, Dominion Securities, and Mid Mountain Group.

_______ 7. The cost of financing capital investments at the present time is very high therefore Avionics' managers may elect to postpone certain expansion projects.

_______ 8. If interest rates reach as high as 18 percent the cost of borrowing becomes prohibitive and many businesses are forced to reconsider or abandon projects that require financing.

Apostrophes (2.20–2.22)

2.20 Basic Rule. The apostrophe is used to show ownership, origin, authorship, or measurement.

Ownership:	We are looking for *Brian's keys.*
Origin:	At the *president's suggestion,* we doubled the order.
Authorship:	The *accountant's annual report* was questioned.
Measurement:	In *two years' time* we expect to reach our goal.

a. **Ownership words not ending in *s*.** To place the apostrophe correctly, you must first determine whether the ownership word ends in an *s* sound. If it does not, add an apostrophe and an *s* to the ownership word. The following examples show ownership words that do not end in an *s* sound:

the employee's file	(the file of a single employee)
a member's address	(the address of a single member)
a year's time	(the time of a single year)
a month's notice	(notice of a single month)
the company's building	(the building of a single company)

b. **Ownership words ending in *s*.** If the ownership word does end in an *s* sound, usually add only an apostrophe:

several employees' files	(files of several employees)
ten members' addresses	(addresses of ten members)
five years' time	(time of five years)
several months' notice	(notice of several months)
many companies' buildings	(buildings of many companies)

A few singular nouns that end in *s* are pronounced with an extra syllable when they become possessive. To these words, add *'s.*

my boss's desk the waitress's table the actress's costume

Use no apostrophe if a noun is merely plural, not possessive:

All the sales representatives, as well as the assistants and managers, had their names and telephone numbers listed in the directory.

2.21 Names Ending in *s* or an *s* Sound. The possessive form of names ending in *s* or an *s* sound follows the same guidelines as for common nouns. If an extra syllable can be pronounced without difficulty, add *'s* . If the extra syllable is hard to pronounce, end with an apostrophe only.

Add apostrophe and *s*	**Add apostrophe only**
Russ's computer	New Orleans' cuisine
Bill Gates's business	Los Angeles' freeways
Mrs. Jones's home	the Morrises' family
Mr. Lopez's desk	the Lopezes' pool

Individual preferences in pronunciation may cause variation in a few cases. For example, some people may prefer not to pronounce an extra *s* in examples such as *Bill Gates' business*. However, the possessive form of plural names is consistent: *the*

Joneses' home, the Burgesses' children, the Bushes' car. Notice that the article *the* is a clue in determining whether a name is singular or plural.

2.22 Gerunds. Use *'s* to make a noun possessive when it precedes a gerund, a verb form used as a noun:

> Ken Smith's smoking prompted a new office policy. (Ken *Smith* is possessive because it modifies the gerund *smoking.*)
>
> It was Betsy's careful proofreading that revealed the discrepancy.

Review Exercise K—Apostrophes

Insert necessary apostrophes and corrections in the following sentences. In the space provided for each sentence, write the corrected word. If none were corrected, write C. When you finish, compare your responses with those provided. For each item on which you need review, consult the numbered principle shown in parentheses.

________ 1. In five years time, Lisa hopes to repay all of her student loans.

________ 2. All the employees personnel folders must be updated.

________ 3. The Harrises daughter lived in Halifax for two years.

________ 4. Both companies headquarters will be moved within the next six months.

________ 5. Some of their assets could be liquidated; therefore, a few of the creditors received funds.

________ 6. The package of electronics parts arrived safely despite two weeks delay.

________ 7. According to Mr. Parvez latest proposal, all employees would receive an additional holiday.

________ 8. His supervisor frequently had to correct Jacks financial reports.

________ 9. Mr. Jackson estimated that he spent a years profits in reorganizing his staff.

________ 10. The contract is not valid without Mrs. Harris signature.

---

1. years' (2.20b) 3. Harrises' (2.21) 5. C (2.20b) 7. Parvez's (2.21) 9. year's (2.20a)

GRAMMAR/MECHANICS CHECKUP—10

Possessives

Review Sections 2.20–2.22. Then study each of the following statements. Underline any inappropriate form. Write a correction in the space provided, and record the number of the Handbook principle(s) illustrated. If a sentence is correct, write C. When you finish, compare your responses with those on page 417. If your answers differ, carefully study again the principles shown in parentheses.

years' (2.20b) **Example** In just two years time, the accountants and managers devised an entirely new system.

________ 1. Two supervisors said that Mr. Ruskins work was excellent.

________ 2. None of the employees in our Electronics Department had taken more than two weeks vacation.

________ 3. All the secretaries agreed that Ms. Lanhams suggestions were practical.

________ 4. After you obtain your boss approval, send the application to Human Resources.

_________ 5. Despite Kaspar grumbling, his wife selected two bonds and three stocks for her investments.

_________ 6. In one months time we hope to be able to complete all the address files.

_________ 7. Marks salary was somewhat higher than David.

CUMULATIVE EDITING QUIZ 5

Use proofreading marks (see Appendix B) to correct errors and omissions in the following sentences. All errors must be corrected to receive credit for the sentence. Check with your instructor for the answers.

1. Mark Zuckerberg worked for years to build Facebook however it was years' before the company made a profit.
2. E-businesses has always been risky, online companys seem to disappear as quick as they appear.
3. According to a leading data source three of the top European entertainment companys are the following Double Fusion, Jerusalem, Israel, Echovoc, Geneva, Switzerland, and IceMobile, Amsterdam, The Netherlands.
4. By the way Tess email was forwarded to Mr. Lopezes incoming box in error and she was quite embarrassed.
5. The OSCs findings and ruling in the securitys fraud case is expected to be released in one hours time.
6. Only one hospitals doctors complained that they were restricted in the time they could spend listening to patients comments.
7. Any one of the auditors are authorized to conduct an independent action however only the CEO can change the councils directives.
8. Charles and Les mountain bicycles were stole from there garage last night.
9. Five of the worst computer passwords are the following your first name, your last name, the Enter key, *Password,* and the name of a sports' team.
10. On January 15 2015 we opened an innovative full equipped fitness centre.

Other Punctuation (2.23–2.29)

2.23 Periods

a. **Ends of sentences.** Use a period at the end of a statement, command, indirect question, or polite request. Although a polite request may have the same structure as a question, it ends with a period:

Corporate legal departments demand precise skills from their workforce. (End a statement with a period.)

Get the latest data by reading current periodicals. (End a command with a period.)

Mr. Rand wondered whether we had sent any follow-up literature. (End an indirect question with a period.)

Would you please re-examine my account and determine the current balance. (A polite request suggests an action rather than a verbal response.)

b. **Abbreviations and initials.** Use periods after initials and after many abbreviations.

R. M. Johnson	c.o.d.	Ms.
p.m.	a.m.	Mr.
Inc.	i.e.	Mrs.

The latest trend is to omit periods in degrees and professional designations: BA, PhD, MD, RN, DDS, MBA.

Use just one period when an abbreviation falls at the end of a sentence:

Guests began arriving at 5:30 p.m.

2.24 Question Marks. Direct questions are followed by question marks:

Did you send your proposal to Datatronix, Inc.?

Statements with questions added are punctuated with question marks.

We have completed the proposal, haven't we?

2.25 Exclamation Points. Use an exclamation point after a word, phrase, or clause expressing strong emotion. In business writing, however, exclamation points should be used sparingly:

Incredible! Every terminal is down.

2.26 Dashes. The dash (constructed at a keyboard by striking the hyphen key twice in succession) is a legitimate and effective mark of punctuation when used according to accepted conventions. As a connecting punctuation mark, however, the dash loses effectiveness when overused.

a. **Parenthetical elements.** Within a sentence a parenthetical element is usually set off by commas. If, however, the parenthetical element itself contains internal commas, use dashes (or parentheses) to set it off:

Three top salespeople—Tom Judkins, Gary Templeton, and Mona Yashimoto—received bonuses.

b. **Sentence interruptions.** Use a dash to show an interruption or abrupt change of thought:

News of the dramatic merger—no one believed it at first—shook the financial world.

Ship the materials Monday—no, we must have them sooner.

Sentences with abrupt changes of thought or with appended afterthoughts can usually be improved through rewriting.

c. **Summarizing statements.** Use a dash (not a colon) to separate an introductory list from a summarizing statement:

Sorting, merging, and computing—these are tasks that our data processing programs must perform.

2.27 Parentheses. One means of setting off nonessential sentence elements involves the use of parentheses. Nonessential sentence elements may be punctuated in one of three ways: (a) with commas, to make the lightest possible break in the normal flow of a sentence; (b) with dashes, to emphasize the enclosed material; and (c) with parentheses, to de-emphasize the enclosed material. Parentheses are frequently used to punctuate sentences with interpolated directions, explanations, questions, and references:

The cost analysis (which appears on page 8 of the report) indicates that the copy machine should be leased.

Units are lightweight (approximately 1 kg) and come with a leather case and operating instructions.

The latest laser printer (have you heard about it?) will be demonstrated for us next week.

A parenthetical sentence that is not embedded within another sentence should be capitalized and punctuated with end punctuation:

The Model 20 has stronger construction. (You may order a Model 20 brochure by circling 304 on the reader service card.)

2.28 Quotation Marks

a. **Direct quotations.** Use double quotation marks to enclose the exact words of a speaker or writer:

"Keep in mind," Kelly Frank said, "that you'll have to justify the cost of networking our office."

The boss said that automation was inevitable. (No quotation marks are needed because the exact words are not quoted.)

b. **Quotations within quotations.** Use single quotation marks (apostrophes on the keyboard) to enclose quoted passages within quoted passages:

In her speech, Marge Deckman remarked, "I believe it was the poet Robert Frost who said, 'All the fun's in how you say a thing.'"

c. **Short expressions.** Slang, words used in a special sense, and words following *stamped* or *marked* are often enclosed within quotation marks:

Jeffrey described the damaged shipment as "gross." (Quotation marks enclose slang.)

Students often have trouble spelling the word "separate." (Quotation marks enclose words used in a special sense.)

Jobs were divided into two categories: most stressful and least stressful. The jobs in the "most stressful" list involved high risk or responsibility. (Quotation marks enclose words used in a special sense.)

The envelope marked "Confidential" was put aside. (Quotation marks enclose words following *marked*.)

In the four preceding sentences, the words enclosed within quotation marks can be set in italics instead, if italics are available.

d. **Definitions.** Double quotation marks are used to enclose definitions. The word or expression being defined should be underscored or set in italics:

The term *penetration pricing* is defined as "the practice of introducing a product to the market at a low price."

e. **Titles.** Use double quotation marks to enclose titles of literary and artistic works, such as magazine and newspaper articles, chapters of books, movies, television shows, poems, lectures, and songs. Names of major publications—such as books, magazines, pamphlets, and newspapers—are set in italics (underscored).

Particularly helpful was the chapter in Smith's *Effective Writing Techniques* entitled "Right Brain, Write On!"

John's article, "Email Blunders," appeared in *The Globe and Mail*; however, we could not locate it online.

f. **Additional considerations.** Periods and commas are always placed inside closing quotation marks. Semicolons and colons, on the other hand, are always placed outside quotation marks:

Mrs. James said, "I could not find the article entitled 'Cellphone Etiquette.'"

The director asked for "absolute security": All written messages were to be destroyed.

Question marks and exclamation points may go inside or outside closing quotation marks, as determined by the form of the quotation:

Sales Manager Martin said, "Who placed the order?" (The quotation is a question.)

When did the sales manager say, "Who placed the order?" (Both the incorporating sentence and the quotation are questions.)

Did the sales manager say, "Ryan placed the order"? (The incorporating sentence asks a question; the quotation does not.)

"In the future," shouted Bob, "ask me first!" (The quotation is an exclamation.)

2.29 Brackets. Within quotations, brackets are used by the quoting writer to enclose his or her own inserted remarks. Such remarks may be corrective, illustrative, or explanatory:

My professor said that "CSIS [the Canadian Security Intelligence Service] is becoming one of the most controversial and secretive of the federal government agencies."

Review Exercise L—Other Punctuation

Insert necessary punctuation in the following sentences. In the space provided for each item, indicate the number of punctuation marks that you added. Count sets of parentheses, dashes, and quotation marks as two marks. Emphasis or de-emphasis will be indicated for some parenthetical elements. When you finish, compare your responses with those provided. For each item on which you need review, consult the numbered principle shown in parentheses.

______ 1. Will you please send me your latest catalogue

______ 2. (Emphasize) Three of my friends Irina Volodyeva, Stan Meyers, and Ivan Sergo were promoted.

______ 3. Mr Lee, Miss Evans, and Mrs Rivera have not responded.

______ 4. We have scheduled your interview for 4 45 p m

______ 5. (De-emphasize) The appliance comes in limited colours black, ivory, and beige, but we accept special orders.

______ 6. The expression de facto means exercising power as if legally constituted.

______ 7. Who was it who said "This, too, will pass

______ 8. Should this package be marked Fragile

______ 9. Did you see the Macleans article titled How Far Can Wireless Go

______ 10. Amazing All sales reps made their targets

---

1. (1) catalogue. (2.23a) 3. (2) Mr.; Mrs. (2.23) 5. (2) colours (black, ivory, and beige) (2.26a) 7. (3) said,; pass"? (2.28f) 9. (4) *Maclean's*; "How Go?" (2.28e)

GRAMMAR/MECHANICS CHECKUP—11

Other Punctuation

Although this checkup concentrates on Sections 2.23–2.29, you may also refer to other punctuation principles. Insert any necessary punctuation. In the space provided, indicate the number of changes you make and record the number of the Handbook principle(s) illustrated. Count each mark separately; for example, a set of parentheses counts as 2. If you make no changes, write *0*. When you finish, compare your responses with those provided on page 417. If your responses differ, carefully study again the specific principles shown in parentheses.

<u>2 (2.27)</u> **Example** (De-emphasize.) The consumption of cereal products is highest in certain provinces (Manitoba, Saskatchewan, Alberta, and Newfoundland), but this food trend is spreading to other parts of the country.

______ 1. (Emphasize.) The convention planning committee has invited three managers Yu Wong, Frank Behr, and Yvette Sosa to make presentations.

______ 2. (De-emphasize.) A second set of demographic variables see Figure 13 on page 432 includes nationality, religion, and race.

______ 3. Recruiting, hiring, and training these are three important functions of a human resources officer.

______ 4. Have any of the research assistants been able to locate the article entitled How Tax Reform Will Affect You

______ 5. Have you sent invitations to Mr Kieran E Manning, Miss Kathy Tanguay, and Ms Petra Bonaventura?

______ 6. James said, "I'll be right over" however he has not appeared yet.

______ 7. Because the work was scheduled to be completed June 10 we found it necessary to hire temporary workers to work June 8 and 9.

______ 8. Hooray I have finished this checkup haven't I

GRAMMAR/MECHANICS CHECKUP—12

Punctuation Review

Review Sections 1.19 and 2.01–2.29. Study the groups of sentences below. In the space provided write the letter of the one that is correctly punctuated. When you finish, compare your responses with those on page 417. If your responses differ, carefully study again the principles in parentheses.

______ 1. (a) Our accounting team makes a point of analyzing your business operations, and getting to know what's working for you and what's not.

(b) We are dedicated to understanding your business needs over the long term, and taking an active role when it comes to creating solutions.

(c) We understand that you may be downsizing or moving into new markets, and we want to help you make a seamless transition.

______ 2. (a) The competition is changing; therefore, we have to deliver our products and services more efficiently.

(b) Although delivery systems are changing; the essence of banking remains the same.

(c) Banks will continue to be available around the corner, and also with the click of a mouse.

________ 3. (a) We care deeply about the environment; but we also care about safety and good customer service.

(b) The president worked with environmental concerns; the vice president focused on customer support

(c) Our website increases our productivity, it also improves customer service.

________ 4. (a) All secretaries' computers were equipped with Excel.

(b) Both lawyers statements confused the judge.

(c) Some members names and addresses must be rekeyed.

________ 5. (a) The package from Albany, New York was never delivered.

(b) We have scheduled an inspection tour on Tuesday, March 5, at 4 p.m.

(c) Send the check to M. E. Williams, 320 Summit Ridge, Elizabethtown, Ontario K6T 1A9 before the last mail pickup.

________ 6. (a) If you demand reliable, competent service, you should come to us.

(b) We could not resist buying cookies from the enthusiastic, young Girl Guide.

(c) Our highly trained technicians, with years of experience are always available to evaluate and improve your network environment.

________ 7. (a) Their wealthy uncle left $1 million to be distributed to Hayden, Carlotta, and Susanna.

(b) Their wealthy uncle left $1 million to be distributed to Hayden, Carlotta and Susanna.

(c) Our agency will maintain and upgrade your computers, printers, copiers and fax machines.

________ 8. (a) We specialize in network design, however we also offer troubleshooting and consulting.

(b) We realize that downtime is not an option; therefore, you can count on us for reliable, competent service.

(c) Our factory-trained and certified technicians perform repair at your location, or in our own repair depot for products under warranty and out of warranty.

CUMULATIVE EDITING QUIZ 6

Use proofreading marks (see Appendix B) to correct errors and omissions in the following sentences. All errors must be corrected to receive credit for the sentence. Check with your instructor for the answers.

1. We wondered whether Ellen Hildago PhD would be the speaker at the Kingston Ontario event?
2. Our operating revenue for 2014 see Appendix A exceeded all the consultants expectations.

3. Four features, camera, text messaging, Web access, and voice mail—are what Canadians want most on there cellphones.
4. Serge Laferia CEO of Imperial Tobacco said "We're being socially responsible in a rather controversial industry.
5. Kym Andersons chapter titled Subsidies and Trade Barriers appears in the book How to Spend $50 Billion to Make the World a Better Place.
6. Wasnt it Zack Tesar not Ellen Trask who requested a 14 day leave.
7. Was it Oprah Winfrey who said that the best jobs are those we'd do even if we didn't get paid.
8. The word mashup is a technology term that is defined as a website that uses content from more then one source to create a completely new service.
9. Miss. Rhonda Evers is the person who the employees council elected as there representative.
10. Would you please send a current catalog to Globex, Inc?

STYLE AND USAGE

Capitalization (3.01–3.16)

Capitalization is used to distinguish important words. However, writers are not free to capitalize all words they consider important. Rules or guidelines governing capitalization style have been established through custom and use. Mastering these guidelines will make your writing more readable and more comprehensible.

3.01 Proper Nouns. Capitalize proper nouns, including the *specific* names of persons, places, schools, streets, parks, buildings, holidays, months, agreements, websites, software programs, historical periods, and so forth. Do not capitalize common nouns that make only *general* references.

Proper nouns	**Common nouns**
Peter Mansbridge	well-known news anchor
Mexico, U.S.A.	Canadian trading partners
Algonquin College	a community college
Parc Lafontaine	a park in the city
Rideau Room, Royal York Hotel	a meeting room in the hotel
Family Day, New Year's Day	two holidays
Google, Facebook, Wikipedia	popular websites
Burlington Skyway	a bridge
Consumer Protection Act	a law to protect consumers
Halifax Chamber of Commerce	a chamber of commerce
Billy Bishop Airport	a municipal airport
January, February, March	months of the year

3.02 Proper Adjectives. Capitalize most adjectives that are derived from proper nouns:

Greek symbol	British thermal unit
Roman numeral	Freudian slip
Xerox copy	Hispanic markets

Do not capitalize the few adjectives that, although originally derived from proper nouns, have become common adjectives through usage. Consult your dictionary when in doubt:

manila folder	diesel engine
venetian blinds	china dishes

3.03 Geographic Locations. Capitalize the names of *specific* places such as continents, countries, provinces, mountains, valleys, lakes, rivers, oceans, and geographic regions:

Quebec City	Lake Athabasca
Rocky Mountains	Pacific Ocean
Annapolis Valley	Bay of Fundy
the East Coast	the Prairie provinces

3.04 Organization Names. Capitalize the principal words in the names of all business, civic, educational, governmental, labour, military, philanthropic, political, professional, religious, and social organizations:

Bombardier	Board of Directors, Scotiabank
The Montreal Gazette*	Vancouver Art Gallery
Toronto Stock Exchange	Bank of Canada
United Way	Canadian Union of Public Employees
Al Purdy A-Frame Association	Canadian Association of Retired Persons

*Note: Capitalize *the* only when it is part of the official name of an organization, as printed on the organization's stationery.

3.05 Academic Courses and Degrees. Capitalize particular academic degrees and course titles. Do not capitalize general academic degrees and subject areas:

Professor Bernadette Ordian, *PhD*, will teach *Accounting* 221 next fall.

Mrs. Snyder, who holds *bachelor's* and *master's degrees*, teaches *marketing* classes.

Jim enrolled in classes in history, business English, and management.

3.06 Personal and Business Titles

a. Capitalize personal and business titles when they precede names:

Vice President Ames	Uncle Edward
Board Chairman Frazier	Councillor Herbert
Premier Thurmond	Sales Manager Klein
Professor Mahfouz	Dr. Samuel Washington

b. Capitalize titles in addresses, salutations, and closing lines:

Mr. Juan deSanto	Very truly yours,
Director of Purchasing	
Space Systems, Inc.	Clara J. Smith
Madoc, ON K0K 2K0	Supervisor, Marketing

c. Generally, do not capitalize titles of high government rank or religious office when they stand alone or follow a person's name in running text.

The prime minister conferred with the armed forces council and many senators.

Meeting with the chief justice of the Supreme Court were the senator from British Columbia and the mayor of Vancouver.

Only the cardinal from Montreal had an audience with the pope.

a. Do not capitalize most common titles following names:

The speech was delivered by Robert Lynch, *president*, Academic Publishing.

Lois Herndon, *chief executive officer*, signed the order.

b. Do not capitalize common titles appearing alone:

Please speak to the *supervisor* or to the *office* manager.

Neither the *president* nor the *vice president* could attend.

However, when the title of an official appears in that organization's minutes, bylaws, or other official document, it may be capitalized.

c. Do not capitalize titles when they are followed by appositives naming specific individuals:

We must consult our *director of research*, Ronald E. West, before responding.

d. Do not capitalize family titles used with possessive pronouns:

my mother	your father
our aunt	his cousin

e. Capitalize titles of close relatives used without pronouns:

Both *Mother* and *Father* must sign the contract.

3.07 Numbered and Lettered Items. Capitalize nouns followed by numbers or letters (except in page, paragraph, line, and verse references):

Flight 34, Gate 12	Plan No. 2
Volume I, Part 3	Warehouse 33-A
Invoice No. 55489	Figure 8.3
Model A5673	Serial No. C22865404-2
Provincial Highway 10	page 6, line 5

3.08 Points of the Compass. Capitalize *north, south, east, west*, and their derivatives when they represent *specific* geographical regions. Do not capitalize the points of the compass when they are used in directions or in general references.

Specific Regions	**General References**
from the South	heading north on the highway
living in the West	west of the city
Easterners, Westerners	western Ontario, southern Saskatchewan
going to the Middle East	the northern part of province
from the East Coast	the east side of the street

3.09 Departments, Divisions, and Committees. Capitalize the names of departments, divisions, or committees within your own organization. Outside your organization capitalize only *specific* department, division, or committee names:

The inquiry was addressed to the Legal Department in our Consumer Products Division.

John was appointed to the *Employee Benefits Committee.*

Send your résumé to their *human resources division.*

A *planning committee* will be named shortly.

3.10 Governmental Terms. Do not capitalize the words *federal, government, nation*, or province unless they are part of a specific title:

Unless *federal* support can be secured, the *provincial* project will be abandoned.

The *Council of the Federation* promotes inter-provincial cooperation.

3.11 Product Names. Capitalize product names only when they refer to trademarked items. Except in advertising, common names following manufacturers' names are not capitalized:

Magic Marker	Lululemon pants
Kleenex tissues	Swingline stapler
Q-tip swab	ChapStick lip balm
Levi's 501 jeans	Excel spreadsheet
DuPont Teflon	Roots sweatshirt

3.12 Literary Titles. Capitalize the principal words in the titles of books, magazines, newspapers, articles, movies, plays, songs, poems, and reports. Do not capitalize articles (*a, an, the*), short conjunctions (*and, but, or, nor*), and prepositions of fewer than four letters (*in, to, by, for*) unless they begin or end the title:

Jackson's *What Job Is for You?* (Capitalize book titles.)

Gant's "Software for the Executive Suite" (Capitalize principal words in article titles.)

"Performance Standards to Go By" (Capitalize article titles.)

"The Improvement of Fuel Economy With Alternative Fuels" (Capitalize report titles.)

3.13 Beginning Words. In addition to capitalizing the first word of a complete sentence, capitalize the first word in a quoted sentence, independent phrase, item in an enumerated list, and formal rule or principle following a colon:

The business manager said, "*All* purchases must have requisitions." (Capitalize first word in a quoted sentence.)

Yes, if you agree. (Capitalize an independent phrase.)

Some of the duties of the position are as follows:

1. *Editing* and formatting Word files
2. *Arranging* video and teleconferences
3. *Verifying* records, reports, and applications (Capitalize items in a vertical enumerated list.)

One rule has been established through the company: No smoking is allowed in open offices. (Capitalize a rule following a colon.)

3.14 Celestial Bodies. Capitalize the names of celestial bodies such as *Mars, Saturn*, and *Neptune*. Do not capitalize the terms *earth*, *sun*, or *moon* unless they appear in a context with other celestial bodies:

Where on *earth* did you find that manual typewriter?

Venus and *Mars* are the closest planets to *Earth*.

3.15 Ethnic References. Capitalize terms that refer to a particular culture, language, or race:

Asian	Hebrew
Caucasian	Indian
Latino	Japanese
Persian	Judeo-Christian

3.16 Seasons. Do not capitalize seasons:

In the *fall* it appeared that *winter* and *spring* sales would increase.

Review Exercise M—Capitalization

In the following sentences, correct any errors that you find in capitalization. Underscore any lowercase letter that should be changed to a capital letter. Draw a slash (/) through a capital letter that you wish to change to a lowercase letter. In the space provided, indicate the total number of changes you have made in each sentence. If you make no changes, write *0*. When you finish, compare your responses with those provided.

5 **Example** Bill McAdams, currently Assistant Manager in our Compensation division, will be promoted to Manager of the Employee Services division.

______ 1. The copyright modernization act, passed in 2011, has been seen as taking away rights from content creators.

______ 2. Marilyn Hunter, mba, received her bachelor's degree from Queen's university in kingston.

______ 3. Please ask your Aunt and your Uncle if they will come to the Lawyer's office at 5 p.m.

______ 4. Once we establish an organizing committee, arrangements can be made to rent holmby hall.

______ 5. Either the President or the Vice President of the company will make the decision about purchasing xerox copiers.

______ 6. Some individuals feel that canadian companies do not have the sense of loyalty to their employees that japanese companies do.

______ 7. The prime minister recently said, "we must protect our domestic economy from Foreign competition."

______ 8. All marketing representatives of our company will meet in the empire room of the red lion motor inn.

______ 9. The special keyboard for the Dell Computer must contain greek symbols for Engineering equations.

______ 10. In the Fall our organization will move its corporate headquarters to the franklin building in downtown winnipeg.

---

1. (3) Copyright Modernization Act (3.01) 3. (3) aunt uncle lawyer's (3.06e, 3.06g)
5. (4) president vice president Xerox (3.06e, 3.11) 7. (2) We foreign (3.10, 3.13)
9. (3) computer Greek engineering (3.01, 3.02, 3.11)

GRAMMAR/MECHANICS CHECKUP—13

Capitalization

Review Sections 3.01–3.16. Then study each of the following statements. Underscore any lowercase letter that should be changed to a capital letter. Draw a slash (/) through any capital letter that you wish to change to lowercase. Indicate in the space provided the number of changes you made in each sentence and record the number of the Handbook principle(s) illustrated. If you made no changes, write *0*. When you finish, compare your responses with those provided on page 417. If your responses differ, carefully study again the principles in parentheses.

4 (3.01, 3.06a) **Example** After consulting our Attorneys for Legal advice, Vice president Fontaine signed the Contract.

________ 1. Personal tax rates for japanese citizens are low by International standards; rates for japanese corporations are high, according to Iwao Nakatani, an Economics Professor at Osaka university.

________ 2. Did you see the *Maclean's* article entitled "Careers in horticulture are nothing to sneeze at"?

________ 3. Although I recommend Minex Printers sold under the brand-name MPLazerJet, you may purchase any Printers you choose.

________ 4. According to a Federal Government report, any development of Provincial waterways must receive an environmental assessment.

________ 5. My Mother, who lives near Plum Coulee, reports that protection from the Sun's rays is particularly important when travelling to the South.

________ 6. Next week, Editor in Chief Mercredi plans an article detailing the astounding performance of the euro.

________ 7. To reach Terrasee Vaudreuil park, which is located on an Island in the St. Lawrence river, tourists pass over the vanier bridge.

________ 8. On page 6 of the catalogue you will see that the computer science department is offering a number of courses in programming.

CUMULATIVE EDITING QUIZ 7

Use proofreading marks (see Appendix B) to correct errors and omissions in the following sentences. All errors must be corrected to receive credit for the sentence. Check with your instructor for the answers.

1. I wonder whether ceo Jackson invited our Marketing Vice President to join the upcoming three hour training session?
2. Our Sales Manager said that you attending the two day seminar is fine however we must find a replacement.
3. The boston marathon is an annual Sporting Event hosted by the City of Boston, Massachusetts on the third monday of April.
4. Steve Chen one of the founders of YouTube hurried to gate 44 to catch flight 246 to north carolina.
5. Jake noticed that the english spoken by asians in hong kong sounded more british than north american.
6. Good Friday is a Statutory holiday therefore banks will be closed.

7. Because the package was marked fragile the mail carrier handled it careful.
8. Money traders watched the relation of the american dollar to the chinese yuan, the european euro and the canadian dollar.
9. My Aunt and me travel South each Winter to vacation in the okanagan with our friends the Perry's.
10. Jim Balsillie former Co-CEO of Research in motion now serves as Chair of the Board of the centre for Interntional Governance Innovation in waterloo.

Number Style (4.01–4.13)

Usage and custom determine whether numbers are expressed in the form of figures (e.g., 5, 9) or in the form of words (e.g., *five, nine*). Numbers expressed as figures are shorter and more easily understood, yet numbers expressed as words are necessary in certain instances. The following guidelines are observed in expressing numbers in written sentences. Numbers that appear on business forms—such as invoices, monthly statements, and purchase orders—are always expressed as figures.

4.01 General Rules

a. The numbers *one* through *ten* are generally written as words. Numbers above *ten* are written as figures:

The bank had a total of *nine* branch offices in *three* suburbs.

All *58* employees received benefits in the *three* categories shown.

A shipment of *45,000* lightbulbs was sent from *two* warehouses.

b. Numbers that begin sentences are written as words. If a number beginning a sentence involves more than two words, however, the sentence should be revised so that the number does not fall at the beginning.

Fifteen different options were available in the annuity programs.

A total of 156 companies participated in the promotion (not *One hundred fifty-six companies participated in the promotion*).

4.02 Money. Sums of money $1 or greater are expressed as figures. If a sum is a whole dollar amount, omit the decimal and zeros (whether or not the amount appears in a sentence with additional fractional dollar amounts):

We budgeted *$300* for a digital camera, but the actual cost was *$370.96*.

On the invoice were items for *$6.10*, *$8*, *$33.95*, and *$75*.

Sums less than $1 are written as figures that are followed by the word *cents*:

By shopping carefully, we can save *15 cents* per unit.

4.03 Dates. In dates, numbers that appear after the name of the month are written as cardinal figures (*1, 2, 3*, etc.). Those that stand alone or appear before the name of a month are written as ordinal figures (*1st, 2nd, 3rd,* etc.):

The Workplace Safety Committee will meet *May 7*.

On the *5th* day of February and again on the *25th*, we placed orders.

In Canadian business documents, dates generally take the following form: *January 4, 2012*. An alternative form, used primarily in military and foreign correspondence, begins with the day of the month and omits the comma: *4 January 2012*.

4.04 Clock Time. Figures are used when clock time is expressed with *a.m.* or *p.m.* Omit the colon and zeros in referring to whole hours. When exact clock time is expressed with the contraction o'clock, either figures or words may be used:

> Mail deliveries are made at 11 *a.m.* and 3:30 *p.m.*
>
> At *four* (or 4) *o'clock* employees begin to leave.

4.05 Addresses and Telephone Numbers

a. Except for the number *one*, house numbers are expressed in figures:

540 Queen Street	17802 8th Avenue NW
One René Lévesque Boulevard	2 Highland Street

b. Street names containing numbers *ten* or lower are written entirely as words. For street names involving numbers greater than *ten*, figures are used:

330 Third Street	3440 Seventh Avenue
6945 East 32nd Avenue	4903 West 23rd Street

c. Telephone numbers are expressed with figures. When used, the area code is placed in parentheses preceding the telephone number:

> Please call us at (*519*) *347-0551* to place an order.
>
> Mr. Sims asked you to call (*604*) *554-8923*, Ext. 245, after 10 a.m.

4.06 Related Numbers. Numbers are related when they refer to similar items in a category within the same reference. All related numbers should be expressed as the largest number is expressed. Thus if the largest number is greater than *ten*, all the numbers should be expressed in figures:

> Only *5* of the original *25* applicants completed the processing. (Related numbers require figures.)
>
> The *two* plans affected *34* employees working in *three* sites. (Unrelated numbers use figures and words.)
>
> Beaver Drilling operated *14* rigs, of which *3* were rented. (Related numbers require figures.)
>
> The company hired *three* accountants, *one* customer service representative, and *nine* sales representatives. (Related numbers under ten use words.)

4.07 Consecutive Numbers. When two numbers appear consecutively and both modify a following noun, generally express the first number in words and the second in figures. If, however, the first number cannot be expressed in one or two words, place it in figures also (*120 70-cent* stamps). Do not use commas to separate the figures.

> Historians divided the era into *four 25-year* periods. (Use word form for the first number and figure form for the second.)
>
> We ordered *ten 30-page* colour brochures. (Use word form for the first number and figure form for the second.)
>
> Did the manager request *150 100-watt* bulbs? (Use figure form for the first number since it would require more than two words.)

4.08 Periods of Time. Seconds, minutes, days, weeks, months, and years are treated as any other general number. Numbers above ten are written in figure form.

Numbers below ten are written in word form unless they represent a business concept such as a discount rate, interest rate, or warranty period.

> This business was incorporated over *50* years ago. (Use figures for a number above ten.)
>
> It took *three* hours to write this short report. (Use words for a number under ten.)
>
> The warranty period is limited to 2 years. (Use figures for a business term.)

4.09 Ages. Ages are generally expressed in word form unless the age appears immediately after a name or is expressed in exact years and months:

> At the age of *twenty-one*, Elizabeth inherited the business.
>
> Wanda Tharp, *37*, was named acting president.
>
> At the age of *4 years and 7 months*, the child was adopted.

4.10 Round Numbers. Round numbers are approximations. They may be expressed in word or figure form, although figure form is shorter and easier to comprehend:

> About *600* (or *six hundred*) stock options were sold.
>
> It is estimated that *1,000* (or *one thousand*) people will attend.

For ease of reading, round numbers in the millions or billions should be expressed with a combination of figures and words:

> At least *1.5 million* readers subscribe to the ten top magazines.
>
> Deposits in money market accounts totalled more than *$115 billion.*

4.11 Weights and Measurements. Weights and measurements are expressed with figures:

> The new deposit slip measures 2 by *6 inches.*
>
> Her new suitcase weighed only *2 pounds 4 ounces.*
>
> Toronto is *60 kilometres* from Oshawa.

4.12 Fractions. Simple fractions are expressed as words. Complex fractions may be written either as figures or as a combination of figures and words:

> Over *two thirds* of the stockholders have already voted.
>
> This microcomputer will execute the command in *1 millionth* of a second. (A combination of words and numbers is easier to comprehend.)
>
> She purchased a *one-fifth* share in the business.*

**Note:* Fractions used as adjectives require hyphens.

4.13 Percentages and Decimals. Percentages are expressed with figures that are followed by the word *percent*. The percent sign (%) is used only on business forms or in statistical presentations:

> We had hoped for a *7 percent* interest rate, but we received a loan at *8 percent.*
>
> Over *50 percent* of the condo owners supported the plan.

Decimals are expressed with figures. If a decimal expression does not contain a whole number (an integer) and does not begin with a zero, a zero should be placed before the decimal point:

> The actuarial charts show that *1.74* out of *1,000* people will die in any given year.
>
> Inspector Norris found the setting to be *.005* centimetre off. (Decimal begins with a zero and does not require a zero before the decimal point.)
>
> Considerable savings will accrue if the unit production cost is reduced *0.1* percent. (A zero is placed before a decimal that neither contains a whole number nor begins with a zero.)

Quick Chart—Expression of Numbers

Use Words	**Use Figures**
Numbers *ten* and under	Numbers *11* and over
Numbers at beginning of sentence	Money
Ages	Dates
Fractions	Addresses and telephone
	numbers Weights and measurements
	Percentages and decimals

Review Exercise N—Number Style

Write the preferred number style on the lines provided. Assume that these numbers appear in business correspondence. When you finish, compare your responses with those provided. For each item on which you need review, consult the numbered principle shown in parentheses.

______	1. (a) 2 alternatives	(b) two alternatives
______	2. (a) sixty sales reps	(b) 60 sales reps
______	3. (a) forty dollars	(b) $40
______	4. (a) at 2:00 p.m.	(b) at 2 p.m.
______	5. (a) at least 15 years ago	(b) at least fifteen years ago
______	6. (a) twelve cents	(b) 12 cents
______	7. (a) ten percent interest rate	(b) 10 percent interest rate
______	8. (a) the rug measures one by two metres	(b) the rug measures 1 by 2 metres
______	9. (a) at eight o'clock	(b) at 8 o'clock
______	10. (a) three computers for twelve people	(b) three computers for 12 people

1. b (4.01a) 3. b (4.02) 5. a (4.08) 7. b (4.13) 9. a or b (4.04)

GRAMMAR/MECHANICS CHECKUP—14

Number Style

Review Sections 4.01–4.13. Then study each of the following pairs. Assume that these expressions appear in the context of letters, reports, or emails. Write *a* or *b* in the space provided to indicate the preferred number style and record the number of the Handbook principle illustrated. When you finish, compare your responses with those on page 417. If your responses differ, carefully study again the principles in parentheses.

a (4.01)	**Example** (a) six investments (b) 6 investments	
______	1. (a) sixteen credit cards	(b) 16 credit cards
______	2. (a) July eighth	(b) July 8
______	3. (a) twenty dollars	(b) $20
______	4. (a) at 4:00 p.m.	(b) at 4 p.m.
______	5. (a) 3 200-page reports	(b) three 200-page reports
______	6. (a) over 18 years ago	(b) over eighteen years ago
______	7. (a) 2/3 of the emails	(b) two thirds of the emails
______	8. (a) two telephones for 15 employees	(b) 2 telephones for 15 employees

CUMULATIVE EDITING QUIZ 8

Use proofreading marks (see Appendix B) to correct errors and omissions in the following sentences. All errors must be corrected to receive credit for the sentence. Check with your instructor for the answers.

1. My partner and myself will meet at our lawyers office at three p.m. on June ninth to sign our papers of incorporation.
2. Emily prepared 2 forty page business proposals to submit to the Senior Account Manager.
3. Of the 235 email messages sent yesterday only seven bounced back.
4. Your short term loan for twenty-five thousand dollars covers a period of sixty days.
5. Each new employee must pick up their permanent parking permit for lot 3-A before the end of the 14 day probationary period.
6. 259 identity theft complaints were filed with the Competition bureau on November second alone.
7. Robertas 11 page report was more easier to read then Davids because her's was better organized and had good headings.
8. Every morning on the way to the office Tatiana picked up 2 lattes that cost a total of six dollars.
9. Taking 7 years to construct the forty thousand square foot home of Olexiy Karpolin reportedly cost more then fifty million dollars.
10. Many companys can increase profits nearly ninety percent by retaining only 5% more of there current customers.

Confusing Words

accede:	to agree or consent
exceed:	over a limit
accept:	to receive
except:	to exclude; (prep.) but
adverse:	opposing; antagonistic
averse:	unwilling; reluctant
advice:	suggestion, opinion
advise:	to counsel or recommend
affect:	to influence
effect:	(n.) outcome, result; (v.) to bring about, to create
all ready:	prepared
already:	by this time
all right:	satisfactory
alright:	unacceptable variant spelling
altar:	structure for worship
alter:	to change

appraise: to estimate
apprise: to inform
ascent: (n.) rising or going up
assent: (v.) to agree or consent
assure: to promise
ensure: to make certain
insure: to protect from loss
capital: (n.) city that is seat of government; wealth of an individual; (adj.) chief
capitol: building that houses U.S. state or national lawmakers
cereal: breakfast food
serial: arranged in sequence
cite: to quote; to summon
site: location
sight: a view; to see
coarse: rough texture
course: a route; part of a meal; a unit of learning
complement: that which completes
compliment: (n.) praise, flattery; (v.) to praise or flatter
conscience: regard for fairness
conscious: aware
council: governing body
counsel: (n.) advice, lawyer; (v.) to give advice
credible: believable
creditable: good enough for praise or esteem; reliable
desert: arid land; to abandon
dessert: sweet food
device: invention or mechanism
devise: to design or arrange
disburse: to pay out
disperse: to scatter widely
elicit: to draw out
illicit: unlawful
envelop: (v.) to wrap, surround, or conceal
envelope: (n.) a container for a written message
every day: each single day
everyday: ordinary
farther: a greater distance
further: additional
formally: in a formal manner
formerly: in the past
grate: (v.) to reduce to small particles; to cause irritation; (n.) a frame of crossed bars blocking a passage
great: (adj.) large in size; numerous; eminent or distinguished
hole: an opening
whole: complete
imply: to suggest indirectly
infer: to reach a conclusion
lean: (v.) to rest against; (adj.) not fat
lien: (n.) a legal right or claim to property
liable: legally responsible
libel: damaging written statement
loose: not fastened
lose: to misplace
miner: person working in a mine
minor: a lesser item; person under age
patience: calm perseverance
patients: people receiving medical treatment
personal: private, individual
personnel: employees
plaintiff: (n.) one who initiates a lawsuit
plaintive: (adj.) expressive of suffering or woe
populace: (n.) the masses; population of a place
populous: (adj.) densely populated
precede: to go before
proceed: to continue
precedence: priority

precedents:	events used as an example
principal:	(n.) capital sum; school official; (adj.) chief
principle:	rule of action
stationary:	immovable
stationery:	writing material
than:	conjunction showing comparison
then:	adverb meaning "at that time"
their:	possessive form of they
there:	at that place or point
they're:	contraction of they are
to:	a preposition; the sign of the infinitive
too:	an adverb meaning "also" or "to an excessive extent"
two:	a number
waiver:	abandonment of a claim
waver:	to shake or fluctuate

160 Frequently Misspelled Words

absence	desirable	independent	prominent
accommodate	destroy	indispensable	qualify
achieve	development	interrupt	quantity
acknowledgment	disappoint	irrelevant	questionnaire
across	dissatisfied	itinerary	receipt
adequate	division	judgment	receive
advisable	efficient	knowledge	recognize
analyze	embarrass	legitimate	recommendation
annually	emphasis	library	referred
appointment	emphasize	license (v.) licence (n.)	regarding
argument	employee	maintenance	remittance
automatically	envelope	manageable	representative
bankruptcy	equipped	manufacturer	restaurant
becoming	especially	mileage	schedule
beneficial	evidently	miscellaneous	secretary
budget	exaggerate	mortgage	separate
business	excellent	necessary	similar
calendar	exempt	nevertheless	sincerely
cancelled	existence	ninety	software
catalogue	extraordinary	ninth	succeed
changeable	familiar	noticeable	sufficient
column	fascinate	occasionally	supervisor
committee	feasible	occurred	surprise
congratulate	February	offered	tenant
conscience	fiscal	omission	therefore
conscious	foreign	omitted	thorough
consecutive	forty	opportunity	though
consensus	fourth	opposite	through

consistent
control
convenient
correspondence
courteous
criticize
decision
deductible
defendant
definitely
dependent
describe
friend
genuine
government
grammar
grateful
guarantee
harass
height
hoping
immediate
incidentally
incredible
ordinarily
paid
pamphlet
permanent
permitted
pleasant
practical
prevalent
privilege
probably
procedure
profited
truly
undoubtedly
unnecessarily
usable
usage
using
usually
valuable
volume
weekday
writing
yield

Key to Grammar/ Mechanics Checkups

Checkup 1

1. Saturdays (1.05a) **2.** cities (1.05e) **3.** turkeys (1.05d) **4.** Nashes (1.05b) **5.** 1990s (1.05g) **6.** editors in chief (1.05f) **7.** C (1.05h) **8.** runners-up (1.05f)

Checkup 2

1. he (1.08b) **2.** him (1.08c) **3.** hers (1.08d) **4.** I (1.08a) **5.** whoever (1.08j) **6.** me (1.08i) **7.** he (1.08f) **8.** us (1.08g)

Checkup 3

1. *are* for *is* (1.10e) **2.** *has* for *have* (1.10c) **3.** *offers* for *offer* (1.10d) **4.** C (1.10f) **5.** chosen (1.15) **6.** *were* for *was* (1.12) **7.** *is* for *are* (1.10c) **8.** b (1.15c)

Checkup 4

1. long-time (1.17e) **2.** quickly (1.17d) **3.** had only (1.17f) **4.** C (1.17e) **5.** better (1.17a) **6.** up-to-the-minute (1.17e) **7.** couldn't have been clearer **8.** feel bad (1.17c)

Checkup 5

1. b (1.19d) **2.** b (1.18e) **3.** b (1.19c) **4.** a (1.19a) **5.** b (1.18a) **6.** a (1.18c) **7.** b (1.18b) **8.** b (1.19b)

Checkup 6

1. (2) not, as a rule, (2.03) **2.** (2) sure, Mrs. Schwartz, (2.02) **3.** (2) reliable, conscientious, (2.01) **4.** (3) Calgary, Alberta, La Salle, (2.04c) **5.** (2) February 4, 2011, (2.04a) **6.** (4) Holmes, Lane, Regina, Saskatchewan S5L 2E2, (2.04b) **7.** (2) supplies, replacing inventories, (2.01) **8.** (1) business, (2.02)

Checkup 7

1. (1) warranty, (2.06a) **2.** (1) market, (2.05) **3.** (2) manufacturer, nameless, (2.06c) **4.** (1) imaginative, (2.08) **5.** (2) Sims, area, (2.09) **6.** (1) buyers, (2.07) **7.** (2) application, Monday, (2.06a, 2.04a) **8.** (2) hand, hard-working, (2.03, 2.08)

Checkup 8

1. (2) name," Etienne, (2.14a) **2.** (4) Cox, PhD, Meridian, MBA, (2.10) **3.** (1) investment, (2.12) **4.** (2) think, however, (2.03) **5.** (2) Collingwood, Laurentians, (2.01, 2.15) **6.** (0) (2.06c) **7.** (2) companies, robots, (2.01) **8.** (2) fact, unprotected, (2.03, 2.08)

Checkup 9

1. (3) months: September, October, (2.01, 2.17a) **2.** (1) money, (2.06a, 2.16b) **3.** (3) short-term credit; manufacturer, however, (2.03, 2.16a) **4.** (1) Canada, (2.05) **5.** (5) customers; for example, retailers, service companies, manufacturers, (2.16e) **6.** (2) Bank, applications to the following: (2.06a, 2.17a) **7.** (2) high; therefore, (2.16) **8.** (2) 18 percent, prohibitive; (2.06a, 2.16c)

Checkup 10

1. Mr. Ruskin's (2.20a, 2.21) **2.** weeks' (2.20b) **3.** Ms. Lanham's (2.21) **4.** boss's (2.20b) **5.** Kaspar's (2.22) **6.** month's (2.20a) **7.** Mark's, David's (2.20a)

Checkup 11

1. (2) managers—Yu Sosa—(2.26a, 2.27) **2.** (2) variables (see Figure 13 on p. 432) (2.27) **3.** (1) training—(2.26c) **4.** (3) "How You"? (2.28e, 2.28f) **5.** (3) Mr. Kieran E. Manning, Miss Kathy Tanguay, and Ms. Petra (2.23b, 2.24) **6.** (2) over"; however, (2.16, 2.28f) **7.** (1) June 10; (2.06) **8.** (3) Hooray! checkup, haven't I? (2.24, 2.25)

Checkup 12

1. c (2.05) **2.** a (2.16a) **3.** b (2.16b) **4.** a (2.20) **5.** b (2.04a) **6.** a (2.08) **7.** a (2.01) **8.** b (2.16)

Checkup 13

1. (6) Japanese international Japanese economics professor University (3.01, 3.02, 3.04, 3.06d) **2.** (5) Horticulture Are Nothing Sneeze At (3.12) **3.** (2) printers printers (3.11) **4.** (3) federal government provincial (3.10) **5.** (2) mother sun's (3.03, 3.06g, 3.08, 3.14) **6.** (1) Euro (3.02) **7.** (5) Park island River Vanier Bridge (3.01, 3.03) **8.** (3) Computer Science Department (3.05, 3.07, 3.09)

Checkup 14

1. b (4.01a) **2.** b (4.03) **3.** b (4.02) **4.** b (4.04) **5.** b (4.07) **6.** a (4.08) **7.** b (4.12) **8.** a (4.06)

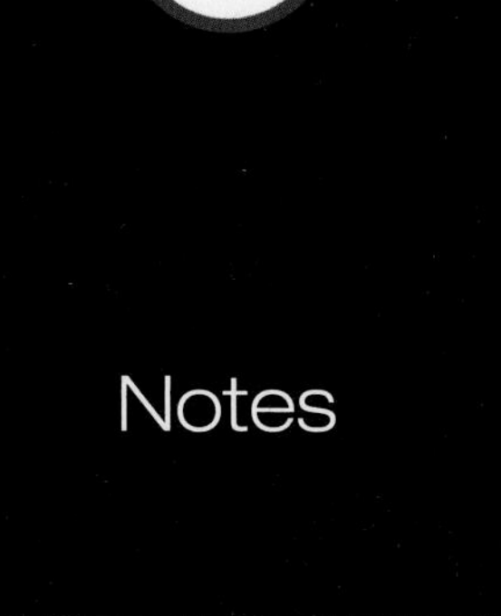

Notes

Chapter 1

1 O'Rourke, J. (2012). *Managerial communication* (5th ed). Upper Saddle River, NJ: Prentice Hall.

2 MetLife. (2011, May). The MetLife Survey of the American Teacher: Preparing students for college and careers. Retrieved from http://files.eric.ed.gov/fulltext/ED519278.pdf

3 Our Work: Livewire Communications. (n.d.). Retrieved June 29, 2017, from http://www.livewireinc.com/our-work/

4 Canavor, N. (2012). *Business writing in the digital age.* Los Angeles: Sage, 1–3; National Writing Project with DeVoss, D. N., Eidman-Aadahl, E., & Hicks, T. (2010). *Because digital writing matters.* San Francisco: Jossey-Bass, 1–5.

5 The Association of American Colleges and Universities/Hart Research Associates. (2009, November). Raising the bar: Employers' views on college learning in the wake of the economic downturn, 5–6. Retrieved from http://www.aacu.org/leap/documents/2009_EmployerSurvey.pdf

6 Appleman, J. E. (2009, October). Don't let poor writing skills stifle company growth. *T+D, 63*(10), 10. Retrieved from http://search.ebscohost.com; Timm, J. A. (2005, December). Preparing students for the next employment revolution. *Business Education Forum, 60*(2), 55–59. Retrieved from http://search.ebscohost.com; Messmer, M. (2001, January). Enhancing your writing skills. *Strategic Finance*, 8. See also Staples, B. (2005, May 15). The fine art of getting it down on paper, fast. *The New York Times*, p. WK13(L).

7 Do communication students have the "write stuff"?: Practitioners evaluate writing skills of entry-level workers. (2008). *Journal of Promotion Management, 14*(3/4), 294. Retrieved from http://search.ebscohost.com; The National Commission on Writing. (2005, July). Writing: A powerful message from state government. Retrieved from CollegeBoard: http://www.collegeboard.com/prod_downloads/writingcom/powerful-message-from-state.pdf; The National Commission on Writing. (2004, September 14). Writing skills necessary for employment, says big business. [Press release]. Retrieved from http://www.writingcommission.org/pr/writing_for_employ.html

8 Survey shows workers shud write better. (2004, September 14). Associated Press. Retrieved from MSNBC at http://www.msnbc.msn.com/id/6000685

9 Employers rank top 5 candidate skills. (2010, January 20). [Weblog post]. Retrieved from http://blog.resumebear.com/2010/01/20/employers-rank-top-5-candidate-skills; Moody, J., Stewart, B., & Bolt-Lee, C. (2002, March). Showcasing the skilled business graduate: Expanding the tool kit. *Business Communication Quarterly, 65*(1), 23.

10 American Management Association. (2010). AMA 2010 critical skills survey: Executives say the 21st century requires more skilled workers. Retrieved from http://www.p21.org/storage/documents/Critical%20Skills%20Survey%20Executive%20Summary.pdf; Vance, E. (2007, February 2). College graduates lack key skills, report says. *The Chronicle of Higher Education*, p. A30.

11 Wong, V. (2013, June 27). Hey job applicants, time to stop the social-media sabotage. *Bloomberg Businessweek*. Retrieved from www.businessweek.com/articles/2013-06-27/for-job-applicants-social-media-sabotage-is-still-getting-worse#r=read

12 Musbach, T. (2009, November 11). Secret weapon in the job hunt today: Personality. FastCompany.com. [Weblog post]. Retrieved from http://www.fastcompany.com/user/tom-musbach; Gallagher, K. P., Kaiser, K. M., Simon, J., Beath, C. M., & Goles, J. (2009, June). The requisite variety of skills for IT professionals. *Communications of the Association for Computing Machinery, 53*(6), 147. doi: 10.1145/1743546.1743584

13 English, A. (2012, October). What makes a great techie? *IBM Systems Magazine*. Retrieved from http://www.ibmsystemsmag.com/aix/trends/whatsnew/great_techie

14 Willmer, D. (2009, April 21). Leveraging soft skills in a competitive IT job market. Computerworld.com. Retrieved from http://www.computerworld.com; Morisy, M. (2008, February 28). Networking pros can avoid outsourcing with soft skills. Global Knowledge. Retrieved from http://www.globalknowledge.com/training/generic.asp?pageid=2119&country=United+States; Stranger, J. (2007, July). How to make yourself offshore-proof. *Certification Magazine, 9*(7), 34–40. Retrieved from http://search.ebscohost.com

15 Marsan, C. D. (2007, December 31). Job skills that matter: Where you can leave a mark. *Network World, 24*(50), 38–40. Retrieved from http://search.ebscohost.com

16 Robinson, T. M. (2008, January 26). Same office, different planets. *The New York Times*, p. B5.

17 Mitchell, G. A., Skinner, L. B., & White, B. J. (2010) Essential soft skills for success in the twenty-first-century workforce as perceived by business educators. *The Delta Pi Epsilon Journal, 52*(1). Retrieved from https://www.scribd.com/document/286348027/Essential-Soft-Skills-for-success-in-the-twenty-first-century-workforce-pdf

18 McEwen, B. C. (2010). Cross-cultural and international career exploration and employability skills. *National Business Education Association Yearbook 2010: Cross-Cultural and International Business Education, 48*, 142.

19 King, J. (2009, September 21). Crossing the skills gap. *Computerworld*, 30. Retrieved from http://search.ebscohost.com; Professional demeanor and personal management. (2004, January). *Keying In*, National Business Education Association Newsletter, 1.

20 King, J. (2009, September 21). Crossing the skills gap. *Computerworld*, 30. Retrieved from http://search.ebscohost.com

21 Wong, V. (2013, June 27). Hey job applicants, time to stop the social-media sabotage. *Bloomberg Businessweek*. Retrieved from www.businessweek.com/articles/2013-06-27/for-job-applicants-social-media-sabotage-is-still-getting-worse#r=read

[22] Rampell, C. (2013, February 19). College premium: Better pay, better prospects. Economix Blogs, *The New York Times*. Retrieved from http://economix.blogs.nytimes.com/2013/02/19/college-premium-better-pay-better-prospects/?_r=0; Crosby, O., & Moncarz, R. (2006, Fall). The 2004–14 job outlook for college graduates. *Occupational Outlook Quarterly, 50*(3), 43. Retrieved from https://www.bls.gov/careeroutlook/2006/fall/art03.pdf

[23] Shah, N. (2013, April 2). College grads earn nearly three times more than high school dropouts. WSJ Blogs. Retrieved from http://blogs.wsj.com/economics/2013/04/02/college-grads-earn-nearly-three-times-more-than-high-school-dropouts

[24] Employers rank top 5 candidate skills. (2011, September 3). Retrieved from http://wildcat-career-news.davidson.edu/internships/employers-rank-top-5-candidate-skillsqualities-sought-in-job-candidates/

[25] Holland, K. (2008, September 28). The anywhere, anytime office. *The New York Times*, p. 14 BU Y.

[26] Telework 2011: A WorldatWork special report, 3. Retrieved from www.worldatwork.org/waw/adimLink?id=53034

[27] Silverman, R. E., & Sidel, R. (2012, April 17). Warming up to the officeless office. *The Wall Street Journal*. Retrieved from http://online.wsj.com/article/SB10001424052702304818404577349783161465976.html; Holland, K. (2008, September 28). The anywhere, anytime office. *The New York Times*, p. 14 BU Y.

[28] Edmondson, A. C. (2012, April). Teamwork on the fly. *Harvard Business Review*. Retrieved from http://hbr.org/2012/04/teamwork-on-the-fly/ar/1

[29] Watzlawick, P., Beavin-Bavelas, J., & Jackson, D. (1967). Some tentative axioms of communication. In: *Pragmatics of human communication: A study of interactional patterns, pathologies and paradoxes*. New York: W. W. Norton.

[30] Birdwhistell, R. (1970). *Kinesics and context*. Philadelphia: University of Pennsylvania Press.

[31] Hall, E. T. (1966). *The hidden dimension*. Garden City, NY: Doubleday, 107–122.

[32] Wilkie, H. (2003, Fall). Professional presence. *The Canadian Manager, 28*(3), 14–19. Retrieved from http://search.ebscohost.com

[33] Nobes, C. (2012, 23 April) Tattoo taboo: Can you ask workers to cover up? Retrieved from http://www.hrmonline.ca/hr-news/tattoo-taboo-can-you-ask-workers-to-cover-up-174725.aspx

[34] Davis, T., Ward, D. A., & Woodland, D. (2010). Cross-cultural and international business communication—verbal. *National Business Education Association Yearbook: Cross-Cultural and International Business Education*, 3; Hall, E. T., & Hall, M. R. (1990). *Understanding cultural differences*. Yarmouth, ME: Intercultural Press, 183–184.

[35] Chaney, L. H., & Martin, J. S. (2011). *Intercultural business communication* (5th ed.). Upper Saddle River, NJ: Prentice Hall, 93.

[36] Beamer, L., & Varner, I. (2008). *Intercultural communication in the global workplace*. Boston: McGraw-Hill Irwin, 129.

[37] Sheer, V. C., & Chen, L. (2003, January). Successful Sino-Western business negotiation: Participants' accounts of national and professional cultures. *The Journal of Business Communication, 40*(1), 62; See also Luk, L., Patel, M., & White, K. (1990, December). Personal attributes of American and Chinese business associates. *The Bulletin of the Association for Business Communication*, 67.

[38] Gallois, C., & Callan, V. (1997). *Communication and culture*. New York: Wiley, 24.

[39] Ibid., 29.

[40] Copeland, L., & Griggs, L. (1985). *Going international*. New York: Penguin, 94; See also Beamer, L., & Varner, I. (2008). *Intercultural communication in the global workplace*. Boston: McGraw-Hill Irwin, 340.

[41] Copeland, L. & Griggs, L. (1991). *Going international*. New York: Penguin, 12.

[42] Klass, P. (2012, January 9). Seeing social media more as portal than as pitfall. *The New York Times*. Retrieved from http://www.nytimes.com/2012/01/10/health/views/seeing-social-media-as-adolescent-portal-more-than-pitfall.html

[43] Aragon, S. R. (2003, Winter). Creating social presence in online environments. *New Directions for Adult and Continuing Education, 100*, 59.

[44] Carter, J. F. (2010, October 14). Why Twitter influences cross-cultural engagement. Mashable Social Media. Retrieved from http://mashable.com/2010/10/14/twitter-cross-cultural

[45] McGrath, C. (2009, August 5). Five lessons learned about cross-cultural social networking. ThoughtFarmer. Retrieved from http://www.thoughtfarmer.com/blog/2009/08/05/5-lessons-cross-cultural-social-networking/#comments

[46] Intercultural Innovation Award. (2017, August 25). Crack in the Wall. Retrieved from https://interculturalinnovation.org/crack-in-the-wall/

[47] Martin, J. S., & Chaney, L. H. (2006). *Global business etiquette*. Westport, CT: Praeger, 36.

[48] Quan, D. (2014, June 27) Have Canada's changing demographics made it time to retire the concept of 'visible minority'? Retrieved from http://news.nationalpost.com/news/canada/have-canadas-changing-demographics-made-it-time-to-retire-the-concept-of-visible-minority

[49] Ten Tips for the awkward age of computing. (n.d.). *Microsoft accessibility, technology for everyone*. Retrieved from http://silverinnings.in/wp-content/uploads/2016/10/Ten-Tips-for-the-Awkward-Age-of-Computing.pdf

[50] Hansen, F. (2003, April). Tracing the value of diversity programs. *Workforce*, 31.

[51] Carbone, J. (2005, August 11). IBM says diverse suppliers are good for business. *Purchasing*, 27. Retrieved from http://search.ebscohost.com

[52] Schoemaker, P. J. H., & Day, G. S. (2009, Winter). Why we miss the signs. *MIT Sloan Management Review, 50*(2), 43.

[53] White, M. D. (2002). *A short course in international marketing blunders*. Novato, CA: World Trade Press, 46.

Chapter 2

[1] Lasswell, H. (1948). *The structure and function of communication in society: The communication of ideas*. New York: Institute for Religious and Social Studies.

[2] McLuhan, M. (1964). *Understanding media: The extensions of man*. New York: McGraw-Hill.

[3] Employee communications during times of change linked to job satisfaction: report. (2013, July 5). *Canadian HR Reporter*. Retrieved from http://www.hrreporter.com/article/17937-employee-communications-during-times-of-change-linked-to-job-satisfaction-report/

[4] Google. (personal communication with Mary Ellen Guffey, January 30, 2012).

[5] Be positive. (2009, March). *Communication Briefings*, 5. Adapted from Brandi, J. Winning at customer retention at http://www.customercarecoach.com

[6] Link, S. (2012, May 2). Use "person first" language. [Letter to editor]. *USA Today*, p. 6A.

Chapter 3

[1] Based on Quan, K. (2015, April 20). How Amex Canada built an office for a mobile-first workforce. Retrieved from http://www.canadianbusiness.com/leadership/office-space/amex-canada-mobile-first-workforce-hotelling/; and Titleman, N. (2016). Attracting millennials. *Canadian HR Reporter, 29*(11), 34. Retrieved from http://search.proquest.com.ezproxy.torontopubliclibrary.ca/docview/1799364377?accountid=14369

[2] Head, A., & Eisenberg, M. (2009, February 4). What today's college students say about conducting research in the digital age. Project Information Literacy Progress Report, University of Washington. Retrieved from http://www.educause.edu/library/resources/what-today%E2%80%99s-college-students-say-about-conducting-research-digital-age

[3] Rindegard, J. (1999, November 22). Use clear writing to show you mean business. *InfoWorld*, 78.

[4] Goddard, R. W. (1989, April). Communication: Use language effectively. *Personnel Journal*, 32.

[5] Booher, D. (2007). *The voice of authority*. New York: McGraw-Hill, 93.

Chapter 4

[1] Sword, H. (2012, July 25). Zombie nouns. Retrieved from http://www.3quarksdaily.com/3quarksdaily/2012/07/zombie-nouns.html

[2] Photo essay based on Al-Greene, B. (2013, May 23). 30 overused buzzwords in digital marketing. Mashable. Retrieved from http://mashable.com/2013/05/23/buzzword-infographic/

Chapter 5

[1] Statistics Canada. (2010). Business and government use of information communication technologies. Retrieved January 24, 2011, from http://www.statcan.gc.ca/tables-tableaux/sum-som/l01/cst01/econ146a-eng.htm

[2] Foster, D. (2010, November 10). How to write better emails. WebWorkerDaily. Retrieved from https://gigaom.com/2010/11/12/how-to-write-better-emails/

[3] Seeley, M. quoted in Palmer, M. (2011, December 19). The end of email? *Financial Times* (ft.com/management). Retrieved from https://www.ft.com/content/5207b5d6-21cf-11e1-8b93-00144feabdc0

[4] Plantronics. (2010). How we work: Communication trends of business professionals. Retrieved from http://www.plantronics.com/media/howwework/brochure-role-of-voice.pdf

[5] Middleton, D. (2011, March 3). Students struggle for words. *The Wall Street Journal*, Executive edition. Retrieved from http://online.wsj.com/article/SB10001424052748703409904576174651780110970.html

[6] Ibid.

[7] Gill, B. (2013, June). Vision statement: E-mail: Not dead, evolving. *Harvard Business Review*. Retrieved from http://hbr.org/2013/06/e-mail-not-dead-evolving

[8] Tugend, A. (2012, April 21). What to think about before you hit 'Send.' *TheNew York Times*, p. B5.

[9] Orrell, L. quoted in Tugend, A. (2012, April 21). What to think about before you hit 'Send.' *The New York Times*, p. B5.

[10] Kupritz, V. W., & Cowell, E. (2011, January). Productive management communication: Online and face-to-face. *Journal of Business Communication*, *48*(1), 70–71.

[11] Allen, P. (2011, November 30). One of the biggest information technology companies in the world to abolish e-mails. Mail Online. Retrieved from http://www.dailymail.co.uk/news/article-2067520/One-biggest-IT-companies-world-abolish-emails.html

[12] Radicati, S. (2012, November 15). Statistics anyone? Retrieved from http://www.radicati.com/?p=8417

[13] Plantronics. (2010). How we work: Communication trends of business professionals. Retrieved from http://www.plantronics.com/media/howwework/brochure-role-of-voice.pdf

[14] Pazos, P., Chung, J. M., & Micari, M. (2013). Instant messaging as a task-support tool in information technology organizations. *Journal of Business Communication*, *50*(1), 78.

[15] Marketing News Staff. (2010, March 15). Digital dozen. AMA.org. Retrieved from https://archive.ama.org/archive/ResourceLibrary/MarketingNews/Pages/2010/3_15_10/Digital_Dozen.aspx

[16] (2016, July 29) Discontinuation of SMS (text messaging) for emergency notifications. (2016, March 1). Retrieved from https://uwaterloo.ca/watsafe/news/discontinuation-sms-text-messaging-emergency-notifications

[17] Skinner. C. A. (2008, July 16). UK businesses ban IM over security concerns. CIO. Retrieved from http://www.cio.com/article/437910/UK_Businesses_Ban_IM_over_Security_Concerns

[18] Flynn, N. (2012, May 23). Social media rules: Policies & best practices to effectively manage your presence, posts & potential risks. The ePolicy Institute. Retrieved from http://www.epolicyinstitute.com/social-media-risks-rules-policies-procedures

[19] Based on The Emily Post Institute. (n.d.). Texting Manners. Retrieved from http://emilypost.com/advice/texting-manners/

[20] Majchrzak, A., Wagner, C., & Yates, D. (2006). Corporate wiki users: Results of a survey. CiteSeer. Retrieved from http://citeseerx.ist.psu.edu/viewdoc/summary?doi=10.1.1.97.407

[21] The five main uses of wikis based on Nations, D. (2009). The business wiki: Wiki in the workplace. About.com: Web Trends. Retrieved from http://webtrends.about.com/od/wiki/a/business-wiki.htm

[22] Barnes, N. G., Lescaut, A. M., & Wright, S. (2013). 2013 Fortune 500 are bullish on social media: Big companies get excited about Google+, Instagram, Foursquare and Pinterest. Center for Marketing Research, Charlton College of Business, University of Massachusetts Dartmouth. Retrieved from http://www.umassd.edu/cmr/socialmediaresearch/2013fortune500

[23] Pearson, M. (2016, August 2). Why corporate blogging is on the rebound. *Globe and Mail*. Retrieved from http://www.theglobeandmail.com/report-on-business/small-business/sb-managing/why-corporate-blogging-is-on-the-rebound/article10003057/

[24] Westergaard, N. (2013, August 18). Social media: Don't fear negative content. *The Gazette*. Retrieved from http://thegazette.com/2013/08/18/social-media-dont-fear-negative-content

[25] Devaney, T., & Stein, T. (2012, December 19). How to turn your online critics into fans. *Forbes*. Retrieved from http://www.forbes.com/sites/capitalonespark/2012/12/19/how-to-turn-your-online-critics-into-fans

[26] Live blog: Wildfire in Fort McMurray, AB. (2016, August 2). Retrieved from http://blog.allstate.ca/cat_events/wildfire-in-fort-mcmurray/

[27] Lindstrom, M. (2012, July 3). How many lives does a brand have? Fast Company. Retrieved from http://www.fastcompany.com/1841927/buyology-martin-lindstrom-lives-of-brands-china-marketing

[28] Brogan, C. (2012, July 13). Become a dream feeder. Retrieved from http://www.chrisbrogan.com/dreamfeeder

[29] WestJet Doesn't Overbook. (2017, May 23). Blog posting and selected comments and responses. Retrieved from https://blog.westjet.com/westjet-doesnt-overbook/#comment-3324936542

[30] Millennials: A portrait of Generation Next. (2010, February 24). *Pew Research Center*. Retrieved from http://www.pewsocialtrends.org/2007/01/09/a-portrait-of-generation-next/; How digital behavior differs among Millennials, Gen Xers and Boomers. (2013, March 21). eMarketer. Retrieved from http://www.emarketer.com/Articles/Print.aspx?R=1009748

[31] Smith, A., & Brenner, J. (2012, May 31). Twitter use 2012. Pew Internet & American Life Project. Retrieved from http://pewinternet.org/files/old-media//Files/Reports/2012/PIP_Twitter_Use_2012.pdf

[32] Barnes, N. G., Lescaut, A. M., & Wright, S. (2013). 2013 Fortune 500 are bullish on social media: Big companies get excited about Google+, Instagram, Foursquare and Pinterest. Center for Marketing Research, Charlton College of Business, University of Massachusetts Dartmouth. Retrieved from http://www.umassd.edu/cmr/socialmediaresearch/2013fortune500

[33] Twitter statistics. (2013). *Socialbakers.com*. Retrieved from http://www.socialbakers.com/twitter

[34] Laughren, C. (2015, June 3). The social approach turns Wells Fargo employees into "relationship investors." Retrieved from https://smbp.uwaterloo.ca/2015/06/the-social-approach-turns-wells-fargo-employees-into-relationship-investors/

[35] Parekh, R. (2012, September 17). Internal affairs: Social media at the office. *Ad Age*. Retrieved from http://adage.com/article/digital/internal-affairs-social-media-office/237207

[36] Li, C. (2016, August 2). Why no one uses the corporate social networks. *Harvard Business Review*. Retrieved from https://hbr.org/2015/04/why-no-one-uses-the-corporate-social-network

[37] Mullaney, T. (2012, May 16). Social media is reinventing how business is done. *USA Today*. Retrieved from http://usatoday.com/money/economy/story/2012-05-14/social-media-econony-companies/55029088/1

[38] Success Story: Driving in-restaurant sales (2016, August 2). Retrieved from https://www.facebook.com/business/success/a-w-canada

[39] Conlin, M., & MacMillan, D. (2009, June 1). Managing the tweets. *BusinessWeek*, 20.

[40] Cisco. *2013 annual security report*, 23-25. Retrieved from https://www.cisco.com/web/offer/gist_ty2_asset/Cisco_2013_ASR.pdf

[41] Flynn, N. (2012, May 23). Social media rules: Policies & best practices to effectively manage your presence, posts & potential risks. *The ePolicy Institute*. Retrieved from http://www.epolicyinstitute.com/social-media-risks-rules-policies-procedures

[42] Ibid.

[43] Ibid.

[44] Nova Scotia Leglislature. (n.d.). Human Rights Act. Retrieved August 25, 2017, from http://nslegislature.ca/legc/statutes/human%20rights.pdf

Chapter 6

[1] White, E. (2008, May 19). Art of persuasion becomes key. *The Wall Street Journal*. Retrieved from http://online.wsj.com/article/SB121115784262002373.html; McIntosh, P., & Luecke, R. A. (2011). *Increase your influence at work*. New York: American Management Association, 4.

[2] Jones, J. P. (2004). *Fables, fashions, and facts about advertising: A study of 28 enduring myths*. Thousand Oaks, CA: Sage Publications (Kindle Edition), Chapter 2; Rosseli, F., Skelly, J. J., & Mackie, D. M. (1995). Processing rational and emotional messages: The cognitive and affective mediation of persuasion. *Journal of Experimental Social Psychology, 31*, 163.

[3] Fogg, B. J. (2008). Mass interpersonal persuasion: An early view of a new phenomenon. In: *Proceedings. Third International Conference on Persuasive Technology 2008*. Berlin, Germany: Springer.

[4] Discussion based on Perloff, R. M. (2010). *The dynamics of persuasion: Communication and attitudes in the twenty-first century* (4th ed.). New York: Routledge, 4–5.

[5] Halperin, S. (2012, December 19). "X Factor" sees significant social media strides. *The Hollywood Reporter*. Retrieved from http://www.hollywoodreporter.com/live-feed/x-factors-social-media-strategy-405485

[6] Perloff, R. M. (2010). *The dynamics of persuasion: Communication and attitudes in the twenty-first century* (4th ed.). New York: Routledge, p. 9.

[7] Ibid.

[8] Howard, T. (2008, November 28). E-mail grows as direct-marketing tool. *USA Today*, p. 5B.

[9] Reynolds, C. (2015, June 8). Direct mail vs. email—Who is king? *Socialmediaweek.org*. Retrieved from https://socialmediaweek.org/blog/2015/06/direct-mail-vs-email-king/

[10] McGee, M. (2012, April 5). 77 percent of us want to get marketing messages via email & there's no close second place, study says. *MarketingLand*. Retrieved from http://marketingland.com/77-percent-of-us-want-to-get-marketing-messages-via-email-theres-no-close-second-place-study-says-9420

[11] Kopecky, J. (n.d.). An investigation into the ROI of direct mail vs. email marketing. *Hubspot Marketing*. Retrieved from https://blog.hubspot.com/blog/tabid/6307/bid/34032/an-investigation-into-the-roi-of-direct-mail-vs-email-marketing-data.aspx

[12] Cited in Rubel, S. (2010, August 9). Hot or not: Email marketing vs. social-media marketing. *Advertising Age*. Retrieved from http://adage.com/digital/article?article_id=145285

[13] Stone, B. (2010, September 22). Facebook sells your friends. *BusinessWeek*. Retrieved from https://www.bloomberg.com/news/articles/2010-09-22/facebook-sells-your-friends

[14] Burson-Marsteller. Asia-Pacific social media study. (2010, October 28). Retrieved from http://www.burson-marsteller.com/press-release/burson-marsteller-asia-pacific-social-media-study-reveals-that-only-40-of-top-asian-companies-have-a-branded-social-media-presence/

[15] Ibid.

[16] Hewlett Packard Enterprise. (2017). Community Blogs. Retrieved from https://community.hpe.com

[17] Weinberg, T. (2009) *The new community rules: Marketing on the social web*. Sebastopol, CA: O'Reilly Media, 129.

[18] Edwards, L. (2012, March 5). Are brands turning people into adverts with social media? *Socialmedia Today*. Retrieved from http://socialmediatoday.com/laurahelen/462175/are-brands-turning-people-adverts-social-media

[19] Tong, V. (2007, November 26). Tattoos: A new favourite of advertisers. *Boston.com*. Retrieved from http://www.boston.com/news/education/higher/articles/2007/11/26/tattoos_a_new_favorite_of_advertisers/?page=full

Chapter 7

[1] Rodger, R. (2011, June 30). Communicating in a Crisis. *Step Two Designs*. Retrieved July 23, 2013, from http://www.steptwo.com.au/papers/kmc_crisis/index.html

[2] Webber, L. (2013, July 18). Text from the boss: U R fired. *The Wall Street Journal*. Retrieved July 23, 2013, from http://blogs.wsj.com/atwork/2013/07/18/text-from-the-boss-u-r-fired

[3] Canavor, N. (2012). *Business writing in the digital age*. Thousand Oaks, CA: Sage, 62.

[4] Mascolini, M. (1994, June). Another look at teaching the external negative message. *Bulletin of the Association for Business Communication*, 47.

[5] Schweitzer, M. E. (2006, December). Wise negotiators know when to say "I'm sorry." *Negotiation*, 4. PDF file retrieved from http://search.ebscohost.com

[6] Brodkin, J. (2007, March 19). Rating apologies. *Networkworld*, *24*(11), 14. Retrieved from http://search.ebscohost.com

[7] Tjan, A. (2017, April 12). This is how you apologize to your flyers. Retrieved from https://www.linkedin.com/pulse/how-you-apologize-your-fliers-anthony-tjan

[8] Letters to Lands' End. (1991, February). *1991 Lands' End Catalogue*. Dodgeville, WI: Lands' End, 100.

[9] Forbes, M. (1999). How to write a business letter. In K. Harty (Ed.), *Strategies for business and technical writing*. Boston: Allyn and Bacon, 108.

[10] Dorn, E. M. (1999, March). Case method instruction in the business writing classroom. *Business Communication Quarterly*, 51–52.

[11] Browning, M. (2003, November 24). Work dilemma: Delivering bad news a good way. *Government Computer News*, 41; and Mowatt, J. (2002, February). Breaking bad news to customers. *Agency Sales*, 30.

[12] Engels, J. (2007, July). Delivering difficult messages. *Journal of Accountancy, 204*(1), 50–52. Retrieved from http://search.ebscohost.com; see also Lewis, B. (1999, September 13). To be an effective leader, you need to perfect the art of delivering bad news. *InfoWorld*, 124. Retrieved from http://books.google.com

[13] Bristol-Smith, D. (2003, November). Need to deliver bad news? How & why to tell it like it is. *HR Focus*, 3. Retrieved from http://search.ebscohost.com

[14] Granberry, M. (1992, November 14). Lingerie chain fined $100,000 for gift certificates. *Los Angeles Times*, p. D3.

[15] Bristol-Smith, D. (2003, November). Need to deliver bad news? How & why to tell it like it is. *HR Focus*, 3. Retrieved from http://search.ebscohost.com

[16] Gartner identifies top ten disruptive technologies for 2008 to 2012 [Press release]. (2008, May 28). Retrieved from http://www.gartner.com/newsroom/id/681107

[17] Woodward, L. (20106, December 7) Shopify tops tech-heavy ranking of best places to work in 2017. http://www.bnn.ca/shopify-tops-tech-heavy-ranking-of-best-places-to-work-in-2017-1.625348

[18] Based on SUV surprise. (2004, June 15). *The Wall Street Journal*, p. W7.

Chapter 8

[1] Photo essay based on Eksteen, L. (2013, September 12). Six reasons why Survey Monkey is the bomb. The Media Online. Retrieved from http://themediaonline.co.za/2013/09/six-reasons-why-survey-monkey-is-the-bomb; Helft, M. (2011, September 15). SurveyMonkey turns online surveys into a hot business. Fortune Online. Retrieved from http://fortune.com/2011/09/15/surveymonkey-turns-online-surveys-into-a-hot-business/

Chapter 9

[1] Union Pearson Express. (n.d.). *Metrolinx*. Retrieved August 6, 2013, from http://www.metrolinx.com/en/projectsandprograms/upexpress/upexpress.aspx

[2] Buck Institute for Research on Aging. (n.d.). Architecture. Retrieved from http://www.buckinstitute.org/architecture

[3] Holtz, H. (1990). *The consultant's guide to proposal writing*. New York: Wiley, 188.

[4] Conference Board of Canada. About Us. (n.d.). Retrieved January 28, 2017, from http://www.conferenceboard.ca/about-cboc/default.aspx

[5] Suzukamo, L. B. (2002, July 3). Search engines become popular for fact-finding, game playing. *Knight-Ridder/Tribune News Service*, p. K6110.

[6] Berfield, S. (2009, August 17). Howard Schultz versus Howard Schultz. *BusinessWeek*, 31.

[7] Writing Tutorial Services, Indiana University. (2011). Plagiarism: What it is and how to recognize and avoid it. Retrieved from http://www.indiana.edu/~wts/pamphlets/plagiarism.shtml

[8] Saylor, Michael. (2012) The Mobile Wave: How Mobile Intelligence Will Change Everything. New York: Vanguard Press.

[9] Broadbent Institute. (September 2015). *The Economic Benefits of Infrastructure Spending in Canada*. Retrieved from https://d3n8a8pro7vhmx.cloudfront.net/broadbent/pages/4555/attachments/original/1441907687/The_Economic_Benefits_of_Public_Infrastructure_Spending_in_Canada.pdf?1441907687

Chapter 10

[1] Buhler, P. M. (2003, April 20). Workplace civility: Has it fallen by the wayside? *SuperVision*. Retrieved June 24, 2008, from ProQuest database.

[2] Johnson, D. (n.d.). Dine like a diplomat [Seminar script]. The Protocol School of Washington, 1998–2006.

[3] Albrecht, K. (2005). *Social intelligence: The new science of success*. San Francisco: Pfeiffer, 3.

[4] Molloy, J. T. (1988). *New dress for success*. New York: Warner Books, 13–14.

[5] Evans, L. (2013, June 21). Will work for biscuits: Celebrating Take Your Dog to Work Day. *Canadian Business*. Retrieved March 30, 2014, from http://www.canadianbusiness.com/lifestyle/will-work-for-biscuits

[6] Hughes, T. (n.d.). Being a professional. *Word Constructions*. Retrieved June 16, 2008, from http://www.wordconstructions.com/articles/business/professional.html; and Grove, C., & Hallowell, W. (n.d.). The seven balancing acts of professional behavior in the United States: A cultural values perspective. *Grovewell*. Retrieved July 18, 2008, from http://www.grovewell.com/pub-usa-professional.html

[7] Brent, P. (2006, November). Soft skills speak volumes. *CA Magazine, 139*, 112. Retrieved June 16, 2008, from ProQuest database

[8] Laff, M. (2006, December). Wanted: CFOs with communications skills. *T+D, 60*(12), 20. Retrieved July 28, 2011, from http://www.pecktraining.com/articles.html

[9] Duke, S. (2001, Winter). E-Mail: Essential in media relations, but no replacement for face-to-face communication. *Public Relations Quarterly*, 19; Flaherty, L. M., Pearce, K. J., & Rubin, R. B. (1998, Summer). Internet and face-to-face communication: Not functional alternatives. *Communication Quarterly*, 250.

[10] Drolet, A. L., & Morris, M. W. (2000, January). Rapport in conflict resolution: Accounting for how face-to-face contact fosters mutual cooperation in mixed-motive conflicts. *Journal of Experimental Social Psychology*, 26.

[11] Miculka, J. (1999). *Speaking for success.* Cincinnati: South-Western,19.

[12] Plantronics. (2010). How we work: Communication trends of business professionals. Retrieved from http://www.plantronics .com/media/howwework/brochure-role-of-voice.pdf

[13] McHugh, E. (2013, March 11). Canadians still love their landlines—But for how long? *The Chronicle Herald* (Halifax). Retrieved August 7, 2013, from http://thechronicleherald .ca/bcw/942869-mchugh-canadians-still-love-their-landlines -but-for-how-long; Smith, A. (2010, July 7). Mobile access 2010. *Pew Research Internet Project.* Retrieved from http:// www.pewinternet.com/Reports/2010/Mobile-Access-2010 .aspx; and Lanman, S. (2005, July 9). Mobile-phone users become a majority. *San Francisco Chronicle*, p. C1.

[14] Brown, M. K., Huettner, B., & James-Tanny, C. (2007). *Managing virtual teams: Getting the most of wikis, blogs, and other collaborative tools.* Plano, TX: Wordware Publishing; and Lipnack, J., & Stamps, J. (2000). *Virtual teams: People working across boundaries with technology* (2nd ed.). New York: Wiley, 18.

[15] Cutler, G. (2007, January/February). Mike leads his first virtual team. *Research-Technology Management, 50*(1), 66. Retrieved June 17, 2008, from ABI/INFORM database.

[16] Ruffin, B. (2006, January). T.E.A.M. work: Technologists, educators, and media specialists collaborating. *Library Media Connection, 24*(4), 49. Retrieved June 20, 2008, from EBSCO database.

[17] Katzenbach, J. R., & Smith, D. K. (1994). *The wisdom of teams.* New York: HarperBusiness, 45.

[18] Gale, S. F. (2006, July). Common ground. *PM Network*, 48. Retrieved June 17, 2008, from EBSCO database.

[19] Callahan, D. (2009, April 21). Breaking the ice: Success through teamwork and partnerships. Retrieved from http://greatlakes.coastguard.dodlive.mil/2009/04/ breaking-the-ice-success-through-teamwork-and-partnerships

[20] Phillips, A. (2012, May 9). Wasted time in meetings costs the UK economy £26 billion. Retrieved from http://www .bmmagazine.co.uk/in-business/wasted-time-in-meetings-costs -the-uk-economy-26-billion/; Herring, H. B. (2006, June 18). Endless meetings: The black holes of the workday. *The New York Times.* Retrieved from http://www.nytimes .com/2006/06/18/business/yourmoney/18count.html?mcubz=3

[21] Herring, H. B. (2006, June 18). Endless meetings: The black holes of the workday. *The New York Times.* Retrieved from http://www.nytimes.com/2006/06/18/business/ yourmoney/18count.html?mcubz=3

[22] Shellenbarger, S. (2012, May 16). Meet the meeting killers—In the office, they strangle ideas, poison progress; how to fight back. *The Wall Street Journal.* Retrieved from http://search .proquest.com

[23] Rogelberg, S. G., Shanock, L. R., & Scott, C. W. (2012). Wasted time and money in meetings: Increasing return on investment. *Small Group Research, 43*(2), 237. doi: 10.1177/1046496411429170

[24] Bruening, J. C. (1996, July). There's good news about meetings. *Managing Office Technology*, 24–25.

[25] Cook, J. K. (1995, April). Try these eight guidelines for more effective meetings. *Communication Briefings*, Bonus Item, p. 8a; See also Stettner, M. (1998, October 8). How to manage a corporate motormouth. *Investor's Business Daily*, p. A1.

[26] Lohr, S. (2008, July 22). As travel costs rise, more meetings go virtual. *The New York Times.* Retrieved from http://www .nytimes.com/2008/07/22/technology/22meet.html?mcubz=3

[27] Ibid.

[28] Schlegel, J. (2012). Running effective meetings: Types of meetings. Salary.com. Retrieved from http://www.salary.com/ running-effective-meetings-6; Cohen, M. A., Rogelberg, S. G., Allen, J. A., & Luong, A. (2011). Meeting design characteristics and attendee perceptions of staff/team meeting quality. *Group Dynamics: Theory, Research, and Practice, 15*(1), 100–101; Schindler, E. (2008, February 15). Running an effective teleconference or virtual meeting. CIO. Retrieved from www.cio.com; See also Brenowitz, R. S. (2004, May). Virtual meeting etiquette. Article 601, *Innovative Leader.* Retrieved from http://www.winstonbrill.com

[29] Tips on meetings: Two rules for making global meetings work. (2011, April 11). *Harvard Business Review.* Retrieved from http://hbr.org/web/management-tip/tips-on-meetings

Chapter 11

[1] Maes, J. D., Weldy, T. G., & Icenogle, M. L. (1997, January). A managerial perspective: Oral communication competency is most important for business students in the workplace. *The Journal of Business Communication, 34*(1), 67–80. Retrieved October 6, 2013, from http://home.bi.no/fgl96053/orgcom/ oral.pdf

[2] Barrington, L., & Casner-Lotto, J. (2008, May). *Are they really ready to work?* Report of The Conference Board. Retrieved October 6, 2013, from http://www.p21.org/storage/ documents/FINAL_REPORT_PDF09-29-06.pdf

[3] Dassanayake, D. (2013, October 2). Just Google it: Britons lose ability to remember key dates because of search engines. Retrieved October 6, 2013, from http://www.express.co.uk/ news/science-technology/433898/Just-Google-it-Britons-lose -ability-to-remember-key-dates-because-of-search-engines

[4] Morrison, J., & Vogel, D. (1998). The impacts of presentation visuals on persuasion. *Information & Management, 33*(3), 125–35. Retrieved October 6, 2013, from ScienceDirect database.

[5] Booher, D. (2003). *Speak with confidence: Powerful presentations that inform, inspire, and persuade.* New York: McGraw-Hill Professional, 126; See also Paradi, D. (2009, March 3). Choosing colors for your presentation slides. Retrieved from http://www.indezine.com/ideas/prescolors.html

[6] Arts and Science Support of Education through Technology (ASSETT), University of Colorado. (n.d.). Prezi vs. SlideShare. Retrieved October 6, 2013, from http://assett.colorado.edu/ prezi-vs-slideshare

[7] Bates, S. (2005). *Speak like a CEO: Secrets for commanding attention and getting results.* New York: McGraw-Hill Professional,113.

[8] Sommerville, J. (n.d.). The seven deadly sins of PowerPoint presentations. *About.com: Entrepreneurs.* Retrieved October 6, 2013, from http://entrepreneurs.about.com/cs/ marketing/a/7sinsofppt.htm

[9] Burrows, P., & Grover, R., with H. Green. (2006, February 6). Steve Jobs' magic kingdom. *BusinessWeek.* Retrieved from https://www.bloomberg.com/news/articles/2006-02-05/ steve-jobs-magic-kingdom; See also Gallo, C. (2006, April 6). How to wow 'em like Steve Jobs. *BusinessWeek.* Retrieved October 6, 2013, from http://www.businessweek.com/ stories/2006-04-05/how-to-wow-em-like-steve-jobs

[10] See TLC Creative Services Inc. (n.d.). PowerPoint pre-show checklist. Retrieved October 6, 2013, from http://www .tlccreative.com/images/tutorials/PreShowChecklist.pdf

[11] Ellwood, J. (2004, August 4). Less PowerPoint, more powerful points. *The Times* (London), 6.

Chapter 12

[1] Social media vs.job boards — The future of recruiting (2015, March 11). Onrec. Retrieved from http://www.onrec.com/news/statistics-and-trends/social-media-vs-job-boards-the-future-of-recruiting

[2] Korkki, P. (2007, July 1). So easy to apply, so hard to be noticed. *The New York Times*. Retrieved October 10, 2013, from LexisNexis database.

[3] Marquardt, K. (2008, February 21). 5 tips on finding a new job. *U.S. News & World Report*. Retrieved October 10, 2013, from http://www.usnews.com/articles/business/careers/2008/02/21/5-tips-on-finding-a-new-job.html

[4] Haun, L. (2013, March 22). Source of hire report: Referrals, career sites, job boards dominate. *ERE.net*. Retrieved October 10, 2013, from http://www.ere.net/2013/03/22/source-of-hire-report-referrals-career-sites-job-boards-dominate

[5] Pratt, Siofra. (2016, May 7), Source of hire 2016 (Infographic). Retrieved from https://www.socialtalent.co/blog/source-of-hire-2016-infographic

[6] Adams, S. (2013, February 5). New survey: LinkedIn more dominant than ever among job seekers and recruiters, but Facebook poised to gain. Retrieved from http://www.forbes.com/sites/susanadams/2013/02/05/new-survey-linked-in-more-dominant-than-ever-among-job-seekers-and-recruiters-but-facebook-poised-to-gain

[7] McConnon, A. (2007, August 30). Social networking graduates and hits the job market. *BusinessWeek*. Retrieved October 10, 2013, from http://www.businessweek.com/stories/2007-08-30/social-networking-graduates-and-hits-the-job-marketbusinessweek-business-news-stock-market-and-financial-advice

[8] Feldman quoted in Marquardt, K. (2008, February 21). 5 tips on finding a new job. *U.S. News & World Report*. Retrieved from http://www.usnews.com/articles/business/careers/2008/02/25/5-tips-on-finding-a-new-job.html

[9] Adams, S. (2012, March 27). Make LinkedIn help you find a job. Retrieved from http://www.forbes.com/sites/susanadams/2012/04/27/make-linkedin-help-you-find-a-job-2

[10] Swallow, E. (2011, October 23). How recruiters use social net works to screen candidates. Retrieved from http://mashable.com/2011/10/23/how-recruiters-use-social-networks-to-screen-candidates-infographic

[11] Burns, K. (2009, September 30). Chronological vs. functional resumes. *U.S. News & World Report*. Retrieved October 10, 2013, from https://money.usnews.com/money/blogs/outside-voices-careers/2009/09/30/chronogical-vs-functional-resumes

[12] Blackburn-Brockman, E., & Belanger, K. (2001, January). One page or two? A national study of CPA recruiters' preferences for résumé length. *The Journal of Business Communication*, 29–57. Retrieved October 10, 2013, from Sage Journals Database.

[13] Isaacs, K. (n.d.). How long should my resume be. *Monster*. Retrieved October 10, 2013, from http://career-advice.monster.com/resumes-cover-letters/resume-writing-tips/how-to-decide-on-resume-length/article.aspx

[14] Fisher, A. (2007, March 29). Does a resume have to be one page long? *CNNMoney.com*. Retrieved October 10, 2013, from http://money.cnn.com/2007/03/28/news/economy/resume.fortune/index.htm

[15] Hansen, K. (n.d.). Your job-search resume needs a focal point: How job-seekers can add focus to resumes. Retrieved from https://www-cms.livecareer.com/quintessential/resume-objectives

[16] Enelow, W.S. quoted in Korkki, P. (2007, July 1). So easy to apply, so hard to be noticed. *The New York Times*. Retrieved from http://www.proquest.umi.com

[17] Diaz, C. (2013, December). Updating best practices: Applying on-screen reading strategies to résumé writing. *Business Communication Quarterly*, *76*(4), 427–445; See also Nielsen, J. (2006, April 17). F-shaped pattern for reading web content. Retrieved from http://www.nngroup.com/articles/f-shaped-pattern-reading-web-content

[18] Struzik, E., IBM expert quoted in Weber, L. (2012, January 24). Your résumé vs. oblivion. *The Wall Street Journal*, p. B6.

[19] Optimalresume.com. (n.d.). Optimizing your résumé for scanning and tracking. Retrieved from https://admin.optimalresume.com/upload/ResourceFile_university_keywords.pdf

[20] Ibid.

[21] Saltpeter, M. (2012, August 17). How a good video resume leads to a good job. *U.S. News & World Report*. Retrieved October 29, 2013, from http://money.usnews.com/money/blogs/outside-voices-careers/2012/08/17/how-a-good-video-resume-leads-to-a-good-job

[22] Nale, M. (2008, February 8). 10 things that make up a good video resume. *ERE.net*. Retrieved October 29, 2013, from http://www.ere.net/2008/02/08/10-things-that-make-up-a-good-video-resume

[23] Krum, R. (2012, September 10). Is your resume hopelessly out of date? Retrieved from http://infonewt.com/blog/2012/9/10/infographic-resumes-interview-by-the-art-of-doing.html

[24] Larsen, M. (2011, Nov. 8). Infographic resumes: Fad or trend? Retrieved from http://www.recruiter.com/i/infographic-resumes

[25] Ibid.

[26] Augustin, H. (1991, September). The written job search: A comparison of the traditional and a nontraditional approach. *The Bulletin of the Association for Business Communication*, 13.

[27] Korkki, P. (2007, July 1). So easy to apply, so hard to be noticed. *The New York Times*. Retrieved from http://www.nytimes.com/2007/07/01/business/yourmoney/01career.html?mcubz=3

Chapter 13

[1] Bergey, B. (2009, December 10). Online job interviews becoming more popular. *WKOW.com*. Retrieved from http://www.wkowtv.com/Global/story .asp?S=11655389; Kennedy, J. L. (2008). *Job interviews for dummies*. Hoboken, NJ: Wiley, 20.

[2] Wilmott, N. (n.d.). Interviewing styles: Tips for interview approaches. *About.com*. Retrieved November 19, 2013, from http://humanresources.about.com/cs/selectionstaffing/a/interviews.htm

[3] Smith-Proulx, L. (2011, November 12). Five tips to ace the panel job interview. Retrieved from https://www.hcareers.com/article/career-advice/5-tips-to-ace-the-panel-job-interview

[4] Cristante, D. (n.d.). How to succeed in a group interview. *Career FAQs*. Retrieved November 19, 2013, from http://www.careerfaqs.com.au/careers/interview-questions-and-tips/how-to-succeed-in-a-group-interview

[5] Bergey, B. (2009, December 10). Online job interviews becoming more popular. *WKOW.com*. Retrieved November 19, 2013, from http://www.wkowtv.com/Global/story.asp?S=11655389

[6] Ovsey, D. (2013, July 29). Study shows job interviews done via video conference put both applicants and interviewers at a disadvantage. *Financial Post*. Retrieved from http://business

.financialpost.com/executive/business-education/study-shows-job-interviews-done-via-video-conference-put-both-applicants-and-interviewers-at-a-disadvantage

[7] Rossheim, J. (n.d.). Do your homework before the big interview. *Monster.* Retrieved November 21, 2013, from http://career-advice.monster.com/job-interview/interview-preparation/do-your-homework-before-interview/article.aspx

[8] Bowles, L. (n.d.). How to research a company for a job search. *eHow*. Retrieved November 21, 2013, from http://www.ehow.com/how_7669153_research-company-job-search.html

[9] Ryan, L. (2006, February 9). Job-seekers: Prepare your stories. *Ezine Articles*. Retrieved November 21, 2013, from http://ezinearticles.com/?Job-Seekers:-Prepare-Your-Stories&id=142327

[10] CareerBuilder. (2016, April 28). Number of employers using social media to screen candidates has increased 500 percent over the last decade. Retrieved from http://www.careerbuilder.ca/share/aboutus/pressreleasesdetail.aspx?sd=4%2F28%2F2016&id=pr945&ed=12%2F31%2F2016

[11] Guiseppi, M. (2010, April 30). Microsoft study finds online reputation management not optional. *Executive Career Brand*. Retrieved November 21, 2013, from http://executivecareerbrand.com/microsoft-study-finds-online-reputation-management-not-optional

[12] Finder, A. (2006, June 11). For some, online persona undermines a résumé. *The New York Times*. Retrieved November 21, 2013, from http://www.nytimes.com/2006/06/11/us/11recruit.html?mcubz=3

[13] Ibid.

[14] CareerBuilder. (2016, April 28). Number of employers using social media to screen candidates has increased 500 percent over the last decade. Retrieved from http://www.careerbuilder.ca/share/aboutus/pressreleasesdetail.aspx?sd=4%2F28%2F2016&id=pr945&ed=12%2F31%2F2016

[15] Wright, D. (2002, August/September). Tell stories, get hired. *OfficePro, 64*(6), 32–33. Retrieved November 29, 2013, from Business Source Premier (EBSCO).

[16] Lublin, J. (2008, February 5). Notes to interviewers should go beyond a simple thank you. *The Wall Street Journal*, p. B1. Retrieved November 29, 2013, from ProQuest database.

[17] Green, A. (2010, December 27). How to follow up after applying for a job. *U.S. News & World Report.* Retrieved November 29, 2013, from http://money.usnews.com/money/blogs/outside-voices-careers/2010/12/27/how-to-follow-up-after-applying-for-a-job

[18] Korkki, P. (2009, August 25). No response after an interview? What to do. *The New York Times*. Retrieved November 29, 2013, from http://www.nytimes.com/2009/08/23/jobs/25searchweb.html?_r=0

Index

Page numbers followed by an f *indicate illustrative information in figures.*

C

D

E

F

G

H

I

J

K

L

M

N

O

P